THE OFFICIAL

LUXOLOGY® MODO® GUIDE

VERSION 301

Dan Ablan

Course Technology PTR
A part of Cengage Learning

Australia, Brazil, Japan, Korea, Mexico, Singapore, Spain, United Kingdom, United States

The Official Luxology® modo® Guide, Version 301
Dan Ablan

Publisher and General Manager, Course Technology PTR:
Stacy L. Hiquet

Associate Director of Marketing:
Sarah Panella

Manager of Editorial Services:
Heather Talbot

Marketing Manager:
Jordan Casey

Executive Editor:
Kevin Harreld

Project Editor and Copy Editor:
Kim Benbow

Technical Reviewer:
Greg Leuenberger

PTR Editorial Services Coordinator:
Erin Johnson

Interior Layout Tech:
Bill Hartman

Cover Designer:
Mike Tanamachi

DVD-ROM Producer:
Brandon Penticuff

Indexer:
Larry Sweazy

Proofreader:
Sandy Doell

Library of Congress Control Number: 2007938239

ISBN-13: 978-1-59863-497-6

ISBN-10: 1-59863-497-6

Course Technology
25 Thomson Place
Boston, MA 02210
USA

Cengage Learning is a leading provider of customized learning solutions with office locations around the globe, including Singapore, the United Kingdom, Australia, Mexico, Brazil, and Japan. Locate your local office at:
international.cengage.com/region

Cengage Learning products are represented in Canada by Nelson Education, Ltd.

For your lifelong learning solutions, visit **courseptr.com**

Visit our corporate website at **cengage.com**

Printed in the United States of America
1 2 3 4 5 6 7 11 10 09 08

Acknowledgments

I think it's best to point out that none of you would be reading this book if it weren't for my beautiful, talented, generous, and completely understanding wife Maria. When I was putting in 16- and 17-hour days working at the studio, dealing with clients, an office move, and lawyers who didn't want to pay for the contracted animation work, she was right there supporting me.

Then, there is Brad, Dion, Bob, David, and the rest of the development team at Luxology. Since the beginning, they have supported my efforts in getting up to speed with the latest version of the software and took time to answer questions throughout the book process. And I can't thank Phillip Obretenov enough for the outstanding cover image he graciously supplied. Awesome work and a testament to the power of modo. Special thanks goes out to Brad Peebler. I've known Brad for many years, and he and I have been down this "book" road before. Thanks for all of the support and help, Brad!

When it came to technical editing this book, I knew who to trap, uh...I mean ask, right from the start—Greg Leuenberger from Sabertooth Productions (www.sabpro.com). Greg's efforts as a technical editor were nothing less than stellar in the modo 201 book, and I can't thank him enough for his work on this guide to modo 301. He really knows his stuff! Additional thanks goes out to Andrew Brown who was instrumental in answering some questions I had in the beginning stages of the book. Thanks, Andy! I can't forget to thank Philip Lawson for his excellent models, which he graciously donated to the book for all of you to use. You'll use his slick martini glass scene to learn some interesting rendering techniques.

I certainly can't wrap up this section without a big thanks to Kevin Harreld at Course Technology, Cengage Learning for getting this book off the ground and putting up with my delays. Thank you to Kim Benbow who edited this book and made my text flow! How does she do it? Thank you to the entire team at Course Technology, Cengage Learning for the opportunity to write this book. Lastly, thanks to the Luxology community. Everyone has been exceedingly supportive on the forums and in personal e-mails as this book process ended up taking nearly a year. Thank you for all your well wishes. I hope you enjoy the book.

About the Author

Dan Ablan is president of AGA Digital Studios, Inc., a 3D animation and visual effects company in the Chicago area. AGA Digital has produced 3D visuals for corporate, legal, and architectural clients since 1994, as well as post-production services in conjunction with Post Meridian, LLC. His recent work includes 3D animation for United Airlines, Abbott Labs, NASA, Lockheed Martin, Blue Cross and Blue Shield, Allstate, and many others.

This represents Dan's twelfth book in the computer software industry. His many best-selling international books include such subjects as LightWave and After Effects software, cinematography, directing, and digital photography for 3D imaging.

Dan is also the founder of 3DGarage.com (www.3dgarage.com), a website dedicated to high-quality video training for various software applications, such as LightWave 3D, modo 3D, Adobe Photoshop and Lightroom, as well as various Mac software. In the early days of 3D, Dan Ablan was in the forefront writing columns and articles for *LightWave Pro* magazine, *Video Toaster User* magazine, *3D Design* magazine, *3D World* magazine, and *NewTek Pro* magazine. Dan has been teaching LightWave seminars since 1995 across the country and at AGA Digital Studios, Inc. Some of the companies Dan has provided training for include Fox Television, ABC-TV New York City, CBS-TV Indianapolis, WTTW-TV PBS Chicago, Lockheed Martin, NASA, and many others. More recently, Dan continues to create 3D animations for various clients, while developing new video training for 3DGarage.com. He also is an accomplished photographer, and you can view his imagery at www.danablan.com, while also checking out his daily blog at www.danablan.com/blog.

Contents

Introduction xi

PART I
GETTING STARTED WITH MODO 301/302

Chapter 1
Interface Configurability 3

Understanding the Basics 4
Viewports 5
Splitting a Viewport 9
Tabbed Viewports 11
Custom Layouts 12
Roll Your Own Interface 20

Chapter 2
Editors, Action Centers, and Work Planes 31

Preferences 31
Input Preferences 32
Display Preferences 35
Data Preferences 40
modo Configuration Files 42
Form Editor 44
Input Editor 50
Action Centers 52
Work Plane 56

Chapter 3 Working with the Tools 59

Selections 59

Working with Selections 60

Selection Methods 65

Item Selection Mode 73

Quick Access Selection 74

Falloffs 76

Pipeline 85

Chapter 4 modo 301/302 Jump Start 89

Model Preparation 89

Model Manipulation 94

Selecting and Editing Geometry 97

Adding and Blending Geometry 104

Surfacing and Rendering Geometry 109

PART II BASIC CREATION METHODS

Chapter 5 Basic Building Blocks 121

Building Blocks, Literally 121

Automating with Macros 133

Additional Macro Use 138

Editing the Shape 143

Cutting the Shape 148

Chapter 6
Working with Layers 153

Items Tab Navigation 153
    Building in Layers 155
    Adding Mesh Layers 162
    Using Background Layers as Reference 166
    Adding Scenes to the Items Tab 170
    Merging Scenes in the Items Tab 180

Chapter 7
Shader Tree Fundamentals 185

Introduction to the Shader Tree 186
Using the Shader Tree 192
    Setting Materials 194
    Setting Image Materials 202
    Masking Effects 207
Your Next Few Steps 212

Chapter 8
Inside the Shader Tree 213

Masks 213
    Item Masks 213
    Polygon Masks 219
    Vertex Masks 221
Additional Material Layers 226
Groups 228
The Next Phase 232

Chapter 9
Animating in modo 233

Animation Basics 233
    Interface and Controls 233
    Channel Keyframes 237
Understanding Keyframing 238
modo 301/302 Graph Editor 244

PART III
WORKING PROJECTS

Chapter 10
Hard-Surface Modeling 249

Working from References 249
Modeling Details 268

Chapter 11
Creating and Painting Textures 279

Understanding the Paint Tools 280
Painting Surfaces. 294

Chapter 12
Subdivision Surface Modeling 301

Understanding Sub-Ds 301
Building a Product in Sub-Ds 303
    Starting with a Cube for a Detergent Bottle 305
    Sharper Edges with Subdivisions. 311
    Advantages of Subdivisions. 315
The Next Step. 326

Chapter 13
Sculpting Techniques 327

Building a Landscape 327
Displacements. 332
Morph Maps 337
Modeling with Sculpt Tools 345

PART IV
LIGHTING AND RENDERING

Chapter 14
Lighting and Rendering in modo 353

Lighting in modo 353
Lighting Concepts 358
Quality of Light 359
Other Light Sources 359
Creating a Lit Scene in modo 362
Rendering Introduction 372
    Frame 374
    Setting 375

Chapter 15
Rendering with Global Illumination 379

Global Illumination 379
Ray Tracing 381
Ray Tracing and Global Illumination Combined 383
Noise and Render 396
What's Next 397

Chapter 16
Output Options 399

Animation 400
    Render and Render Current View 402
    Render Selected 402
    Render All 402
    Render Turntable 403
    Render Animation 403
    Open Preview Render 403
    Open LAN View 404
    Bake 404
    Render Items 404

Saving Single Images 405
Auto Save Single Frame Renders 406
Outputting Models 406
Your Next Step 408

PART V
APPENDIXES

Appendix A Reference Materials 411

Web Sites 411
Reflection Properties 412
Refraction Properties 413

Appendix B What's on the DVD 419

DVD Contents 419
Video List 419
Using the Video Files 420
System Requirements 420

Index 421

Introduction

3D imagery is everywhere. In fact, there's more 3D work in television, movies, and the Internet than you realize. Many mobile phones now use 3D graphical icons! A good majority of "non-effects" films actually include quite a bit of visual effects. Filmmakers use 3D imagery to add digital sets, open windows on buildings, add leaves to trees, or simply add birds to a scene. With the advances in technology and improvements in software performance, digital content creators have been able to visualize their dreams while controlling budgets.

In 2004, a new product hit the ground running, allowing 3D modelers and animators to reach even higher goals. Formed by the originating programmers and team that built LightWave 3D, Luxology, LLC created what was, and still is, considered the best 3D modeling package on the market. modo 103 not only made 3D modeling easy, but also more fun than people ever imagined. A user coined the phrase "Model at the Speed of Thought," and Luxology has adopted it because it truly describes the power of the program. With the release of modo 201 and 202, the user had even greater power. 2007 saw the release of modo 301, which not only included animation capabilities, but also sculpting and enhanced creative control, all of which I'll cover in this book. Evolution is inevitable, and it hasn't been more clear than with this current release from Luxology.

Getting the Most from This Book

The Official Luxology modo Guide, Version 301 is designed to help you understand the power of the world's most robust 3D modeler. This second-generation program now offers 3D painting and texturing, as well as advanced rendering capabilities. This book will hold your hand through starting the application to saving your final render. Unlike many books that simply talk about concepts and functionality, this book will have you actually working in the program. The book is divided into four sections: Part I, Getting Started with modo 301/302; Part II, Basic Creation Methods; Part III, Working Projects; and Part IV, Lighting and Rendering. To maximize this printed resource, it's recommended you start at the beginning and work your way through to the end. You'll begin with an introduction to the program, and before long, you'll create a small project. I'll break down modo's core concepts and, from there, take you through the entire program. So even if you're experienced with modo, it's not a bad idea to take some time and go through the book from the beginning because you might pick up a tip or a trick you weren't aware of.

About the Creation of This Book

The Official Luxology modo Guide, Version 301 was written on a MacBook Pro, 2.33 Intel Core Duo with 2 GB of RAM and an ATI x1600 video card. The operating system used was Mac OS 10.5, Leopard. Tutorials were tested for this book on a Macintosh G5 desktop PowerPC, a Sony Vaio Pentium 4 PC running the Windows XP operating system. Luxology has created an application that runs identically on both PC and Macintosh computers. The only difference you'll experience is based on the processor, RAM, and video graphics card you have installed on your system. There are a few keyboard variances, which will be noted throughout the book.

Read the modo Manuals

This book is designed to be a companion to the modo manual supplied with your purchased software. Read through the information provided by Luxology, and you'll get the greatest bang for your buck when it comes to mastering modo.

Experiment and Practice

Every once in a while, you might find yourself with some free time—either at work in the afternoon, waiting for a render or for a client to call, or perhaps at home, late at night. Use those times to experiment with modo. Simply take a look around you and model what you see. How about starting with the computer monitor on your desk? There's no better reference than a physical object directly in front of you! Pay attention to the bevels, the depth of the buttons, and how the light reacts to these areas. Practice modeling the details and discover how easy modo handles the task. Feel like sculpting something completely organic and unique? Go for it. If you get stuck, keep going and work through the kinks. Before you know it, you'll be zipping through the interface and modeling just about anything you can imagine, while no longer worrying about finding the right tool. Before long, you'll be modeling, sculpting, and animating at the speed of thought.

Now, I've tried to make this book as informative as possible, but as you know, no single resource can be the only information you use. While modo is a young product and this book is one of the first on the market, there certainly will be more coming, as it happens with any software release. Another excellent way to get a grasp of this powerful software is with Internet discussions and training videos. The Luxology.com website has an excellent forum where you can not only ask questions, but also view others' work and expand your knowledge of what modo can do. As an adjunct to the discussion forums, Luxology has created Luxology.tv, a great place to find video tutorials. Additionally, you can visit 3DGarage.com for up-to-date video training courseware for modo, such as the 301 Signature Courseware, a 15-hour course I created to help people learn modo from the ground up. But don't just look to modo-specific software books and videos. There are many more resources for learning animation, lighting, texturing, and rendering than you may realize. Principles in camera techniques, lighting techniques, and more, all can be applied in modo. I've compiled a list of additional resources, which you'll find in the book's appendixes.

Conventions Used in This Book

One thing to remember—always work with the Caps Lock key off! Throughout this book, you will come across many keyboard shortcuts, and there are significant differences between a lowercase shortcut and an uppercase shortcut. The essential and immediate shortcuts used regularly are assigned to lowercase keys, while less-used commands are assigned to uppercase keys. What's important to remember is that some of the uppercase commands are more complex functions, and if you're not prepared to execute such a command, you may get odd and unexpected results.

Lastly, when it comes to conventions and usage, I'll give you one piece of advice—stop clicking! Yes, that's right. Stop clicking! When someone is learning software, any software, and they're not quite seeing the results they expect, or there's no response from a tool, users tend to click. They click anywhere, and in modo, this could be a problem. For example, you've selected a group of polygons and would like to rotate them all. However, after you thought you selected the Rotate tool, when you click and drag, something else happens entirely. You click some more, and in your haste, deselect the polygons. Now, you can undo and get back to your selection without much trouble. But the point is, work deliberately. Select a vertex, edge, polygon, light, or camera. Select a tool, click, and go. You'll find that not only will you learn the software more quickly, you'll do so with fewer problems. And while you're at it, stop pressing the spacebar—that changes things, too, and it doesn't make your scene move. Animation in modo will be explained in depth—I promise!

System Considerations

Ah yes, the system question. People are always asking what's the best to get. Should you spend $10,000 on a custom-built 3D workstation? Yes. You should. Order the best system you can from Apple or Boxx, then send it to me. Oh, my editors say I can't ask you to do that. Okay, then what about dual 64-bit machines or quad processors? In the end, it comes down to your wallet and what works for you. But what is crucial, and often a mistake made by many—don't overdo the processor and forget the memory. You're better off getting an old Pentium 4 2.7 GHz or a Mac G5 1.67 with two or three gigabytes of RAM, rather than the latest 4.0 GHz processors with only 512 KB or 1 GB of RAM. Think of it this way: RAM (memory) is like money—you can never have too much. What's more, and very important for modo's best functionality, is the video card you use. Do you need to go out and spend $3000 on the latest and greatest video card? No, not at all. If you've got it, by all means go for it. For the rest of us, a top-notch ATI or nVidia card with at least 128 MB of video memory will serve you quite well. Try to go for 256 MB on the video card if you can. Be sure to check the compatibility and recommended video cards and drivers with Luxology at www.luxology.com.

Why This Book?

Unlike Adobe Photoshop, which has more books published about it than any one bookstore can shelve, this modo book is the first (well, second) of its kind. This is a follow-up to the first ever modo book, *The Official Luxology modo Guide* (for 201). As a relatively new application, modo has already saturated the 3D market from hobbyists to professionals alike, in small studios and large, even to the likes of Pixar. Certainly, what you can create in modo is entirely up to you, and with version 301's new texturing and rendering capabilities, the possibilities are endless. You don't need to know 3D modeling to use this book; but if you do, you're a step ahead of everyone else. This book was created to introduce you to modo 301 and help guide you through the tools, interface, and controls available. In order to maximize these pages, I'll use projects to help you learn and understand. Luxology has done a tremendous job creating the modo 301 manual and additional learning materials, but this book was created to give you a succinct workflow through modo. This book was written so that you can learn the tools and what to do with them.

Who Am I?

Today, computer books are written by just about anyone. Some are good, and some are not. I always tell people my books can be found in the bookstore right near the real books! In most cases, it doesn't matter who's writing the book—what matters is the content. Well, maybe the author has something to do with it!

Before I entered the glamorous and fascinating world of 3D animation, I worked in the not-as-much-fun world of video production. After graduating college with a bachelor's degree in broadcast journalism and a minor in photojournalism, I promptly went to work for a very small CBS affiliate. Let me tell you, holding an Ikagami 79A video camera on your shoulder in the November cold, smack in the middle of an Indiana cornfield is a joy. It's a reason to get up in the morning. Actually, I'd rather have multiple root canals. You see, for me, I wanted more, and I moved up to a program manager position for a large cable television outfit. There, I discovered 3D animation via NewTek's LightWave 3D and an Amiga computer. It was 1989, and you have to remember that, back then, 3D was only prevalent in hugely expensive systems in the top video production studios and mostly in an experimental state. Getting into 3D meant you were really smart or really rich. A 3D system from Bosch or Alias could run you over $100,000. With Video Toaster and LightWave, a goofy schlub like me could create 3D imagery. One look at a small red apple rendering one pixel at a time (I think it took an hour or so), and I was hooked. From there I produced corporate video for a couple of years and, along the way, submerged myself in 3D. In 1994, I went to work for an Amiga dealership, selling and training Video Toaster and LightWave systems. Also in 1994, I was fired from the Amiga dealership because Commodore stopped making Amigas. However, I had started doing 3D work on the side, and with the help of unemployment checks from the state of Illinois, I was able to forge ahead with my own business, AGA Digital Studios.

While creating 3D animations for corporate accounts like Bosch and Kraft Foods, I also began submitting articles to the only LightWave publication at the time, *LightWave Pro* magazine. From there, I wrote tutorials every month and also contributed to their sister publication, *Video Toaster User*. I was "Dr. Toaster" and would answer questions for readers (I did not choose the name of the column, by the way). Avid Media Group, publishers of *Video Toaster User* and *LightWave Pro*, were bought out by Miller Freeman Publishing, and so I started writing for a new magazine called *3D Design*. Around 1995, I met with a representative from Macmillan Publishing, and we discussed the idea of a LightWave book. They knew who I was through my articles in the trade magazines, and in 1996, the first book on LightWave was published, *LightWave Power Guide* from New Riders Publishing.

Now, 12 years later, AGA Digital Studios, Inc. creates animations for corporate and industrial clients. In addition to daily animation work, in 2003, I founded a new division to AGA Digital, dedicated to 3D learning courses. 3DGarage.com is a training source with material presented as project-based courses. (Visit www.3dgarage.com for more information.) For more on my other books and photography, visit my website at www.danablan.com.

Words to Work By

It's truly amazing what you can do with a simple desktop computer (or laptop) and a few key software packages. Today's technology has grown beyond anyone's imagination, and it's only getting better—modo 301 is proof of that.

Whether you're a hobbyist or professional in the field of 3D modeling and animation, you're in it because you enjoy what you do. You have a passion for creating. And while you may have a job or a client along the way who makes you want to quit the whole thing, deep down you know you can't. You know that your best work is yet to come, and *The Official Luxology modo Guide, Version 301* is here to help.

Part I

Getting Started with modo 301/302

1

Interface Configurability

Trying to learn computer software is often a lot of fun, but as you might know, it can also be frustrating. Compounded in your quest for mastering a new software application, such as modo 301/302, is the element of 3D. This adds even more facets to the amount of information you'll need to absorb to create anything more than a blob of 3D geometry—or so you think! While Luxology's modo is an easy-to-use application, it does take a little getting used to. But within the next few pages, you'll soon be seeing results and realizing that this killer application from Luxology is not as difficult to learn as you once thought.

Here's the deal—an old story, but a good one just the same (and true). I had just returned from the bookstore and was skimming through the new line of books on various topics. I looked at the Maya books, the Flash books, the general 3D graphics books, and, while the information was good, there was so much talk! Argh! You don't want that, do you? Granted, you don't want a point-and-click book, but rather a book that will help you understand the tools. I first came upon this situation when writing *Inside LightWave 8* (New Riders Press, 2004). At the time, I was looking into using Flash more, and all of the books I found talked about the same thing. They all started out the same way, either covering the tools of the interface or having you build silly little character shapes. Somehow it was left to me to sift through 500 pages and then figure out how to make some simple interactive menus. Because of this frustrating structure I find in most software books, I want my books to help you learn differently. For example, if you were to sit down with me right now in my studio, I'd show you modo. We'd start with a "hey, check this out" and "here's how this works" type of approach. Would you ever sit down in a training session with someone and have them talk about theory and the history of 3D and blah, blah, blah? No, you want to learn the software! Or what if you went to a trade show to see modo in action? Imagine Luxology's Brad Peebler sitting there and discussing coordinates, the history of 3D, or the principles of lighting. You'd walk. You'd be there to see the software and what it can do. So why should a book on the subject be any different? Therefore, to quickly advance you from a novice to a somewhat dangerous 3D modeler, this jump-start chapter has been created. It is designed to take you through the entire process of creating, surfacing, and rendering a model in modo 301/302 without much effort. Note that this chapter will not discuss workflow, tools, or the interface in detail. Rather, it will provide a show-and-tell method of learning that quickly walks you through the necessary steps to gain a keen understanding of the modo 301/302 process. And with that, you'll be able to work in the program and get results right away. The idea is not to have you read 30 or 40 pages only to find that you created a ball, moved and rotated it, and copied it to three layers. I know you're smarter than that!

Built around a unique architecture, modo allows the user to create a completely custom interface. While colors and fonts remain primarily the same, modo's strength comes from the ability to rearrange panels and tool palettes in any way possible. Most 3D programs have some ability to customize the interface. There are others that only allow you to add a button or change a color. But Luxology's modo is an entirely different breed.

With modo, you have the flexibility of quickly duplicating panels or starting with a completely blank interface and building your own from the ground up. What's more is that modo is capable of displaying lists of information in several different formats, depending on the space available. When you shrink or expand a panel, modo will switch the list format on the fly to the one that best fits the space available.

This chapter will introduce you to the modo 301/302 interface and run through a few different ways in which the program can not only be configured but used. You'll learn how to create your own custom interfaces and save them.

Understanding the Basics

By this point, you most likely have worked with modo a bit. Perhaps you've simply clicked through the interface and tried a few tutorials from the resources provided from Luxology when you purchased the software. In any case, this chapter will start you off assuming you've not used the program at all and ramp up from there.

When you start up modo 301/302, you're presented with a default interface, as shown in Figure 1.1.

To begin understanding the interface, you first need to understand viewports.

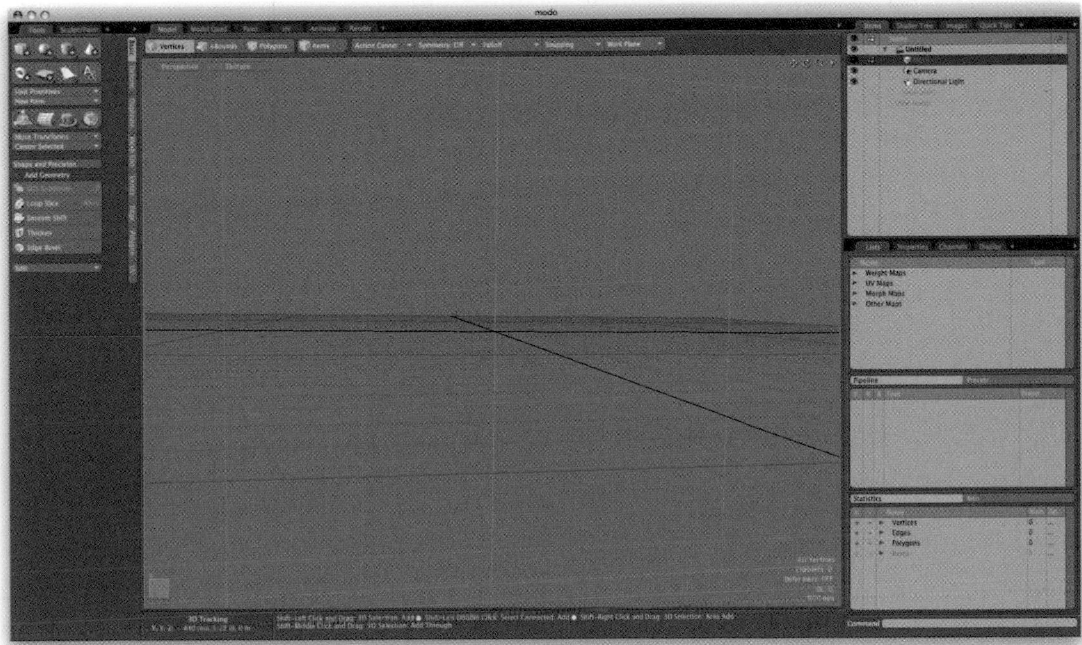

Figure 1.1 The default modo 301/302 interface is simple, yet powerful. Here on Mac OSX, the interface looks no different than its Windows counterpart.

Viewports

Viewports are literally your window to the world when it comes to modo. You can have as many as you like, and you are not limited to where you place them. A viewport can contain a model view, such as the large main work area you see in Figure 1.1. Or a viewport can contain lists for objects, textures, or images. Everything in modo's interface is built within a viewport.

3D Model View

3D workspaces, toolbars, Mesh lists—what does it all mean? Well if you consider that at first you have a viewport, you can understand that you have the ability to add whatever view you want to that viewport. Take for example the main workspace in the default view shown in Figure 1.2. This is a viewport with a 3D Model view applied. There are viewport position, rotation, and zoom controls automatically added to the top-right corner, and a 3D orientation icon is automatically added to the bottom-left corner.

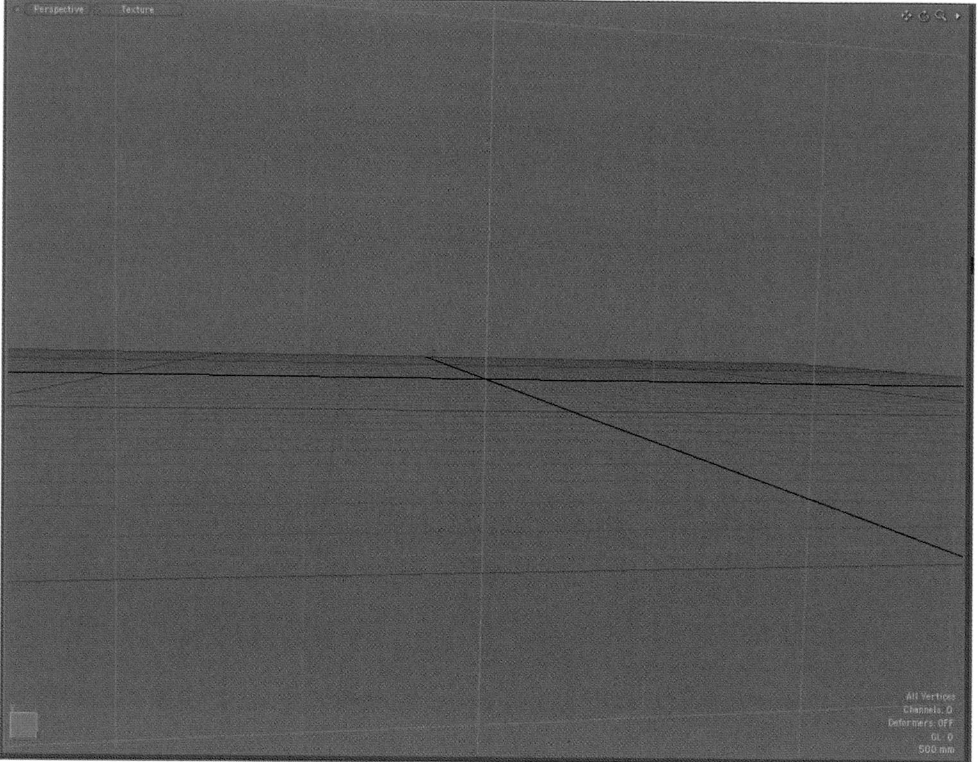

Figure 1.2
A typical viewport in modo, set to a 3D Model view.

Viewports contain all of the functions available to you in modo 301/302. But the primary use for a viewport is a 3D Model view. This is where you create your models and scenes.

- **The 3D orientation** icon that appears in a 3D Model view is your visual compass to axis control in modo. Here you can determine which axis is primary, X, Y, or Z—that is, it will help you model in one large viewport using modo's ingenious Work Plane. For example, in most 3D applications, if you want to build a box that is flat on the ground, you'd work in a top, or Y-axis, view. In modo, you can do that, but a faster way to work is to rotate your view so that the 3D orientation icon in the bottom left of the viewport is highlighted to Y axis. When you draw out a flat box, it will be lying flat on the X and Z axes. This might sound confusing, but as soon as you start working with the tools in Chapter 3, it will make perfect sense. And you'll wonder how you got along without it!
- **The Viewport Style** buttons appear at the top left of the 3D Model view. There are two buttons, and if you click either, you'll be presented with viewport style choices. The first button on the left currently reads Perspective (see Figure 1.3), informing you that you're working in a Perspective view. This is the Viewport Type

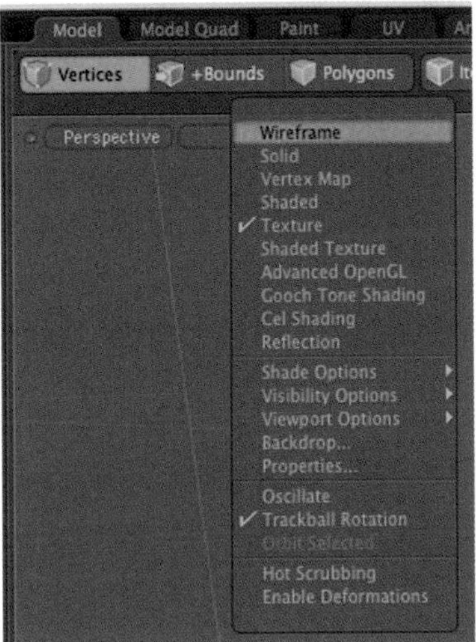

Figure 1.3
You can access all of the viewport's various options by clicking, then selecting from the top left of the viewport.

list. With a Perspective view, you can rotate around the entire 3D scene and also have control of your tools on all axes. The second button just to the right sets your viewport style. You can view your work as wireframes, solid objects, textured, or even cell shaded for a cartoon like look. Note that all of the viewport visibility options are available from this menu as well.

There are quite a few viewport styles to choose from, and each will be appropriate at some point in your modo career, many of which you'll use through the tutorials in this book. Figure 1.3 shows the choices available for both viewport style buttons at the top left of the 3D Model view.

A 3D Model view also has viewport style controls. The first list on the left chooses your viewport type, while the list on the right determines your viewport style, such as wireframe or shaded.

The grids you see in the 3D Model view are your references for modeling, rotating, moving, and more. There are two grids in view: The darker grid is horizontal (along the X,Y axis) extending to the horizon, and the lighter grid is the work plane, which changes positions depending on how the view is rotated. You'll see how these are used in Chapter 2.

Tool Viewports

A viewport is nothing more than a blank panel—sort of a canvas that you can assign work elements to. At the top left of the modo default interface, you'll see a panel labeled Tools, as shown in Figure 1.4. This viewport is currently set to a tabbed viewport with a modo Tools tab and a Sculpt/Paint tab.

The tab to the right of the Tools tab is labeled Sculpt/Paint. (We'll get to that a bit later on.) But perhaps for some reason you don't want a viewport to be a modo Tools tab. No problem! Let's say you want to change the modo Tools tab to a Preferences Editor. Look to the very top-right corner of the desired viewport, as Figure 1.5 shows you. There's a little right-facing triangle. Click it, and as you can see in Figure 1.6, there is a slew of things you can change this panel into. If you go down the list and select Editor, then Preferences Editor, you'll see the viewport change over, as in Figure 1.7.

As you can see, it's pretty easy to change viewports to anything you like. You can even make this small modo Tools tab into an additional 3D Model view, as you see in the main window of the interface. Set the interface back to its default by going to the File menu and choosing Reset. Conversely, you can also do this by simply going to the Layout menu at the very top of the interface, then to Layouts, and choose 301/302 Default Layout.

Figure 1.4 One of the main work areas within modo is the Tools viewport.

Figure 1.5 To change a viewport, click the right-facing triangle in the upper-right corner of the desired viewport.

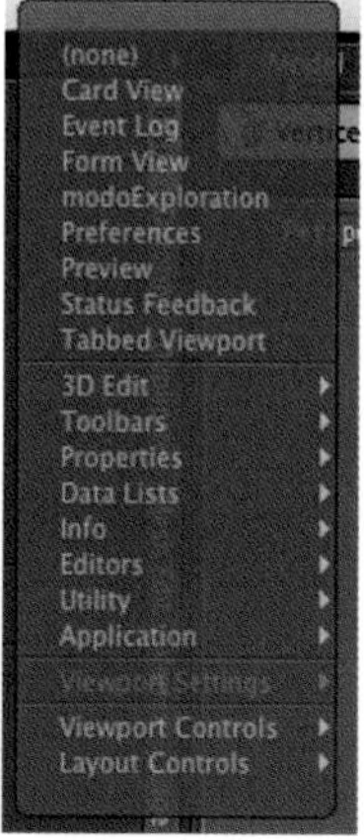

Figure 1.6 When you click the triangle, you see a huge list of options for your viewport.

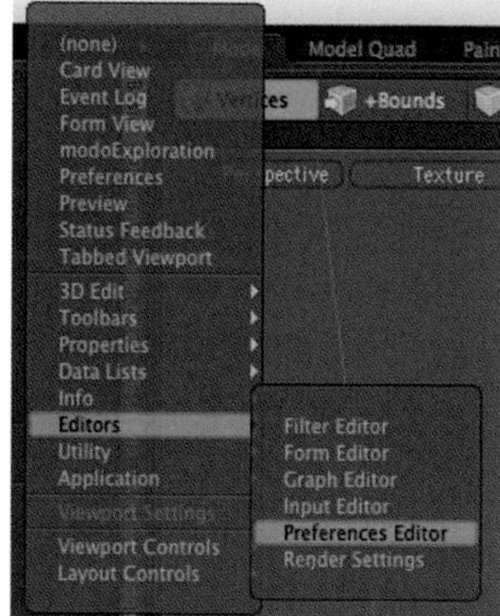

Figure 1.7 Choosing one of these options, such as Editor, then Preferences Editor, changes the viewport.

Splitting a Viewport

Perhaps you want to have a copy of a viewport, or perhaps you'd like to have two sets of the Mesh list, found on the right side of the interface. You can either add a viewport and change it to what you like or simply split the existing viewport. Try this out: In the main view of the interface, you'll see the large 3D Model view, as shown earlier in Figure 1.2. This is the scene area where you'll build your models. Hold the Ctrl key on your keyboard, and click the tiny dot in the top left of the viewport, also known as a *thumb*, as shown in Figure 1.8.

As soon as you Ctrl-click the thumb in a downward motion, you'll split the viewport vertically. Ctrl-click the thumb to the left or right, and you split the viewport horizontally., Or right click and choose Copy, and you'll automatically get an instant floating copy of the panel. Figure 1.9 shows the duplicate placed just to the right of the original.

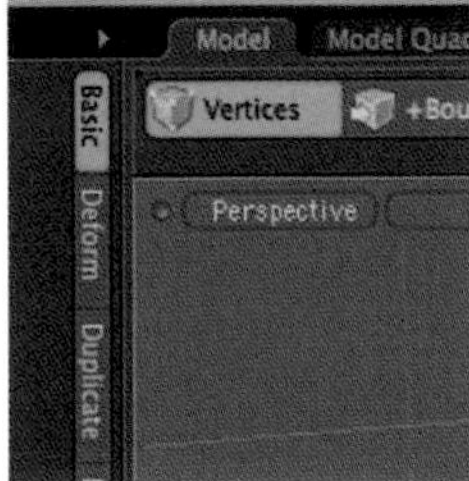

Figure 1.8 The little dot at the top left of the viewport is pretty powerful.

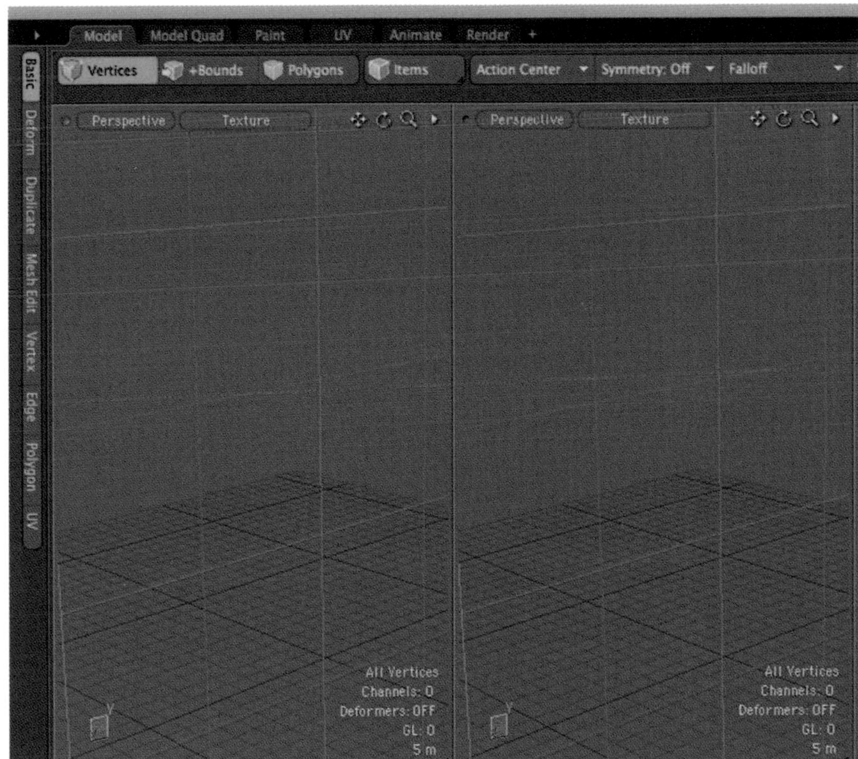

Figure 1.9 Holding the Ctrl key and clicking downward on the tiny dot (thumb) in the upper-left corner of the viewport splits it vertically.

Note

Holding the Ctrl key and then clicking with a downward swipe on the dot in the upper-left corner places the duplicated viewport below the original rather than to the right.

Note

You cannot undo a viewport copy with a traditional Ctrl-Z or Command-Z function. Instead, right-click on the tiny dot in the upper-left corner and choose Delete.

Once this copy is made, you can click the right triangle in the upper-right corner, as already mentioned, and change the viewport to anything you like, perhaps a list of images you'll use for texturing objects. This is a super fast way of looking at your model through a different camera. Say you're looking at your model in Perspective view and you want to see a top view at the same time. Do a horizontal swipe Ctrl-click to split the viewport, then change the camera to a top view using the viewport menu mentioned earlier.

Now, one more thing to know about the tiny dot in the top left of the viewports. Well, two things really! First, right-click on this dot, and you'll see a list of options, as shown in Figure 1.10.

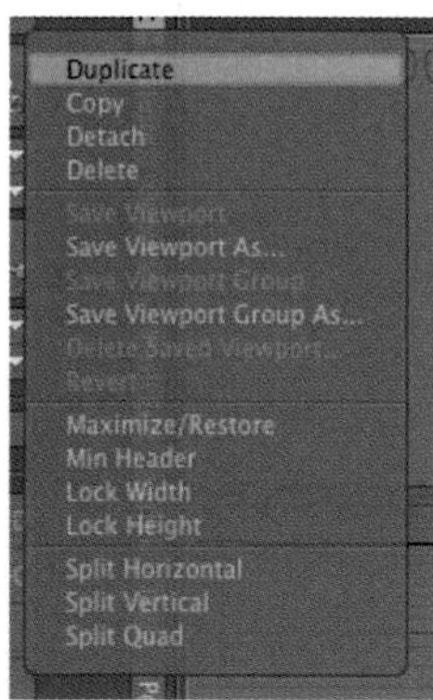

Figure 1.10 Right-click on the tiny dot in the upper-left corner of the viewport, and you'll find a list of options.

Look closely at the list. You'll see that you can duplicate, copy, detach, or even delete a viewport. What's more, you can save the viewport, too, which is pretty cool. Take some time and click these different options to see the results. Remember, you can always go back to the original viewport by returning to the 301/302 default layout from the Layout menu at the top of the interface.

Tip

If you happen to change to a viewport style that eliminates the dot in the upper-left corner, don't think that you'll be unable to access the options. You can still right-click to get to the options; however, you'll have to right-click directly on the upper-left corner of the viewport. The trick is to move your mouse to the upper edge of the viewport and, when you see an orange rim highlight the viewport, you're good to go! Right-click at that point and access the options.

Tabbed Viewports

Take a close look at the top right of the modo interface. Assuming your modo interface is set to a 301/302 default layout, you should see an orange highlighted tab named Items. To the right of it is Shader Tree, and next to that is Images, then Quick Tips (see Figure 1.11). These headings are called tabbed viewports.

You can have as many tabbed viewports as you like. For example, Figure 1.11 shows two default tabbed viewports that allow you to change your viewport from an Items tab to Shader Tree and more, with the click of the mouse. The benefit of tabbed viewports is that you don't need to have multiple viewports open to access tools. For example, you're not always going to be using render settings, so why have the viewport taking up valuable screen real estate? Figure 1.12 shows the default tabbed viewports in the middle right of the interface. Here, you can see the Lists tab, along with Properties, Channels, and Display.

As you might have guessed, clicking any one of these tabbed viewports changes the viewport they're assigned to. But by using a tabbed view here, you have access to areas whenever you need them, such as the Lists view; however, if it's not an area you need often, you're not wasting precious screen real estate.

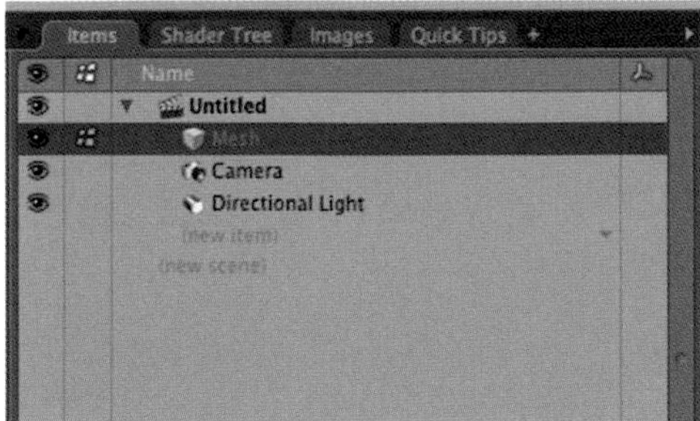

Figure 1.11 Tabbed viewports are noticeable in the 301/302 default layout, such as those at the top right of the interface for Items, Shader Tree, and more.

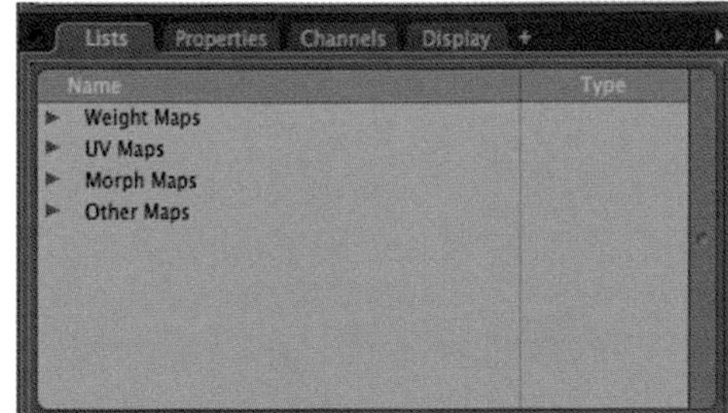

Figure 1.12 The default tabbed viewports at the right of the interface show four tabbed areas: Lists, Properties, Channels, and Display.

Custom Layouts

Now that you are somewhat familiar with the viewport panels in modo 301/302, you should also be aware of how to arrange them. This section will guide you through rearranging the interface; then you'll follow along with a project to build your own interface from the ground up, and learn how to save your viewport configuration.

1. Make sure you're working with a default modo 301/302 interface. Go to the Layout menu, then to Layouts, and choose 301/302 Default Layout.
2. Click the Tools tab at the top left of the modo interface, if it's not already selected.
3. Hold the Ctrl key, and click any of the primitives, such as the torus (or donut, if you're a south side cop named Dave from Chicago). What you'll see is a quick perfect ring added to the main viewport. This Ctrl-click command on primitives is a really easy way to add instant boxes, balls, discs, and so on for further modeling, or in this case, interface testing.

   Holding modifier keys, like Shift or Ctrl, gives you alternative icons for different variations of the command or tool.
4. With the torus in the viewport, press the a key. The object fits to view, as shown in Figure 1.13.

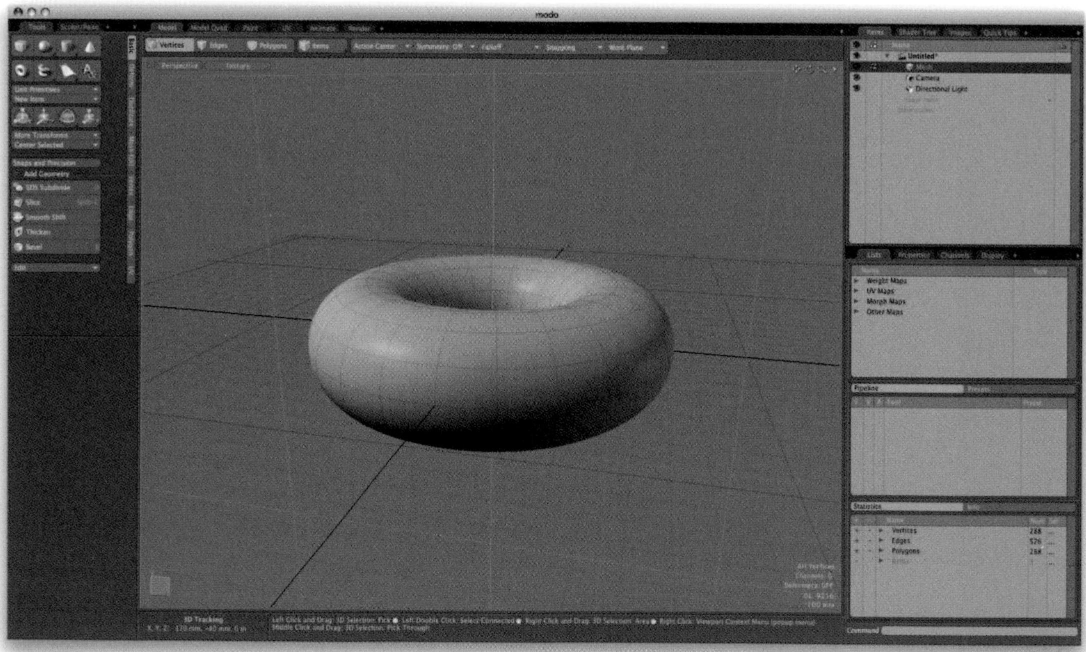

Figure 1.13 Holding the Ctrl key and then clicking on a primitive shape instantly creates an object in the 3D Model viewport. Pressing the a (lowercase) key fits that object to view.

Note

Unless otherwise told, all keyboard equivalents should be done in lowercase.

5. Now that there is some geometry in the 3D Model viewport, click the right-facing triangle at the top-right corner of the 3D Model viewport, as shown in Figure 1.14.

Figure 1.14 Click the right-facing arrow in the upper-right corner of the 3D Model viewport to change the viewport layout.

6. When you click the triangle, you'll see a long list of viewport options. Here, you can change a viewport to a Tool Properties panel, or an Input Editor—whatever you like. And this triangle lives in the upper-right corner of all viewports, so you can change them just as easily. For now, in the list that appears, choose the Render Tri setting, as shown in Figure 1.15.

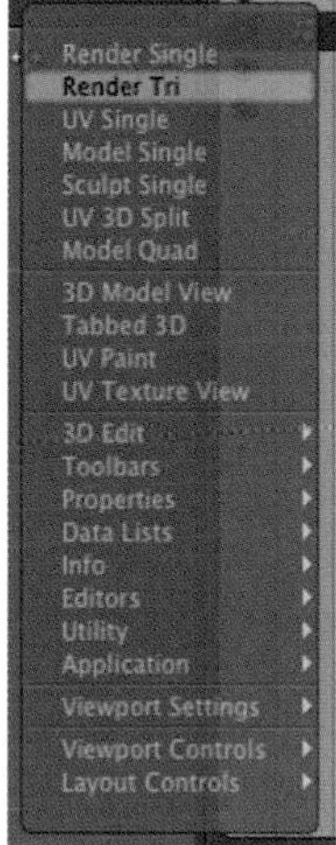

Figure 1.15 Clicking the right-facing triangle in the upper-right corner of a viewport offers a range of viewport choices, such as the Render Tri option.

When you click the Render Tri viewport option, your current 3D Model viewport changes to three views. A Preview viewport at the top left showing a real-time render, a Camera view at the top right, and a Perspective view in the larger centered window. Figure 1.16 shows the change.

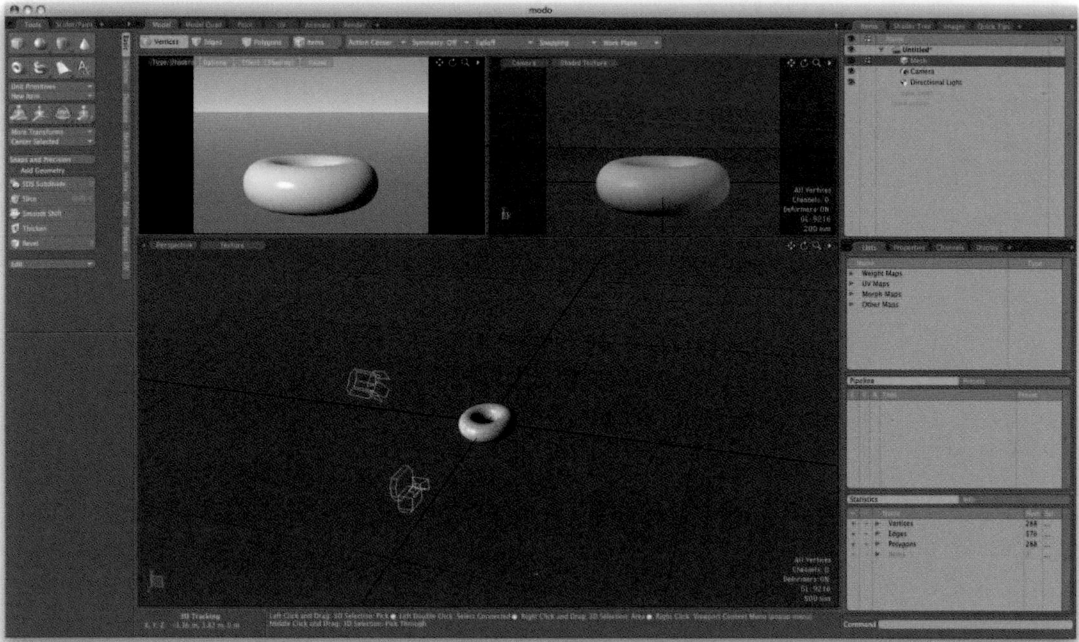

Figure 1.16 The Render Tri viewport setting changes your current viewport (in this case the 3D Model view) to a Preview (render), Camera, and Perspective view all in one.

> **Tip**
>
> If your render preview doesn't appear right away, click and drag the Zoom, Rotate, or Move tool in the upper-right corner of the Camera view. You can also click the pause and then reset in the top of the Preview window.

> **Tip**
>
> If you don't see the camera and light icons in the Perspective view, as shown in Figure 1.17, press the letter o (not zero) key on your keyboard to open the viewport options, then click the Visibility tab on the right side of the panel. There, you'll see the options to turn on Show Lights and Show Cameras, among other things. If you move the mouse off the panel, it will automatically close. Just press o again to reopen. With that said, you can also find these option from the viewport type list mentioned earlier.

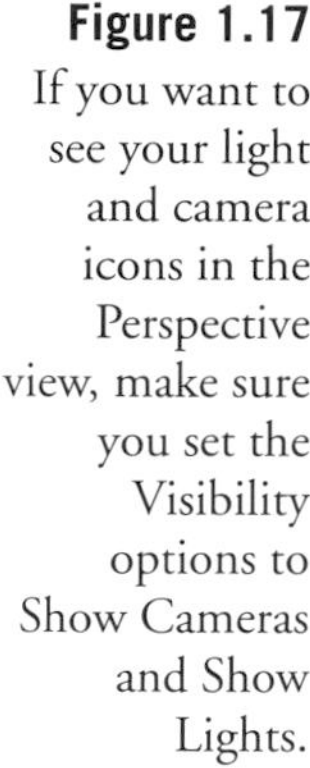

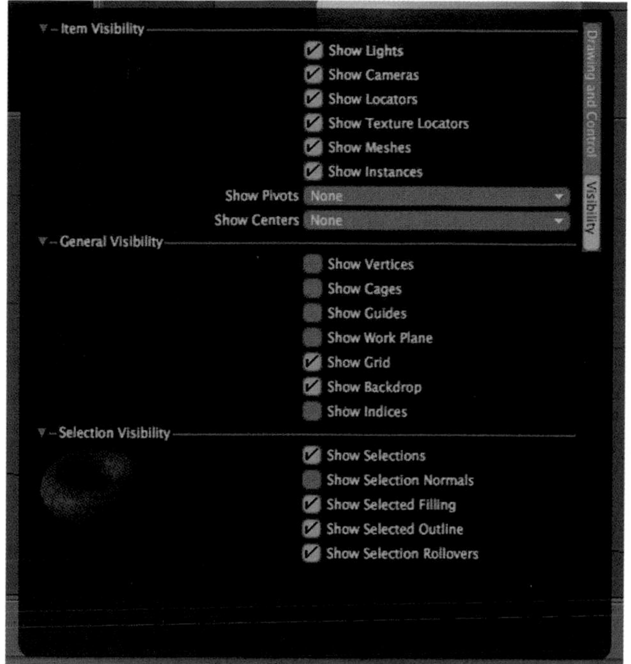

Figure 1.17
If you want to see your light and camera icons in the Perspective view, make sure you set the Visibility options to Show Cameras and Show Lights.

The layout you've created so far is good, but it could be better. And in most realistic working conditions, you'll want to have access to more of modo's features.

1. Click the Items tab at the top right of the modo interface, and drag it over to the left, between the main viewport and the current tabbed viewports. You'll see an orange line appear between the viewport panels when you're locked in, as shown in Figure 1.18. Note that you may need to drag the edge back a little to the right after you let go of the mouse.
2. When you see the orange line, let go of the mouse and your viewport will appear in its new location. Figure 1.19 shows the relocated viewport.

If you look carefully at the top of the original tabbed viewport, you'll notice that the other tabbed viewports remain (Shader Tree, Images, and Quick Tips). But let's say you want the properties for selected items to appear beneath the Items tab? You can easily change this as well.

1. Click on the Properties tab at the center right of the interface.
2. Then, click and hold the mouse on the Properties tab and drag it underneath the newly positioned Item List (or anywhere else you like). You'll see that familiar orange line appear, indicating where your new viewport will be positioned. Release the mouse and voilà! Your Properties panel is now its own viewport outside of the tabbed viewports. Clicking an item in the Item List now shows its properties directly below (see Figure 1.20).

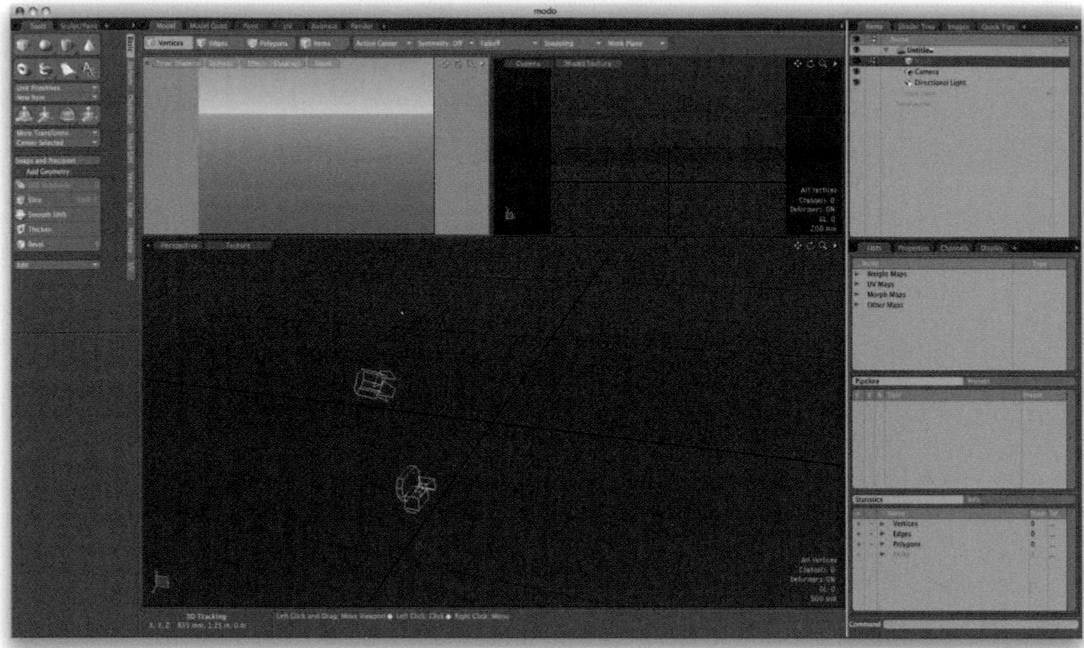

Figure 1.18 Click and drag the Items tab off of the existing tabbed viewports.

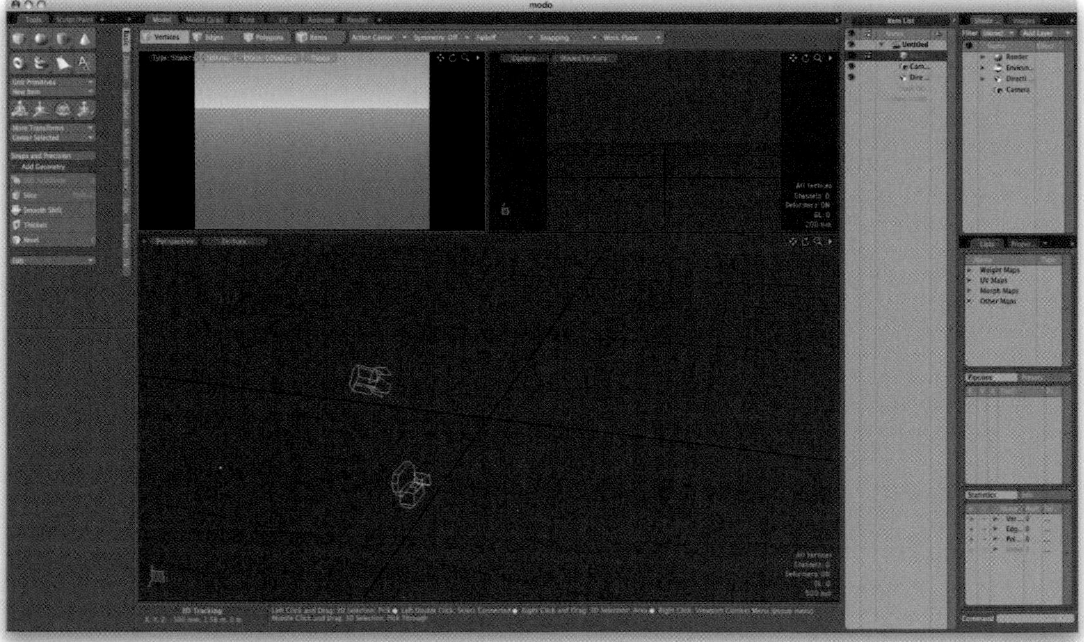

Figure 1.19 An orange line appears, identifying where you're placing the panel.

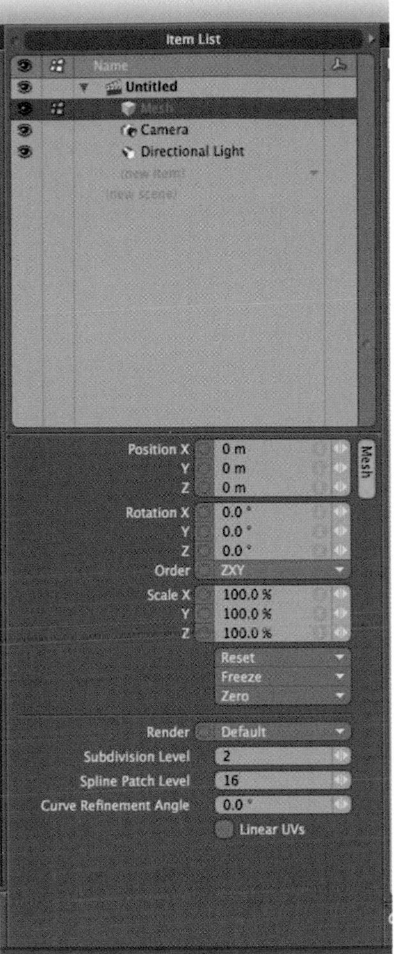

Figure 1.20 Sometimes you just want to have the viewports and tabs set to how you work, and modo makes it easy for you to do as shown here.

3. Finally, you can click and drag on the edge of a viewport to size it within the interface. Figure 1.21 shows the moved viewport.

> **Tip**
>
> So what if you want to make a nontabbed viewport list a tabbed viewport? Click that right-facing triangle at the top right of the panel, and go down to the Applications category, then choose Tabbed Viewport.

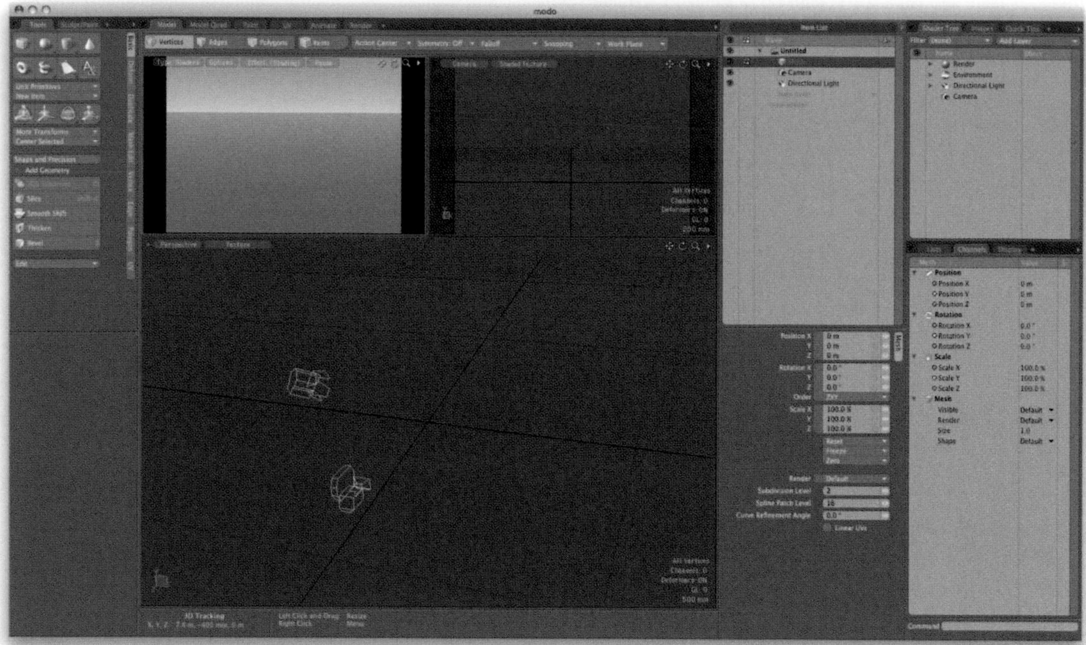

Figure 1.21 You can click and drag the Properties viewport into the Item List.

Oh no! You wanted to keep that Item List as part of the tabbed viewport after all? Perhaps your client has called and suddenly your work has changed. The cool interface you just set up isn't going to work for you, and you need to change it. Not to worry.

1. Back over at the Lists, Channels, Display viewport, click on the plus sign to the right of the tabbed listings, as shown in Figure 1.22. A list of options will appear.

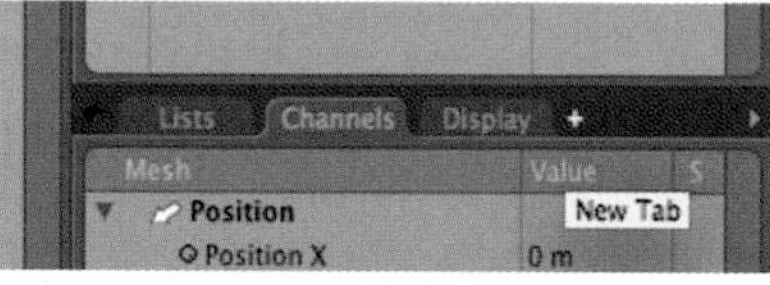

Figure 1.22 When you move the mouse over the plus sign of a tabbed viewport, you'll see a New Tab option appear.

2. Choose Properties, and then Item Properties, as shown in Figure 1.23.

Tip

Remember that when you add tabs to a viewport, you might need a bigger viewport. To adjust the size of a viewport, simply click and drag on any edge of the viewport. The panels will shift around accordingly.

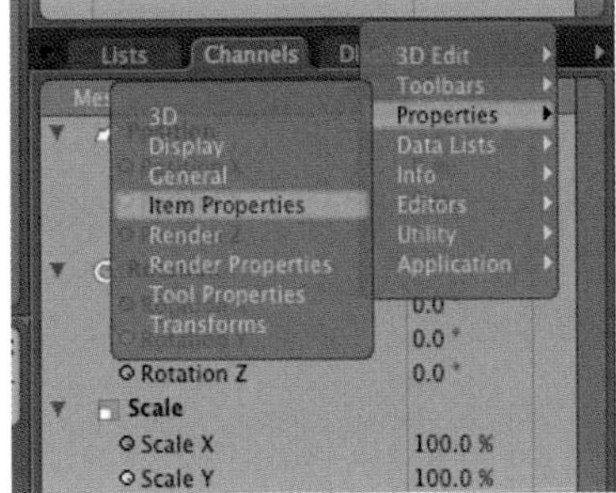

Figure 1.23
To add another tab to a tabbed viewport, just click the plus sign at the top right of the column and choose what you like.

You've invested some time getting your interface to look the way you want. Now that your new layout is in place, how about saving it? The last thing you'd want is to have to redo it all. So read on to learn about saving the layout.

1. Go up to the Layout menu and choose Save As, shown in Figure 1.24.

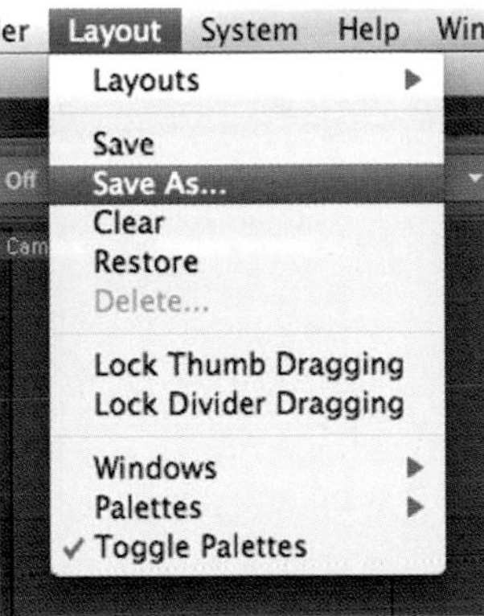

Figure 1.24
To save your new layout, click the Layout menu and choose Save As.

2. In the Save Layout dialog box that appears, enter a name such as My Cool Layout and click OK, as shown in Figure 1.25.

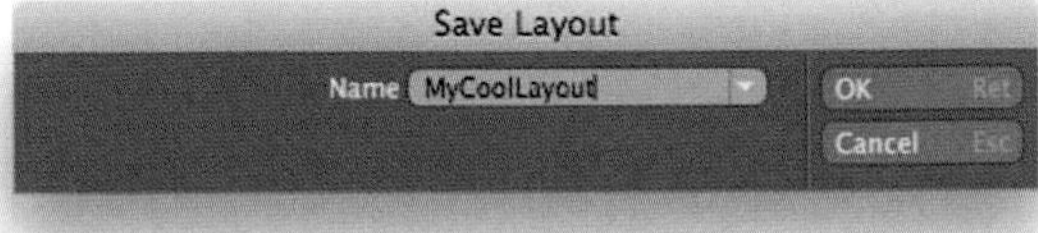

Figure 1.25
Save your new custom layout with a unique name.

Any time you want to recall this layout, go to the Layout menu, then to Layouts, and choose My Cool Layout, as shown in Figure 1.26.

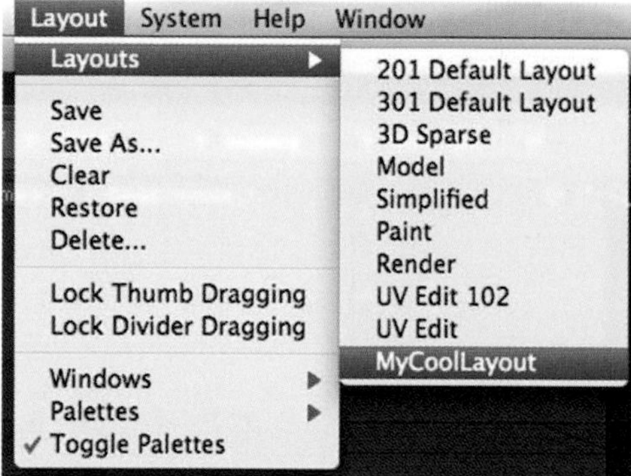

Figure 1.26
Any time you wish to recall the layout you've created, just choose it from the Layout menu, or go back to the 301/302 default layout.

Tip

Try choosing other layouts that the Luxology team has provided for you. You can always go back to the 301/302 default 301/302layout by selecting it from the Layout menu. However, if you make a change to the default layout, modo remembers. Here's the trick: Select the 301/302 Default Layout option twice! That's right, select it once, then select it again. The layout will go back to the default settings before you modified them.

As you can see, configuring viewports is not that difficult. It's actually kind of fun rearranging panels and tools to fit your own workflow, which is especially good for those cool extra wide monitors. But what if this entire setup is just not for you? Maybe you're sort of a roll-your-own type of person? No problem. Read on to configure your own custom interface. Well, it won't be your custom interface, it'll actually be mine—but the next section will show you how to create a modo interface from the ground up.

Roll Your Own Interface

Now let's say you're the type of person who doesn't like to order what's on the menu—you want the special. You're a person who takes the road less traveled, or who simply wants things your own way. Luxology has designed modo so you can configure it how you like. Perhaps you have a smaller workspace and only use a few modeling tools? No problem. Or maybe you're lucky enough to be working on a new 30-inch LCD display? modo can accommodate.

1. Start up modo and don't worry about what Layout you're currently using. From the Layout menu at the top of the interface, select Clear, as shown in Figure 1.27. Selecting Clear from the Layout drop down menu clears your interface, obviously! But now you have a blank slate to work with. Figure 1.28 shows the empty workspace.

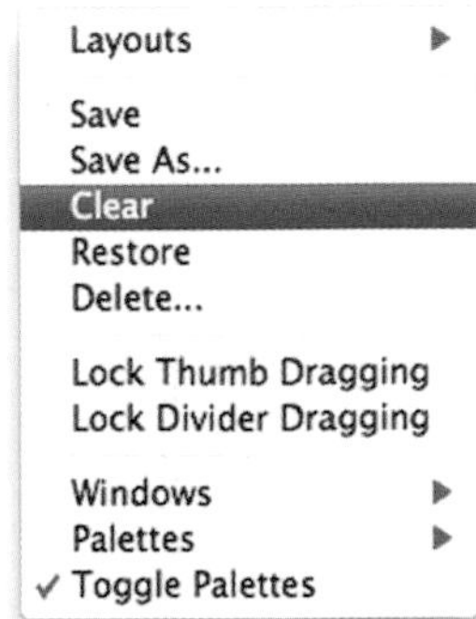

Figure 1.27 Select Clear from the Layout menu.

Figure 1.28 Choosing Clear from the Layout menu does what it says—it clears your interface!

2. When you build your own interface, you need to take into consideration what tools you need most. And remember, you can make as many interface options as you like, such as a power modeling interface with only your key modeling tools, or a power render interface with just a few render buttons and an item Preview window, or one just for animation and sculpting. It's up to you. For now, you can begin by first adding a new window from the Layout menu, as shown in Figure 1.29. You'll be presented with a blank viewport, as shown in Figure 1.30.

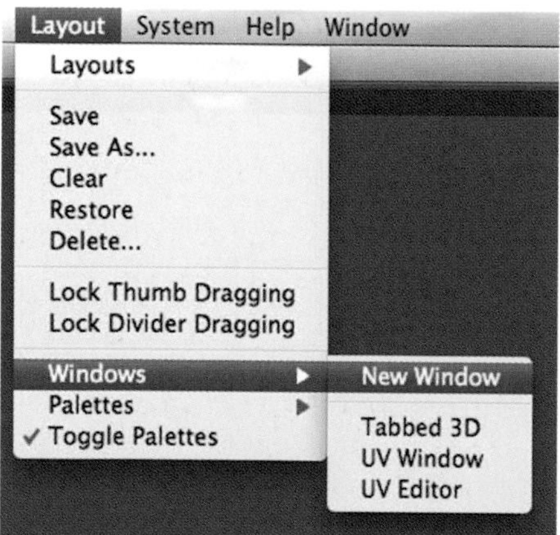

Figure 1.29 To begin making your own interface, select Windows, New Window from the Layout menu.

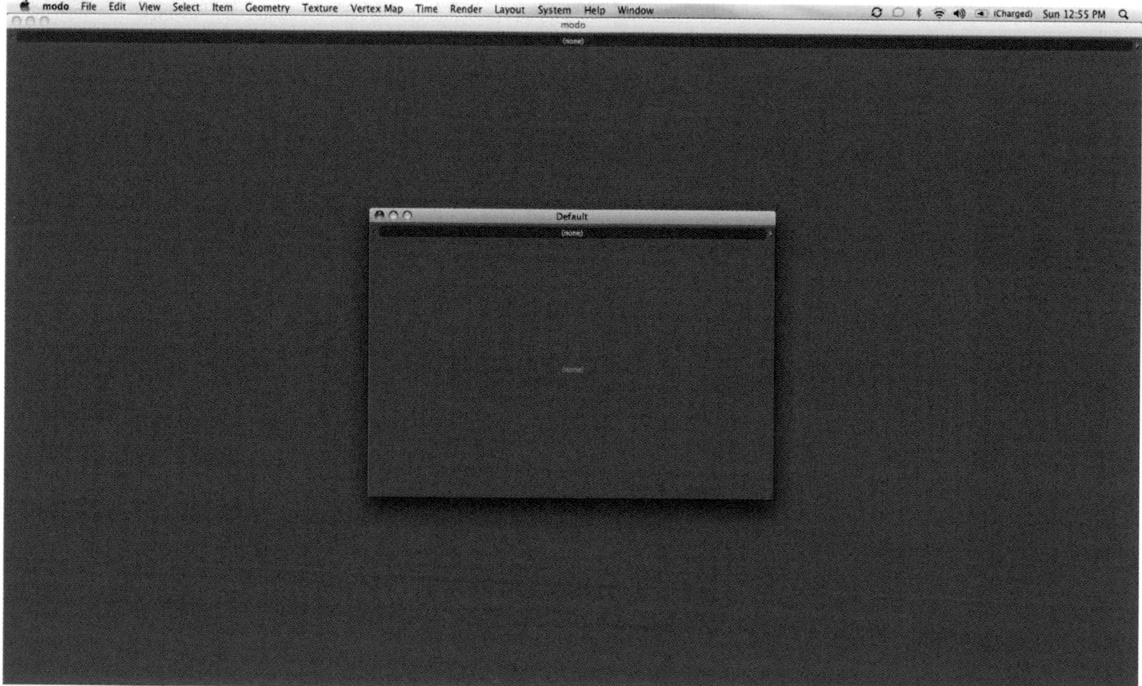

Figure 1.30 Adding a new window from the Layout menu presents you with a blank viewport.

> **Tip**
>
> In the Layout menu, you'll also see a New Palette option (in the Palettes submenu). The only difference between a palette and a window is that palettes can be instantly hidden by pressing the grave accent (`) key, directly to the left of the number 1 key at the top of your keyboard. It shares the tilde (~) key.

3. One of the first things you usually do in modo is build a basic primitive shape or curve. So click the right-facing triangle in the top right of the empty viewport, and choose Toolbars, then modo Tools, as shown in Figure 1.31. Figure 1.32 shows how the panel looks once the modo Tools are added.
4. Now that you have a viewport to work with, you can start positioning it within your interface. Move the mouse to the tiny dot in the upper-left corner of the new modo Tools viewport. You'll see an orange frame appear around the viewport. Click and drag the viewport up to the very left of the modo main interface, until you see an orange line appear around the viewport, as shown in Figure 1.33.
5. To set the viewport position in place, let go of the mouse. The modo Tools viewport will be placed into the interface, as shown in Figure 1.34.

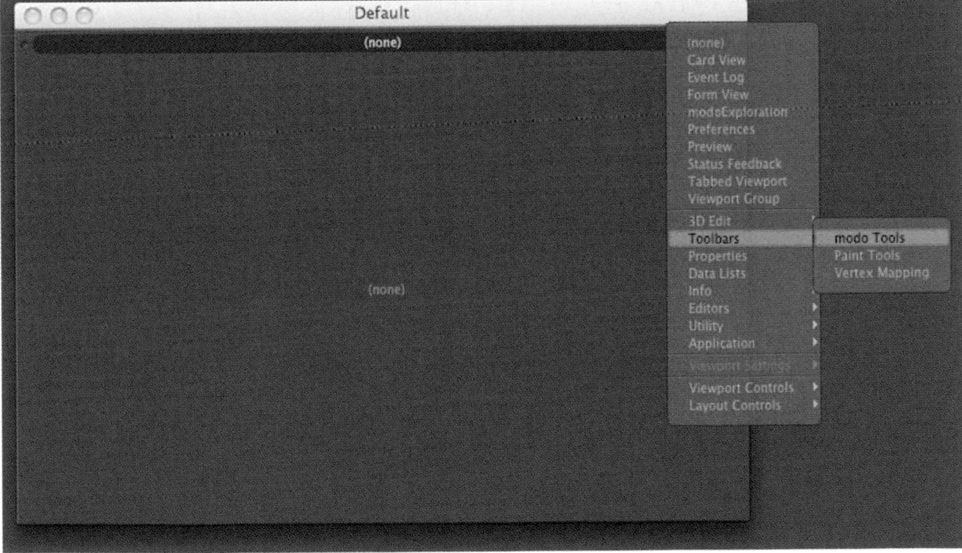

Figure 1.31 To begin creating your own interface, add a modo Tools viewport.

Figure 1.32
Now the modo Tools viewport has to be configured into the interface.

Figure 1.33
Moving the modo Tools viewport to the left of the interface is easy. Just look for the orange line to appear around the new panel, then click and drag for placement.

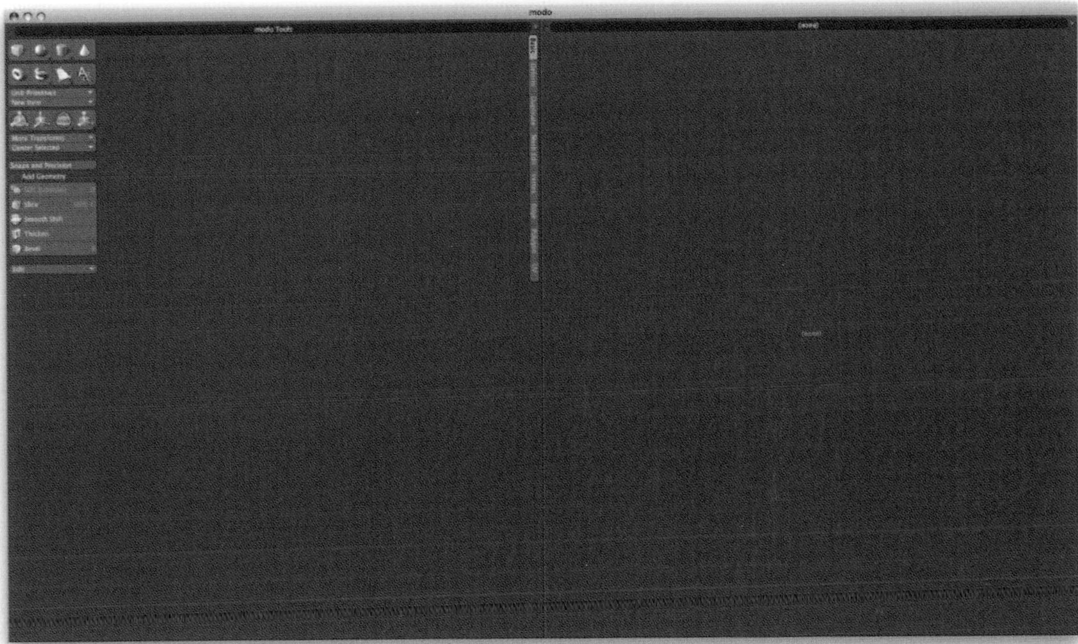

Figure 1.34 Moving the modo Tools viewport to the left of the interface and letting go of the mouse positions the viewport into the interface.

6. Click in the main interface, then move the mouse to the right edge of the modo Tools viewport. Your mouse will change to a left and right arrow icon. Click and drag to decrease the width of the modo Tools viewport.
7. Because the modo interface currently has no other viewports, you only will have the option to move the viewport to the top, left, bottom, or right side of the interface. You'll see that the viewport you added in step 2 still exists, floating on top of the modo interface. Click the right-facing triangle at the upper right of the floating viewport, and choose Properties, then Tool Properties, as in Figure 1.35. It will be blank at this point because no tools are selected. When you select a tool, such as the Move tool (press w on the keyboard), the Tool Properties viewport will become active.

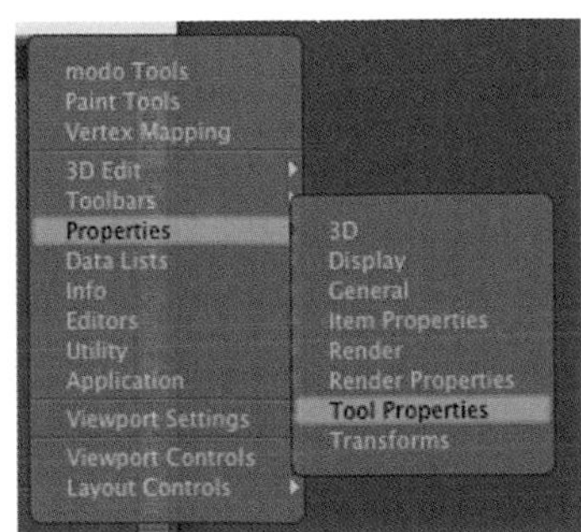

Figure 1.35 Your original viewport still remains floating outside of the main interface, so change this to a Tool Properties viewport.

8. As you did in steps 4 and 5, click and drag the added viewport to a position within the interface. Remember not to let go of the left mouse button until you see that familiar orange line appear. This will help you align the viewport. Size the panels by dragging the edge of each. Figure 1.36 shows the Tool Properties viewport positioned to the right of the modo Tools viewport.

> **Note**
>
> The Tool Properties panel will appear blank until you actually turn on a tool.

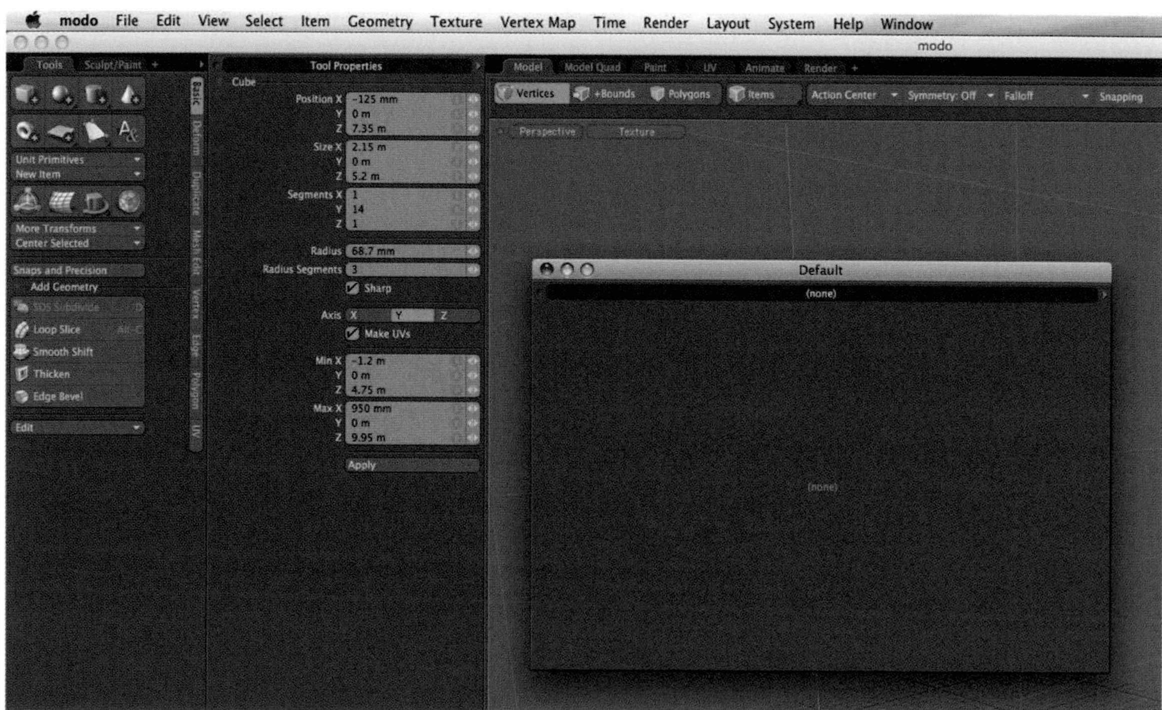

Figure 1.36 The Tool Properties viewport is positioned within the interface next to, rather than under, the modo Tools viewport.

9. Now that you have a few viewports in place, close the added viewport that's still floating.

10. In Figure 1.36, you can see that the modo Tools and Tool Properties viewports are placed on the left side of the interface. On the right side is a blank viewport. Click the right-facing triangle at the top right of this blank viewport and choose 3D Edit, then 3D Model view, as shown in Figure 1.37.

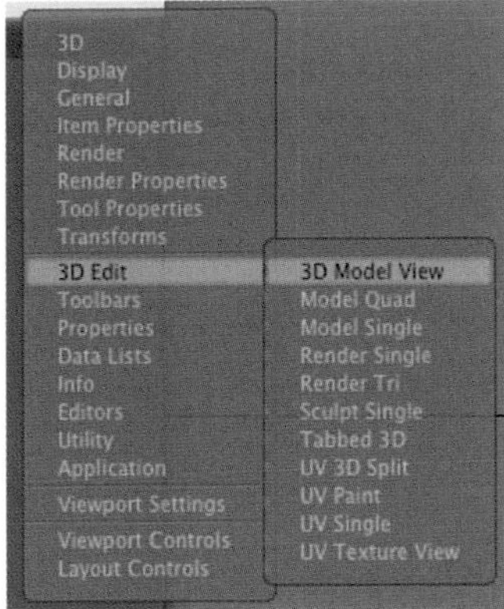

Figure 1.37 You can choose to add a 3D Model view to the large viewport within the interface.

11. Choosing 3D Model view converts this large blank viewport into a 3D Model view. You can also change the viewport style here to Camera, Top, Side, and so on at the top left of the panel. It currently defaults to Perspective view with a Shaded view type. The viewport Move, Rotate, and Zoom controls are automatically loaded with this particular viewport at the top right. Figure 1.38 shows the addition.

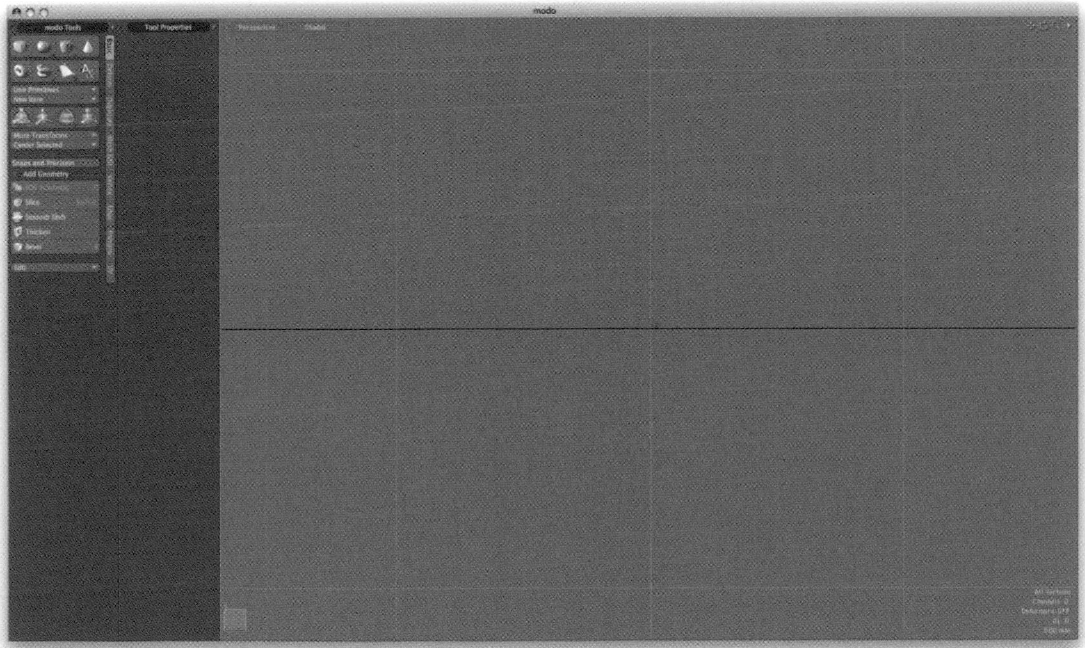

Figure 1.38 Changing the large blank viewport within the interface to a 3D Model view creates a nice large workspace for modeling.

Instead of adding a new window like you did last time, you can also Ctrl-click with a downward swipe to split the 3D viewport vertically, then change the top viewport to an Items list using the little triangle. It's sometimes faster to split viewports on the fly, then add windows and drag them in place. But it's also handy to build a new layout from the ground up. The choice is yours.

12. You could use an Item List to see what object, lights, and cameras you have in your scene. Add a new window from the Layout menu at the top of the screen. Make this new window a Mesh list by clicking the right-facing triangle at the top-right corner of the panel, choosing Data Lists, then Item List, as shown in Figure 1.39.

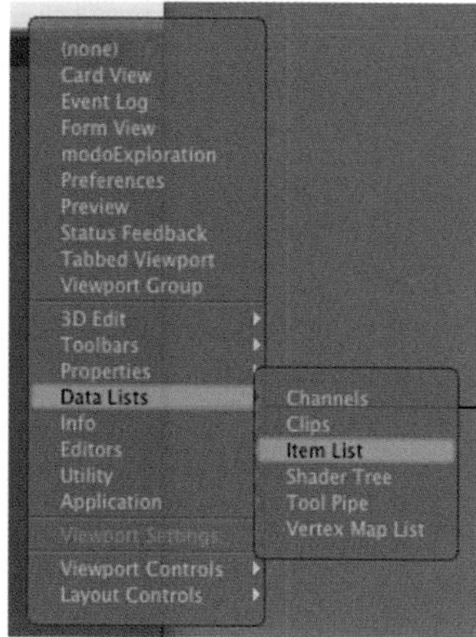

Figure 1.39
Create a new viewport and make it an Item List to see what objects, lights, and cameras are in your setup.

13. Position the new Item List interface to the left of the 3D Model view, as shown in Figure 1.40.

14. Scale the size of the Items List by clicking and dragging on the separation bar between it and the 3D Model view.

15. How about one more viewport? Add a new window from the Windows submenu of the Layout menu. Click the right-facing triangle at the top right of the new window and select Application, Preview. Then position this new Preview viewport on top of the Tool Properties panel. When you click and drag the viewport, you'll see the familiar orange bar appear; but if you carefully move the mouse, you'll see the bar jump between the left side of the Item List and the top of the Tool Properties. Size the viewports as you like by clicking and dragging between them. Figure 1.41 shows the newly positioned viewport.

16. If a smaller new window viewport is floating above your main interface, close it. Then go ahead and choose Save As from the Layout menu and give your new custom layout a name.

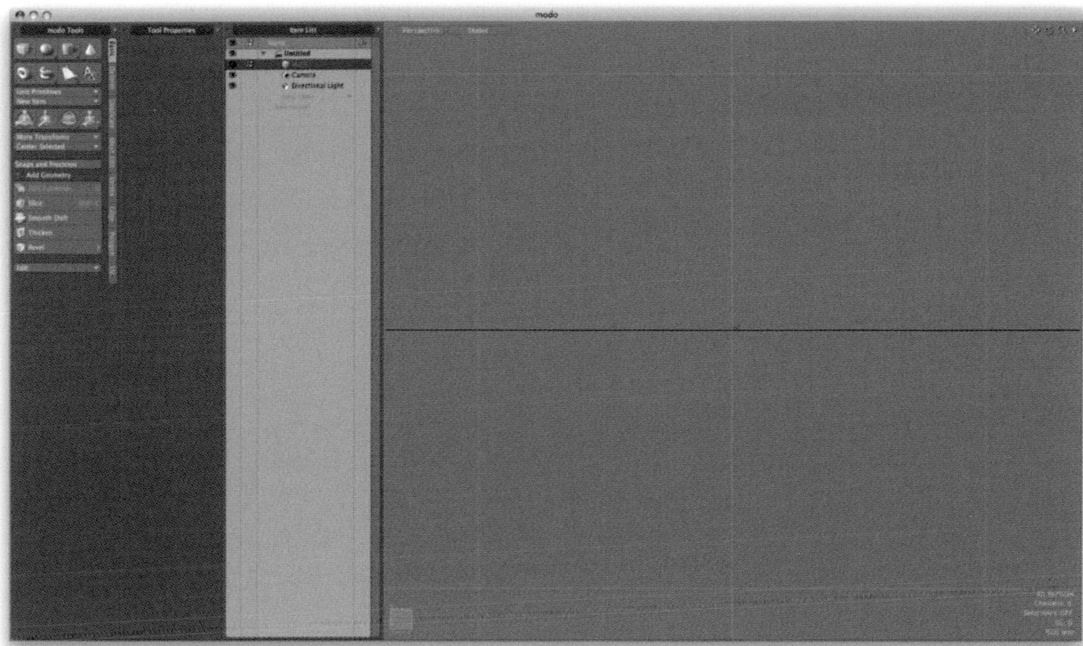

Figure 1.40 Position the new viewport into the layout by dragging it to the left of the 3D Model view.

Figure 1.41 Create one more viewport and position it to the right of the Item List.

Tip

If you'd like to share your configs with other modo users, go to the File menu and choose Config Export. To import a different configuration, choose Config Import from the File menu. You can develop different layouts and share them with co-workers, or give them out for free on the Luxology.com forums!

As you can see, creating and rearranging viewport panels in modo is pretty easy. The interface setup I've created here is not really that exciting, but you can probably do much better on your own! Remember that you can add a color picker, a Clips list, and more. And if you want to save space within a particular viewport, create a tabbed viewport. Additionally, remember that you can right-click on the little dot at the top left of a viewport to detach it, delete it, copy it, and so on.

As mentioned earlier, you can create a new palette rather than a new window. The only difference is that the palette can be instantly hidden with the ` key (one left of the number 1 key). So if you create an entirely new interface, you can have a toolbar in a viewport that floats, rather than locks to the interface. To do this, create a new palette from the Layout menu, and then add the desired tool to it. Then don't put it into the interface. When you want to hide the panel, press the ` key. It's kind of a cool way to work—you can pull up one or many viewports with the click of a button. Again, it all depends on what you like, what screen real estate you have, and so on.

You've only scratched the surface of modo 301/302's configurability, so read on to Chapter 2 to learn about the customization you can make with Form Editors, Key Editors, Pie Menus, and much more.

2

Editors, Action Centers, and Work Planes

Chapter 1 highlighted the ease of configurability with modo 301/302. But simply adding, changing, and rearranging viewports is just the tip of the iceberg when it comes to customizing your work flow. Rearranging the interface is great, no doubt, but to really get under the hood and make some modifications to the program to fit your specific likes and dislikes, you need to learn about the Input Editor and Form Editor. Additionally, there are certain Preferences you can modify to fit your needs. This chapter will cover these options. From there, you'll learn about Action Centers and the Work Plane. The next step in your modo career is to understand how modo 301/302 allows you to have complete control over your vertices, edges, and polygons.

Preferences

Preferences in most programs are simple things such as file save locations, menu bar inclusions, and so on. In modo, there's a lot more to the preferences than you might think. But this section will give you an overview of the Preferences panel and suggest when and why you should visit these controls. You can also refer to your modo 301/302 manual supplied to you from Luxology.

Take a look at Figure 2.1, which shows the Preferences panel. You can access it by going to the System menu at the top of the interface, and then selecting Preferences.

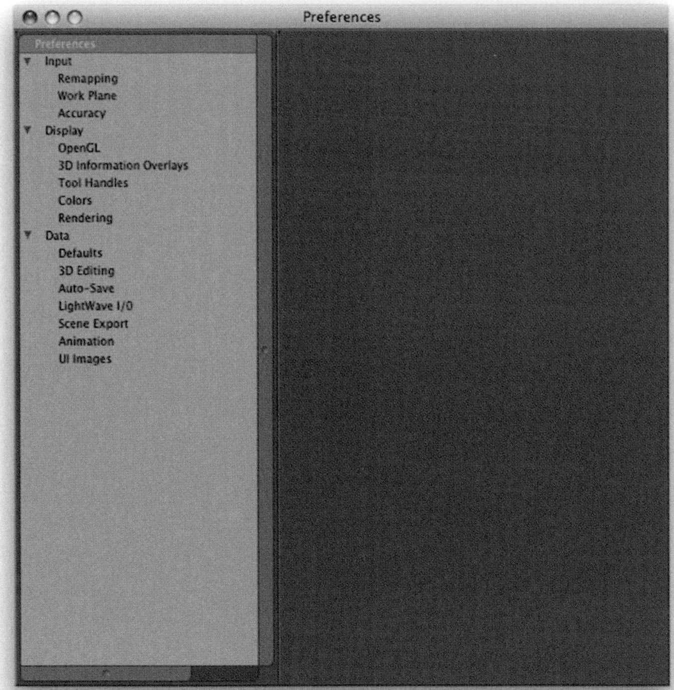

Figure 2.1
The Preferences panel upon opening, selected from the System menu at the top of the modo 301/302 interface.

Input Preferences

On the left side of the panel, you'll see three categories: Input, Display, and Data. These three main categories give you the power to change underlying preferences, which can truly change the way you work. Normally, you're going to keep most of these at their defaults; but on occasion, you may need a tweak or two, so this section will quickly give you the rundown on each category.

Remapping

Click the Remapping listing under the Input category. You'll see variables pop up on the right side of the Preferences panel, as shown in Figure 2.2.

Here you can change preferences, such as the maximum undo levels, or select the type of input device you're using, such as a mouse or tablet. Another key preference here is the Mouse Input Presets selection. Click this drop-down menu, and you'll be able to change modo's keyboard input commands to that of your favorite program, such as LightWave, Silo, Maya, and others, as shown in Figure 2.3.

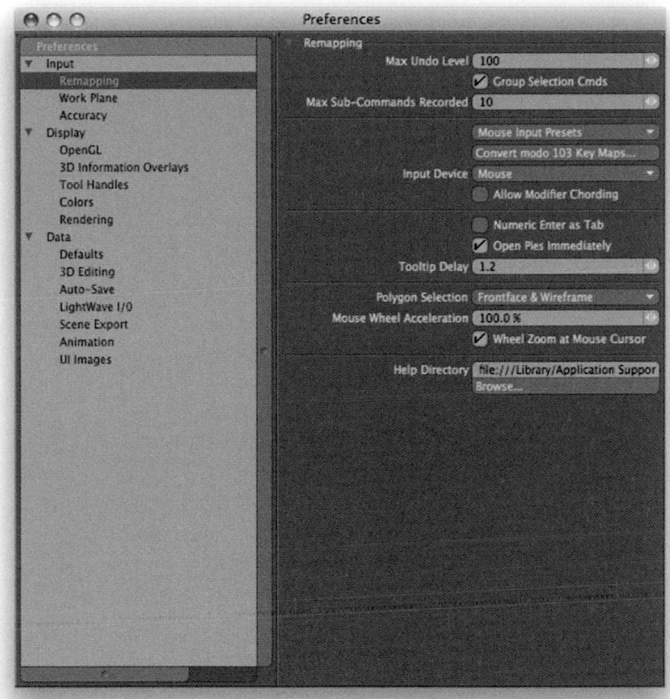

Figure 2.2
When you click the remapping listing, you'll see additional variables.

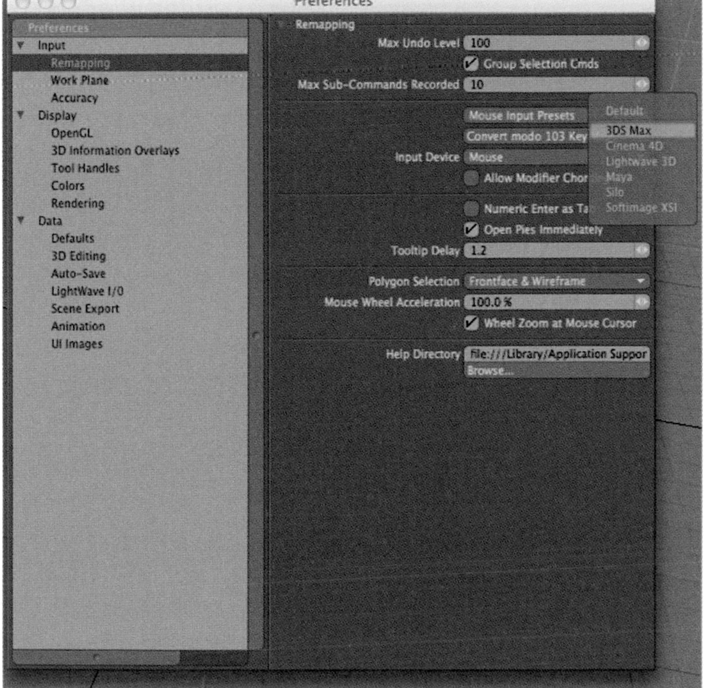

Figure 2.3
With so many options available in modo's presets, there's one initial preference you might be interested in—the Mouse Input Preset setting.

However, we're not going to be changing these input presets in the book—we're working strictly with modo's own default input presets. Why? It's often better to learn a program natively so that you fully understand the tools and workflow. Then, once you're comfortable with the program, you can configure it any way you like.

Work Plane

Another key area within the Input category in the Preferences panel is the Work Plane options. Here you can set a Preferred Plane Bias, as well as lock the plane. You're probably asking yourself, what's a work plane? Ah, good question, young grasshopper! The Work Plane is a powerful workflow enhancement that will be discussed in detail later in this chapter. But, to give you an introduction, the Work Plane in modo affects all mesh editing you do. It gives you control over the alignment of various operations, such as Align to Selection or Align to Geometry. You may have seen many modo demos either in person or as preview videos on the Internet. In those videos, you probably saw that the demo person was working in a single viewport. While most 3D modeling programs work in a quad view, and modo offers that to you, the Work Plane is what enables you to work in a large single viewport.

Accuracy

Depending on how you like to work, modo gives you the ability to work in measurements of metric, English, or SI (system internationale). Figure 2.4 shows the available options.

When you choose a specific Unit System setting, such as Metric, modo allows you to choose a default unit to work with. In the case of Figure 2.4, the unit value is set to Meters. This means that overall measurements throughout the program are based on this, such as the size of a cube, the movement of a mesh on the Y axis, and so on.

The Accuracy controls also give you Light Unit System options: Radiometric or Photometric. Photometric measurements of light are based on luminance values, whereas Radiometric measurements are based on radiance values. With Photometric values, every wavelength is measured according to how visible it is, such as a bright white box or a light bulb. Radiometric measurements are based on what is called *unweighted power*. The human eye responds better to green light than red. This means that a green source in your scene will have a higher luminous value than the same red source. The calculations modo performs when it comes to photometric or radiometric Light Unit Systems can also be understood between the difference of watts (radiometric) and lumens (photometric).

The Accuracy settings allow you to change how coordinates are rounded off when set throughout the program: None, Normal, Fine, and Fixed. Depending on what you're modeling, you might want to work with specific values. modo has many values that you

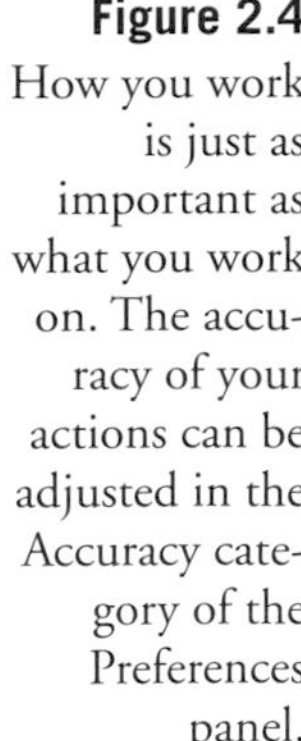

Figure 2.4
How you work is just as important as what you work on. The accuracy of your actions can be adjusted in the Accuracy category of the Preferences panel.

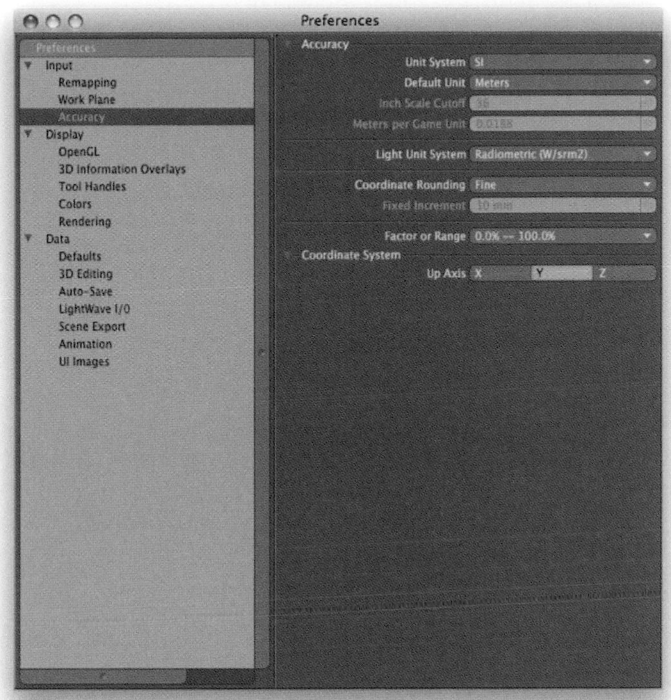

can adjust, obviously. You can tell the program to use a 0% to 100% scale or 0 to 1.0, if you like.

Finally, you can see that you have the ability to set the default coordinate system by choosing X, Y, or Z.

Display Preferences

Probably one of the most used settings you'll often change are the Display preferences, as shown in Figure 2.5.

Many of the variables here can change often, depending on what you're working on. Also, depending on the strength of your computer, you might want to adjust some of these values.

OpenGL

OpenGL is an open graphics language method for computer displays. This widely distributed multiplatform function is an industry standard for computer games, 2D and 3D graphics, and even basic operating system functions. modo's OpenGL settings allow you to set a default texture resolution from 64 × 64 pixels up through 8192 × 8192.

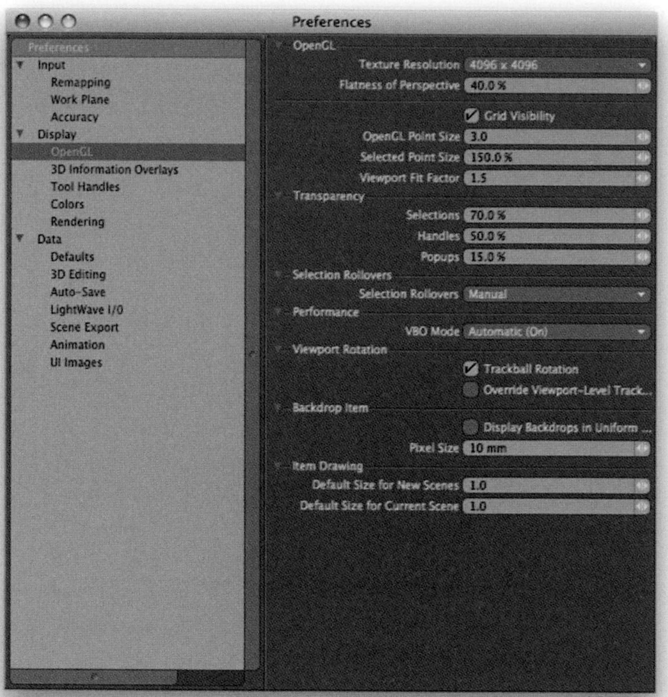

Figure 2.5
The Display category of the Preferences panel offers more of the most common controls for your everyday modo workflow.

The more powerful your video card, the higher you can set this value. When you use textures and images in your 3D scene, applied to models either as texture maps, normal maps, bump maps, and so on, the quality of the display is set here. This setting does not affect the render quality, only the display. The default is 4096 × 4096.

You can control the Flatness of Perspective value within the OpenGL settings in the Preferences panel. Essentially what this setting does is change the amount of perspective in modo's Perspective viewport. Figure 2.6 shows a teapot in the Perspective view with a Flatness of Perspective value set to 0%. Figure 2.7 shows the same view with a Flatness of Perspective value set to 100%.

Other OpenGL settings allow you to turn the grid on and off with the Grid Visibility option. You can change the OpenGL Point Size value as well as the Selected Point Size value. Again, these values don't affect your final render or model, simply their display. When it comes to OpenGL transparency in modo, you can change preference values for Selections, Handles, and Popups. The default values work quite well, but perhaps you'll want your control handles, such as those for move and rotation, to be less visible. If so, change the transparency for them here.

Figure 2.6 A Flatness of Perspective value set to 0% creates a wide-angle view in a Perspective viewport.

Figure 2.7 A Flatness of Perspective set to 100% drastically changes the Perspective viewport.

You might have noticed when working in modo that moving your mouse over parts of an object automatically highlights the vertices, edges, and polygons, giving you easy direction for selecting the right element. The way this selection rollover happens can also be changed in the Preferences panel.

Your system might not be the latest and greatest, or maybe it is! But even so, at times you might find your performance lacking. modo offers control of the VBO, or Vertex Buffer Objects, with the VBO Mode settings. Here you can tell modo to turn off this feature. VBOs work by keeping your item data in the graphic card's memory, allowing for faster transformations. Some older cards (or drivers) do now allow VBOs to function correctly. If you are experiencing odd behavior or bad performance, then turn the VBOs off and quit modo so the setting is saved. Then, restart modo. However, rather than turning this value on or off, you might try setting it to Automatic. This value doesn't usually need to be changed unless you're having some trouble with your video card performance, which in many cases happens with nVidia cards on a PC. modo 301/302 will run much faster with VBOs on. Leave this set to Automatic, and modo will handle the rest for you, regardless of what system you're working on.

3D Information Overlays

A simple selection of preferences in this list allows you to turn on or off the overlays for Current Selection, Current Tool, Grid Size, and Morph Map. What this means is that if you look at the bottom right of the viewport when working on a model, you'll see values, such as the number of polygons, vertices, or edges selected, as well as the tool you're using, and so on. If these values annoy you while you're working, you can always turn them off.

Tool Handles

Tool handles are a very important part of the modo workflow, as you'll see throughout this book. They give you access to specific axis control for tool operations. Because of this, there are a number of preferences you can set for them. You have the ability to change the size of the points on tool handles, including Large Points (Pixels) and Small Points (Pixels). Additionally, you can change the Handle Line Width and the Handle Line Hit Width options. The Hit value within these preferences is the pixel area that defines the handle. A large Hit size makes it a little easier to select a tool handle when you move the mouse over it. The Handle Scale values change the visible size of the tool handles in the 3D viewports. If you selected the Rotate tool for example, and changed the Handle Scale value, the rotational rings defining the rotate values would be adjusted.

Finally, the Draw Style for Tool Handles option can be set to Invisible, Basic, or Advanced. If you set it to Advanced, you'll see the amount of your movement, rotation, scale, and so on in the 3D viewport. This will help you make specific adjustments if needed.

Colors

Figure 2.8 shows the Colors preferences. Here you can change the colors to various schemes or create a new one. Additionally, you can change the colors of pretty much everything in modo, from the Background to Selection options all the way down to the color of display text. Goof around with these and have some fun making up different color schemes for your modo interface. While changing colors might be fun, it can also be helpful if your eyesight is not the best or you're color blind. This is just one more area where modo excels in its flexibility. It should be noted that you are just setting up color palettes here. To actually apply any of these palettes to a screen (unless you're adjusting the default), you have to do it through the View, Viewport Color Scheme menu.

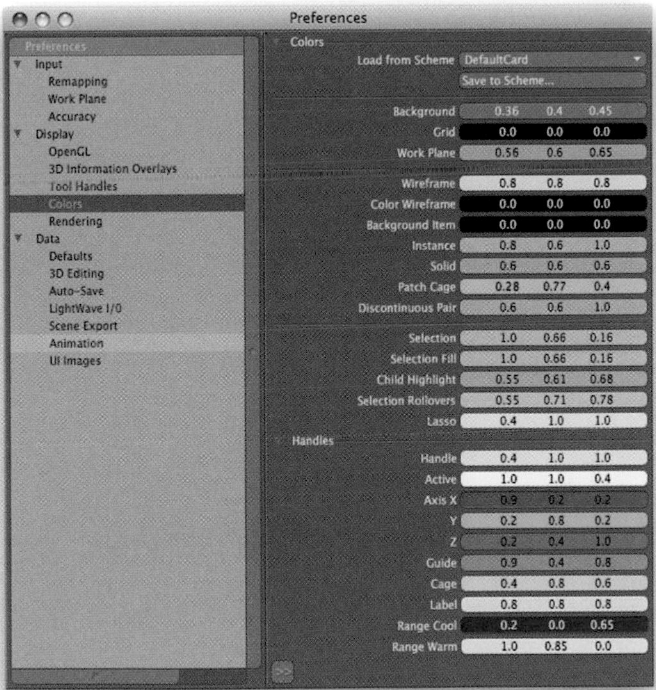

Figure 2.8 Preferences for Colors allow you to work with different schemes or create your own.

Rendering

Rendering preferences give you the flexibility to tell modo how many render threads to work with. However, you can keep the Render Threads setting at Automatic, and modo will determine if you have one, two, four, and even sixteen processors in your computer and use them accordingly for rendering. You can set the Cache Size for Geometry option, giving you flexibility for larger modeling projects. Therefore, the more memory you have in your system, the better, and the higher you can set this value. What's important to know in modo 301/302 is that you now have the ability to set up network rendering, and in order to do so, you need to check on Use Network Render Nodes. That is, you can use modo on another system in your network to aid in rendering a single animation.

The default output gamma will apply this gamma correction to your image before saving it. The display gamma will apply this gamma setting to your image as it is shown in the Preview and Render viewports. These are independent, so you can view a gamma correction that may be applied later on during compositing while still saving the image uncorrected. There is no "right" value for gamma correction, but the default value of 1.6 is a good starting place. Because modo's rendering is physically accurate, you will almost certainly need to apply a gamma correction to your image, since physically accurate light values tend to come out too dark when viewed on a monitor (as opposed to real life). Also for rendering, you can set the Bake UV Border Size value to something other than the default value of 3. This default value works quite well in most situations, but at times, depending on the UV map, you might need to increase or decrease this value. Baking a UV map means that you're rendering an image map based on a model's shape (which you've determined) and record data into that map such as color, light, and shadows.

Data Preferences

Data preferences are specific controls for 3D editing, saving, exports, and user interface images.

Defaults

In most cases, it's a good idea to keep default names set to Default so you know what it is. The Defaults Preferences settings allow you to change the default name to anything you like for the Default Materials, Default Parts, or Default Texture Maps options. You can also tell modo to Auto Create Item Masks. Depending on the type of texturing you're applying in the Shader Tree, you may enjoy having this option turned on to help save you a step. (The Shader Tree will be discussed in Chapter 7.)

On of modo's most powerful features is the ability to create instances. Instances can be applied to textures, objects, lights, and even cameras. An instance by definition is a suggestion or request. Unlike a copy of an object, for example, an instance does not duplicate the geometry, but rather, references it. You would use instances for creating large copies of items to better manage your system resources. Using the MeshPaint tool to create grass or leaves could benefit from instances. In the Preferences panel, you can tell modo that when creating instances, it should create them as bounding boxes. This will help the redraw time, especially when you have hundreds, even thousands, of instances. There are basically two reasons to use instances instead of copies: (1) You will save RAM, and (2) the instance will not be able to have any independent properties, but it will inherit all properties from its master (the original object you instanced). This is helpful if you need to make a change that will affect all the instances at once. For example, you build a single screw or bolt. You then create dozens of instances and place the bolts all over a model. Later, you realize you need to change the bolt. Instead of remodeling all of them, you can edit the original model, and instances will be changed as well, at the same time.

Although modo is an excellent subdivision surface modeler, you also have the ability to build with spline curves. You can set default values for the Patch Display Level, Curve Display Level, and Curve Display Angle, as well as the New Spline Patch Display Level. Like many values throughout the Preferences, the default values here work quite well. Finally, modo allows you to set a Default Image Format. This is especially useful when creating images for painting on 3D models.

3D Editing

With only two preferences to set within this heading, they give you control over the flatness limit of your geometry, and Vertex Deletion options. When deleting a vertex, you have the option to Remove Line Polygons or Keep All Polygons. Depending on your model and what you're intending to create, you would change this preference. But in many cases, you'd use the default setting of Remove Line Polygons. What this means is that when you delete a vertex (a point), you are telling the model to remove the line polygons connected to it, rather than removing the entire polygon.

Auto-Save

For some, Auto-Save options are a life saver. For others, they are a tool of destruction. The Auto-Save feature in modo is not enabled by default. You can turn it on in the Preferences panel, set the time interval for saves, a backup directory, and the number of revisions. The reason an Auto-Save feature might be destructive is that, if you make a change to your model that you don't like and the Auto-Save kicks in, you could very easily overwrite your existing model. When using any automated operation, make sure you're aware that it's on and what's its doing.

LightWave I/O

LightWave 3D has been around since 1990, and the developers of modo have a history with that program. Because of the way LightWave handles geometry, special preferences have been created to handle LightWave models, such as Load SubPatch as Subdivided, and Save Subdivided as Subpatched. LightWave models, when textured with images, point to a specific directory. Therefore, modo has the option to set a content directory for LightWave models. What this means is that when a LightWave model with applied texture maps is loaded, modo will know where to look for the images.

You can also turn on the following options: Save Flat Transforms and either Convert Imported Textures or Lock Imported Textures.

Scene Export

When you build objects in modo and create a cool render scene, you might be inclined to put your name on it. The Scene Export preference allows you to set an author name, a copyright, and an absolute path.

Animation

Now that modo animates, you have preferences for this feature as well, such as the Time System option, be it Frames, Seconds, SMTE, or Film. You can choose your default frames per second, such as 24FPS for film, or 30FPS for NTSC video. There are also options for default scene lengths and more. You'll learn all about animation in Chapter 9.

UI Images

Perhaps your models are all cartoon characters, and you never need image maps. No problem! But for everyone else who uses a lot of images for textures, lighting, or reference, the preferences for UI images offer a good amount of control, allowing you to sort by age or alphabetically. You can also give modo a Maximum Images number, which will help you control your system resources. And as with other geometry preferences, you can also set image preferences, such as Cache Size and Thumbnail Size. Lastly, the UI Images preferences give you the ability to clear images from throughout modo, such as the backdrop or paintbrushes.

You may never have the need to open the Preferences panel for modo 301/302. That's fine. The Luxology team has done a pretty darn good job anticipating what will work best for most users and has set the preferences accordingly. If you do need to adjust them, and if at some point they get completely screwed up, you can revert back to defaults. To do so, simply delete your configuration files.

modo Configuration Files

Sometimes you need a fresh start, a clean slate. When it comes to modo, that might mean deleting your configuration, or config, files. They are located in different places on the Mac and PC. Configuration files are written when you close modo, so any changes you make to your preferences, layouts, or other user interface options are recorded in a configuration file. By deleting them, you are erasing those settings and creating a brand new file when you restart modo. It's a great way to get back to the original installed version of the program without reinstalling the entire program.

Mac Configs

To reset modo to all of its default values on a Mac running the OS X operating system, you can delete the config files found in the Preferences folder of your user account. Go to your user:Library:Preferences:com.luxology.modo301/302, as shown in Figure 2.9.

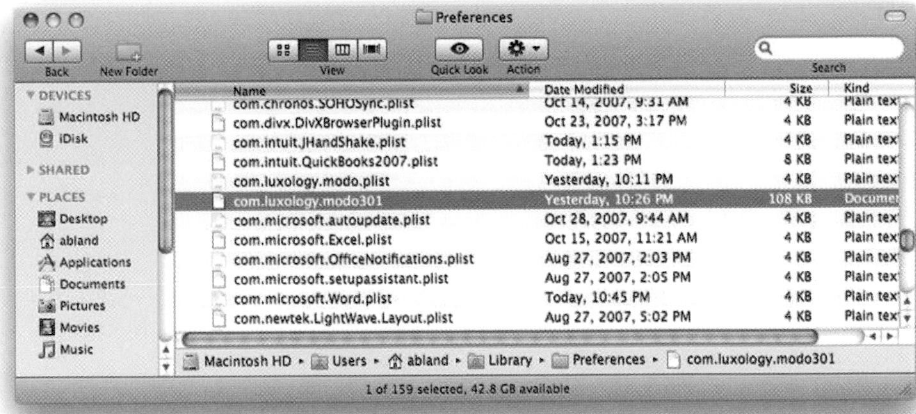

Figure 2.9
At times, you might want to delete this file to reset modo to its full defaults. Here is the location where modo stores its configuration files on an Apple Macintosh.

With modo shut down, just drag this file to your trash. Restart modo, and you're good as new.

PC Configs

To reset modo to all of its default values on a PC running the Windows XP operating system, you delete the config files found within the Documents and Settings folder (see Figure 2.10).

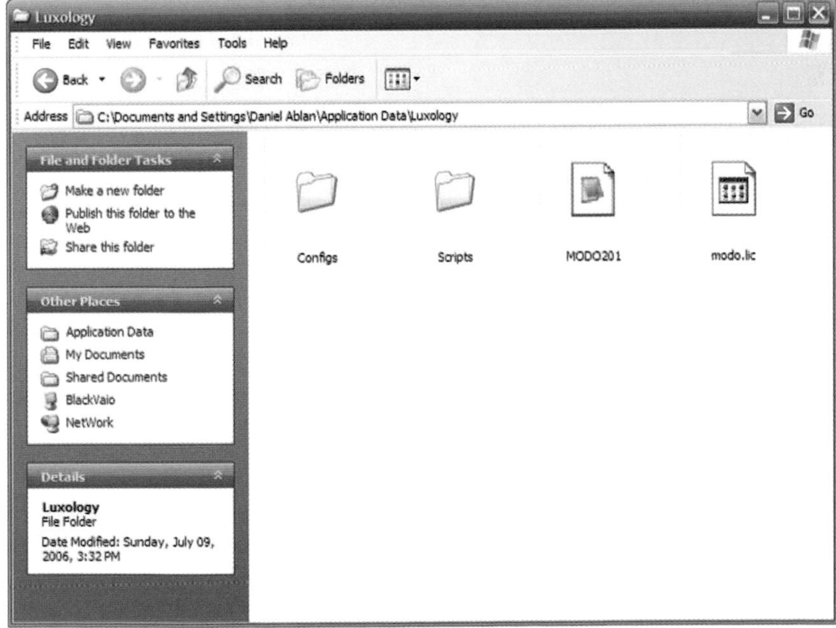

Figure 2.10
modo's config files are located within the Document and Settings folder on a Windows-based PC.

> **Note**
>
> *You* have to choose Show Hidden Files, look inside the Application Data folder, and then the Luxology folder. The file is Modo301.cfg.

Form Editor

Under the System menu at the top of the modo interface is a selection for the Form Editor. Selecting this calls up a panel with a lot of information, as show in Figure 2.11.

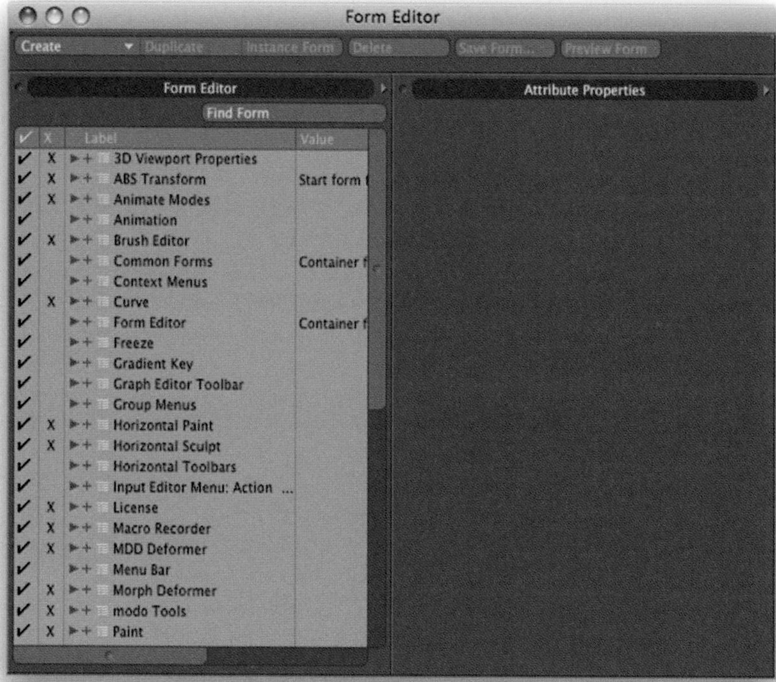

Figure 2.11 The Form Editor upon opening looks daunting, but is easy to use and quite powerful.

In many ways, the Form Editor is a deeper set of preferences for modo's many variables. But while the Preferences panel allows you to adjust certain values, the Form Editor actually allows you to create or duplicate specific operations. One of modo's unique capabilities is allowing the user to change key commands or add alternate commands to various functions. Take a quick tour of the Form Editor to familiarize yourself with the panel and how it works. If you look at Figure 2.11, you'll see two main panels with the headings Form Editor and Attribute Properties. The Form Editor section on the left side of the panel gives you access to all of the forms in modo, such as the modo tools buttons you commonly use to create basic primitive shapes. The basic tutorial coming up will show you how to quickly find a particular form to edit. When you find a form and select it, the Attribute Properties panel becomes active on the right. For example, Figure 2.12 shows the modo Tools form selected, and what you see on the right under the Attribute Properties are Common Properties values, such as the Label, Description, and Help URL settings. You can set many of these values to aid in your workflow. You'll also see Form Properties options, such as if the form is exported, which means that it's available to use in the modo interface. You can also choose for a particular form to be laid out vertically or horizontally whether the form should have an icon and, if so, what size. Go ahead and play with some of these values to see for yourself how they change your modo setup.

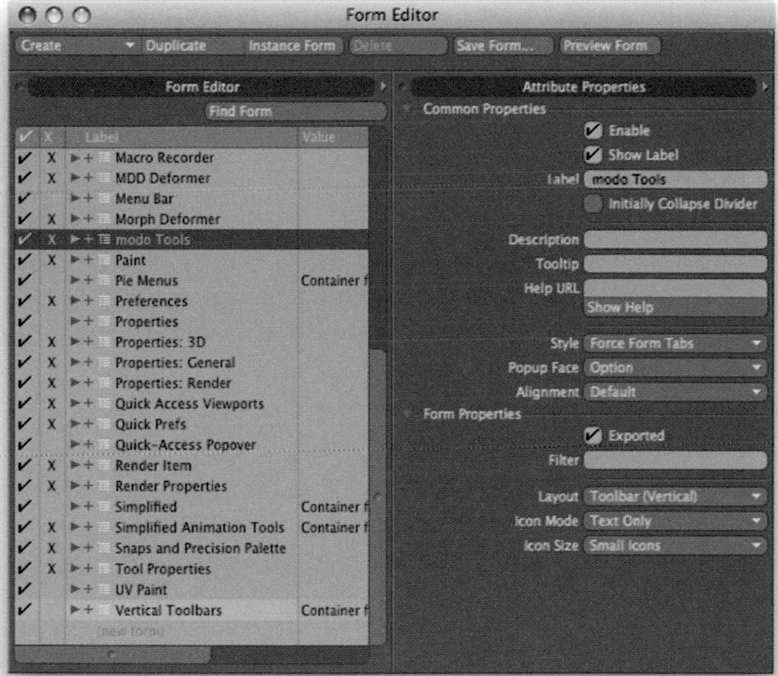

Figure 2.12
The Form Editor lets you find a form you want to edit on the left side of the panel, which then activates its attributes on the right side of the panel.

The Attribute Properties for modo's forms are very similar; some, however, have slight variations. Rather than listing all of the features in the Form Editor, these next few steps will guide you through creating an alternate command in modo 301/302 utilizing the Form Editor.

1. For this project, you're going to add an alternate command for a modo tool. In the modo interface, select the Tools tab on the left side of the screen to view the modo tools, as shown in Figure 2.13. Note that this is found within the Basic tab (which is placed vertically within the Tools tab.)

Figure 2.13
Navigate to the modo Basic tab, found under the Tools tab.

2. Holding the Shift key, click on the Torus tool to make a quick toroid to create a model in a new mesh layer. You'll see a donut shape appear in the viewport. Press the a key to fit it to view, then hold the Alt/Option key and click and drag in the interface to rotate your view. Note that you should be in a Perspective viewport, as shown in Figure 2.14.

3. Now that you have created an object, you can do something to it, such as move it. If you place your mouse over the Move tool under the Transform listing, you'll see a popup menu telling you what the tool is, its keyboard equivalent, and its alternate commands, as shown in Figure 2.15.

Tip

Placing the mouse over just about any button or tool in modo will display additional commands, names, and features when appropriate.

4. Make sure the Form Editor is open by choosing Form Editor from the System menu at the top of the modo interface or by pressing F3.

5. In the Form Editor, click Find Form from the top center of the panel, and then click on the Move tool back in the Tools tab. The Form Editor will instantly open to that selected tool, making your search absolutely painless. Figure 2.16 shows the panel after choosing Find Form.

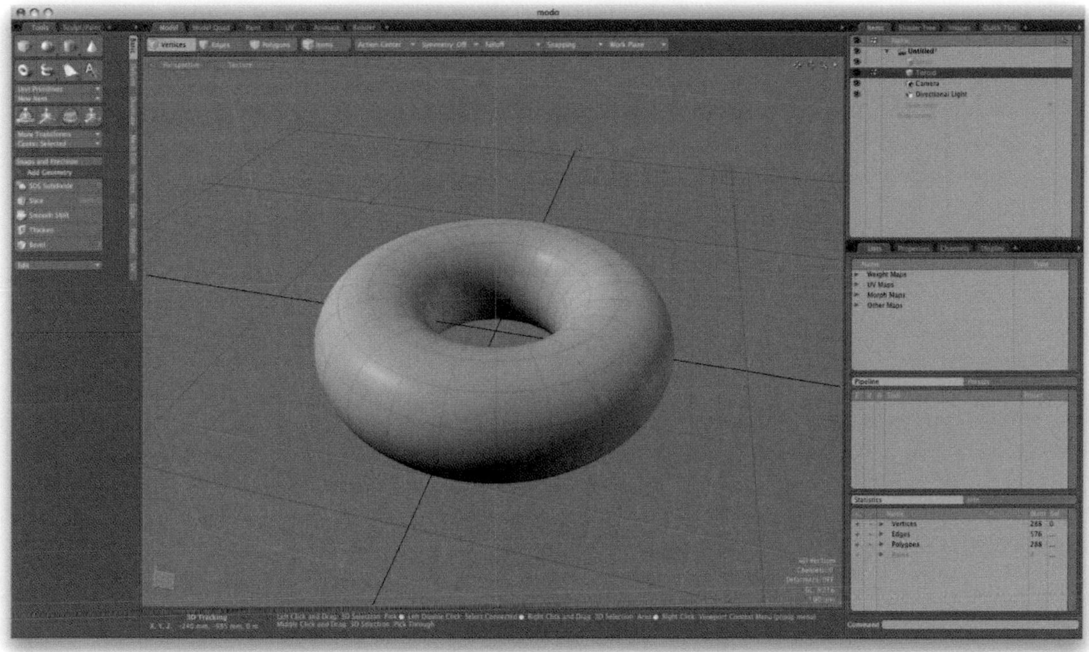

Figure 2.14 Shift-clicking on a primitive shape creates that basic shape in a new mesh layer.

Figure 2.15 Holding the mouse over a tool for a few seconds in modo calls up its commands.

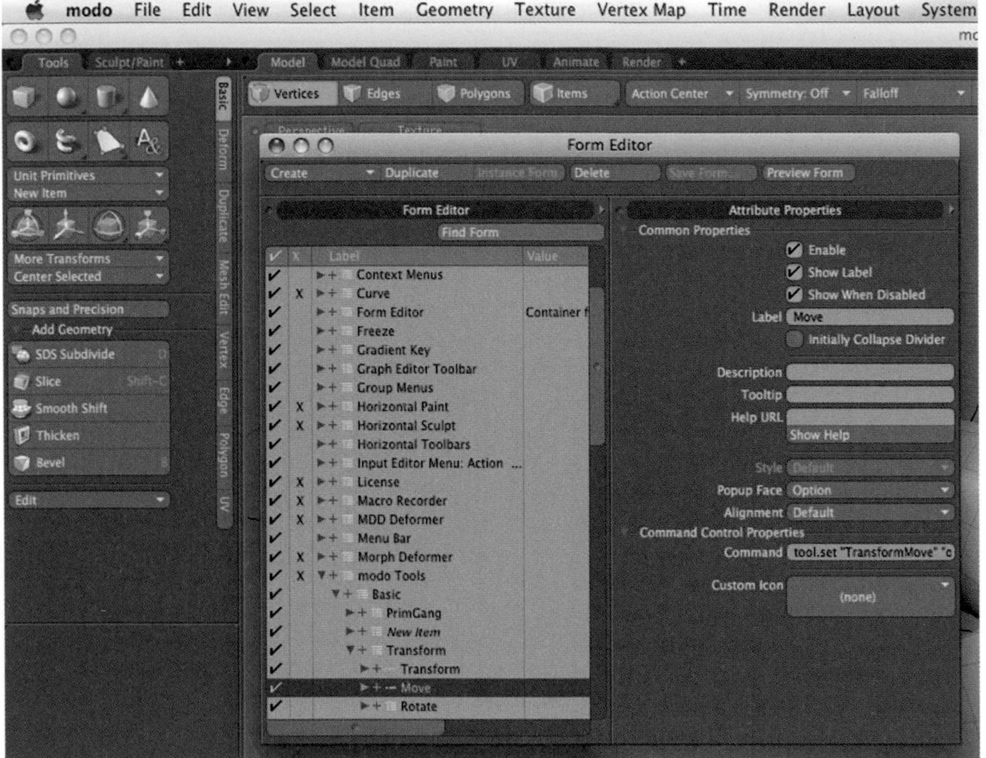

Figure 2.16
Rather than searching through a plethora of forms in the Form Editor, use the Find Form function to quickly select the form you want to edit.

6. Looking at the Form Editor, you'll see that the modo Tools category is expanded to the Basic category, which displays the Transform category. There you can see that the Move tool is selected. Click the small triangle to the left of the Move listing to expand its commands. You'll see that there is an Alternate Commands listing. Expand that, as shown in Figure 2.17.
7. From Figure 2.17, you can see that a Soft Move has a value of Alt, meaning the Alt key is the modifier to make the alternate happen. This is the Option key on a Mac. Similarly, you'll see Soft Drag assigned to Shift, and Element Move (a fantastic tool) assigned to Ctrl. Right-click on the Element Move command (Apple key and click on single-button Macs).
8. When you right-click, you'll see options for Create Alternate Command, Edit, and Delete. For this tool, there are quite a few alternate commands already, but perhaps you'd like to change one? Easy. With the right-click, select Edit.

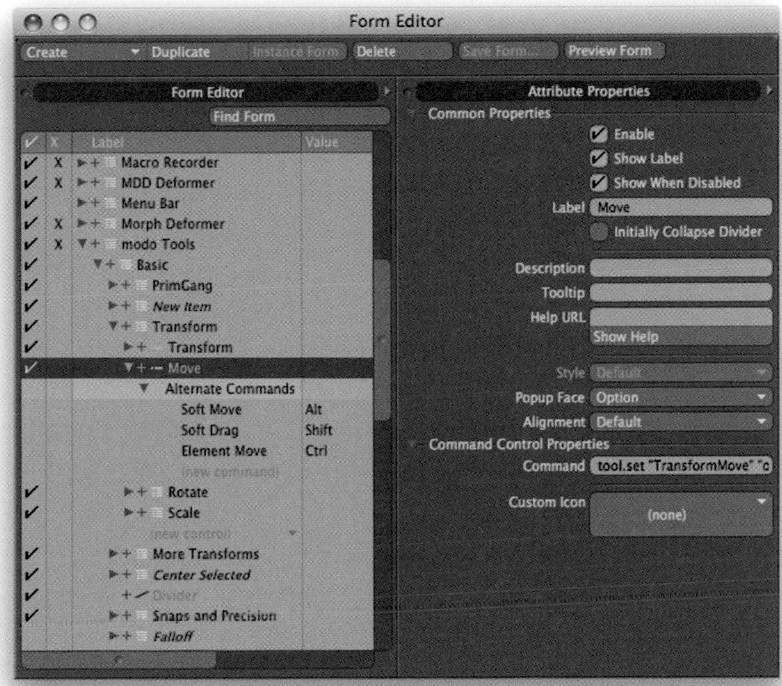

Figure 2.17 Expand the Move listing, and the Form Editor displays its alternate commands.

9. In the Create Alternate Command dialog box that appears, you can see that the modifier is Ctrl, the Command is tool.set "elementMove" "on" and the Label setting is Element Move. Of course, you can relabel your tool here, but for now, hold the Shift and Ctrl keys at the same time, and you'll see the modifier keys update, as shown in Figure 2.18.

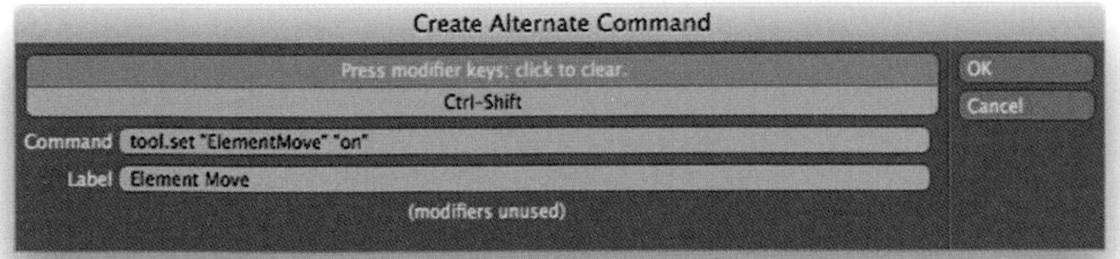

Figure 2.18 Holding the Shift and Ctrl keys at the same time tells modo to use those together as an alternate command for the Element Move tool.

10. Click OK, and you'll see your new alternate command modifiers listed in the Form Editor.

11. Close the Form Editor, and then press the Shift and Ctrl keys. Look at the Move tool as you do, and you'll notice that the icon changes to represent the Element Move tool. Choose it, and then click and drag on your object in the viewport.

Congratulations! You just modified your first tool! Obviously, this is just the beginning when it comes to modifications, and I could probably write an entire book on using the Form Editor, modifying keys, and creating new ones. But this quick tutorial helped familiarize you with the Form Editor and what you can do with it. A few notes you should know:

- To revert back to your existing settings after modifying, you can edit the command again. Or you can delete your modo configuration files, as described earlier.
- Other attribute properties allow you to create your own icon. At the bottom of the Attribute Properties panel within the Form Editor, you can set a custom icon. Click the blank icon and then select Load Image from the popup menu that appears. Add your own image, and away you go!
- From the top of the Form Editor, you can create instances of forms (such as the modo Tools), as well as create new forms and commands and save them.
- Using the Form Editor, you can create your own custom interface tools. If you click on the Layout menu, then choose Layouts, Paint, you'll see a variation of the Form Editor's capabilities. The Horizontal icons across the top of the interface were assembled using the From Editor and Attribute Properties. Be sure to click and drag the viewport windows down a bit to reveal the Paint layout icons.

Input Editor

The Form Editor is cool, but so is the Input Editor. Also accessed from the System menu at the top of the modo interface, or by pressing F2, the Input Editor is your home for keyboard shortcuts and commands (see Figure 2.19).

Across the top of the Input Editor panel, you can see the Modifiers listings: All, Unqualified, Ctrl, Alt, and Shift. Select any one of these, such as Ctrl, and you'll reveal all of the commands in modo that use Ctrl as a modifier. Figure 2.20 shows the Ctrl modifiers selected, and at the very top is Ctrl-A for the Trigger listing.

The next column shows the command. You'll see that Ctrl-A controls viewport.alignSelected, and the Description column to the right shows that the tool aligns a selected viewport. Additionally, take a look beneath the Ctrl-A listing, and you'll see that the command acts differently in different viewports.

Similarly to the Form Editor, if you right-click on a command, you are offered controls to vary its use. Most of these are something you may or may not wish to change, but if you do, remember what you've changed so that you can get back to the default settings.

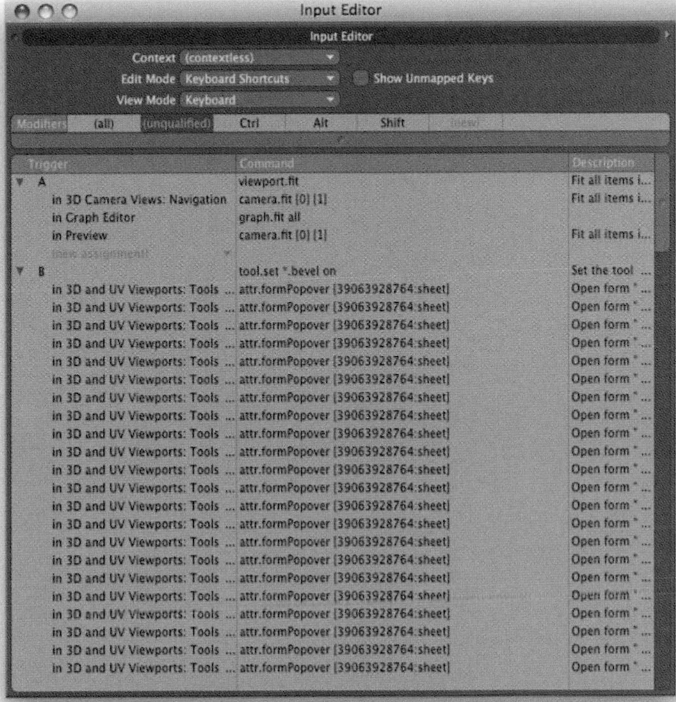

Figure 2.19 The Input Editor gives you access to all of your keyboard commands.

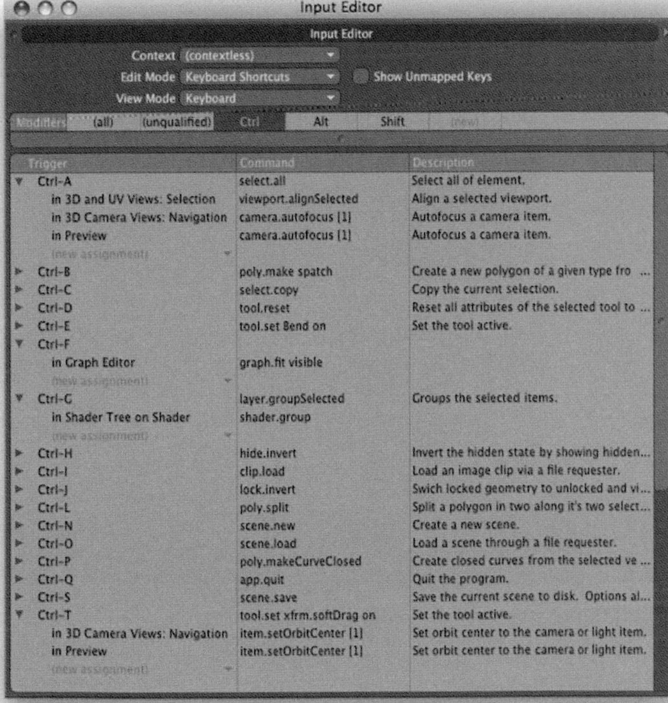

Figure 2.20 Selecting Ctrl from the Modifiers list shows all of modo's commands that use the Ctrl key.

At the top of the Input Editor is the Edit Mode selection. By default, you see Keyboard Shortcuts, but clicking the drop-down list shows that you can view key commands for viewports and tools. And as you might expect, you can modify, add, or delete any number of these commands. It's important to note that you can assign specific shortcuts on a per-viewport or per-tool basis. For instance the f key in a 3D viewport flips polygons, but in the Item List it finds the currently selected Item.

You may never feel the need to use the Input Editor, and that's just fine. It was important to show it to you now so we can forget about it! Really though, you should be aware of the Input Editor and the Form Editor, and as powerful as they are, there often is not really a need to use them unless you specifically need to change a command or keystroke. The Luxology team has done a pretty good job assigning keyboard equivalents and alternate commands to the toolset. For more specific info on these areas, view your modo manual and check out the forums at www.luxology.com. I want to make sure there's enough room in this book for model creation, texturing, and rendering!

Action Centers

There's nothing more frustrating in 3D modeling than not being able to control your mouse movements in the direction you want. This is especially true when trying to move or rotate a selected edge or polygon. But never fear, Action Centers are here! Okay, that was lame, but Action Centers are not, so follow along with this simple operation to see how they work. First, close any panels that might be open, such as the Input or Form Editor.

1. From the File menu, select Reset to bring modo back to its original state.
2. From the Basic category, under the modo Tools tab, hold the Ctrl key and click the Sphere icon. This will create a unit (1 meter) sphere in the currently selected mesh item.
3. Press the a key to fit the ball to view.
4. Press the t key to activate the Element Move tool. Run your mouse (without selecting) over the ball, and you'll see the edges and polygons highlight soft blue as you breeze over them.
5. When you feel the urge, move over any edge or polygon and click and drag. Figure 2.21 shows the movement.

Tip

An *element* is either a vertex (point), edge, or polygon.

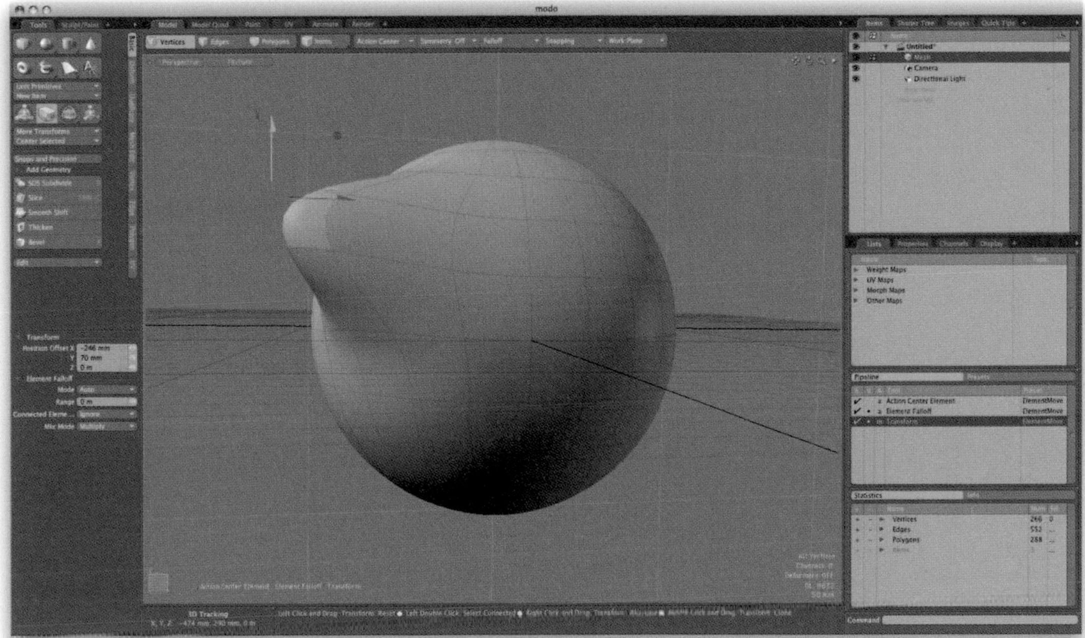

Figure 2.21 Element Move is a powerful tool that saves you time. You can click and drag on a vertex, edge, or polygon and move it.

At certain times when modeling, the object might need specific movement or adjustment on an edge or polygon. Traditional modeling tools often make it difficult to exactly align the selection as you want it. However, modo makes it easy to do by adjusting a few settings.

1. Notice that when you move an edge or polygon around, it's hard to give it a specific direction. Okay then, click and drag on one of the handles, such as the green Y-axis handle, and the current element moves up.
2. But perhaps you need to move that edge directly out from the ball. That is to say, you need it to move along the surface normal. The *surface normal* is simply which way the polygon is facing. Polygons are one sided. From the top of the modo interface, select the Action Center drop-down list, then choose Element, as shown in Figure 2.22.
3. Once you choose Element as the Action Center, go back to the viewport, click on an edge or polygon, and look at the handles—they're aligned to the selection. Click on the blue handle and drag, and you'll be able to pull the polygon directly away from the object, as shown in Figure 2.23.

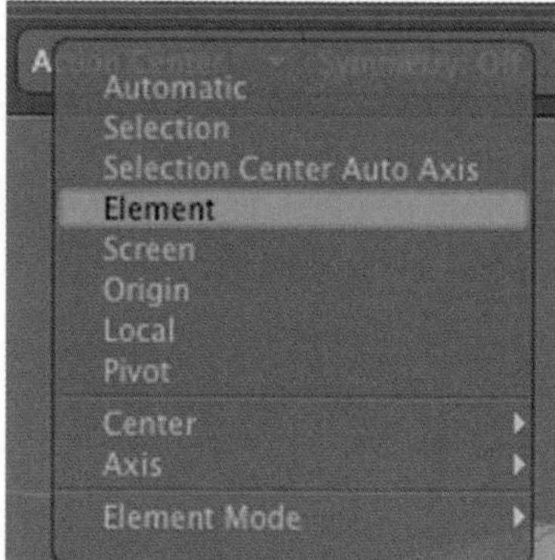

Figure 2.22 There are a number of Action Centers to choose from.

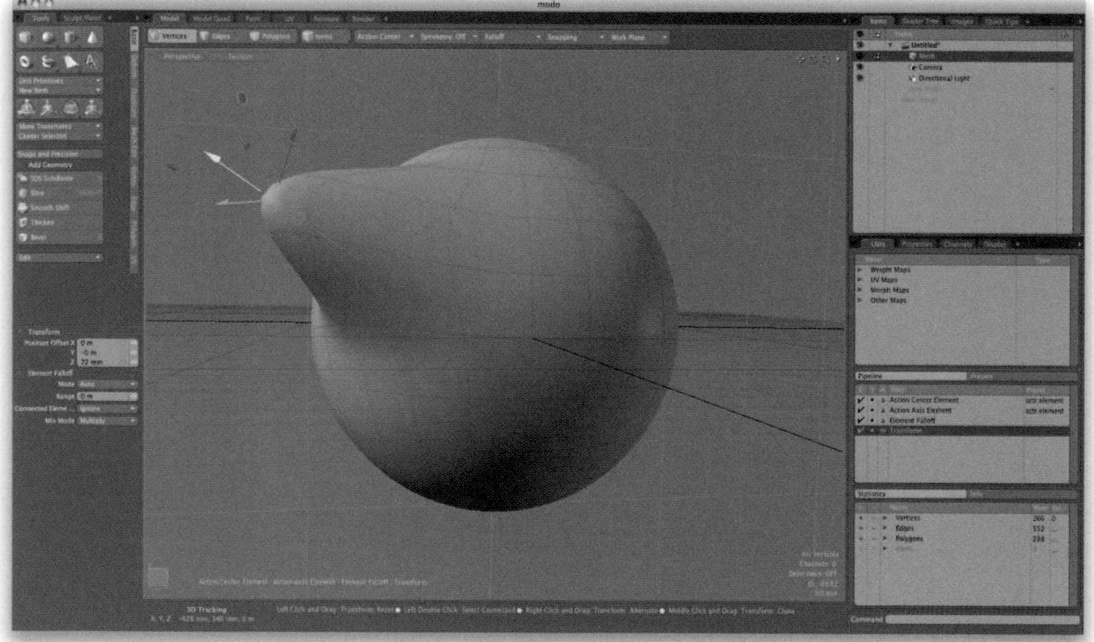

Figure 2.23 Once an Element Action Center is set, you can move the selected edge (or vertex or polygon) deliberately on a specific axis equal to the surface normal.

Action Centers allow any action to be oriented to a desired specification you set. Generally, 3D modeling programs tend to use the pivot point or mouse position for the Action Center. modo uses these Action Centers, but also many others, enabling you to customize the axis and center for tool handles. Other Action Centers include Automatic (the default), Selection, Screen, Origin, and others. Action Centers are a combination of a center and an axis. The presets will give you a center and an axis at once, viewable in the Tool Pipe and the viewport at the lower left by the orientation axis. The reason you can move the element out from the ball is not really due to the Action Center, but the action axis. The center is still just the element that's selected. However, the default element move tool only has an Action Center (element) and not an axis predefined, so it uses the world axis. You can just as easily go to the Action Center drop-down menu, choose Axis, and select Element. You will notice that in both the Tool Pipe and the viewport you now have an Action Center and an action axis. It's the axis that the tool aligns to, and the center is where the tool handles appear. Now that you have seen how the Action Center can affect an action or transformation, here's a quick list of the Action Centers and their uses:

- **Automatic**—Uses the current geometry as its guide, and center of the tool (such as Move or Rotate) on it. This Action Center axis is aligned to the world space in modo.
- **Selection**—Uses the selected geometry as its guide. The selected tool will align itself to the selected geometry.
- **Selection Center Auto Axis**—Similar to the Selection Action Center, but changes the tool alignment to the major axes.
- **Element**—As you've seen, aligns a tool to a selected elements normal.
- **Screen**—Pretty cool in that it realigns the tool based on the current screen. Therefore, if you're modeling in a Perspective view, then switch to a side view while using, say, the Move tool, it will be aligned based on your changing viewports.
- **Origin**—Useful for things like scaling objects. It aligns the tools and places the handle at the origin of the universe rather than the object.
- **Local**—Good for those times when you have multiple elements selected. Say you have two eyeballs selected in a character and need to move each one. Setting the Action Center to Local would allow you to apply an action to each selection on its local axis.
- **Pivot**—Simply uses the selected mesh item's pivot as its Action Center.

You can also set Auto, Selection, Element, Screen, Origin, and Pivot for the center and axis as well, directly from the Action Center drop-down menu. This additional level of control in modo 301/302 enables you to set the same Action Center type controls described previously, but directly to the center and axis.

Each is useful in its own respect and chosen based on the modeling task at hand. Remember that the Action Center applies to all of the modo tools, from Move to Rotate, Scale, and so on. You'll choose and use these Action Centers throughout the book's projects.

Tip

To really see how Action Centers work, check out the free video from 3D Garage.com called Action Centers.mov on the book's DVD-ROM.

Work Plane

Last but not least is the Work Plane. By now you've clicked around modo enough to be familiar with the interface, but one thing might be weighing on you—what the heck is that vertical grid? Until you understand how useful that second grid is to your modeling, it will only appear as a visible nuisance.

No matter what 3D program you're working in, you can only control up to two axes at a time, such as X and Z. But with modo's Work Plane, the alternate gray grid plane you see in the Perspective viewport gives you a third axis to work in. The reason is that the Work Plane adjusts to your geometry or selected element. Rotating your viewport makes the Work Plane snap to the major axis, such as ZY, XZ, or XY. The Work Plane is used to assist and set the center and axis of tools you use to build and edit your 3D models. Step through the following instructions to get a feel for the Work Plane.

1. From the File menu, select Reset to bring modo back to its original state.
2. Then from the Basic category within the Tools tab, select the Unit Primitives drop-down menu, then choose In Current Mesh, and click the Teapot primitive, as shown in Figure 2.24.

Figure 2.24 modo offers access to a few additional primitive shapes, such as the industry standard Teapot.

3. With the teapot in the viewport, press the a key to fit it to view. Then hold the Alt/Option key and click and drag the viewport from left to right. Pay attention to the vertical light gray grid, and watch what it does. You'll see it snap based on the axis as it changes.

   What's happening here is the Work Plane is adjusting to the dominant axis. By rotating the view, you're changing that axis. How can you tell what the axis is? Take a look at the bottom-left corner of the viewport. Do you see the XYZ representation, as shown in Figure 2.25? Notice that it's highlighted in gray between two axes. This represents the Work Plane and will change as you rotate. If you were to build an object and needed it to lie flat on the Y axis as you created it, you would rotate the Perspective viewport until this icon showed the Work Plane between the Z and X. You'll do this later in the book as you build objects.

Figure 2.25 Pay attention to the icon at the bottom left of the modo viewport. The gray highlight between two axes shows your dominant axis.

4. Select the Polygons button from the top of the modo interface. This tells modo you want to work with polygons.
5. Click and drag over some polygons on the corner of the handle to select them.
6. If you choose a tool such as Move or Rotate at this point, you can control how the selected polygons would be adjusted through an Action Center setting. But what if you wanted even more control, perhaps to build additional objects from the selection? At the top right of the modo interface is a Work Plane drop-down menu. Click it and choose Align Work Plane to Selection, as shown in Figure 2.26.
7. The adjusted Work Plane will constrain the selected tool to the new position set by the axis of the Work Plane.

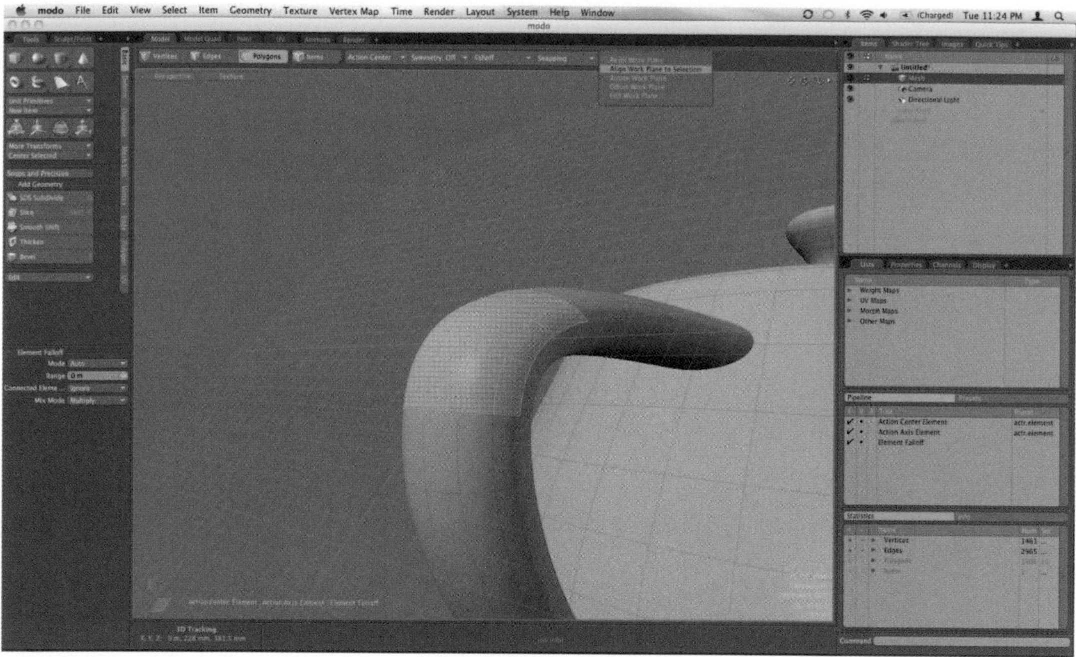

Figure 2.26 You can align the Work Plane to your selection, allowing you to have greater control over your tools and how they interact with your model.

> **Note**
>
> With the Work Plane drop-down menu, you can also choose to reset the Work Plane, offset, or rotate it based on your needs. Experiment with these settings, then check out the video called WorkPlanes.mov on the book's DVD-ROM to learn more.

As you can see, a few key areas within modo are quite powerful. This chapter guided you through some of their uses, but not all. The best way to understand how each of these key areas work is to see them in action in a full-blown project. But before you get to that, read just one more chapter to learn about selections, falloffs, and the amazing modo Pipeline, also known as the Tool Pipe.

3

Working with the Tools

To get the most out of modo, it's important to understand how the tools work. While you can get by just clicking around in the program until you build something you like, you'll save a lot of time with a clear knowledge of how the key tools function inside modo 301. Specifically, this chapter is about working with selections, falloffs, and the Tool Pipe.

Selections

Like most 3D applications, modo's selections and tools work in a similar fashion—you choose a selection mode, click and select particular geometry, and modify the selection in some way. And like most applications, if nothing is selected, what you do (such as move or rotate) applies to everything. But modo goes a step farther by making selection and deselection easier than you thought possible. In the end, your workflow is greatly improved. There are five selection modes available to you in modo 301: Vertices, Edges, Polygons, and Items. By clicking and holding within the Items selection mode, you can choose Materials, Pivot, and Center selections as well. You'll use the Items selection more later in the book when it's time to get things in motion with modo's animation capabilities.

Take a look at Figure 3.1 which shows the various selection modes available at the top of the modo interface. You see the four selection modes available: Vertices, Edges, Polygons, and Items. What is discussed here primarily focuses on the three selection modes you'll use most often, Vertices, Edges, and Polygons. Note that the default 301 layout is used here.

Figure 3.1
Across the top of the modo interface are the four selection modes.

Working with Selections

The best way to understand how modo's selections work is by trying them out for yourself. This next tutorial will instruct you on creating an object and using it to work through various selections.

1. Start up modo and make sure you're working with a default 301 layout, which you can set from the Layout menu at the top of the interface.
2. Next, in the Tools tab on the left side of the screen, hold the Shift key and select the Torus primitive. This is within the Primitives category of the modo Tools panel (see Figure 3.2).

> **Note**
>
> If you Shift-click, you get a new mesh item that is automatically given the name of the primitive you clicked. If you Ctrl-click, then the primitive is added to the currently selected mesh item, which happens to be named Mesh in a newly opened scene.

Figure 3.2
In order to start working with selections, you need to have some geometry!

3. Next, press the a key to fit the new primitive shape to view.
4. To begin working with selections, start with the most common selection type, Polygon. Click the Polygons button at the top of the modo interface (see Figure 3.3) to tell the program you want to work with Polygons. This means that when you click on your model, you'll be selecting the polygonal geometry, or the surface of the model.

> **Note**
>
> It's important to pay attention to the mode buttons at the top of the modo interface. This will tell you what selection mode you're working in. Additionally, you can repeatedly press the spacebar to toggle through the three main selection modes.

> **Note**
>
> You can switch selection modes by pressing the 1 through 7 keys on your keyboard.

5. With the Polygons mode button selected, click and drag over a few polygons on the torus shape with the left mouse button. Before you select, as you mouse over the polygons, you'll see them highlight a light blue. This is not a selection, but a guide to help you select the right element, in this case, polygons. Now, when you click the mouse to select, you'll see the selected polygons highlight orange. Figure 3.3 shows the selection.

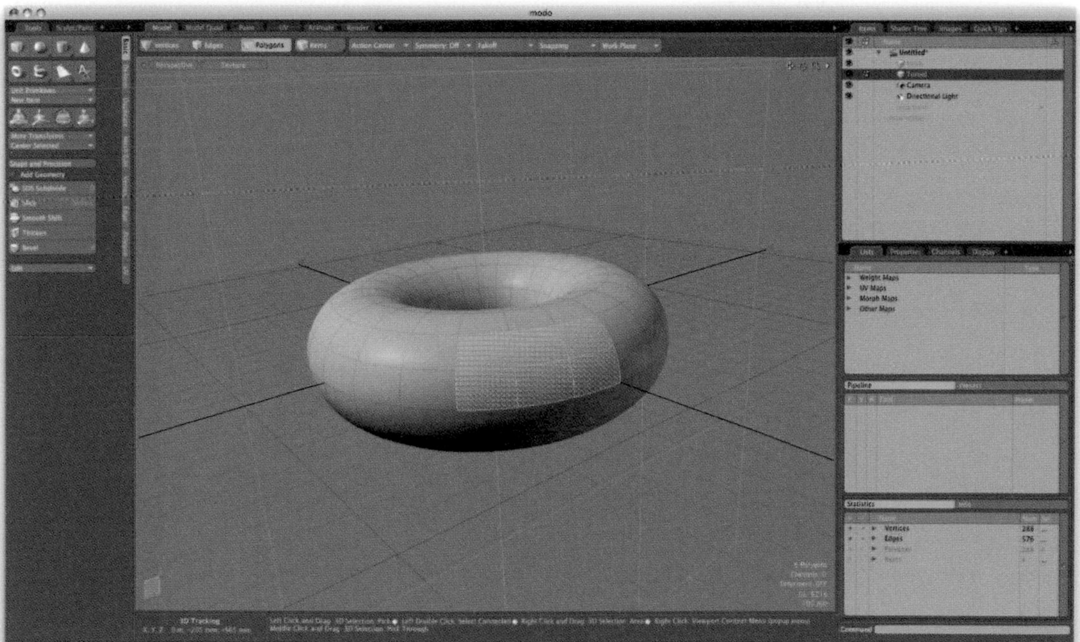

Figure 3.3 When you click to select a single polygon or multiple polygons while in Polygons mode, the selected geometry highlights as bright orange.

6. With a few polygons selected, press the Shift key and the a key at the same time. The selected polygons will now fit to view. Consider this keyboard shortcut when working on specific areas of models, whether you have polygons, edges, or vertices (points) selected. Now press just the a key to fit the model to view, rather than the selection.

Note

Be sure to note the heads-up display (HUD) visible in the bottom right of the layout interface. This will tell you how many vertices, edges, polygons, or materials are selected (in this case, it displays "6 Polygons"). If none are selected, the HUD will display "All Polygons" for Polygons mode. The other modes will be displayed as appropriate.

7. With these polygons selected, whatever tool you choose will apply to just these. With that said, press the b key on your keyboard to activate the Bevel tool. You can find this tool under the Mesh Edit tab on the left side of the interface. When you turn on the Bevel tool, the Tool properties become visible at the bottom left of the interface, as shown in Figure 3.4. But it will also appear within the Basic category under the Add Geometry heading.

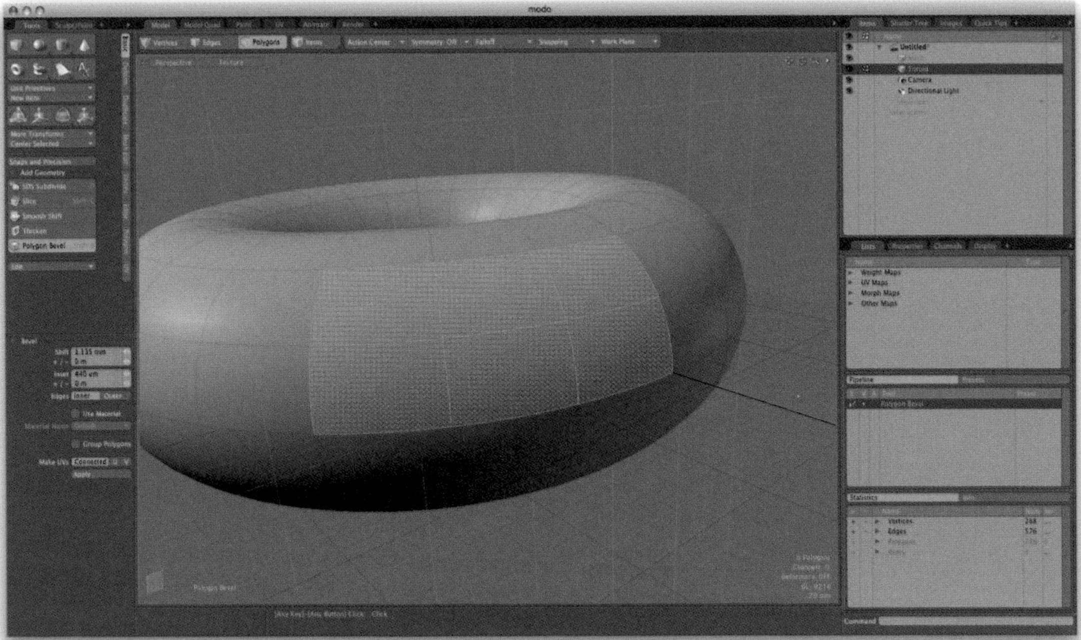

Figure 3.4 When you activate a tool, the Tool properties become visible. Here the Bevel tool is active.

8. With the Bevel tool active, click once in the layout. You'll see a red and blue handle appear, as shown in Figure 3.5.

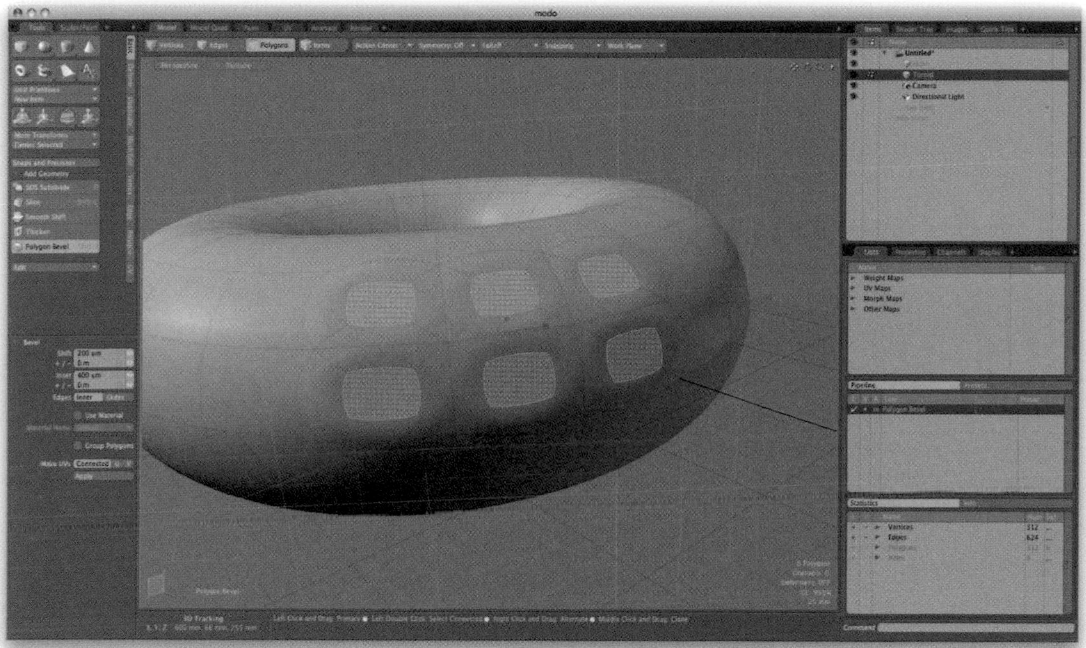

Figure 3.5 Turning the Bevel tool on and then clicking in the layout activates the tool's control handles.

9. If you click and drag the red handle to the right or left, you change the Inset value of the bevel. Try it.
10. If you click and drag the blue handle, you change the Shift value of the bevel.
11. After you've played around with these tools, press Ctrl-Z on the keyboard to undo. Then, click and drag in the layout, making sure not to click on either handle. You can perform a change to the Inset and Shift values for the bevel at the same time.
12. One thing you might have noticed is that each of the selected polygons bevels independently. This is fine in some situations, but mostly you'll want to bevel these together as one. To do so, press Ctrl-Z a few times to undo your bevels, returning to just the selected polygons. Then, in the Tool properties panel for Bevel, on the left of the interface, click the Group Polygons button.
13. Click and drag in the layout, either free form or directly on one of the handles. Figure 3.6 shows the bevel operation with Group Polygons on.

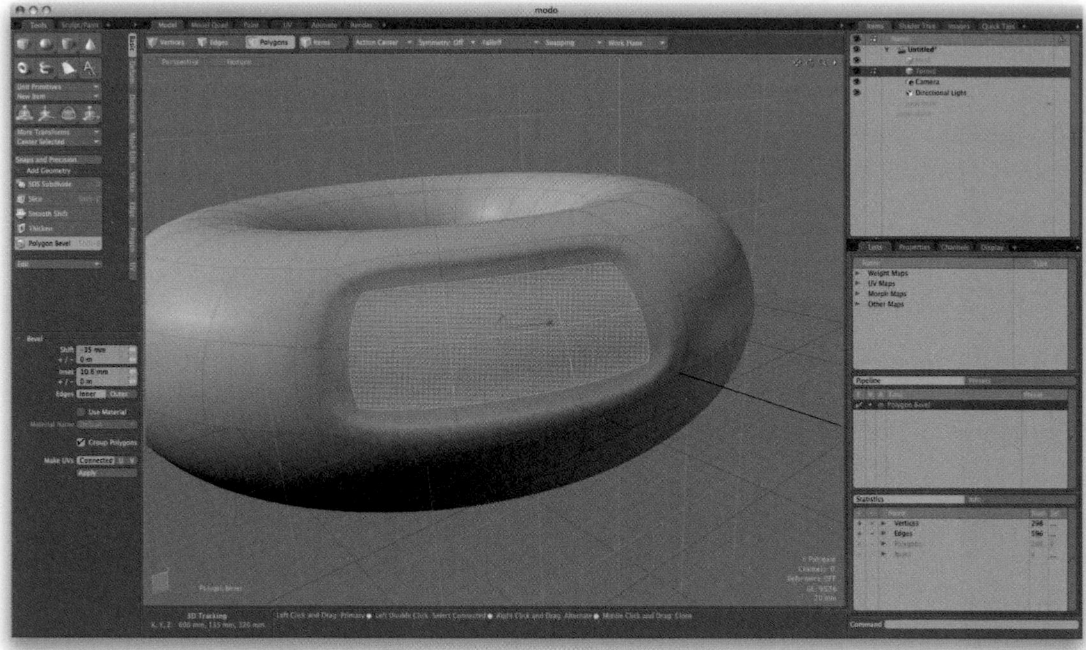

Figure 3.6 With Group Polygons selected in the Tool properties panel, selected polygons bevel as one.

> **Note**
>
> You can also enter values numerically in the Tool Properties panel.

14. If you now turn off the Bevel tool by pressing the b key again, or clicking on the Bevel tool, then turn it on again, you activate a new bevel. And because your polygons are still selected, you're now beveling from your existing bevel. But a better way to quickly bevel again is to hold the Shift key and click once in the layout. Make an adjustment, beveling more, then hold the Shift key and click, and bevel again. The process can continue to create complex and interesting shapes very easily.

> **Note**
>
> One standard operating procedure in modo is to Shift-click with a tool active, and you'll reset that tool.

You'll use the bevel process a lot in your modeling tasks, and you'll see this firsthand later in the book. Let's try a few more selection tasks and then move on to a few more complex controls.

Selection Methods

Probably one of the best things about working in modo is how easy it is to select vertices, edges, polygons, or materials. Unlike a lot of other 3D applications, modo allows you to get down to business quickly because you're not spending a lot of time selecting the necessary elements to edit. Take a quick look at this next section to see the various ways you can select geometry.

1. In modo, go to the File menu at the top of the interface and select the Reset command, as shown in Figure 3.7. This clears the layout and resets it back to its default views. Note that you'll get a message asking if you want to save your work. Choose what's right for you.

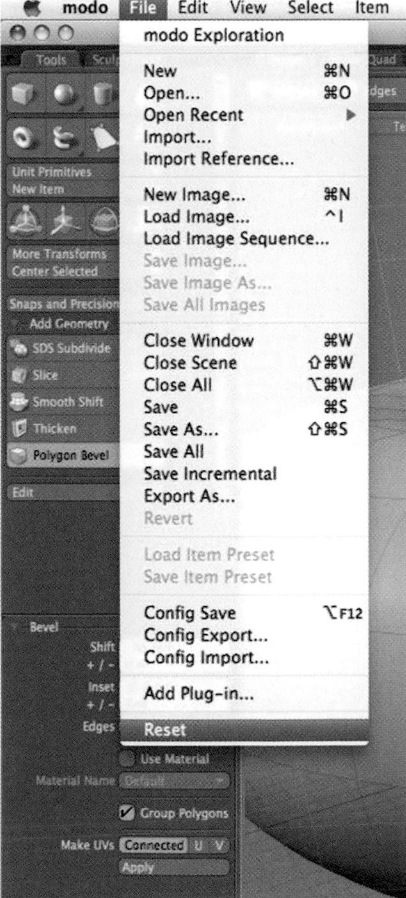

Figure 3.7 To clear out your work and start fresh, choose the Reset command from the File menu.

2. Click the Basic tab on the left side of the modo interface to access the primitives. Click the Unit Primitives drop-down menu, then choose In Current Mesh and select the Teapot primitive.
3. Once the Teapot primitive is loaded into the layout, press the spacebar to toggle to the Edges selection mode, visible at the top of the interface. Then press the a key to fit the model to view. Feel free to press the period (.) key on the keyboard to zoom in or the comma (,) key to zoom out.

Note

Remember that you can hold the Alt key and click directly in the layout to rotate the view. Conversely, you can hold the Alt and Shift key at the same time, then click in the layout to move it around, or use Alt and Ctrl to zoom.

4. When you move your mouse over an edge while in Edges selection mode (or any other mode, for that matter), you'll see the element highlight. This helps you choose the selection. Figure 3.8 shows a highlighted edge as the mouse moves over it.

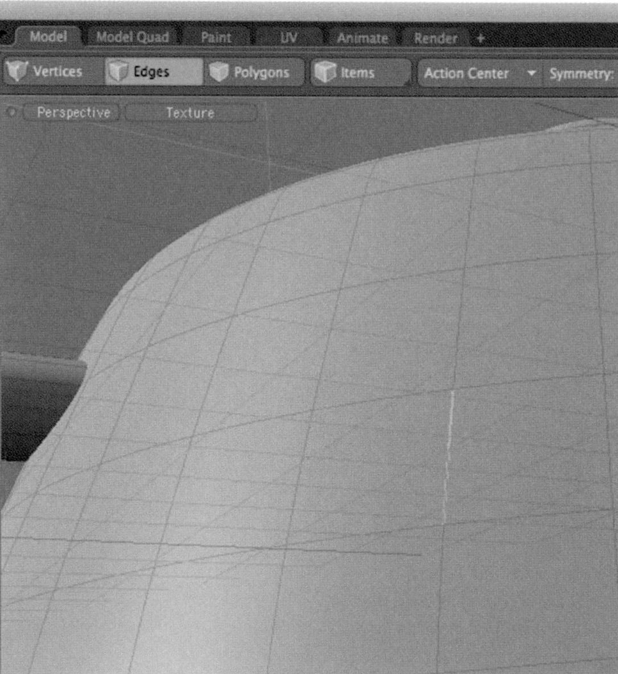

Figure 3.8
When you move your mouse over any element, modo helps you select that particular element by highlighting it in light blue.

Note

If you don't like the selection rollovers, you can disable it. Press the o (not zero) key on your keyboard to open the View and Shading options. Click the Visibility tab, and at the bottom, you can uncheck Show Selection Rollovers (see Figure 3.9).

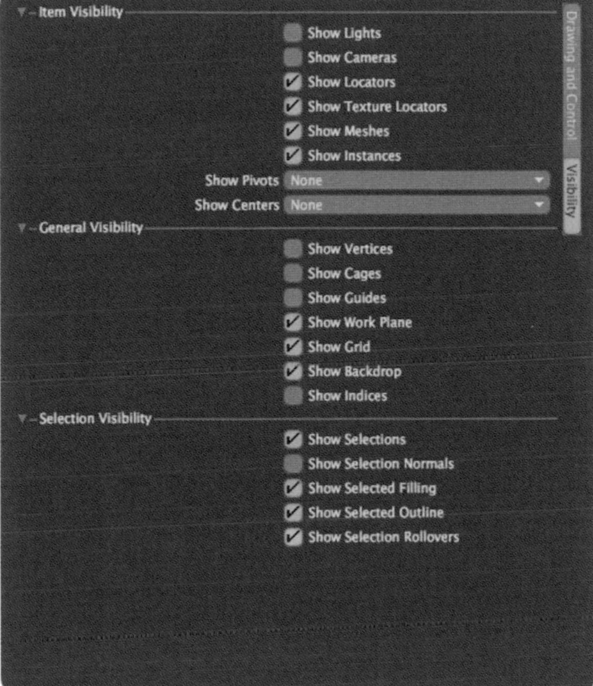

Figure 3.9 On modo's Visibility tab in the View and Shading panel, you can choose not to use selection rollovers if you like.

5. When the mouse highlights an edge you want to select, simply click on it. The edge will be selected and turn orange. You can hold the mouse down and select more than one edge by dragging the mouse over the desired selection. Try clicking and dragging over a few edges to select them.
6. If you accidentally select extra edges, hold the Ctrl key and click on the edge you don't want in order to deselect it. To continue adding to a selection, hold the Shift key and choose the edges you want to select. Note that this method applies to all selection modes.

7. But the great thing about modo is the quick way you can select elements. Find an edge in the middle of your Teapot primitive and double-click it. One click will select the particular edge, while the double-click will select the entire edge loop, as shown in Figure 3.10. Try it out!

Figure 3.10
Double-clicking on an edge will select the entire edge loop.

8. Once this edge is selected, you can slide it, move it, size it, bevel it, extend it, and so on. Go ahead and press the b key to select the Bevel tool as you did earlier. Then click and drag in the layout to bevel the selected edge. Figure 3.11 shows the result.
9. A cool option is how you can change from one selection mode to another. After you've beveled the single edge, as Figure 3.11 shows, you are left with multiple edges selected—the original edge, plus the new ones created with the operation. But what if now you wanted to multiply the polygons created by the edge bevel? Rather than deselecting the edges, then reselecting polygons, simply hold the Alt key on your keyboard, and look at the selection types across the top of the interface, as shown in Figure 3.12. They each now say "Convert." So if you have a group of selected edges, as in Figure 3.11, hold the Alt key and click the Vertices selection mode. You will convert the selected edges to selected Polygons. Figure 3.13 shows the result.

10. You can see that by starting with a simple edge selection, you've quickly added geometry and converted the selection to polygons in a matter of clicks. Now you can choose a tool, such as Bevel (press the b key), and click and drag to bevel out the selected polygons. Make sure Group Polygons is on in the Bevel tool properties panel.
11. Bevel the selected polygons two or three times, similar to the process you performed earlier in the chapter. After you've beveled once, hold the Shift key and click on the layout to start a new bevel. Figure 3.14 shows a few bevels on the selected polygons.

Figure 3.11 After a quick and easy edge selection, you can bevel the selection to add more geometry.

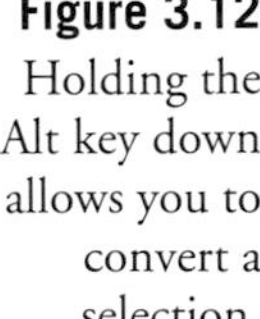

Figure 3.12 Holding the Alt key down allows you to convert a selection.

Figure 3.13 Selected edges are quickly converted to selected polygons.

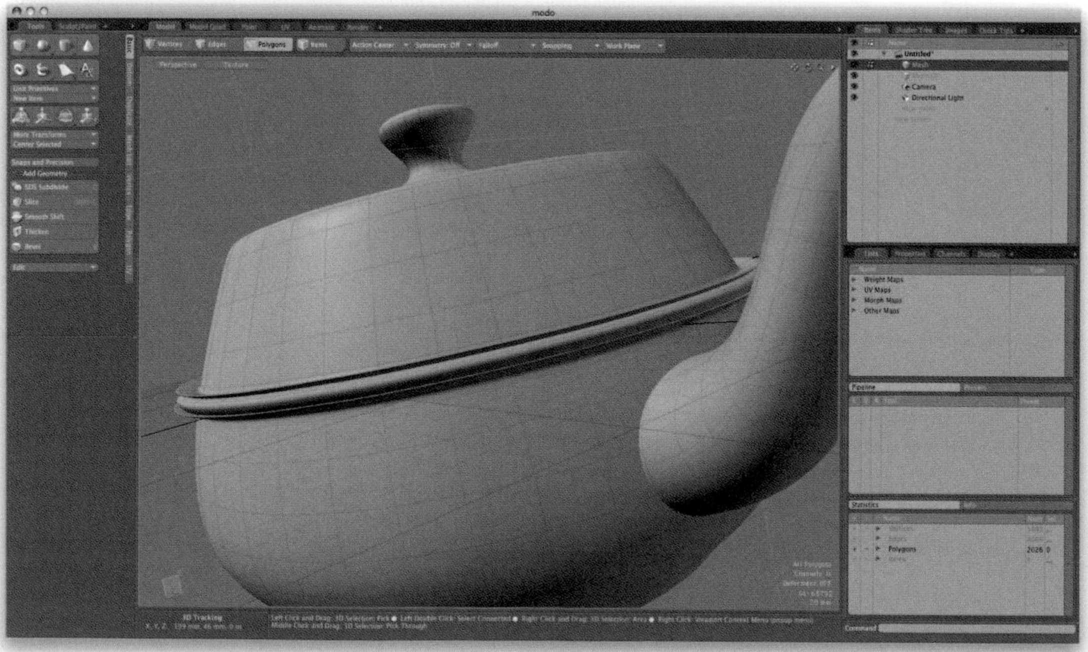

Figure 3.14 Because the conversion from edges to polygons was easy, you can now bevel the polygons to modify the geometry.

As you can see, working with selections in modo is pretty painless. This chapter, although not too exciting, is important to understand because it is the foundation of all the work you will do in the program. You will continually be selecting and deselecting any time you work with a model. This is especially true when you start working with multiple objects or an object with multiple parts.

Note

As your modeling skills progress and you begin making more complex models, you can create Selection Sets. This is a way to tell modo that you want to save a selection of vertices, edges, or polygons. Why? Well, perhaps the desired selection is intricate and encompasses multiple surfaces. Or perhaps it's a group of edges that need to be adjusted often based on a client's needs. Why go back and worry about selecting the exact element every time? Instead, select the desired vertices, edges, or polygons, then from the Select menu at the top of the modo interface, choose Assign Selection Set. Give it a name, and click OK. Then any time you want to select that same group of elements, simply choose Use Selection Set from the Select menu.

Here are a few more ways you can select in modo 301:

- Select two elements in order (vertices, edges, or polygons), and then press the up arrow on your keyboard. This will allow you to continue selecting in the same direction.
- Using the down arrow on your keyboard deselects in succession.
- Select one polygon or edge and press the left or right arrow on the keyboard to quickly select a selection loop.
- Hold the right mouse button, or Apple key and mouse button on the Mac, and you can lasso select. This method allows you to quickly draw around an element you want to select. This works for vertices, edges, or polygons. If you take a look at the Select menu, you can change Lasso style to a Rectangle, Circle, or Ellipse shape.
- Double-clicking on a polygon will select all attached polygons.
- Double-clicking on an edge will select the edge loop.
- Double-clicking on a vertex will select all attached vertices.
- Holding the mouse key down while you pass the cursor over the model will select everything in the path. This is a paint-style selection. Releasing the mouse, then holding it down again while you pass over the model, will deselect everything in its path. Remember that what is selected depends on the selection mode you're in, set at the top of the interface—Vertices, Edges, or Polygons.

- Selecting one element, then letting go of the mouse button and selecting another deselects the first selection. To continue a selection after releasing the mouse button, hold the Shift key.
- To deselect an undesired selection without deselecting everything, hold the Ctrl key and click on that unwanted selection.
- To deselect anything selected, click into the layout, off of the model itself.
- For faster selections, right-click on an element to quickly change to that particular selection mode. So if you are working in edges, and want to work with polygons, and pressing the spacebar is just to taxing on you, right-click on a polygon and you'll instantly change selection modes.
- Another way to quickly change selection modes is to right-click away from the model to get an instant popup menu (see Figure 3.15).
- Also try pressing Alt and the q key to call up a selection pie menu, as shown in Figure 3.16.

> **Note**
>
> When you have a full model to select, an easy way to make selections is to use the Select Connected feature. It's often easier to select just a few polygons, then press the left bracket key ([). This will select every element connected to the selection.

Figure 3.15 Right-clicking in the layout gives you a quick popup menu to change selection modes.

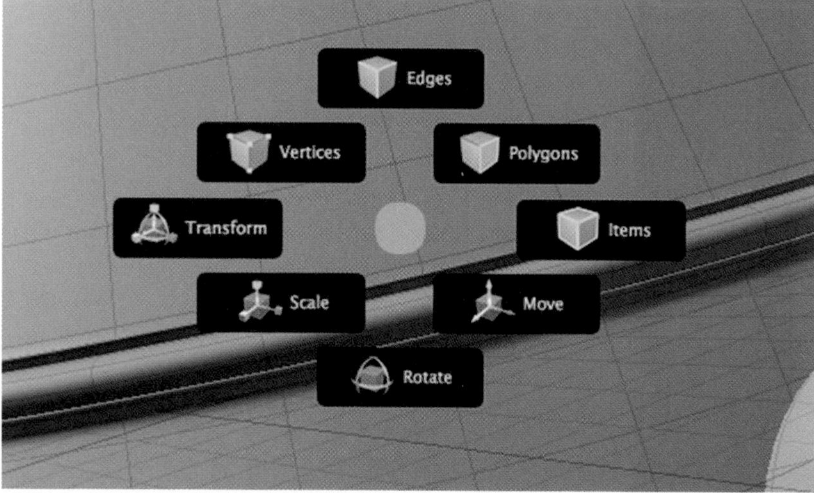

Figure 3.16 Pressing Alt and the q key calls up a pie menu for changing selection modes.

> **Note**
>
> When you select an element while the layout is set to a shaded mode (default), you will only select what's visible to you. That is to say, you won't select elements on the other side of the model. If, however, you're working in a wireframe view, what you select in front of the model will also select what's in back. Here's a tip though: If you have a three-button mouse, use the middle mouse button to select through the model in a shaded mode. This works great for a lasso-style selection. If, however, you're in wireframe mode, using the middle mouse button only selects those elements facing the camera.

Item Selection Mode

You'll see at the top of the interface another selection mode labeled Items. Because modo 301 offers cameras and lights in addition to models (or meshes), you have the ability to select these various items. This mode will also be important when you learn about animation a little later in the book.

Using the selection modes Vertices, Edges, or Polygons allows you to select elements within a particular model, as does the Materials selection mode (found by holding down the Items selection mode button.) But the Items selection mode gives you the freedom to select different items in the modo layout. So how would you use this selection mode? Easy. Say you had a large scene with two cameras, six objects, and four lights. By choosing the Items selection mode, you can just click on whatever item you want in the layout, then choose a tool to adjust it, such as Move or Rotate.

Items selection mode makes it easy to work on multiple items without a lot of thinking. You don't have to worry about heading over to the Mesh list, choosing an item, editing the item, and so on. Just use Items selection mode!

Now, in modo 301 there's a bit more to the Items selection mode. Click and hold the Items button, and you'll see additional options to select, such as Materials, Pivots, and Center, as shown in Figure 3.17. Here you can select and work with these elements in your scene. For example, modo 301 gives you the ability to animate a pivot. Why is that

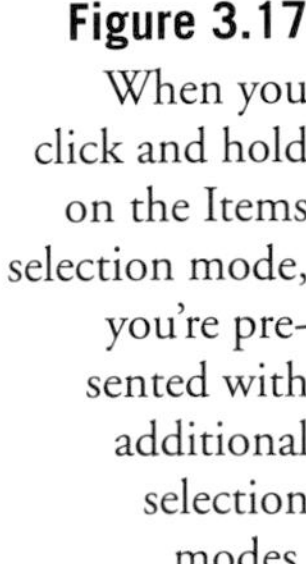

Figure 3.17 When you click and hold on the Items selection mode, you're presented with additional selection modes.

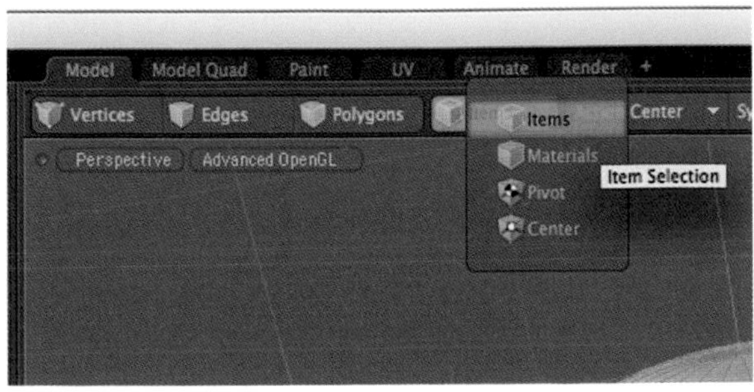

important? Imagine that you're animating a tumbling block. As that block rolls along the floor, it needs to rotate and pivot on various edges and corners. By animating the pivot over time, you can set where that rotation happens with each frame. There are times you won't animate a pivot at all, but you might move it for things like swinging doors or rotating mechanical arms.

Note

A quick way to get to Items selection mode is to press the Shift key and spacebar at the same time.

Quick Access Selection

There's one more thing to learn about selections, and that is the Quick Access Selection bar. This is a really cool way to work with selections, especially if you're not good at remembering keyboard equivalents. It's an easy way to see the available options in one place.

1. Working with the same model you were using earlier (or any primitive shape), mouse over a group of polygons to select them, as shown in Figure 3.18.

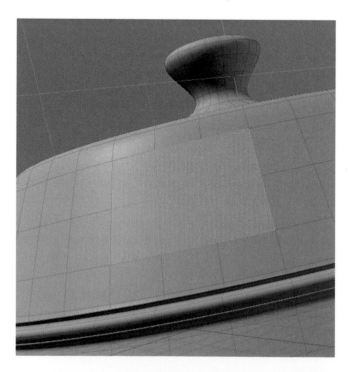

Figure 3.18
Select a group of polygons, remembering to first switch to Polygons selection mode at the top of the interface.

2. Then press the Alt key and the spacebar. You'll be greeted with the Quick Access Selection bar, as shown in Figure 3.19.

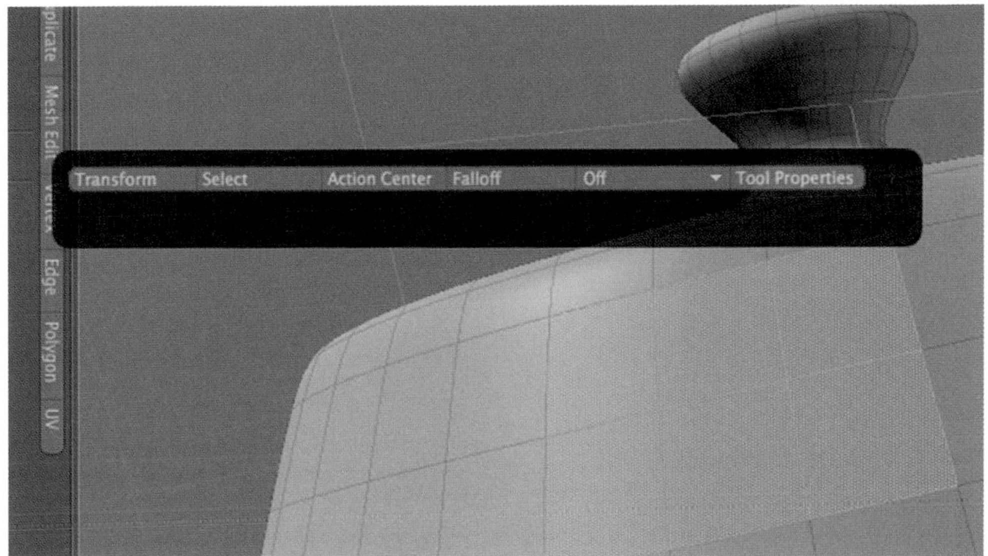

Figure 3.19 Pressing the Alt key and spacebar calls up the Quick Access Selection bar.

3. By pressing the Select button in the Quick Access Selection bar, you can choose what to do with the selected elements. You can invert the selection, select Connected, and so on, as shown in Figure 3.20.

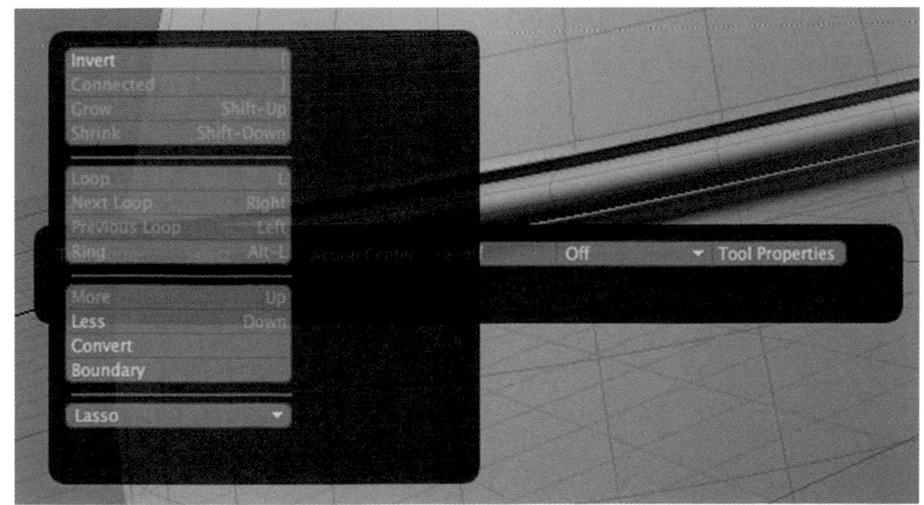

Figure 3.20 From the Quick Access Selection bar, you can choose what to do with your selected elements, all in one handy location.

Experiment with these various selection modes using just simple primitive shapes, as we've done here in these few pages. There are multiple ways to change selection modes, as you can see, and which method to use is completely up to you. Get comfortable with this process and try the different methods.

Falloffs

You might have heard about modo's advanced feature set, and even probably heard something about falloffs. More than just a term, falloffs are important to the way you control how a tool works in modo 301/302. *Falloffs* allow you to ramp a tool's effect based on the falloff type you choose. By doing this, you can create great effects with less effort. To grasp this cool concept, follow along with this quick tutorial.

1. From the File menu, choose Reset to restore modo to its default views and clear out the primitive shapes you've worked with.
2. Because you've not yet created any models, use the Teapot primitive for this exercise, as you did previously. The goal of these few steps is to gain an understanding of the falloffs available in modo 301. Holding the Shift key, click the Teapot primitive from the Tool Bar tab on the left side of the interface. Press the a to fit the model to view.
3. From the top of the modo interface, choose Automatic, from the Action Center drop-down list.
4. Then, from the Falloff drop-down list, choose Radial as shown in Figure 3.21.

Figure 3.21
Set the falloff type to Radial from the Falloff drop-down list at the top of the modo interface.

5. Press the w key to quickly select the Move tool, which is located in the Basic vertical category.

6. Now click and drag in the layout. The Move tool will affect the region within the Radial falloff. You'll see a large purplish ring around the model. This represents the falloff. Click directly in the middle of this ring and drag it over to the spout of the teapot, as shown in Figure 3.22.

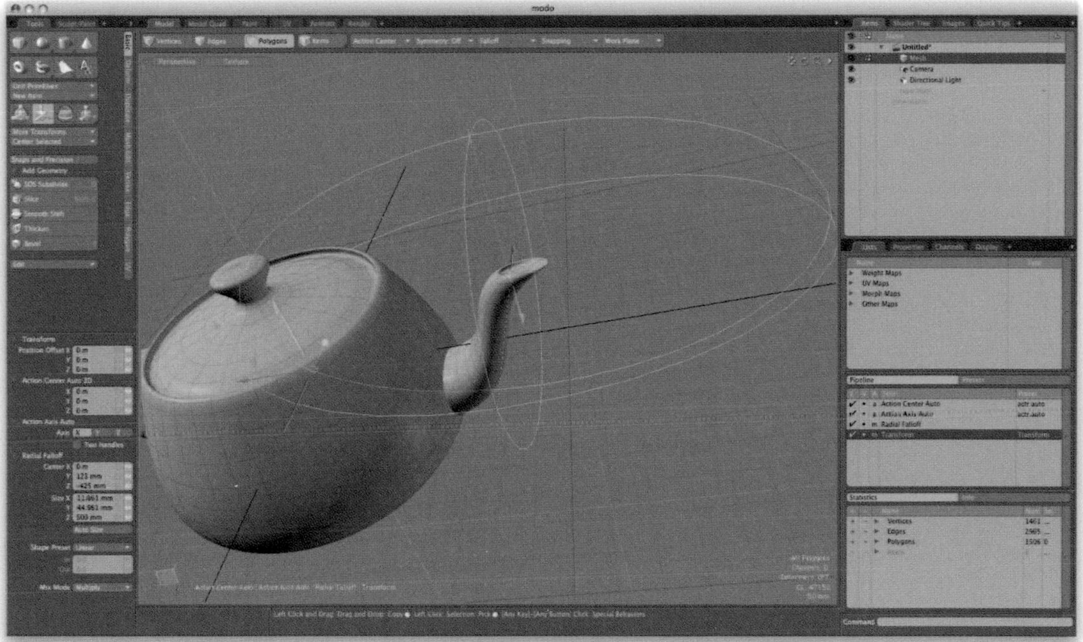

Figure 3.22 When a falloff is active, you'll see the falloff handles.

7. You'll see small red (X axis), blue (Z axis), and green (Y axis) controls for the size of the falloff, represented as small plus signs. These are located on the edges of the falloff ring. Click and drag each to change the amount of the falloff, as shown in Figure 3.23.
8. Now, within the falloff region, click and drag to use the Move tool. But notice how the move is applied—just within the Radial falloff (see Figure 3.24).

   As you can see in Figure 3.23, the falloff is affecting how the Move tool applies to the mesh. At the center of the falloff, you have 100% of the Move tool applied. With the outer edge of the region of the Radial falloff, you have 0% of the Move tool applied, hence the term *falloff*.

Figure 3.23 You can easily adjust the size of the falloff and the amount of its influence by dragging each ring.

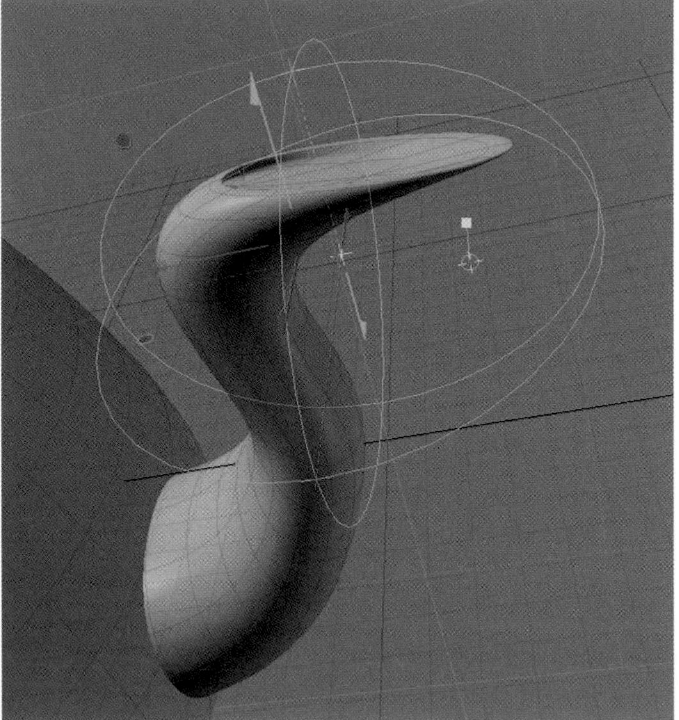

Figure 3.24 With a Radial falloff applied to the Move tool, you can specifically change a shape to something a little less traditional.

Note

You can click and drag with the middle mouse button to change the influence of the tool while using falloffs.

9. Now try something cool. Click and drag the light blue square that is located in the center of the Radial falloff. Drag it around, and you'll see the falloff can shape your model simply by moving it. Remember that this Radial falloff is combined with the Move tool to gain this effect. Figure 3.25 shows the falloff moved to the top of the spout, essentially flattening it out.

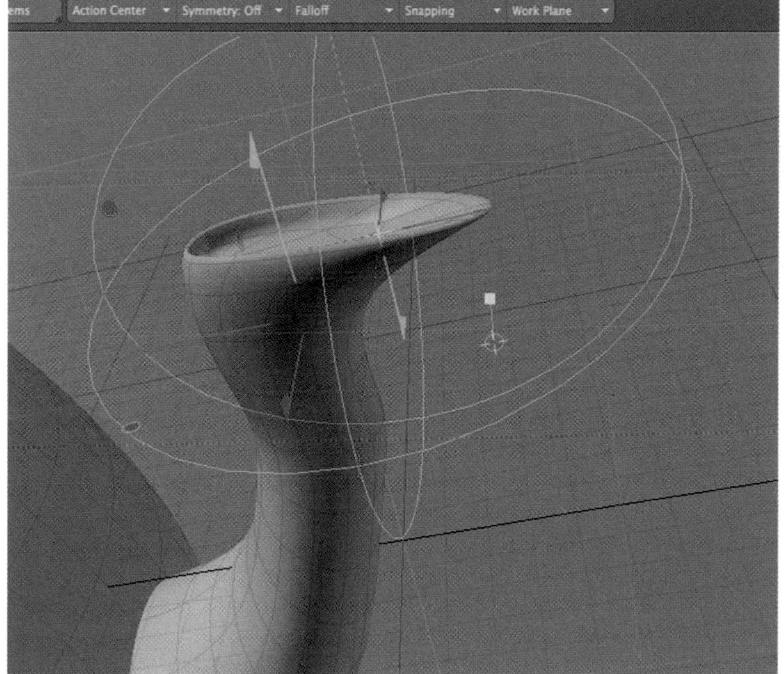

Figure 3.25 The Radial falloff type applied with the Move tool can shape and deform your model simply by moving it around.

Like anything, seeing something in action often helps drive a point home. Learning to use modo's falloffs is no exception. These next few steps will guide you through using falloffs so you gain a better understanding of how they work.

1. Here's one other example to see falloffs in action. Press the spacebar to turn off the Move tool. Then from the Falloff drop-down menu, select Linear.
2. Click with the left mouse button at the top corner of the teapot spout and, keeping the mouse button depressed, drag to the bottom of the spout, as shown in Figure 3.26. You'll see a light colored elongated triangle of sorts, representing the Linear falloff.

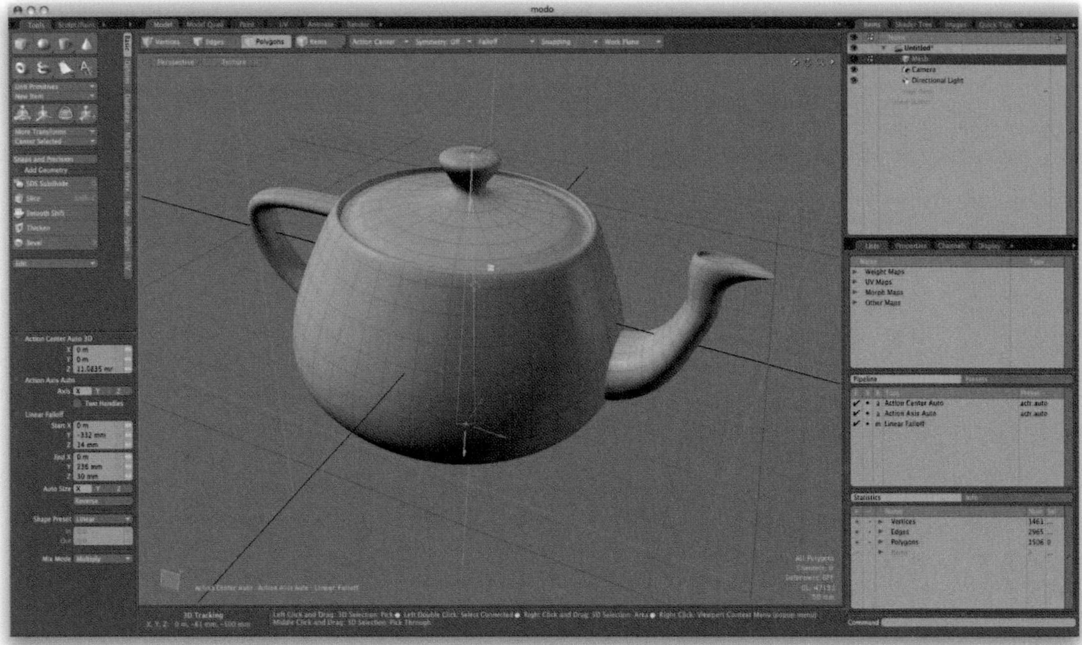

Figure 3.26 A Linear falloff is set by clicking in one spot, then dragging out.

3. Press the e key on your keyboard to turn on the Rotate tool.
4. Click toward the bottom of the spout at the joint, where it extends out from the teapot. You'll see the rotation handles appear, as shown in Figure 3.27.
5. Now click and drag the red rotational handle to the right to rotate the object. Notice what happens? You're deforming the object. Only a portion of it is rotating. This is because the Linear falloff is telling modo to apply 100% of the tool at the bottom and 0% at the top—the narrow end of the falloff tool. Figure 3.28 shows the deformation.
6. Now click and drag on either of the center crosshairs from either end of the Linear falloff and drag them around. You'll see how the model deforms, similar to the Radial falloff movement you did earlier.

You can see that by using the Falloff tools in modo, you have even greater flexibility for creating organic shapes. Imagine trying to actually model a bent, ugly teapot from scratch. It would be as easy as using a few tools with falloffs applied. But there are more than just the two falloffs described here. Take a look at the Falloff drop-down list and try the same steps you've just performed with different falloff types. See what you can come up with.

Figure 3.27 Selecting the Rotate tool and clicking in the layout in a specific area determines where the rotation control handles will appear.

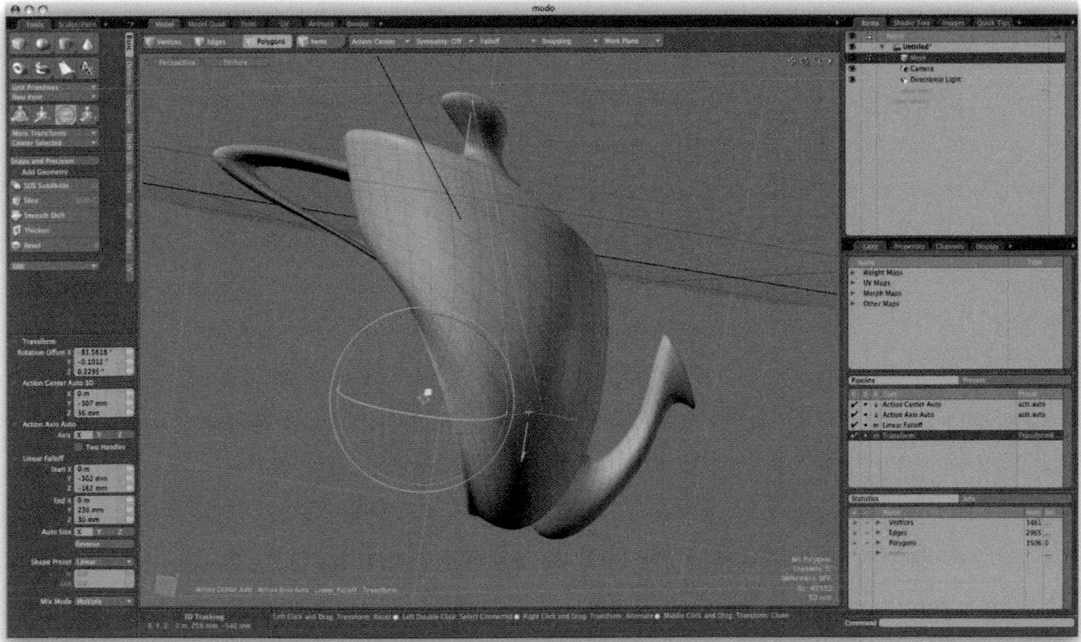

Figure 3.28 Rotating the object with a Linear falloff results in a deformation of the object.

This next project will show you a pretty powerful combination of tools to create some cool shapes.

1. Using the Teapot primitive from the previous exercise, press the spacebar to turn off any tool that might be on. You can also press Ctrl-Z to undo your deformations and return to a less deformed shape. Or feel free to reset your program from the File menu and create a new primitive shape.
2. From the Falloff drop-down list, select None.
3. Press the spacebar until your selection mode is set to Edges. Look for this at the top of the interface.
4. Now press the t key to activate one of modo's most powerful tools, the Element Move tool. This tool allows you to simply click and drag on any element to move it. It's excellent for shaping objects. This tool is located under the Deform vertical category list, as shown in Figure 3.29.

Figure 3.29
Select the Element Move tool from the Deform vertical category.

5. Find an edge on the model, and then click and drag it (see Figure 3.30). The Element Move tool allows you to click and drag on any element, saving you the trouble of selection, choosing a tool, performing the action, dropping the tool, dropping the selection, and then repeating. This saves huge amounts of time when modeling.

   Notice in Figure 3.31 that the edge is moved. It looks like a little bump in the object. What if you wanted to really dent the object? How would you do that? There are some other modeling tools you could apply, but one easy way is to add a falloff to the Element Move tool.

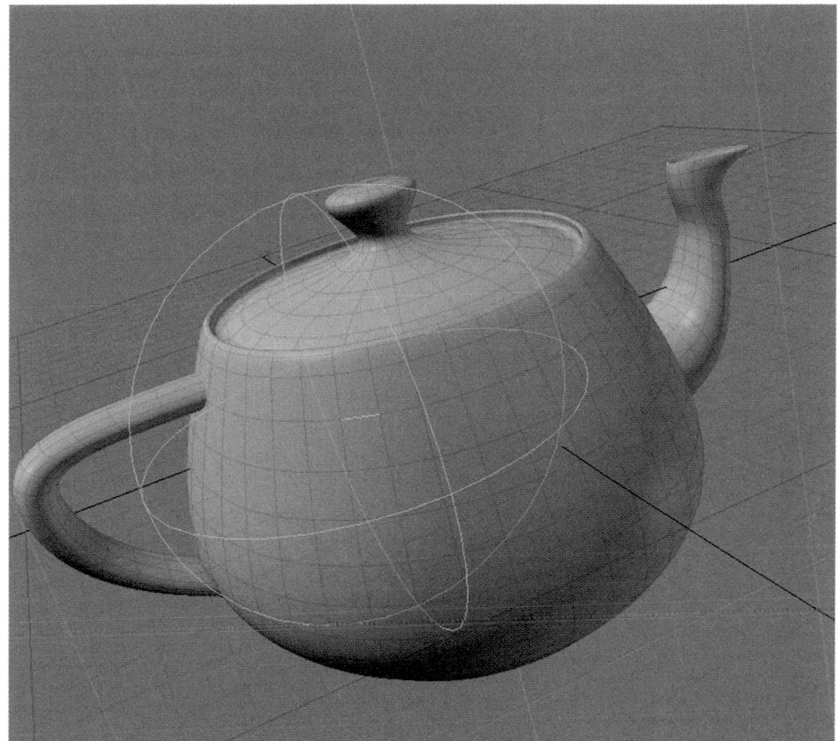

Figure 3.30 Using the Element Move tool makes it easy to pull and shape elements such as edges.

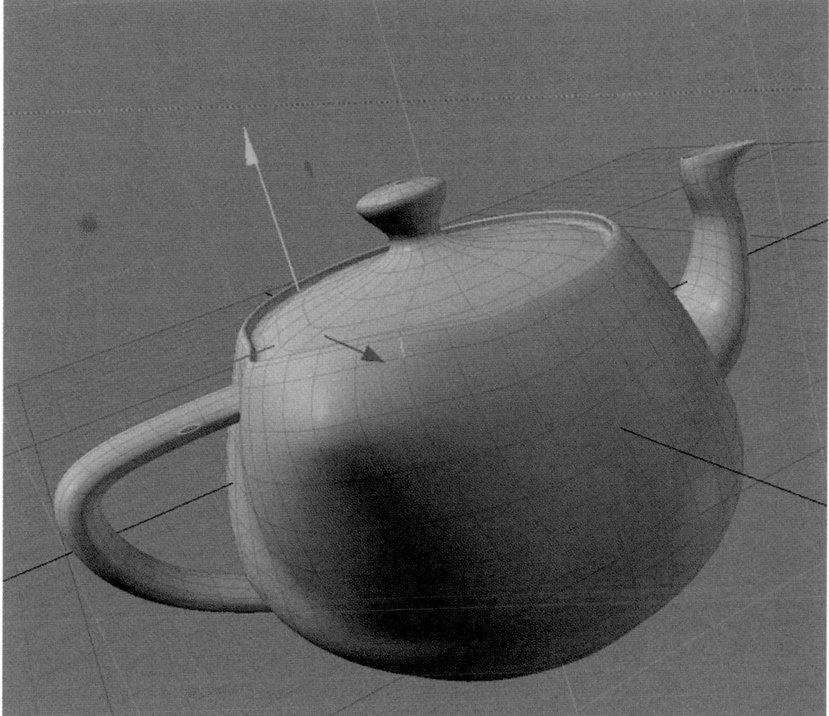

Figure 3.31 Once the falloff is set, moving a single edge pulls the surrounding edges but the effect falls off based on the region you define.

6. Press Ctrl-Z to undo your previous Element Move operation. From the Falloff drop-down list, select Element.
7. Press the t key again to turn on the Element Move tool. Then, with the right mouse button, draw out a falloff region as you did earlier. Figure 3.29 shows the result.
8. Click and drag on an edge of the model. Now instead of just the edge moving, you'll see that the edge takes a lot more of its neighboring geometry with it. Figure 3.32 shows the deformation.

You can see that by using a simple falloff you can achieve great results. Once you've set up a tool like this, you can rotate around the view (hold the Alt key, then click and drag) and start dragging edges, polygons, or vertices to shape the model. Figure 3.31 shows a dented up teapot using just the Element Move tool with an Element falloff type.

At any point, you can change the falloff region. To do this, use the right mouse button (hold the Apple key on those single-button Macs) and then set your falloff region. Then with the left mouse, click and drag on an element. Rinse and repeat until you have the model you want.

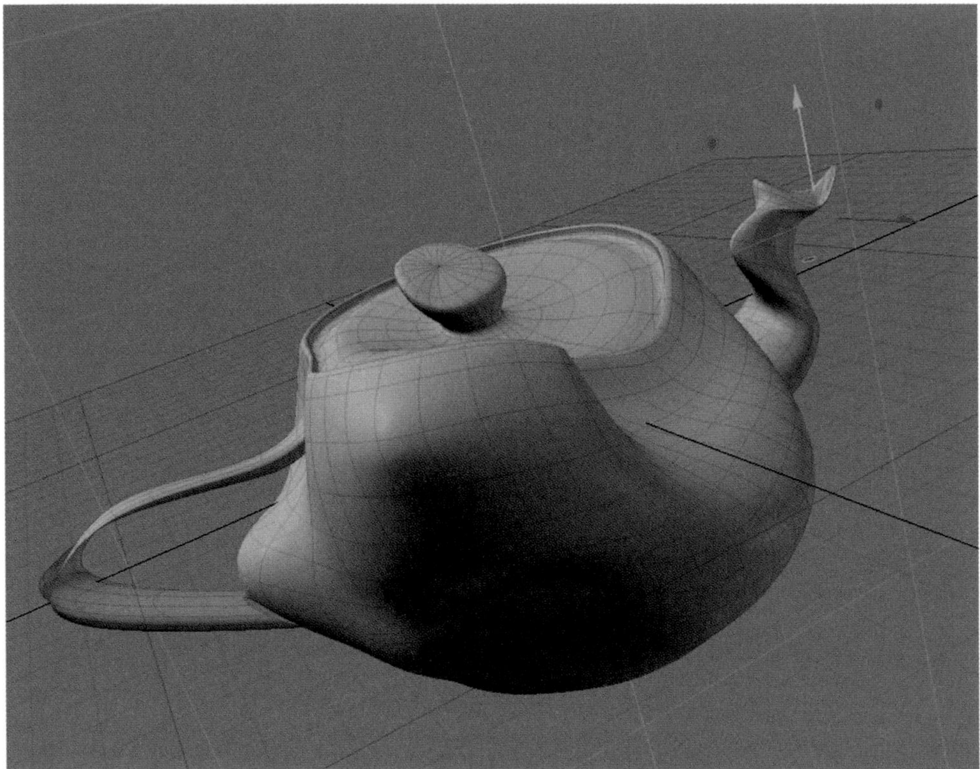

Figure 3.32
Using just the Element Move tool with an Element falloff, you can take out your frustrations on a defenseless teapot.

> **Note**
>
> Remember that using the Element Move tool doesn't mean you're stuck moving just edges. You can click and move on any element of your model, vertex, edge, or polygon. That's the beauty of the tool.

Falloffs are quite powerful and, combined with the right tools, who knows what you can create! But while I could go on and on with different crazy examples, there's one other important area you should learn about before heading into the project chapters.

Pipeline

Finally, in this chapter we come to the Pipeline, also known as the Tool Pipe. You might have heard this term passed around on a forum or two or perhaps in some marketing material. Contrary to what you might think, the Tool Pipe has nothing to do with a pipe or modeling one; rather, it's a melting pot of components and tools. With the Tool Pipe, you're able to take falloffs, for example, further by combining them with other modeling and creation tools. Tools in many programs have limited falloffs, but modo is different. The Pipeline is where all actions come together by joining modifiers and tools. Figure 3.33 shows the Tool Pipe at the bottom right side of a default modo 301 interface. Here, you can see the Element Move tool combined with an Element falloff type.

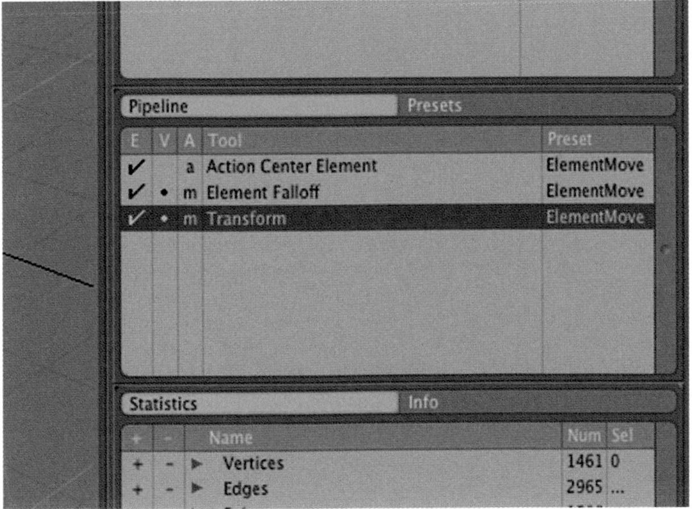

Figure 3.33
The Tool Pipe is where all modo actions and modifiers come together, creating more powerful commands and presets.

Taking a closer look at Figure 3.33, you can see that the tools being used to deform the teapot are all listed. There are two Move commands (Transform and Element Falloff), along with an Automatic Action Center set to Element. The end result is a tool that does more than meets the eye.

The Tool Pipe is not something you really ever have to worry about working in, but you can if you choose. It's the Tool Pipe that makes modo's functions so powerful. For example, by choosing an Airbrush falloff, and then choosing the Bevel tool, modo's Tool Pipe combines these to give you a more powerful modeling operation.

1. Using an object like the teapot, or another model or primitive, select the Airbrush falloff from the Falloff drop-down menu.
2. If you're using the Teapot primitive, press the d key one time to subdivide the entire model. This creates more geometry to work with.
3. Then click on the Polygon category from the vertical list on the left side of the interface, and choose Bevel (or just press the b key).
4. With the right mouse button (hold the Apple key on single-button Macs) click and drag out a range of influence for the tool. Figure 3.34 shows the result.

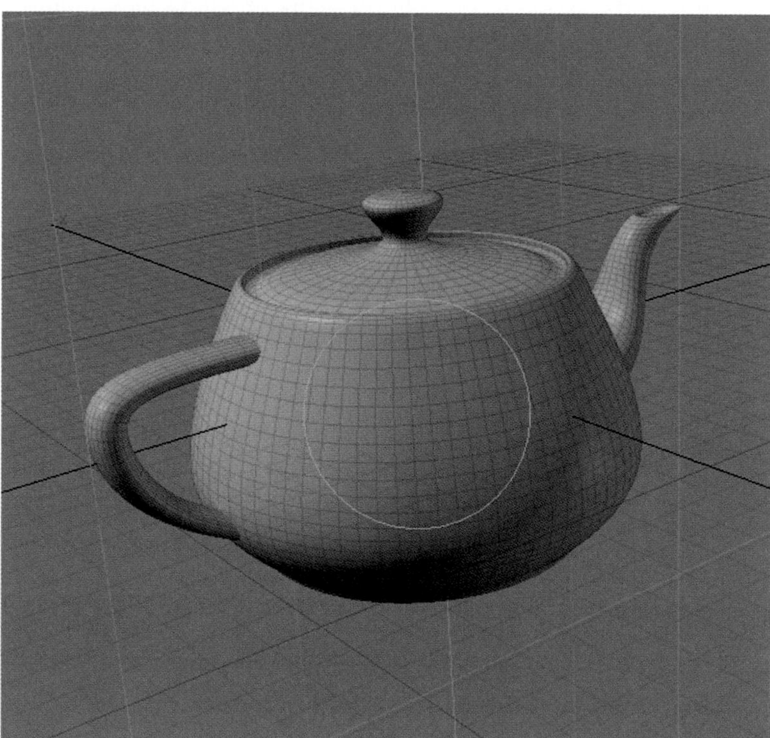

Figure 3.34
As with the other falloff types, you select the falloff you want, choose a tool, then right-click in the layout to set a range of influence. The Tool Pipe remembers your combination of tools.

5. Making sure that the Shift value has a setting of about 1 cm or so in the Tool Properties panel on the bottom left of the interface, click and drag on your model.
6. The Tool Pipe has combined the Polygon Bevel tool with the Airbrush falloff. The result is that not only can you change the way your modify tools work (as shown earlier in the chapter), but you can also change the way geometry is created. Figure 3.35 shows the airbrushed bevel operation.

Figure 3.35 The Tool Pipe not only combines modify functions, but geometry creation as well. Here an Airbrush falloff type is combined with the Polygon Bevel tool. The result is the ability to "paint" on the bevels.

This poor teapot has had enough abuse for one chapter, don't you think? But hopefully the examples have shown you what the core modo tools can do. The combinations of Action Centers and falloffs all come together in the Tool Pipe, and in the end, you have ultimate control. While at first it may seem a bit daunting, you'll soon come to learn that there is a method for this madness. As the next chapters progress, you'll see all of these core tools in action. You'll use them for yourself, creating objects and scenes that are definitely more attractive than a busted old teapot. So if you're ready, grab a snack and head on Chapter 4 to begin the basic modeling chapters.

4

modo 301/302 Jump Start

You've been briefly introduced to modo in the previous chapters, and read about modo's exceedingly customizable interface, Action Centers, falloffs, and the Pipeline. From here, you'll head into the projects, which will utilize the information you've read about in the first three chapters. With that said, on to the Jump Start project!

Model Preparation

Before getting started, be sure you're using the default modo 301/302 interface setting. Remember, you can find this by going to the Layout menu, then choosing Layouts, 301/302 Default Layout, as shown in Figure 4.1.

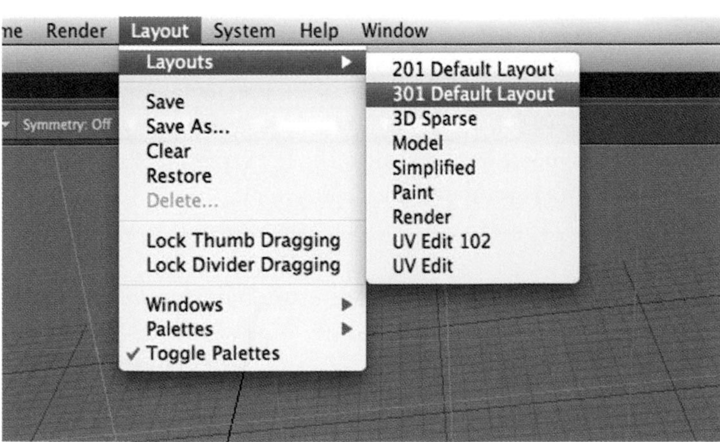

Figure 4.1 To set your modo 301/302 interface to its natural state, choose the default setting from the Layout menu.

The project you'll be embarking upon in this chapter will give you a working knowledge of modo 301/302. What you'll create is simple, but along the way, you'll get a feel for how to approach most projects in the program. Figure 4.2 shows the final 3D render you'll create in the upcoming pages.

Figure 4.2
Simple and effective, modo's tools make modeling and rendering an object like this a piece of cake.

1. Start up modo 301/302 with a default interface. Then make sure you're in the Model tabbed view, with a Perspective viewport.
2. Click the Tools tab on the top left of the interface (see Figure 4.3).
3. In the Tools tab, select the Cylinder primitive, as shown in Figure 4.4.

Note

If you look closely at the corner of the Cylinder icon, there's a black triangle. You'll see this in a few other primitive tools as well. This is telling you that the tool has more options. Click and hold with the left mouse button, and you'll see a variation of the tools. If you did this for the Cylinder primitive, you'd find the Capsule tool.

4. Hold the Alt/Option key, then with the left mouse button, click and drag in the Perspective view to rotate it. Rotate the view so that the Work Plane is set to the Y axis, as shown in Figure 4.5. You can view this icon in the bottom left of the interface, and this tells modo that the Y axis is the primary axis when you begin building your model. You'll see this work in the next step.

> **Note**
>
> While it might not look like the icon representing the Work Plane looks like it's on the Y axis, it is. To explain the Work Plane further, watch the Work Plane movie on the book's disc.

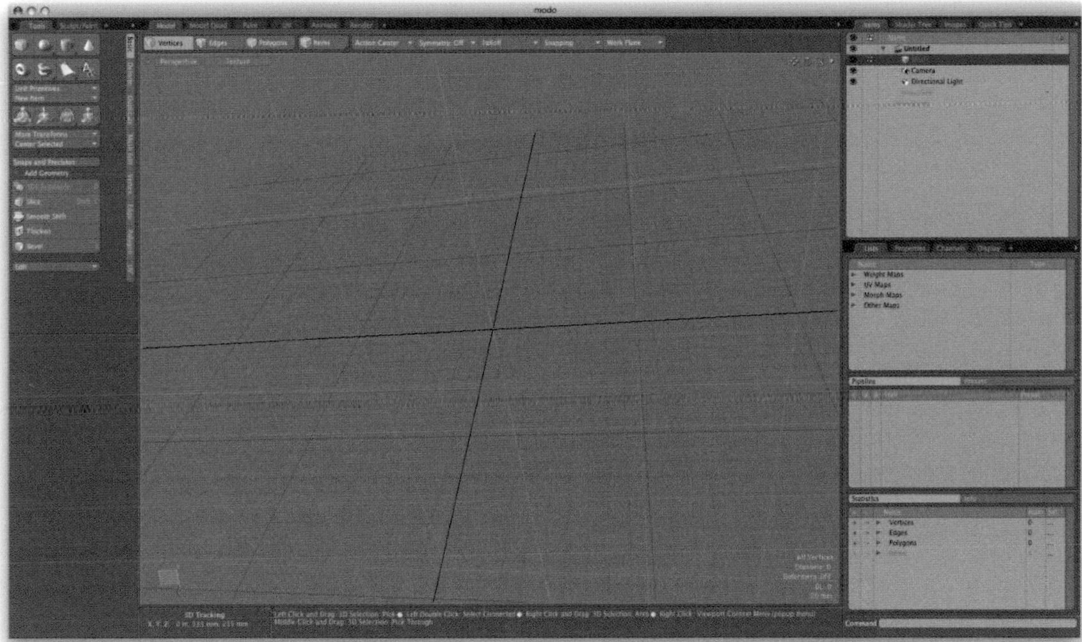

Figure 4.3 To begin modeling your mug, just be sure you're working in a default 301/302 interface, similar to this.

Figure 4.4 Select the Cylinder primitive from the Tools tab to begin modeling your mug.

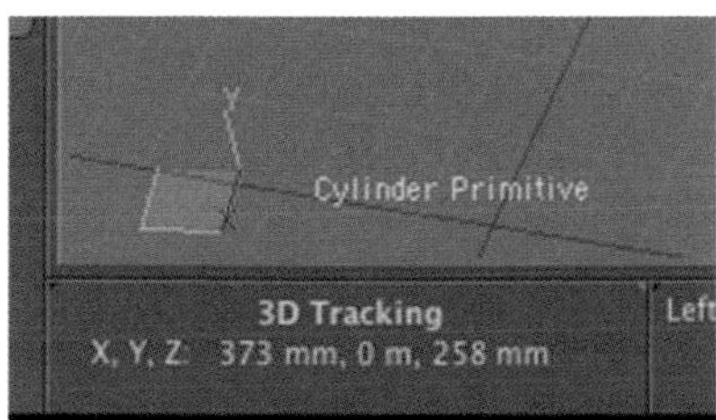

Figure 4.5 Make sure that your Work Plane is set to the Y axis.

5. Now that the Work Plane is set to the Y axis, click and drag in the viewport. You should see a flat cylinder, as shown in Figure 4.6.

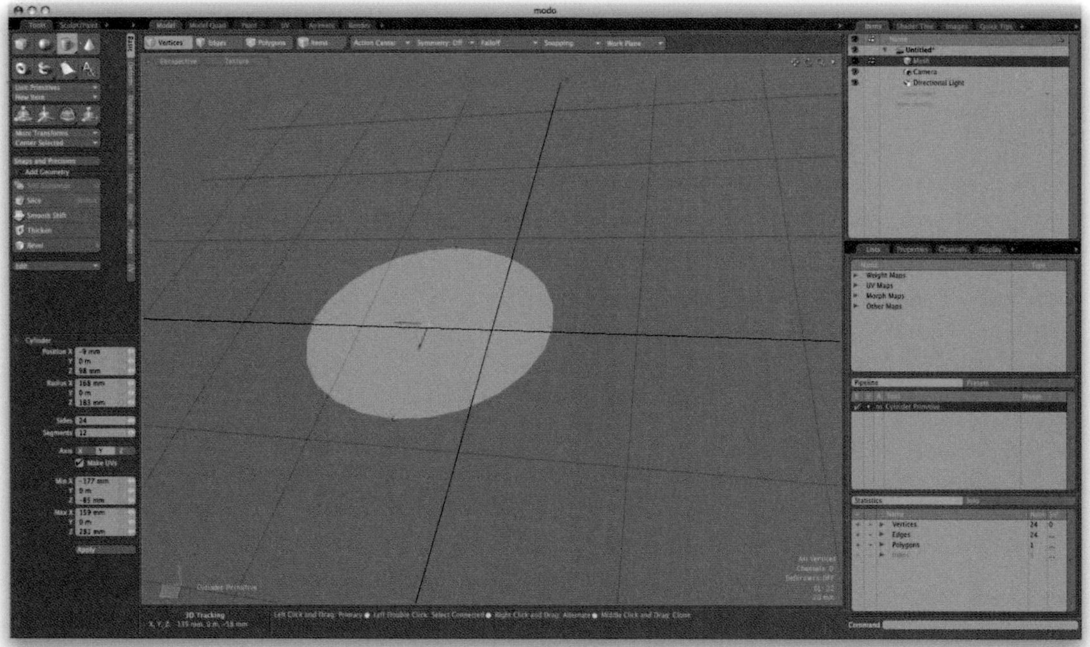

Figure 4.6 Begin creating the mug with a flat cylinder.

6. Now before you go any further, take a look at the Cylinder tool properties that appear on the left of the interface (refer to Figure 4.6). You can see that modo recorded the position, radius, and axis for the newly created disc. Because you've not yet turned off the tool, you can still make changes to the model, either interactively in the viewport or numerically in the properties. Go ahead and set the Sides value to 48 and Segments to 24, as shown in Figure 4.7.

   Your radius might not be equal, which it should be in this case, because you don't want to create an oval mug. Maybe you do, but let's go with an evenly shaped version for this round. In the Radius setting for the Cylinder tool, you'll notice a small icon to the right of the numbered value. This is not the arrow icon used to adjust the value, but rather, the icon to the left of the arrow. Place your mouse over this value and leave it there for a moment. You'll see some options appear, as shown in Figure 4.8.

   What you see in Figure 4.8 is modo 301/302's new Gang select feature. It's a tremendous time-saver. There are four options to it, however. The first is Independent, which is the default setting. You then have Copy, where changes are

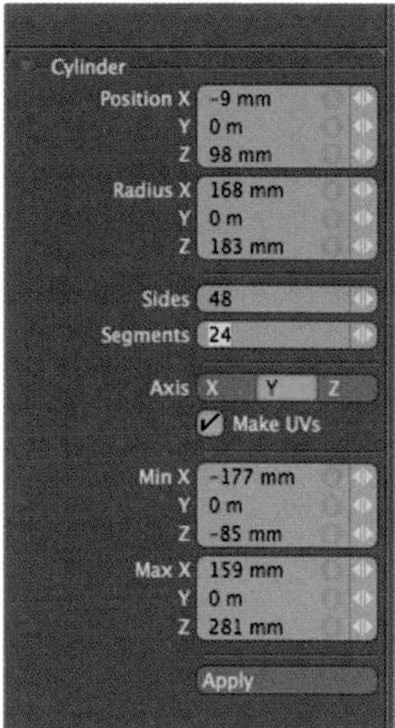

Figure 4.7 You can numerically change values for a primitive tool while the tool is still active.

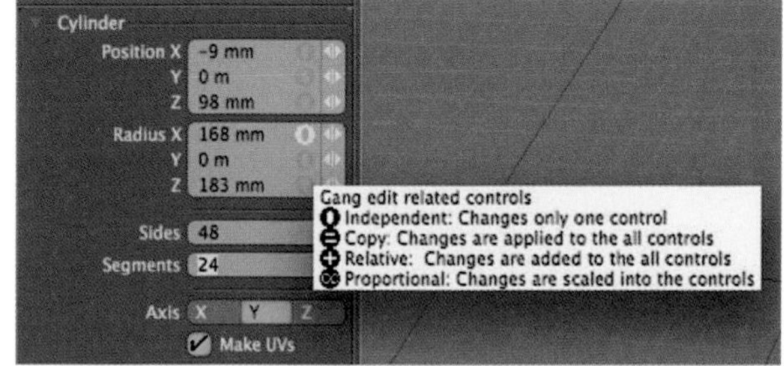

Figure 4.8 Hover your mouse over the icon to the right of the numeric entry in the tool properties to see the Gang select variations.

applied to all values. Next is Relative, where changes are added to all controls. Finally there is Proportional, where changes are scaled into the controls. It all sounds more complex than it really is, but you'll see in a moment how handy this feature is. You'll find these Gang select options throughout value settings in modo 301/302.

7. Click the Gang select for the X value of Radius one time to change to Gang select Copy mode. As soon as you do, you'll see the value highlight. Simply type in a new value, such as 250 mm, and press Return. You'll see all three values instantly change to that amount, as shown in Figure 4.9.

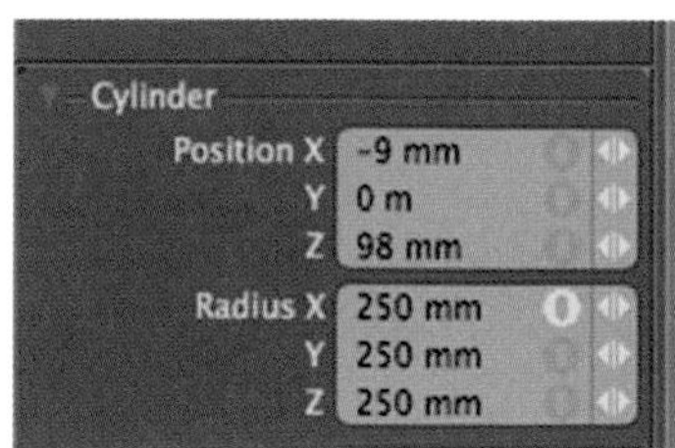

Figure 4.9 The new gang select feature in modo 301/302 makes setting three values fast and easy.

8. Press the q key to turn off the Cylinder tool. Your primitive object is ready to be turned into something more then a chunk of polygons. Note that you can also press the spacebar to turn off a tool; however, this can be confusing if you're not aware because the spacebar also changes between the various selection modes.

Model Manipulation

With a simple primitive object created, you can use it to generate all kinds of new shapes by editing vertices, edges, or points. This next section will show you how to create the inside of the mug, along with fine-tuning some details.

1. First things first—save your work! You're probably saying, "What work?" While creating a Cylinder primitive isn't all that complex, remember that the goal of this chapter is to help you learn how modo works and understand the workflow. With that said, you can go to the File menu, then select Save. Since you haven't saved at this point, choosing this option is the same as choosing Save As. Pick a location and save your work as Mug.
2. Now, go to File menu again, and choose Save Incremental. Your model is now saved as a new version. Why did you do this? You saved the original cylinder block as Mug. By then saving an incremental version, that original model is intact should you ever need to start over. Get it? With every significant change you make, save an incremental version. You might find that at some point you just completely mess up your model, and because you've been saving incrementally, you never have to completely start over.
3. Press the spacebar a couple of times so that you're in Polygons selection mode.
4. Hold the Alt/Option key and then click and drag in the viewport so that you can see the top of your cylinder-soon-to-be-coffee-mug object.
5. Click once on the top of the model to select the large round polygon that makes up the top of the object, as shown in Figure 4.10.
6. With the top polygon selected, you can start shaping the inside of the mug. Now you're going to get tired of hearing this, but press the b key on your keyboard to activate the Bevel tool.
7. Once the Bevel tool is selected, click once in the layout to activate it. You'll see blue and red handles appear, as shown in Figure 4.11.
8. With the tool on, you'll notice the Bevel tool properties available on the left side of the screen, just as you did when working with the Cylinder tool. The Bevel tool offers a set of controls, as do most tools. However, modo allows you to work interactively, which is what the red and blue handles are for. Click and drag the red handle to about 20 mm. You can see the value change in the Bevel tool properties. The red handle changes the Inset value, or how far "in" the bevel will go.

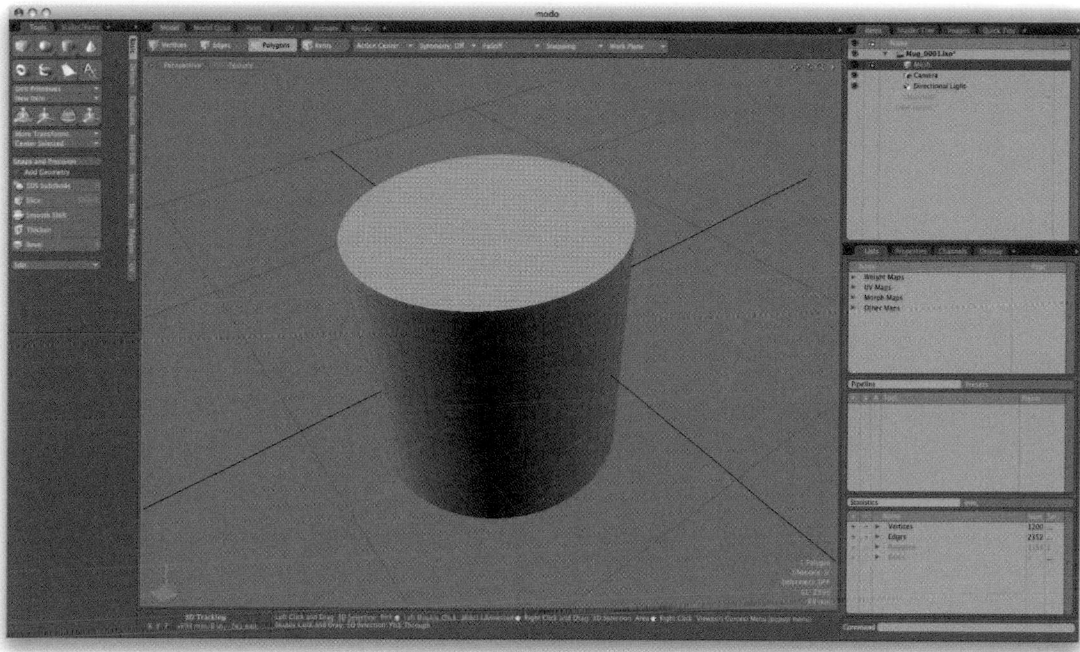

Figure 4.10 To begin shaping the mug, work in Polygons selection mode, and then select the top polygon.

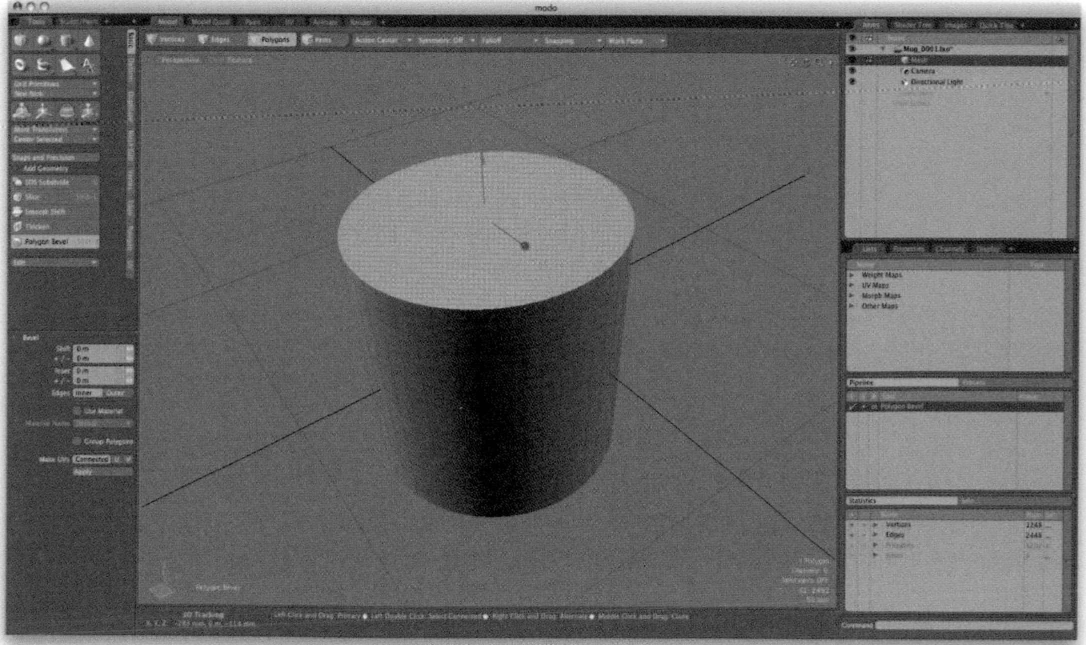

Figure 4.11 To use the Bevel tool, first select it by pressing the b key on your keyboard, then clicking in the viewport to activate it. This is the same procedure for most of modo's tools.

9. Next you want to shift the polygon down into the mug itself. However, if you did that now, you'd get a very sharp-edged mug. This is because you've only inset the polygon. You need another polygon to build the inside of the mug. Therefore, hold the Shift key and click once in the layout. You've just reset the bevel, essentially copying the selection. If you look at the Bevel tool properties, the Inset value is now back to 0 mm.
10. With this newly created polygon, click and drag the blue handle to pull the selection down into the mug, about –460 mm. This changes the Shift value, as shown in Figure 4.12.
11. At this point, save your scene. Mac users, press Command/Apple and the s key. PC users, press Ctrl and the s key. You can also use the File menu, and choose Save.
12. So, big deal, right? A cylinder with an inside. True, it's not very exciting. But wait! We're not finished. Press the q key to turn off the Bevel tool. Then click once in an empty area of the layout to deselect the polygon. That is, don't click on the model itself.
13. Press the Tab key. The model looks a little different, right? But the top edge got very sharp, as it appears in Figure 4.13.

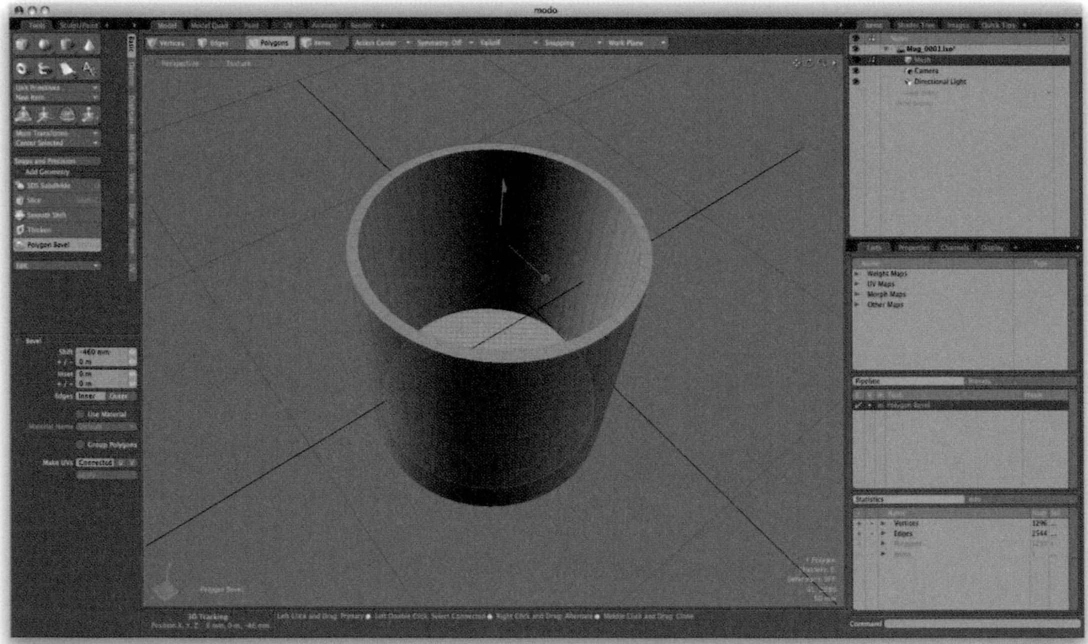

Figure 4.12 Dragging the blue handle changes the Shift value for the selected polygon.

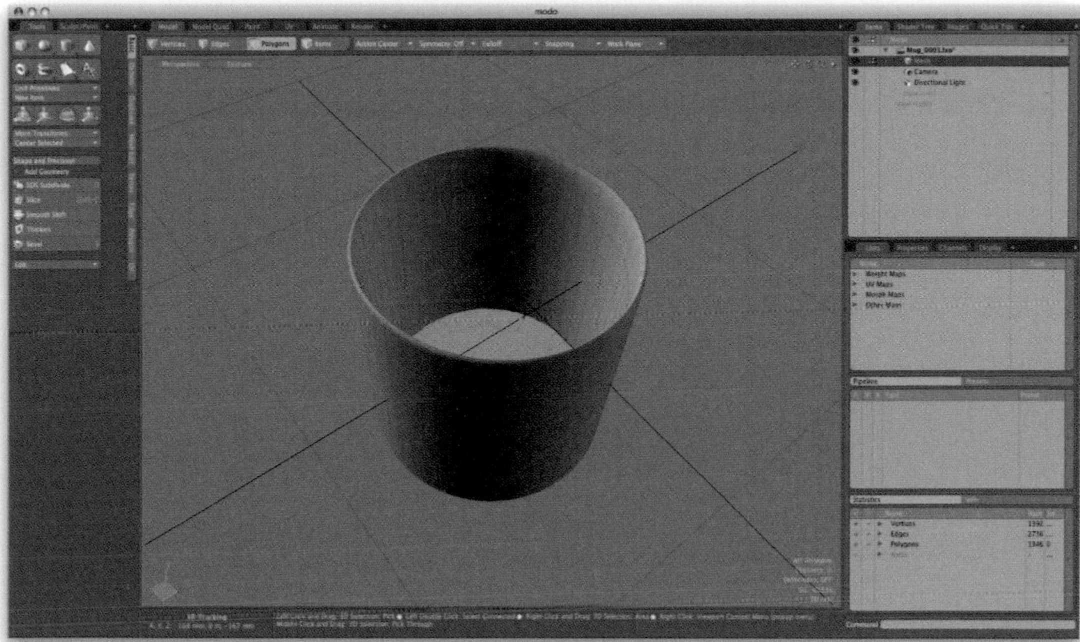

Figure 4.13 Pressing the Tab key changes the model from polygons to subdivision surfaces.

By pressing the Tab key, you've changed your model from ordinary polygons to subdivision surfaces. Or, for a better explanation, the model is now made up of smooth curves. So why the sharp edge at the top of the mug? Because there was not enough geometry there to hold the curve in place. If you've ever worked with Bezier curves in Adobe Illustrator, you know that you need more points for areas within your curve that should be more detailed. The same goes for subdivisions in 3D. In this next section, you'll begin working with edges to shape the model even more.

Selecting and Editing Geometry

When it comes to editing geometry, modo makes it pretty easy. You can add, delete, slice, or even remove points (vertices), edges, and polygons. This section will show you how to edit the mug to have a cleaner, smoother appearance.

1. Working with the mug you started earlier, press the spacebar until you're in Edges selection mode, as shown in Figure 4.14.

Figure 4.14 Switch to Edges selection mode at the top of the modo interface.

2. Remember that in the previous section, you pressed the Tab key to turn the model into a subdivision model. Be sure to keep it that way. Then place your mouse over the top-most edge on the outside of the mug. The edge will be highlighted, as shown in Figure 4.15. Feel free to hold the Alt/Option key, and then click and drag to rotate the view to get better access to the edge.

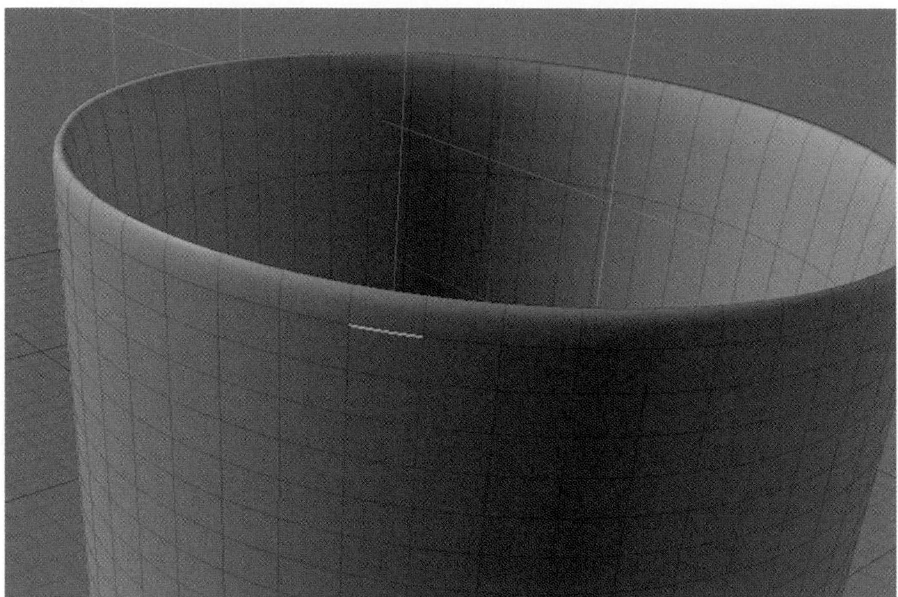

Figure 4.15
Hover the mouse over the top-most edge, and it will become highlighted.

Note

If you're working in Vertices, Polygons, or Items mode, hovering the mouse over geometry will highlight it, as you've seen with the Edges selection mode.

3. Once the edge is highlighted, double-click it. This will instantly select the entire edge loop. Figure 4.16 shows the selection.
4. With the edge selected, press the b key to turn on the Bevel tool.
5. Click and drag in the viewport to bevel the edge, about 6 mm or so, as shown in Figure 4.17.

Figure 4.16 Double-click the top-most edge to select the entire edge loop.

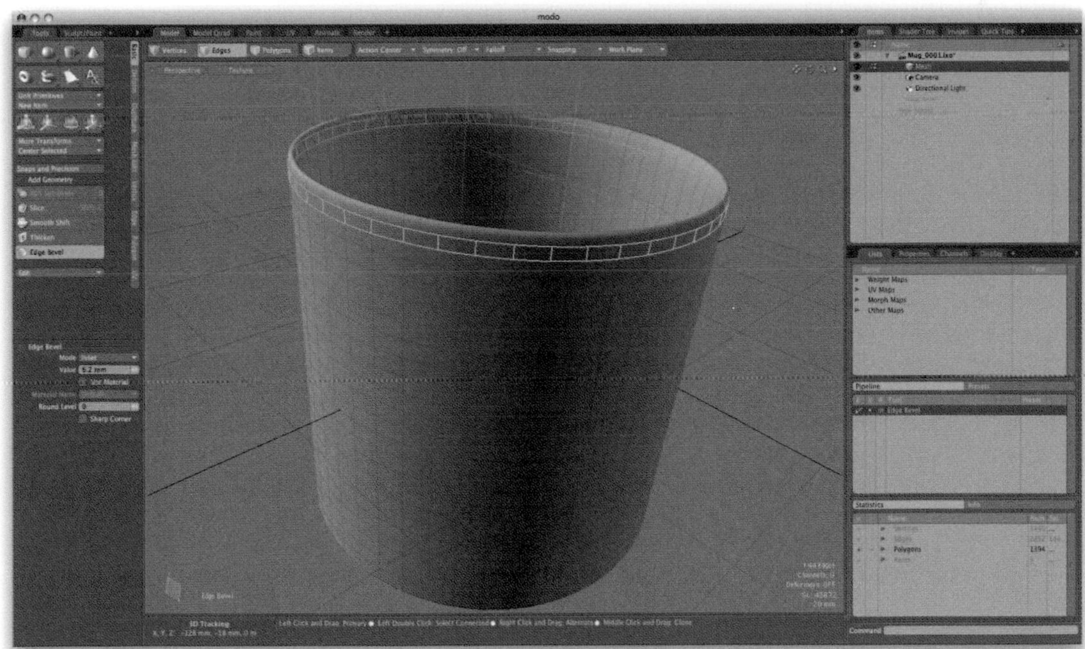

Figure 4.17 Bevel the selected edge.

6. While the beveled edge is still selected, hold the Alt/Option key and watch the selection mode buttons. They change from Vertices, Edges, and Polygons to read "Convert." So, while holding the Alt/Option key, click the Polygon Convert option. The beveled edge selection is now a polygon selection, as shown in Figure 4.18.

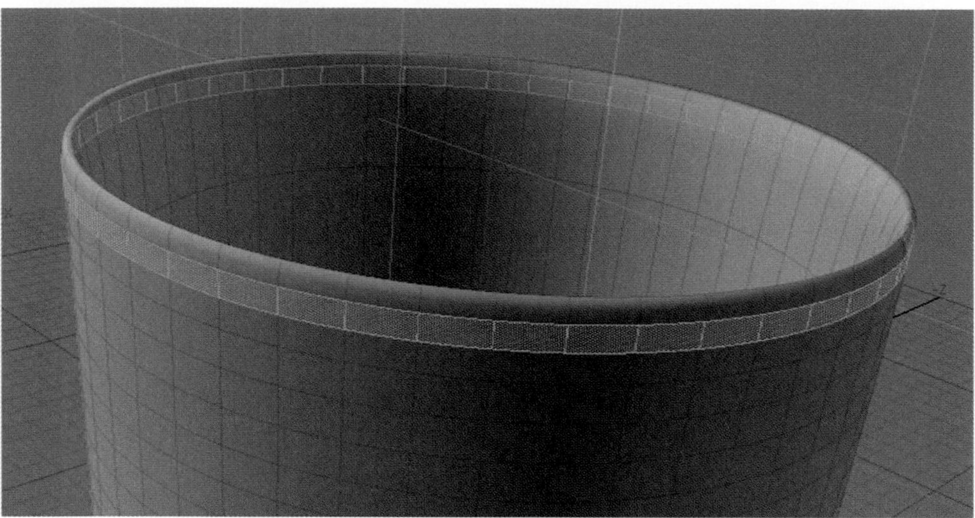

Figure 4.18
Using the Convert selection option, it's easy to change between selections.

7. Using the Convert selection option will come in very handy when you have more complex selections. For now, press the r key to turn on the Scale tool. Then carefully click on the center blue crosshair and drag to scale up the selection to about 107%, as shown in Figure 4.19.
8. Press the q key to turn off the Scale tool, then click off of the model to deselect the polygons.
9. Save your work, but perform an incremental save as you did earlier in the chapter.
10. Now the sized up polygons don't really look so good, do they? In fact, how would you even drink coffee out of this thing? You can smooth out this shape by removing some unneeded edges.
11. Making sure you're in Edges selection mode, start with the edge just below the polygons you've beveled—that is, the edge below the top curve. Double-click it to select the entire loop.
12. Now, to add to your selection, hold the Shift key, and double-click the next edge down on the model.
13. Then, still holding the Shift key, double-click the next edge down the model, and so on. Select all the edges, leaving about five edge loops unselected at the bottom of the model, as shown in Figure 4.20. Note that you can hold the Shift key, and then use the right arrow on the keyboard to add the edge loops.

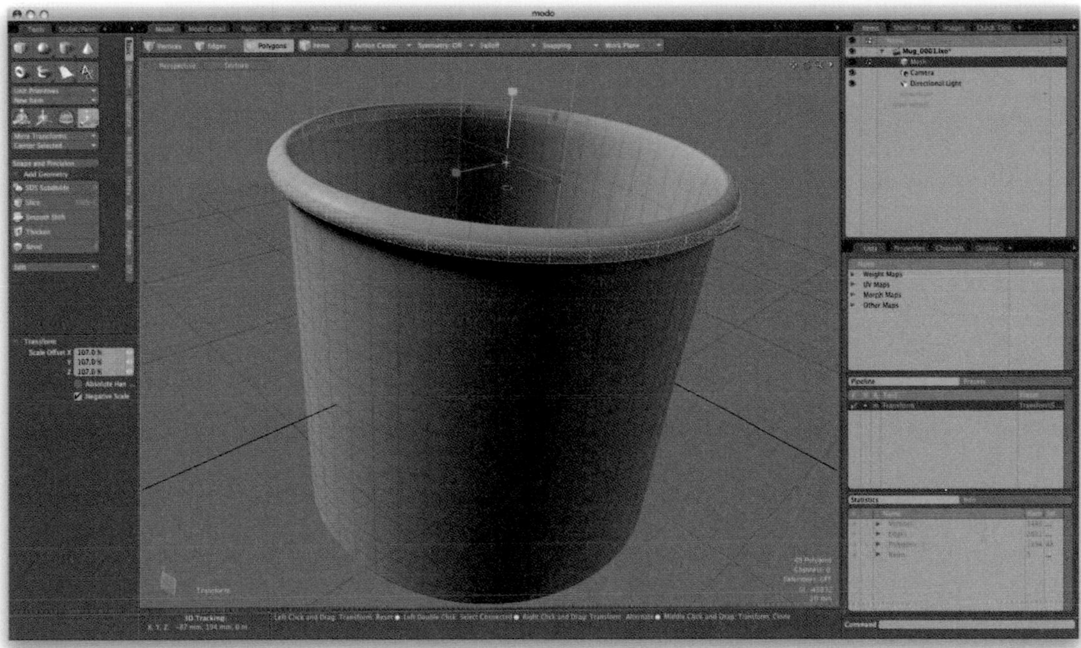

Figure 4.19 Using the r key for Scale, click on the center blue crosshair and drag the scale up to 107%.

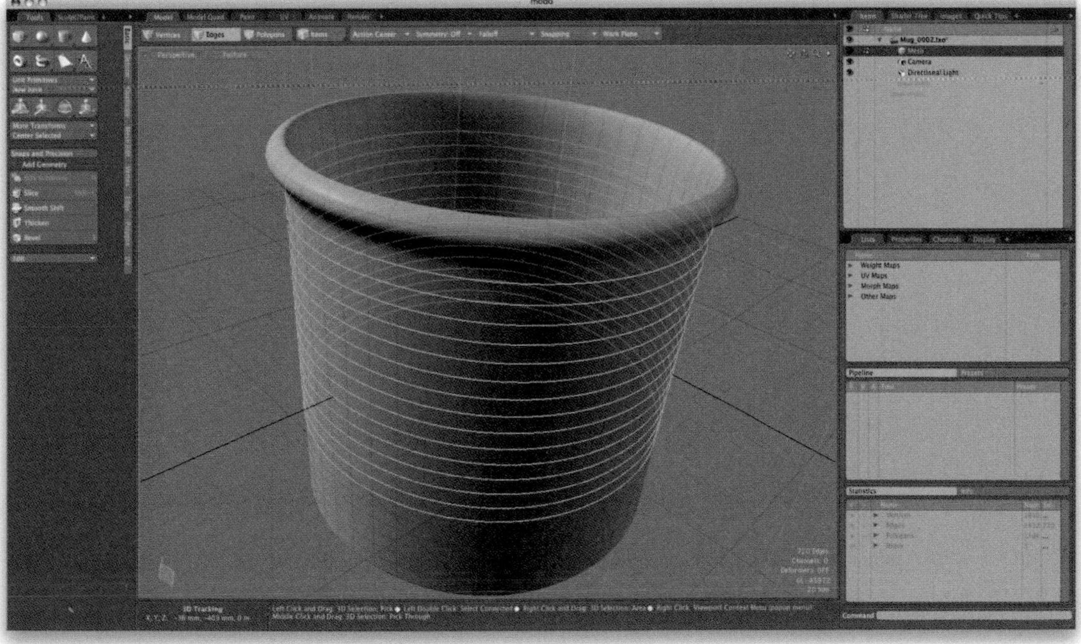

Figure 4.20 Select multiple edges by pressing the Shift key while you select.

Note

To remove an unwanted selection without deselecting everything, hold the Ctrl key and click on the vertex, edge, or polygon you want to deselect.

14. With all of those edges selected, go to the Edge vertical category in the Tools tab, and click Remove, as shown in Figure 4.21. Note that you can also use the Backspace key on your keyboard. Mac users, this is Delete on some of your keyboards, but it's the Backspace key. Really. It is.

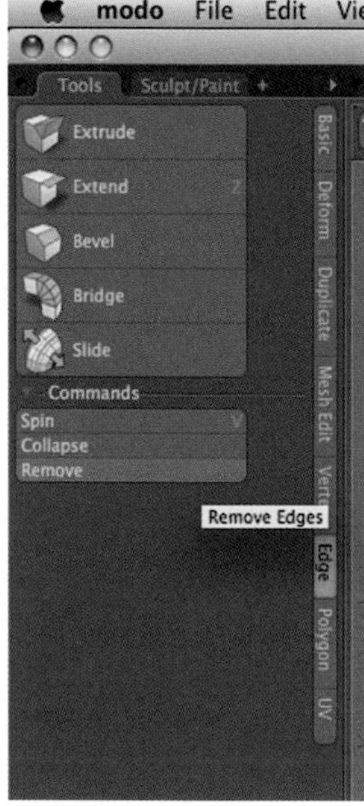

Figure 4.21
Remove the selected edges.

15. Figure 4.22 shows how the model looks without those messy edges. Now it's looking a bit more like a mug. But you can do a little better. Select the edge on the top ring of the beveled polygons from earlier, as shown in Figure 4.23.

16. With this top edge selected, press the b key again and bevel out the edge about 10 mm. Also add a Round Level value, which will add additional edges to the bevel. Set the Round Level to 1 (in the tool properties for the bevel), as shown in Figure 4.24.

17. With your new-found knowledge of beveling and removing edges, feel free to experiment. Save your model. You can also select edges, use the Move tool (press w), the Scale tool (press r), and so on.

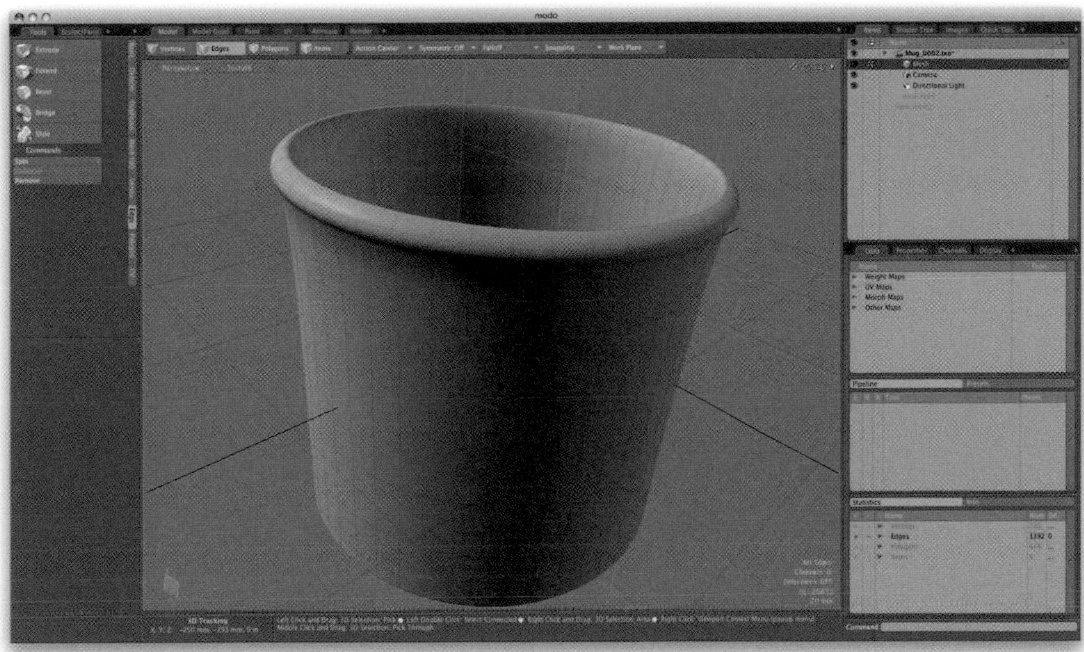

Figure 4.22 After removing some unwanted edges, the model shapes up.

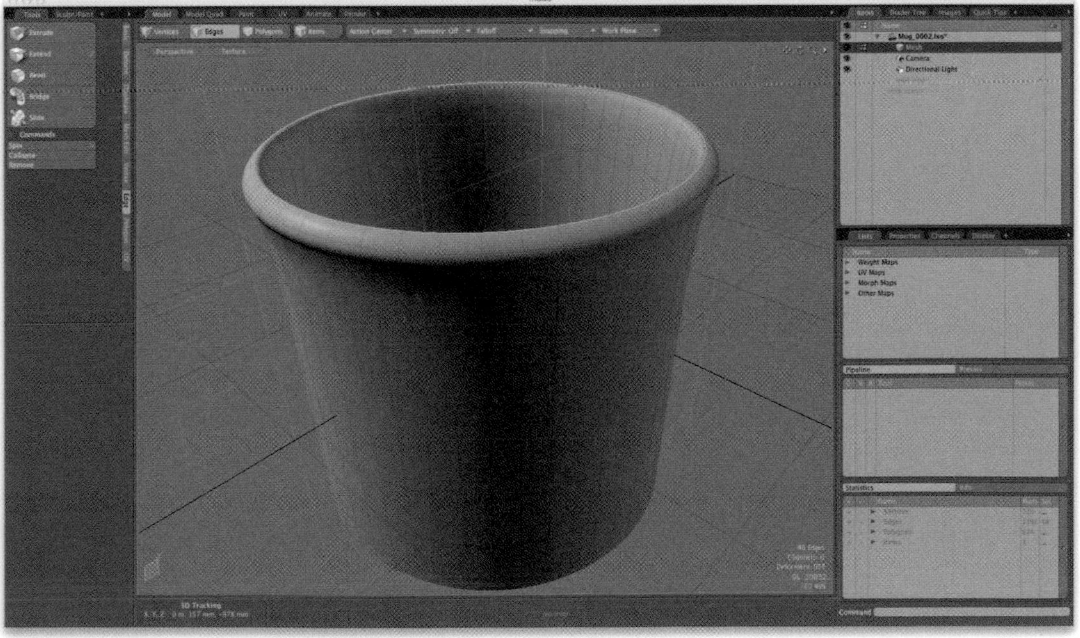

Figure 4.23 Select the top edge.

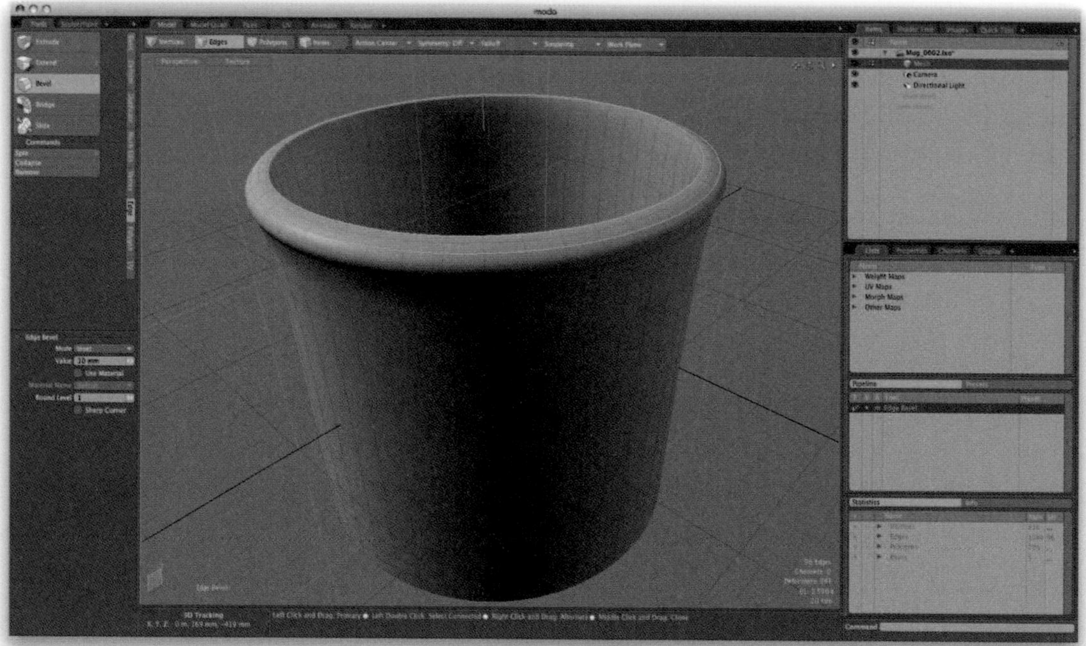

Figure 4.24 Bevel the top edge to add more detail, but add a Round Level value as well.

Adding and Blending Geometry

Japanese food is great. There's nothing like some fresh spicy tuna rolls and a hot cup of tea. And you know what that tea has in common with this tutorial? Not much. But their teacups don't have handles. So if you want to model a hot cup of Japanese tea, consider this next section null and void. But for those of you who like coffee or hot chocolate, or you just can't hold onto a mug without a handle, this section is for you.

1. Use your model from the previous section, but save it again as an incremental version. This way, the changes you make this time around can be scrapped if you want, and you have the model (the previous incremental version) available at any time should you want to start over. But why would you?
2. To create the handle, you'll be working with polygons. Select four polygons on the bottom side of the mug, as shown in Figure 4.25. You'll need to be in Polygons selection mode to select polygons, so press the spacebar to change modes.
3. In the Tools tab, click the Duplicate vertical category. Then choose the Curve Extrude tool.

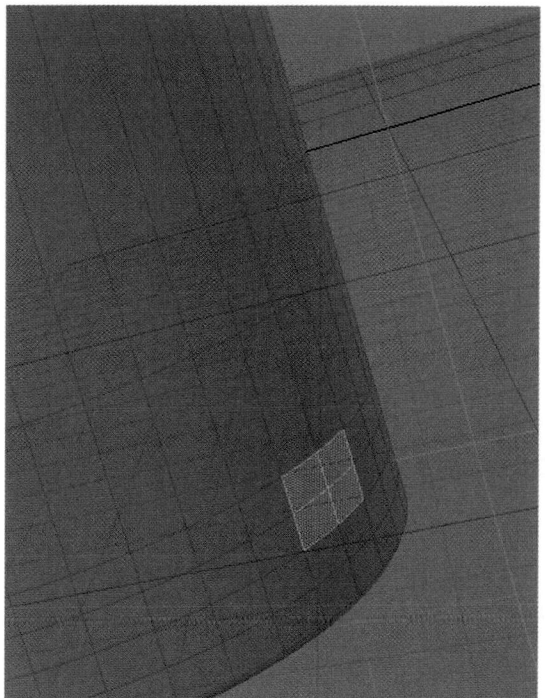

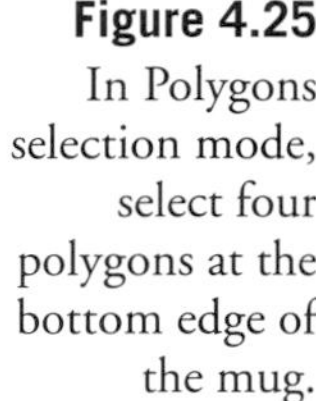

Figure 4.25
In Polygons selection mode, select four polygons at the bottom edge of the mug.

4. Hold the Alt/Option key and click and drag to rotate the view around so the selection is about at the center of your screen but facing toward the right.
5. With the Curve Extrude tool selected, click once just in front of the selected polygons. Then click again just to the right. You'll see a curve start to develop, represented by a series of small dots. The larger squares are the key points where you've placed your mouse clicks. Make sure that the Automatic option is checked in the Tool Properties area for the Curve Extrude tool. Figure 4.26 shows the two points and the tools.
6. Click four more times to build out the mug's handle. Now this is a bit tricky, and you'll find that rotating your view helps. Figure 4.27 shows the progress.
7. In the tool properties for the Curve Extrude tool, change the Mode setting under Curve Path to Edit. Its default is set to Add. Figure 4.28 shows the option.
8. Now click and drag on any of the key points you created for the Curve Extrude tool, and you'll be able to shape the handle. Be sure to rotate the view around to make sure you're lined up from all angles. Figure 4.29 shows the shaped handle.
9. Press the spacebar to turn off the Curve Extrude tool. Save your work by pressing Command and the s key (Mac), or Ctrl and the s key (PC).

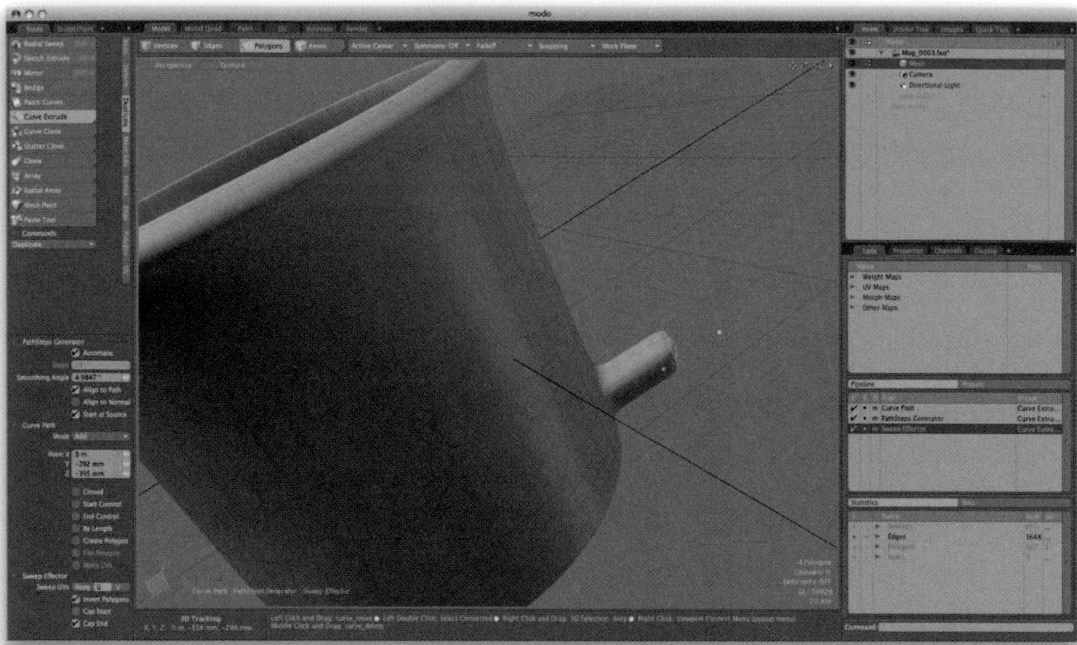

Figure 4.26 Using the Curve Extrude tool, you can begin creating the handle to the mug.

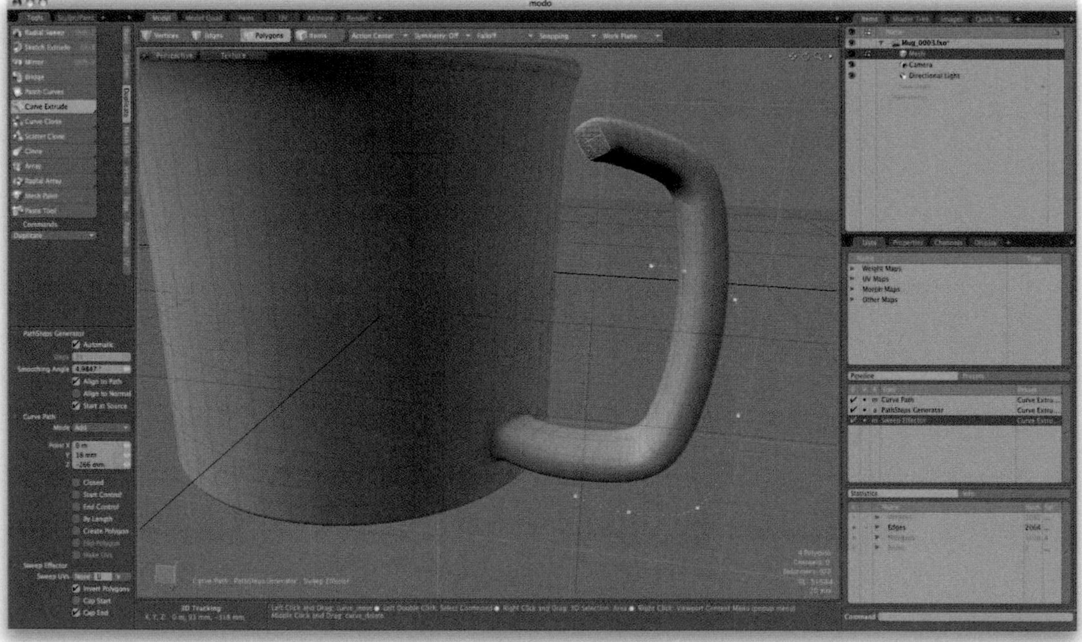

Figure 4.27 Click four more times in the shape of the handle to build out the polygons.

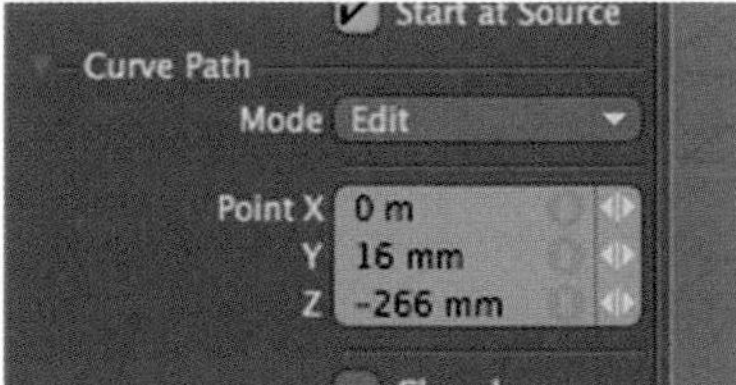

Figure 4.28 Change the Curve Path Mode setting to Edit.

Figure 4.29 Use the Edit mode to adjust the curve path.

10. Now you need to attach the end of this handle to the top part of the mug. Just pushing the end of the handle into the mug could work, but ideally you'd like to see the handle modeled into the mug, as it is at the bottom where you began the curve extrude. First, make sure the four end polygons are selected, as shown in Figure 4.30.
11. Hold the Shift key to add to the selection, and select the top three polygons right in front of the end of the handle, as shown in Figure 4.31.
12. From the Polygon vertical category in the Tools tab, select the Bridge tool, as shown in Figure 4.32.
13. Click and drag in the layout and watch the selected polygons merge. The more you drag, however, the more segments you add. In this case, just one segment is necessary, although you might like the look of more, depending on your model. Figure 4.33 shows the change.
14. Save your work.

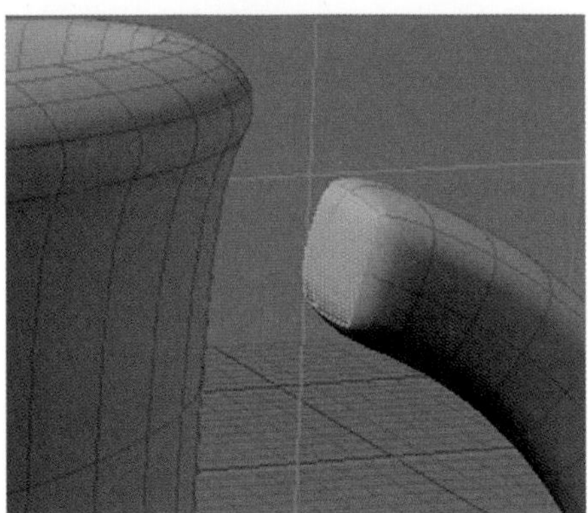

Figure 4.30 Make sure the top end polygons are selected for the handle.

Figure 4.31 Holding the Shift key, select three polygons on the mug itself, just behind the handle's selected polygons.

Figure 4.32 To join the selected polygons, use the Bridge tool from the Polygon vertical category.

Figure 4.33 Click and drag to bridge the selected polygons together.

You may find that you might need to do a little more editing to shape the handle to your liking. Remember that you can press Ctrl-Z or Command-Z (Mac) to undo your steps. This is a simply operation, but don't be fooled; the Bridge tool is quite powerful and will come in very handy on many modeling projects. For now, you should have a good idea of how to create some basic geometry, as well as selecting and editing edges and polygons. But go on to the final section to add a material and see a render of your project.

Surfacing and Rendering Geometry

Part of modo's strength is in its material and rendering capabilities. Certainly, the modeling tools make creating 3D objects easy, but it's the materials, lighting, and rendering that will bring the model to life. This next section will quickly introduce you to setting up materials and rendering.

1. Working from your previous model, save an incremental version.
2. Without any polygons selected, press the m key on your keyboard. This calls up the Polygon Set Material option. Here you can define surfaces for your models. But here's the big rule: If nothing is selected, your material will be applied to the currently selected mesh items. In this case, you have only one surface to worry about. In upcoming tutorials, you'll set multiple materials on the same model.
3. In the Polygon Set Material option, enter the name Mug, and press the Return key on your keyboard or click OK. Figure 4.34 shows the setup.

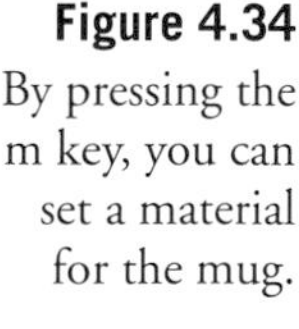

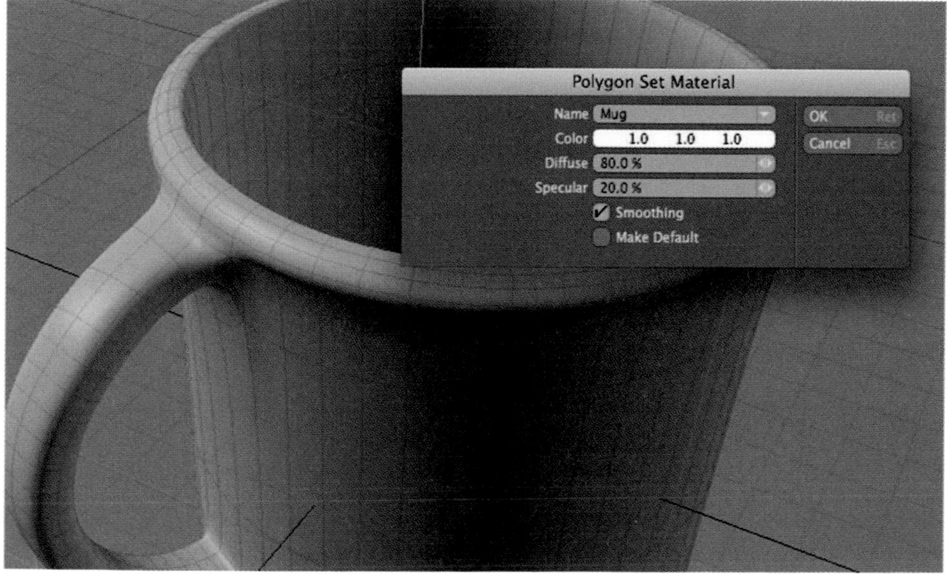

Figure 4.34
By pressing the m key, you can set a material for the mug.

4. Now that a material is set for the object, you can set up some basic parameters. Click the Shader Tree tab at the top right of the interface. Then click the triangle in front of the Render listing to see the current scene's materials, as shown in Figure 4.35.

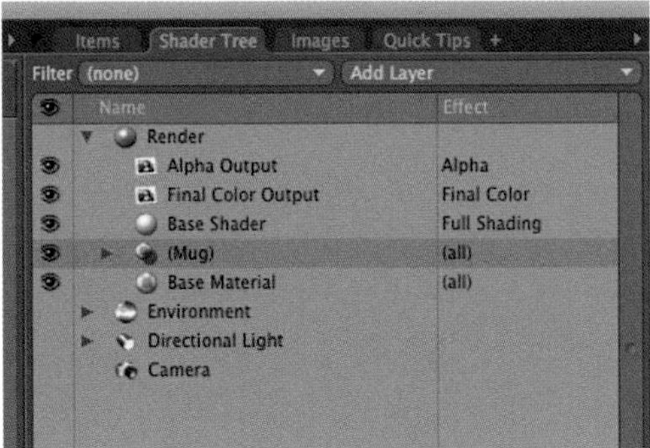

Figure 4.35
Click the Shader Tree tab to edit the newly created material.

5. You'll see that within the Render category of the Shader Tree is your new material group called Mug. Click the triangle to the left of Mug to expand it, and you'll see the Material icon. Select it.

> **Note**
>
> Because you've created a material group already, the Base Material setting that lives in the Render category within the Shader Tree does not affect anything in the scene.

6. Once the Material icon is selected, click the Properties tab located below the Shader Tree to see the material settings. Figure 4.36 shows the options.

7. Later in Chapter 7, you'll learn all about the Shader Tree and setting material properties. So for now, change the color to a pale orange by clicking on the Diffuse Color setting. This will call up your system's default color palette. Figure 4.37 shows the operation.

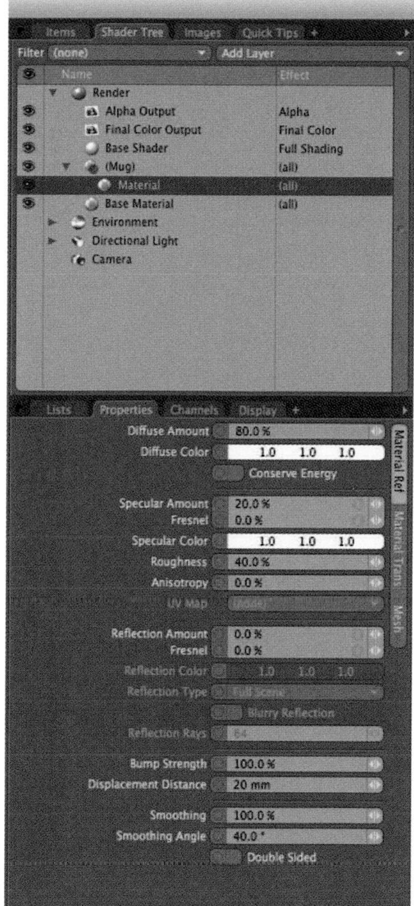

Figure 4.36 Once a material is selected, you can open the Properties tab to change the settings.

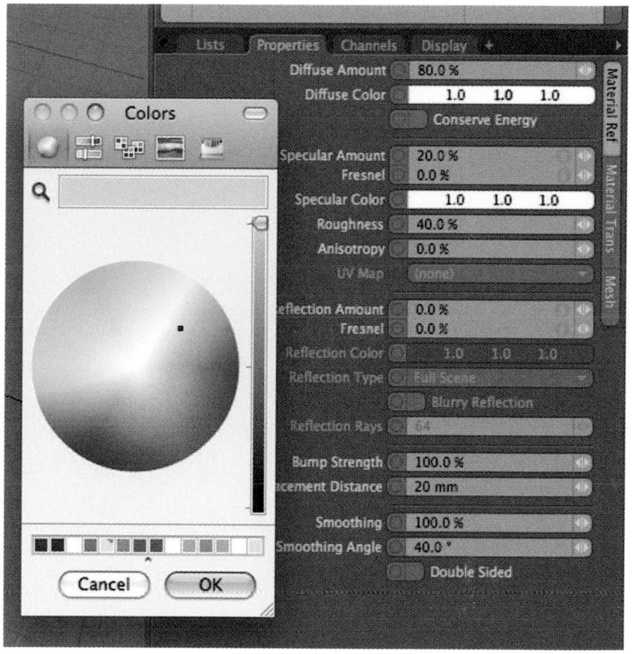

Figure 4.37 Change the color for the Mug material.

8. Next, you'll want to add a little shine and reflection to the mug. But to get a better idea of what these settings look like, change to a different view. In the modo interface, click the Render tab at the top of the screen. You should see a preview on the top left, a Camera view on the top right, and a Perspective view on the bottom, as shown in Figure 4.38.
9. At the very top right of the Camera viewport, click and drag on the Zoom icon, as shown in Figure 4.39.

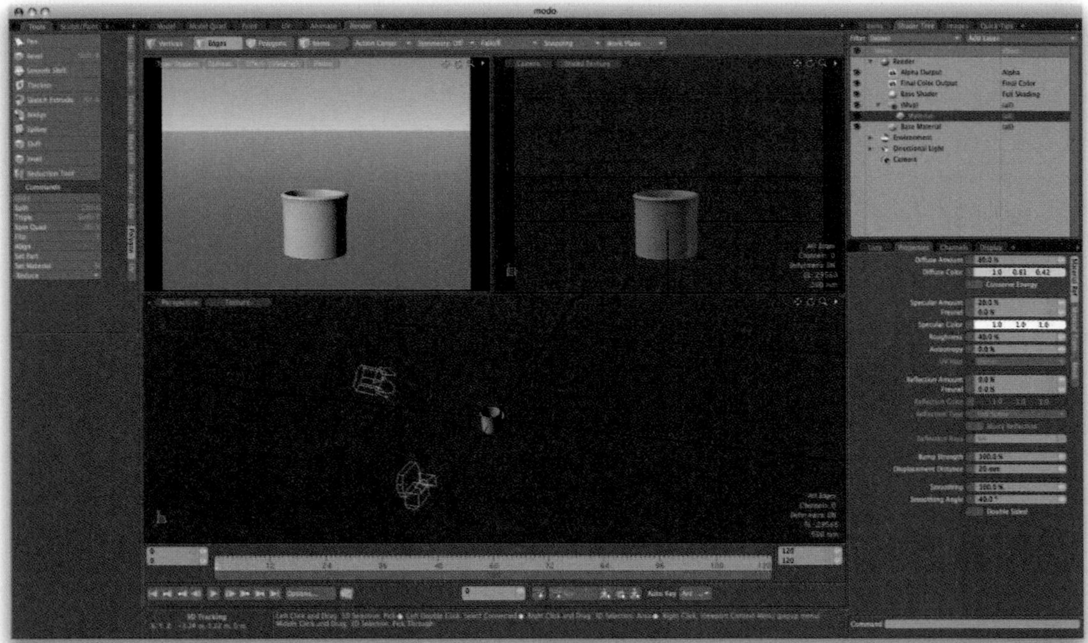

Figure 4.38 Click the Render tab at the top of the interface to see your mug's surfaces in real time.

Figure 4.39 Use the Zoom icon to push the camera in closer to the object.

10. Zoom into the mug to see it closer. Also, you can click and drag on the Rotate icon (the middle of the tree icons) in the top right of the Camera viewport to angle the view. Figure 4.40 shows the new view.
11. Your mug needs a little something to sit on rather than having it just floating. In the Tools tab, click the Basic vertical category and, while holding the Shift key, click the Plane icon. Note that this icon doesn't show by default, but it's located with the Tube primitive.
12. Your added plane might be smack dab in the middle of your mug when added. In the Items tab, which is to the left of the Shader Tree tab, select this new Mesh item, which will be called Plane.
13. Press the r key, and then click and drag on the center blue crosshair to scale the plane larger.
14. Then press the w key, and click and drag on the green handle to move the flat plane just beneath the mug. Figure 4.41 shows the changes.

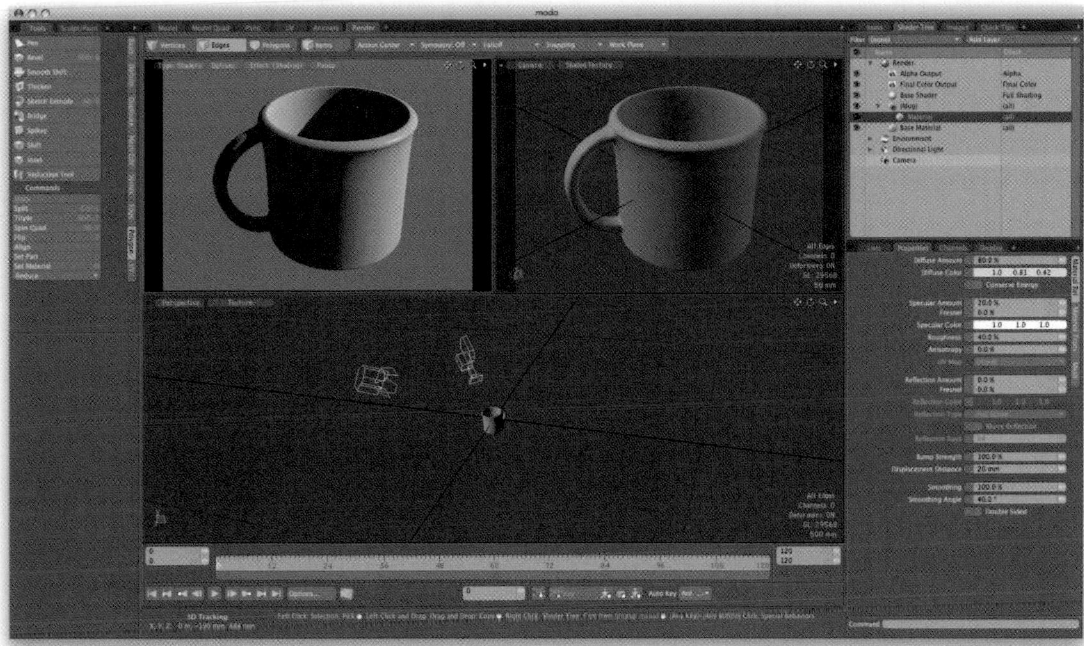

Figure 4.40 Move and rotate the view around to see a closer view of the mug.

Figure 4.41 Scale the flat plane larger, then position it beneath the mug.

15. Press m to call up the Polygon Set Material option, and set a material name for the flat plane, such as Floor.
16. Click back over to the Shader Tree. Expand the Floor material group and select the Material icon.
17. In the Properties tab for the material set the color of the floor to an off-white.
18. Keep the other settings at their defaults, but change the Reflection value to 20%, as shown in Figure 4.42.

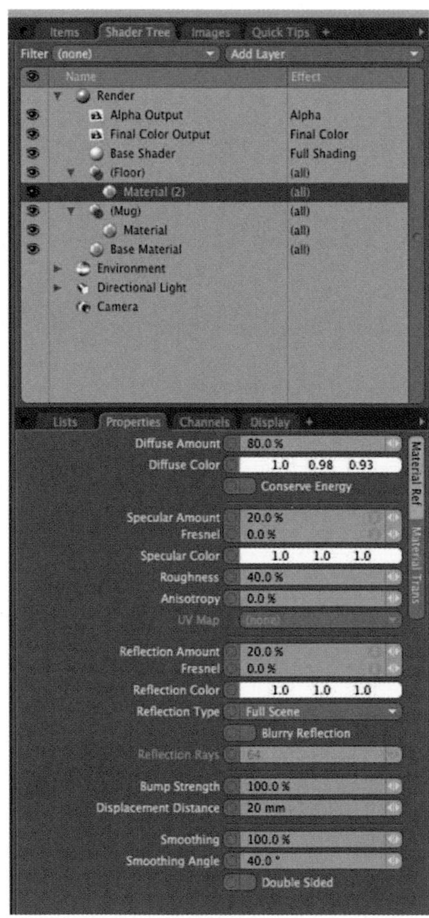

Figure 4.42
Set a reflection of about 20% for the floor.

19. Now go back to the Mug material, and set the Specular Amount value to 40%. Change the Roughness to 60%. Roughness is similar to a gloss value. Then set the Reflection Amount to 10%. Figure 4.43 shows the full interface with the material settings and a preview render view.

Figure 4.43 A few more surface changes to the mug, and the scene is coming together nicely.

20. Save your work! Saving at this point saves the change in camera position and the material settings.
21. Finally, in the Shader Tree, select the Directional Light listing.
22. In the Properties tab for the selection, change the Spread Angle value to 45, and Samples to 32. This will soften the shadow for the default light and also give it a bit more quality. Figure 4.44 shows the change.
23. Click the Render listing in the Shader Tree, and then in the Properties tab, click the Global Illumination vertical category.
24. In the Global Illumination tab, simply click Enable. What you'll see is that modo now calculates the environment and the surroundings as part of the illumination for the scene. The default environment is a green to blue value, representing a ground to sky. Figure 4.45 shows how good your simple model looks with these few tweaks.
25. Save your work.

Figure 4.44 Add a spread angle and increase the Samples value of the default directional light.

Figure 4.45 Softening the light, and turning on Global Illumination makes the simple mug look pretty nice!

Clearly, this only scratches the surface of what modo can do. You've probably seen the awesome renders on the Luxoloy.com site and wonder just how those were made. Well, guess what? You just took your first steps in that direction. The process you've used throughout this chapter will be the basis for most of your work in modo. Later in the book, you'll learn more about surfacing, lighting, and rendering. You'll also see how you can set up animation to make even a simple scene like this coffee (or hot tea) mug look even cooler.

When you're ready, turn the page and move on to Chapter 5 and learn about more modeling tools.

Part II

Basic Creation Methods

5

Basic Building Blocks

By now you should have a general idea of how modo 301/302 approaches the creation process. But what is better than actually creating something to see the process for yourself? The first four chapters, Part I of the book, introduced you to the program, the interface, the tools, how to select and deselect, and how the key tool controls work with a simple project. Part II will take you through four more chapters, introducing you to modeling with modo and a bit more. With each chapter, you'll learn how to create models from the ground up. You'll also learn all about the Shader Tree and how to texture your models.

Building Blocks, Literally

You probably thought that because this chapter was titled "Basic Building Blocks" you'd learn about fundamentals of the program, tools to create models, and so on. No way! You're through with those introductory chapters! In this chapter, you're actually going to build blocks! In the next few pages, you'll learn more about the basic modeling tools and how to navigate your way around the Items tab.

1. You'll start building many objects with simple primitive shapes when using modo. Begin with a default 301/302 layout (see Figure 5.1) by selecting the option from the Layout menu at the top of the modo interface.
2. On the left side of the interface under the Tools tab, select the Cube primitive. When you do, the properties for the cube appear on the bottom left of the screen, as shown in Figure 5.2.

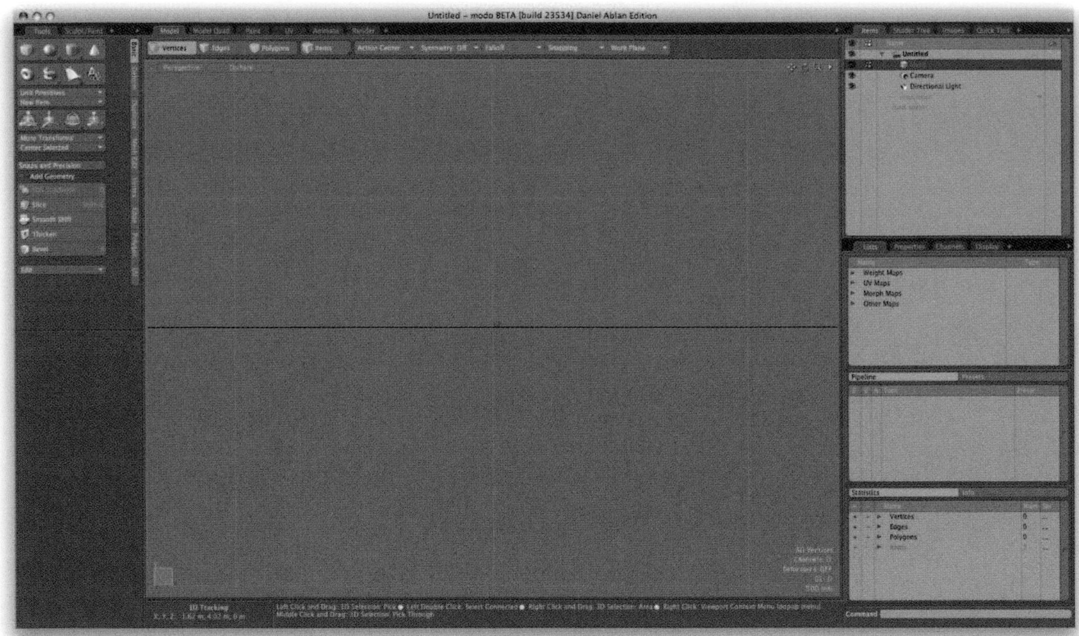

Figure 5.1 modo's default layout.

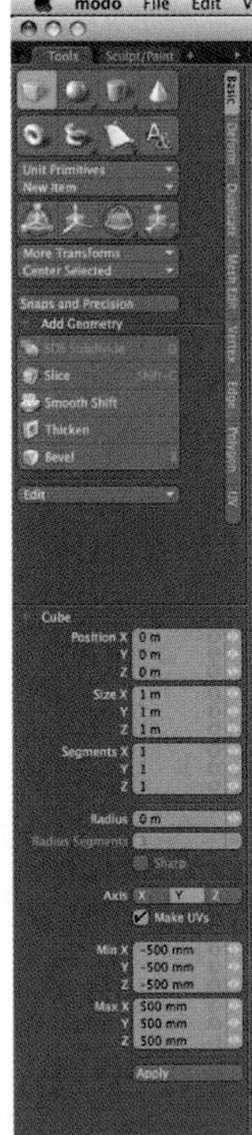

Figure 5.2 You'll begin with a Cube primitive, using the specific numeric controls to start the basic shape.

3. Rather than drawing out a box in the layout viewport, you can create one more specific for your modeling task. Set the Cube primitive settings to the following:

Position	X	0
	Y	0
	Z	0
Size	X	1.8 m
	Y	350 mm
	Z	1.1 m
Segments	X	10
	Y	2
	Z	7
Radius	0	
Axis	Z	

4. After you've entered the settings, click the Apply button at the bottom of the Cube properties panel. If you can't see it, simply click and drag the panel upward from the top edge of the panel. Figure 5.3 shows the Cube primitive with the applied settings.

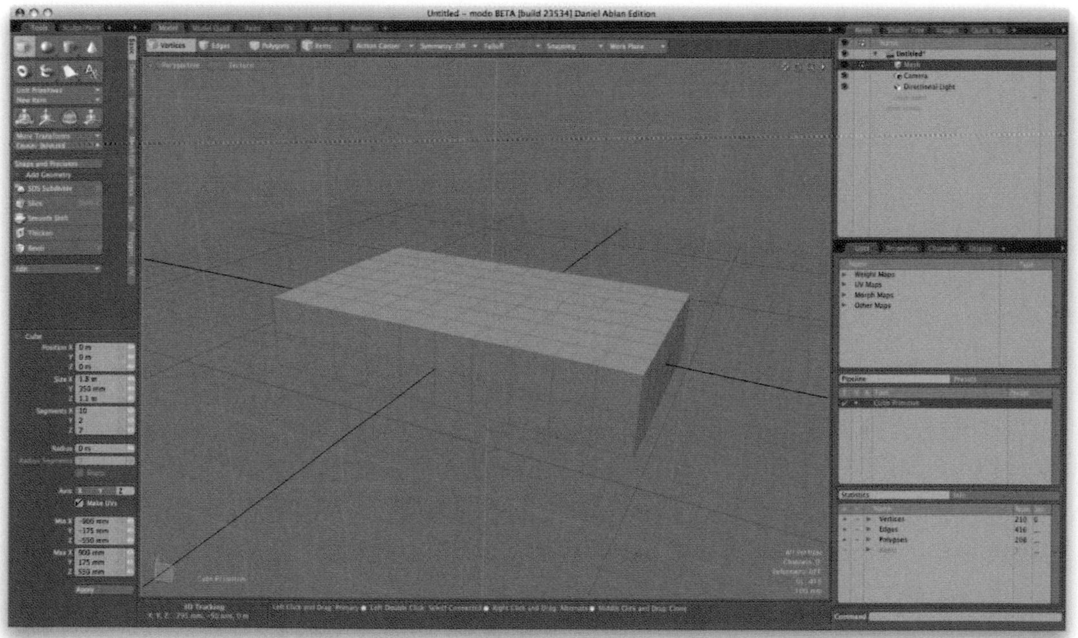

Figure 5.3 A specific Cube primitive shape is created numerically. The segments play a key role in the creation of the toy block.

5. Press the q key to deactivate the Cube primitive.
6. In the Items tab to the right, you'll see that the new cube you've created is listed just as Mesh. Since you only have one object created in one layer, this is more than fine. However, it's a good idea to get in the habit of naming your models as you build them, regardless of how complex or simple they are. Select the name Mesh in the Items tab, right-click, and select Rename, as shown in Figure 5.4. Rename the mesh to Toy Block or something similar.

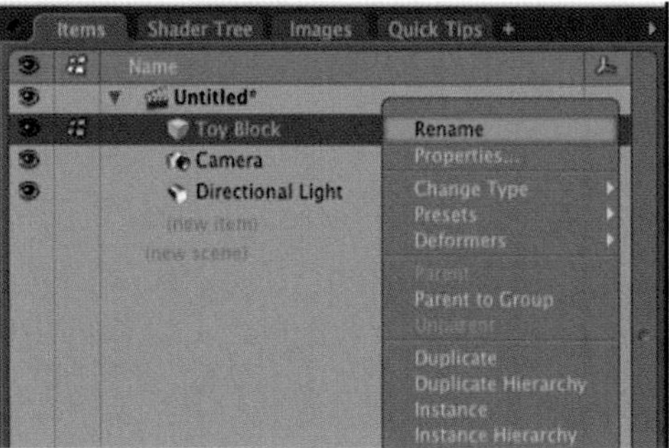

Figure 5.4
Any time you create a new mesh, right-click on its name in the Items tab and rename it to stay organized.

Note

When you right-click on an item in the Items tab, not only can you rename the item, but also duplicate, delete, and more. Pay close attention to the options when you right-click here and anywhere throughout modo.

7. Now is a good time to save, so if you're on a Mac, press the Apple key and s key at the same time. Choose a name and a place to save your current mesh. If you're on a PC, press Ctrl and the s key.

   This project will give you a good idea of how powerful the modo tools are, even on the simplest level. You've created a basic cube with a specific number of segments for a reason. With the subdivided top surface of the mesh, you can select specific polygons and edges to create more detail. This same principal applies to just about anything you'll create.
8. If you press the Tab key, you'll see the cube round out. The Tab key turns on subdivision surfaces, as shown in Figure 5.5.

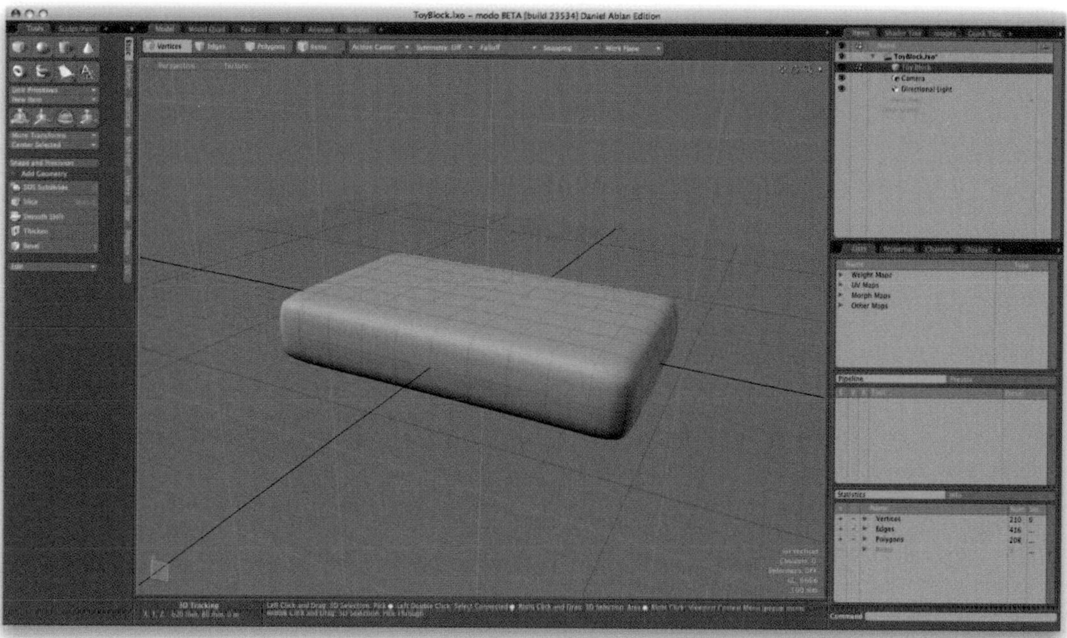

Figure 5.5 Pressing the Tab key to turn on subdivision surfaces for your model shows that it's too smooth at this point.

9. You'll want your final model to be a subdivision model, but as you can see here, it's too smooth. This often is a good thing, as you want to always be adding more detail rather than trying to take it away. By saying the model is too smooth, it means that there is not enough geometry to obtain the right amount of dctail. It's easier to add more geometry than to take away. Go ahead and press the Tab key again to return to your original square cube.
10. Rather than adding unnecessary geometry to your entire model by creating more polygons, you can work with just the edges to create the sharp lines your model needs. Select the Edges mode button at the top of the interface to tell modo you want to work with edges. Also, adding additional edges can help tighten up the curvature of the model. Another way is to use the Edge Weighting features in modo.
11. If you double-click on the closest edge, you'll select the entire length of that edge. Figure 5.6 shows the example.
12. By pressing the up arrow multiple times (on your keyboard), you'll begin selecting the contiguous edge. Keep pressing until your selection loops around, encompassing the object. Then repeat the process until you have selected all outer edges. This includes the corners. Figure 5.7 shows the full selection. Note that you should see a listing of 76 edges in the bottom right of the viewport when all the outer edges are selected. And don't forget that you can hold the Alt key, then click and drag the view to rotate around to select the edges on the other side of the cube.

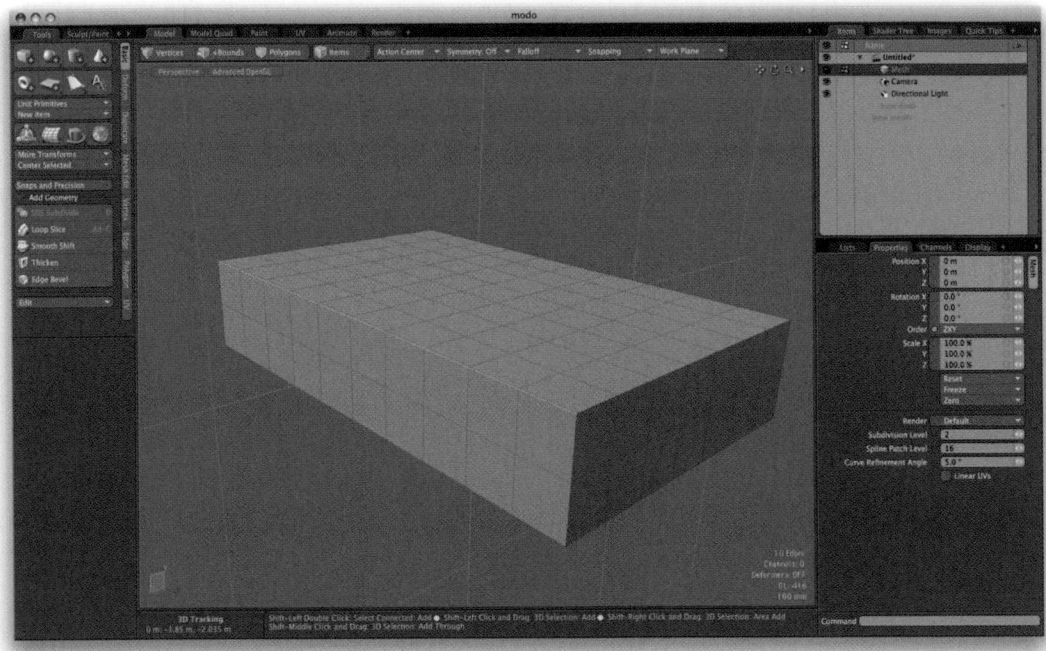

Figure 5.6 Double-clicking on an edge selects the entire length of that edge.

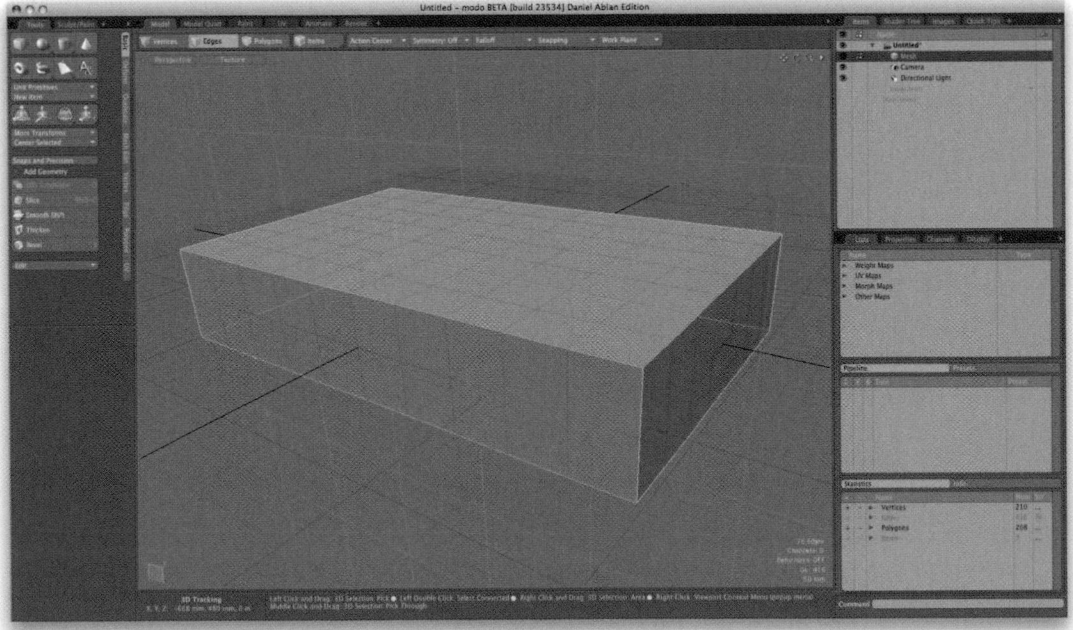

Figure 5.7 Select all outer edges of the cube.

Note

You can also hold the Shift key, and double-click on each edge length that you want to select.

13. Now that the outer edges are selected, press the b key to activate the Bevel tool. Click and drag on the model to bevel the selected edges. Take a look at the Bevel tool properties on the left side of the interface. Bevel mode should set to Inset with a value of 17 mm. You can manually enter this value if you like and also add a Round Level of 2. Figure 5.8 shows the result.

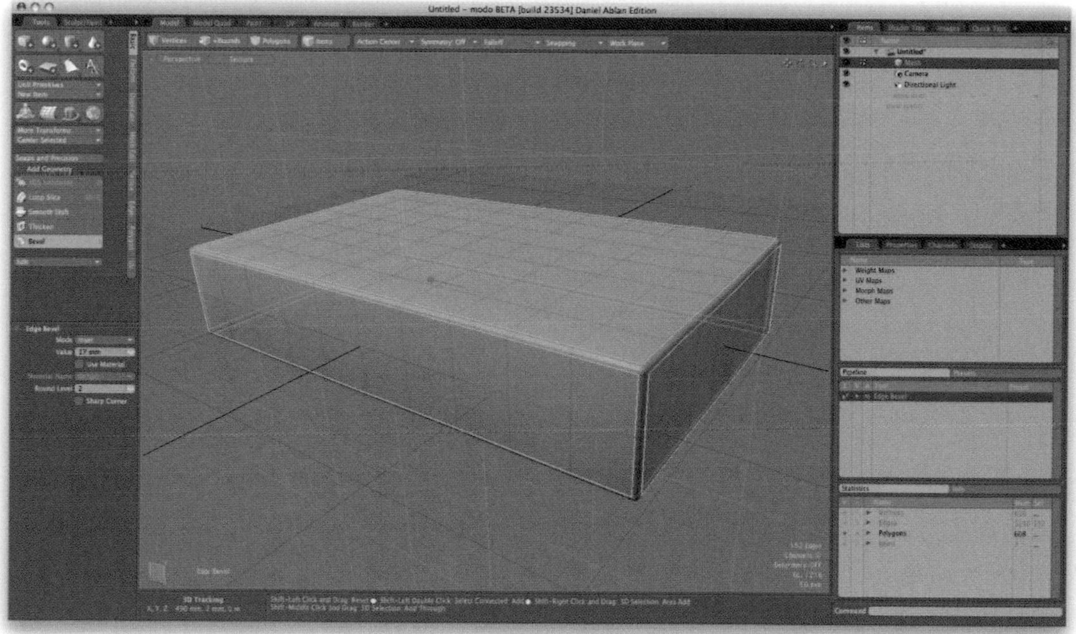

Figure 5.8 Bevel the edges of the cube and also add a little rounding to them.

14. Press the q key to drop the Bevel tool. Then click a blank area of the layout to deselect the edges.
15. Save your work by pressing Ctrl/Command and the s key.

Note

If you look at the name of your model in the Items tab at the top right of the interface, you might notice a little asterisk (*) after it. When this appears, it means that a change has happened, such as a move or bevel. When you save your work, the asterisk will go away. It's a good idea to keep your eye on this to make sure you're saving often. That is, of course, if you're the forgetful type.

16. Now if you press the Tab key to toggle subdivision surfaces, the model holds its shape, but the edges have a very slight, smooth rounding. By beveling the edges, you've added more geometry to those specific areas, and when the subdivision surfaces are applied (Tab key), there is greater control over the shape.

    The toy block you're building doesn't have round edges, but if you were to look at just about any object in the real world, the edges are never straight lines. They have smoothness, and it's this edge detail that will help give your models realism.

17. Choose Polygons mode from the top of the modo interface, and select four polygons on the top of the model at the left corner. But make the selection one row in from each edge, as shown in Figure 5.9.

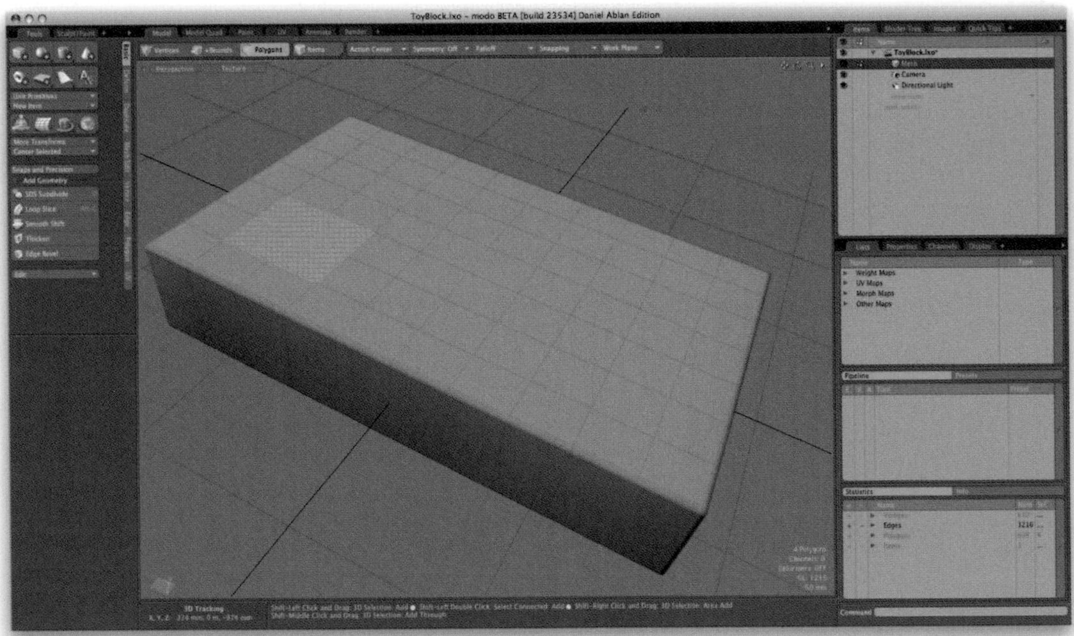

Figure 5.9 Select just four polygons on the top of the model, making sure to select one row in from each edge.

18. Press the Shift key and the a key to fit the selection to view.
19. Press the Shift key and the t key to triangulate the selected polygons. This command activates the Triple function found under the Polygon vertical menu listing.
20. If your model looks like Figure 5.10, you have subdivision surfaces on. For now, you don't want this, as it helps keep things simple. If it is on, deselect these polygons by left-clicking on each of them, or simply click a blank space within the viewport to deselect everything. When nothing is selected, press the Tab key to turn off the subdivisions. Then select the four polygons again. Your selection should look like Figure 5.11.
21. Now select Edges mode from the top of the modo interface, and then, holding the Shift key, select the two separate edges that run parallel with the two contiguous edges, as shown in Figure 5.12.
22. When the edges are selected, press the v key to spin them. This command is also found in the Edges vertical category. Figure 5.13 shows the result.
23. After you've spun the edges so they are contiguous, switch to Vertices mode at the top of the modo interface. Then select the single point in the center of the edges you've been working with, as shown in Figure 5.14.

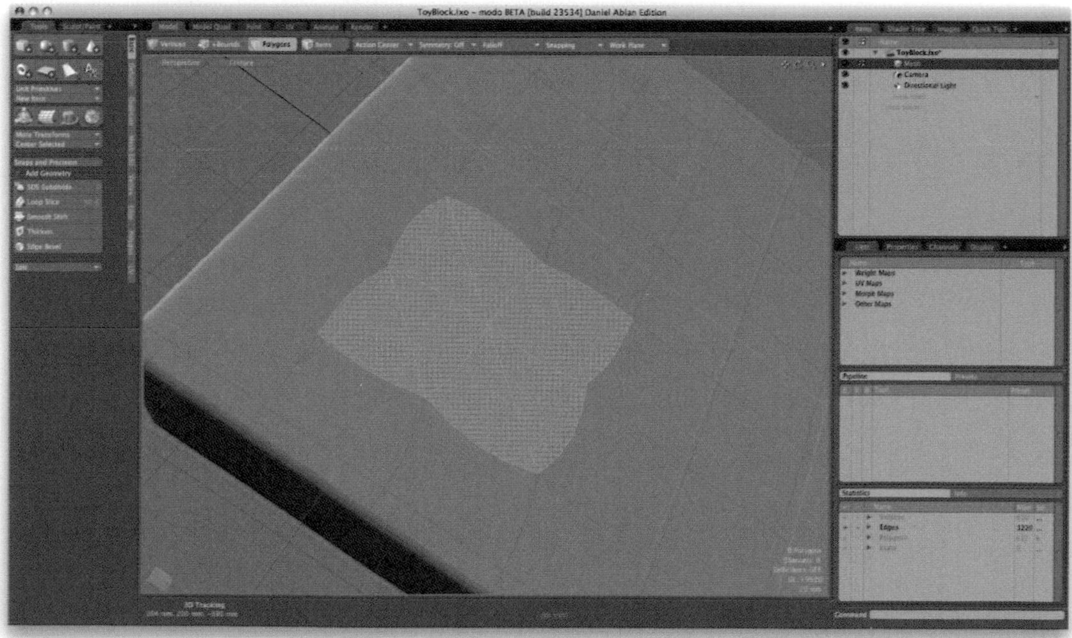

Figure 5.10 If you select and triple these four polygons and the mesh looks distorted, you're in subdivision surface mode.

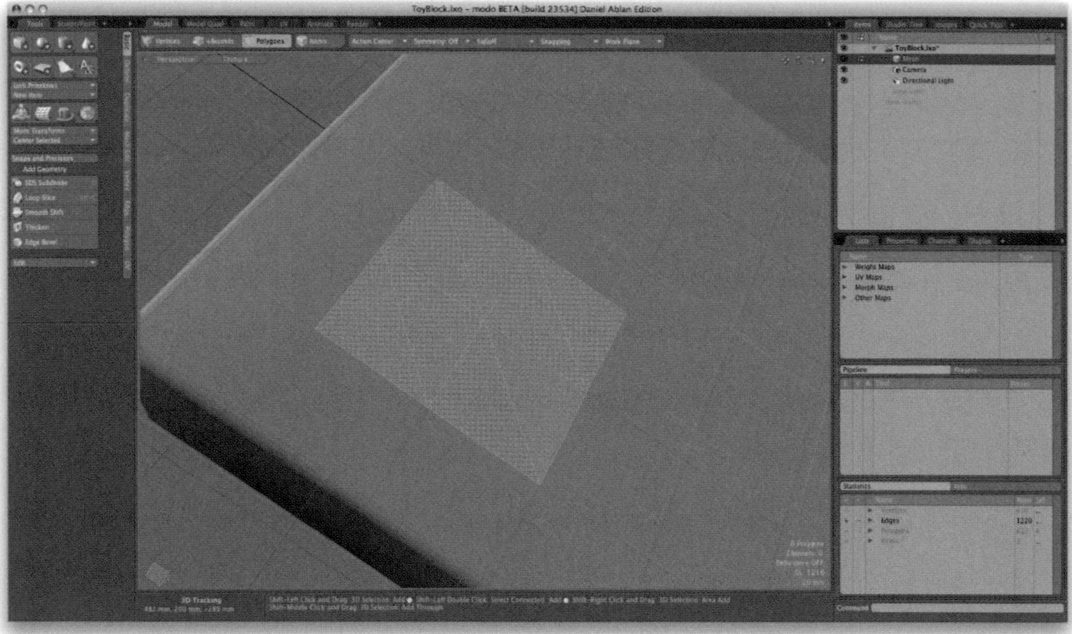

Figure 5.11 With subdivision surfaces turned off for this model, the selected and tripled polygons remain squared.

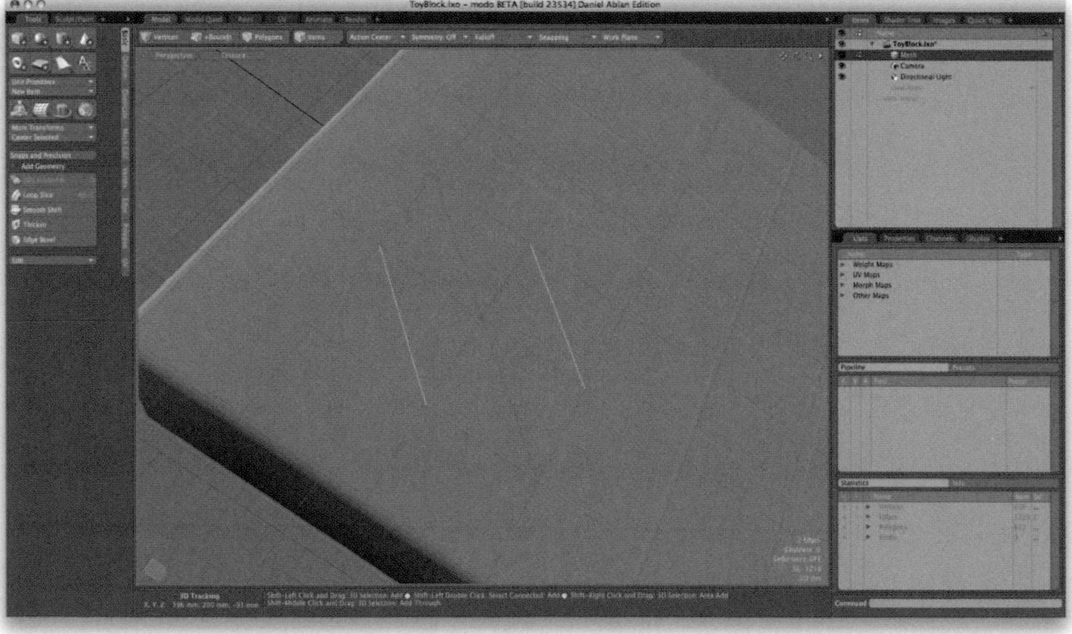

Figure 5.12 Select the two edges that are parallel to the contiguous edges.

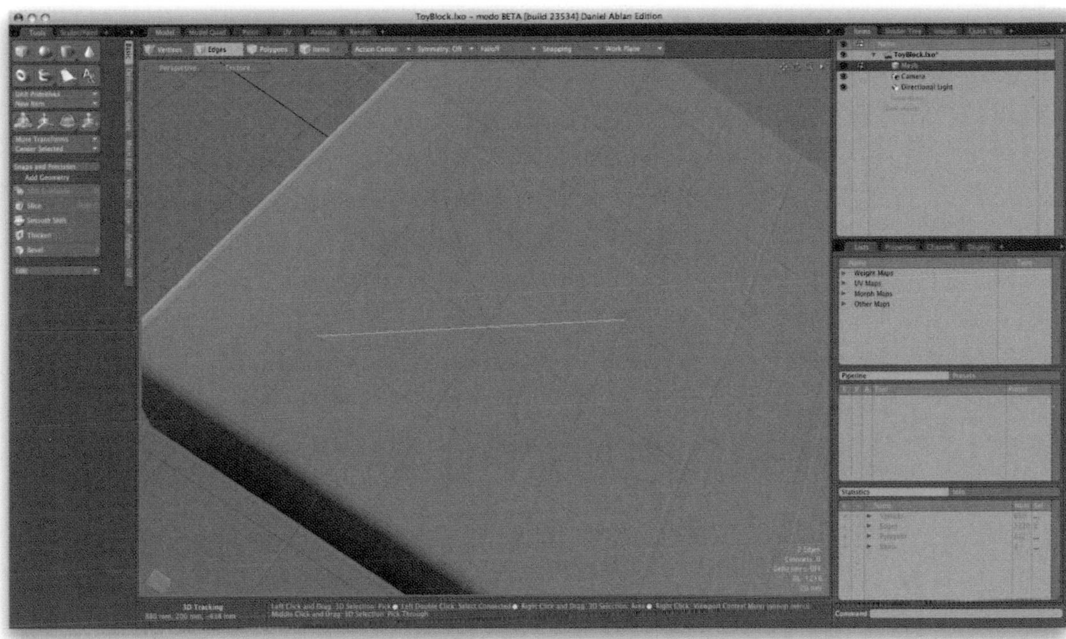

Figure 5.13 Pressing the v key activates the Spin Edges command.

Figure 5.14 Once the edges are spun, select the point in the center of them while in Point selection mode or by pressing the number 1 on your keyboard.

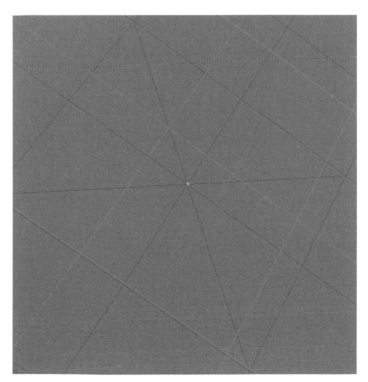

24. Press the b key to activate the Bevel tool. Make sure that Use Material is unchecked, and Round Level set to 0. The Round Level might have a value from the last time you used it, so be sure to clear it out to 0; otherwise, you'll generate a different look, almost a spider web effect. If you try this out, be sure to undo (Ctrl-Z, PC, or Command-Z, Mac.)
25. When ready, simply click and drag in the viewport to bevel the selected edges to about 130 mm. You can see the value in the Tool Properties area changing as you bevel. You don't want the bevel to cross over any edges. Figure 5.15 shows the operation.
26. Once the bevel is complete, press the q key to turn off the Bevel tool.
27. Next, change to Polygons mode at the top of the modo interface, then click to select the center of the eight-sided disc, as shown in Figure 5.16.
28. Save your model!

The process you've completed so far is nothing glamorous—you're simply working with edges and cubes to create a more organic shape. The next few steps will start adding detail to the building block and show you a way to simplify the process.

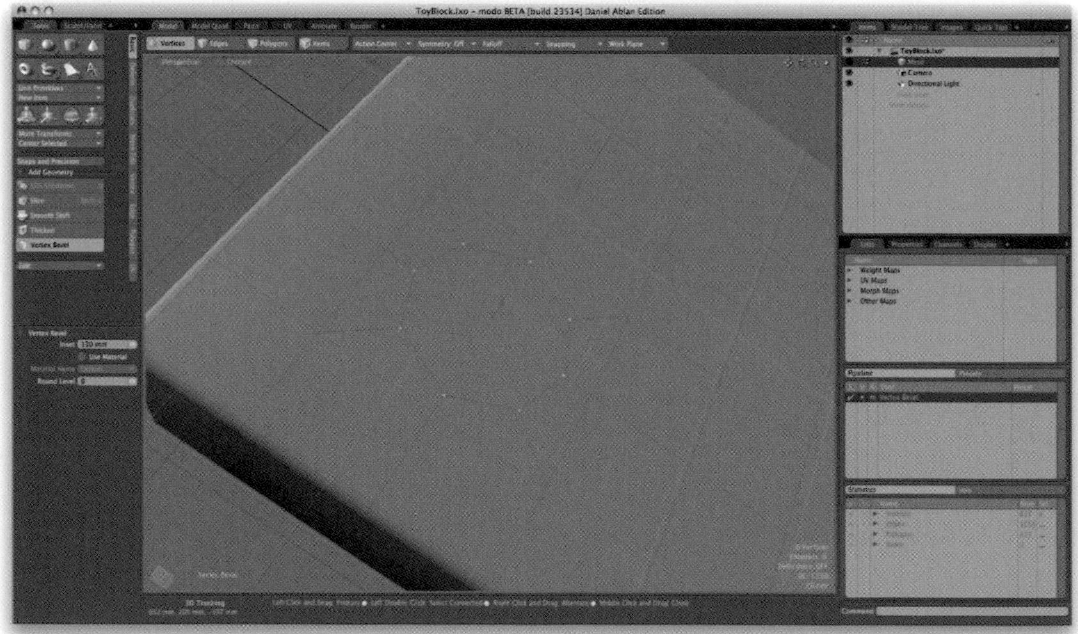

Figure 5.15 Bevel the selected edges, being careful not to overlap them by beveling too much.

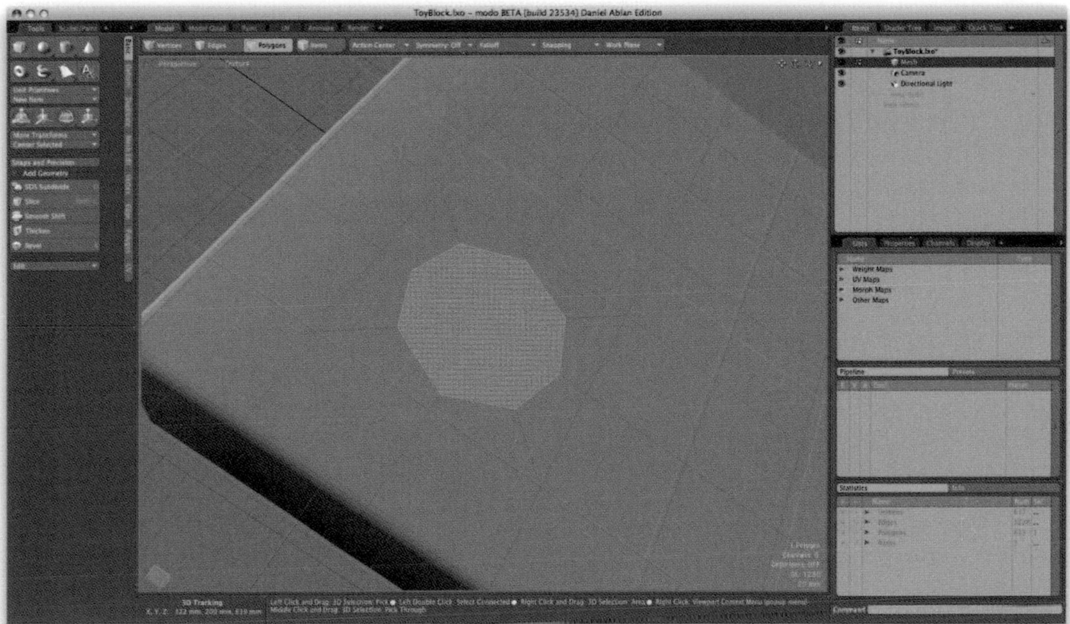

Figure 5.16 In Polygons mode, select the center of the eight-sided disc, which is the result of the beveled edges.

Automating with Macros

From this point, you'll be creating six large tubes that stand out from the base of the block. And while you could easily repeat the steps shown earlier, or attempt to perform them at the same time, this next section of the project will make it easier. Using macros is a way to automate repetitive tasks for all kinds of modeling jobs. You'll use them here to record your bevel operations so that every tube you need to create will be identical. You can use this process for creating things like windows or doors as well.

1. Using the same eight-sided polygon from the previous exercise, select Record Macro from the System menu at the top of the modo interface, as shown in Figure 5.17.
2. At this point, modo's Macro function is recording your steps. With the same eight-sided polygon still selected, press the b key to activate the Bevel tool. Click on the polygon, and you'll see the red and blue bevel handles. Click and drag the red handle to inset the bevel about 5 mm. You can see the Inset value change in the Tool Properties panel on the left side of the interface. Then, click and drag the blue handle up a little to change the Shift value of the bevel also about 5 mm. These values don't have to be exact, so any approximation is fine. Figure 5.18 shows these operations.

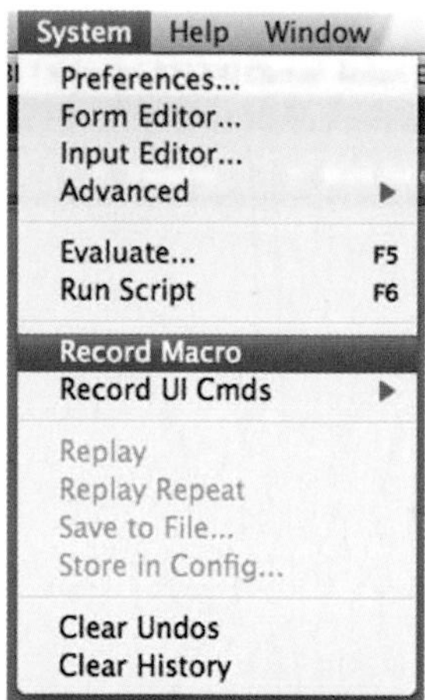

Figure 5.17 To start creating a macro, select Record Macro from the System menu.

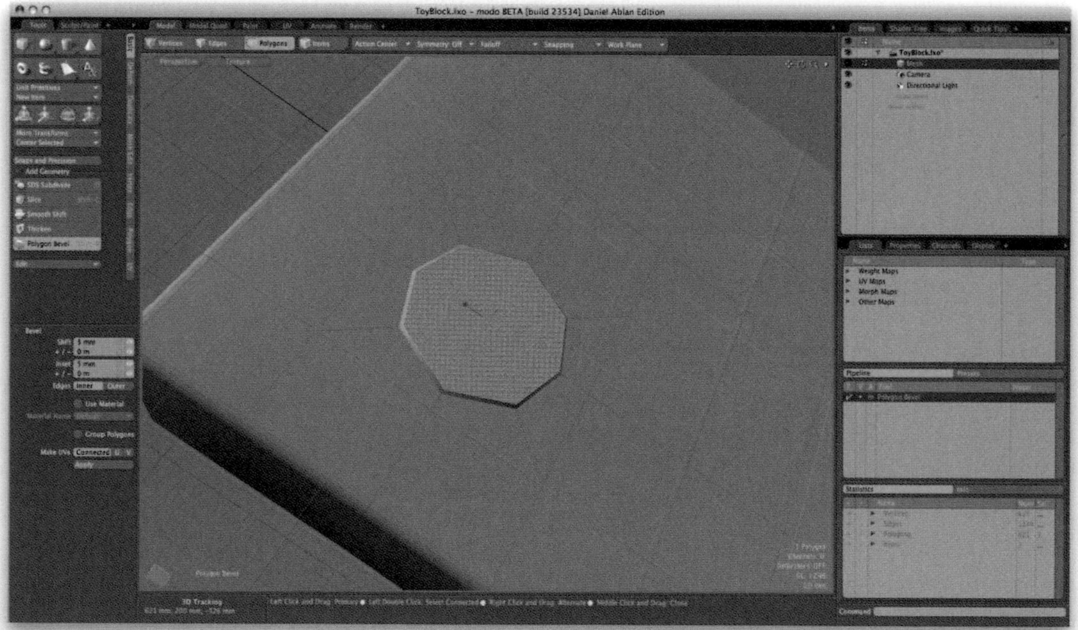

Figure 5.18 Inset and shift the selected polygon about 5 mm or so.

3. Because the polygon is still selected, you can bevel again to create more detail. The best way to do this is to hold the Shift key, then click on the polygon once. This effectively "resets" the Bevel tool, which you can tell by noticing that the values in the Tool Properties area are zeroed out.
4. Now bevel again, with an Inset value of about 5 mm or so and a Shift value of 160 mm. Figure 5.19 shows the operation.

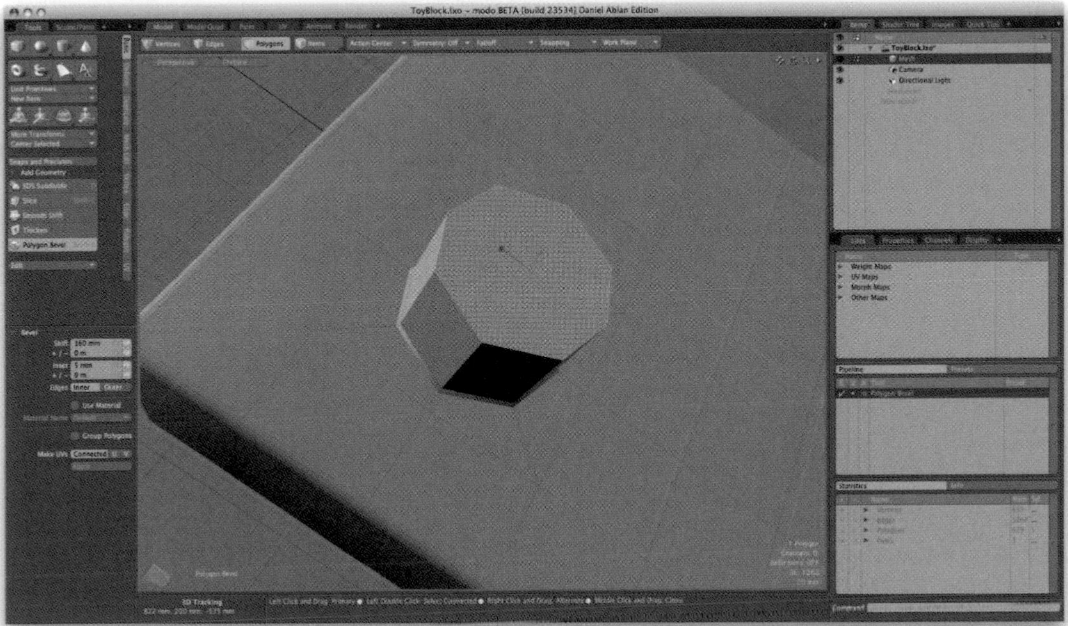

Figure 5.19 Inset and shift the selected polygon to extend it up and away from the block.

5. Hold the Shift key and click on the selected polygon to reset the Bevel tool. Then, bevel again with an inset of about 6 mm for both the Shift and Inset values. Figure 5.20 shows the result.
6. Finally, hold the Shift key, click on the polygon to reset the Bevel tool, and bevel just one more time with only an Inset value of about 30 mm.
7. After this last bevel, go back up to the System menu and select Recording Macro, which now has a check mark next to it, as shown in Figure 5.21.
8. You can save this macro for use any time in the future. It will work now without saving, as it's sitting in modo's memory. However, should you quit the program for any crazy reason, the recorded macro is lost forever. So back in the System menu, select Save to File. Then give your recorded macro a cool little name and a place to live. You'll come back to this shortly.
9. Back in the viewport, press the q key to turn off the Bevel tool. Then click off of the model to deselect the geometry.
10. Save your work! Command and the s key on the Mac, or Ctrl and the s key on the PC.
11. Now press the m key to assign a material to this block.

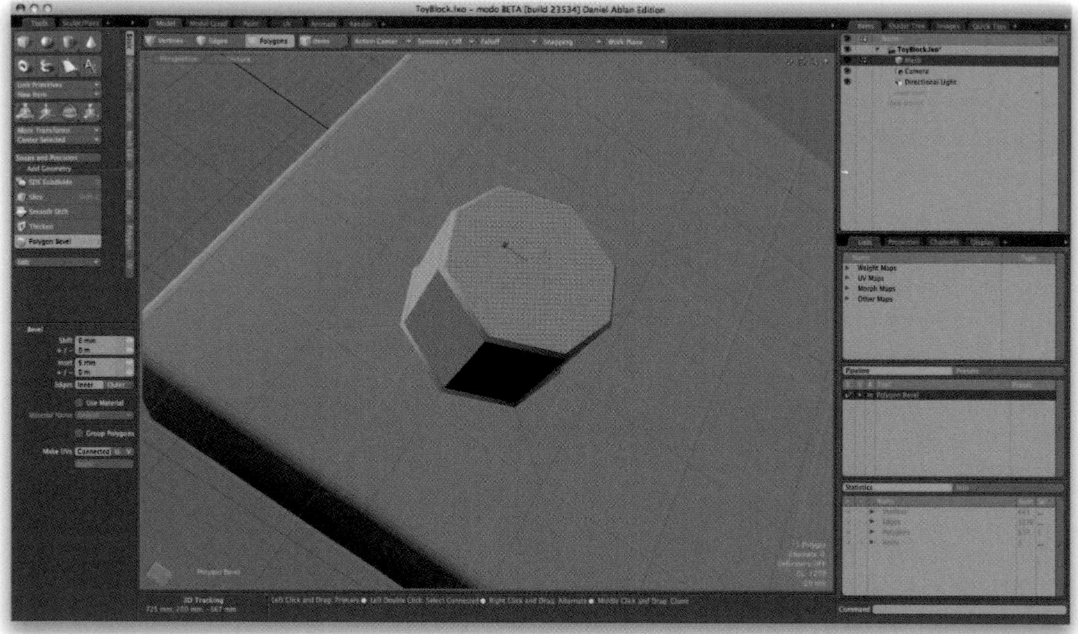

Figure 5.20 Bevel the selected polygon again, but this time with about 6 mm for both the Inset and Shift values.

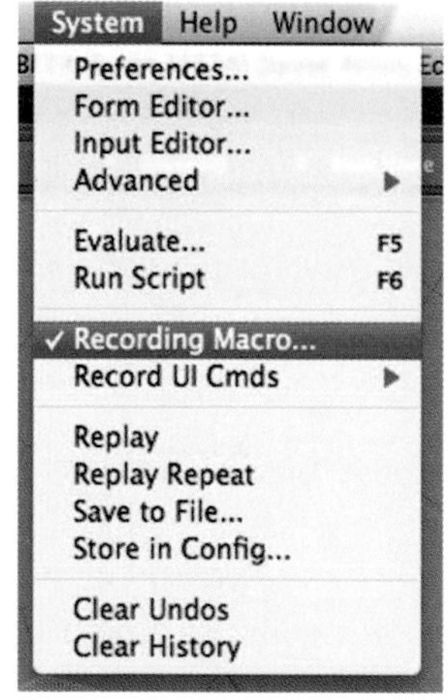

Figure 5.21 Once you've finished your bevel operations, turn off the Record Macro function.

12. In the Polygon Set Material dialog box that appears, give your model a slick name, add a little color, and up the specularity a bit for maximum visual impact (see Figure 5.22). Well, OK, it won't be anything to write home about, but it'll help make it shine!

Figure 5.22
Press the m key to set a material name for the model.

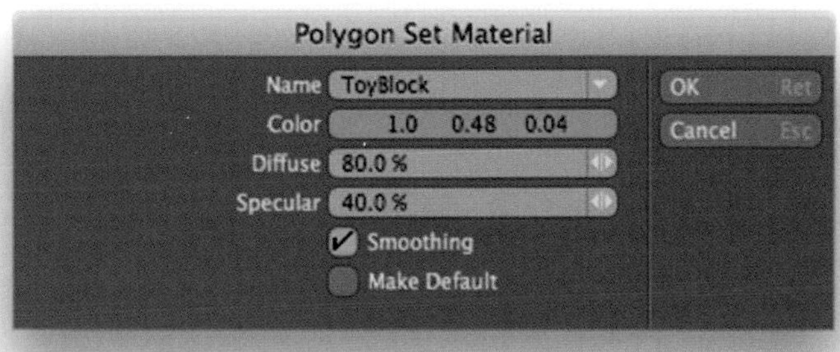

> **Note**
>
> Remember the rule: If nothing is selected, what you do applies to everything. In this case of setting a material, nothing is selected—so by pressing m to call up the Polygon Set Material dialog box, you're applying a surface name to the entire model.

13. Click OK to set the material and close the Polygon Set Material dialog box.
14. Then back in the main viewport, press the Tab key to activate subdivision surfaces. Notice how the tube, although extending out of the base model, is cleverly attached? It has a smooth edge, which was the goal of all those little bevels. The bevels are what picks up the light and adds that nice detail every model should have. Figure 5.23 shows the detail.
15. Save your work! Tired of hearing that? Good. Then you're getting it.

It's important to point out that what you've created, a round tube blending smoothly out of a box is not normally an easy task in most modeling programs. By working with edges, spinning and beveling them as needed, you've created an initial polygonal shape that, when subdivided, is round and smooth.

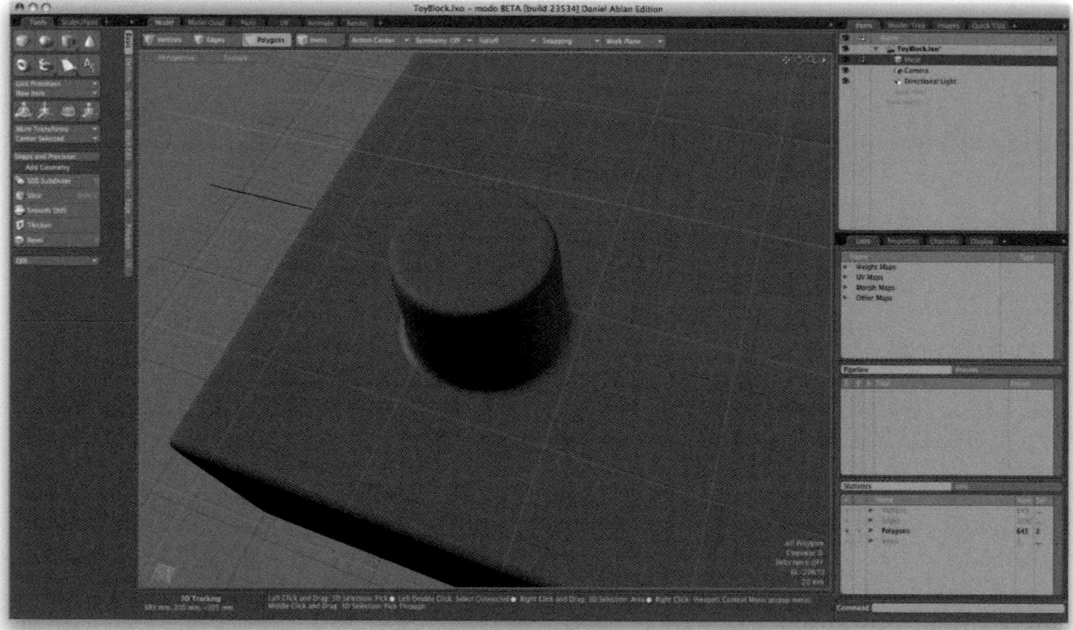

Figure 5.23 Once you press the Tab key, you can see how the bevels add necessary detail to the model.

Additional Macro Use

Creating the identical tubes throughout the rest of the model is not as arduous a task as the previous one. Follow along now to see how to use your marvelous macro on the rest of the model.

1. Press the Tab key to turn off the subdivision surfaces. Then, one row over from the first tube you've created, select four polygons, as shown in Figure 5.24.
2. You'll repeat the same steps you performed earlier in the chapter: First press Shift and the t key to triple the selected polygons.
3. Once tripled, switch to Edges mode at the top of the modo interface. Then, select the two parallel edges, as shown in Figure 5.25.
4. With the two edges selected, press the v key to spin them so they face in toward the center of the four polygons.
5. Switch to Vertices mode, then select the center point of those edges, as shown in Figure 5.26.

Figure 5.24 To begin creating additional tubes out of your block, select the four polygons opposite the original.

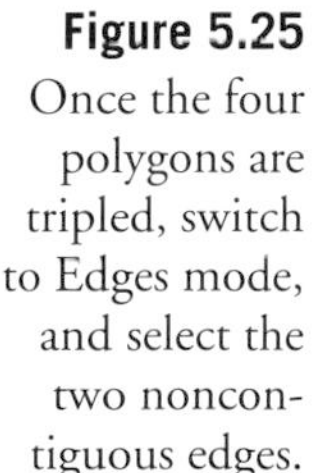

Figure 5.25 Once the four polygons are tripled, switch to Edges mode, and select the two noncontiguous edges.

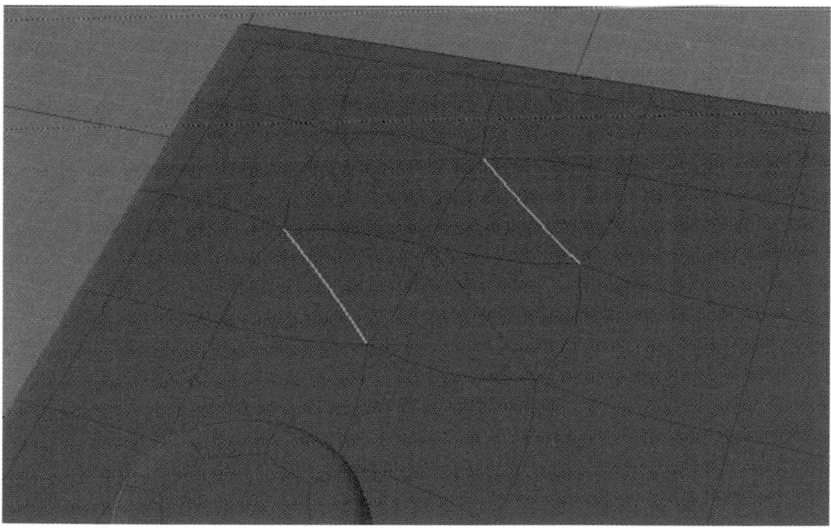

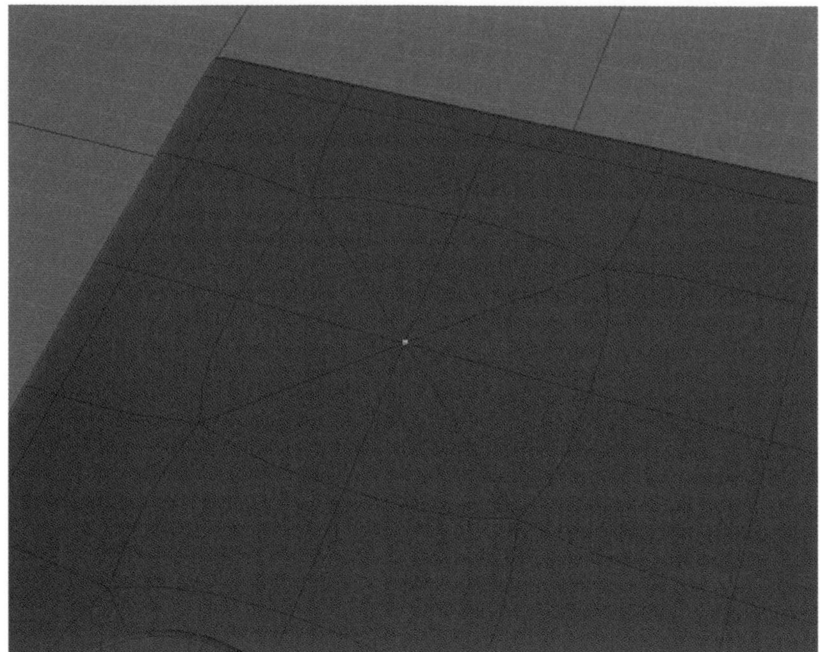

Figure 5.26
After the two edges are spun, select all of the edges within the four polygons.

6. With the center point selected, press the b key to activate the Bevel tool. Click and drag in the layout to bevel the selected edges. The first bevel was set to 130 mm. Bevel this selection to the same value, being careful not to overlap the edges.
7. Once you've beveled, press the q key to turn off the Bevel tool.
8. Press the spacebar to jump to Polygons mode. Then, click on the center eight-sided polygon, which is the result of the beveled edges, as shown in Figure 5.27.
9. Save your work!
10. Now comes the fun part! From the System menu, select Run Script.
11. Select the macro script you saved earlier. Or use the one from this chapter, saved on the book's DVD. It's called ToyBlockBevels.lxm. Remember, you need to do this with the polygon selected first. After you select the Run Script, all of the bevel operations you applied to the first tube are instantly applied to this selected polygon, as shown in Figure 5.28. Pretty cool!

Note

The macro you've recorded does not need to be applied to the same exact number of polygons. You can use this macro on one polygon, two, or as many as you like. And, there's one available on the book's DVD for you in the Chapter 5 folder.

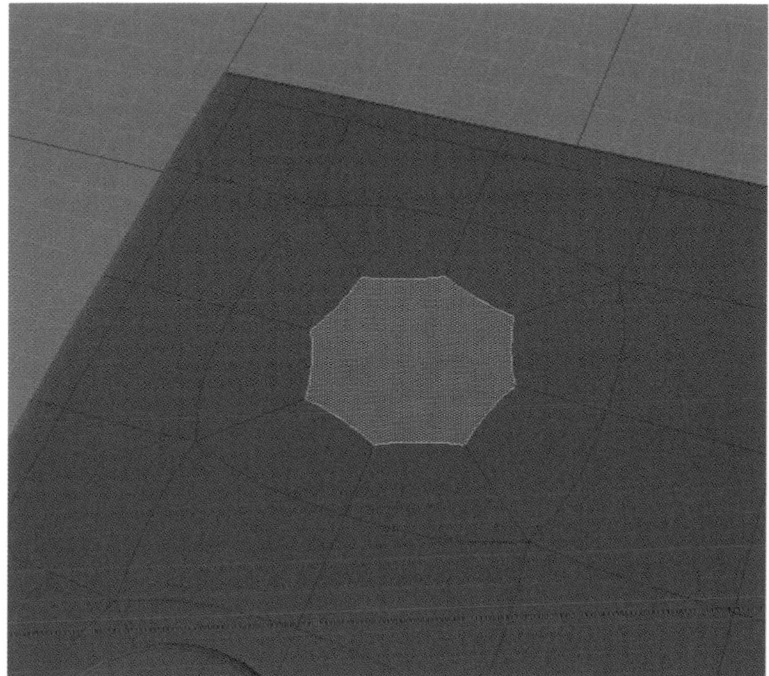

Figure 5.27
After the edges are beveled, switch to Polygons selection mode and select the eight-sided polygon.

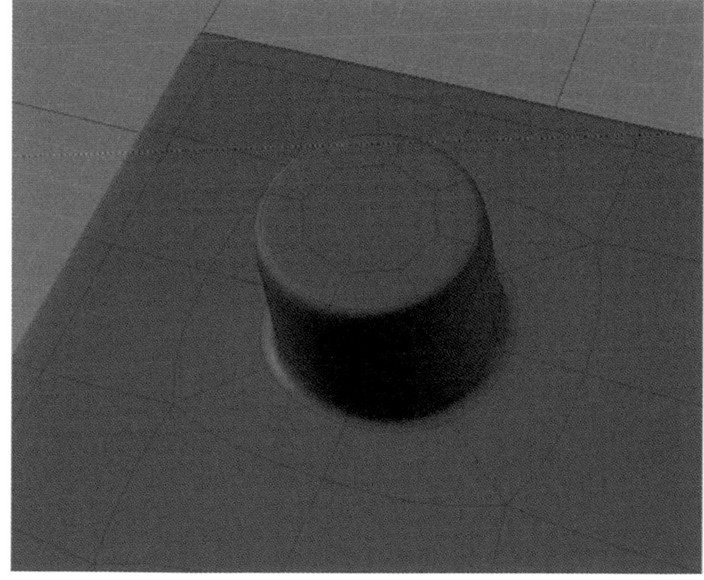

Figure 5.28
By applying the saved macro to the selected polygon, the bevel operations from the first beveled tube are instantly applied to the second.

12. Press the spacebar to turn off the active tool, then click away from the model in the viewport to deselect the polygon.
13. Press the Tab key to see how the model looks in subdivision surface mode. Figure 5.29 shows the model this far.

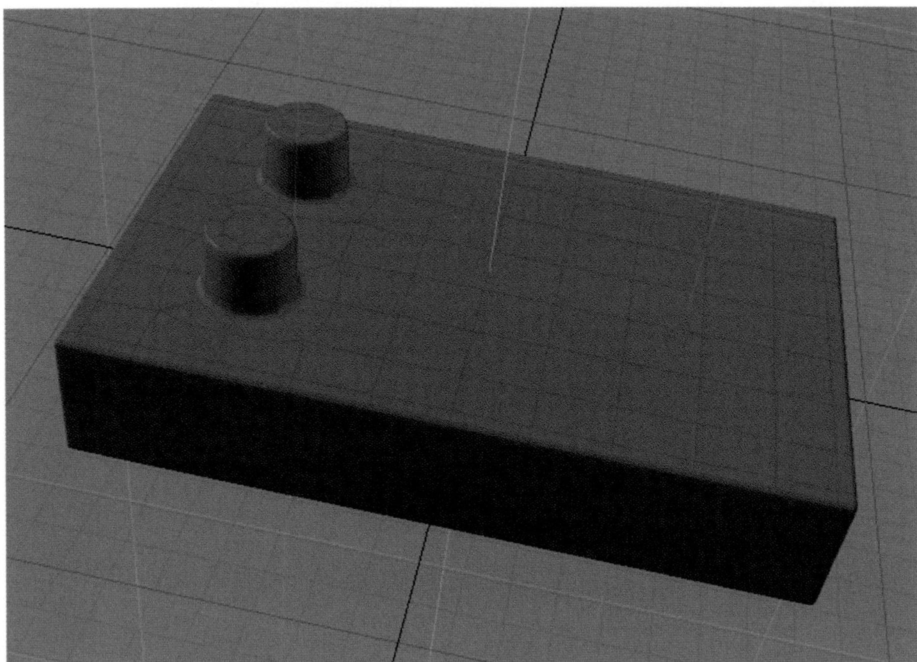

Figure 5.29
After the Macro function is applied, any polygons are deselected. When you press the Tab key, the model turns to a smooth subdivided model.

14. Save your work!
15. Go ahead and repeat the process of selecting four polygons, tripling, spinning and beveling the edges, and then running the macro script on the resulting polygon. Figure 5.30 shows the final six tubes extended from the original cube.

> **Note**
>
> You can work on multiple selections at the same time in modo. Select the polygons you want to triple throughout the model, and then triple them. Select all of the edges you want to spin, and spin them at once. The same applies to beveling the edges, and running the Macro script as well. Simply select the polygons you want to run the recorded Macro on, and bam! Instant bevels!

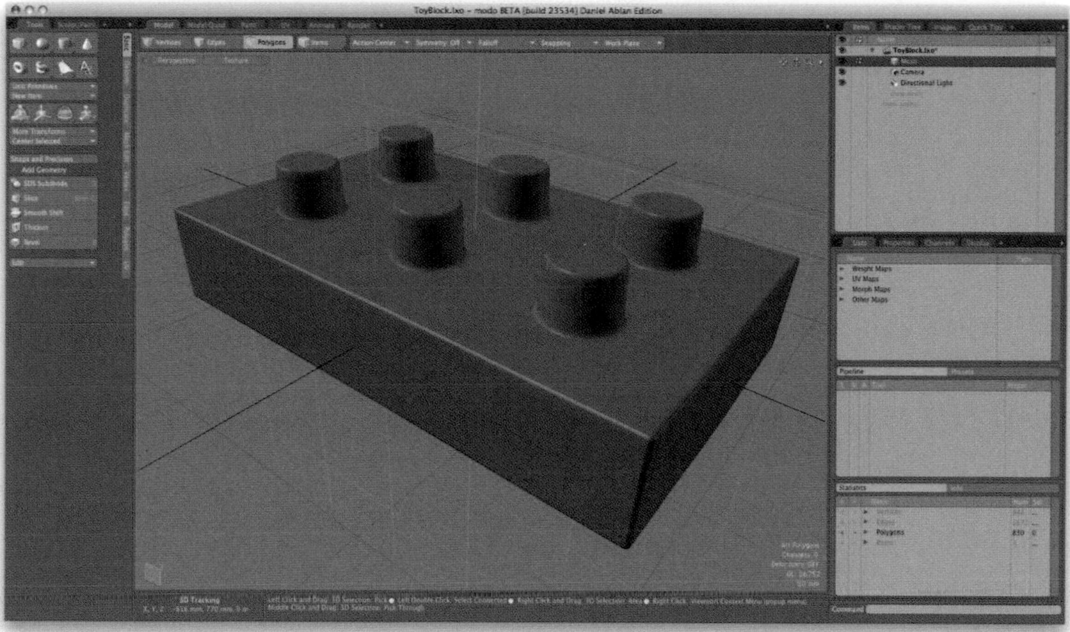

Figure 5.30 The steps described in this chapter are performed again on other sections of the cube, along with the recorded macro applied.

Editing the Shape

You can see that without a huge amount of work, you can create some good looking models, even on the simplest level. But what if you've built your toy block and all of a sudden realize that the tubes are just a little too small? Do you start over? How do you size just the tubes without affecting the rest of the object? This next section will show you how to edit the size of the tubes without disrupting the base of the model.

1. First and foremost, make sure your model is saved. And, it's even a good idea to make a secondary copy of the model as a backup. You can choose Save As from the File menu and give your object a new name, or just add a version number to it.

2. Making sure you're in Polygons selection mode, found at the top of the modo interface, select the top polygon of each tube, as shown in Figure 5.31.

3. Next, hold the Shift key and press the up arrow on your keyboard continually to select all the polygons that make up the tubes, about four times. Figure 5.32 shows the full selection.

4. You should now have 198 polygons selected, as shown by the display in the bottom right corner of the modo interface (see Figure 5.33). Be sure not to select into the base of the model, beyond the tube itself. Save your work.

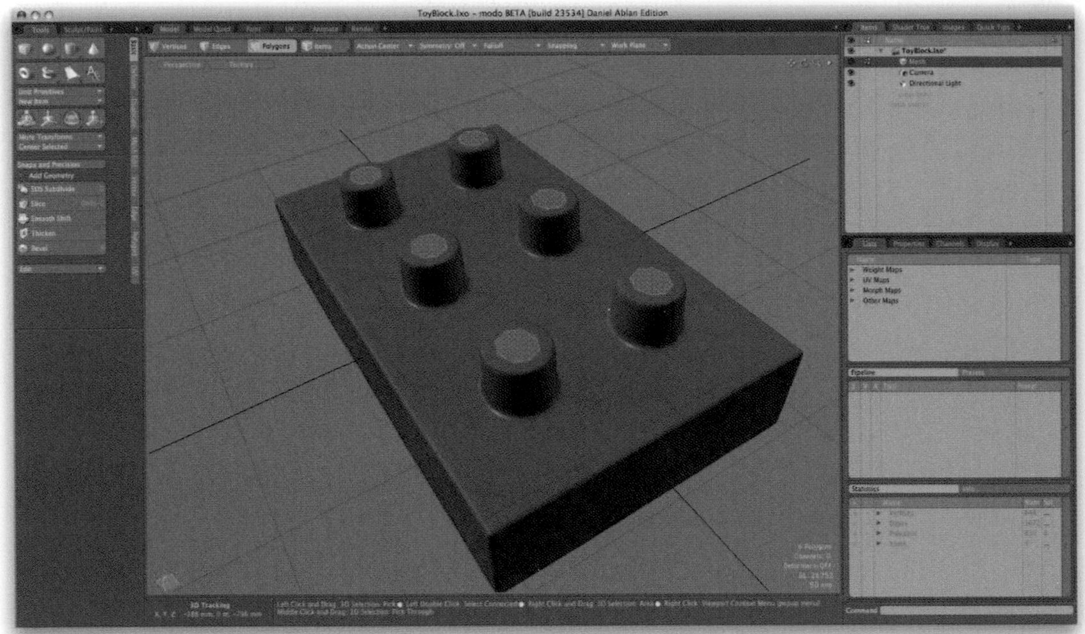

Figure 5.31 To begin adjusting the size of the tubes, select the top polygon of each tube.

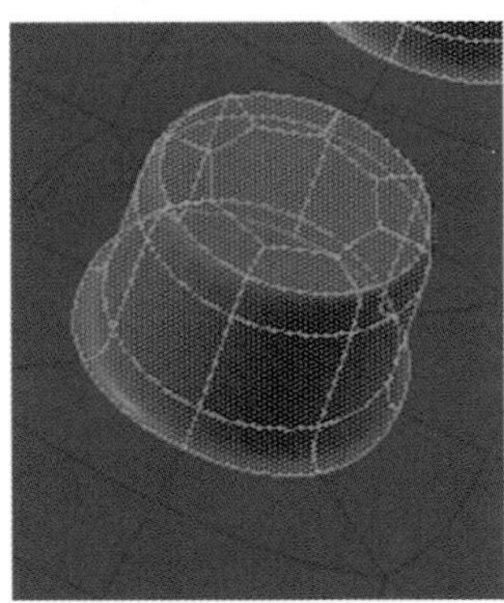

Figure 5.32 Hold the Shift key and press the up arrow multiple times to select the entire set of polygons that make up the tubes.

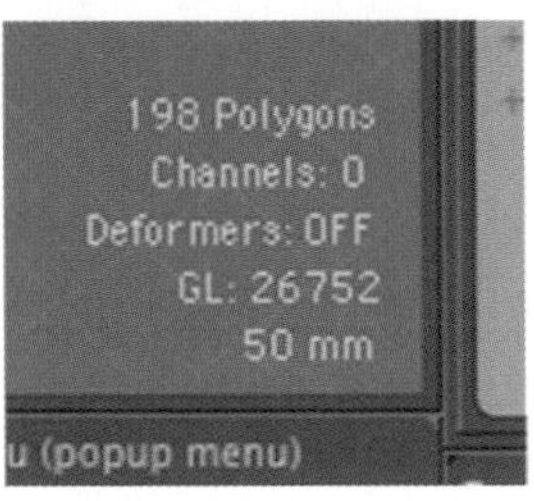

Figure 5.33 Once all the polygons of the tube are selected, you should have 198.

5. Before you do anything else, assign a selection set to these polygons. You can do this from the Select menu at the top of the interface, and choose Assign Selection Set, as shown in Figure 5.34. In the dialog box that appears, choose Assign Selection Set, give the polygons a name, choose Add, and then click OK. Then any time you need to reselect these polygons, you can choose Use Selection Set from the Select menu.

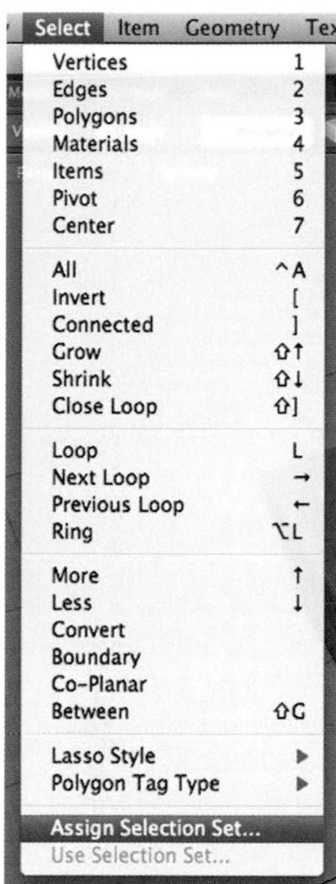

Figure 5.34
Assign a selection set to the selected polygons.

The advantage of a selection set is that you won't have to reselect these polygons if you accidentally deselect them or want to continue working later. On a larger scale, a selection set works well for more complex objects when creating morph maps or if there are areas of a complex model you need to edit often.

6. If you've accidentally deselected the polygons, be sure they are selected, either manually, as described earlier using the Shift key and up arrow, or by recalling your saved selection set. Figure 5.35 shows all of the tubes selected as they should be for the next few steps.

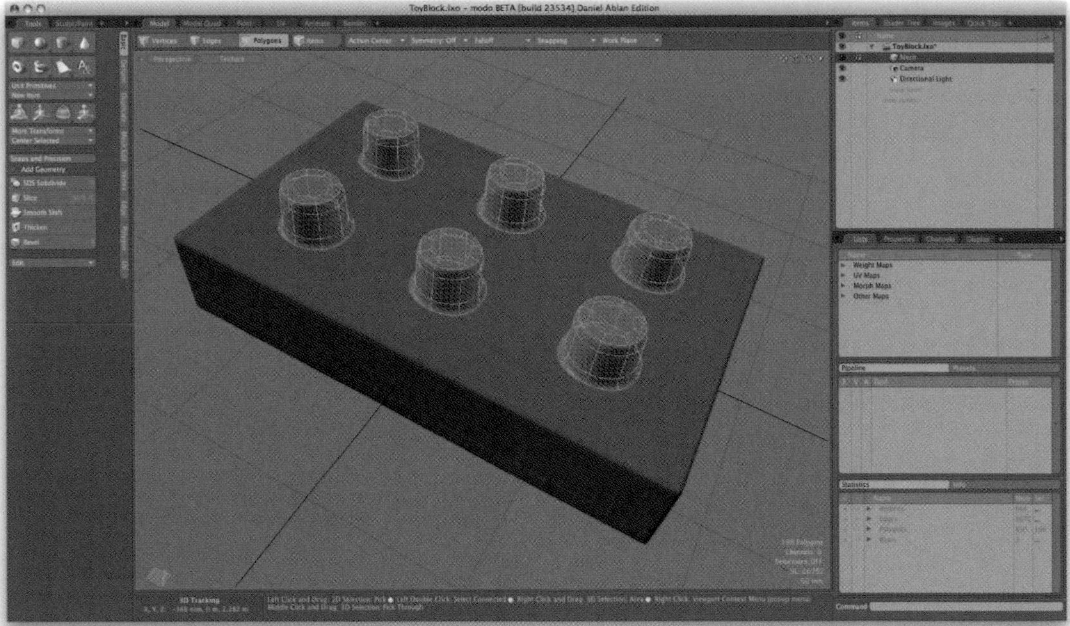

Figure 5.35 Select all of the tube polygons throughout the model.

> **Note**
>
> Remember, in order to add to your existing selection, be it polygons, edges, or vertices, hold the Shift key, then click the new selection. If you accidentally click a new polygon and deselect something you've already selected, simply undo it by pressing Ctrl-Z on the PC or the Apple (Command) key and z on the Mac. And if you accidentally select a polygon you don't want, remember to hold the Ctrl key, then click on the unwanted polygon to deselect.

7. Because you have multiple polygons selected, sizing them normally would result in their being sized as one unit. This means they would push away from the center origin. Instead, you want each selected tube to size based on the selection, not on the entire model. No problem for modo! From the Action Center drop-down menu at the top of the interface, select Local.
8. Press the r key to activate the Scale tool. Then click and drag on the blue circle to scale constrained to two axes so the pegs get fatter, but not taller. Paying attention to the tool properties on the left side of the interface, scale the selections up with a factor of about 135%, as shown in Figure 5.36.

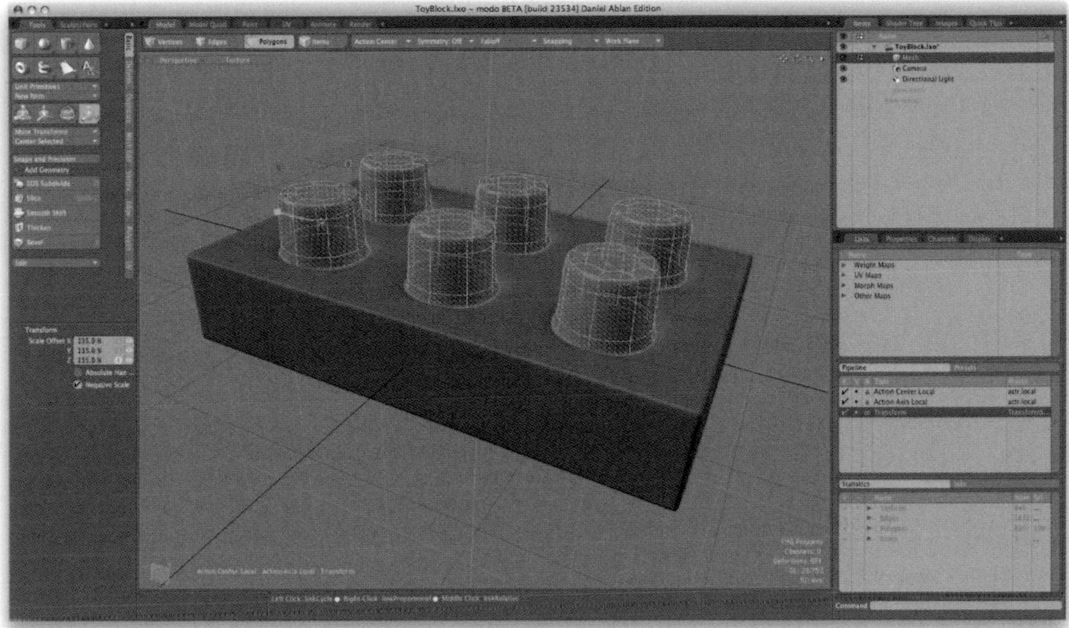

Figure 5.36 With Action Center set to Local, you can scale each selection to two axes.

9. Press the spacebar or q key to deactivate the Scale tool.
10. You can see, because the selections scaled up upon themselves, they stayed in place. This is good for the most part, but they pushed themselves into the base of the cube a bit. No worries! Simply press the w key to activate the Transform tool, and then click and drag the vertical handle to move the selections up about 60 mm. Now because the Action Center is set to Local, the axis will read as Z, and the handle will be blue. Normally the Y axis is up and the handle is green. Figure 5.37 shows the move.

> **Note**
>
> Depending on how much you scale your selections, polygons at the base of the tubes might pinch a bit with neighboring geometry. You can scale the polygons less, or after you've scaled them to the desired amount, press the t key to activate the Element Move tool, and click and drag the pinched edges to fix them. But using the blue circle within the tool as you did earlier helps scale equally.

11. Save your work! Then press the spacebar to turn off any active tools.

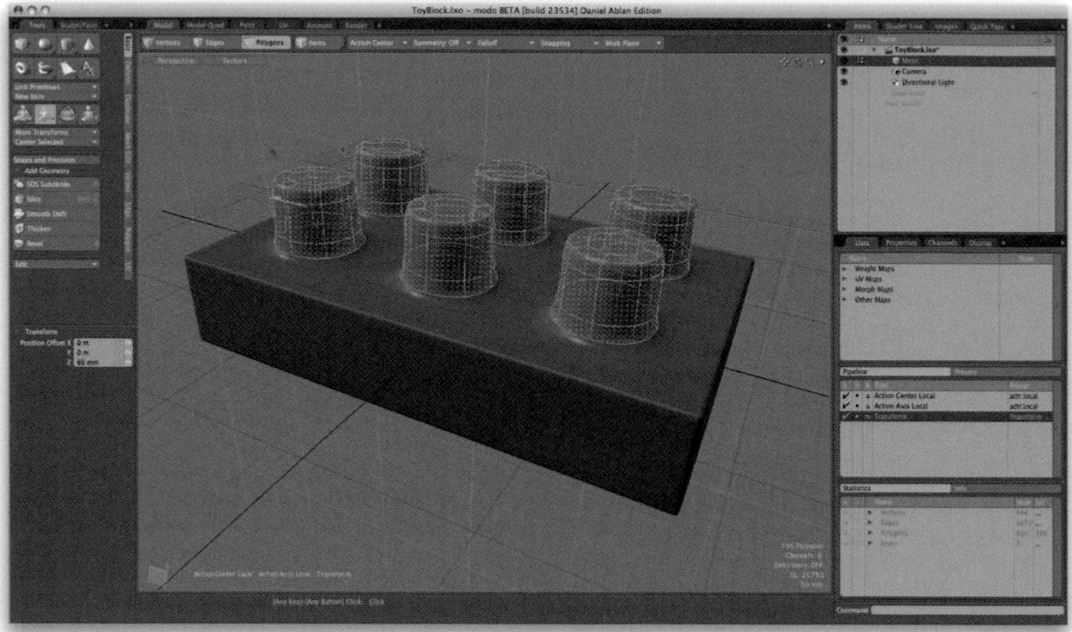

Figure 5.37 Using the Transform tool, move the selection up away from the base of the model.

Cutting the Shape

Your model is now looking much better, and there's only one thing left to do. If you hold the Alt key and click and drag in the viewport, you can rotate around to look at the base of your model. The bottom is solid, so if these were real building blocks, they wouldn't be able to stack. So you need to cut the bottom to match the top. This is easy to do with a Boolean function, but first you need a copy of the model.

1. With your model saved, move over to the Items tab on the right side of the interface. Right-click on the model name and choose Duplicate. You'll see a copy of your model added to the Items tab, as shown in Figure 5.38.
2. The first thing you want to do is size one of the objects down slightly. Click the small eyeball icon to the left of the first Toy Block item in the Items tab to hide this model from view. Then, select the duplicate mesh [Toy Block (2)]. Make sure all of the tubes are selected by choosing Use Selection Set from the Select menu at the top of the screen. Choose the selection set you created for the selected tube polygons.
3. Once the tubes are selected, press Shift and the r key to set a uniform scale by a factor of 90%. To do this, click once on the small icon to the right of the Scale Offset values in the Transform tool properties. Type in 90, and press Return. All fields will change to this value (see Figure 5.39). The selected tubes will equally size down.

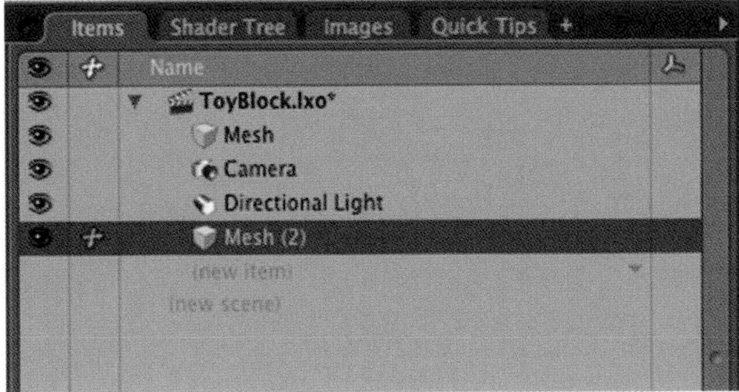

Figure 5.38 Right-click the Toy Block in the Items tab and choose Duplicate. You'll see another copy of your object added to the list named Toy Block (2).

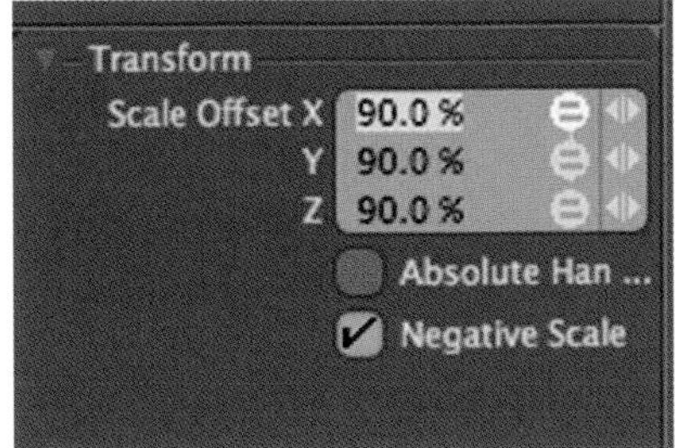

Figure 5.39 To uniformly scale the selected tubes, press the Shift and r keys, and enter a value of 90% in the Tool Properties panel.

4. Before you deselect the tubes, press the left bracket key ([) to invert the selection. You can also select Invert from the Select menu at the top of the interface.
5. Press the spacebar one time to turn off the Scale tool, then press Shift and the r key to reactivate the tool. Turning the tool off and on again resets its values as well. Scale the selected geometry about 95% this time. Press the spacebar to turn off the tool, then click off of the model in the viewport to deselect the geometry. Figure 5.40 shows the full-scaled model.

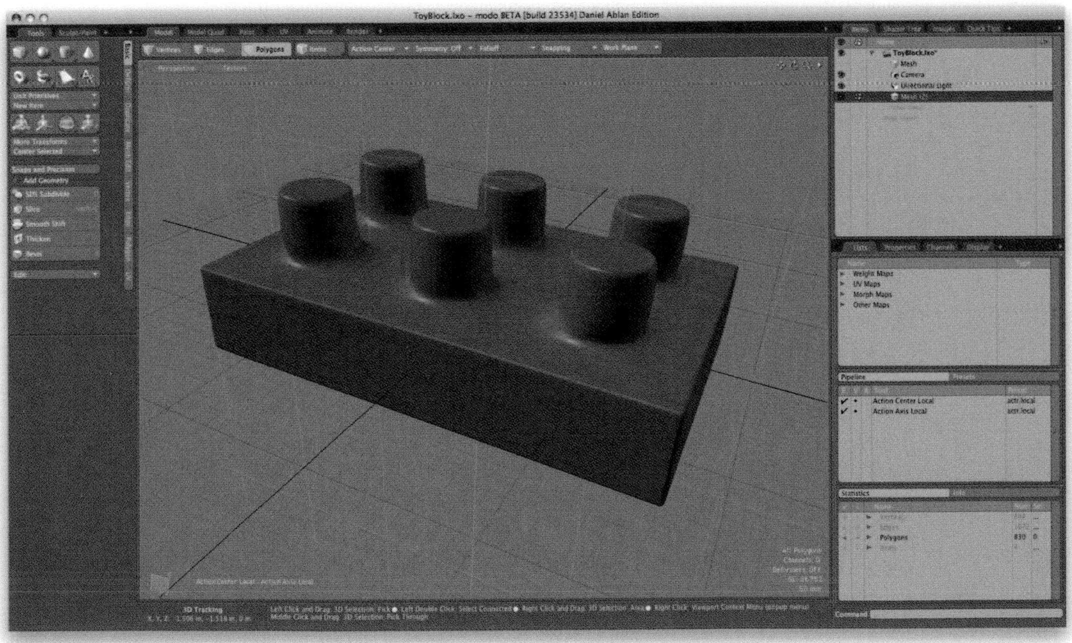

Figure 5.40 By uniformly scaling the entire model, one copy is now smaller than the other.

6. Save your work. Click the eyeball for the first Mesh item to make it visible again. You'll see a blackout line floating outside of the shaded model. This is the first model in the background.
7. Press the w key and move the scaled down copy [Toy Block (2)]of the object about –28 mm. Move it down enough so the bottom hangs out beneath the original version, visible as a background layer.

> **Note**
>
> You should be able to see your background layer by default. If you don't, first select the main item you're working with in the Items tab. Then, make sure that the small eyeball icon on the left of the item listing is checked for the background object—in this case, the duplicate copy. Also, you can change your background view style by clicking the render style button at the top left of the viewport (which reads Texture in Figure 5.40), and then going to Shade Options, Background Item. You can choose Wireframe, Flat Shade, or Same as Active Layer.

8. Press the single quote key (') to reverse the layers in the Items tab, putting the smaller, adjusted block into the background and the larger original into the foreground.
9. Then from the Geometry menu at the top of the interface, select Boolean as shown in Figure 5.41. In the Boolean CSG dialog that appears, choose Subtract and click OK. The background layer will be used to effectively cut away the foreground layer. Figure 5.42 shows the result—a hollowed out building block.

> **Note**
>
> CSG stands for Constructive Solids Geometry.

10. Reverse layers again (press the ' key) and then in the Items tab, right-click on the smaller block and select Delete. Save your model.
11. Feel free to undo and adjust the scale of the background mesh as needed. Perhaps, depending on your model, the smaller mesh might cut into the sides of the first mesh when the Boolean function is performed. If this happens, use the Selection Set to scale the tubes a bit more. You can even scale the body of the block manually, as you see fit.

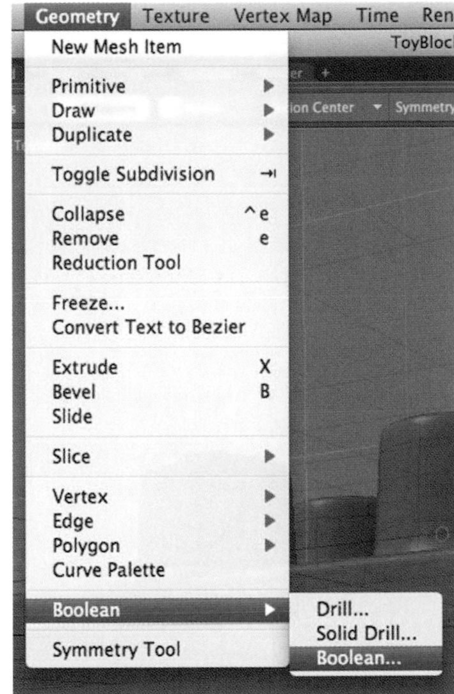

Figure 5.41 The Boolean CSG function allows you to use one layer to cut away another.

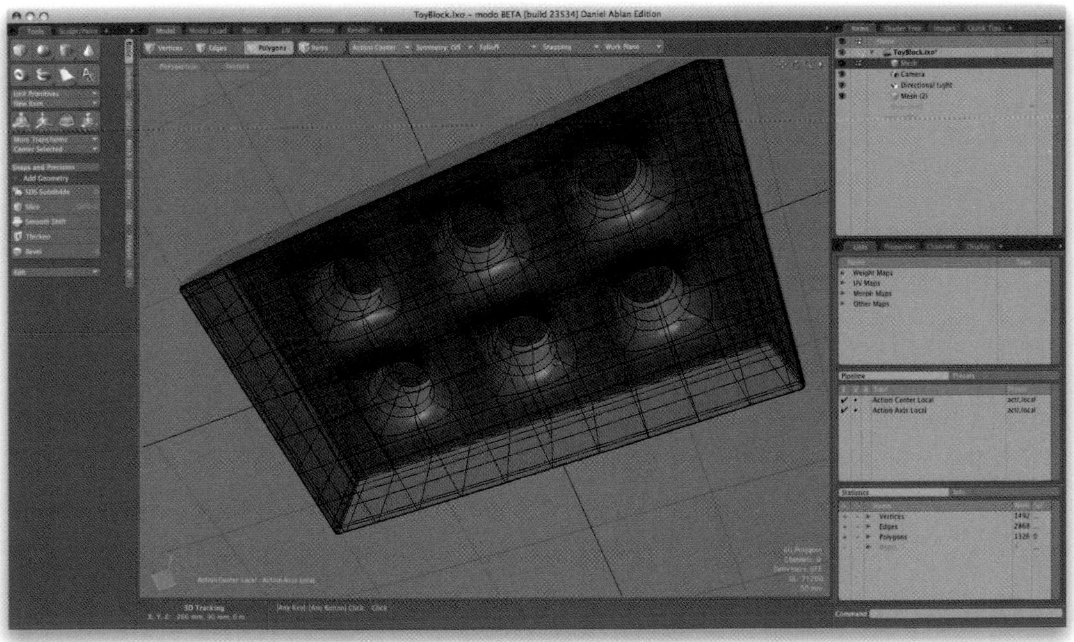

Figure 5.42 After the Boolean function is performed, the smaller block is used to cut out the inside of the larger block, resulting in a hollow shape.

The goal here is to make a smaller model on a different layer in the Items tab, which you use as a cutting tool. By using the Shift-r command for Uniform Scale, you're able to scale the entire selection together uniformly. That in combination with a slight move will enable you to easily scale the cutting model.

Note

You can change your viewport (at the top left of the screen) to a left or front view to make selections easier.

Remember you can use the right mouse button to lasso select the geometry. And if you want to select in an orthogonal view, like the front or side, change to a Wireframe shade to make sure you're selecting all the way through the model.

You don't necessarily need to cut out the bottom of the model. In fact, you won't even see that if you're only showing the tops of the models in the render. Ideally, this type of model, a subdivision surface model, can cause issues with Boolean operations. However, this model enabled you to see how the Boolean operations worked and how you can use them. This feature is great for cutting holes in things, such as a doorway or a window. Perhaps you need to build a keyhole into an old-fashioned door. Just build the door in one layer, and in another, build the keyhole. Extrude it through the door and use the Boolean command to cut that shape out of the door, just as you did with the two blocks in this chapter.

As an alternative, instead of using Boolean operations, you could select the bottom polygons on the mesh, bevel them inward and then upward with Group Polygons checked in the Tool Properties panel. Now just make pegs as you did earlier, but bevel them up instead of down.

So there you have it. Basic building blocks—literally. While the chapter didn't show you how to model anything outrageous or super-cool looking, it did show you the basics of general modeling and how modo handles each task; it also showed you various scaling tools, Action Centers, and Booleans. This foundation is crucial to everything you do in modo, so keep in mind what you've done here for the next chapter.

6

Working with Layers

Chapter 5 introduced you to more modeling tools, and also might have piqued your interest regarding the Items tab and how the layers within it work. This chapter will outline how the layers work with a cool project. Later in the book, you'll texture and render the layered model you build in this chapter.

Layers are powerful for a number of reasons. First and foremost, it's a way to work on scenes that encompass multiple elements. For example, in Chapter 5, you built a single toy block. If you wanted to create a scene with many of these objects, and perhaps a toy truck to go along with the block, you'd create the truck in another layer. The advantage here is that you can build the second object without disrupting the original model. If you've ever used Photoshop, you've worked with layers, using a different layer for separate parts of the image. The idea is the same here in modo, and the amount of layers you can use is unlimited.

You can also use layers for creating shapes with functions, like a Boolean subtract from Chapter 5. One layer is used to cut away another layer. All of your layer controls are available in the Items tab, so read on to learn more.

Items Tab Navigation

The Items tab is located at the top right of the interface, as you have already seen throughout the book. But there is more to this handy little panel than meets the eye. Figure 6.1 shows the Items tab upon startup.

> **Note**
>
> Your Items tab grouping on the right side of the interface might be shortened, depending on your screen size. Be sure to place your mouse on the left edge of the panel, then click and drag to widen the panel and view it in all of its glory.

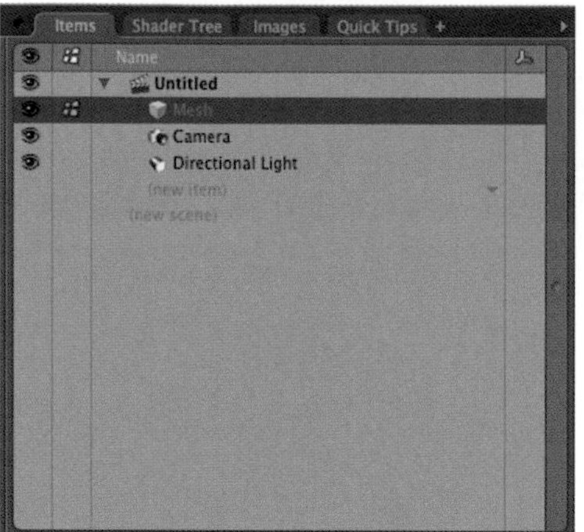

Figure 6.1
The Items tab is home to all of your scene elements, from objects to cameras, lights, and more.

By default, a mesh layer is selected in the Items tab. You can tell it's blank because the name is grayed out. You'll also see a listing for Camera and Directional light. These are the default items in modo. You may not actually see a light and a camera in the layout, depending on how you've set up your interface. You can make the camera and lights visible by pressing the letter o on your keyboard (not zero). This opens the viewport options panel. Then go to the Visibility tab and choose Show Cameras and Show Lights (see Figure 6.2).

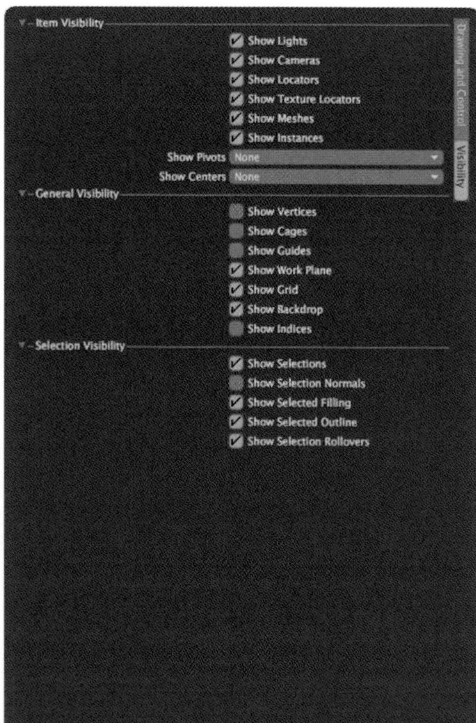

Figure 6.2
You can make the camera and lights visible by choosing them from the vertical Visibility tab.

Though the Items tab is easy to navigate and understand, it's crucial to your workflow and you have to remember it's there. You use it to select items in the modo layout. You use it to rename and group items, and even create instances or duplicates of your 3D objects. But another key feature of the Items tab is the layering capability—the focus of this chapter's project, which will give you a more thorough understanding of the Items tab.

Building in Layers

Normally, when someone mentions working in layers, people think of programs like Adobe's Photoshop or something similar. Each layer contains an element of the current project. In modo, you need to think of the Items tab in the same way. As you create a 3D object, you can build up the layers for it in the same way you would for a Photoshop document. In this project, you'll create a message board that contains many elements, such as a thumbtack, Post-it Notes, and a photograph. (In the next chapter, you'll be introduced to the Shader Tree and learn how to apply image maps to the objects you create in this chapter.) The idea for this project came from this book's excellent technical editor and artist, Greg Leuenberger. The Items tab will help you not only create the scene setup with objects and lights, but help you organize as well. To begin creating this scene, think of what you'll need to complete it. You're creating a message board, like a corkboard used in a college dorm room or kitchen, or perhaps an office. The message board will hang on a wall. On the corkboard are sticky notes and a thumbtack holding a photograph. What do you create first? Truly, it doesn't matter. But to help you with workflow, build from the back forward. You'll start by creating the corkboard, and from there add the notes and other elements.

1. Begin this project with a default modo layout. If you have a project you've been working on, now is a good time to save it. You can then go to the File menu and select Reset to return to the default modo workspace.

> **Note**
>
> Unlike Adobe's Photoshop, or modo's Shader Tree, the order of the layers in the Items tab does not matter. You can build a 3D object, and it can be listed above or below another object in the Items tab. This will have no affect on its visibility in your final render.

2. Make sure your main view in the modo layout is set to Perspective. You can set this from the top left of the modo viewport; or better, with the mouse in the viewport, press the o key to call up the viewport options (as shown in Figure 6.3).

> **Note**
>
> When pressing o for viewport options, simply moving the mouse off of the options panel will remove it. To call it back up, press the o key again.

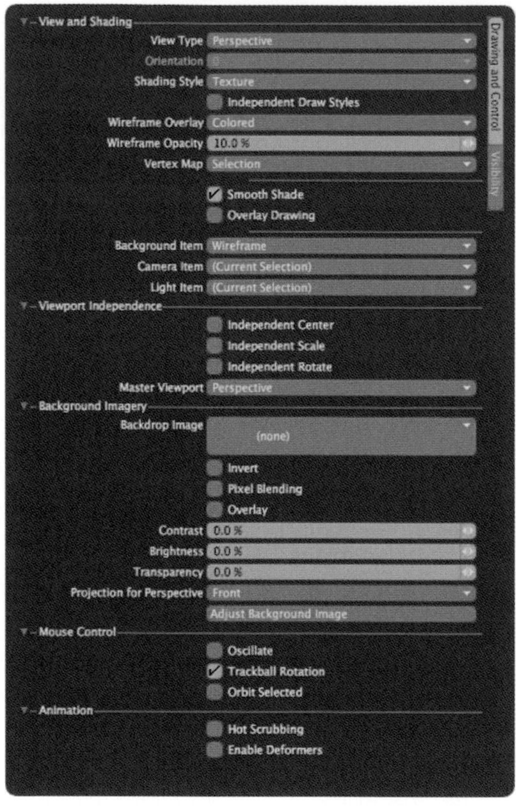

Figure 6.3
You can press the letter o to open the viewport options.

3. In the viewport options, set the View Type option (at the top of the panel) to Perspective. Move the mouse away from the options panel, and it will close.
4. Hold the Alt key on your keyboard and rotate the Perspective view until the work plane is XY, as shown in Figure 6.4. This icon is visible in the bottom left of the viewport.

Figure 6.4
To begin making the corkboard, set the dominant axis to XY.

5. Select the Cube primitive on the Tools tab; also make sure the Basic tab is selected. Then in the Perspective view, draw out a flat box to fill the majority of the view, about 10 × 6 meters in size, as shown in Figure 6.5.
6. Before you turn off the Cube primitive tool, click the blue center crosshair in the middle of the object and pull it forward to give the box some depth. (Note that this is not the blue arrow.) Pull it about 400 mm, as shown in Figure 6.6.

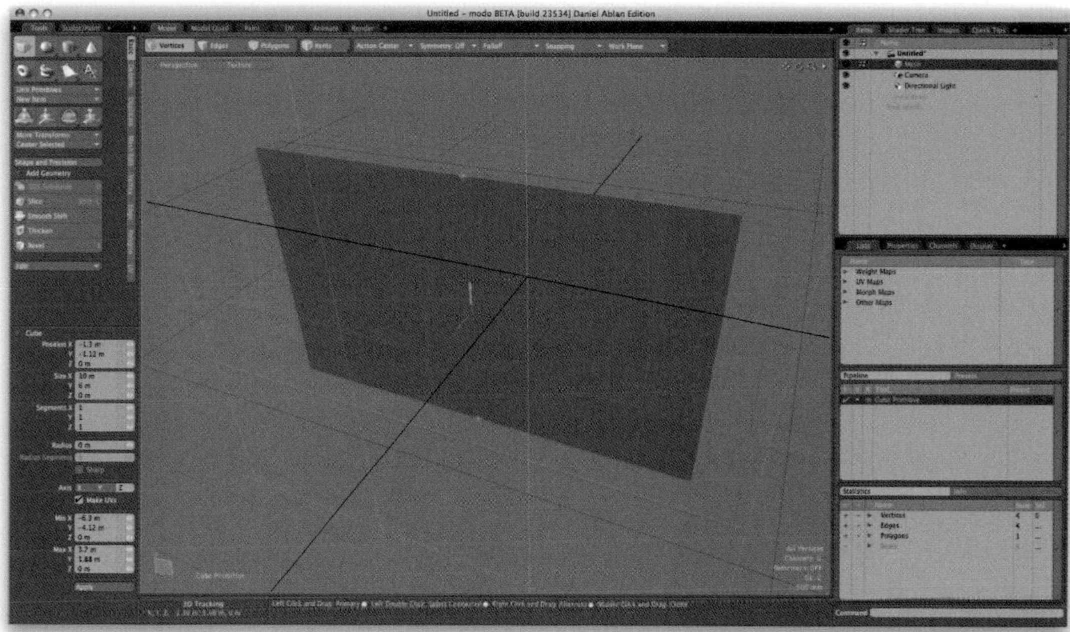

Figure 6.5 You can start the corkboard with a Cube primitive.

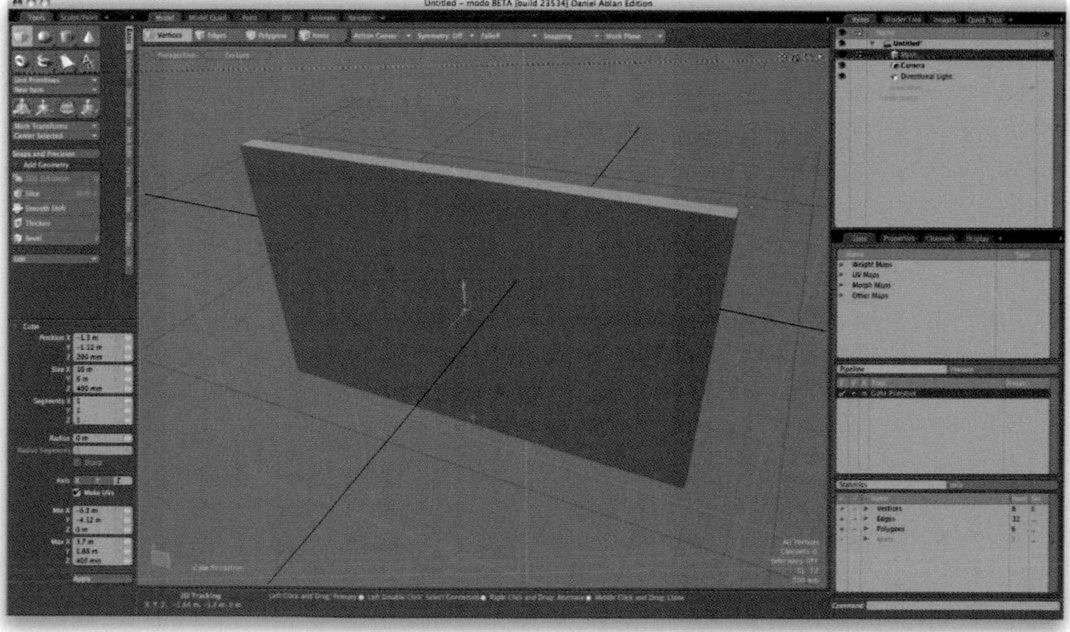

Figure 6.6 Give your corkboard some depth on the Z axis, about 400 mm.

7. Press the spacebar to turn off the Cube primitive tool, and then save your object as Corkboard.

> **Note**
>
> Remember that you can see the specific measurements of your tools in the Tool Properties panel, which appears at the bottom left of the modo interface within the Tools tab when a tool is selected.

8. Making sure you're in Polygons mode at the top of the modo interface, click to select just the front-facing polygon on the corkboard.
9. Press the b key on your keyboard to turn on the Bevel tool. Then click on the selection to activate the tool. At this point, the control handles will appear.
10. Grab the red handle for the Inset value, and drag it in about 140 mm, as shown in Figure 6.7.
11. Hold the Shift key and click on the selection to reset the bevel. Then, drag the blue handle in toward the object to shift the selection –140 mm. Figure 6.8 shows the operation.

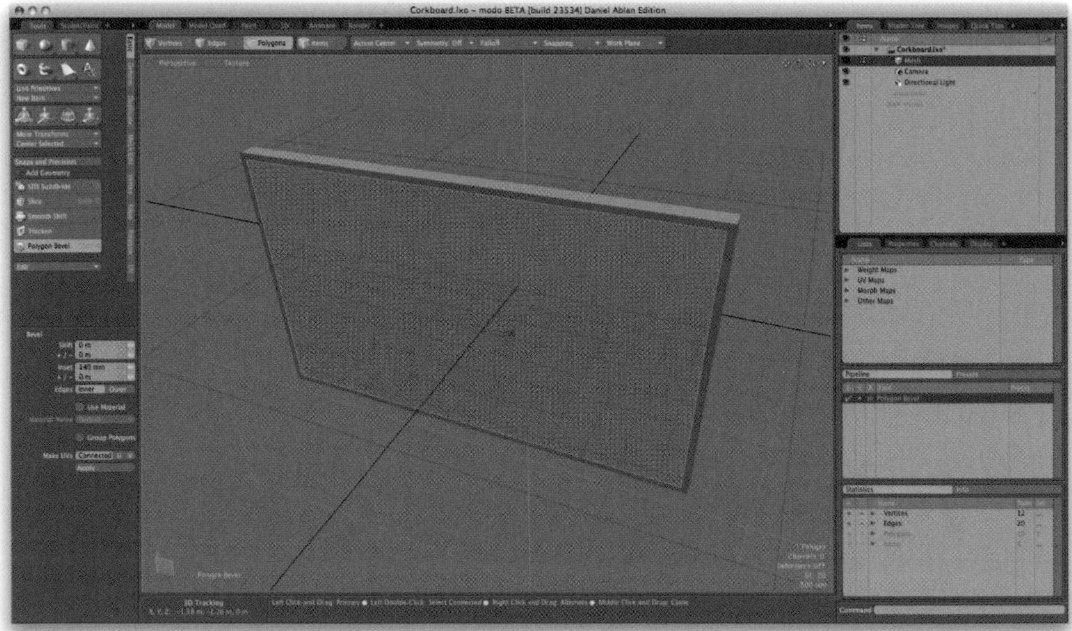

Figure 6.7 Bevel just the inset of the selected front polygon about 140 mm.

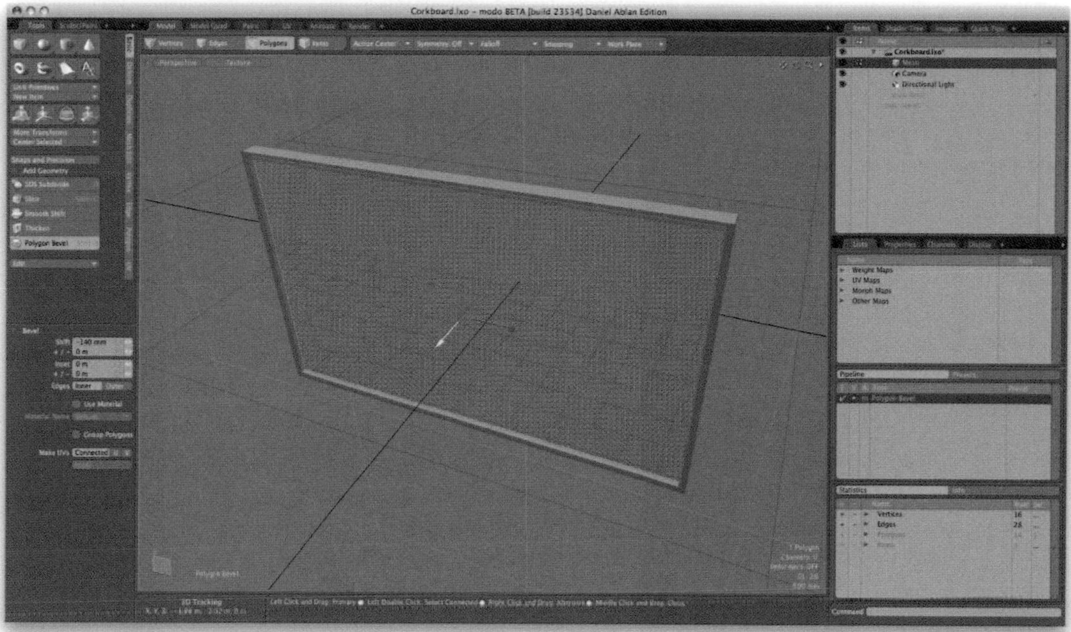

Figure 6.8 Bevel the Shift value by clicking and dragging the blue handle to bring the selected polygon in about –140 mm.

12. Press the spacebar to turn off the Bevel tool, then click off of the model to deselect the polygon.
13. Take a look over at the Items tab on the right of the interface. If you've saved your scene, the name you chose will appear in bold at the top of the list. Beneath that you'll see listings for Camera and Directional Light. The Mesh is your object. Right-click on it and select Rename from the popup that appears. If you're on a Mac, remember to hold the Apple key and click.
14. Rename the mesh to Corkboard and click OK. Figure 6.9 shows the Item Name dialog box.
15. Now is as good a time as any to save your work.

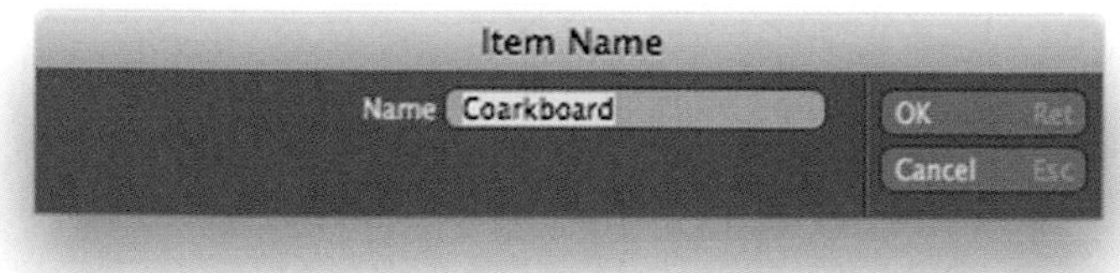

Figure 6.9 Right-click on a mesh in the Items tab to rename it. You can do the same for cameras and lights.

16. Most message boards aren't as basic looking as the one you've built here. They have some roundness to them, which is easy to do in modo. With the existing corkboard in your viewport, choose Edges selection mode to tell the program you want to work with edges.
17. Double-click on the outer front edge of the corkboard to select the entire edge loop, as shown in Figure 6.10.
18. Once the edge is selected, press the b key to call up the Bevel tool.
19. In the properties panel for Edge Bevel, set the Round Level value to 3. Then click and drag in the viewport to bevel the selected edge roughly 40 mm. You can see the Edge Bevel Value setting in the Tool Properties panel. Feel free to zoom in closer to see the detail after you bevel by pressing the period (.) key on your keyboard. Hold the Alt key and click and drag in the view to rotate it to get a closer look. Figure 6.11 shows the rounded edge.
20. Press the spacebar to turn off the Bevel tool, then click away from the object to deselect the edges. Save as necessary.
21. Now you need to bevel the inside edge in the exact way you did the outer edge. Double-click the edge to select the entire loop, press b for the Bevel tool, and bevel it out about 40 mm. Figure 6.12 shows the inside edge nicely beveled. (Note that you could also have beveled both sets of edges at the same time.)

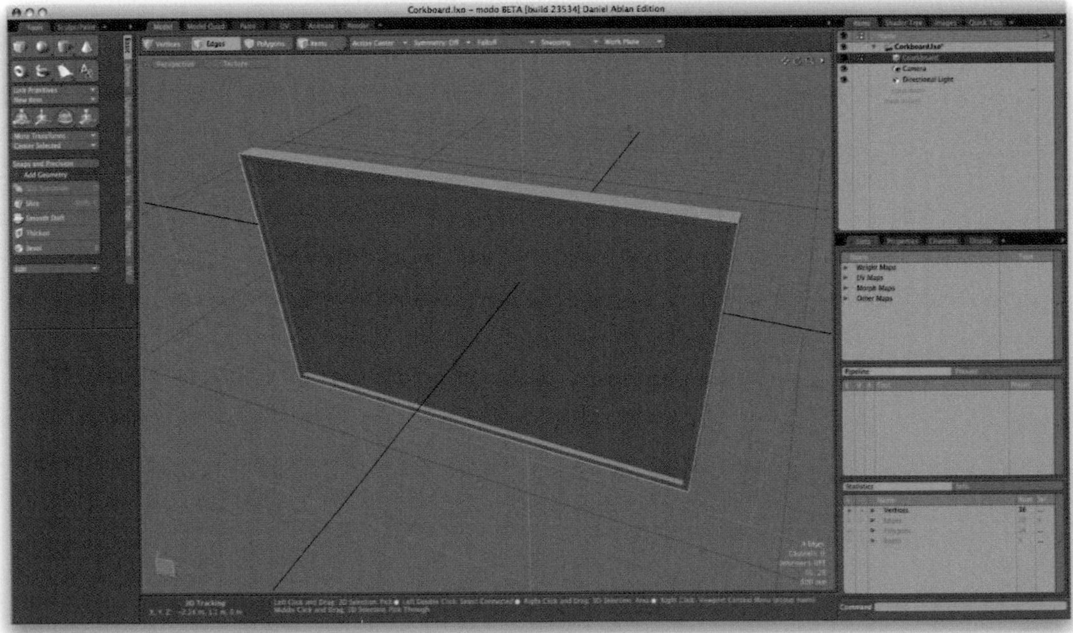

Figure 6.10 Double-click the outer front edge to select the edge loop.

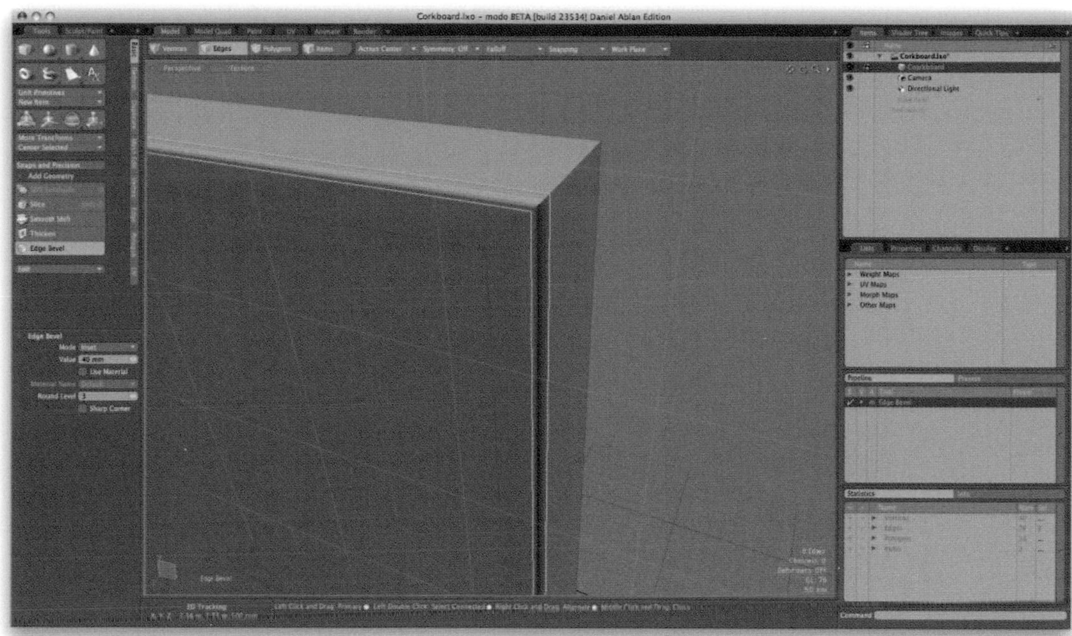

Figure 6.11 Bevel the selected edge with an added Round Level setting to smooth it out.

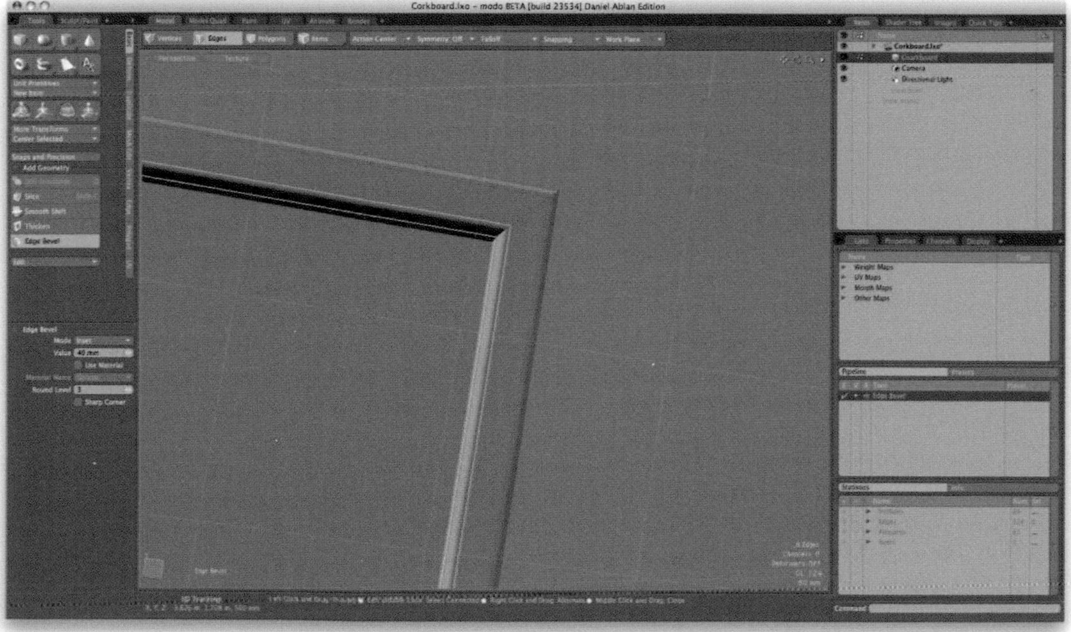

Figure 6.12 Bevel the inside edge of the corkboard to match the roundness of the outside edge.

Of course you can vary this to suit your taste, but doesn't modo do an excellent job of beveling these edges? You can use this technique in just about every model you build. Go ahead and save your model. It's time to create some things to hang on it!

Adding Mesh Layers

So what if you wanted to create more elements in the scene? Would you build them in the same mesh layer? Or should the new objects be in their own layers? Truth be told, it really depends on the project at hand; however, you can't go wrong with building in layers, which is what this chapter is all about. So let's take that approach.

1. With the corkboard scene saved, head over to the Items tab and click New Item. This is beneath the current items of Camera, Directional Light, and your Corkboard mesh. It's slightly grayed out.
2. When you click New Item, modo will give you an option to choose between a new mesh, new light, new camera, and so on. Choose Mesh, as shown in Figure 6.13.
3. If you're working with a default modo layout, the existing corkboard will become a black wireframe, signifying that it's in the background. You don't have to keep it this way for long. Press the a key to fit the mesh to view.
4. Click the Unit Primitives down arrow, select In Current Mesh, and then click the Plane primitive, as shown in Figure 6.14. In Current Mesh builds the object in the selected mesh in the Items tab. If you chose In New Mesh, a new mesh would be created with the plane object. Also note that by holding the Shift key, you'll see the Tube primitive icon change to a Plane primitive. Clicking on it creates a new Plane in a new mesh layer.

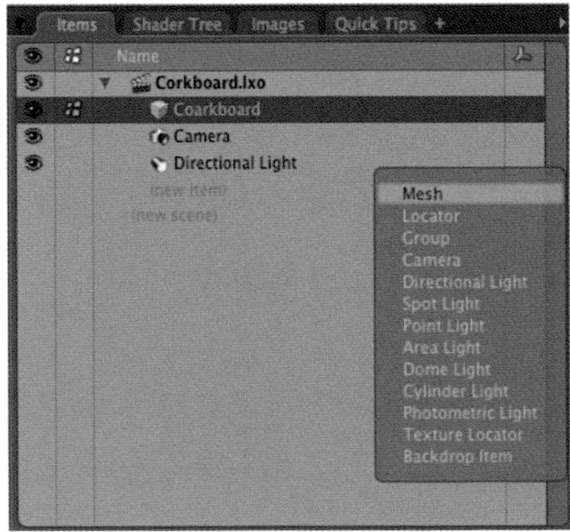

Figure 6.13 To add additional layers of objects to your scene, click New Item in the Items tab and choose Mesh.

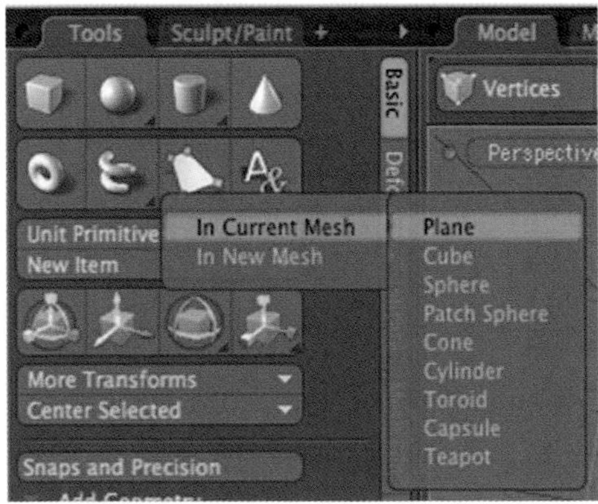

Figure 6.14 Hold the Shift key to view the alternate primitives, and then select the Plane icon, which creates a new object and mesh layer.

You'll notice now in your Items tab that the new mesh is placed in the new mesh layer. If you chose to create the Plane primitive in a new mesh layer, the name Plane is automatically generated for you. This is a handy little feature in modo 301/302 when creating primitives with the Shift key depressed.

5. Taking a look at Figure 6.15, you can see that the Plane primitive is a flat square mesh centered in the viewport. Press the y key to activate the Transform tool, and click and drag on the red ring to rotate the plane upward, as shown in Figure 6.16.

Note

Using the Transform tool by pressing the y key is sort of a one-stop shop for transforming your object. This one tool allows you to control position, rotation, and scale. Note that position, rotation, and scale are also available on their own.

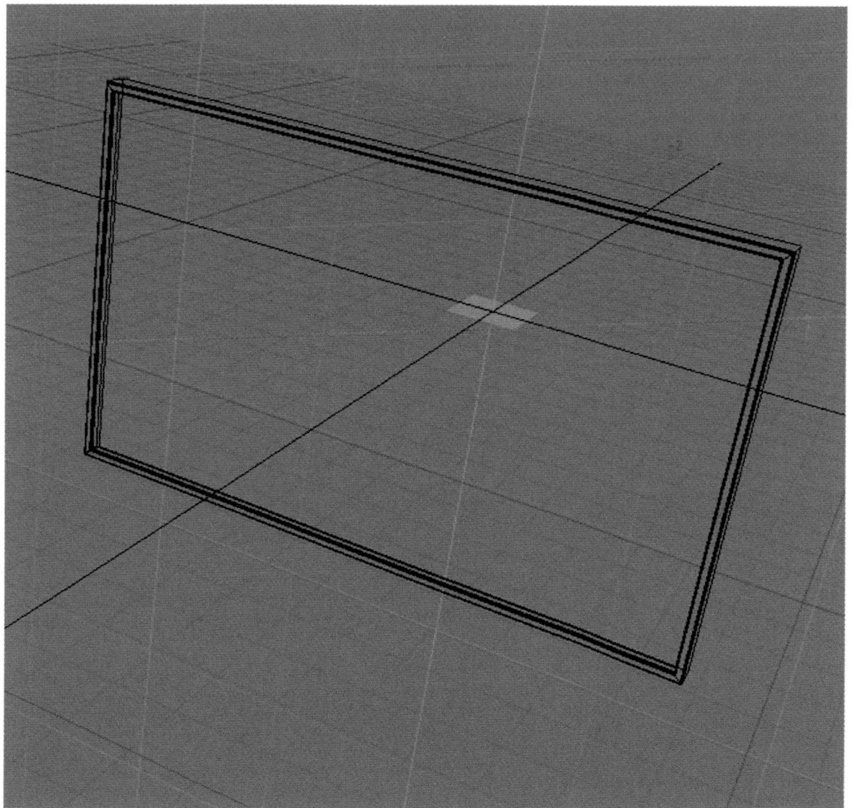

Figure 6.15 Creating a Plane primitive creates a flat mesh in the middle of the viewport.

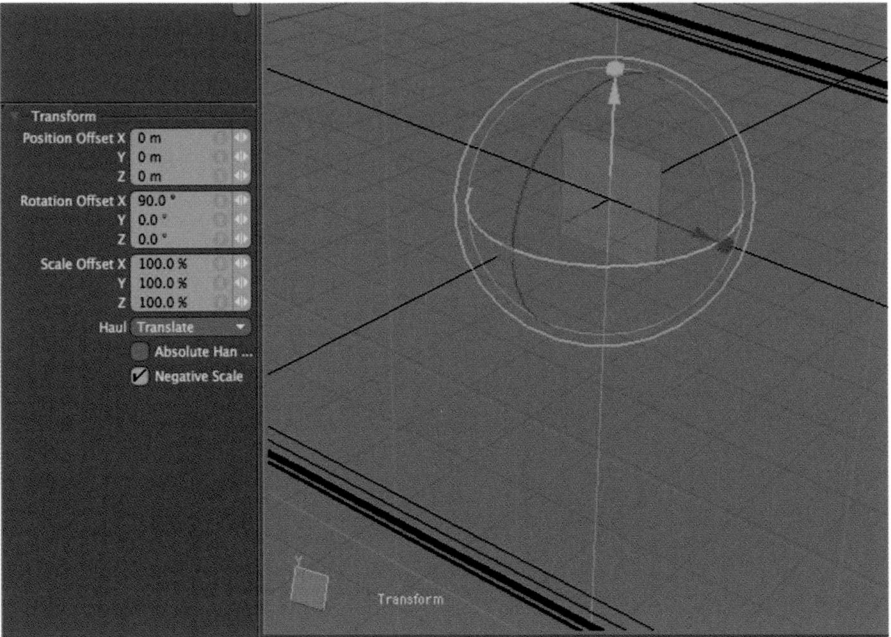

Figure 6.16
Using the Transform tool, click and drag the render handle to rotate the Plane primitive.

6. This first flat plane will be a Post-it Note, so you're going to use the Bend tool to shape it, making it curl out from the corkboard. But in order to bend it, it needs to be subdivided to be more pliable. Press the Shift key and d on your keyboard. This calls up the Subdivide Polygons command. Choose Faceted for the Subdivision Method option. Other methods are Smooth, and Subdivision Surface, or SDS. Since this is not a subdivided object, Faceted is fine for flat objects. Leave the other settings at 0, and click OK. Your flat plane will be subdivided, and you'll now have four polygons instead of one (two on each axis).
7. Repeat the previous step to subdivide one more time.
8. Select the Bend tool from the Deform vertical category within the Tools tab.
9. Once the Bend tool is on, click at the top of the Post-it Note in the viewport. When you do, you'll see a control handle—a blue ring. You'll also see a thin line extending out to the right with a plus sign (+) on the end. Click and drag the plus sign to the bottom of the Post-it Note object. This sets the falloff for the Bend tool. This is not the light-blue square that extends out the back from the control ring. Dragging this square sets the Action Axis, although you can do this by just clicking Action Axis to X in the Tool Properties panel.
10. Now click and drag the blue ring to bend the Post-it Note. Notice that just the bottom of the object bends and not the entire thing? It bends from the point in which you clicked to set the Bend tool. Figure 6.17 shows the operation and settings.

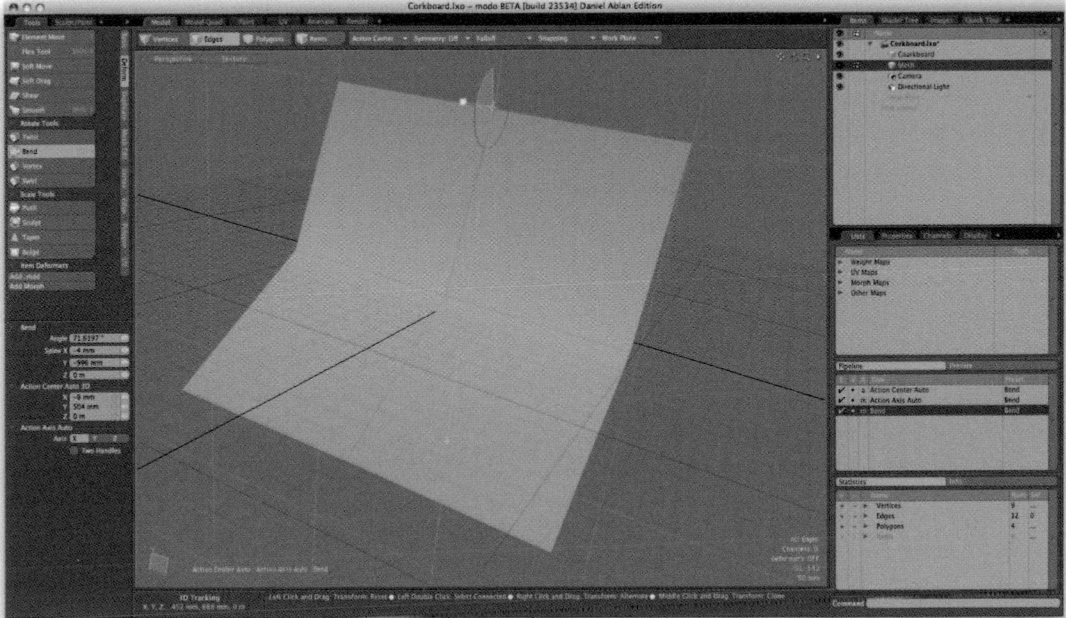

Figure 6.17 Using the Bend tool with a falloff, the Post-it Note quickly curls.

11. Press the spacebar to turn off the tool. Next, press Shift and the d key again for Subdivide Polygons. Subdivide the note again to smooth it out a little bit more.
12. Now select the Twist tool. You're going to give a little imperfection to the object.
13. Click at the top of the object, close to where you did with the Bend tool. You'll see two falloff handles. Before you mess with those, click and drag the blue ring (control handle) to twist the object. Figure 6.18 shows the effect.
14. The falloff of the Twist tool applies the effect more at the fat end of the falloff and less at the narrow end. The result is a curl in the Post-it Note object. Before you turn off the tool, feel free to move the falloff around to see the various results. Just click and drag the control handles around either of those light-blue squares—they'll become yellow when selected. When finished, press the spacebar to turn off the tool.
15. Save your work.
16. Once you have the shape the way you like it, subdivide it one more time by pressing Shift and the d key. But this time, instead of Faceted, choose Smooth.
17. After the subdivision, press m on your keyboard to set the polygon material. Give the item a name, such as Post-it Note, and change the color to a pale blue or something else you might like.

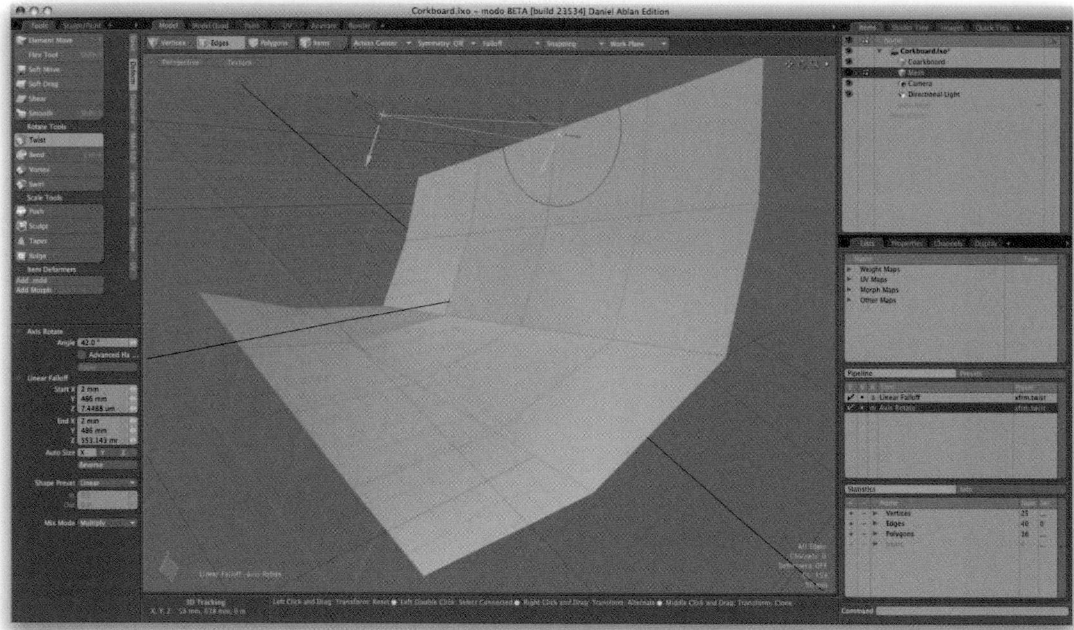

Figure 6.18 With the falloff of the Twist tool, you can bend or curl up just one corner of the object.

Using Background Layers as Reference

So far what you've done is fairly straightforward. You've not modeled anything outrageous or award-winning. What you have done is build in layers, which is a key operation for just about anything you do in modo. Each layer is part of an overall scene, and that means you'll need to reference the other layers to line things up for the final render. This section will quickly show you how to work with multiple layers as reference.

1. With the Post-it Note object selected in the Items tab, your background object should be the original corkboard object. It most likely appears as a black outline. Instead, change it to a solid by first pressing the o key while your mouse hovers in the viewport.
2. Pressing o calls up the viewport shading options. Toward the top of the panel is an option for Background Item. Change it from Wireframe to Same as Active Mesh, as shown in Figure 6.19.
3. Now that background objects are solid shaded, you'll have an easier time aligning other objects in the scene. From the Items tab, select the Post-it Note mesh.

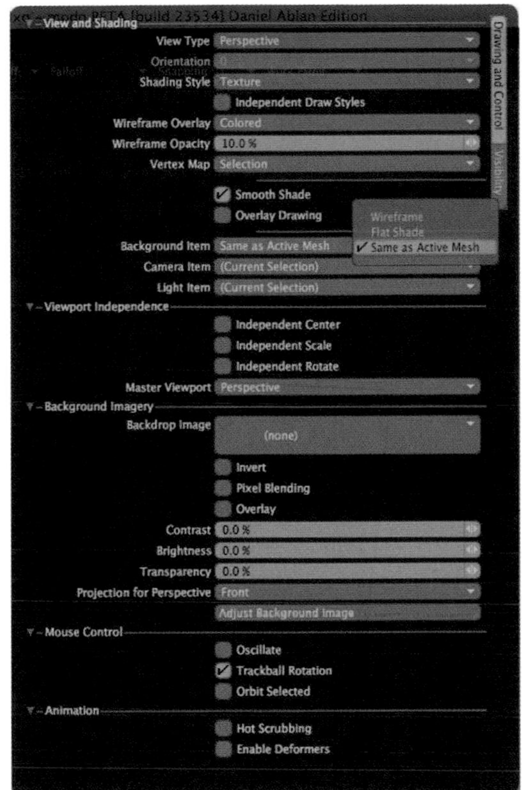

Figure 6.19 Changing the viewport options to see the background as a solid versus a wireframe will help you align objects.

Note

To stay organized, right-click on the new mesh in the Items tab to rename it. Instead of Plane, rename the object to Post-it Note.

4. Press y on the keyboard to select the Transform tool. Then click the various control handles to rotate and position the Post-it Note on the corkboard. Place it so that the top end (which would be the sticky part of the note) is touching the corkboard. Figure 6.20 shows a similar setup.

Note

To add a little more precise positioning, use the Element Move tool. Press the t key to activate the tool. Make sure you're in Polygons selection mode, and remember to right-click and drag to set the size of the Element Move tool influence. Then, click and drag with the left mouse button on any point, polygon, or edge to adjust it. Be sure to view the Element Move video on the book's disc to learn more.

5. You may want to scale the Post-it Note a bit. Press the r key, then click on the center light-blue crosshair and drag to scale evenly. Also, press the w key to select the Move tool and move it over to one edge of the corkboard. Figure 6.21 shows the model at this point.

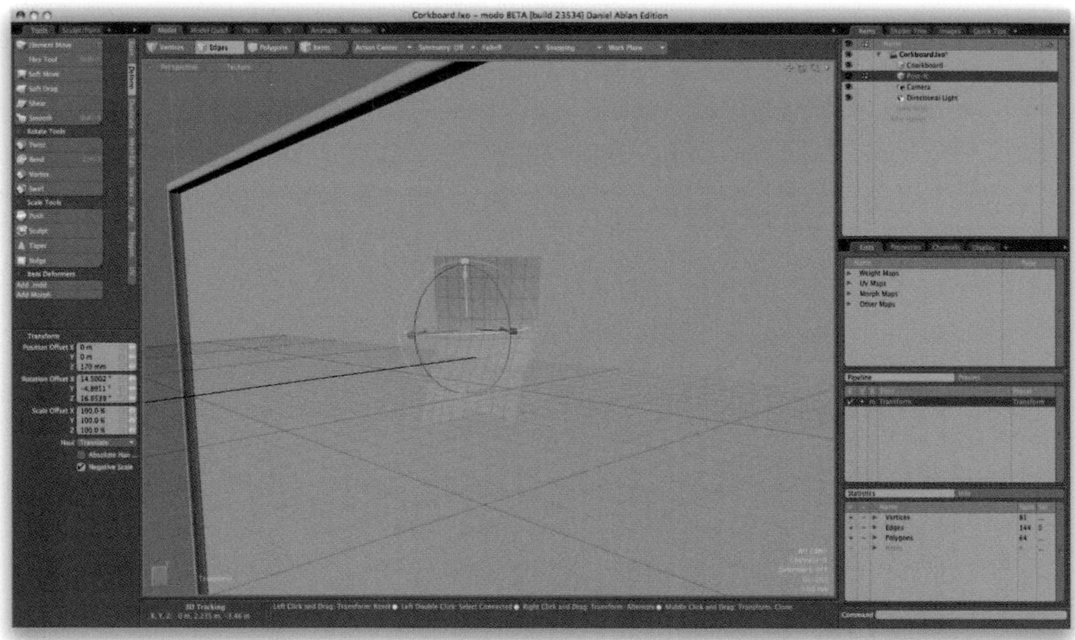

Figure 6.20 Using the Transform tool is a great way to position objects.

Figure 6.21 The Post-it Note on the corkboard, positioned and scaled.

6. Finally, repeat these steps to create new Post-it Notes, or simply right-click on the object in the Items tab and select duplicate. Position them throughout the corkboard, bending, scaling, and rotating them as needed for variation. Remember that with each copy you create, double-click to select, and press m for material to give that note its own unique surface. Feel free to use the Element Move tool by pressing t on the keyboard to shape the objects so they are not completely identical. (You'll be surfacing these next in Chapter 7.) Save your work.
7. Now you'll add a few other interesting things to the corkboard. First, a simple photograph. Create a new mesh layer in the Items tab by clicking New Item in the list.
8. With the new mesh layer selected, rotate the view so the work plane is set the YX. Remember that this is identified by the small white square between the axis markings in the bottom-left corner of the viewport, as shown in Figure 6.22.
9. Draw out a flat cube in the shape of a standard photograph, as shown in Figure 6.23. Remember that as you draw it out, if you can't see it, you can click and drag directly on the blue and red handles to position the object.
10. When the object is made, press the spacebar to turn off the tool.
11. Press m on your keyboard to call up the Set Polygon Material dialog box, and give this new object a surface name of Photo or something similar.

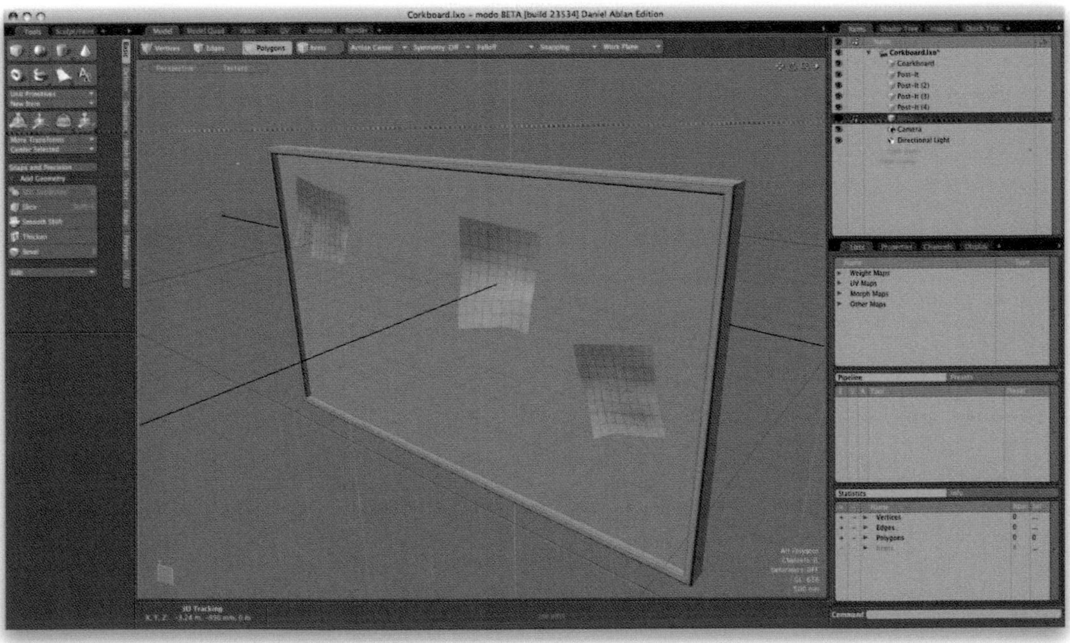

Figure 6.22 To set the work plane axis, hold the Alt key, then click and drag in the viewport to rotate. When rotating, watch the icon in the bottom-left of the viewport to see where the white square lines up.

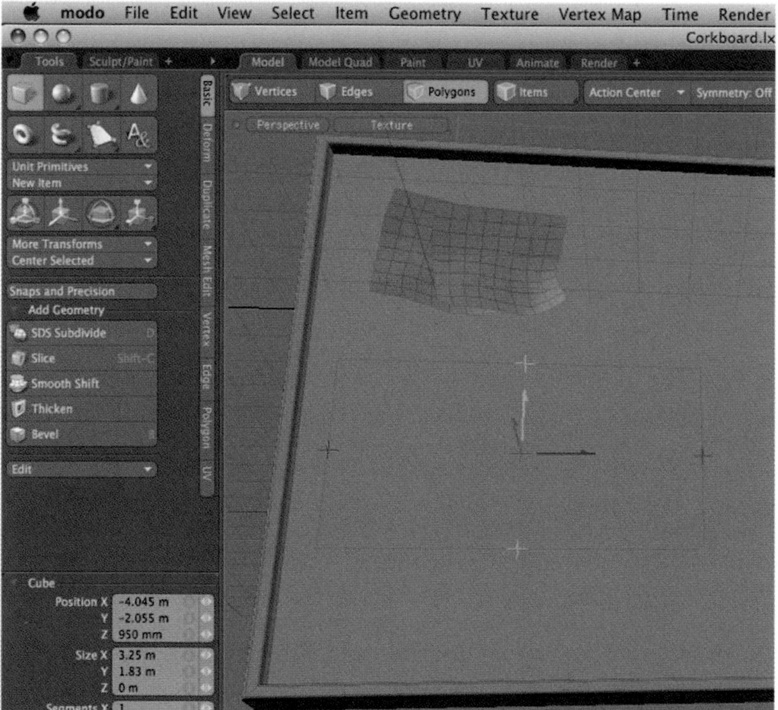

Figure 6.23 When drawing out a Cube primitive, remember to click and drag on the control handles to position it wherever you like.

While the goal is not to irritate certain readers with reminders (you know who you are), it is important to stress that you should make sure you save your work at this point. Go ahead and make other copies of objects if you wish, or simply continue on to the next section. However, if you do build more objects on your own, just remember to press m on your keyboard to give each new object its own unique surface name. If you build objects in the same layer, just remember to select the specific polygons for which you want to create a separate surface material.

Adding Scenes to the Items Tab

By now you should see your message board forming. Adding a few Post-it Notes and a photograph are getting you closer to the final render. As mentioned previously, you'll be texturing and image mapping all of these objects in the next chapter. But there is one thing missing from this message board, and that's thumbtacks! While Post-it Notes have their own adhesive, photographs need to be pinned up. This next section will show you how to build a thumbtack and apply it to the existing scene.

1. In this section, rather than building in a new layer, you'll start an entirely new scene. The reason is to show you that you can work on multiple scenes at the same time in modo. From the File menu, select New. On the Items tab, you'll see a new untitled scene, along with a blank Mesh layer and Camera and Directional Light listings. Figure 6.24 shows modo after the operation.

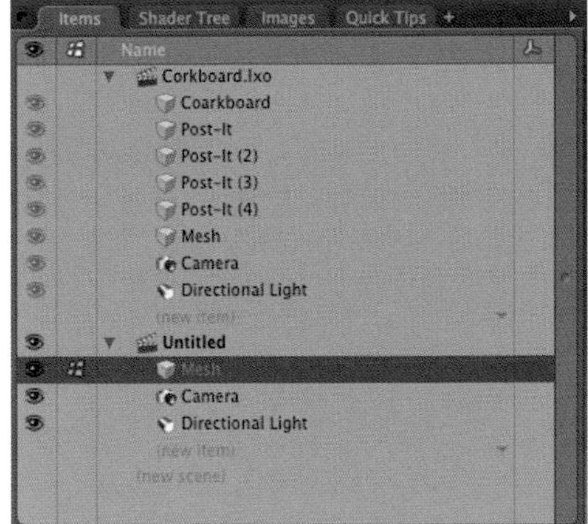

Figure 6.24
Selecting New from the File menu creates a new scene, clearing out the viewport; but it still leaves your existing scene intact.

This is a new scene. But if you look at the top of the Items tab, you'll see that your original Corkboard object is still there. You can select it, and it will appear in the viewport.

2. Select the empty Mesh layer in the new scene, and then in the Tools tab, hold the Ctrl key on the keyboard and click the Cylinder primitive. You'll see that modo creates a perfectly round cylinder in the mesh layer, as shown in Figure 6.25. Feel free to right-click on this new mesh and rename it to Thumbtack.

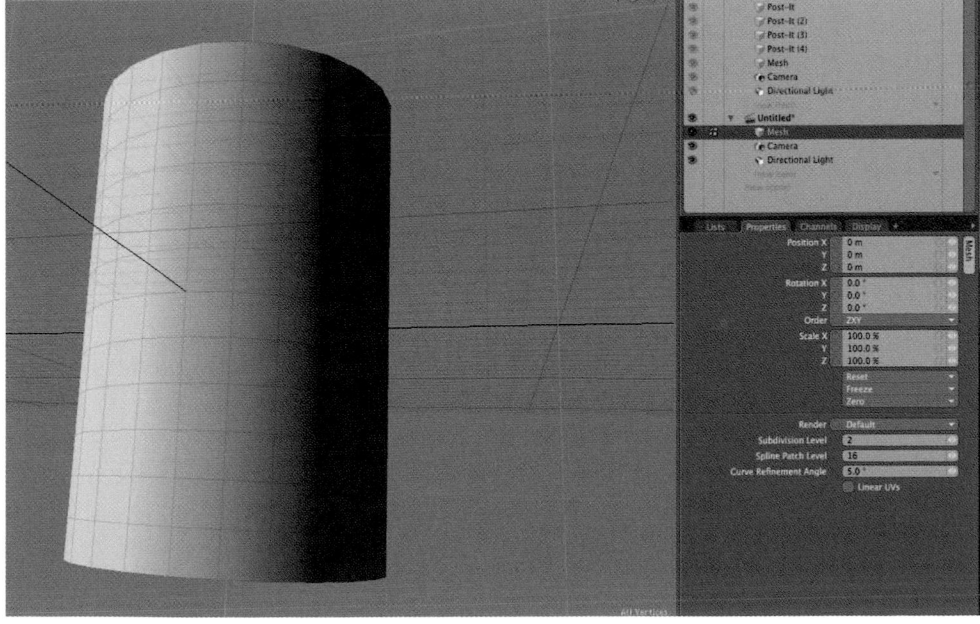

Figure 6.25
Holding the Ctrl key while selecting a primitive, such as the Cylinder, creates a perfectly shaped object instantly.

3. Holding the Ctrl key, select the Scale tool, as shown in Figure 6.26.
4. Next, from the top of the interface, select Linear from the Falloff drop-down menu, as shown in Figure 6.27.

Figure 6.26 To select the Scale tool, hold the Ctrl key on your keyboard and select it.

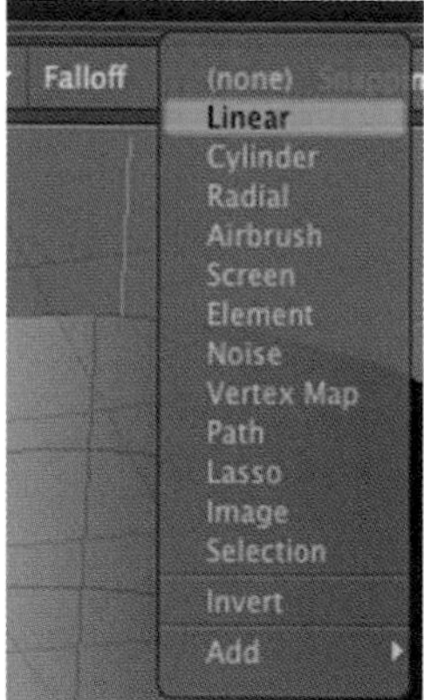

Figure 6.27 Set a Linear falloff from the top of the modo interface.

5. You'll see a triangular outline appear within the object, as shown in Figure 6.28. When the falloff is turned on, you'll see additional controls appear within the Tool Properties panel for the Scale tool. Change the Auto Size setting from X to Y.
6. In the Tool Properties panel, drag the Factor for Scale value down to 60%. Remember that you can gang select the values by clicking the small icon to the right of the value, allowing you to enter the setting in one axis but have it affect all. You'll see the cylinder bend inward, but only toward the larger end of the falloff. Figure 6.29 shows the result.

> **Note**
>
> If you like, click and drag the falloff handles to see how their affect changes the shape of the model. Also, view the Falloffs movie on the book's disc to get a better feel for this powerful control.

7. Now press the spacebar until your selection mode is set to Polygons. Back under the Falloff menu, change the setting to None.
8. Hold down the Alt key, and then click and drag in the viewport to rotate around to see the top of the object. Click on it once to select it.
9. Press the b key to activate the Bevel tool. Click on the polygon to bring up the Bevel tool handles.

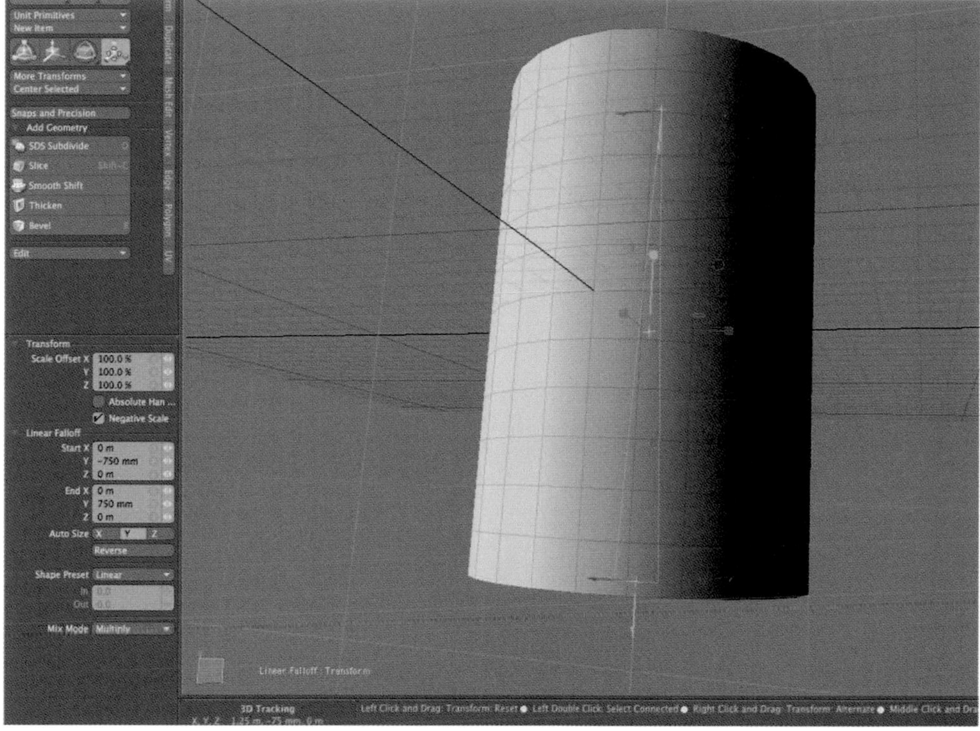

Figure 6.28 When you apply a Linear falloff to an object, you'll see the representational outlines appear in the view.

Figure 6.29 Using a Linear falloff along with the Scale tool will taper the effect of the tool toward the fat end of the falloff.

10. Click and drag the red handle to bevel the Inset value to about 50 mm, as shown in Figure 6.30.
11. Hold the Shift key and click on the beveled polygon to reset the Bevel tool. Then, click and drag the blue handle up about 65 mm for the Shift value.
12. Hold the Shift key and click the selected polygon again to reset. Bevel the Inset value back in about –60 mm by dragging the red handle. Figure 6.31 shows the results.
13. Continue beveling the selected polygon a few more times, as in the previous steps, until you have another wedge in the object. Figure 6.32 shows the result.
14. For the bottom of the thumbtack, select the base polygon on the rounded edge. Figure 6.33 shows the selection.
15. Now, bevel the selected polygon to create another wedge in the thumbtack similar to the way you created the top portion. This time set the Inset value to about 260 mm.
16. Bevel again and shift the polygon down, then bevel once more to set the Inset value to about 20 mm. Then bevel one more time, setting Shift to about 575 mm and Inset to 12 mm. Figures 6.34 and 6.35 show the idea.

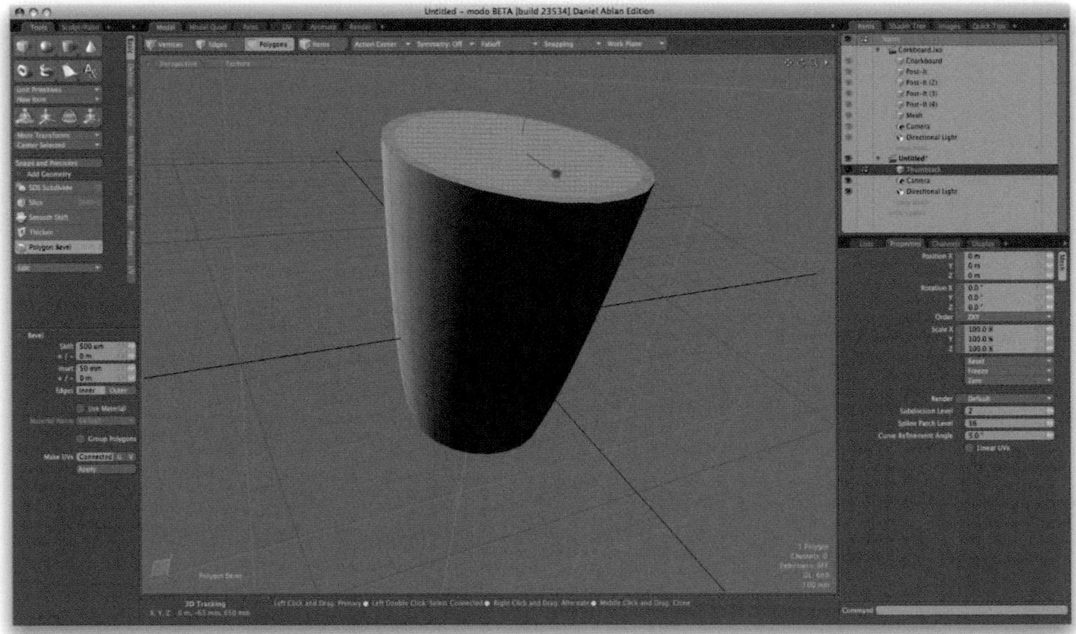

Figure 6.30 Begin shaping the thumbtack by beveling the top polygon of the cylinder.

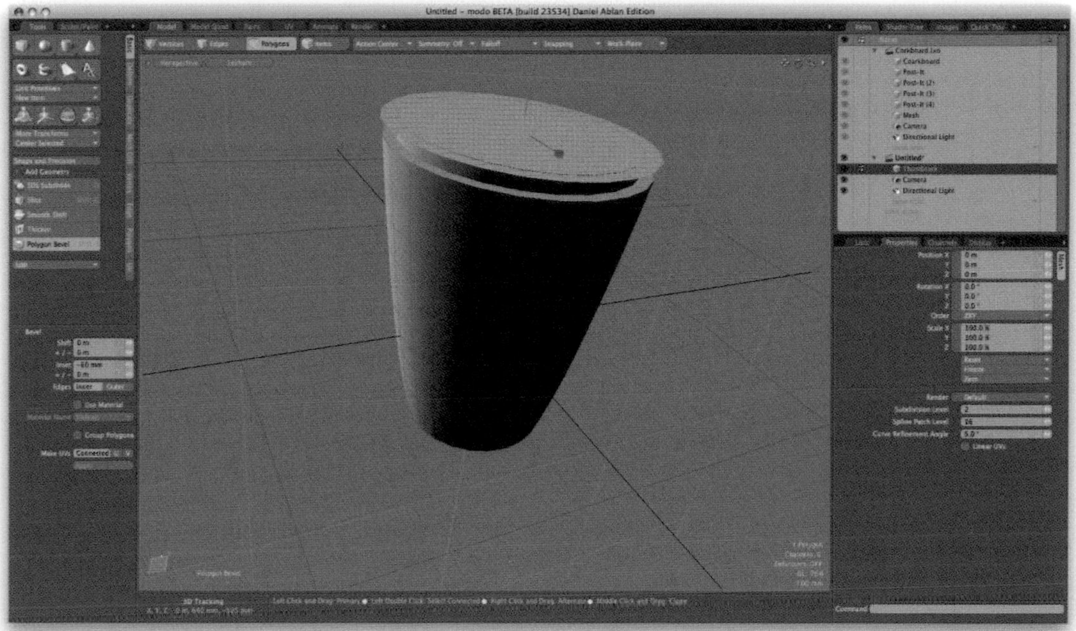

Figure 6.31 Holding the Shift key and clicking once on the selected polygon resets the Bevel tool.

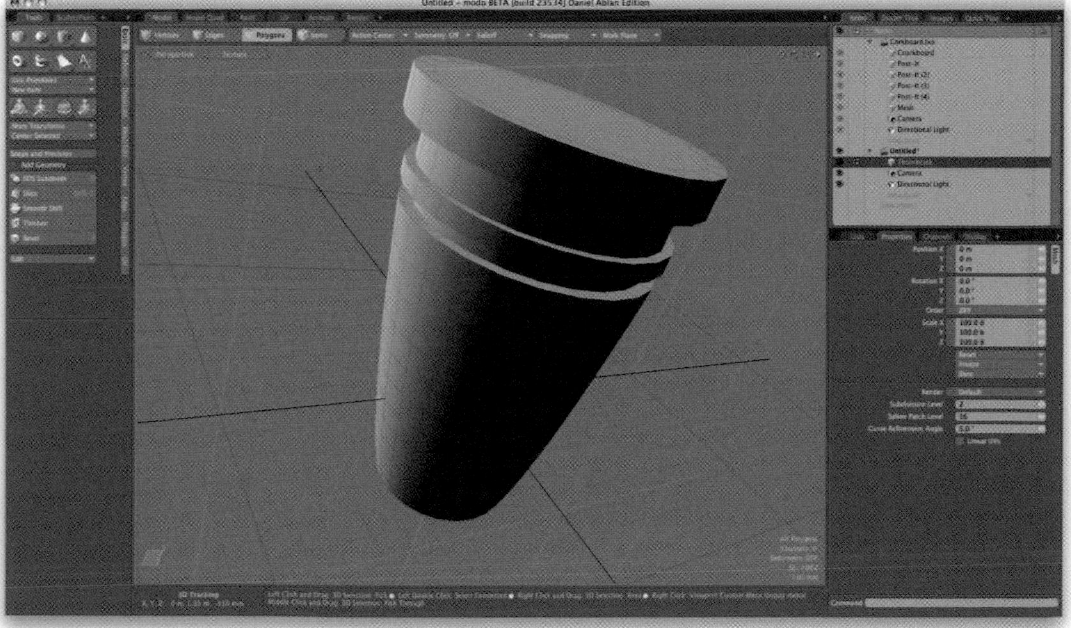

Figure 6.32 Continue beveling the polygon to create an additional wedge for the top of the thumbtack.

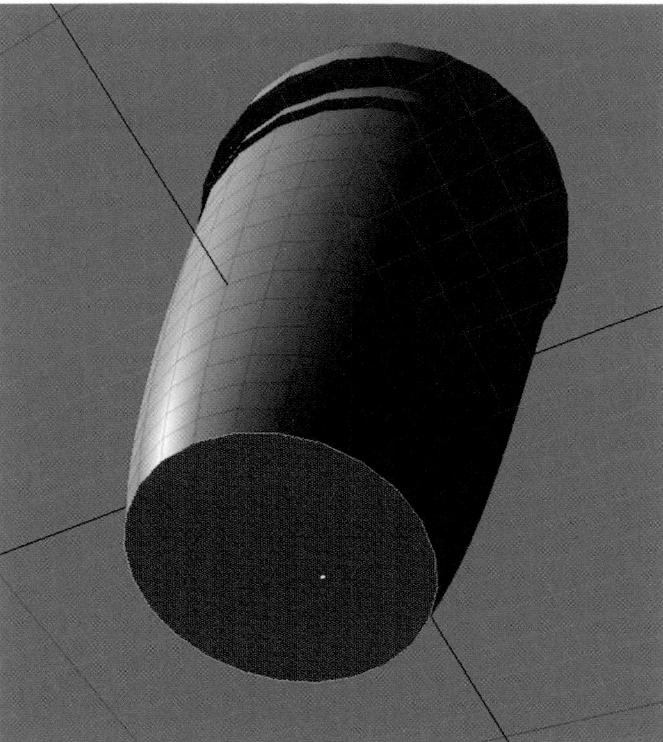

Figure 6.33 Select the bottom rounded polygon, similar to the top polygon selection method performed earlier.

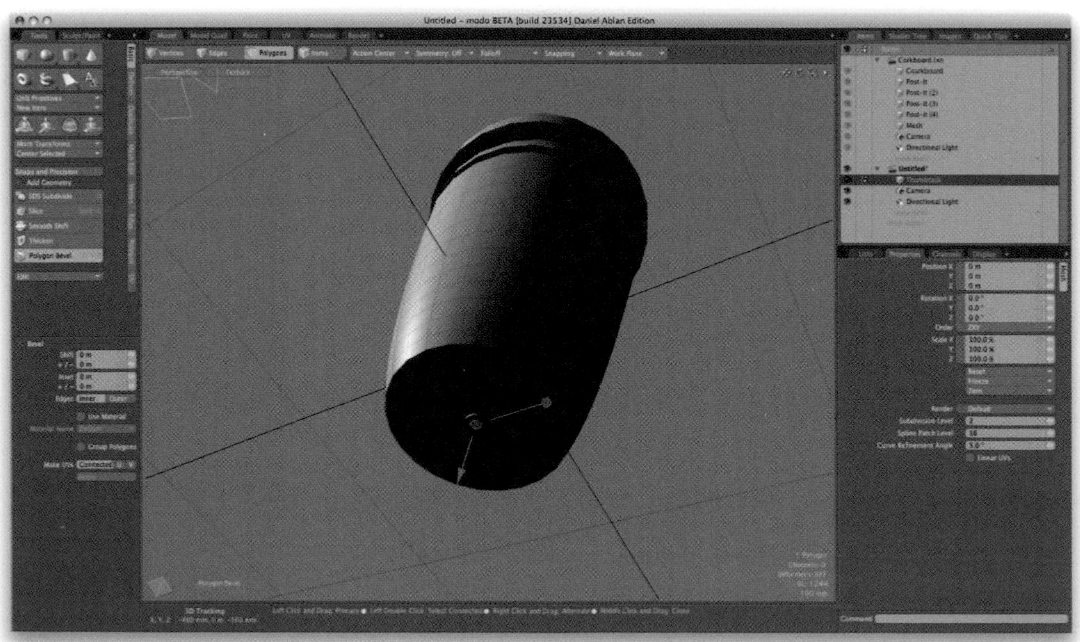

Figure 6.34 Bevel out the bottom of the thumbtack, as with the top, but set the Inset value a bit smaller this time.

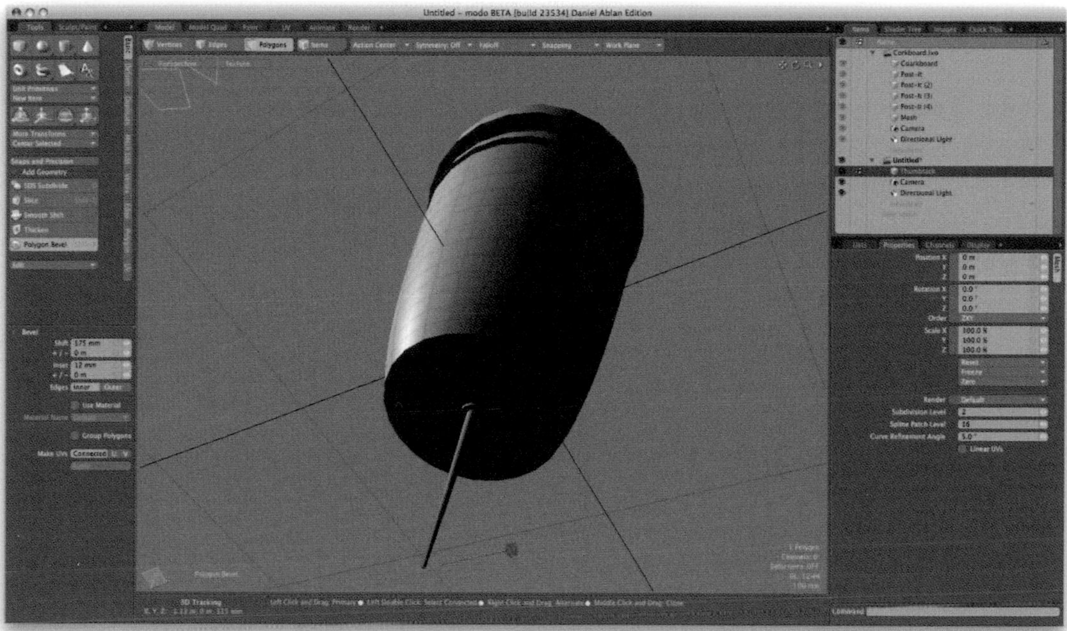

Figure 6.35 Bevel again, but this time use both the Inset and Shift settings to create the pin of the thumbtack.

17. Save your work! Press the q key to turn off the Bevel tool.

    Next press the Tab key to activate subdivision surfaces. You can see that the thumbtack smoothes out—perhaps a little too much, as shown in Figure 6.36. You can fix this with a few edge adjustments.

18. Press the Tab key to turn off subdivision mode. This is not necessary to perform the next steps, but it makes selection a bit easier in this case. Making sure you're in Edges selection mode, select the edges that revolve around the Y axis, including the very small pin tip and the edges underneath each wedge, as shown in Figure 6.37.

19. With the edges selected, go ahead and bevel them.

Note

Remember when selecting in modo, you can double-click on an edge to select the entire edge loop. To add to the selection, hold the Shift key. To deselect an unwanted selected edge without deselecting everything, hold the Ctrl key and click on that edge.

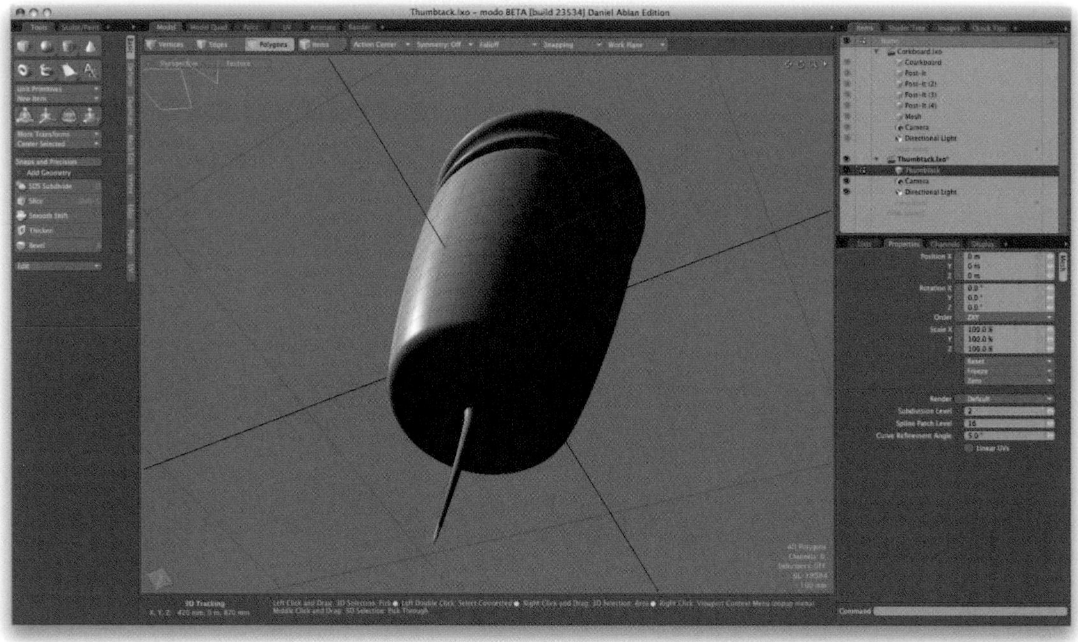

Figure 6.36 Pressing the Tab key to activate subdivision surfaces smoothes out the object, but a little too much.

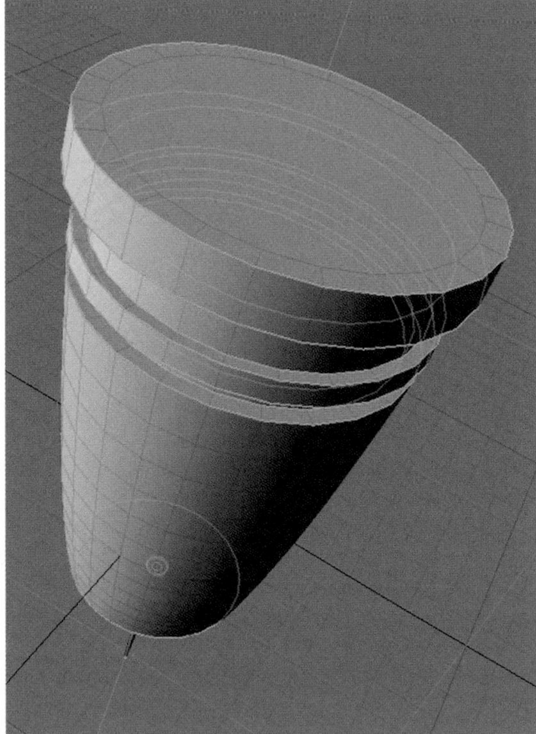

Figure 6.37 Select all of the horizontal edges of the object, from top to bottom. These are the circular edges created from the bevel operations.

20. After a slight bevel on the edges, this added geometry will help hold the shape of the object when subdivided. Press the spacebar to turn off the Bevel tool, then click off of the object to deselect the edges. Next, press the Tab key to see the change beveling the edges has made to the object when subdivided. Figure 6.38 shows the result.

Figure 6.38 After the edges of the object have been beveled, more geometry is added. When subdivided by pressing the Tab key, you can see that the shape is clean and sharp, without being too smooth.

21. Feel free to undo and tweak the edges and their shape if you like. The goal here is to round out the edges a bit and to show you how a few bevels to a cylinder's polygons and edges can create a cool object.
22. Making sure you're in Polygons selection mode, select the polygons that make up just the pin area of the thumbtack.
23. Press m on your keyboard to set the material to thumbtack metal or similar.
24. Instead of deselecting, simply press the left bracket ([) key on your keyboard. (It's located to the right of the P key.) This will invert your selection, and since the remaining polygons are just the plastic portion of the thumbtack, press m again and name these selected polygons thumbtack plastic.

25. Deselect the polygons, then feel free to shape the polygons by selecting and sizing them as you see fit. Figure 6.39 shows the final thumbtack.

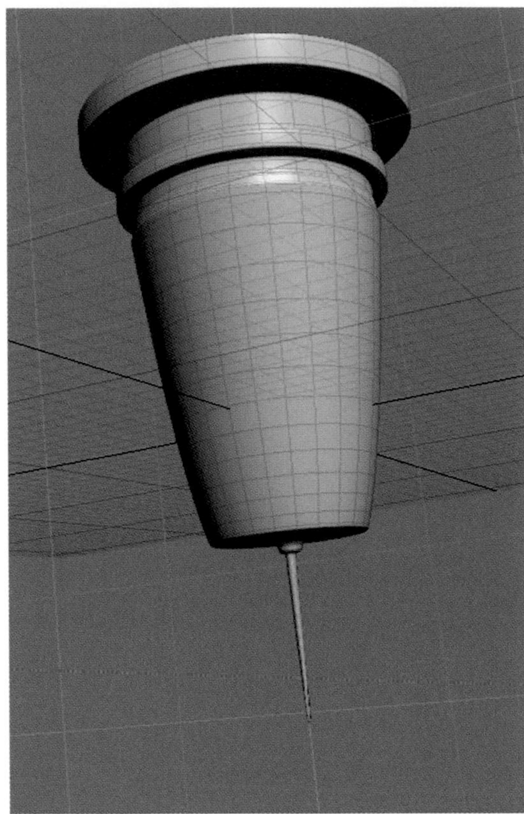

Figure 6.39
The finished thumbtack model.

Merging Scenes in the Items Tab

The previous exercises have given you a lesson or two in working with the Items tab, building really simple objects, and using the key tools to do so. You've also learned how to add a new scene to the Items tab to build new objects. But what if you want to merge that new object into an existing scene?

Figure 6.40 shows the Items tab with the corkboard scene and the thumbtack scene loaded into modo.

Because there are two scenes, you need to combine parts of one into the other. In many cases, you will already have set up your lighting and your environment in a particular scene. With the corkboard and thumbtack here, neither scene has had any work done to the lighting. But because the corkboard scene contains four objects, it will be easier to move the thumbtack into it than the other way around.

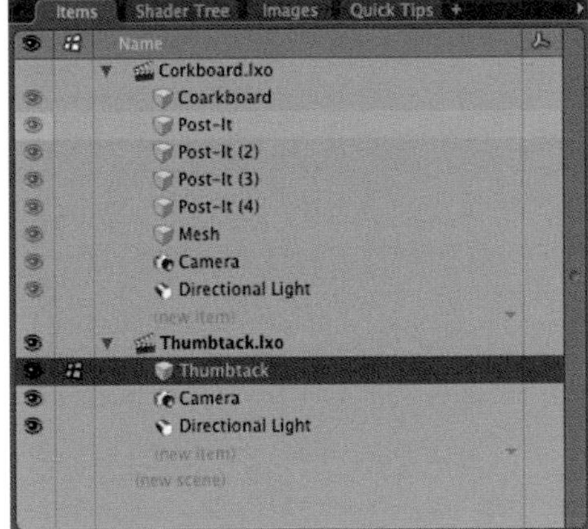

Figure 6.40
Two scenes loaded into modo are visible in the Items tab.

1. Select the Thumbtack object listing in the Items tab, then click and drag it up into the corkboard scene. You can drop it anywhere you like at this point, as shown in Figure 6.41.

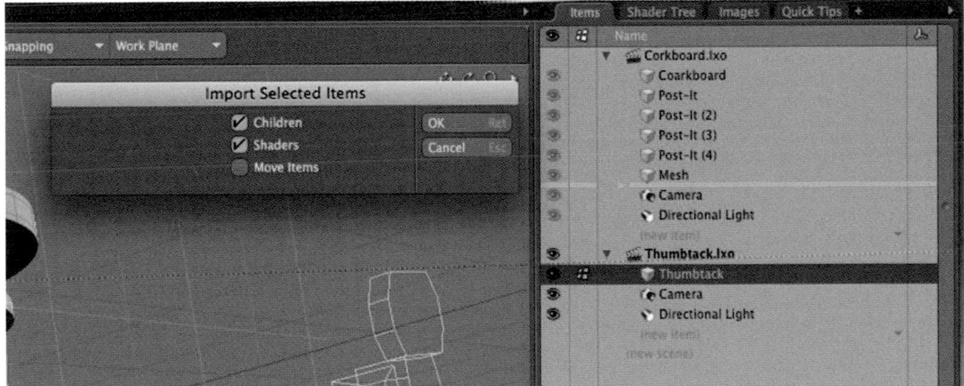

Figure 6.41
To bring an object from one scene into another, simply drag it.

2. As soon as you drag and drop the object from one scene to the other, a dialog pops up giving you the options to import Children (child objects) and Shaders, and asking if you'd like to move the layer. By default, the first two options are checked on, so you can go ahead and click OK to import the thumbtack object into the corkboard scene.
3. You'll notice from Figure 6.42 that the thumbtack is significantly larger than the corkboard. No problem! Press the r key, and then click on the light-blue crosshair in the center of the control handles. Click and drag to size the thumbtack down to about 10% of its original size and move it out in front of the corkboard, as shown in Figure 6.43.

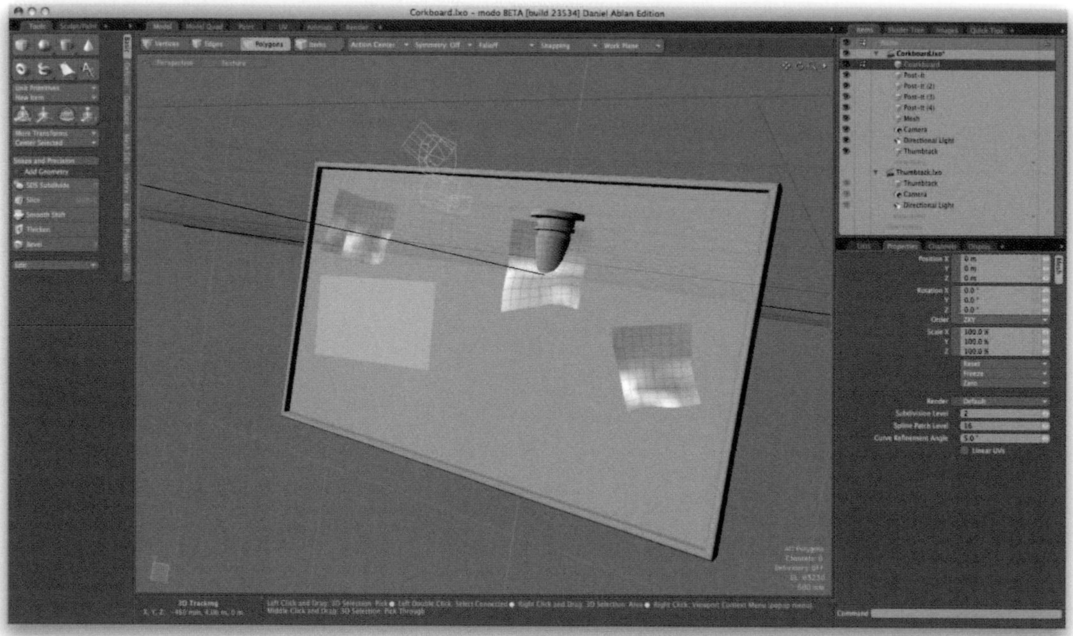

Figure 6.42 Bringing the thumbtack object into the corkboard scene was easy. But it's too big!

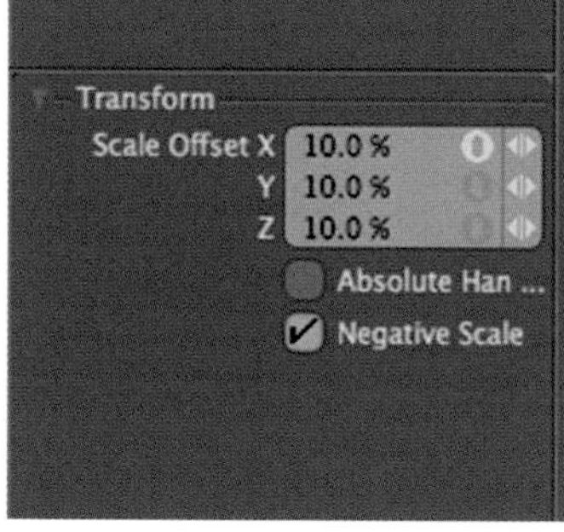

Figure 6.43 Using the Scale command (r key), it's easy to scale down the object to fit the scene.

4. Press the spacebar to turn off the Scale tool.
5. Rotate the view to see the front of the corkboard. You can do this by holding the Alt key and then clicking and dragging in the view. You can also use the controls in the upper right of the viewport—just click on one of the icons, hold your mouse down, and drag.
6. Making sure the thumbtack object is still selected in the Items tab, press the w key to select the Move tool.

7. Click and drag the handles to move the object to the front of the corkboard. Note however that, depending on where your model is, you might need to move it in toward the corkboard rather than pulling it from the back. Either way, use the Move tool to position the thumbtack over the note object you created earlier (see Figure 6.44).

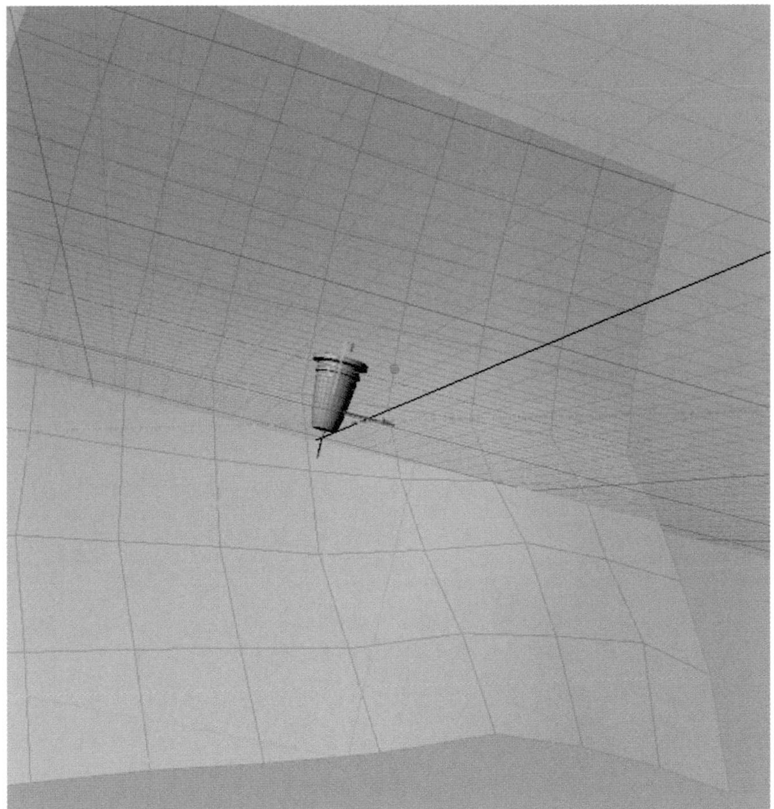

Figure 6.44
Use the Move 3D tool to position the thumbtack.

8. Once you've moved the thumbtack into position over the photo object, press the e key to select the Rotate tool. Grab the red handle (depending on your setup) and rotate the thumbtack so its sharp end is sticking into the photo on the corkboard. Also, rotate it on the heading a bit—most thumbtacks in the real world are not pushed in completely straight, so angle yours a bit for a better look. You might need to press w again to use the Move tool to align it more after you rotate it. You can also press y and get rotation and position (and size) all in one tool. Move the thumbtack to the corner of the photo object. Figure 6.45 shows the final thumbtack position.
9. Save your work!

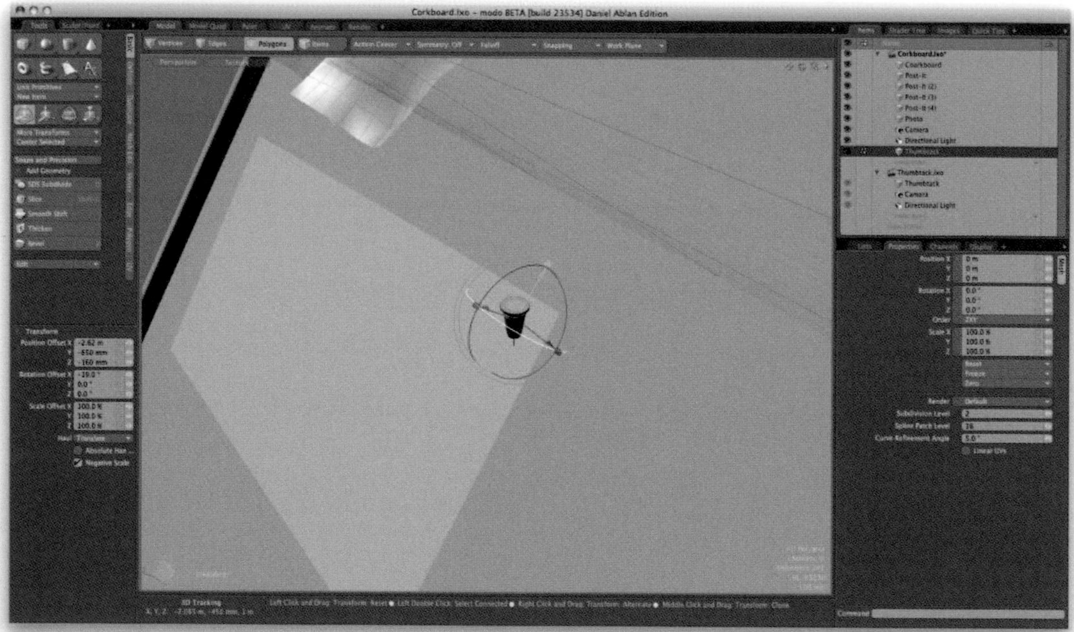

Figure 6.45 Finally, use the Rotate tool (e key) to rotate the thumbtack into a natural position.

So there you have it! You've navigated your way through the Items tab, making new objects, new scenes, and adding objects from one scene into another. These simple operations are the same no matter what you're making in modo, be it something as simple as a corkboard or as complex as a jet airliner.

You're encouraged to add more notes and items to your corkboard. The objects you've made in this chapter should give you a really good idea of how the process works and how to use the tools. Other object ideas are pendants from colleges. Simply make an elongated triangle, adding a little thickness to it. Or how about a flat round disc, slightly beveled with a hole cut out in the center to create a CD? Copy your thumbtack object to look as if it's holding up the CD on the corkboard. Use your imagination and have fun with what you build.

When ready, read on to the next chapter where you'll learn about the Shader Tree, using everything you've built here as the ingredients for cooking up a full-textured scene.

7

Shader Tree Fundamentals

In Chapter 6, you modeled something a little untraditional in a corkboard with Post-it Notes. While most projects work through modeling a full 3D object, it's a good idea to think beyond the norm. The corkboard project was a lesson in working with the Items tab, but it was also designed to trigger your thought process. While most of us head into a 3D modeling program to create cars, character heads, or telephones, the project in Chapter 6 was a little less conventional, but a cool project just the same, and we'll put our own twist on it here.

In the previous chapter, you learned how to build objects and work with the Items tab. You learned how to rename an object in the Items tab and how to create materials. You also learned that if you press the Shift key and click on a primitive shape (such as a cube), you get a new mesh item called Cube. By pressing m and entering a name, you are assigning a material to these polygons. What modo is actually doing is two things:

1. **Creating a polygon material selection set out of these polygons**—You can see them in the Info list under Polygon, Material.
2. **Creating a new group layer in the Shader Tree that is linked to this selection set**—This linkage of a group layer and a set of polygons (or an item or item hierarchy) is called a *mask*. A mask makes sure that all the material and texture layers in that group are applied only to those linked polygons or item(s). If you choose a material from the drop-down menu that already exists, then you are just adding those polygons to the existing selection set and its associated mask.

Note

It's important to understand that a *material* is a selection set of polygons, and a *mask* is a group layer that references these polygons (or an item or hierarchy of items).

Keep in mind that the Items tab covered in Chapter 6 gets precedence when it comes to naming. If you name an item Material in the Items tab, it will result in a Material(1) name. That material then appears as Material(2) in the Shader Tree. With that said, try not to overthink this process. Those numbers are one of the first things you'll see, and they can be confusing. But what's more important right now is selecting the right material and learning how to apply the right effects. If you explicitly name an item Apple and add a new group layer via the right-click drop-down menu in the Item List and rename it Apple, you will get Item=Apple(1) and group layer=Apple (2). But whichever one you create first gets precedence. So if you add a group layer named Apple and rename an item to Apple afterwards, the item is now Apple(2).

Introduction to the Shader Tree

You've worked with the Tools tab quite a bit up until this point, visible at the top left of the modo interface. If you look to the right, just next to the Items tab, you'll see another tab labeled Shader Tree, as shown in Figure 7.1.

Figure 7.1
The Shader Tree tabbed viewport is visible at the top right of the modo interface.

When you click the Shader Tree tab, you're presented with a viewport that has four items, Render, Environment, Directional Light, and Camera (see Figure 7.2). You'll also see a selection for Filter and Add Layer at the top. You'll come back to these later.

To the left of three of those listings is a small triangle. Click the triangle next to the Render listing to expand it. You'll see four items—Alpha Output, Final Color Output, Base Shader, and Base Material, as shown in Figure 7.3.

Note

To introduce you to the Shader Tree, you'll work with a default modo interface with no geometry loaded. The best way to set this is to make sure modo is closed, then restart. Or if you have modo already running, from the File menu choose Reset to clear the viewports. Make sure you save any work first.

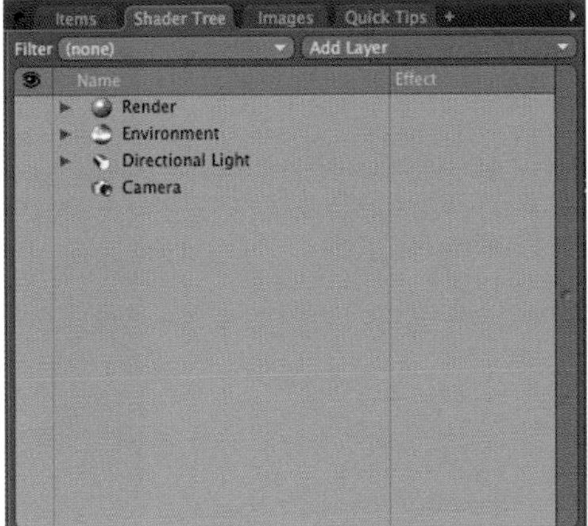

Figure 7.2 The default Shader Tree tab is your home for all surfacing and render control.

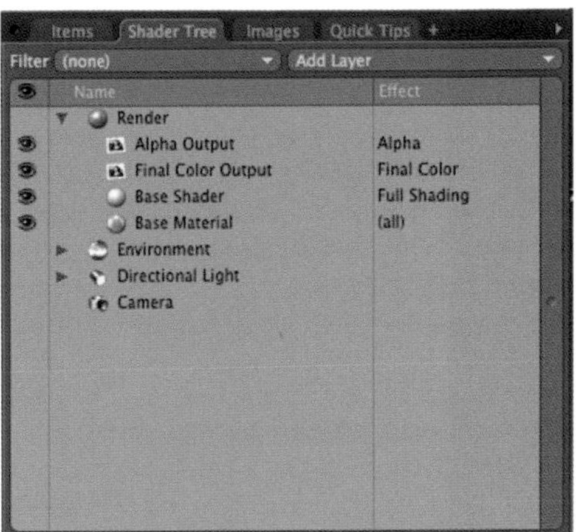

Figure 7.3 Expanding the Render listing in the Shader Tree shows the default material and shader.

The base material in the Shader Tree is what drives everything above it. The material feeds information into the Shader, which then takes that information and feeds it into the renderer, taking with it color and alpha values. The alpha value is used for layering and keying in post-processing programs. The renderer then adds the appropriate settings you apply. While this might sound a bit confusing at first, don't worry. This chapter will break it down, and then you'll see first-hand how this clever little panel works.

Click the Base Material listing. You'll see a slew of controls appear beneath the Shader Tree in the Properties tab. By selecting a layer in the Shader Tree list, you activate the controls for that listing. Now even though there is no geometry in modo, you can still see the Base Material settings, such as Diffuse Color, Specular Amount, and so on, as shown in Figure 7.4.

> **Note**
>
> Be sure to check out the Shader Tree video on the book's disc to get a quick overview of the process.

As you build objects and add surface materials, as you did with the project in Chapter 6, the material names you specify will appear here in the Shader Tree. But there's more to this area than meets the eye. This next project will show you how to work with a few settings in the Shader Tree. From there, you'll texture the objects you created in Chapter 6.

1. In the Shader Tree, click the Render listing. You'll see the Render properties appear beneath the Shader Tree, as shown in Figure 7.5.

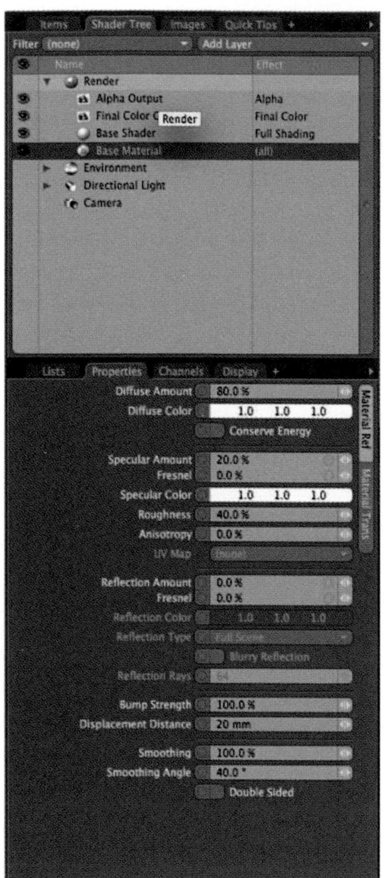

Figure 7.4
By selecting any listing in the Shader Tree, you activate the controls for that listing in the Properties tab. Here, Base Material is selected and its Render properties appear below.

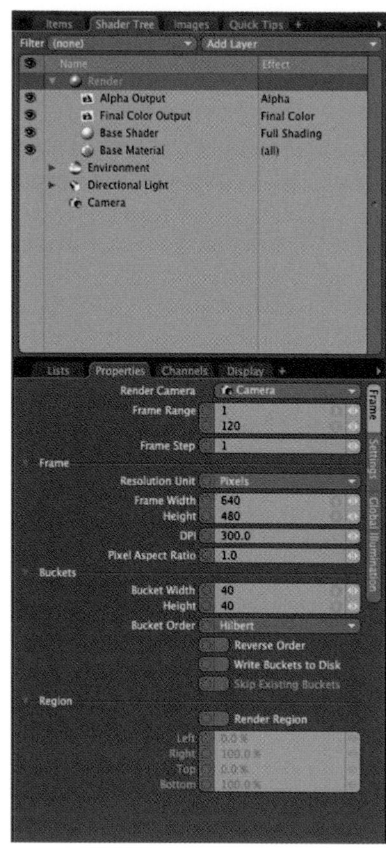

Figure 7.5
By selecting the Render listing in the Shader Tree, you gain access to all of the render controls, such as resolution, render settings, and more.

On the right side of the Properties tab, you'll see vertical tabs. The top selection is Frame, as shown in Figure 7.5. Here you can set the Resolution Unit value in Pixels or Inches. You can also change the size of your render, the default being a resolution of 640 × 480. The other settings apply to how modo renders, which you'll learn more about later in the book. For now, leave all of these settings at their defaults. The other vertical category listings include antialias settings, subdivision rates, and displacement rates. You'll also see a category for Global Illumination, a powerful way to render your scenes with added realism. Take a look at these areas to familiarize yourself with their location, but leave the settings at their defaults for now.

2. Back up in the Shader Tree, select the Environment listing. When selected, you'll see a few options below in the Render properties, such as Visible to Camera, Visible to Reflection Rays, and so on. These are all checked on by default.
3. When you expand the Environment listing, you'll see Environment Material. Select this and you'll gain access to the colors of the modo render environment from four-color gradients to physically based daylight. Figure 7.6 shows the selection.

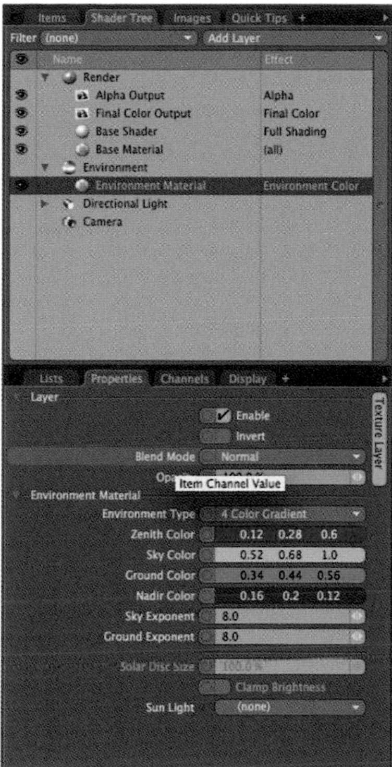

Figure 7.6 The Environment Material selection within the Environment setting of the Shader Tree is where you can control the color of the modo background for renders.

4. In the Environment Material Properties tab, you can see that the Environment Type is set to 4 Color Gradient by default. Press F8 on your keyboard to render a preview frame. Figure 7.7 shows the result. Notice how the render shows the same color gradient structure as listed in the Environment Material.
5. Change the Environment Type to 2 Color Gradient, Nadir Color to pale orange, and Zenith Color to a deep blue. Do this by simply clicking on the color swatch to call up your system's color palette, or you can click and drag on the number RGB values. When done, press F8 again to render a preview of the scene, if your preview window is not still open. Figure 7.8 shows the result.
6. Click the triangle next to Directional Light in the Shader Tree listing. You'll see that the default is set to Light Material, as shown in Figure 7.9.
7. Now select the Directional Light listing itself in the Shader Tree. You'll see the properties change to some basic but important light settings, as shown in Figure 7.10. The settings here allow you to change the light intensity (Radiant Exitance), the shadow type, position, and so on.

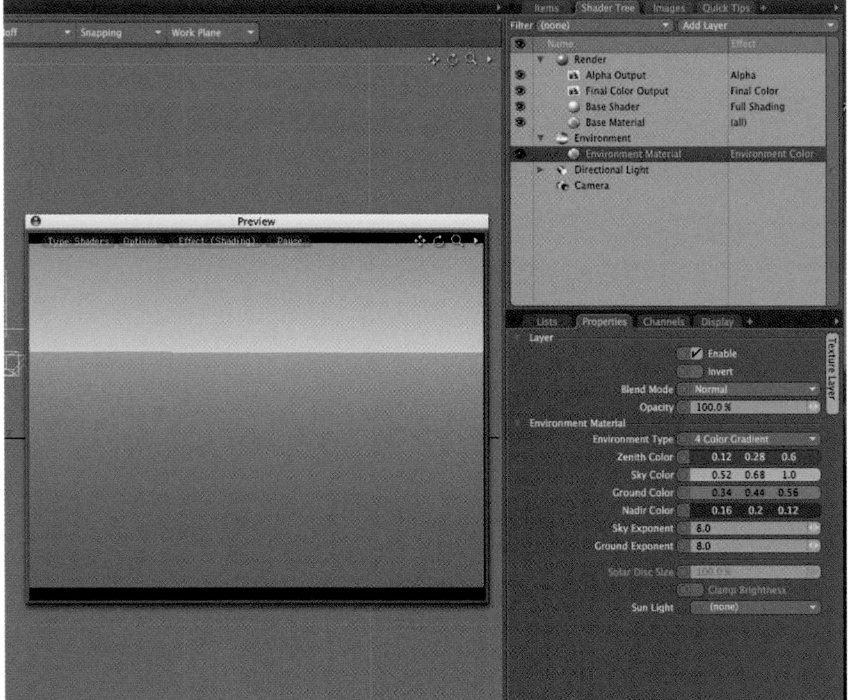

Figure 7.7
A quick render of a default modo scene shows the result of the Environment Material settings.

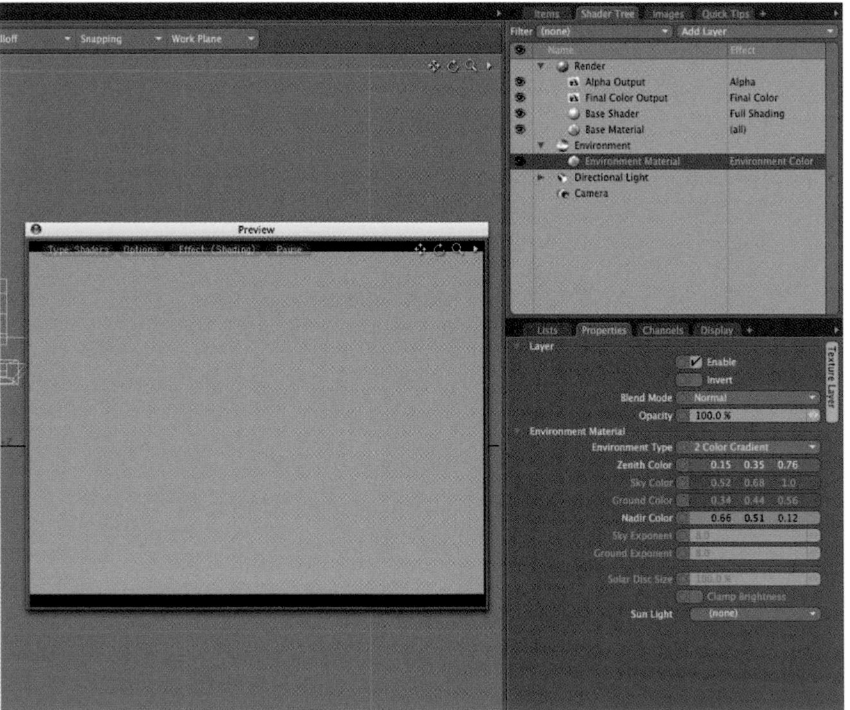

Figure 7.8
A two-color gradient removes the horizon line in the rendered scene.

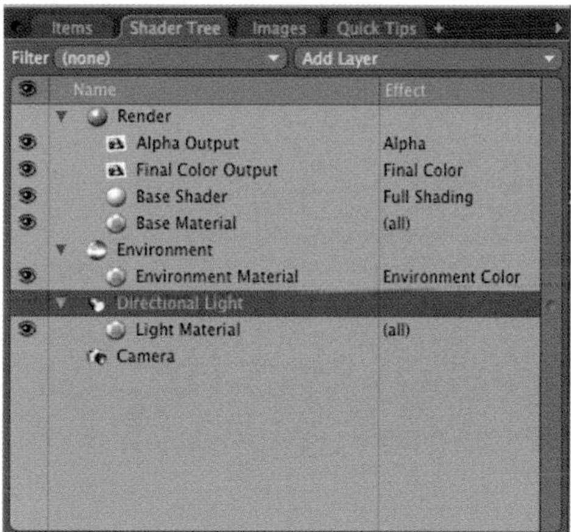

Figure 7.9 A default light in modo also has a default material.

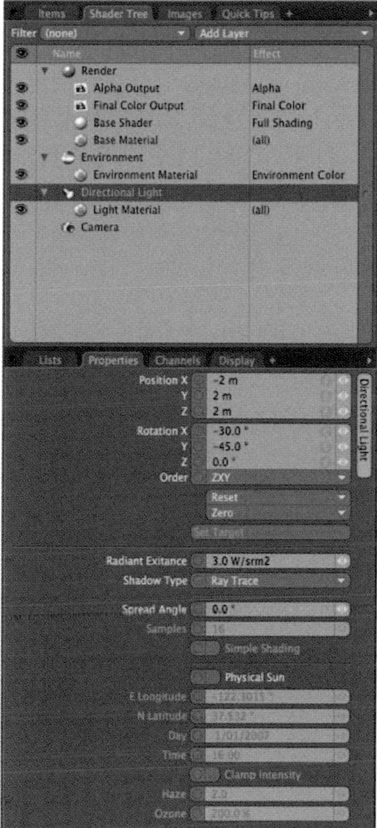

Figure 7.10 Selecting Directional Light in the Shader Tree, rather than Light Material, calls up basic but important light settings in the Render Properties tab.

These are just a few steps to familiarize you with the basic information in the Shader Tree. While you've not yet created anything, you can see how to access the various properties for Shader Tree items. Select the item, and the properties for that item appear below the Shader Tree in the Properties tab. Within the Properties tab, there can also be vertical tabs for additional tools. Remember this as you're setting variables for textures, camera render settings, and so on. Now move forward to see the Shader Tree in action by applying textures and image maps to the corkboard model you created in the previous chapter.

Using the Shader Tree

There are still many areas of the Shader Tree yet to be explored. But in order to do that, you'll need to have some geometry to work with. This geometry, of course, will need to have materials set. But wait! You did that already in Chapter 6. This next project will help you apply both image maps and computer-generated textures to your scene.

1. Load up the corkboard object you created in Chapter 6. Or if you like, use the one from the book's disc. Figure 7.11 shows the model. Note that a few more items have been added. A large flat plane was created that will become an element you'll use in a moment for image mapping, and the thumbtack you created was copied a few additional times to hang up the new items on the corkboard.
2. With the corkboard scene loaded, click the Shader Tree tab. Then, expand the Render listing by clicking the triangle icon.
3. Unlike earlier in this chapter when all you saw was Base Material and Base Shader in the Shader Tree, you now see all of the materials created for the objects. Remember, you pressed the m key after you built the Post-it Note and set a polygon material name. This name is what you now see in the Shader Tree (see Figure 7.12).

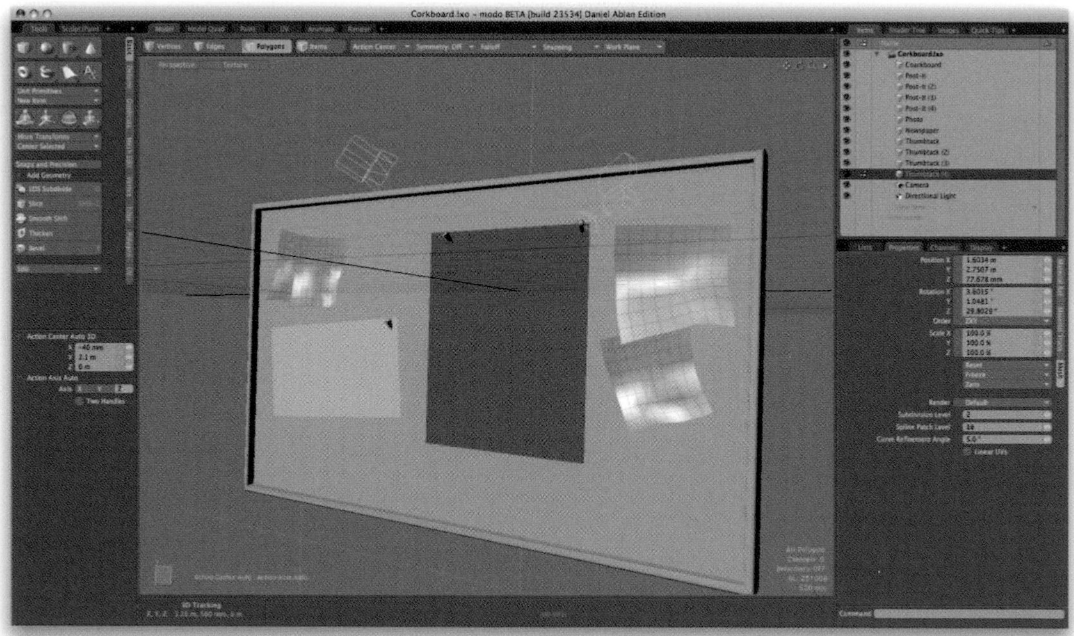

Figure 7.11 The corkboard object from Chapter 6 with additional items added to populate it.

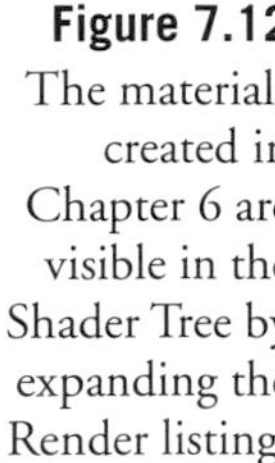

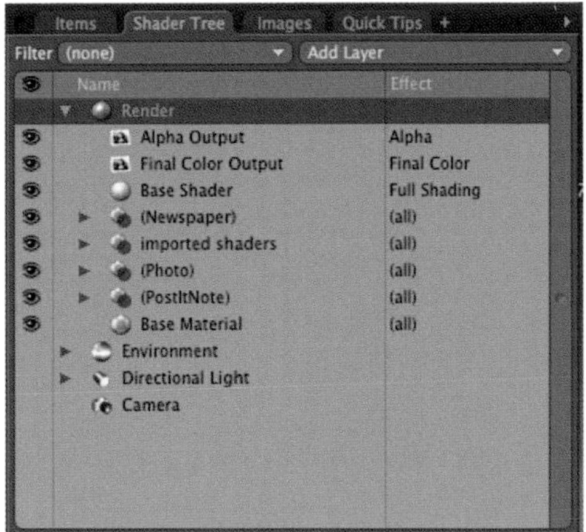

Figure 7.12 The materials created in Chapter 6 are visible in the Shader Tree by expanding the Render listing.

In Figure 7.12, you can see the materials that have been created. The column on the left shows a little eyeball. This is the material visibility. Clicking this eyeball toggles the material on or off. This is helpful because at times textures might be set but they distract you while you are setting other materials. They also might take up valuable video memory, so by toggling them off, you can save resources and work faster. To the right is the name of the mask, which was set when you created it. As a refresher, you can do this by selecting the polygons you want to surface, pressing the m key on your keyboard, and giving those polygons a material name. A material name is just a name for that set of polygons you have selected. modo then creates a group layer in the Shader Tree that is linked to those polygons. modo also gives the group layer the same name as the material, only enclosed in parentheses. This combination of a group layer and its link to the polygons defined in the material set is called a mask.

Last is the Effect column in the Shader Tree. Right now, the Base Shader listing has a Full Shading effect. Remember that this shader feeds the renderer—therefore, having it set to Full Shading allows all of the shading options to be applied. But what other types of effects are there? If you right-click (Command-click on a Mac), you'll see the other shading options, such as Diffuse Shading, Luminous Shading, Reflection Shading, and more. You'll use these various shadings throughout the book. The rest of the materials' effects read (All). If you right-click (Command-click on a Mac), you'll see that all of these materials can be set to any type of effect you want, from a bump to displacement to even a mask. You'll learn how and when to use these different effects shortly.

But what if you don't see your material in the Shader Tree? Perhaps you forgot to set a material surface to some geometry in your scene. Can it still be added? Absolutely.

1. To see how easy it is to add a material to the Shader Tree, set your selection mode to Polygons at the top of the modo interface.
2. Next, select the corkboard mesh from the Items tab.

3. Then, click on the center polygon of the corkboard to select it.
4. Press the m key and set the material name to Corkboard. Give it a slight orange color and click OK. You'll see the mask instantly added to the Shader Tree, since it's a combination of a group layer and a link to a material set, as shown in Figure 7.13.

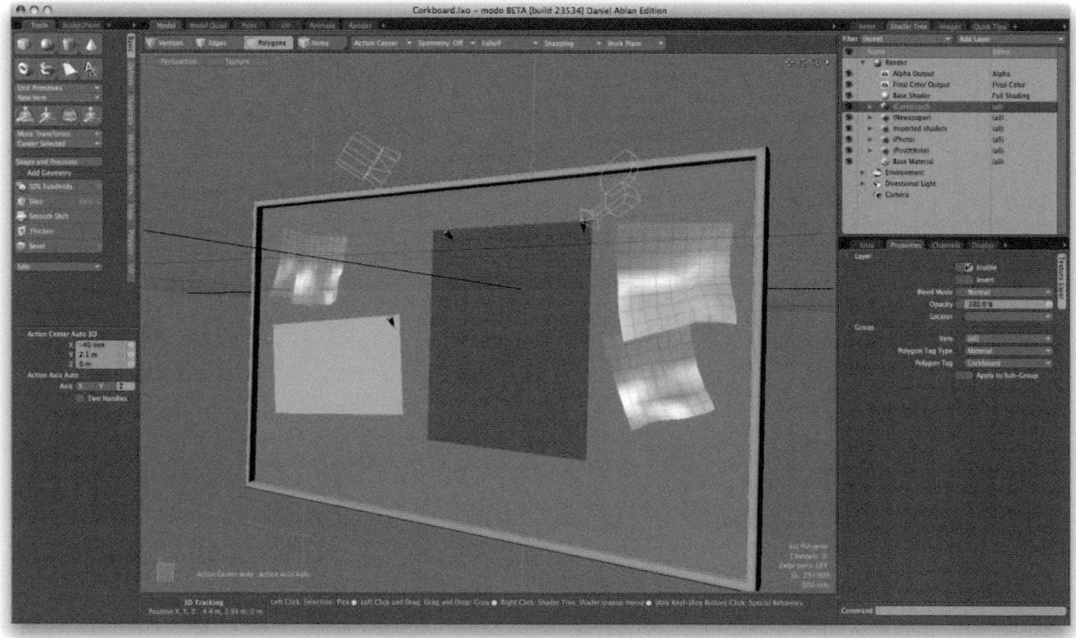

Figure 7.13 Materials can be added to the Shader Tree at any time. Assigning a material to selected geometry instantly adds a mask to the Tree.

5. Press the left bracket key ([) to reverse the selection. This will select the frame of the corkboard.
6. Press the m key and set the material name for these selected polygons to Corkboard Frame or something similar. You'll see the mask also added to the Shader Tree.

You can see that it's easy to get materials into the Shader Tree, whether they are imported with an existing object or created on the fly. But what to do with these materials once they're available in the Tree?

Setting Materials

Now that the Shader Tree is fully populated with mask names, how about actually setting those material layer properties? Since you built the corkboard first, how about starting there? You'll work your way up from there, applying computer-generated surfaces and image maps.

You might also notice that there are little icons to the left of the material names. Here's how it breaks down. The green dot with a red dot is the *mask*. This is just a group layer set to mask items or polygon selections. A group layer, material, or item will have the same icon with the red dot mask, whether there's a material in there or not. This next section will help explain things further.

1. In the Shader Tree, select the Corkboard layer, as shown in Figure 7.14.

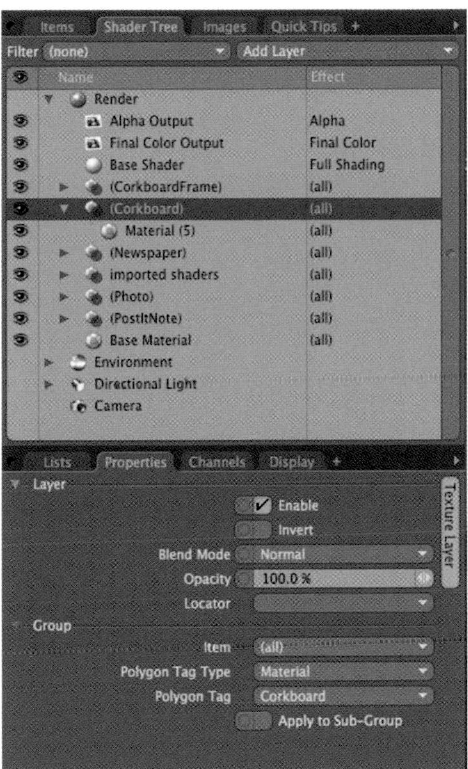

Figure 7.14
Select the Corkboard texture layer in the Shader Tree.

2. It's important to understand the difference between the group layer and the material itself. When selecting the Corkboard mask (the group layer) in the Shader Tree, you'll just see a few Render properties appear below the Tree. This mask texture layer allows you to set the opacity and apply any masking grouping. For now, you don't need to create a grouping for the texture layer. It's already a mask assigned to the corkboard material—you can see it under the Polygon tag. So with the Corkboard mask texture layer expanded in the Shader Tree, select the material layer for it. This is also represented by a green and white checkered ball. The Material Layer listing will be indented, showing that it belongs to the group layer just above it. You'll see the crucial settings appear for this material in the Properties panel, as shown in Figure 7.15.

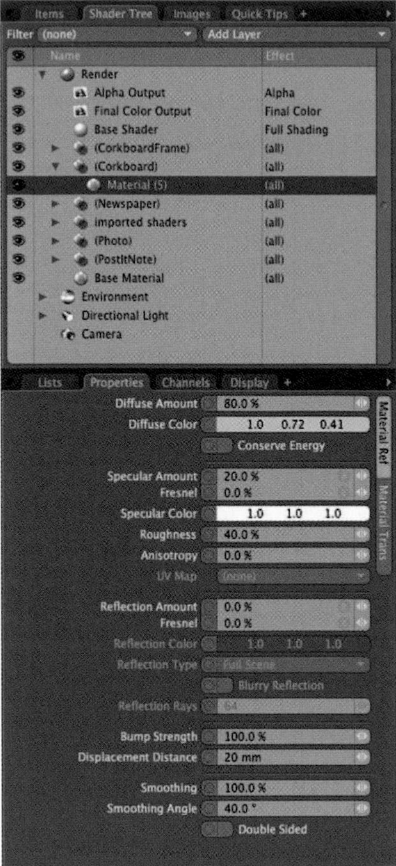

Figure 7.15
Selecting the material layer for the Corkboard mask texture layer displays the most crucial surfacing attributes in the Properties panel.

3. You'll see that in the Properties panel with the material layer selected, there are two vertical category listings. The top is the Material Ref(erence), which contains all of the key color and shading values. The second is the Material Trans(missive), where you can set transparent, subsurface, and luminous values.
4. But for now, in the Material Ref category of the Properties tab, make sure the Diffuse Amount value is set at its default 80%. The Diffuse Color setting should be a pale orange or light brown color, something similar to a corkboard color.
5. Conserve Energy should be unchecked for now. This handy little tool's purpose is to provide physically based shading, given realistic input values. This is especially true for surfaces that have both diffuse and reflective values applied. Shading with Conserve Energy turned on is a bit slower to compute, and if you're just tweaking appearances by eye, you probably don't need it. Pure diffuse or pure reflective surfaces also don't need it. So for now, leave it off.

6. The rest of the settings should be left at their defaults right now. They allow you to control the specularity, amount of gloss (roughness), and more.
7. Back up in the Shader Tree, with the Material Mask listing selected underneath the Corkboard texture, click Add Layer at the top of the Shader Tree, and select the Cellular texture, as shown in Figure 7.16.

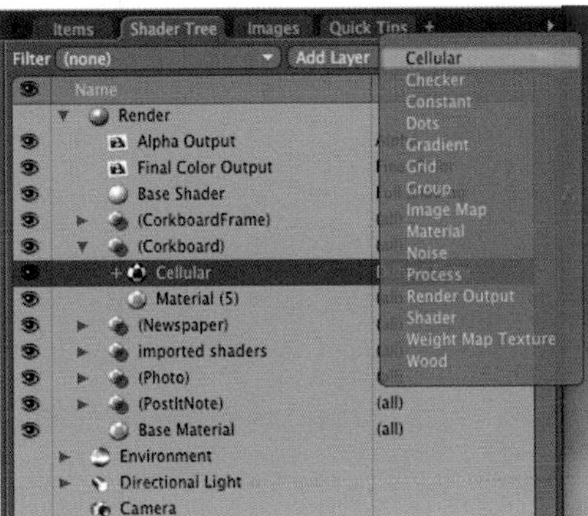

Figure 7.16 Add a layer to the Corkboard material by choosing it from the Add Layer drop-down list.

8. Using the Render tab at the top of the viewport, you'll change your view to a three-panel viewport, one of which is a preview window. When applying procedural computer-based textures, this preview window will allow you to see the texture. Figure 7.17 shows the texture layer added and view change.
9. Notice that in the Shader Tree, the Cellular texture is added above the Corkboard material layer. If it were located below the material layer, you would not see it in the preview window. You'll also see that this added layer has a black-and-white checkered icon. In the Properties tab, click the Texture Locator vertical category listing. This will present you with the size and mapping settings for the Cellular texture.
10. The texture initially is a little too large, so you'll want to size it down. But instead of just randomly guessing a value for the XYZ size settings, you can do some math right in the panel. After the Size X listing, type /.04 to tell modo to divide the value by .04, effectively changing it to 40 mm, as shown in Figure 7.18. You can use the gang select option to change all values at once. Click one time on the small round icon to the right of the values so that you see the little equal (=) sign.
11. Save your scene. You can see how the Cellular texture is now smaller in the preview window, as shown in Figure 7.19.

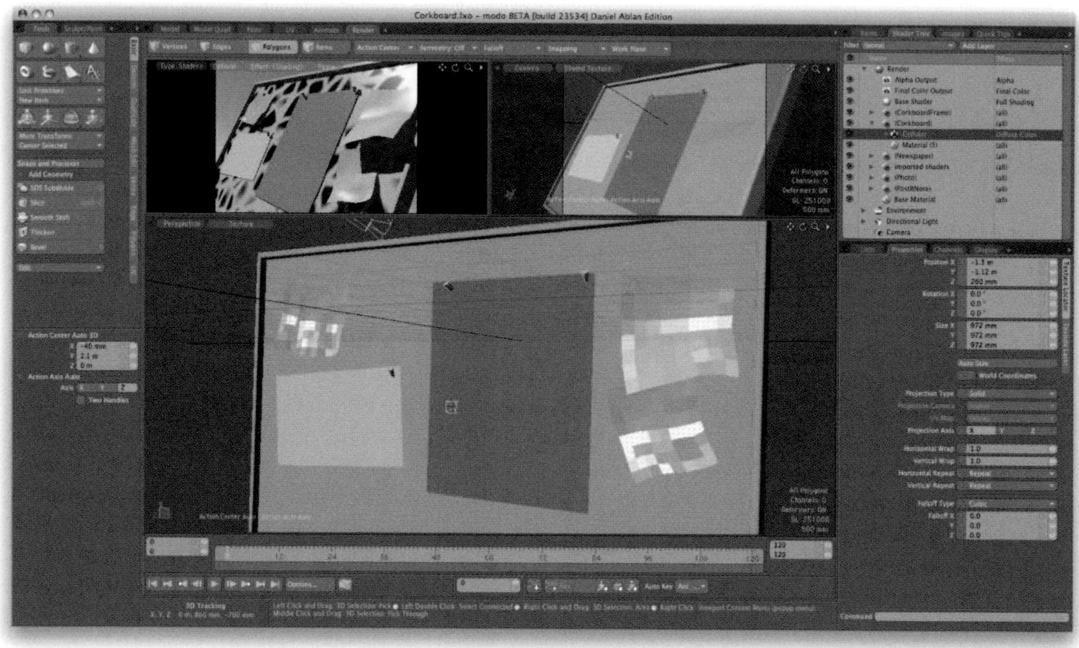

Figure 7.17 Once a computer-generated texture layer is added to the material, you can view it with a preview window.

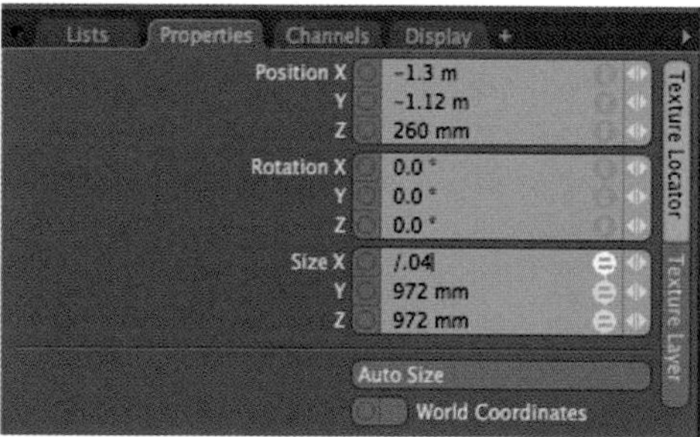

Figure 7.18 You can let modo calculate some math for you. Just add a forward slash (/) for divide and the amount you'd like to set.

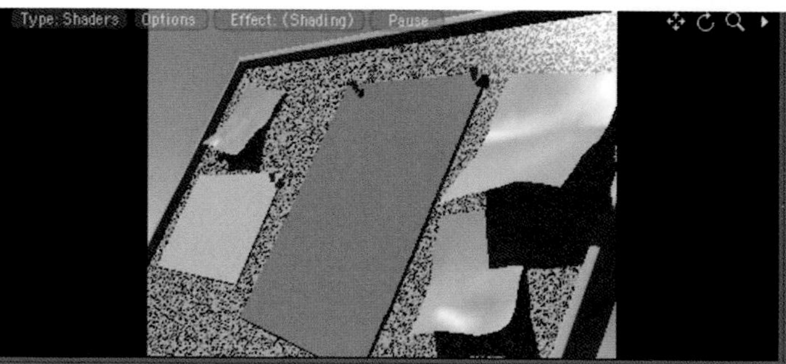

Figure 7.19 The scaled down Cellular texture in the preview window.

12. Right now, the texture is black and white because its effect in the Shader Tree is set to Diffuse Color. Right-click the Effect listing (Command-click on a Mac), and change it to Diffuse Amount. You'll see the same Cellular texture now diffused, or blended, with the material for the corkboard, as shown in Figure 7.20. What you've done here tells modo that the dark parts of the cellular diffuse texture absorb more light than the light parts, giving variation to the material layer's diffuse color setting.

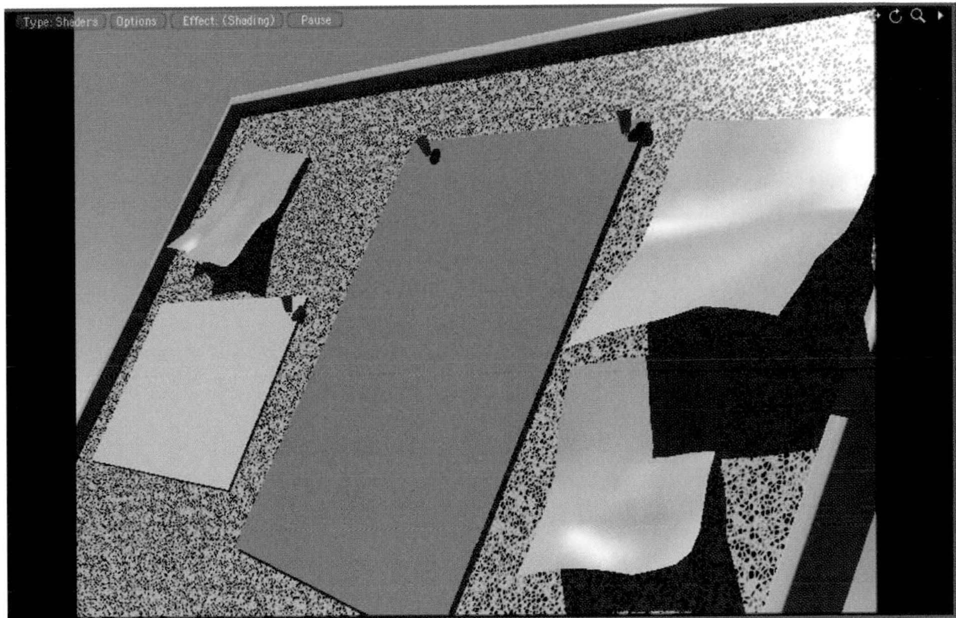

Figure 7.20 The same Cellular texture is now diffused with the material for the corkboard.

13. Maybe you can take this texture to another level? Sure you can! Right-click on the Cellular listing—not the effect, but the name itself in the Shader Tree. In the popup that appears, select Create Instance to create an instance of the Cellular texture. An instance is not so much a duplicate as it is a carbon copy of the original. It simply references the original, saving your computer's memory and processing power. An instance will appear italicized.
14. For the effect of the instanced Cellular texture, right-click on the Diffuse Amount listing and change it to Bump. You'll see the Cellular texture in the preview window appear to have depth, as shown in Figure 7.21.
15. This new bump doesn't quite make the surface look like a corkboard, so select the first, original, nonitalic Cellular texture layer. In the Properties tab, click the Texture Layer vertical tab. Then change Cell Value to 60% and Filler Value to 80%. This will take away some of the heavy contrast by coloring within the cell holes.

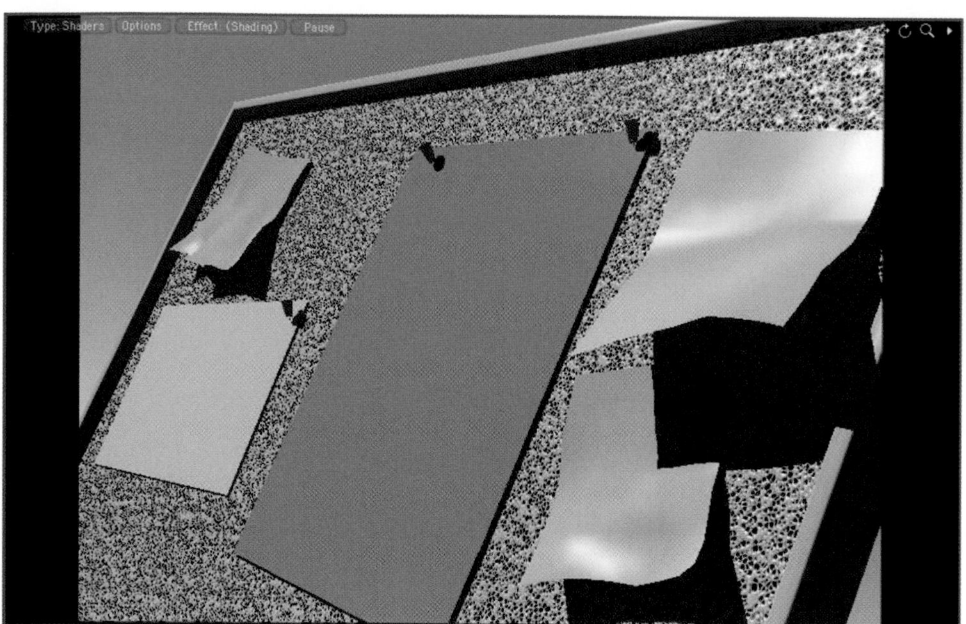

Figure 7.21
An instance of the Cellular texture with a Bump effect gives the material more depth.

16. Back up in the Shader Tree, select the Cellular instance, which has its effect set to Bump.
17. In the Properties tab, click on the Texture Layer tab again, and check the Invert box to reverse the bump map. Change Opacity to 80%. Figure 7.22 shows the difference.
18. Feel free to play with the size and color (Cell Value and Filler Value settings) of the Cellular texture to make it your own. The settings shown previously are subtle, but maybe you see how the texture looks even smaller? Perhaps more or less bump? Play around with the settings, and you can get some cool results. Try one more setting: Select the Cellular(2) layer, the one with the Bump applied. In the Properties tab, uncheck the Invert box in the Texture Layer tab.
19. Click the Texture Locator vertical tab within the Properties tab and bring the overall size down to about 5 mm. Figure 7.23 shows the result in the corkboard.
20. When ready, save your work.

You can see that by adding a procedural texture and making an instance of it, you can quickly create some great looking organic textures. However, trying to create a Post-it Note is not as easy with computer-generated images. While modo is pretty powerful, it can't quite mimic a hand-written note, at least not yet. So that leaves you with the task of importing existing image maps.

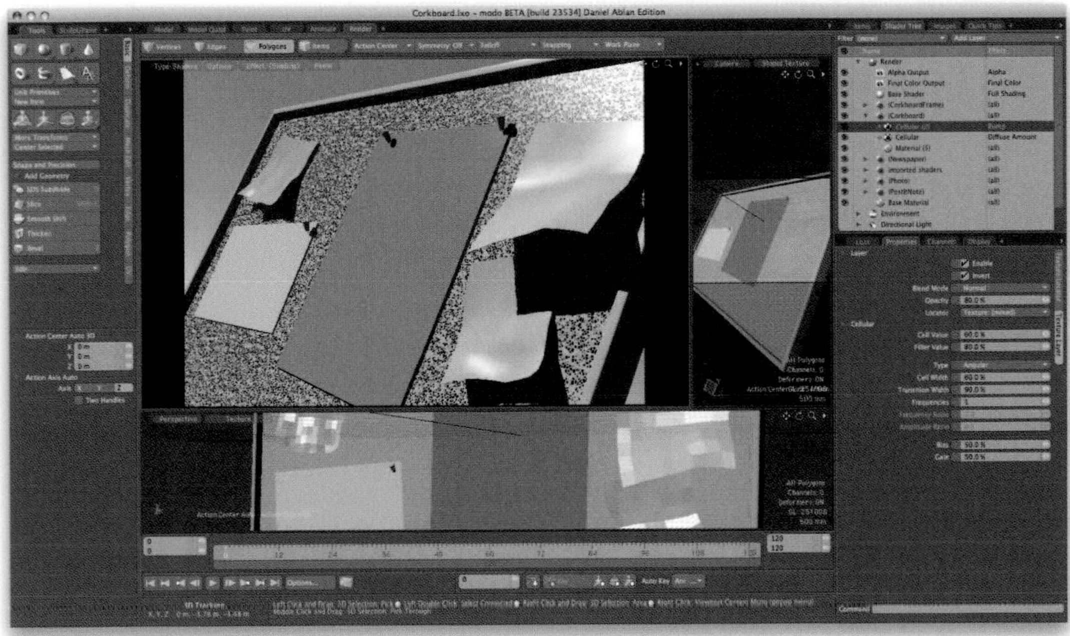

Figure 7.22 The instanced Bump effect is leveled off a bit by changing the original Cellular texture and decreasing the bump opacity.

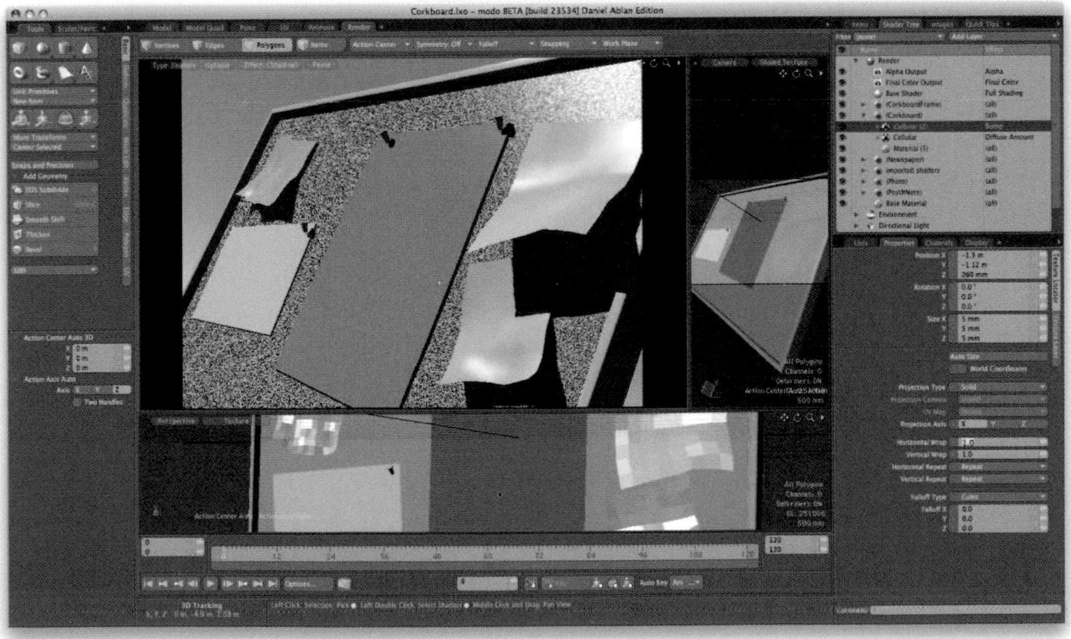

Figure 7.23 By adjusting the Cellular texture to a smaller size and adjusting the bump layer, the resulting texture more closely resembles a corkboard.

Setting Image Materials

While there could be a book all its own about modo texturing, this chapter is only here to get you started with the tools. There are many areas and effects you can try, many of which we'll employ in upcoming tutorials in this book. The previous section guided you through adding a procedural texture layer to the surface of the corkboard. This section will take you a step further by showing you how to add images as textures.

1. Continuing from the previous exercise, select the PostItNote1 mask layer and expand it. Choose its material layer.
2. If you take a look at the Properties panel, either in the Material Ref tab or the Material Trans tab, there's no setting for mapping an image. What gives? You need to add an image layer to the Post-it Note group. Make sure Material layer is selected for the PostItNote1 mask in the Shader Tree.
3. At the top of the Shader Tree, select Add Layer, and choose Image Map, as shown in Figure 7.24. A message box will open allowing you to choose an image.

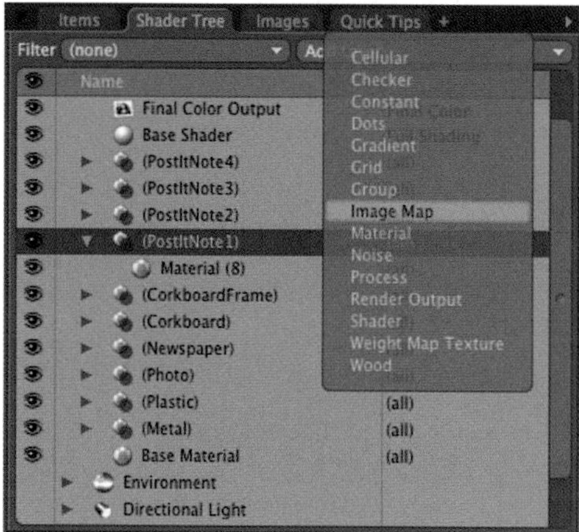

Figure 7.24 Adding an Image Map layer to a material is easy by selecting it from the Add Layer drop-down list.

4. Point your requester to the Projects folder on the book's DVD, and in the chapter 7 folder, choose the PostItNote1.png image.
5. When you select the image, the image map layer will be created in the Post-it Note Mask layer, with its effect set to Diffuse Color. This is fine for now. With the image map layer selected in the Shader Tree, select the Texture Locator vertical tab in the Properties panel, and you can see the image map controls.
6. The Projection Type option is automatically set to UV Map, and if you look at Figure 7.25, you'll see the image mapped on the first Post-it Note. Save your work!
7. If you change Projection Type to Planar, you'll see the image is repeated across the Post-it Note (see Figure 7.26). This is normal, but you're not placing tiles, but rather

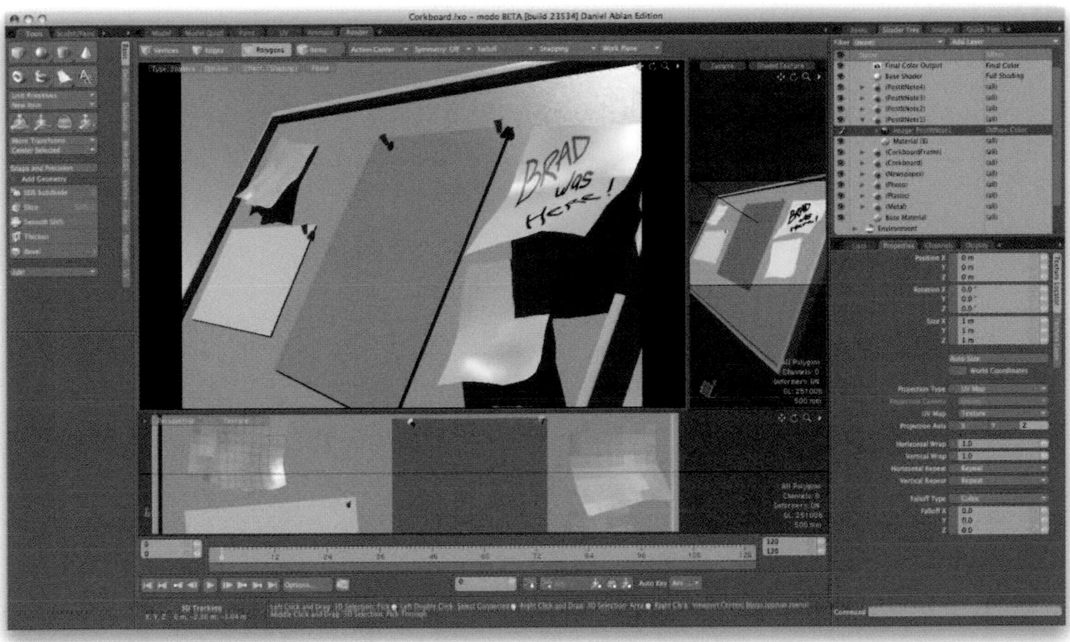

Figure 7.25 By adding an image to a mask in the Shader Tree, it is automatically added to the surface.

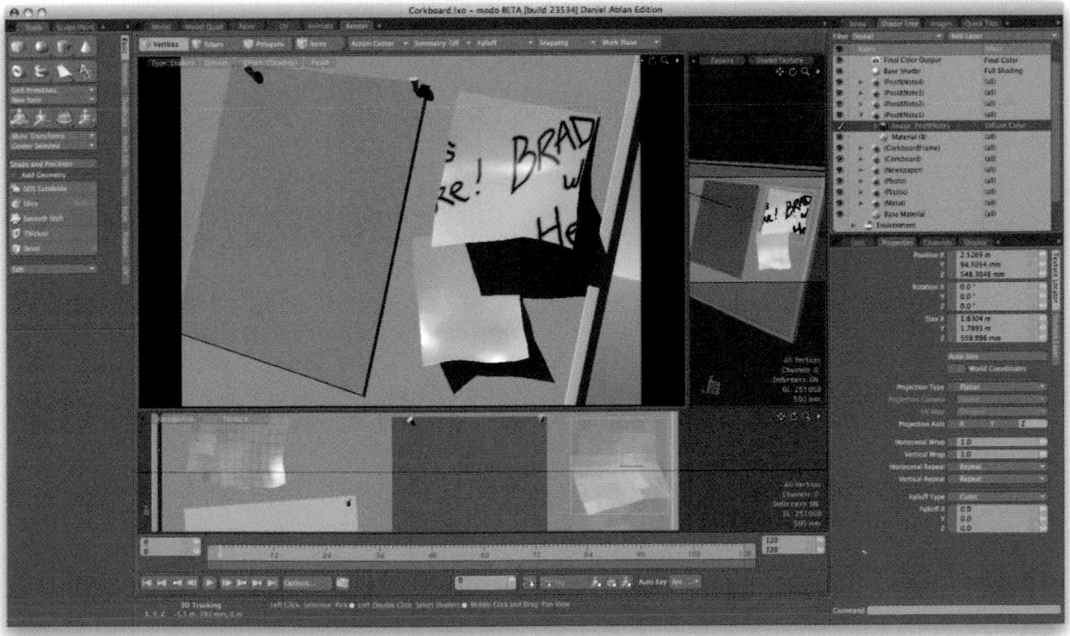

Figure 7.26 The first object has an image map applied, but it can be distorted and not aligned if not mapped correctly.

a single image. Set Projection Axis to Z, and click Auto Size. You might find that the image distorts slightly. This is because the geometry is not completely flat on the Z axis. Rotate your view around in the viewport to get a closer look at the first Post-it Note, now image mapped, as shown in Figure 7.26.

8. You might notice that this Post-it Note could use a little something more. First, change the Projection Type option back to UV. (We'll cover UVs later in the book.) First, save your work by choosing Save from the File menu.
9. Select the Material layer for the Post-it Note group mask, just under the image map layer. This is the base material for this particular group mask. When you select it, you can see the basic properties in the Properties panel. And because the image you just mapped on the mesh was a 32-bit image, the area around the hand-written text is transparent. This means these base settings will show through.
10. Set Specular Amount to 10%. Specular Color can remain at white. Set Roughness to 70%. Since there are no reflections, you don't need to set a value there; and this surface doesn't need a bump, so you're all set. However, change the Diffuse Color value to an off white. You'll see the color of the paper change. Figure 7.27 shows the settings.

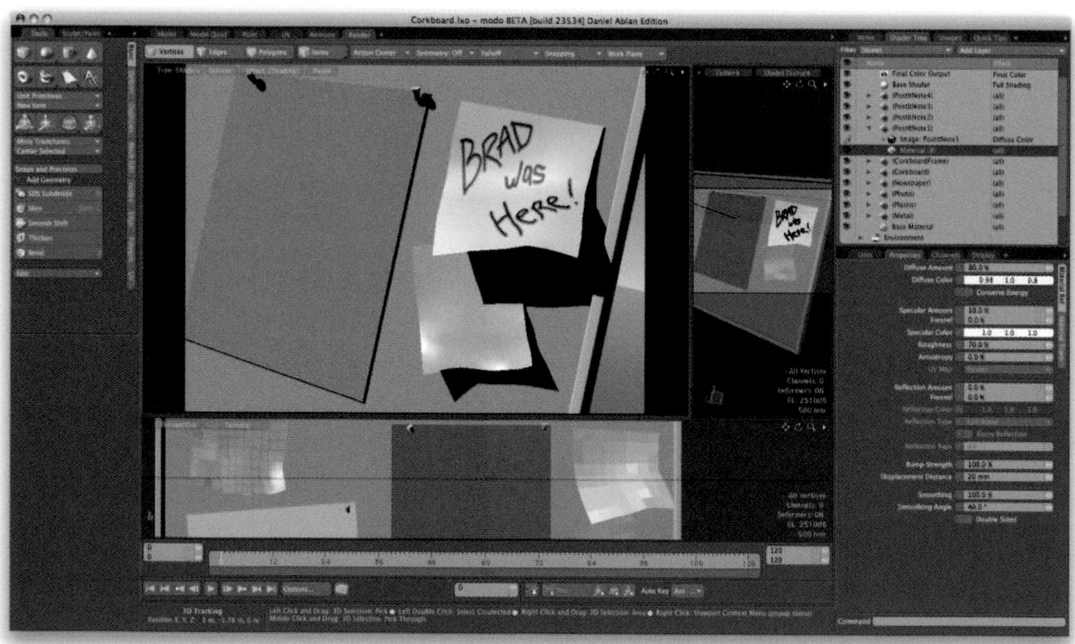

Figure 7.27 By setting a few basic properties, the Post-it Note is now textured.

11. There's another great way to apply an image map. First, click the Images tab and drag it open to see all of the contents. There, you'll see the existing image map you loaded through the Shader Tree. But if you look closely, you can see the Load Image listing. Click it, and select the FallLeaves.jpg image from the Chapter 7 project folder.
12. When loaded, the preview shows just the image, but you can also see the image thumbnail in the Images tab, as shown in Figure 7.28.

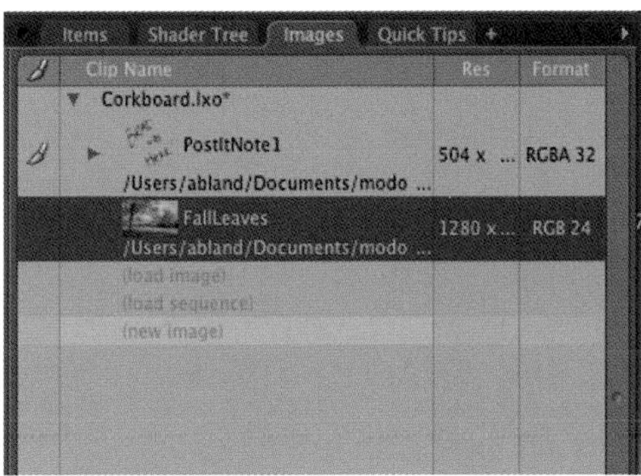

Figure 7.28
Rather than loading an image in the Shader Tree, you can load it directly in the Images tab.

13. In the viewport, click on the photo mesh on the corkboard. You should be in Items selection mode at the top of the modo interface. Then, click and drag the thumbnail of the tree image from the Images tab and drop it on the photo object in the Perspective view. The image should apply itself to the photo, but it might not be lined up properly.
14. In the Shader Tree, expand the Photo material group. You'll see an image map layer just like the one you added to the Post-it Note group. It was automatically added by dragging and dropping the image map. Figure 7.29 shows the applied image.
15. As you did with the Post-it Note properties, change the Projection Type setting from UV Map to Planar on the Z axis for the tree image. Remember that this is under the Texture Locator vertical category. Also remember to click Auto Size. You'll see the image applied to the photo mesh, as shown in Figure 7.30.
16. Save your work.

The Shader Tree can be confusing, with groups and layers, materials and images, but it's easier than you might think. You've already accomplished a lot with the lessons in this chapter, but as always, there's more you can do! This next project will take the texturing capabilities a step further and introduce you to more masking techniques.

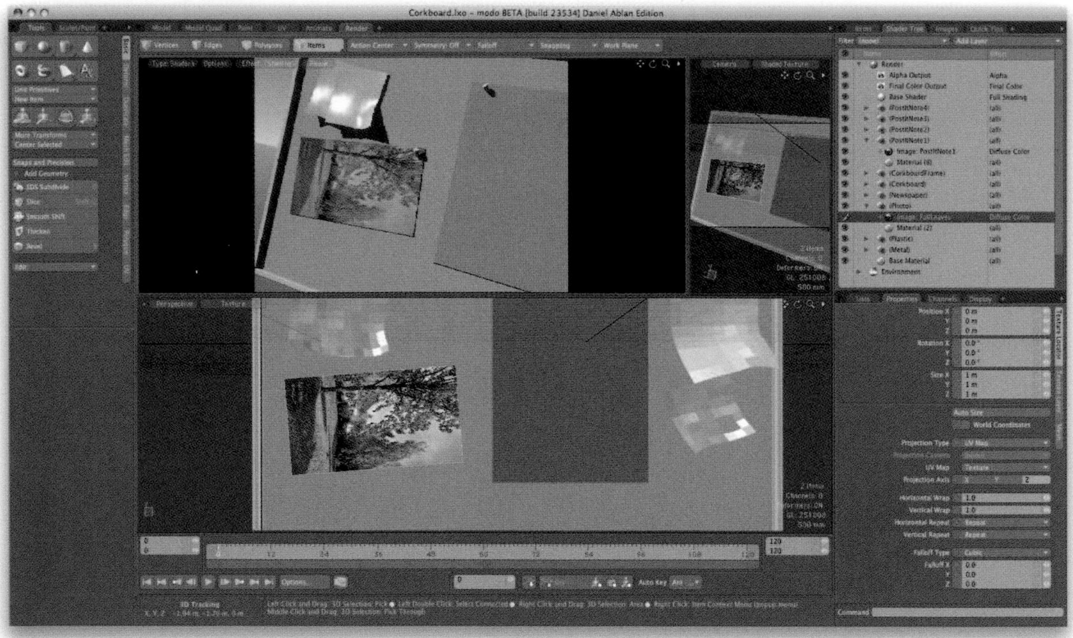

Figure 7.29 Dropping an image on a mesh in the viewport is a quick-and-easy way to add an image map layer to the Shader Tree.

Figure 7.30 Applying the tree image as a planar map on the Z axis with the Auto Size setting perfectly maps it onto the mesh.

Masking Effects

The term *mask* will be used a lot when it comes to modo and the Shader Tree. This section will use one image to mask out another. It's a great way to shape a mesh without actually modeling it.

1. Continuing from the previous exercise and your corkboard object, select the newspaper mesh on the board. You can choose Items mode at the top of the modo interface, and then click in the viewport to select the mesh.

> **Note**
>
> A quick way to jump to Items mode is to press the Shift and spacebar keys at the same time.

2. Click over to the Images tabbed viewport to the right of the Items tab.
3. Select Load Image and, from the book's DVD in the Chapter 7 folder, within the Projects directory, choose the Newspaper.png image.
4. When the image loads, drag and drop it onto the newspaper mesh. Figure 7.31 shows the setup.

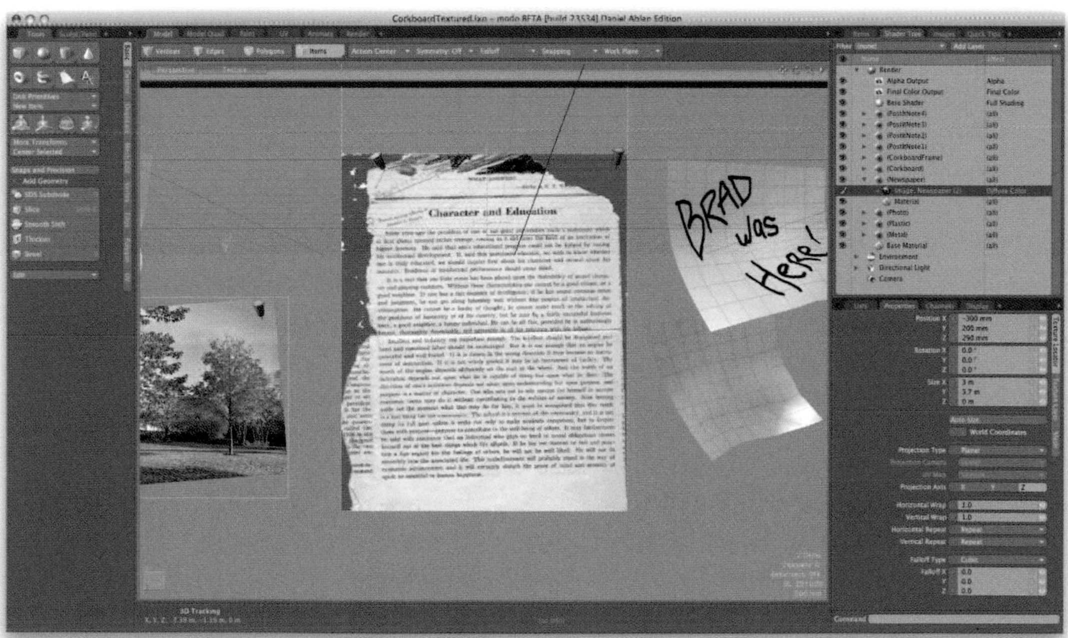

Figure 7.31 Applying a newspaper clipping to the mesh is easy by loading it in the Images tab, then dragging and dropping it onto the mesh.

5. Expand the Render group in the Shader Tree, if it's not already.
6. Expand the Newspaper group, and then select the image layer that was added by dragging and dropping the newspaper clipping image onto the mesh.
7. In the Properties panel, click on the Texture Locator vertical tab.
8. Change Projection Type from UV Map to Planar.
9. Set Projection Axis to Z.
10. Click the Auto Size button. The newspaper clipping is now mapped, but not aligned. Click and drag the Position Y arrows to bring the image up manually on the polygon. You can also just type in roughly 200mm, as shown in Figure 7.32.

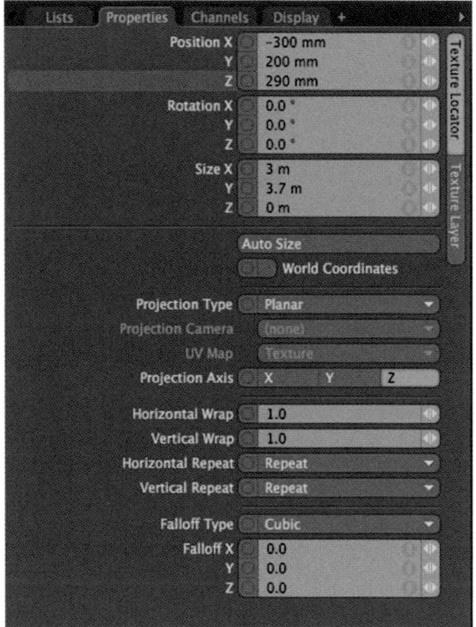

Figure 7.32
Adjusting the newspaper clipping settings in the Texture Locator vertical category of the Properties panel maps it on the mesh.

11. Now you know as well as anyone that newspaper clippings hanging on a corkboard need a ripped edge, right? No one cuts out clippings perfectly. You can see that the image already has rough edges, but the polygons are still showing through. In the Images tab, load the NewspaperMask.png image. This is a 32-bit image with a Photoshop painted rough edge.
12. When the image is loaded, click over to the Shader Tree.
13. Now right-click on the existing image map for the newspaper and duplicate it. Then select the new image within the Newspaper group in the Shader Tree.

14. From the Properties tab, select the Texture Layer vertical tab. Change the image to the Newspaper Mask image. What you've done is duplicate the image map settings you previously applied, merely changing the actual image used. Figure 7.33 shows the properties. Figure 7.34 shows the applied image.

15. You're going to make a few more changes, and then you'll see how this all comes together. Select the Newspaper Mask image in the Shader Tree within the Newspaper layer group. Notice that its effect is set to Diffuse Color. This is fine for the actual newspaper clipping image, but the paper mask image is going to be used to cut away the mesh.

16. Change the effect, right-click on Diffuse Color and select Transparent Amount.

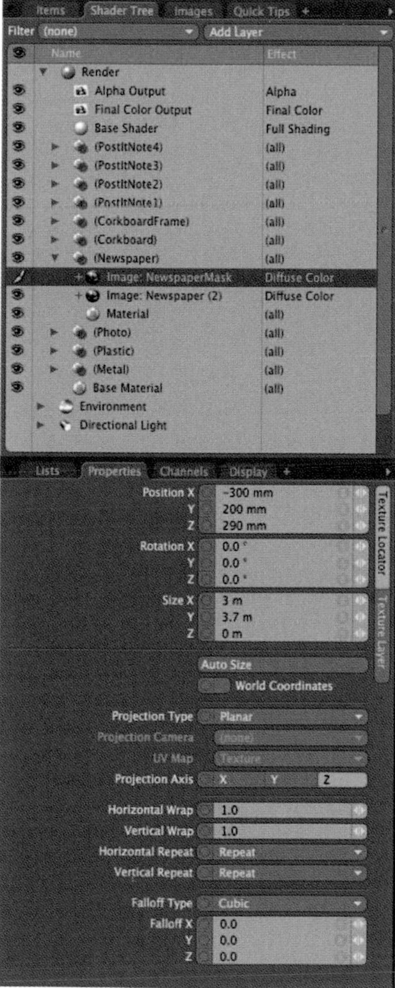

Figure 7.33
By copying an applied image, you can simply change the image used but keep the existing settings.

Figure 7.34 Duplicating images is an easy way to create texture masks.

17. Once the Effect value is set to Transparent Amount, you might not see the correct result. Why? The paper mask image is white on a black background. To effectively clip the mesh and utilize the transparency, open the Texture Layer category in the Properties tab and click Invert.
18. Making sure you have a preview window open, you can see the instant result. Use the Render tab to quickly call up a preview. Figure 7.35 shows the setup.

> **Note**
>
> Remember that the white value of an image or procedural texture will equal a value of 100% for that channel, while a black value equals 0%. In this case, you'll want to invert the transparency map so the white values are around the edges of the newspaper clipping, making them transparent.

19. Save your work! Now all you need to do is move the thumbtacks into place since you've clipped away parts of the newspaper.

Take a look at Figure 7.36. This is how the Newspaper layer group currently looks. Let's break this down so you see what's happening.

Figure 7.35 Changing the effect of the paper mask to Transparent Amount and inverting the image allows you to clip away part of the mesh.

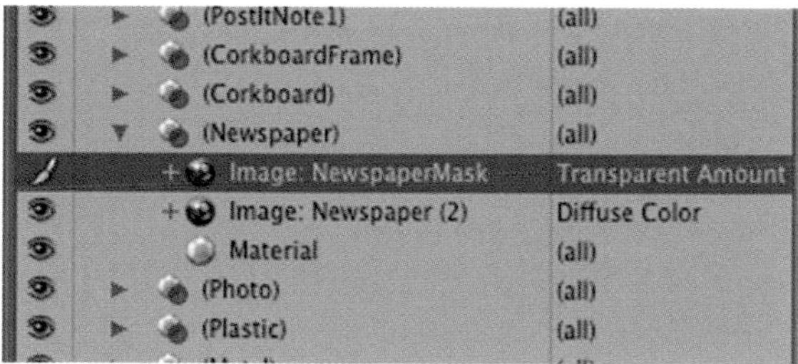

Figure 7.36 The Shader Tree, although simple in appearance is quite powerful. Here, the newspaper mesh is turned into a clipping on a corkboard with a few texture layers.

The Material layer within the Newspaper mask sets constant values for all of the Material layer's attribute channels (Diffuse Color, Specularity, Transparency, and so on). You can alter these constants by adding texture layers above the Material layer. A texture layer can be an image, a procedural texture, or a gradient. These textures can be set to affect any channel (Diffuse Amount, Reflectivity, Transparency Color, and so forth) via the Effect column. In this case, you have added image map texture layers to affect the Diffuse Color and Transparency channels. The values stored in the image maps (the pixel colors) define the values for the channels they are assigned to. So instead of the constant color in the Material layer's Diffuse Color channel, you get all of the colors in the Newspaper image map. And instead of the Material layer's Transparency channel value of 0%, you get the Transparency values defined by the black-and-white pixels of the Newspaper Mask image. These texture layers will override the Material layer channel below them, but they can be mixed with the Material layer values (and with other texture layers) by varying the Texture layer's opacity setting and Blend mode.

Your Next Few Steps

By no means are you done using the Shader Tree. Actually, you're just getting started! But as you can see with these few simple actions, your corkboard model is already taking shape and looking good. You've added a procedural computer-generated texture layer. You've mapped images and applied different effects. So what more could you do? On your own, go ahead and map the other items on the corkboard. Try experimenting with different types of images, remembering that if you create something in Photoshop or another paint package, to do so on a transparent background. There's an additional photo in the Chapter 7 folder, within the Projects folder on the book's DVD. You can use this image, as well as any another Post-it Note. Try making some of your own as well. Save that image as a PNG to retain the 32-bit alpha data that modo will read. Perhaps you can tear off a small piece of the second Post-it Note, using the same effect that you did with the newspaper? Maybe you have a corkboard in your office or home. Take a photo of it, and apply that image to the board rather than using a computer-generated texture.

In Chapter 8, you'll dive even deeper into the Shader Tree. There's much more to this than meets the eye, but you'll soon find that out. Later in the book, as you get into more advanced modeling, you'll also learn how to use modo's powerful painting and sculpting features to create your own unique textures, and then animate them.

8

Inside the Shader Tree

Chapter 7 gave you a good overview of working with the Shader Tree, helping you identify group layers and materials, as well as using images and basic materials. However, the real power of the Shader Tree comes from adding layers and masks. What you've done so far is just the first step to this killer addition to modo. In fact, it's one of the most powerful features of any 3D application on the market. This chapter will further introduce you to the layers, masks, gradients, and UV texturing available in the Shader Tree.

Masks

A good majority of the work you'll do in modo 301/302 might not be more than the projects you created in Chapter 7. But it's important to be aware of and understand the tools available to you under the hood. You never know when a project might creep up that requires the use of these controls and settings. Beyond that, you might just find that you like to experiment to create stunning pieces of art.

Item Masks

An *item mask* is a mechanism that enables you to segment your scene to determine how various materials will be applied to certain elements. There are many ways to set masks in modo, from items, to polygons, vertex maps, and more. Item masks begin at the highest level, which is where this chapter starts. From there, you'll work down to polygon materials.

1. Taking a closer look at the Shader Tree, you'll want to open up modo from the File menu and select Reset. This will bring modo back to a default setup.

2. Rather than modeling in this chapter, you'll work with some preexisting scenes created for you. This object is from the modo 201 book, but will work well for modo 301. There's a tutorial on how to create this key in the form of a video on the book's disc. Note that it's done using 201, but the techniques all apply in 301. You can find the key project files on this book's DVD, in the Chapter 8 folder within the Projects directory. Load up the Key.lxo scene. Press the a key to fit the model to view. Hold the Alt key, and then click and drag in the viewport to see both keys. Figure 8.1 shows the key loaded in a Perspective viewport.

Figure 8.1 The key object loaded from the book's disc is ready to be surfaced.

3. On the right side of the screen, click over to the Shader Tree tab.
4. In the Shader Tree, click the small triangle to the left of the Render listing to expand its contents. Figure 8.2 shows what's there, a base material and a base shader.
5. Go ahead and make another copy of this key by right-clicking on the mesh name in the Items tab and selecting Duplicate.
6. You'll now see Key and Key(2) in the Items tab. In the main viewport, press the y key and move the duplicate key from the original position. Feel free to rotate it some. Don't worry about positioning it just yet; you only need to be able to see both keys. Save the new setup as BlankKey or something similar. Figure 8.3 shows the operation.

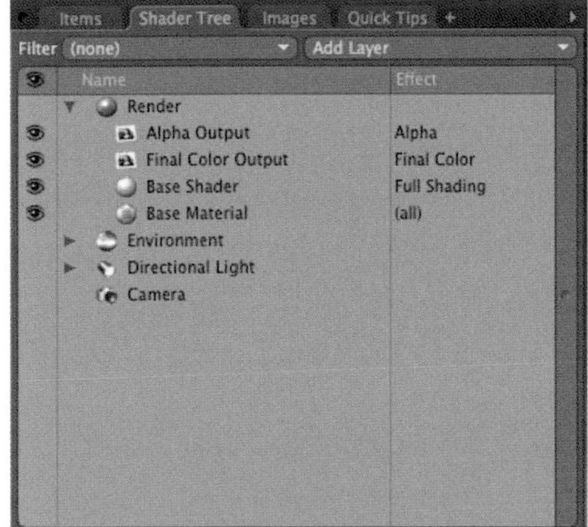

Figure 8.2 The Shader Tree shows the default settings for the key model.

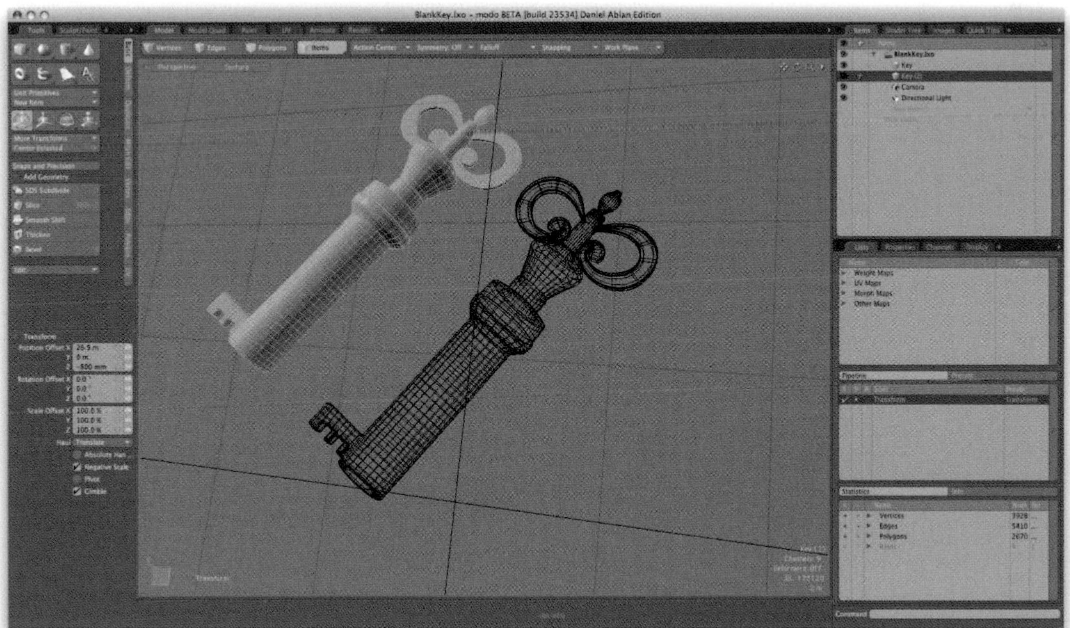

Figure 8.3 A duplicate key is made by right-clicking and selecting Duplicate in the Items tab, then positioning in the viewport.

7. Back over in the Shader Tree, notice that you still only have one base material and one base shader. This is because the original key was duplicated and neither has a mask applied. However, it doesn't really matter that a mask wasn't applied. If you had a material mask (a mask on a polygon material selection set), both items would still be linked to that mask. If you had an item mask on one key and duplicated it, then the new key would get the base material and the old key would still be masked by the item mask. That means if you change the base material, it will affect both models. First, press the o key to call up the viewport options. Set the Background Item option to Same as Active Layer.

Note

The viewport options panel that appears when you press o on your keyboard looks slightly different on a Mac than on a PC. The PC version is more solid, while the Mac's is darker and a little more transparent. Both are identical in function, however.

8. Both keys, although in different layers in the Items tab, will be visible as shaded models. Select Base Material in the Shader Tree, and then change the Diffuse Color setting in the Properties tab to an off-white/soft-brown color.
9. Any other value you change for the base material will affect both keys. This includes transparencies, reflections, and so on. In the Items tab, right-click on Key(2), and select Create Item Mask, as shown in Figure 8.4.

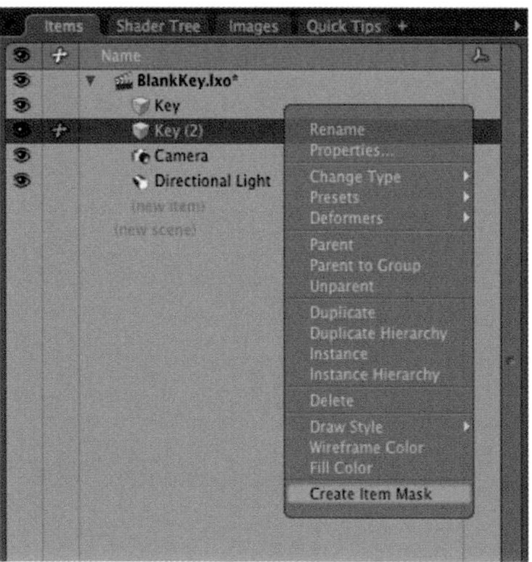

Figure 8.4
You can right-click on the key mesh layer in the Items tab to easily create an item mask.

10. You'll see that the color you applied to the base material in step 8 is now only applied to one key. And, if you look in the Shader Tree, a new item mask is listed, as well as an additional material, as shown in Figure 8.5.

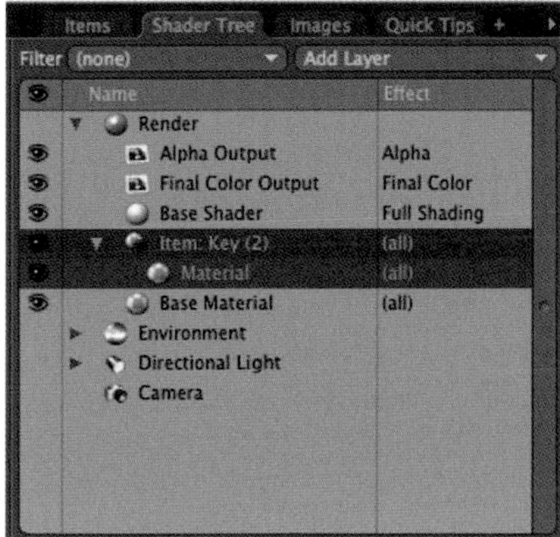

Figure 8.5 Adding an item mask to the duplicate key adds new properties in the Shader Tree.

11. This new item mask you've created allows you to set unique surfaces for the key you created it for. From the Items tab, select the original key and create an item mask for it, just as you did in step 9. Now you'll see another addition to the Shader Tree, as shown in Figure 8.6.

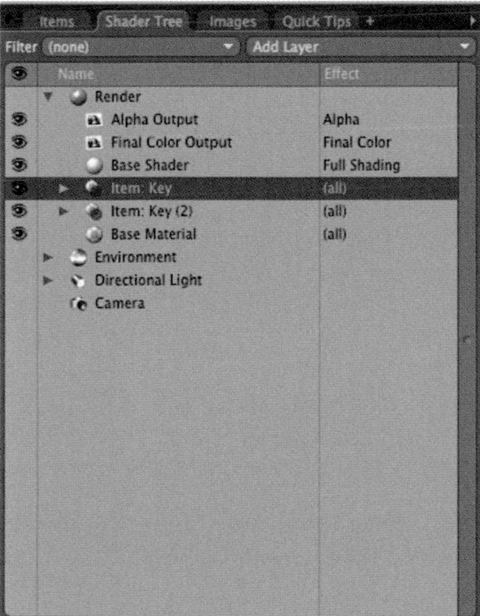

Figure 8.6 Adding an item mask to the original key adds additional settings in the Shader Tree.

Note

When you create an item mask (or a polygon mask, as you'll do shortly) the addition you see added to the Shader Tree is also considered a group. The group contains the materials.

The group layer is made into a mask when it is linked to an item or a selection of polygons. By right-clicking on an item and making an item mask, you simultaneously created the group layer and linked it to the item. If you press m and create a new material called Gold, you will simultaneously create a new group layer in the Shader Tree linked to the material set of polygons called Gold.

12. Save your scene with a new name, perhaps TwoKeys or something similar. (It's a good idea to save your scene in stages so you can always get back to a previous version at any time. You'll want one scene with blank keys and no masks, and another with masks.)
13. By adding the second item mask, you can see that both keys are back to the light gray color, which is what the new materials inside their item masks default to. The base material isn't so much overwritten as it is ignored by the keys. In the Shader Tree, right-click on Item: Key and select Rename. Rename it to just TopKey. Do the same for Item: Key(2), naming it BottomKey. This is only for organization, and you can rename it to anything you like. It has no effect on the scene. Also note that since the keys have item masks that contain their material settings, the base material is not taken into consideration when shading them. It still exists in the scene, however, to give new (unmasked) geometry a default surface.
14. Now, the original base material is overwritten, but it still holds a place in the scene, based on the settings applied in the Shader Tree. Select the Material listing for TopKey. It will be listed as Material or Material (2), depending on which item mask you made first. modo adds the "(2)" to help differentiate between them. If you want, you can rename the material, but it's not necessary. For now, change its Diffuse Color setting to a soft beige.
15. With Material still selected for TopKey, increase the Specular Amount value to 50%. This increases the shininess of the object. Bring the Roughness to about 80% to spread out the shine created by the increased specularity. Figure 8.7 shows the settings.
16. Because you want the base material to be the same for both keys, right-click on the TopKey material listing and select Copy. Then, select the BottomKey material listing, right-click, then choose Paste. You'll see the bottom key in the shaded viewport now match the top key. Save the scene!

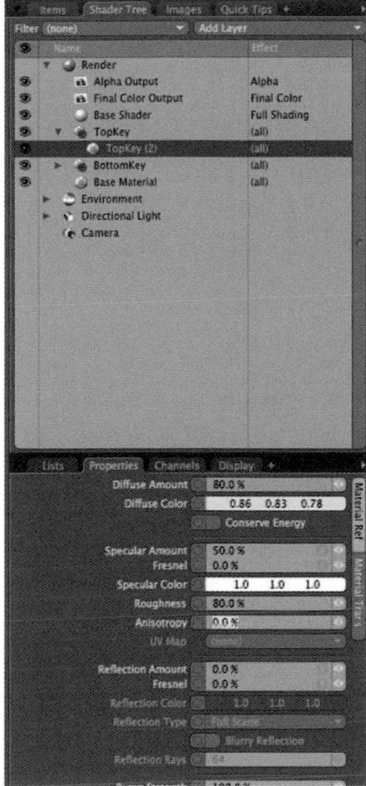

Figure 8.7
With just a few changes to the TopKey materials, the object starts looking better.

Polygon Masks

Similar to an item mask, a *polygon mask* creates a material mask in the Shader Tree. But rather than creating a mask for the entire object, a polygon mask allows you to set a material for a specific set of polygons. For example, the key object you're using in this scene really only needs one surface, and, therefore, an item mask is enough. But perhaps you'll need to create a separate surface for one particular part of the key. This is where a polygon mask is used.

1. Switch to Polygons selection mode at the top of the modo interface. Then select the polygons making up the tip at the end of the top key, as shown in Figure 8.8. A quick way to select this region is to click once on the end, then hold the Shift key, and press the up arrow five times to expand the selection up around the end.
2. Press the m key to call up the Polygon Set Material dialog box. Set the name of the selected polygons to TopKeyTip and press OK. Figure 8.9 shows the Shader Tree with the polygon mask added.

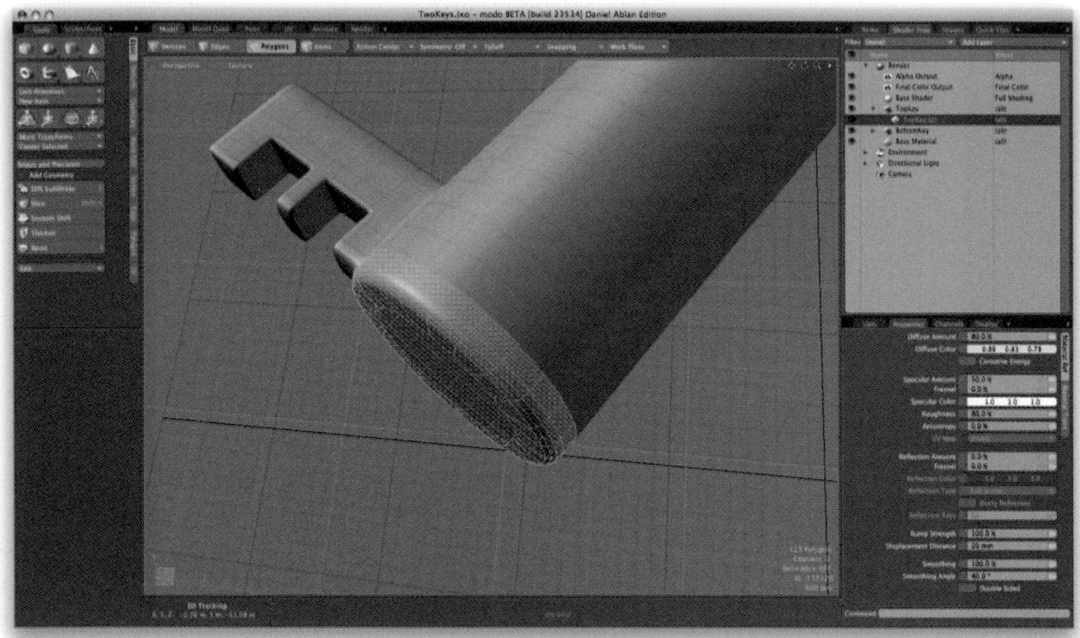

Figure 8.8 The end of the top key's polygons are selected.

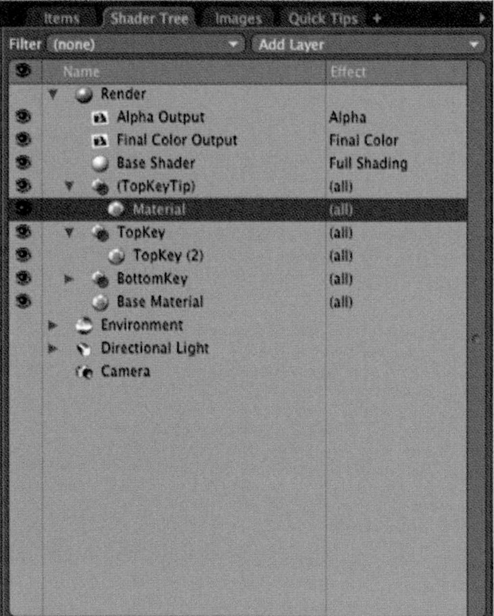

Figure 8.9 Once the selected polygons have a mask applied, a new material name appears in the Shader Tree.

3. Take a close look at the key in the viewport. Notice that the tip is now a default white color again, and does not retain the original surface properties you set. This is because the new polygon mask overrides the original one you created. However, this is only because it is sitting on top of the original surface in the Shader Tree. If you drag it below the Item Mask, then you'd lose the color.

The problem now is that, even though you have an additional material for a specifically controlled surface, you have a sharp crease between the two. Ideally, you'd want the tip material to blend with the rest of the key material. The goal is to create just a variance in the texture to make the key look a little worn at the tip. The way you can blend this tip is by adding a vertex mask.

Vertex Masks

Taking the masking information down one more level, you come to the vertex mask. You can add a vertex map texture layer—but it's not a mask like an item mask or a polygon material mask. It's just a texture layer within one of these masks, and you can set the layer to any effect (including layer mask and group mask). But it's not a mask in and of itself. It's actually just a texture layer. It's important to note that a layer mask and group mask are different than item and polygon masks. This particular mask will allow you to blend the tip of the key and any surfaces you apply to the rest of the key.

1. In the viewport, switch to the Edges selection mode, then carefully select the edge at the top of the tip selection (see Figure 8.10).

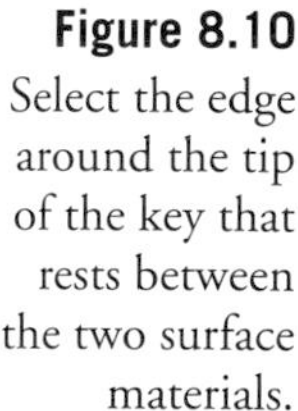

Figure 8.10
Select the edge around the tip of the key that rests between the two surface materials.

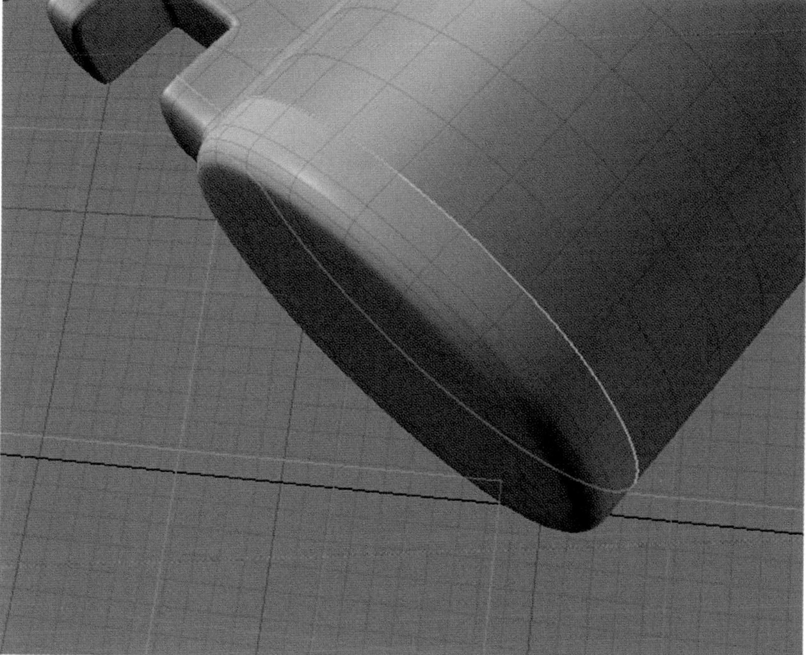

2. Under the Shader Tree tab and to the left of the Properties tab, you'll see the Lists tab. Select it to view the contents. Expand the Weight Maps listing, and underneath the Subdivision listing, choose New Map. The Create New Vertex Map dialog box will appear, as shown in Figure 8.11.

Figure 8.11
You can create a new vertex map for selected vertices and edges within the New Vertex Map dialog box.

3. Set the Vertex Map Name to KeyTipWeight, and Click OK.
4. Change your modo viewport to the Render tab at the top of the viewport. Press Shift and the a key to fit the selection to view. Rotate the camera view if needed.
5. Then, change the viewport style in either the Perspective view or Camera view to Vertex Map. The items in your scene will appear as a flat green color, as shown in Figure 8.12. This color represents the weight applied, and the flat color refers to a neutral value.
6. With the edge still selected in the viewport, select the Weight tool from the Vertex Map drop-down menu at the top of the interface. Or you can simply press Shift and the w key to activate it.
7. Click and drag to the right in the Vertex Map shaded viewport. You should see the selected edges' surrounding areas become red, as shown in Figure 8.13.
8. A red color means that the weight applied to this edge is a positive value. If you click and drag to the left, the weight turns blue and is a negative value. For now, press the k key to call up the numeric entry for the Weight tool, and make sure it's set to 100%.
9. Taking a look at the preview window in the Render Tri view still shows the white tip with a hard edge to the rest of the key. That's because, although you've created a weight map for the selected vertices, you've not applied it anywhere.

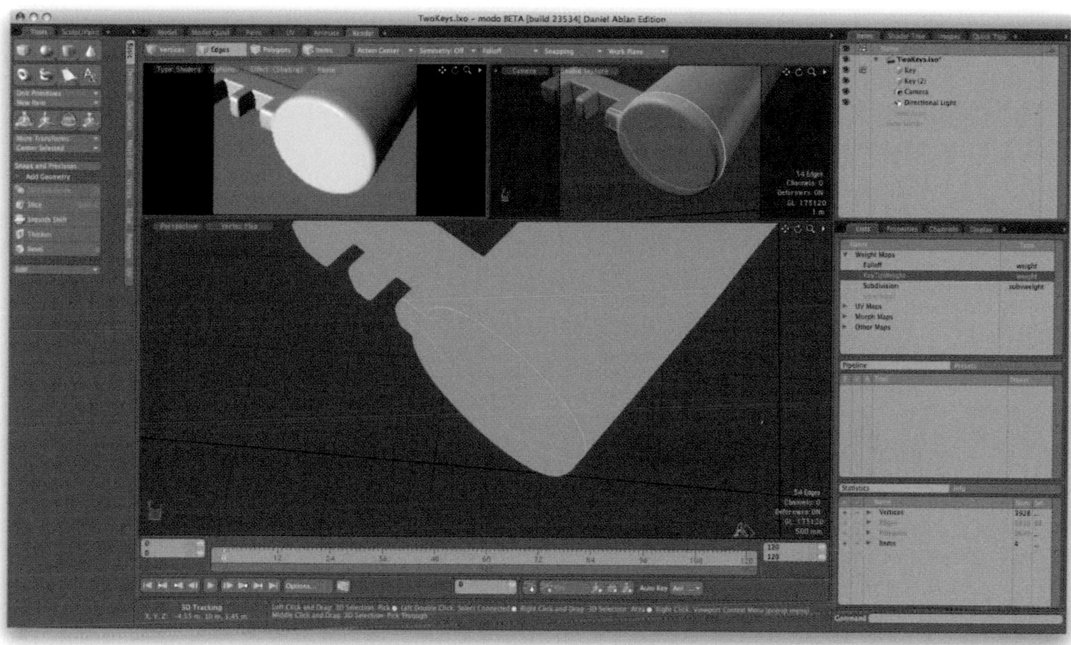

Figure 8.12 Change your viewports to a Render tab, and also make one viewport a Vertex Map style for shading.

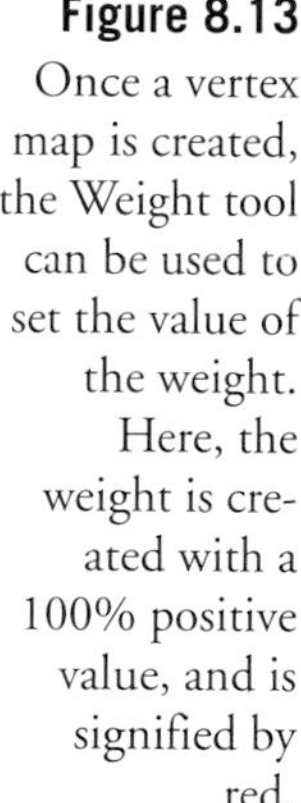

Figure 8.13 Once a vertex map is created, the Weight tool can be used to set the value of the weight. Here, the weight is created with a 100% positive value, and is signified by red.

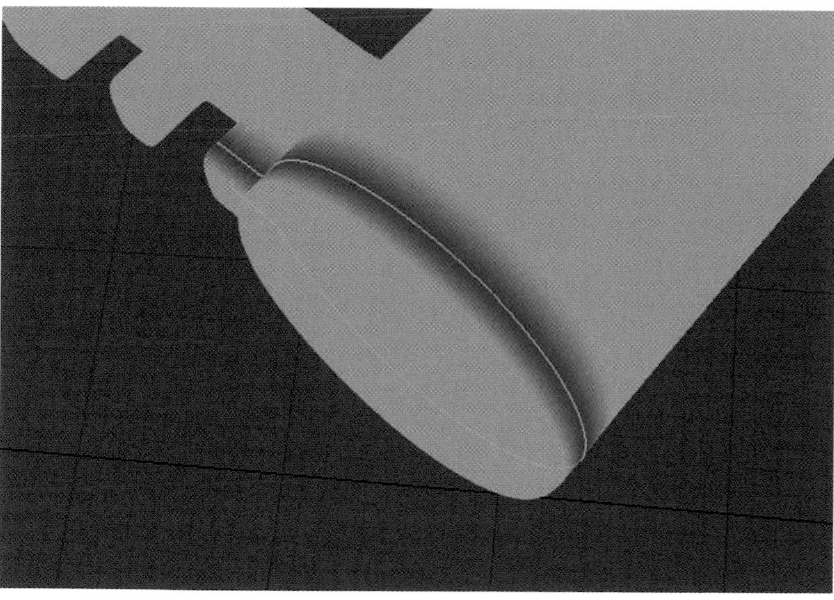

10. Over in the Shader Tree, select the TopKeyTip group, and then from the Add Layer drop-down list at the top of the Shader Tree, select Weight Map Texture. Figure 8.14 shows the setup, along with the preview window. Notice how the tip is now black, except for the weighted edge, which is white.

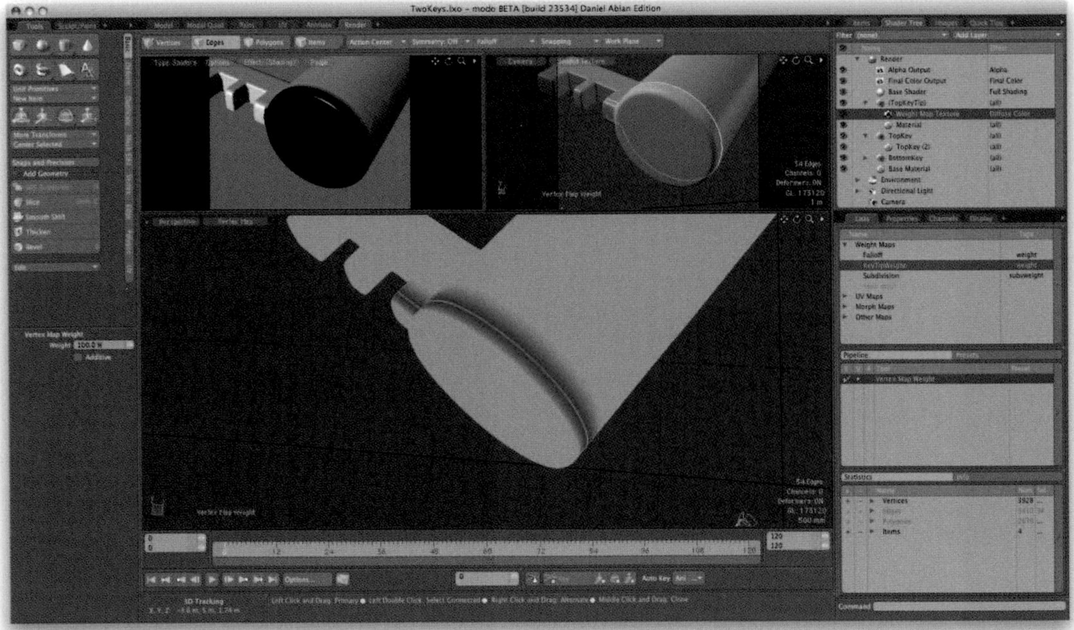

Figure 8.14 Once a weight map texture is applied in the Shader Tree, the material starts to change but does not yet blend.

11. The new weight map texture doesn't blend into the key just yet because its effect is set to Diffuse Color in the Shader Tree. Right-click on this effect listing and change the weight map texture to Group Mask. What you'll now see is that the tip of the key is the same color as the rest of the key, but the edge between the two sets of materials is colored a soft white (see Figure 8.15). This soft white is the vertex mask. But there's a little more to do.

12. Make sure Weight Map Texture is selected in the Shader Tree. By having this material layer selected, additional materials added will be placed directly above. From the Add Layer drop-down menu, select Noise to add a noise layer to the TopKeyTip group. You can see from Figure 8.16 that the noise material layer is concentrated within the edge weight.

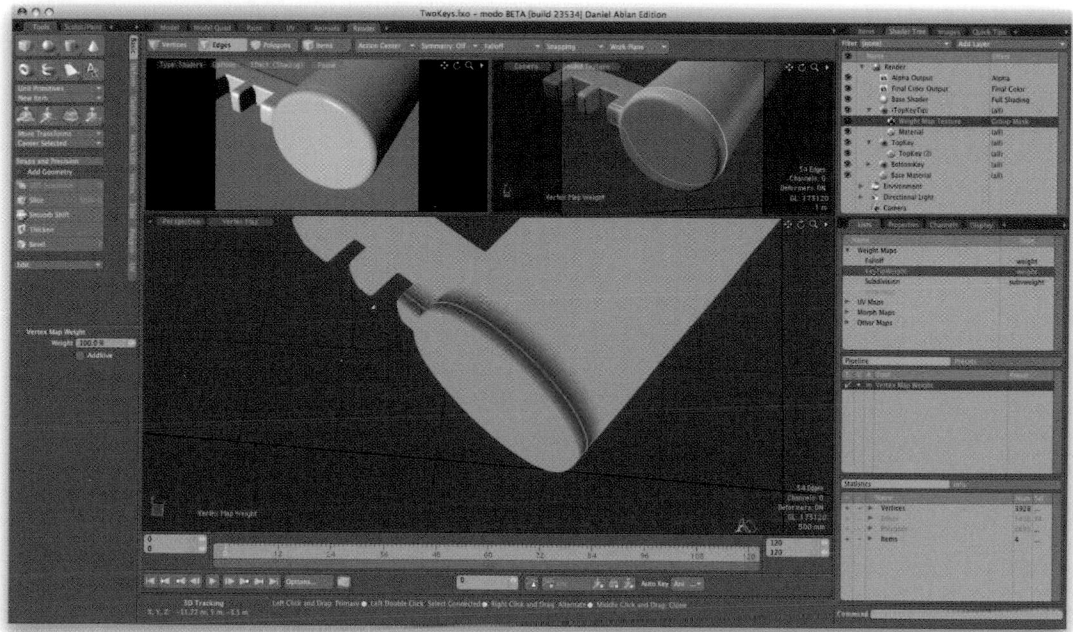

Figure 8.15 As a group mask, the weight map texture applied now uses the vertex mask to blend the materials.

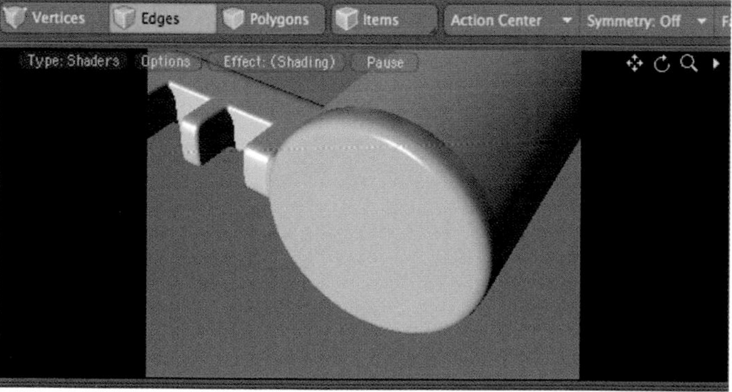

Figure 8.16 Adding a noise layer doesn't exactly get applied to the tip of the key when applied above the Weight Map Texture listing.

13. Select Weight Map Texture, and in the Properties panel, making sure you're in the Texture Layer vertical tab, change Value 1 to 100% and Value 2 to 0%. This essentially inverts the values of the weight map texture. And yes, you could have simply checked the Invert box at the top of the panel. However, it's important to know what you're inverting first. Figure 8.17 shows the noise channel now applied to the tip of the key but blended nicely into the main key material.

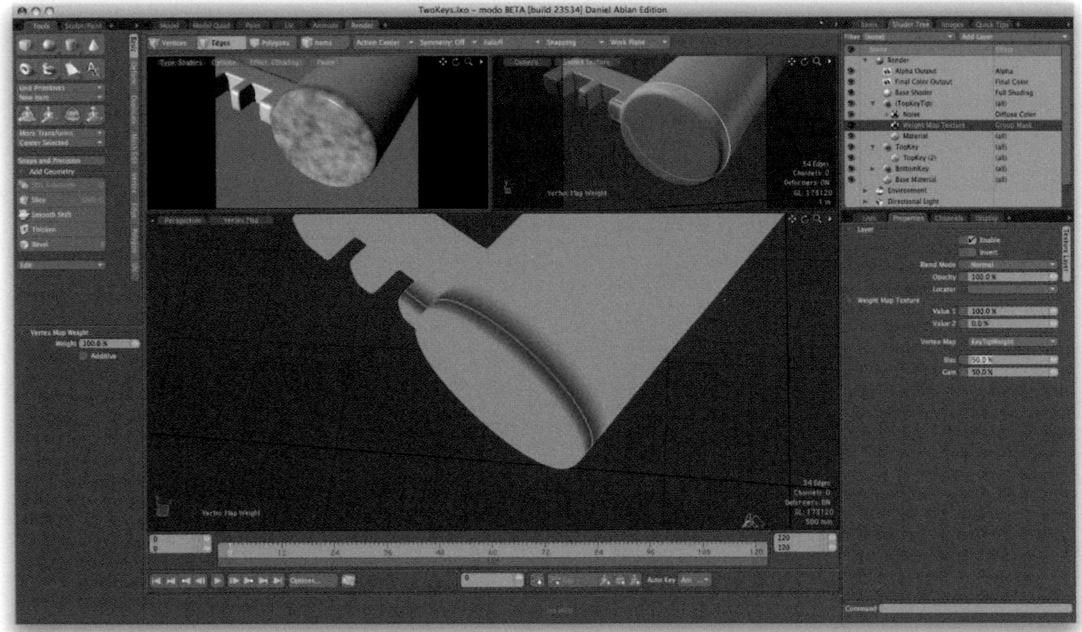

Figure 8.17 Once the Weight Map Texture values are changed, the noise channel blends well with the key materials.

You might ask why you would create two separate masks for the keys if all you were going to do was copy and paste the material settings. That's a good question! You are creating two masks to separate the noise channel, which blends into the tip of the key. However, it still needs a little adjustment. One more thing, you can vary the Vertex Map Weight amount to see the difference in how it blends. Perhaps something around 60% will blend better than 100%. Try it out!

Additional Material Layers

You can see that by weighting the vertices and applying a weight map texture in the Shader Tree, two masks are blended together—an item mask and a polygon mask. With this setup, you can add in any additional materials you like, such as the noise layer you've already added. But this is just the beginning.

1. In the TopKeyTip group in the Shader Tree, select the Material listing. Its Diffuse Color setting is still at its default state of 1.0, 1.0, 1.0, or white. In order to successfully blend the tip of the key with the rest of the mesh, set this base color to the same beige color you applied earlier for the rest of the key. If you're not sure, select the Material listing for either the top or bottom key. You can also just right-click on the top or bottom key Material listing, select Copy, and then select the key tip material; right-click again, and select Paste.

2. Once the key tip material's Diffuse Color option is set, select the noise layer. In the Properties tab, click the Texture Layer vertical tab. Then change Blend Mode to Hard Light. Color 1 should be 0,0,0, or just pure black. Set Color 2 to the same color as the material color, or beige.
3. Finally, change the Type setting to Turbulence. For the other settings, they should be 4 for Frequencies, 2.0 for Frequency Ratio, 0.2 for Amplitude Ratio, and 50% for both Bias and Gain. Figure 8.18 shows the settings and results. Looks a bit like rust, doesn't it?

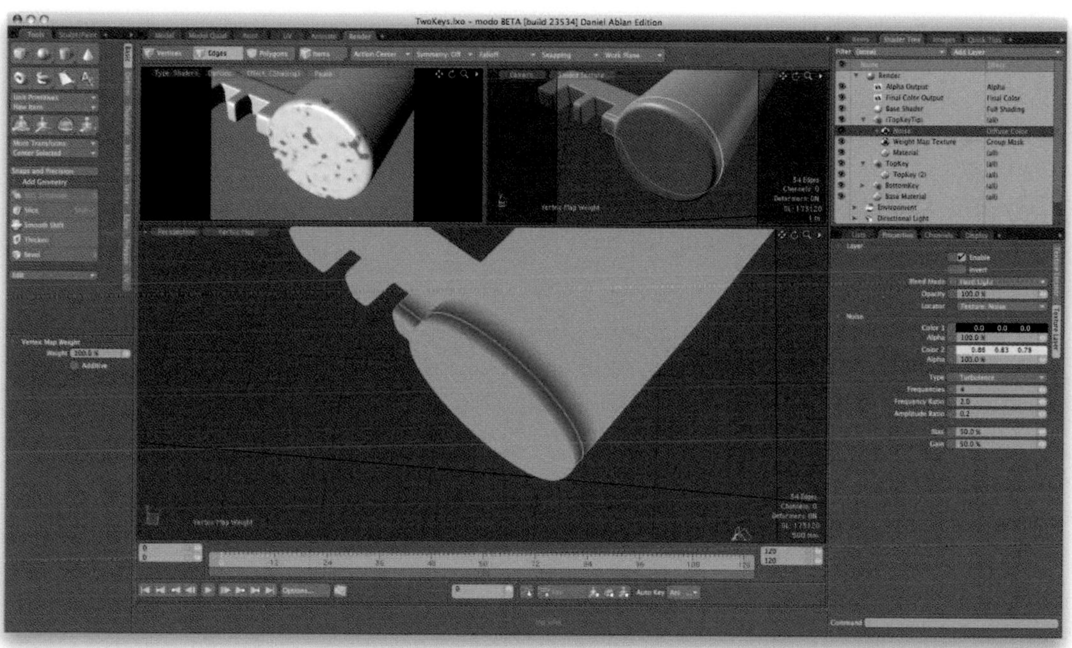

Figure 8.18 Change a few color values and the Blend Mode setting, and they result in a swell looking rust!

> **Note**
>
> Bias will affect the texture to favor the primary color value when setting a positive amount. Setting a negative amount will tell the texture to favor the secondary value. The values here are Value 1 and Value 2, the two colors you just set. Gain, on the other hand, is like a gamma control, which affects the falloff between the two values. A 0% value is a soft falloff, whereas a 100% value is a sharp falloff. You can experiment with these values in the Render tab (or open a preview window by pressing F8) and see the results.

4. With the noise layer values set, save your scene. Then, with the noise layer still selected, right-click on it and choose Create Instance. An *instance* is like a copy or duplicate, but without taxing your system as much as a copy. An instance references the original item, similar to a clone. An instance will be italicized.
5. Select the noise instance after it's created, then right-click on the Effect value in the Shader Tree, changing Diffuse Color to Bump.
6. Select the Material listing for the TopKeyTip, and change Bump Strength to 200%. You might think that because this material is at the bottom of this group, it affects everything above it. But the only reason it affects everything above it is because there's nothing above it. If a channel above it were set to Bump Strength, the material bump strength channel would be overwritten. Plus, there is no way to map bump strength anyway—it's just a multiplier of the values in the Bump texture maps. And because you now set the noise channel (the instance) to Bump, this material value will be applied.

You can see that once you apply a texture layer, you can quickly copy it by making an instance of it, then change a few values and enhance the shading on your model even further. Quite honestly, the possibilities are endless. You'll come back to more shading soon, as you move on to more advanced projects. But first, read on to learn more about groups in modo.

Groups

A group in the Shader Tree contains your material masks, such as the TopKeyTip you just finished surfacing. But what would happen if you or your client wanted this same surface applied to the rest of the key, perhaps with a slight variation? Certainly, you can copy and paste all the values, and on many occasions, you will. However, you can also use groups, which not only allow you the control to make variations to multiple surfaces at one time while still tweaking individual ones, but it also helps keep you organized. Using a group, you'll be able to apply the same surfacing from the tip of the key to the entire key and make adjustments to each.

1. In the Shader Tree, select the Render listing. Choose Group from the Add Layer drop-down menu. This adds a group to the top of the Shader Tree.
2. Ctrl-select the TopKey, BottomKey, and TopKeyTip material groupings.
3. When selected, press Ctrl-g to group them. Figure 8.19 shows the setup.
4. Next, expand the TopKeyTip material listings and select the Noise material listing. Right-click on it and select Duplicate. This will create a Noise(3) layer (the third Noise layer in the scene) in the Shader Tree.

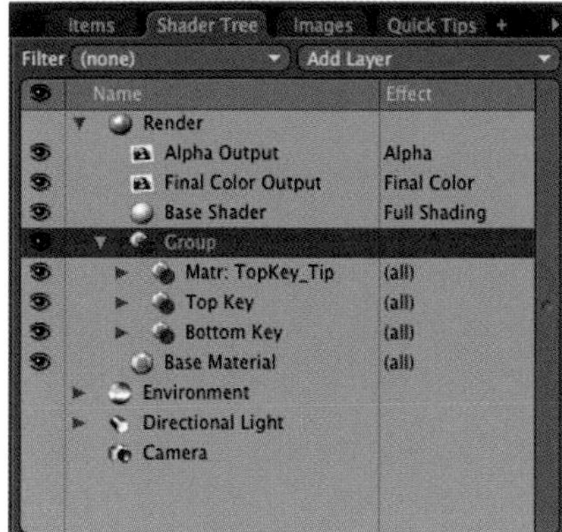

Figure 8.19 Create groups for your materials by selecting and pressing Ctrl-g.

5. As you build and create within the Shader Tree, it's important to stay organized. Groups are helpful for this, so click and drag the Noise(3) material layer up into the new group. Each material, however, can still vary, such as the key tip—it has a texture that falls off due to the group mask. Figure 8.20 shows the change.

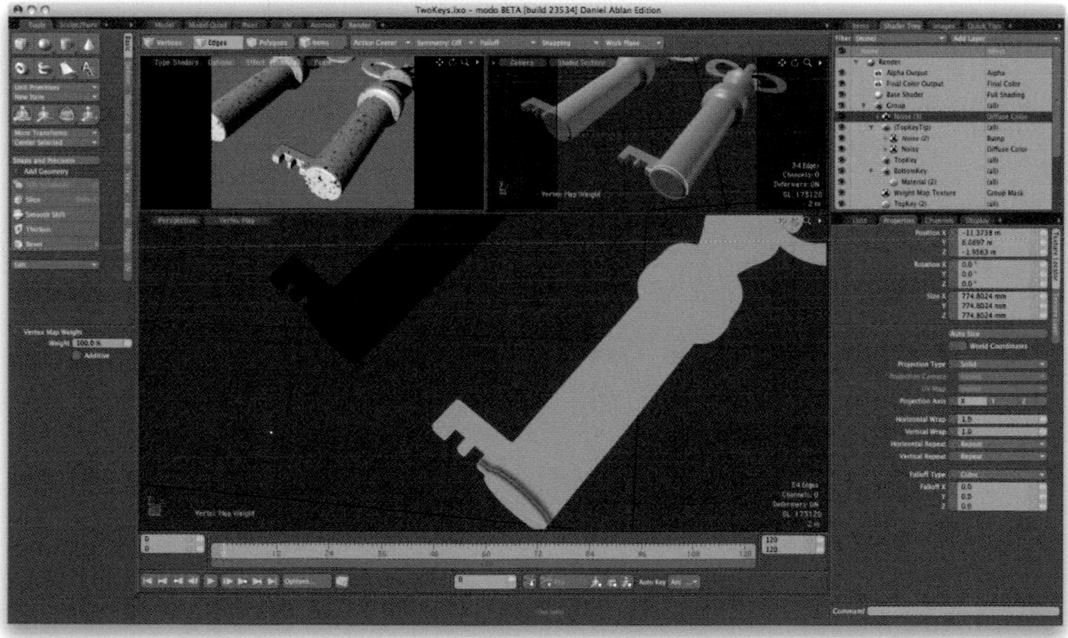

Figure 8.20 The new group is important for organization.

Tip

It's always a good idea to name your material layers, especially after you're starting to duplicate them. You can do this by right-clicking on them and choosing Rename.

6. Because the new noise channel lives above everything else in the group, whatever material you place here blankets the other materials by default. The TopKeyTip noise material was originally set to Diffuse Color for its effect value. By copying this noise channel, you've doubled up on the color for the tip. To fix this, change the Noise(3) effect value by right-clicking and selecting Diffuse Amount.
7. Now let's say you want to wash some additional values over the entire key. The easy way to do this is to add a new material layer from Add Layer menu in the Shader Tree. Select the Cellular material. Then, move it up to the top of the group. You'll see your original surfaces completely covered by the new material, as shown in Figure 8.21. You can see the difference in the Render Preview window at the top left of the interface.

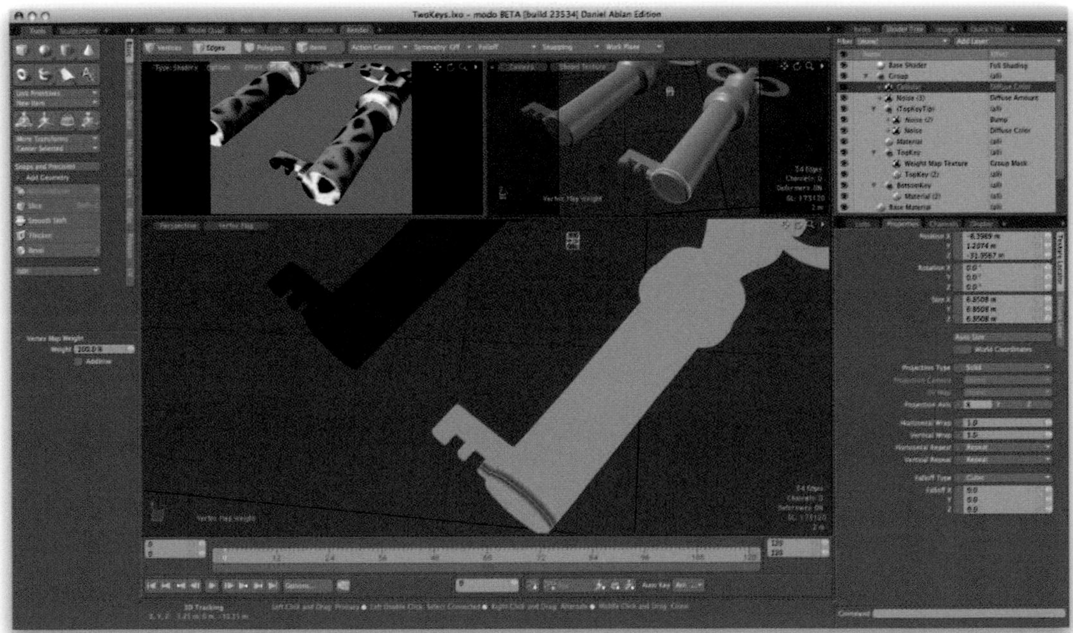

Figure 8.21 A new Cellular material placed at the top of the group overrides every other material!

8. The newly created Cellular texture blankets all other materials because its default effect value is set to Diffuse Color. The noise channels are doing a good job of mucking up the key, so how about making the Cellular texture just some added dirt? You can do this by changing its Blend Mode setting. With the Cellular material selected, change Blend Mode to Multiply in the Texture Layer vertical tab of the Properties panel.
9. Next, change the Cell Color values to a soft brown, but leave Filler Color at white, its default.
10. Change the Type setting to Round for a more dotted appearance. Increase the Cell Width value to about 45% and Transition Width to 90%. Figure 8.22 shows the changes.
11. Click over to the Texture Locator vertical tab in the Properties panel, and change the size to 6 m for the X, Y, and Z axes. Figure 8.23 shows the change.

From this point on, you can vary the existing materials for the keys, such as bringing down the opacity for the Noise(3) and Cellular materials in the main group's Properties tab. This will help soften the look. And by all means, play with these settings to come up with something on your own!

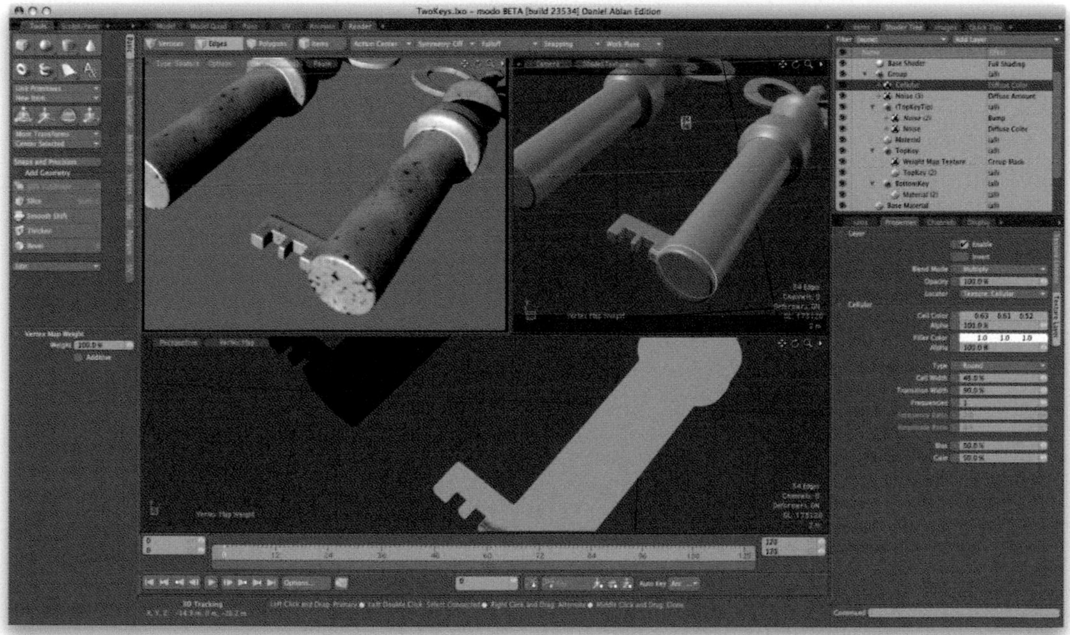

Figure 8.22 After a few changes to the Cellular material in the Properties panel, the added stains to the key are beginning to take shape.

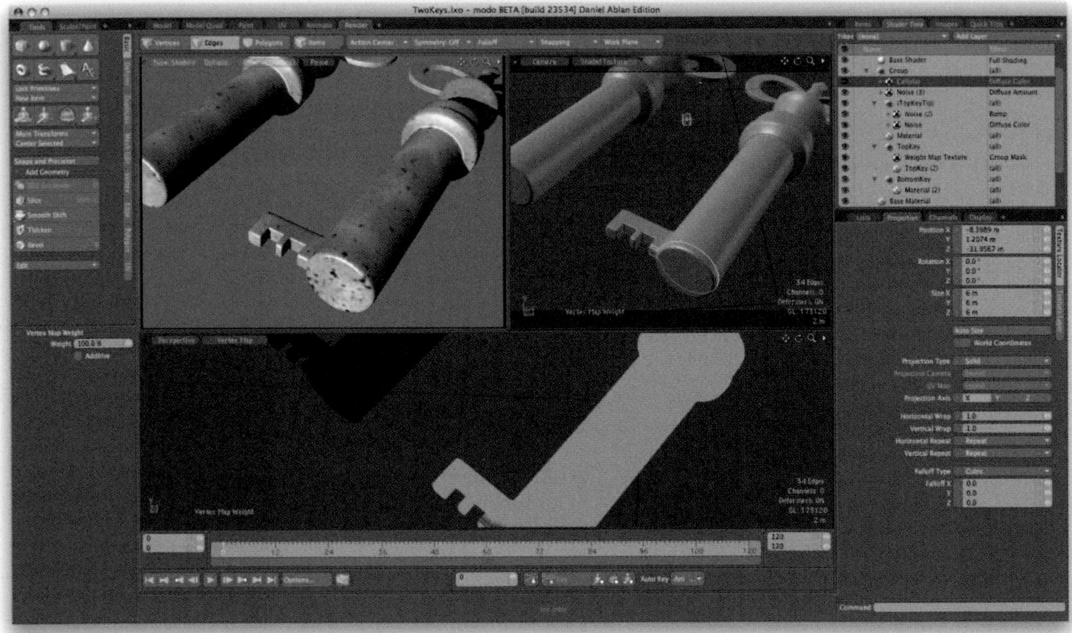

Figure 8.23 By simply increasing the size of the Cellular material, the effect of added dirt is now visible on the keys.

The Next Phase

The information within this chapter gave you a good overview of the types of masking capabilities in modo. The Shader Tree is a powerful feature and, although it appears simple, it can be very complex. The tutorials you've just read through are effective for many projects you will encounter in your modo career. But, alas, there is so much more to learn, grasshopper! The keys in this chapter can be surfaced in a number of ways, and the methods shown here are just a few examples. These methods were also chosen to demonstrate techniques, such as setting up a vertex map to blend different masks.

To go even further, there is a 70-minute video tutorial provided for you on the book's disc, covering modeling, shading, and rendering of the keys used in this chapter. Feel free to watch those when you have a moment to learn some additional techniques.

Now, move on to Chapter 9, where you'll learn about animation in modo. From there, the fun continues when you will start painting and sculpting textures directly onto your models.

9

Animating in modo

One of the most anticipated features of modo 301 is animation. And, as promised, the team at Luxology delivered in this first software release the ability to put items in motion. But modo's animation capabilities go far beyond just moving a camera and an object. This chapter will not only introduce you to the concepts of animating in modo, but also provide you with the understanding of what can be animated and how.

Animation Basics

The animation capabilities in modo are more powerful than they appear. That is to say, while this first iteration of animation in modo is basic keyframing, the flipside is that you can keyframe just about everything. This is something other programs that have been around for many years still lack. To begin your learning, you'll first take a quick peek at the animation tools, then go through a simple project to get your move on.

Interface and Controls

Opening up modo for either modeling or animation is a no-brainer. There are no secondary modules to install, nor are their different versions of the software to animate. You see, some 3D animation programs over the years have offered a basic version, where you can model and perhaps use limited animation. Some are offered to you in two different programs, while others serve up their wares a la carte. But modo is different. If you've used modo 101 or 201, running modo 301 doesn't look all that different, does it? You see, the programmers thought long and hard about how to integrate future elements and future tools. They didn't want to be like the others, and their core system is designed in such a way that they can add features with complete and full integration.

And by full integration, we're not talking about a plug-in that pops open a panel. Rather, we are talking about integration that means a new set of tools and controls for your creative pleasure. With that said, fire up modo and click the Animate tab at the top of the interface. Figure 9.1 shows the view.

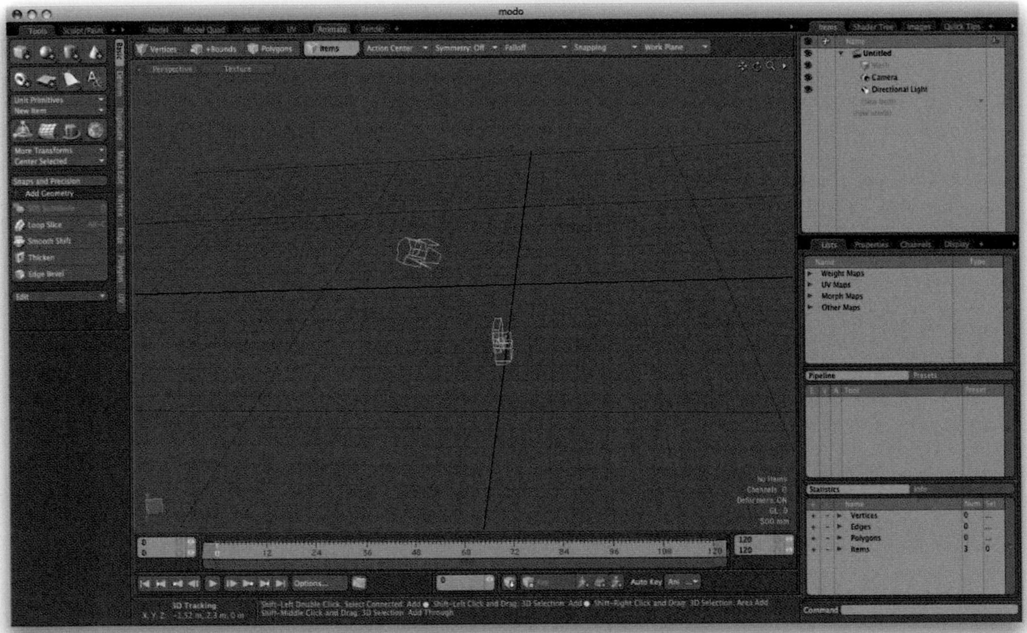

Figure 9.1 To begin using the animation tools in modo 301/302, click the Animate tab at the top of the interface.

You'll see that in the Animate tab, the full interface doesn't look that much different than the rest of the program, except for one area. Take a look at the modo timeline at the bottom of the interface, as shown in Figure 9.2.

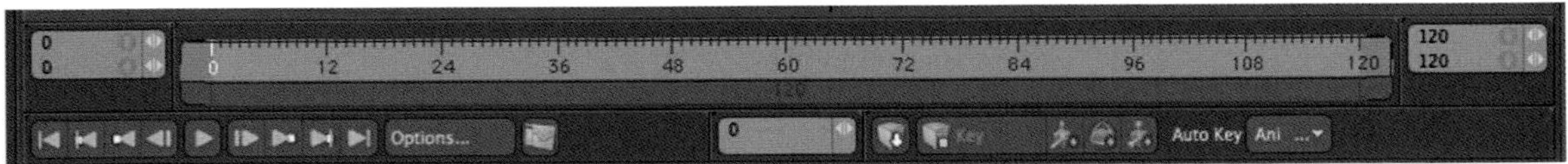

Figure 9.2 The modo timeline offers more features than you might think.

On the left and right of the timeline, you'll see double sets of numbers, which might appear confusing at first. Figures 9.3 and 9.4 show these numeric areas. What are they, you ask? You've probably clicked on them and were not quite sure how they work.

Figure 9.3 The first frame value for the modo animation timeline.

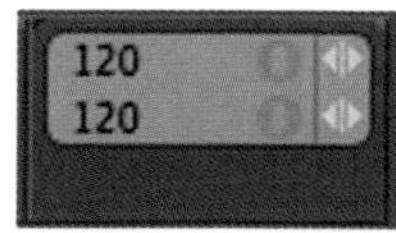

Figure 9.4 The last frame value for the modo animation timeline.

The numbers on the left represent the first frame of your animation timeline. The numbers on the right represent the last frame of your timeline. These two values are the top set of numbers. Figure 9.5 shows the timeline in full with the first frame set to 0 and the last frame to 120.

Figure 9.5 The full modo 301/302 timeline with first and last frames set.

The bottom set of numbers in the left and right regions represent the preview. So, for example, your full animation is 300 frames, or 10 seconds if you're rendering at 30 frames per second. But let's say you only want to preview about 40 frames in the center of your animation. You can set the preview value by entering in the numbers. Figure 9.6 shows the same timeline with a 300-frame animation and the preview set to 40 frames in the middle of the animation.

Figure 9.6 Using the modo timeline, you can set a preview region.

Take a closer look at the bottom of the timeline in Figure 9.6, and you'll see a small scrub bar that reads 40. This is the preview bar, and not only can you click and drag it to view 40 other frames in the animation as a preview, but you can also simply click and drag ends of the bar to change the value. Double-clicking on either end jumps the value to its starting and ending values.

Beneath the timeline itself are the animation controls with common playback icons, like Rewind, Play, Next Frame, Last Frame, and so on (see Figure 9.7).

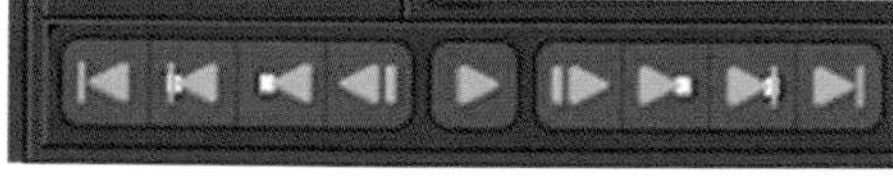

Figure 9.7 The animations you create can be controlled through the playback icons beneath the timeline.

Centered in the timeline is an input value area that shows the current frame. Simply, this allows you to set your timeline to a specific number. You can enter the value, click and drag the arrows to the right, or even just click in the timeline to change the current frame. Figure 9.8 shows an arbitrary position at frame 95.

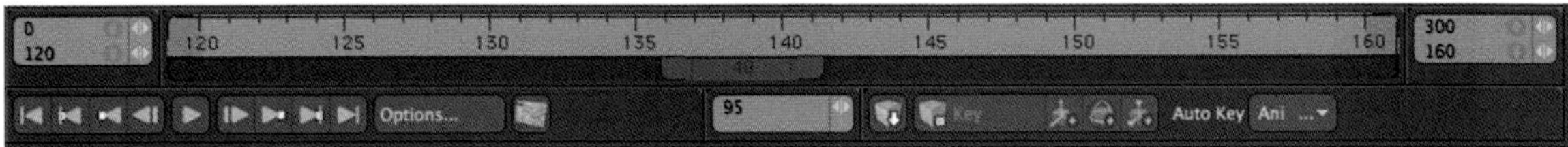

Figure 9.8 The frame area at the center bottom of the timeline not only displays the current frame, but it also allows you to jump to a desired frame.

To the right of the current frame value are your keyframe controls. Here, you can create a keyframe, drop selected channels, or create specific transformation keyframes (see Figure 9.9). In a moment, you'll learn about keyframes and how they are used in modo 301/302.

Figure 9.9 The keyframe controls within the modo timeline are your tools for creating and dropping selected channels.

There's one more area to show, and that's the Options button. You'll find this to the left of the current value area. When you click the Options button, a small panel will appear, as shown in Figure 9.10, that allows you to set the current timeline value, the full scene value, the time format (such as SMPTE time code or film time format), as well as the frames per second of your animation. You can also open the Graph Editor, which is opened by clicking the small envelope icon to the right of the Options button. You'll learn about the Graph Editor a little later in this chapter.

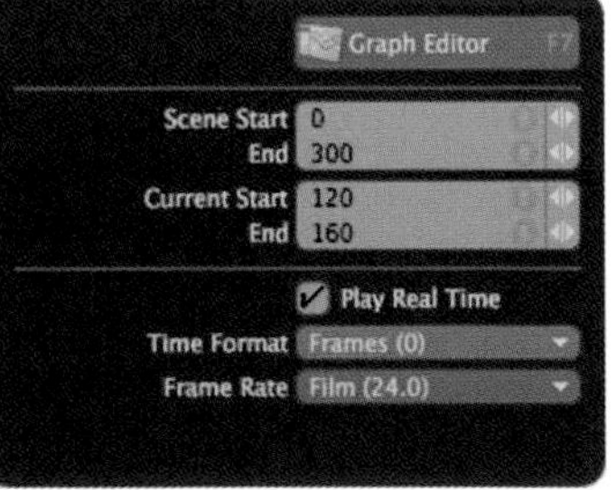

Figure 9.10 Clicking the Options button in modo's timeline offers more specific control over timing and keyframes.

Channel Keyframes

As mentioned earlier, modo 301/302 offers basic keyframing, most of which is controlled through the timeline. However, there are other areas where you can set keyframes. Figure 9.11 shows the Camera listing selected in the Items tab, along with the Properties tab selected. Take a closer look at the areas just to the left of the input values.

The small dots to the left of the values throughout modo represent keyframeable values. Figure 9.12 shows a close-up view of the Position and Rotation values for the selected camera. Position X and Rotation Y are selected, which tells modo that you want to keyframe those selected values.

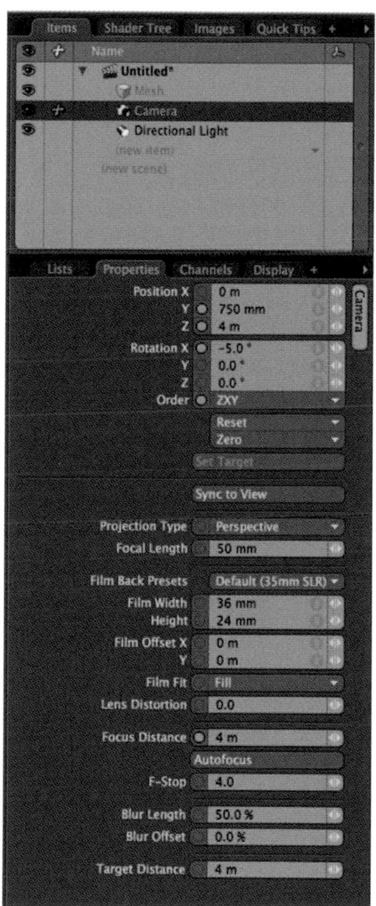

Figure 9.11 While the timeline offers global keyframe control, you can specifically determine keyframes for many values throughout modo.

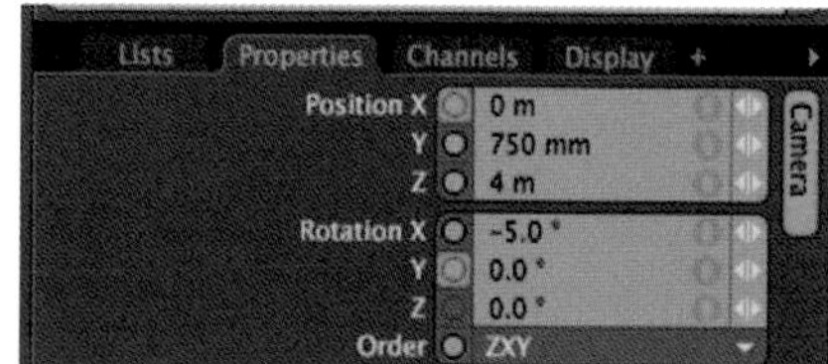

Figure 9.12 With Position X and Rotation Y selected in the Properties panel, you're telling modo that you want to keyframe those values.

Keyframing a Position or Rotation value allows you to put things in motion. But let's say you set a keyframe for Focal Length. What would that do? Well, if the focal length is how wide or zoomed in the modo camera is, setting a keyframe would allow you to animate this property. So again, anywhere you see these dots, that particular value is keyframeable.

Lastly, hold your mouse over one of those dots to the left of a property value. A legend will come up explaining the various options for setting keyframes. Figure 9.13 shows an example.

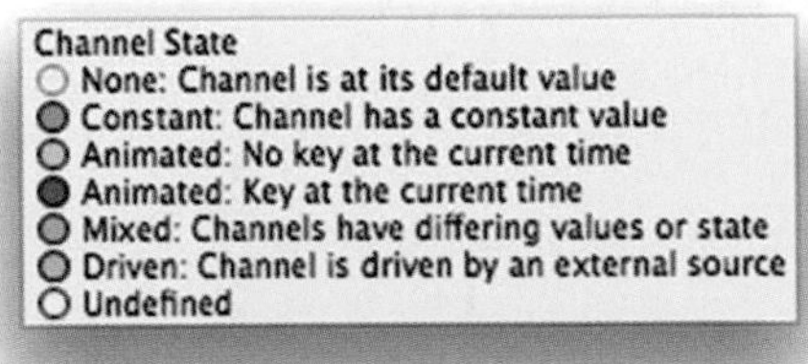

Figure 9.13
Hold your mouse over a keyframe channel (the dot to the left of an input value) and a legend will appear, offering the various keyframe states.

The legend that appears includes the various channel keyframing states: None, Constant, Animated (with no key at the current time), Animated (with key at the current time), Mixed, Driven, or Undefined. The example of two keys set in Figure 9.12 is orange, which simply means they are selected. As you click on the keyframe circle, you will toggle through the keyframe channel states. (These different colors represent the keyframe states as you just saw in Figure 9.13.) As you do so, you will see the color of the dot change. However, the next section, which discusses keyframes, will show you a more practical example of how these channel keyframes work.

Understanding Keyframing

You might be new to animation, and since the term *keyframe* has been mentioned so many times already, you're probably wondering what the heck it is. In generic terms, a keyframe tells a selected item (such as the camera) to be at a specific place or position at a specific point in time. But more specifically, setting a keyframe is telling modo to set a value for a selected channel at a specific time. You'll set up your own keyframes in a moment.

It's important to understand that setting keyframes in modo is more than just moving and rotating an object over time. It's also about setting channel values. Let's say you want an object's color to change from red to blue as it spins and moves across the screen. You set keyframes for that value. Perhaps you want the camera to quickly zoom into an animated race car. To do so, you would set a keyframe for the Focus Distance value.

Follow along with this project to put an object in motion.

1. The easiest way to get working with animation in modo is to do so with a simple object. With an empty scene, hold the Shift key and click the Torus primitive from the Basic vertical tab of the Tools tab. This will create a donut-like object in its own mesh layer. Press the a key to fit the object to view, as shown in Figure 9.14.

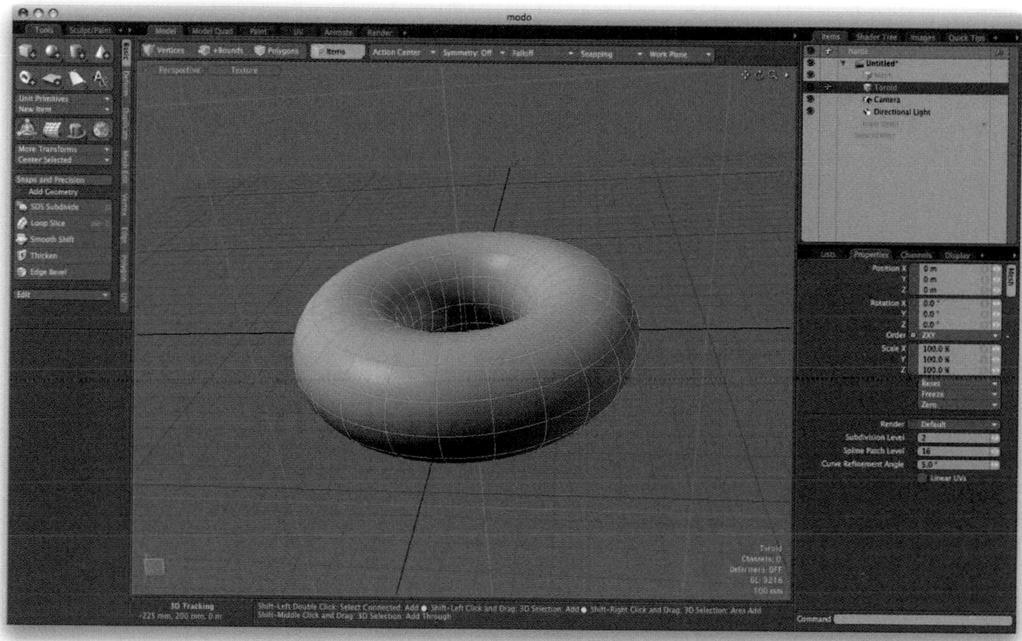

Figure 9.14 Load a Torus primitive, and get ready to set up your first animation.

2. To begin setting up this scene, you'll first animate just the torus itself. From there, you'll animate the camera. Press Shift and the spacebar at the same time to jump to Items mode.

3. Next, click on the torus in the viewport. This automatically selects the key in the Items tab. However, the torus might automatically become selected. The only other items in the scene are a light and a camera. Make sure the Properties tab is visible for the key so you can gain access to the Position and Rotation values. Figure 9.15 shows the selection.

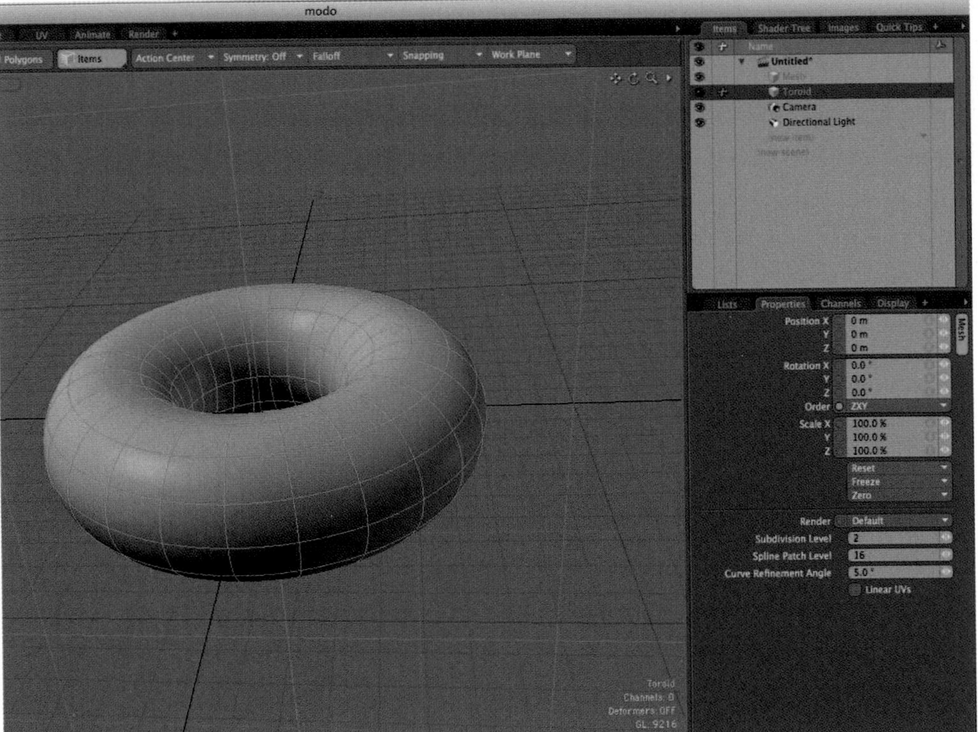

Figure 9.15
In Items mode, select the torus and open the properties for it.

4. It's important to remember that you must select the item in the Items tab that you wish to animate. Click over to the Animate tab at the top of the interface to see your timeline. Next, put a move on the item, from left to right. To do this, first make sure your timeline is set to 0. It should be by default, but to check, click and drag directly in the timeline until the small white line is at 0. You'll also see the current timeline value in the center display, located just beneath the timeline itself. Next, press the y key on your keyboard. This is a terrific tool to use for animating because it offers position, rotation, and scale all in one. However, you don't always want to use this tool because you don't always need to keyframe every value. And, as soon as you press the y key, you'll see the Position, Rotation, and Scale channels highlighted in red in the Properties tab. As described earlier, red signifies that the value is animated, with a key at the current time.
5. Grab the red arrow in the viewport to drag the torus to the left side of the screen, as shown in Figure 9.16.
6. Take a look at Figure 9.16 and notice the channels for the torus item in the Properties tab. They're all colored orange, which means they are selected, but the values, represented by the red dot, mean that a keyframe has been set. Figure 9.17 shows a close-up of the representation.

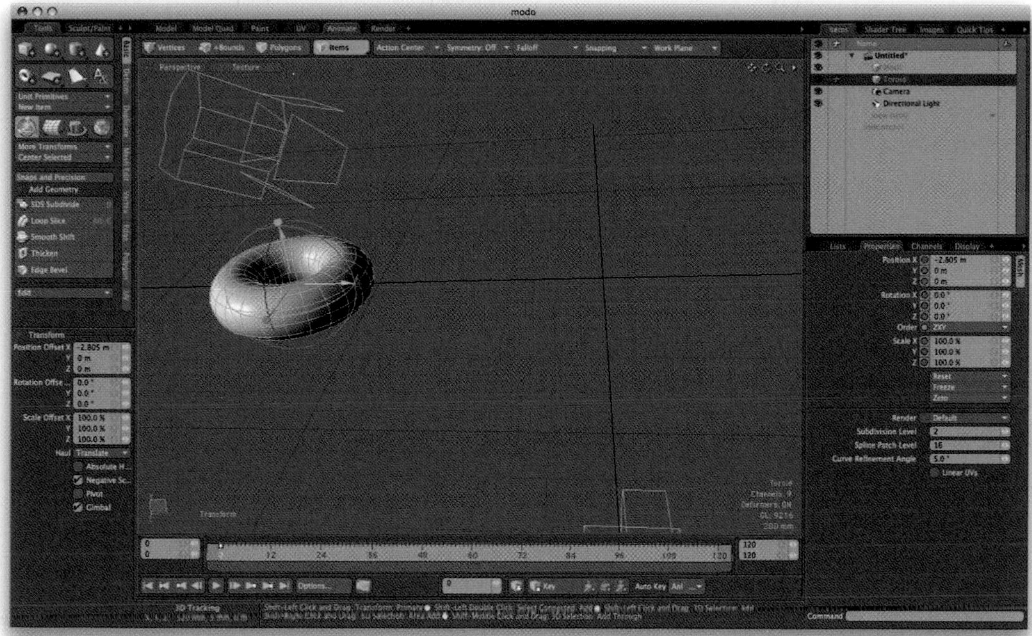

Figure 9.16 To begin a simple animation, use the Transform tool by pressing the y key and move the item over to the left side of the screen.

Figure 9.17 Selected values (orange) now have keyframcs set, represented by the red dot.

7. Now move your timeline slider to frame 60. Press w to choose the Transform tool to move the item. Before you do anything, look at the values in the Properties tab. The Rotation and Scale channels are no longer selected, but all the values are now represented with green dots (see Figure 9.18). Green means the value is animated, but no key is set. Think of a green dot as a green light—you're good to go but have not yet pressed the gas (the gas being a keyframe!). Click and drag the red handle for the X axis, and move the item to the right side of the interface, as shown in Figure 9.19. Notice that the channels for Position turn red.

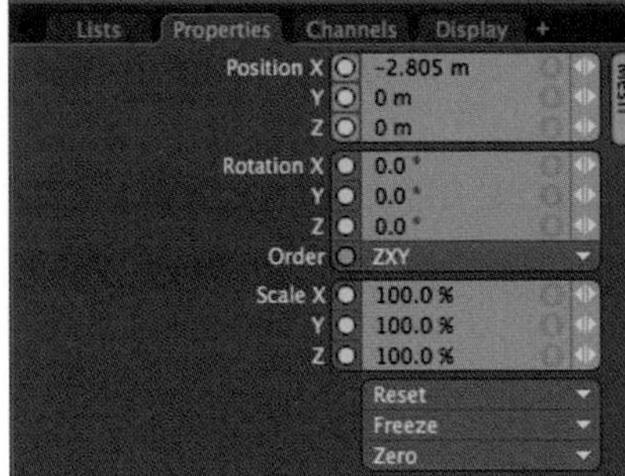

Figure 9.18 When you use the Transform tool, only the Position values are selected.

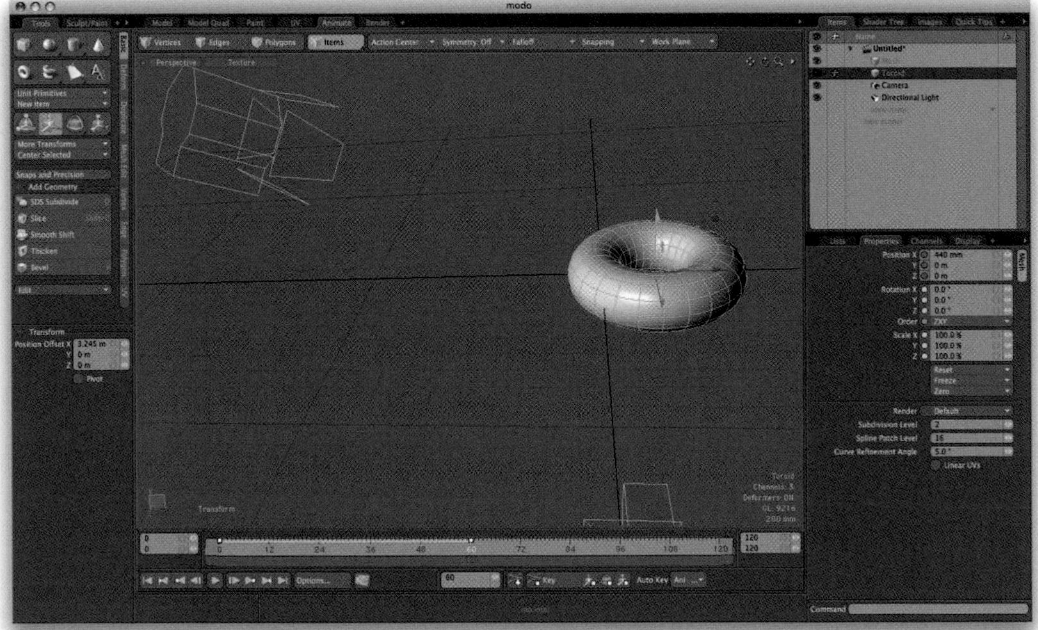

Figure 9.19 Movement at a new point in time is recorded as a keyframe.

The Position channels turn red to signify that a keyframe was created because, by default, Auto Key is set to Animated. This feature is found at the bottom of the interface, beneath the timeline. What this means is that the Animated option will auto-create keyframes when values are changed on previously keyframed channels. If All is selected, modo will create a keyframe on a channel any time the channel's value is changed, even if it has already been keyframed. Figure 9.20 shows the timeline with the two keyframes set at 0 and 60. You'll see that once these keyframes are set, a green line connects them.

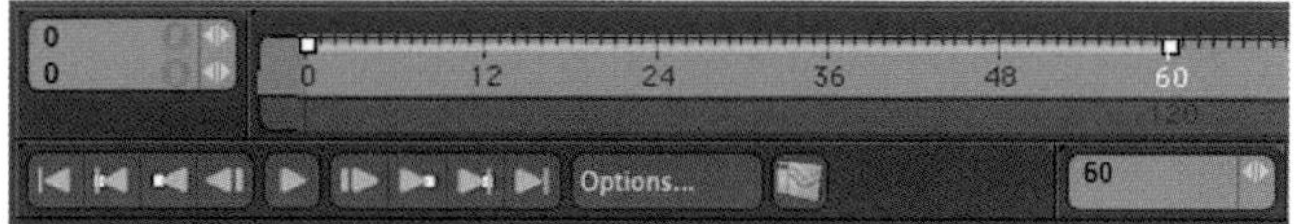

Figure 9.20 When more than one keyframe is created, a green line appears between them in the timeline.

8. Press the Play button at the bottom of the timeline, and you'll see the torus object move from left to right. Exciting, isn't it? It's like getting new teeth when you never had any! Okay, it's not that exciting, so let's spice it up a bit. Go to frame 30.

9. Press the e key to turn on the Rotate tool. You'll see the Rotation values become selected in the Properties panel with their values showing green. Figure 9.21 shows an example. Now rotate the torus on any particular axis.

10. Press the Play button to see the torus animate. It starts out at frame 0, where you first set it, and ends at frame 60. But now, instead of going left to right, it spins along the way, then sort of floats into the last keyframe. The reason for this is that your first and last keyframe had only Position channel keyframes, but the middle keyframe at frame 30 has keyframes set for just the rotational values. In the end, there is a constant motion from frame 0 to 60, with keyframes set to movement. Frame 30 does not have any keyframes set to movement, so the torus' motion is constant.

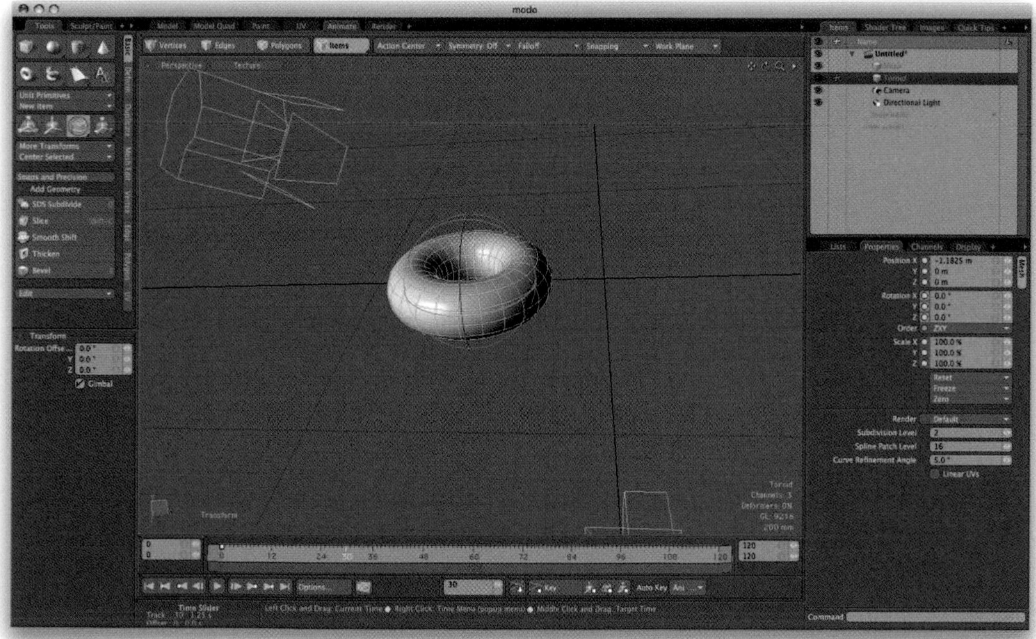

Figure 9.21 Because modo interpolates the motion between keyframes, you can add a keyframe in between the two existing keyframes for more motion.

11. You can experiment more, perhaps by adding more keyframes after frame 60. Let's say you wanted the item to sit for one second at frame 60 before it moves again. Simply create a keyframe at frame 90, with the item in the same position as it is at 60. Go to frame 90, select w for the Move tool, then click the Key button beneath the timeline.
12. You've now set four keyframes, telling the model to have three unique positions over 60 frames (or two seconds in time, using the NTSC video standard); one rotational change, and modo has interpolated the frames in between the keys. That's it! You're animating in modo.

When you play the animation, you might notice that the motion of the item isn't abrupt. It starts out smoothly, and ends the same way. This is because modo automatically adds an Ease In and Ease Out feature to those keyframes. It works great at the start and end frames, but there's too much slow-down in the middle. You can control this through the Graph Editor.

modo 301/302 Graph Editor

The Graph Editor in modo might seem confusing at first, but it's really not. It's where you can individually control all channels, keyframes, and the curves that make up their motions.

1. Click the envelope icon at the bottom of the interface to get to the Graph Editor, as shown in Figure 9.22.

Figure 9.22
Click the envelope icon at the bottom of the modo interface to open the Graph Editor.

2. Figure 9.23 shows the Graph Editor when opened. It looks harmless enough, right? In fact, it's downright boring! But wait, click the first channel for Position X in the left Channels column. Press the a key to fit all curves to view. Figure 9.24 shows the motion curve and keyframes for the selected X channel.
3. You'll see that the red channel, the selected Position X channel, is most prominent in the Graph Editor—you can see its keyframes selected directly on the curve and at the bottom of the timeline within the Graph Editor. You'll see the Position Y channel (green) and Position Z channel (blue) behind the Position X channel. To select them, hold the Ctrl key to select or deselect one value. Or hold the Shift key and with Position X already selected, click on Scale Z, and all channels in between will be selected. They're also visible and editable in the Graph Editor curve window, as show in Figure 9.25.

Figure 9.23
The Graph Editor upon opening.

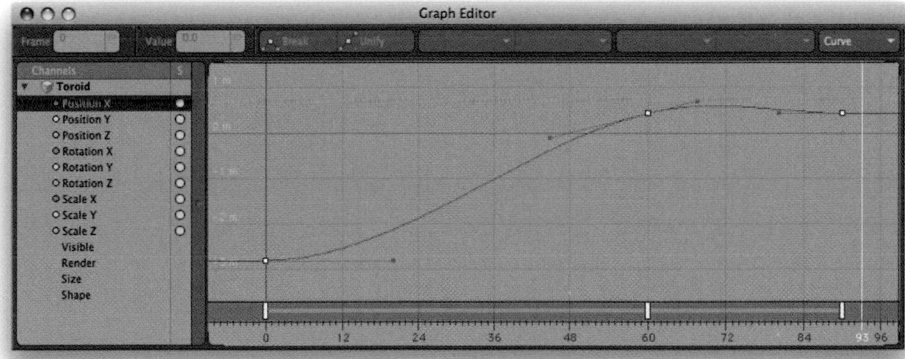

Figure 9.24
Once even a single channel is selected in the Graph Editor, the panel comes to life.

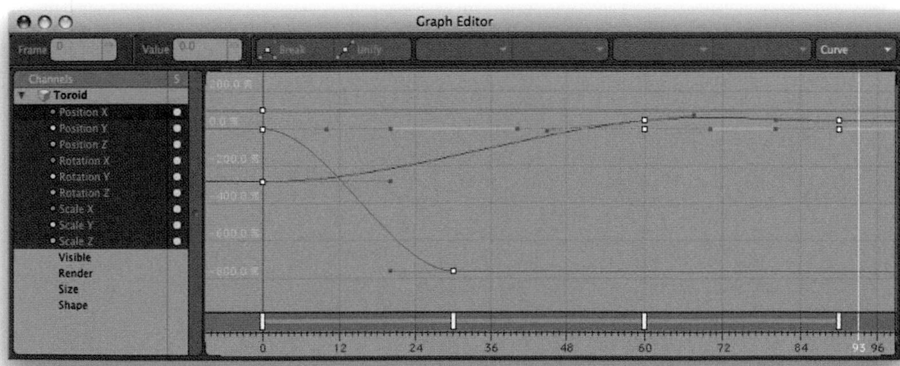

Figure 9.25
You can select and edit more than one channel at a time in the Graph Editor.

4. So let's say you don't like that the motion sort of hovers a bit between frames 60 and 90. You want the item to stay put during these frames. After all, you keyframed the exact position, so why isn't the motion static? It's because of the motion curve here in the Graph Editor. Click once on the key marker at the bottom of the Graph Editor for frame 90. This will select all the keys above it. This is good to do because you won't accidentally move a keyframe in the Graph Editor.
5. Once the keys are selected in the Graph Editor, some more options become available at the top of the panel. You'll see one button that says Slope:Auto. Change this to Manual. This will give you control handles, similar to Bezier curve handles. But it also helps even out the motion of the rotation key in between the two end keyframes. If you're in a hurry, select the keyframes for frame 60. Change the Slope option to Auto Flat. You'll then see the curve ease into frame 60 and then flatten out to frame 90, keeping your motion static. That's it! Animation done.

   You can select the other keys and change their incoming and outgoing curves, and then play the timeline to see your changes.

Animation in modo can be, and often is, much more complex than what's described here in these pages. However, the principles are the same. The Graph Editor can be quite powerful as well, so to help you understand these new features to the fullest, there are video tutorials on the book's DVD-ROM to help further demonstrate the topics in this chapter. You'll find them in the Chapter 9 folder of the Videos folder.

Before you read on, check out those videos, as you'll need to know how to use the animation features later in the book. Then, continue on to Chapter 10 for some hard-surface modeling techniques.

Part III

Working Projects

10

Hard-Surface Modeling

Part of modo's flexibility is the way it handles various tasks, such as hard-surface modeling in addition to organic type shapes. Hard-surface modeling is used for things like electronics, spacecrafts, machinery, and so on. This type of modeling may or may not use subdivision surfaces, but it relies on the use of edge weights and bevels for fine details.

This chapter will guide you through the creation of a realistic traffic light. You'll learn modeling techniques that can be applied to any number of objects you choose to model. In addition, you'll learn to combine the use of instances to build and control the finer details.

Working from References

To begin this project, you'll use references from photographs. Often, 3D artists feel that their work should be unique and that using photos is cheating. Quite the contrary, using photographs as a reference is the leading way that professional 3D artists build their creations. Does this mean that their work is not unique? Not at all. The photographic reference gives you the basis for your model. As much as you think you know what something should look like, you'll be able to create a better model when using a photo reference. The reference image is only the start of your model, as it helps you remember detailed aspects as well as proper proportions. From there, the model is all your own. Change the color, the style, and so on. This applies to modeling cars, furniture, or even characters. Whatever you create, make it your own.

The photo reference you'll be working with is shown in Figure 10.1. You can see in this image details in the glass and the proper curvature of the lens hood for each light, as

Figure 10.1 The stoplight you'll create in 3D will be based on this photograph.

well as the backside shape. Now, you don't need to model the stoplight exactly like this. In fact, it's good to change the model a bit, which you'll do in this tutorial. As stated, the picture is simply a reference to get started. And hey, speaking of getting started…

> **Note**
>
> In the projects folder for this chapter on the book's disc, you'll find a few additional stoplight reference images.

1. Open modo and start with a blank scene. You can do this by saving any previous work, then selecting Reset from the File menu.
2. Hold the Alt key, and then click and drag in the viewport to rotate the view until your work plane is set to the Z axis. Watch the legend in the bottom-left corner of the viewport until a light square is drawn between the X and the Y.
3. Then from the Tools tab, select the Cube primitive. Drag out a flat cube, roughly 1 m for the X and Y axes. Don't add any depth on the Z axis.
4. In the properties for the Cube primitive, change Radius to 50 mm. This will round the corners of the cube. Set Radius Segments to 3. Figure 10.2 shows the setup.

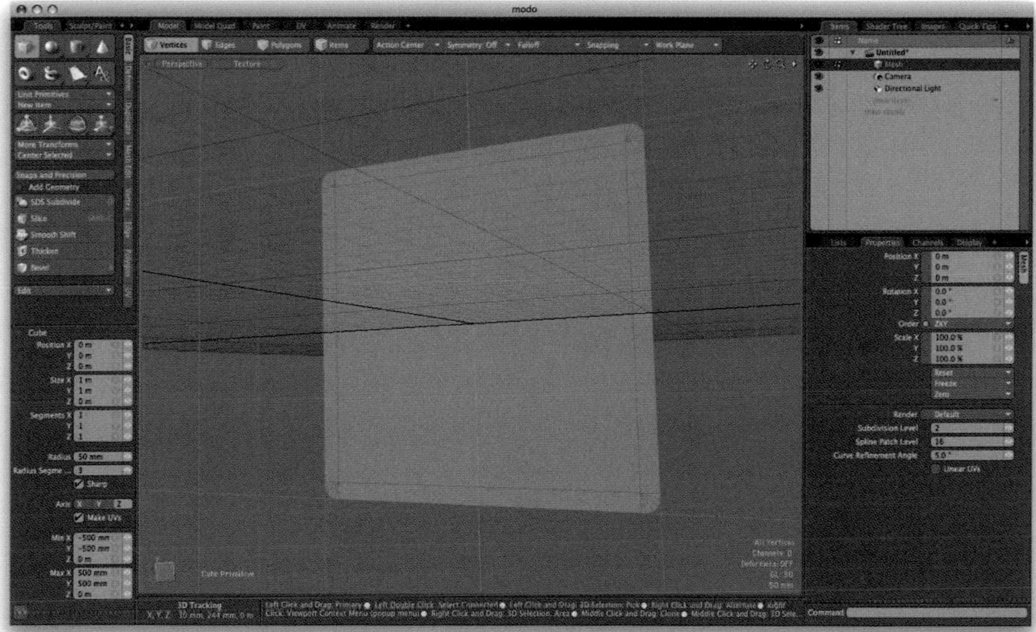

Figure 10.2 Begin building the stoplight with a simple flat cube.

5. Because each of the three lights is the same on the model, you can create one and then duplicate it later. Go to Polygons mode at the top of the interface (you can press the spacebar repeatedly to change modes), then press the x key for Extrude. Click on the object to call up the control handles.
6. Click and drag the blue handle about –70 mm, as shown in Figure 10.3.
7. Press q to drop the Extrude tool. Switch to Edges selection mode, and then double-click on the edge between the sides and the face. Press b for the Bevel tool, then click and drag. Bevel the edge to a value of about 5 mm and set Round Level to 2, as shown in Figure 10.4.
8. Repeat this edge bevel step for the back side of the object as well.
9. Press the a key to fit the model to view.
10. Select the front face polygon by clicking on it. (Make sure you're in Polygons selection mode.) Figure 10.5 shows the initial polygon selection.
11. Hold the Shift key and press the up arrow once to expand the selection. Now the entire face of the object is selected, as shown in Figure 10.6.

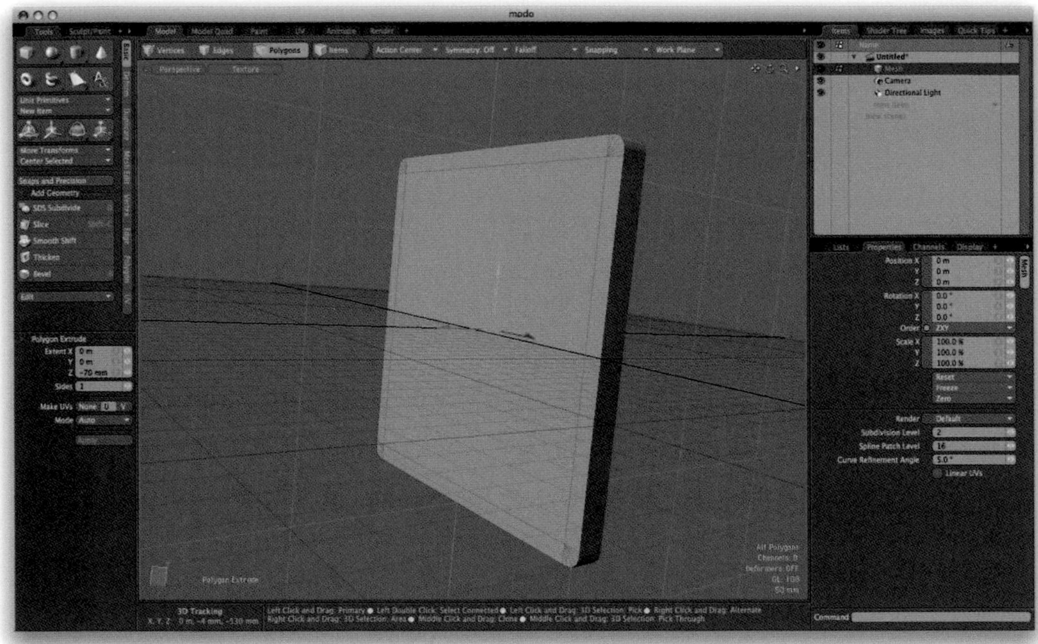

Figure 10.3 Extrude the object on the negative Z axis to give it depth.

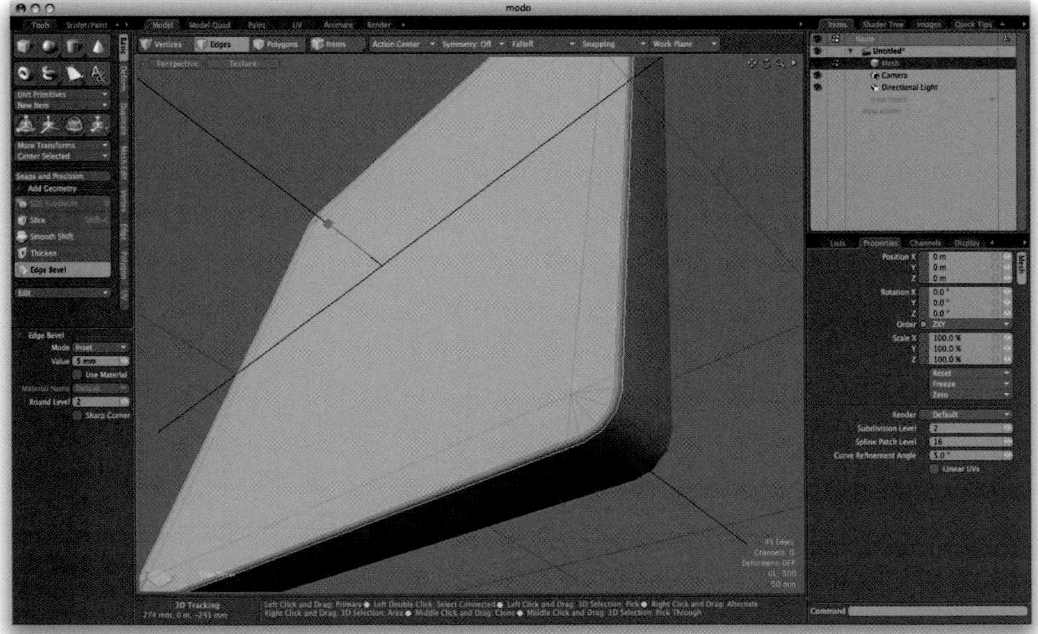

Figure 10.4 Bevel the front edge of the object.

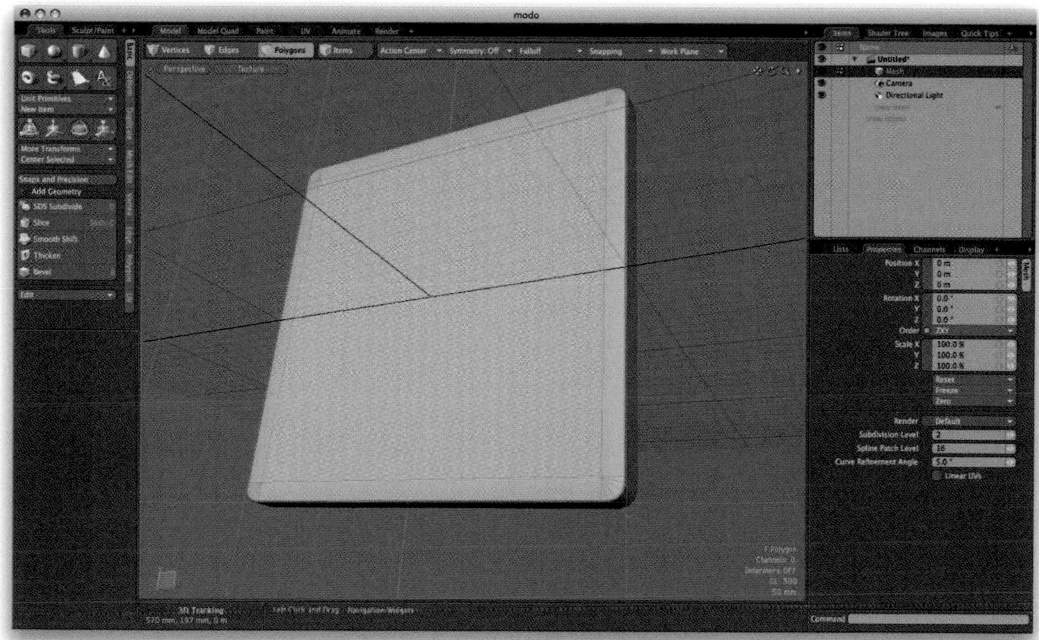

Figure 10.5 Select the large center polygon on the front of the object.

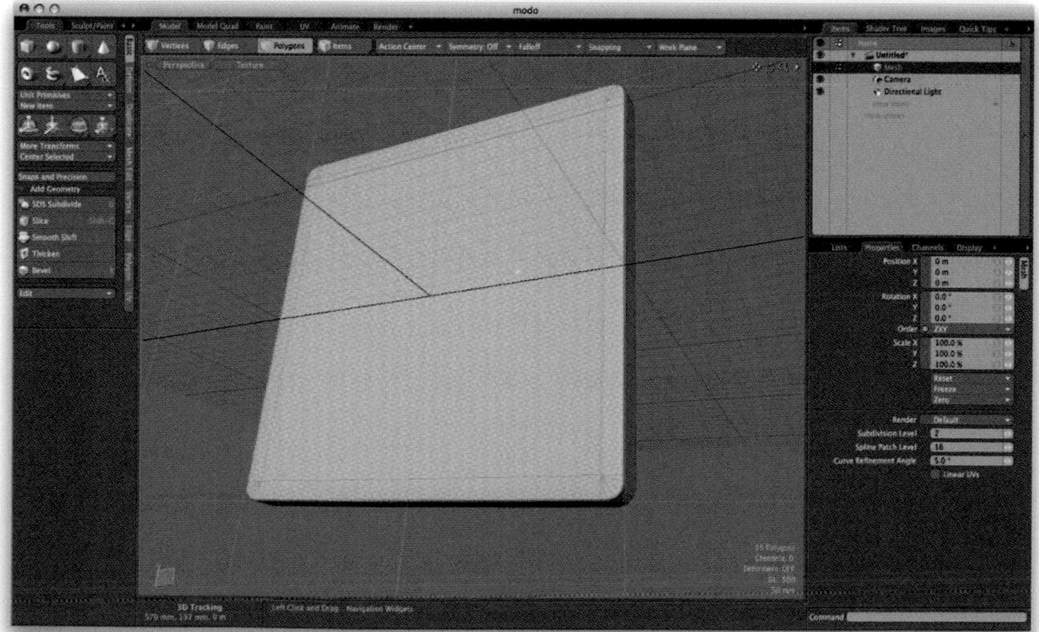

Figure 10.6 Expand the selection by holding the Shift key and pressing the up arrow on the keyboard.

12. With the front face polygon selected, press b for the Bevel tool, and bevel the geometry on the inset only, about 24 mm or so, as shown in Figure 10.7. Also, make sure that the Group Polygons option is selected in the Bevel properties area.
13. Click an empty area of the viewport to deselect the polygons. If you press the Tab key to turn the model into a subdivision surface, you won't notice much change. Unlike more organic models, this edge beveling and detail holds the object together in such a way that subdivisions don't change the shape of the model much. By beveling the polygons, you are putting edges closer together, and this will result in sharper edges when converted to a subdivision surface. Look very closely at the corners. Figure 10.8 shows a side-by-side comparison of the model without subdivisions on and with subdivision applied. The image on the left is the model without subdivision surfaces applied. The image on the right has subdivision surfaces applied, but other than making the model smoother, the process doesn't change the shape of the model.
14. Now you can add more detail to create the lens. First, save your work to this point. Rename the current mesh layer to something other than "mesh," perhaps Base. Then in a new mesh layer in the Items tab, create a flat disc slightly smaller than the flat cube you created earlier. Use the photo presented at the front of this chapter as a size reference. Figure 10.9 shows the flat disc.

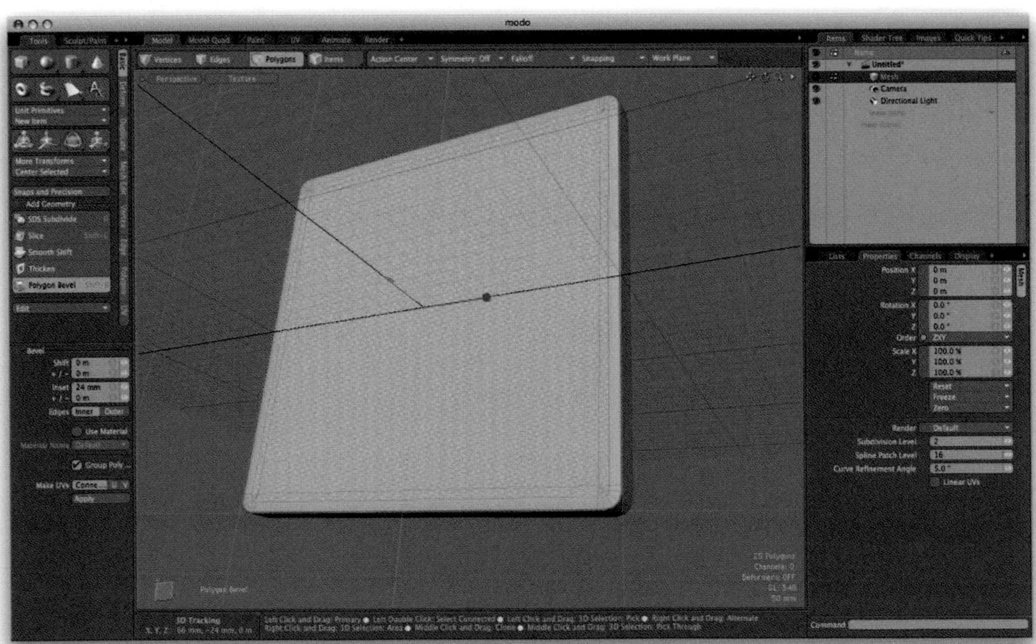

Figure 10.7 Bevel the front face polygon for a little added geometry.

Figure 10.8 By beveling edges, creating clean smooth models is made easy with the help of subdivision surfaces.

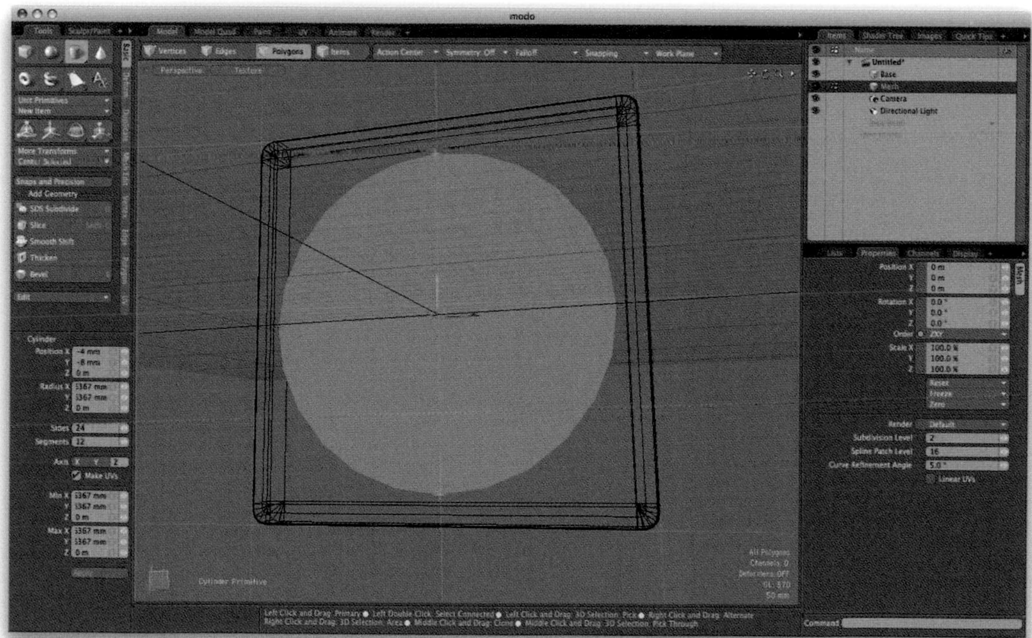

Figure 10.9 Begin creating the housing of the lens with a flat disc.

Note

To help you place the disc evenly, you can center the models. Select the base mesh layer, and from the Basic tab in the Tools tab, select Center Selected, then choose All, as shown in Figure 10.10. Do this again for the disc to center it evenly after it's created.

> **Note**
>
> In this project, the background item visibility is set to Wireframe. Press o for viewport options, and change the setting if you'd like.

15. Press w for the Move 3D tool, then click and drag on the blue handle to position the disc directly on top of the cube. A good trick for doing this is to carefully watch the background layer's wireframes. If the solid object in the foreground active layer is above the background layer, you won't see the wireframes. As you move the flat disc, look for the wireframes coming through the disc. Move the disc very slowly and carefully until the frames are behind it.
16. Select the single flat polygon (make sure you're in Polygons selection mode). Bevel the disc to create two rings. The first bevel should be about 15 mm for the Shift value. Then holding the Shift key, click the selection to reset the bevel. Click and drag again to bevel another 15 mm, but this time just for the Inset value. Figure 10.10 shows the operations. Note that you can grab the blue and red handles of the Bevel tool to easily make the adjustments.

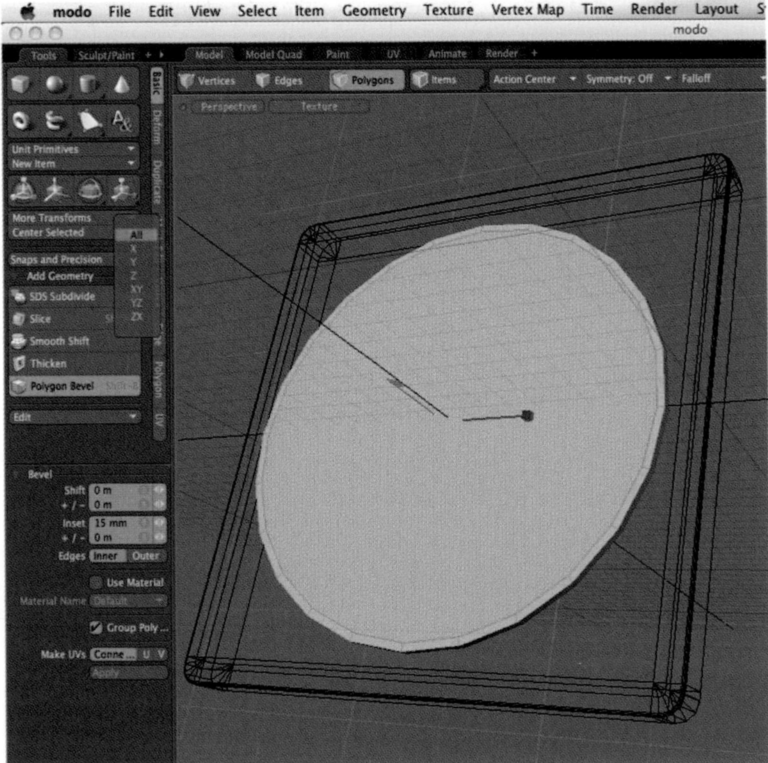

Figure 10.10 Bevel the selected polygon, the flat disc, once for the Shift value and once for the Inset value.

17. With the polygon still selected, bevel two more times, just as in step 16.
18. When finished, press q to turn off the Bevel tool, then click off of the model to deselect the polygons. Next, press the Tab key to view the model with subdivision surfaces. The shape remains, but it's too smooth. Figure 10.11 shows the situation.

Figure 10.11 After the bevel operations and viewing the model with subdivision surfaces applied, the object is clean but too smooth.

19. To sharpen the edges but still leave detail, you'll bevel the edges. Select the four edges that make up the model, starting from the bottom edge (see Figure 10.12) Remember to change to Edges selection mode at the top of the interface, then double-click on the edge to select the edge loop. Conversely, you can select one edge, then press the L key to select the rest of the edge loop.
20. Once selected, bevel the edges (press b) about 2 or 3 mm, with a Round Level setting of 2. What you'll see is a sharp-edged model, but not too sharp or too smooth. Figure 10.13 shows the result.
21. Select the top polygon and bevel again, but this time with a Shift value of 640 mm. This creates the lens hood for the stoplight.
22. The top end of the bevel will look very rounded, like a shriveled up melon. No worries though, just hold the Shift key and click on the model again to reset the bevel. Figure 10.14 shows the two results.

Figure 10.12
Select the four edges that make up the sides of the model.

Figure 10.13
Beveling the edges of the disc results in a sharp, but smooth corner.

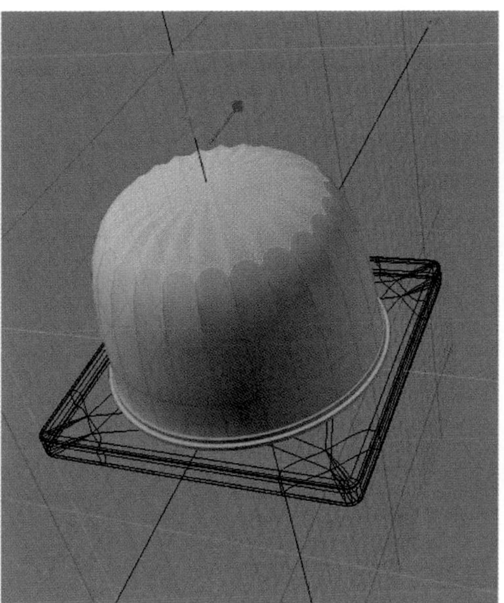
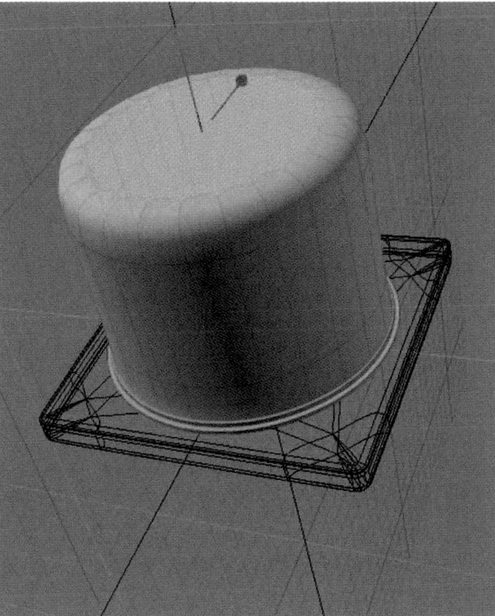

Figure 10.14 When you bevel a subdivision surface, you might think your hard-surface model is losing shape. But with one additional bevel, the shape tightens up. More control to the edges will sharpen the model even more.

23. As you can see in Figure 10.14, the model takes better shape with even just one added bevel. When you're creating hard-surface models, the more control you add to your model's geometry, such as bevels and weights, the sharper it will be. Bevel one more time with just an Inset value of about 140 mm. Deselect the polygon and save your work.
24. Now tighten up some other edges before moving on to the finer details. Select the edge at the base of the stoplight lens hood, as shown in Figure 10.15.
25. While you could bevel this edge, you might want to use an edge weight. Edge weights control the curve in a positive or negative fashion and are especially good when you don't want added geometry. In this spot, you can use either a bevel or an edge weight. But an edge weight will come in really handy for areas like tight corners. For now, make sure the subdivision is selected in the Weight Maps section of the Lists tab. Then, with the edge selected, choose the Edge Weight Tool from the Vertex Map menu, shown in Figure 10.16.
26. With the Edge Weight tool selected, click and drag in the viewport. You'll see the geometry on either side of the edge change shape. Dragging to the left softens the weight, setting a negative value, while dragging to the right hardens the edge with a positive value. Note that you can turn on the Vertex Map render style at the top of the viewport to see the weight. Red shows that the edge weight is positive, while blue shows a negative value. Figure 10.17 shows the edge weight in both Vertex Map as well as Shaded views. On the left, the Vertex Map render style shows the positive edge weight in red. The Shaded render style on the right shows the actual geometry shape with an edge weight applied.

Figure 10.15 Select the edge at the base of the lens hood.

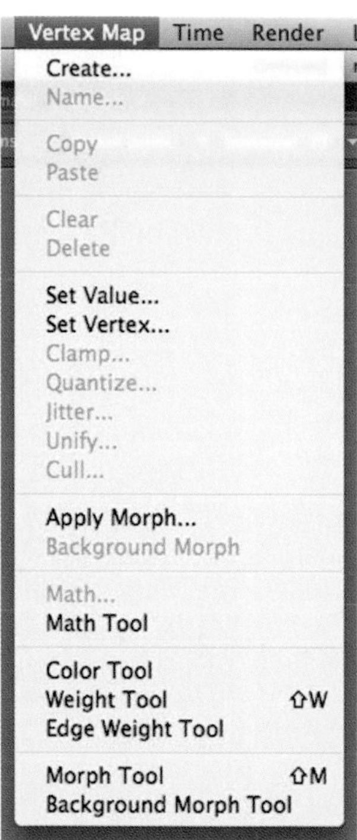

Figure 10.16 Select Edge Weight Tool from the Vertex Map menu.

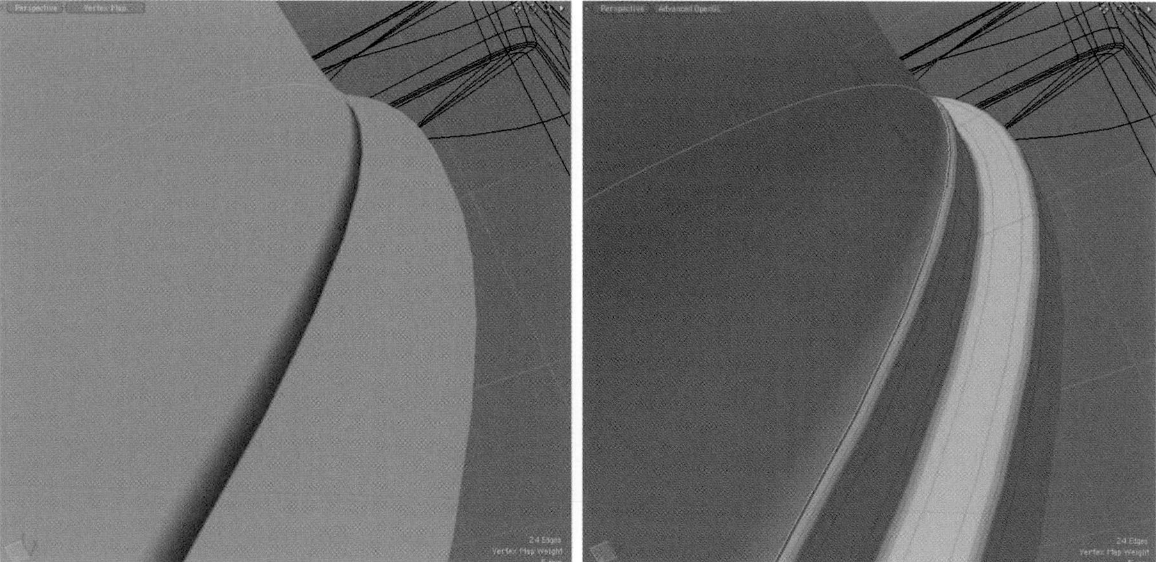

Figure 10.17 Using an edge weight, you can sharpen the effect of a selected edge.

27. Press q to drop the Edge Weight Tool, then click a blank area in the viewport to deselect the edge.
28. Head on back up to the top of the lens hood, and select the polygon. Hold the Shift key, then press the up arrow once to expand the selection. This will select all the polygons that make up the front of the lens hood. You'll want to remove these, and in some cases, you can delete them. But the polygons are only one sided, and modo does not (yet) have a Thicken tool to create the insides. It is not recommended that you use the Double Sided feature in the Surface properties to create inside-facing polygons on the lens hood. So bevel the selection once, with a small Inset value of about 20 mm. You could also use the Thicken tool as well. This new 301/302 feature is pretty great for giving objects more depth. Check out the Thicken video on the book's DVD to see how cool this tool is. It's located in the Chapter 10 folder of the Videos folder.
29. Hold the Shift key, then click to reset the bevel. Bevel the Shift value down inside the lens hood, about –660 mm. Figure 10.18 shows the results.
30. Next, bevel one more time, but all you need to do is Shift-click the selected polygon to sharpen it up. This inside end will be covered with the lens of the traffic light. Save your work.

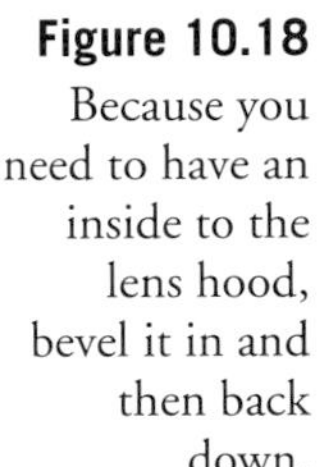

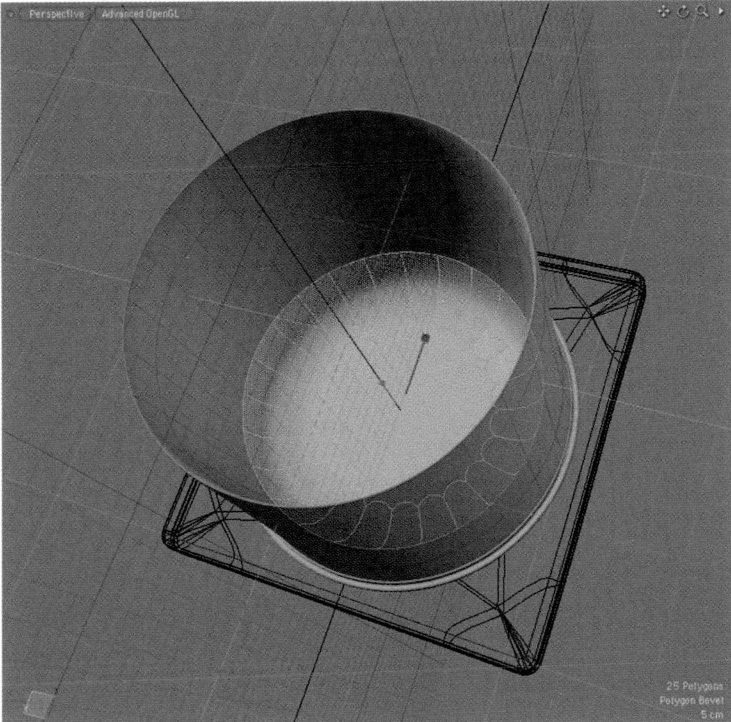

Figure 10.18
Because you need to have an inside to the lens hood, bevel it in and then back down.

31. With a few more steps, the basic housing is complete, and then you'll add the small details, like screws and brackets. Deselect all polygons, and then turn off subdivision surfaces by pressing the Tab key. Click over to the Vertex vertical tab in the Tools tab, and click the Merge button. The Merge Vertices dialog box will open, as shown in Figure 10.19. The default Range setting is Automatic. Make sure that Keep 1-Vertex Polygons is checked. Click OK, and modo will tell how many vertices are merged, if any. What did this do? Often when modeling shapes with tight bevels, you can generate points (vertices) that live right on top of each other. This can cause problems later on. Performing an automatic merge fixes that.

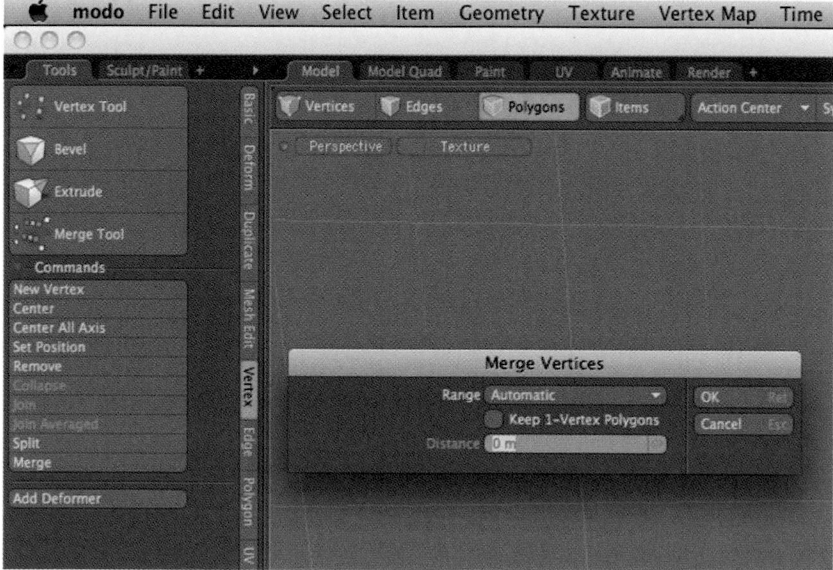

Figure 10.19 From the Vertex category in the Tools tab, select Merge to eliminate unwanted points, if any.

32. After the merge, select the bottom polygons, inside and out, as shown in Figure 10.20. These are the polygons that make up the bottom curve of the lens hood.

33. Rotate the view around to see the bottom outside edge of the lens hood, then press the r key to activate the Stretch 3D command. Click at the base of the lens hood to set the action center, as shown in Figure 10.21.

34. Click and drag directly on the blue handle, then stretch the selected geometry down on the Z axis. Figure 10.22 shows the operation.

35. Feel free to undo if needed, click to reposition the Stretch 3D command, and grab the blue handle to stretch again. Conversely, after you've stretched the geometry, you can press the w key to simply move the selected geometry to sit just above the back of the lens hood.

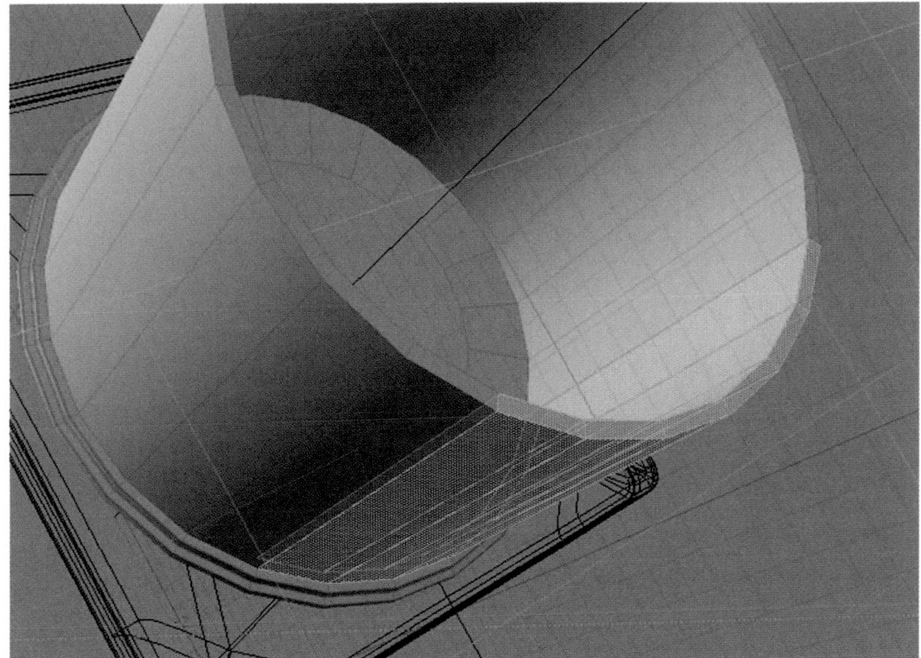

Figure 10.20 Select the polygons that make up the bottom center of the lens hood.

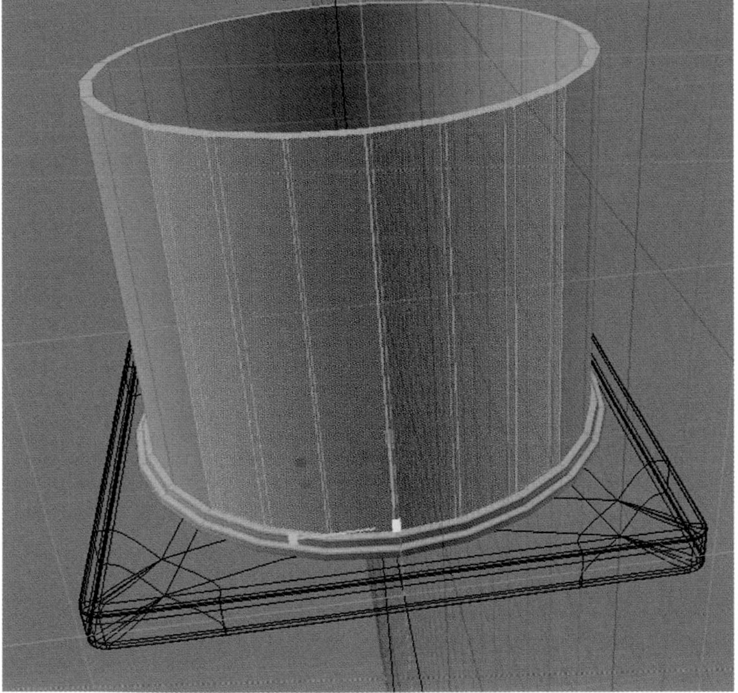

Figure 10.21 Select the Stretch 3D command and click at the base of the selection.

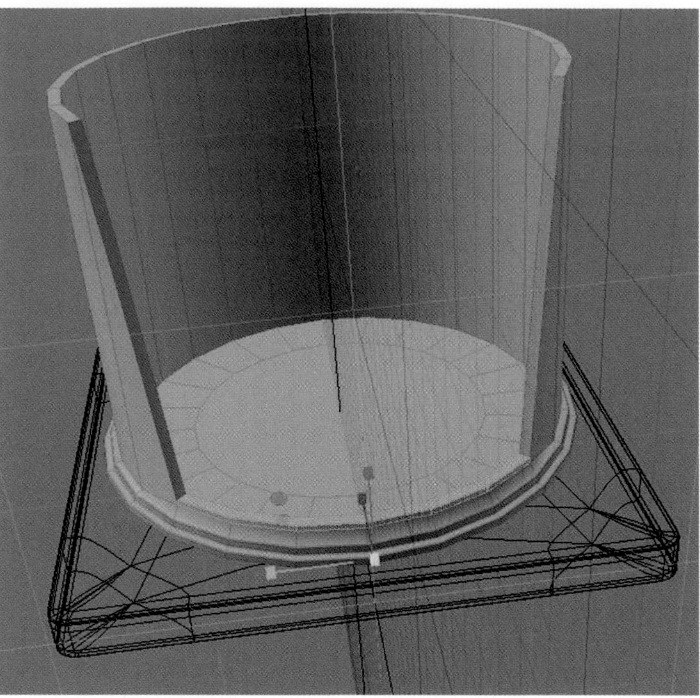

Figure 10.22
Stretch the selected geometry down on the Z axis.

36. Once the stretch is complete, press q to drop the tool. Deselect the polygons. Press the Tab key to view the model in subdivision surfaces, and you should have something like Figure 10.23. Looks good, but it could use a few adjustments.

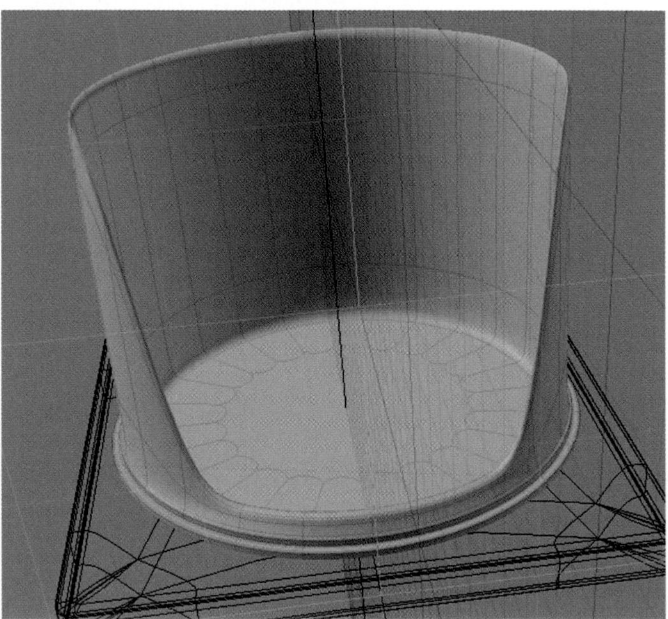

Figure 10.23
Stretching the geometry down looks good, but a little more detail is needed.

37. Turn off the subdivision surfaces by pressing the Tab key. Double-click the outside and inside edges of the lens hood, as shown in Figure 10.24.

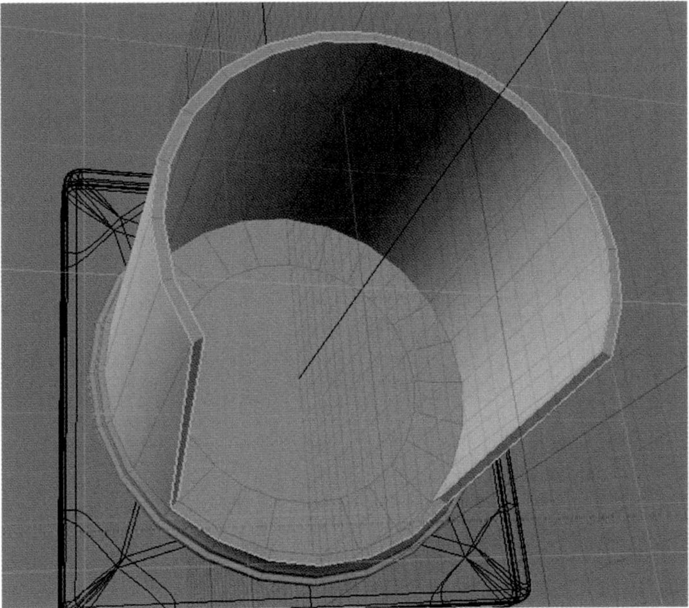

Figure 10.24
Select the outer and inner edges of the lens hood.

38. Bevel the selected edges about 4 mm with Round Level set at 2.
39. Deselect the edges, then press the Tab key to see the model as subdivision surfaces. Ah, much better. But look at the bottom inside edge of the lens hood (see Figure 10.25). A little weirdness going on there? No problem!
40. Click over to the Mesh Edit vertical tab within the Tools tab, and choose the Slice command (or press Shift-C). Rotate your view around to see the bottom of the lens hood, then click on the outside of the hood and drag all the way across through the object to slice in added geometry. Figure 10.26 shows what it looks like.

Note

As mentioned earlier in the chapter, make your model your own, only using the initial image as reference. In studying traffic lights, there seems to be quite a few varieties. For this 3D model, the lens hood sides angle up. In the image, the opening is straight. Yours can be shaped any way you like!

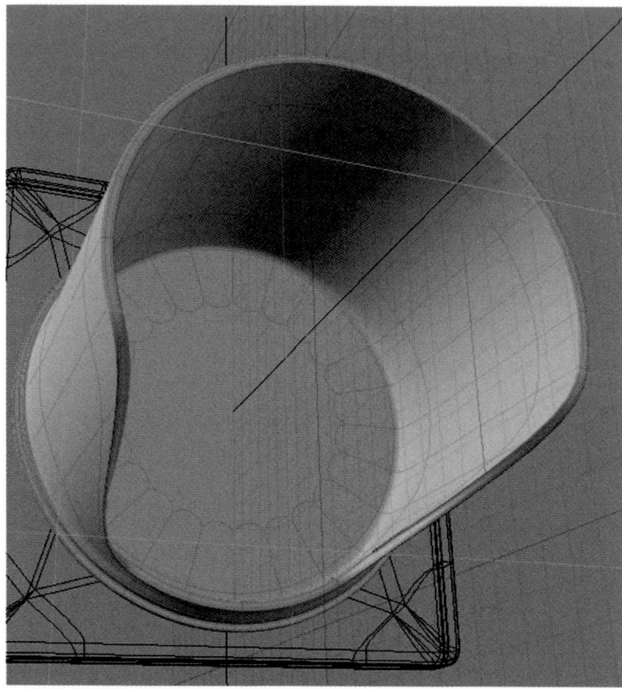

Figure 10.25 With the edges beveled, the lens hood looks much sharper.

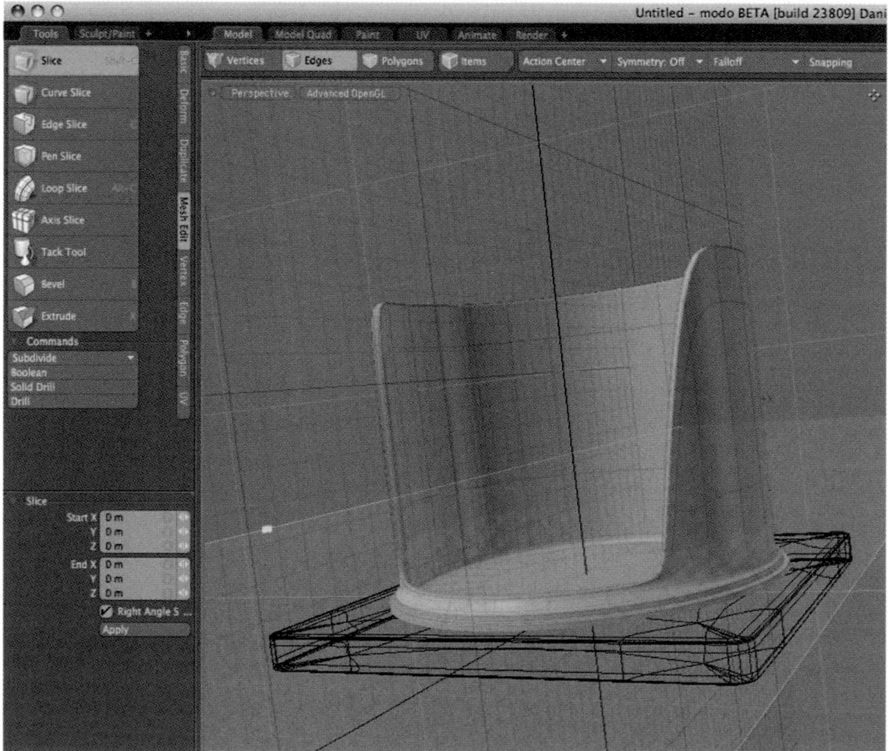

Figure 10.26 Using the Slice tool, you can add geometry to your model in necessary areas.

41. This is a little odd to get the hang of, but it's simple to use after a few tries. Once the slice is through, you can click and drag on the light-blue squares on either side of the slice to position it. Feel free to rotate your view to make sure the slice goes all the way through the model. You want to position the slice slightly above the inset curve of the lens hood, as shown in Figure 10.27.

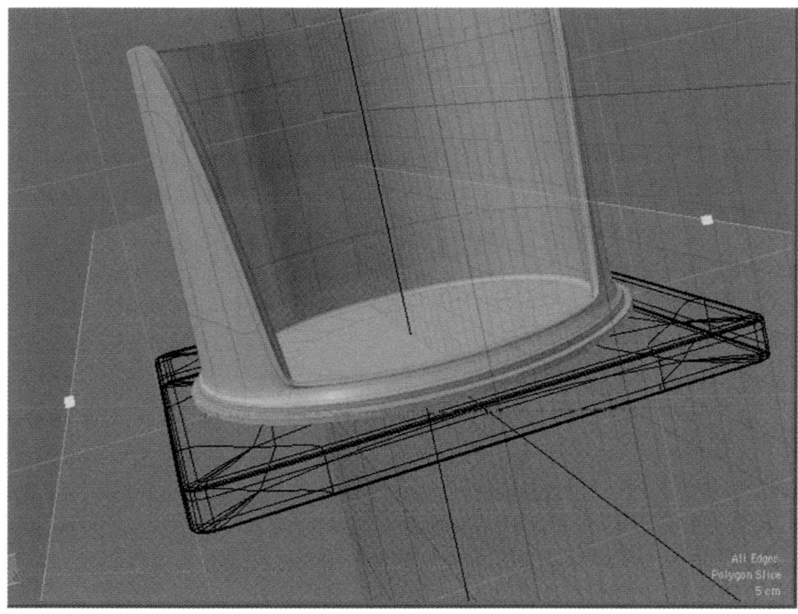

Figure 10.27
Make sure that your slice is positioned just above, not below, the base of the inset curve.

42. When you're finished with the slice, turn off the tool and save your work.
43. Lastly, press m for the Polygon Set Material dialog, and give the lens hood a polygon mask with a name of LensHood with a color of shiny black.
44. Also select the base model that the lens hood rests on and give that a polygon mask name of Base or something similar. Name your mesh layers as well by right-clicking on them. Save your scene.

What you've done here is relatively basic, but you can see with just beveling edges and polygons, using the Stretch, Merge, and Slice commands, that you can create detailed shapes. Just about everything you build can benefit from these tools, which is the reason this tutorial is here! But there's much more that can go into this, so read on!

Modeling Details

Details in your models are what will make them stand out from the rest. The tight beveled edges you've created in the previous exercise are just the first step. It's highly important to make sure the edge bevels are included, but it's also the smaller details that can make or break your final image. This section will get you started making the details of the stoplight, including screws, the lens, and brackets. To begin, you'll finish filling in the lens hood area with the glass lens.

1. Press the Ctrl and spacebar keys at the same time to call up the viewport pie menu. Select the Front view. (When working with round shapes, sometimes it helps to be looking straight on.) Then select the polygons that make up the inside back end of the lens hood, as shown in Figure 10.28. Remember to change to Polygons selection mode at the top of the interface (or press Alt/Option and the q key to call up the pie menu selection modes.)
2. Why create a new disc and worry about shaping it to build the lens? You're halfway there with the existing lens hood! With the selected polygons, press Ctrl-C to copy them. Select a new mesh layer in the Items tab, then press Ctrl-V to paste them down.

Figure 10.28
Select the polygons that make up the back inside end of the lens hood.

3. Press Ctrl and the spacebar to call up the pie menu, and switch back to a Perspective view.
4. Select the new mesh later, and with all of the new disc polygons selected, press Shift and the s key for the Smooth Shift tool. (Remember that pressing just lowercase s is for setting keyframes.) This tool is sort of like Bevel, but it allows you to add scale to the multiplied polygon, which is perfect for creating this lens. This tool, by the way, is located within the Polygon tab in the Tools tab.
5. With Smooth Shift active, click and drag so that you set an Offset value of 30 mm and a Scale of about 95%. Leave Max Smoothing Angle at its default. You can click and drag the red and blue handles just as you do with the Bevel tool, or enter the value numerically in the Tool Properties panel. Figure 10.29 shows the operation.

Figure 10.29 Using the Smooth Shift tool, you can create the lens for the stop-light.

6. Hold the Shift key, then click on the lens to reset the Smooth Shift tool. Smooth Shift again with an Offset of 25 mm and this time with a Scale of 85%.
7. Repeat the process one more time with an Offset of 40 mm or so and a Scale of 80%.

8. Press q to turn off the Smooth Shift tool, and deselect the polygons. Press the Tab key to activate subdivision surfaces if it's not already applied. Figure 10.30 shows the lens created with Smooth Shift.

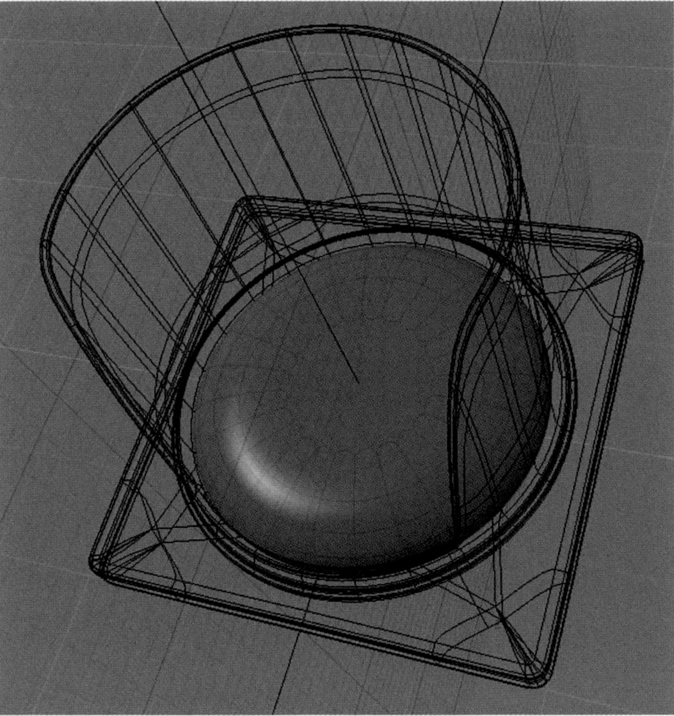

Figure 10.30 Using the Smooth Shift tool, you can add geometry to your model in necessary areas.

9. Press m to create a polygon mask for the lens, giving it a surface name of Lens (or if you're daring, call it Red Lens). Then hold the Shift key and select all mesh layers in the Items tab to see how your model is coming along. Figure 10.31 shows the model so far. It's getting there!
10. Go ahead and finish up the back side of the base of the model, and then it's time for the finer details, like screws to hold it together! Turn off subdivision surfaces for right now by pressing the Tab key. Select the base mesh layer, and rotate the 3D viewport around to see the back side.
11. Select the polygons that make up just the back side. You can do this by clicking in the center, then holding the Shift key and pressing the up arrow to expand the selection. Figure 10.32 shows the selected polygon.

Figure 10.31
Taking a look at all the layers together, the stoplight model is starting to resemble something familiar! Note that the surfaces are set to gray rather than black for visibility.

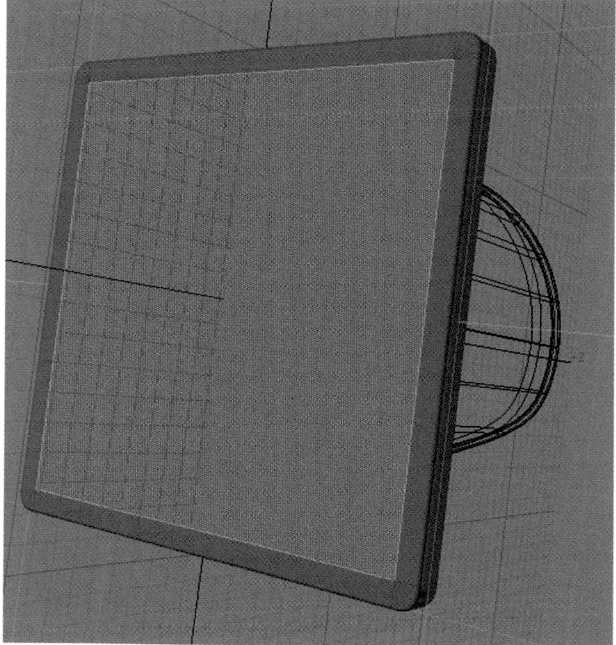

Figure 10.32
Select the polygons that make up the back side of the stoplight base.

12. Press Shift and the d key at the same time to call up the Subdivide Polygons command. The default selection is Faceted, which is for flat geometry, such as you have here. Click OK. The selected single polygon is now four polygons. Repeat the process one more time, and you'll have 16 polygons occupying the same space, as shown in Figure 10.33.

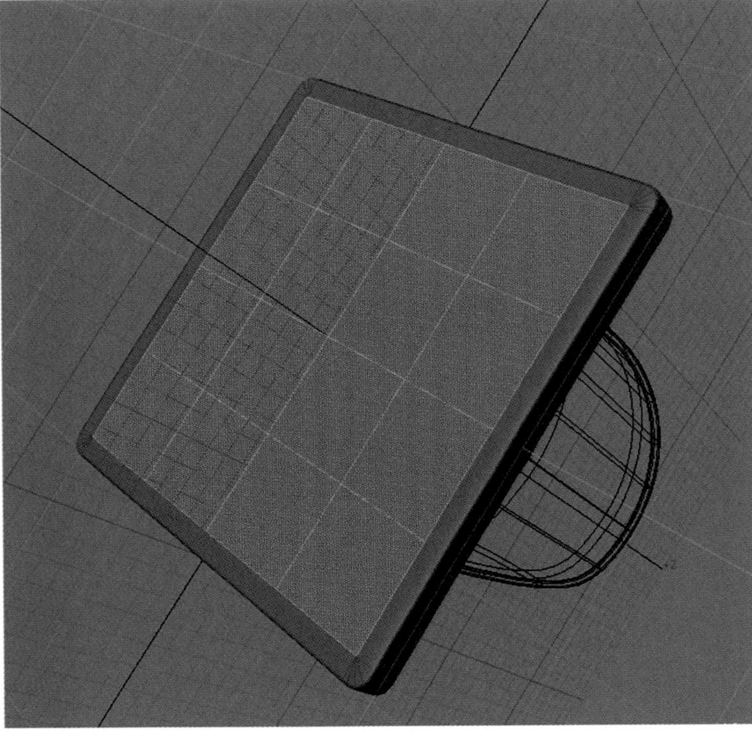

Figure 10.33
Subdivide the selected polygon twice to generate 16 polygons.

13. Switch to Edges selection mode (you can click it, press the spacebar repeatedly, or press the 2 key). Then carefully select the inner square of edges, as shown in Figure 10.34.
14. Press the r key and then click and drag on the light-blue cross hair in the center to scale the selection up equally to about 170%, as shown in Figure 10.35.
15. Press q to drop the Stretch 3D tool, and then select the two crossing edges in the center of the polygons, as shown in Figure 10.36.
16. With the edges selected, press Delete on your keyboard to remove them. At this point, you're probably wondering just what the heck you're doing, right? Don't worry, it'll make sense in a minute. In order to create a round shape out of this square shape, you're generating additional geometry within the model. The next steps will make it more clear.

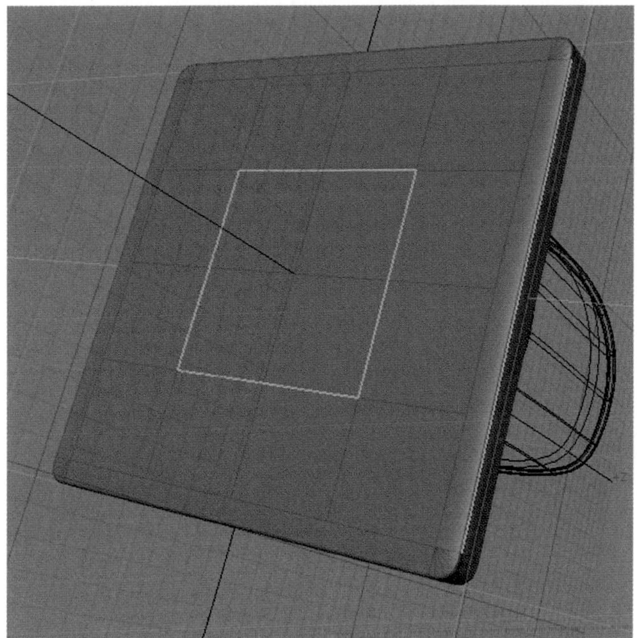

Figure 10.34
Select the edges in the center of the polygons.

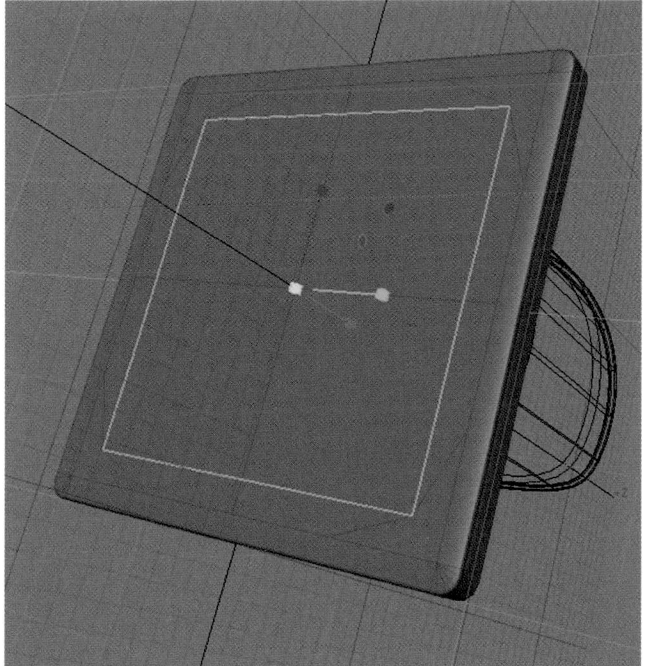

Figure 10.35
Scale up the selected edges.

Figure 10.36
Select the two crossing edges.

17. With the center edges deleted, switch to Polygons selection mode, then select the center polygon. From the Polygon vertical tab in the Tools tab, select the Spikey tool. Click and drag slightly on the selected polygon. You should have pie shapes within the geometry, similar to what's shown in Figure 10.37.
18. As you can see, the subdivisions generated extra geometry so that when it was time to perform the Spikey operation, the tool was able to grab onto the points generated, even though you removed the edges. Cool, eh? But wait. Press q to drop the Spikey tool, then switch to the Vertices selection mode.
19. Select just the center point, directly in the middle of the model. Then press b for the Bevel tool and click and drag. Yes, you can bevel the points of an object, too. And because the extra geometry was there with the Spikey tool, you have enough points to generate a round shape. Figure 10.38 shows a 35 cm bevel on the center point.
20. Switch back to Polygons selection mode, and select the center polygon. You now have a round shape in the center of the square polygon shape. Well, okay, it's not that round yet, so bevel it in about 15 mm on the inset. Bevel again with a 400 mm shift, and finally make another bevel with an Inset value of 15 mm.

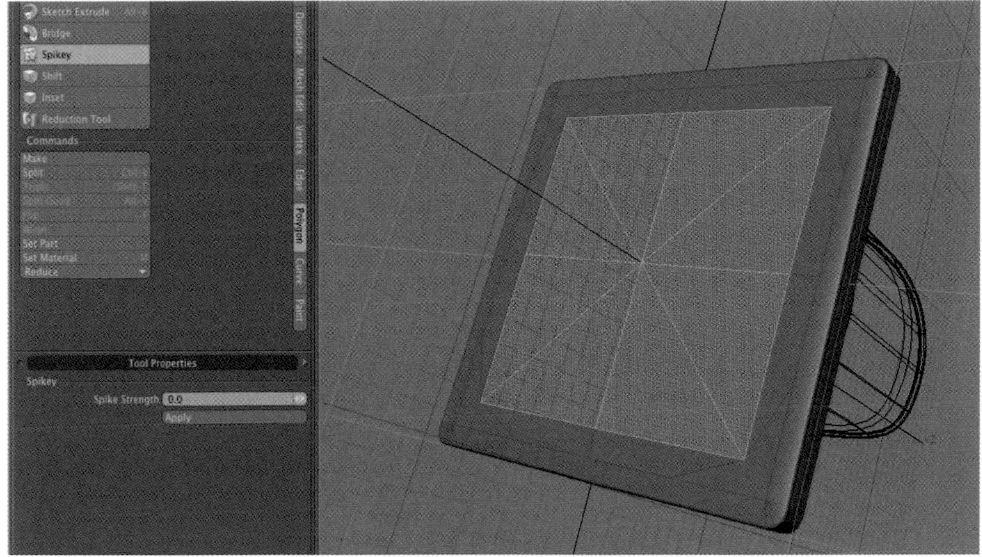

Figure 10.37
Using the Spikey tool, you can subdivide your geometry in a whole different way.

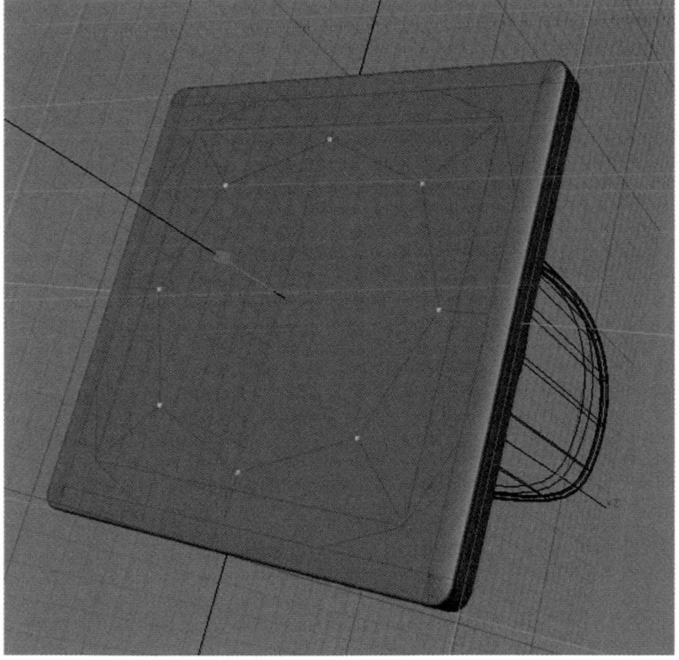

Figure 10.38
Select the center point on the back of the model and bevel it.

21 When the three bevel operations are finished, press q to drop the Bevel tool, then deselect the polygon. Press the Tab key to turn on subdivision surfaces and look! A round shape is coming out of a square shape. Cool. (See Figure 10.39.)

22. Save your work!

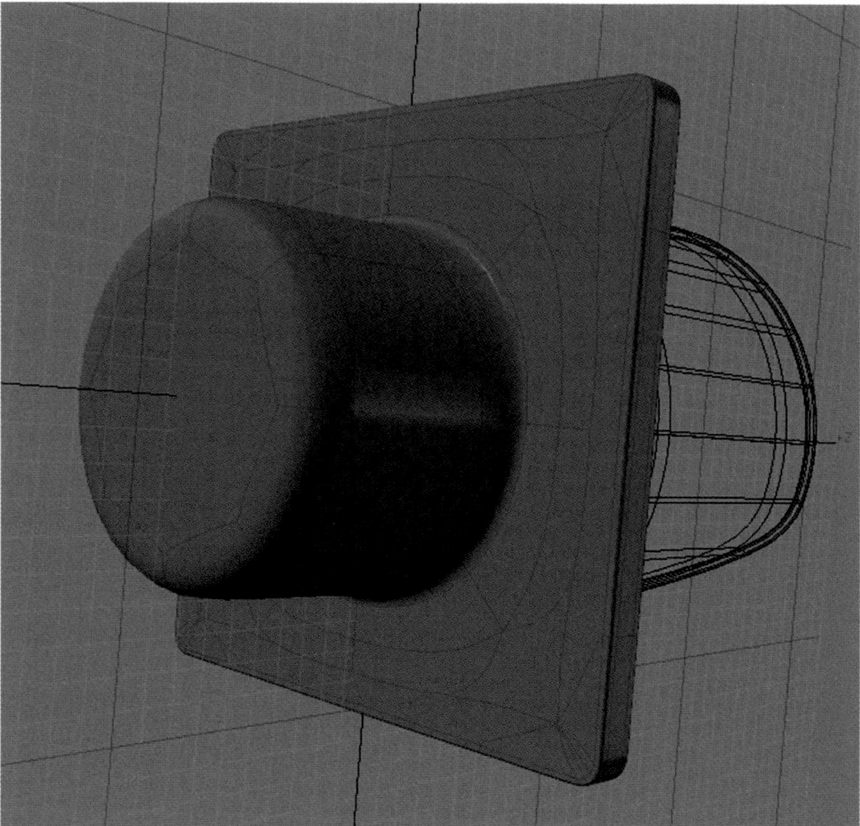

Figure 10.39
With a few bevels and subdivision surfaces applied, the back side of the object, the square base, now has a round shape extruding out of it.

This technique can be used for any number of things, from electronics to cars to spacecraft. Take a look around you—on your desk, in your kitchen, anywhere. You'll often see machine-made objects that have smooth round shapes molded as part of a more squared shape. And the round shape is not just sitting on top of the square; it's truly part of it, as shown in the previous example. The round shape extruding out of the back of the stoplight might be too small, and too long, but by selecting the necessary geometry, you can easily scale and move it as needed.

Hard-surface modeling and subdivision modeling are not as complicated or as separate as you might think. The examples in this chapter have clearly shown that a combination of both methods works well to create sharp detailed models. Applying subdivision surfaces, a model does become smooth, often too smooth, as you saw with the lens hood. But by beveling edges, slicing, edge weighting, and simply adding more geometry to control the flow of the model, you can create very specific details.

But wait, there's more! For the next portion of this tutorial, turn to the Stoplight video on the book's DVD. This video uses modo 201, but the lesson works the same in 301, as the core modeling has not changed from version 201, or even 101! You'll learn how you can further edit the back end and shape the round lens housing behind the lens hood. You'll also clearly see how to build the screws and brackets, as well as discover how instancing can help out. You'll also pick up some other cool tidbits along the way. When you're ready, pop open the book's disc and continue this chapter's projects in the Chapter 10 folder. Then, move on to Chapter 11 to learn how to surface this model with modo's killer paint tools.

11

Creating and Painting Textures

When the new surfacing and painting features were promoted for modo 201 at a SIGGRAPH conference a couple of summers ago, users rejoiced. When modo the product finally shipped, the tools were more than users could ask for. Now modo 301 offers even better painting features, along with sculpting tools (which you'll learn about in Chapter 13).

While many programs have node-based surfacing, the modo team opted for the Shader Tree and a system of masks. This tree-like approach, while appearing quite simple, is actually very easy to use but powerful at the same time. In addition to this cool modeling application adding the ability to paint color and texture directly on your models, you can also brush in bump maps, displacements, and even use images to paint.

This chapter will first introduce you to additional surface properties for glass and ice. Then you'll learn the painting tools, how to use them, and ways they can be altered. From there, you'll work on a project utilizing the painting and bump tools, then take it a step further and apply these techniques to the traffic light you created in Chapter 10. Honestly, these topics can be a book all on their own. However, I've added a few tutorial videos on the book's disc to help you understand the tools covered in this chapter as well as guide you beyond the text.

Understanding the Paint Tools

To begin, it's important to understand a few key tools that make up the powerful painting features in modo. This section will guide you through using and setting up a model for painting. The super talented Philip Lawson has generously provided this book with a cool scene for you to work with. Figure 11.1 shows the model you'll be working with.

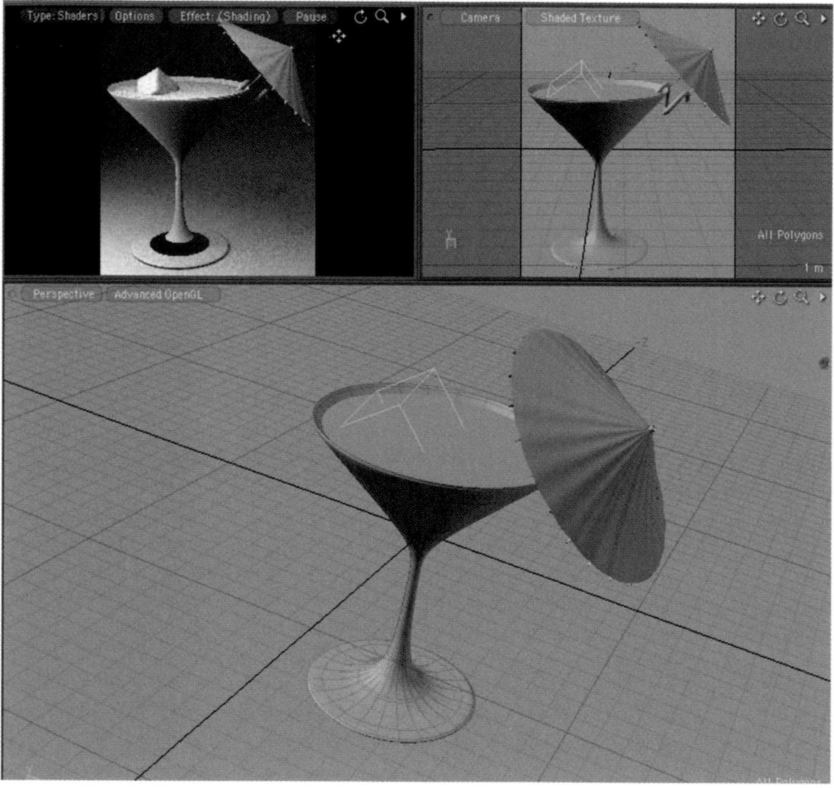

Figure 11.1
Philip Lawson's martini glass model is a perfect launching pad for learning how to create and paint textures.

Since the original scene Philip Lawson created was done so well, it's only right that we paint it with graffiti! Well, probably not graffiti, but rather than painting on a ball or donut shape, it might be fun to paint on a cool model. You can load the glassFinal.lxo scene to take a look at Philip's glass settings and lighting. For now, you'll begin with a blank version of the model, that is, one without textures. You'll resurface this model entirely for yourself. But wait! You'll take it a step further by adding painted textures to the scene.

1. Open up modo and load the glassBlank.lxo scene from the book's disc. It's in the Wineglass folder within the Chapter 11 projects folder.

2. When loaded, click over to the Render tab at the top of the viewport. You should see something like Figure 11.2.

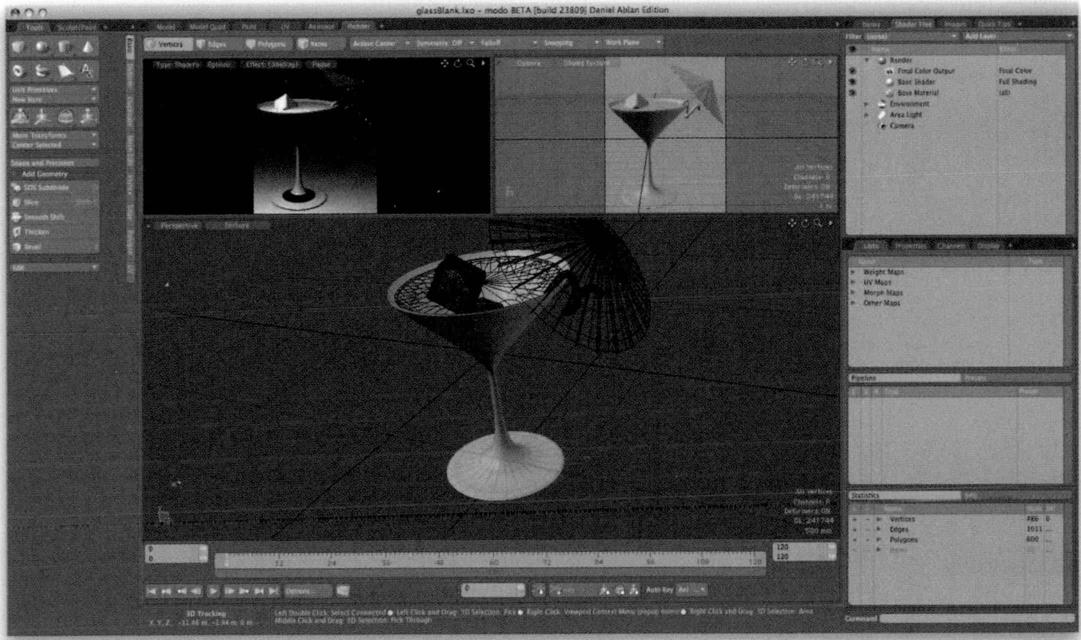

Figure 11.2 Philip Lawson's martini glass model loaded without textures is a little boring without surfaces!

3. To begin, you'll set up the glass surface. You might think this is hard to do, but modo makes it so easy, you'll be surprised how fast you can set it up.

> **Note**
>
> For the projects you've done so far, including the work in this chapter, you'll learn how to light and render these scenes starting with Chapter 14.

4. If you take a look at the Items tab, you'll see that the object layers are all named. However, clicking on the Shader Tree tab and opening up the Render listing, there's only one Base Material and one Base Shader. Their objects in the scene do not have materials set up. Could this have been done for you? Sure it could have! But really, the next few steps will help reinforce a key aspect of using modo. Select the Glass mesh layer in the Items tab.

5. With the Glass mesh layer selected, press m on the keyboard to call up the Polygon Set Material dialog box. Enter the name **Glass** and maybe tint the color a bit. Then click OK. Original name, don't you think? Figure 11.3 shows the material now added to the Shader Tree tab.

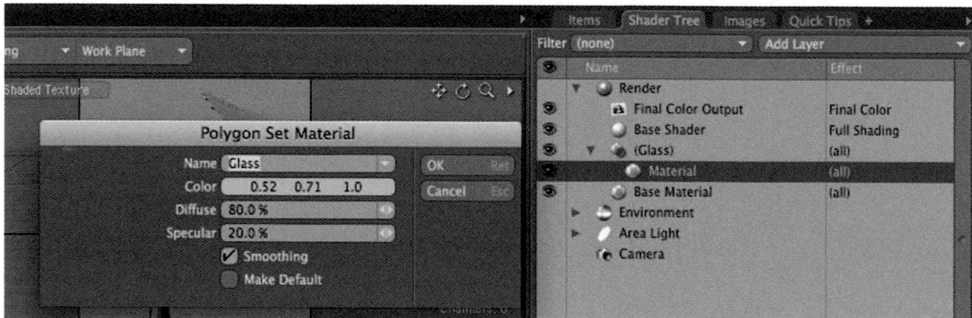

Figure 11.3 Setting a polygon material mask adds specific surface controls to the Shader Tree tab.

6. Next select the Drink mesh layer and again press m to set a material name. Enter the name, oh, perhaps, **Drink**? This now adds the material to the Shader Tree tab as shown in Figure 11.4.

7. Repeat the previous steps for the remaining mesh layers. Figure 11.5 shows the Shader Tree with all of the material masks applied.

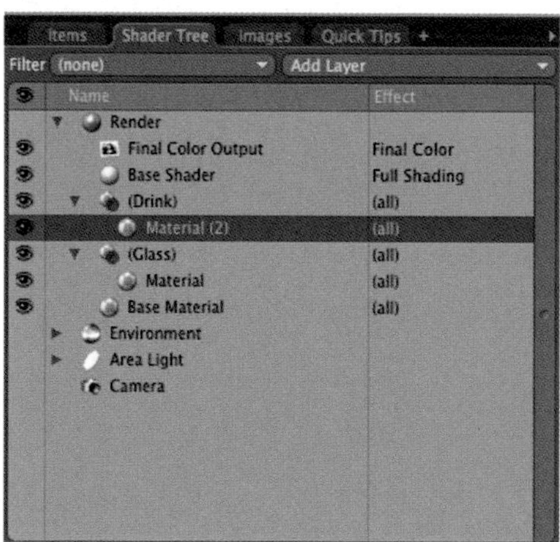

Figure 11.4 Create a material mask for the Drink mesh layer, creating surface controls for the liquid in the glass.

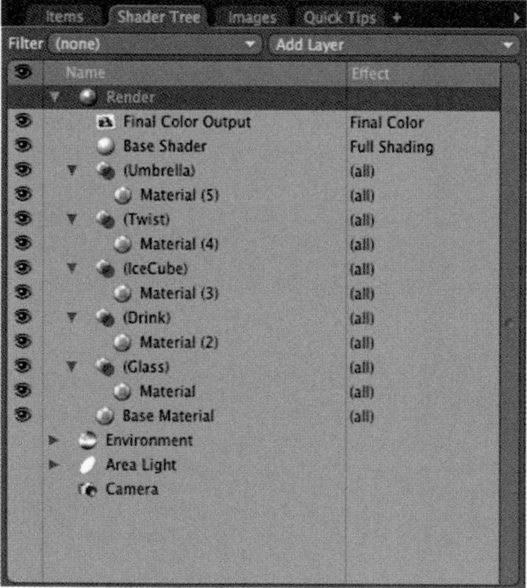

Figure 11.5 Repeat the process of assigning material masks to each of the mesh layers, naming the materials according to their layer name.

> **Note**
>
> If you look at the modo interface in Figure 11.5, you'll see that the names of the materials in the Shader Tree all have a numeric value next to them. This is modo's way of organizing names that are the same within the scene. If you rename the material layer to something different, even changing one character to a capital letter, the numbering will be removed. Having your mesh layers named the same or different as the materials really doesn't matter. It's up to you and how you like to organize your scene and objects. What is important is that the materials are applied to the right objects.

8. Save your scene, perhaps with a new name, so that you do not save over the original glassBlank.lxo scene.
9. Now head over to the Shader Tree tab. Select the Glass material, and feel free to slide the viewports around to increase the size of the preview window. You can do this by clicking and dragging directly on the borders between the views.
10. For the surface of the glass, you can set this up without much effort in modo 301/302. With the glass material selected in the Shader Tree tab, go down to the Properties tab. In the Material Ref vertical tab, set Diffuse Amount to 0% (see Figure 11.6). This tells the surface to not accept any light from the scene. What's that? No light? Yes, no light. Glass surfaces benefit more from reflection and refraction (the bending of light).
11. Set the Fresnel (pronounced Fre-Nel) to 100% for both specularity and reflection. This tells the surface to be more reflective as the glancing angle changes. What does that mean? Well, you sure have a lot of questions! Consider a car window. If you look at the passenger window of a car from the vantage point (the glancing angle) of the front of the car, the window is hard to see through. This is because at that angle, it's very reflective. But if you walk up to the window and stand directly in front of it, the reflection is very slight and you can now see through it. In the case of the glass surface in this scene, the sides of the glass away from your view will be more reflective.
12. Make sure to keep specularity and reflection, as well as the Fresnel specularity and reflection values, the same—that is, Specular and Reflection Amount values should be 5% and the Fresnel values should be 100%. (Specularity is the amount of shininess on the surface.)
13. Set Roughness to 10% (the roughness is how glossy it will be). Add a little bluish tint to the Specular Color setting (see Figure 11.6).

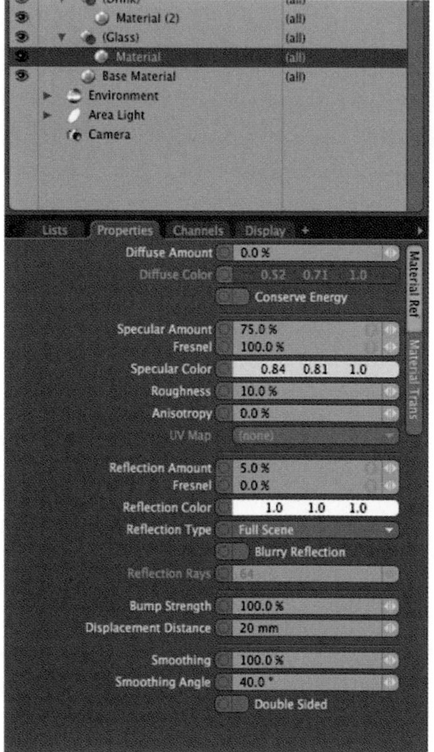

Figure 11.6
A few settings set up for the glass material, and the surface is looking more like a metallic martini glass.

14. Click on the Material Trans vertical tab, and set Transparency to 100% (see Figure 11.7).
15. In order for the glass to look like it should, you need to apply refraction. Set Refractive Index to 1.4. Refraction is what happens to light as it travels through transparent surfaces, such as glass, water, and so on. It essentially bends. Typically, glass has a refraction index of about 1.35, but depending on your model, you can vary this to your liking.
16. Finally, set Absorption Distance to 5 m. What this value does is set the thickness of the transparency. If you set a Transparent Color value, you'll obtain the effect of tinted glass in thicker areas, such as at the base of a drinking glass. The Absorption Distance value determines how far a ray travels before the color becomes 100% of the transparency color. A longer absorption distance will have a lesser effect. Figure 11.7 shows the preview and setup.
17. Now the scene is still quite dull and doesn't have much color. Change that by going to the Environment listing in the Shader Tree tab. Make sure that Environment Type is set to 4 Color Gradient, as shown in Figure 11.8.

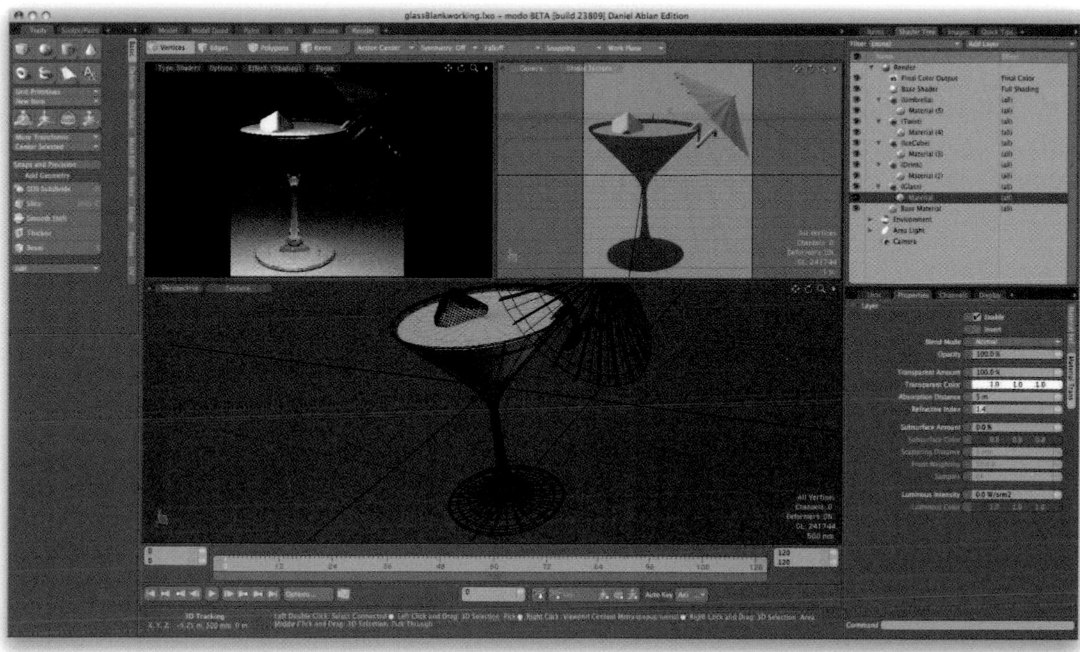

Figure 11.7 Setting a few values in the Material Trans tab helps create the glass effect. You can see how the base and stem of the glass look pretty good!

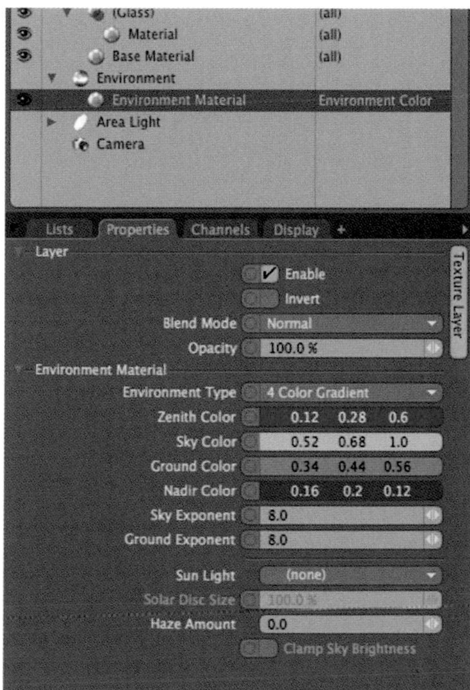

Figure 11.8 Make sure the Environment material has a 4 Color Gradient setting applied.

18. Philip Lawson's original scene used an HDR (high dynamic range) image to light the environment, but for this setup, you'll use something simple. For now, select the Render listing at the very top of the Shader Tree. Then click the Global Illumination vertical tab down in the Properties tab. Click the Enable option under Indirect Illumination. Let your preview window redraw. Now there's color in the scene, as you can see in Figure 11.9.

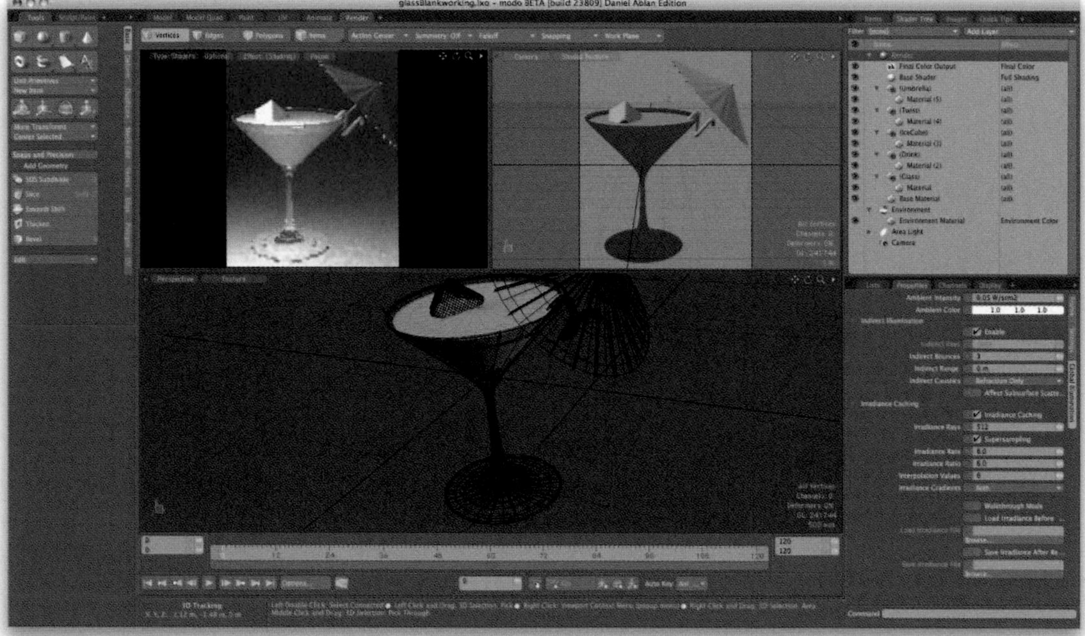

Figure 11.9 By simply turning on Global Illumination, modo uses the colored environment as an added light source, enhancing your surfaces.

> **Note**
>
> While this is not a chapter on rendering or lighting, it's important to understand that these areas play a key role in the surfacing of your objects, especially glass. Therefore, you've cheated and used global illumination before it's officially discussed. Read more about HDR and global illumination in Chapters 14 and 15.

19. Save your work.

20. Now you need to take what you've learned about glass and apply it to the liquid and the ice cubes. First, select the Drink material in the Shader Tree.

21. In the Properties tab, set Diffuse Amount to 0%. Fresnel should be 100%, while Specular Amount is 5% and Roughness 40%. Give the Specular Color and Reflection Color values a slight off white, perhaps 0.82, 0.82, 0.82. A trick is to hold the Shift key, then click and drag on the color values to change them equally. Next, set Reflection Amount to just 2%. You only need a little bit of reflection here. Figure 11.10 shows the settings.

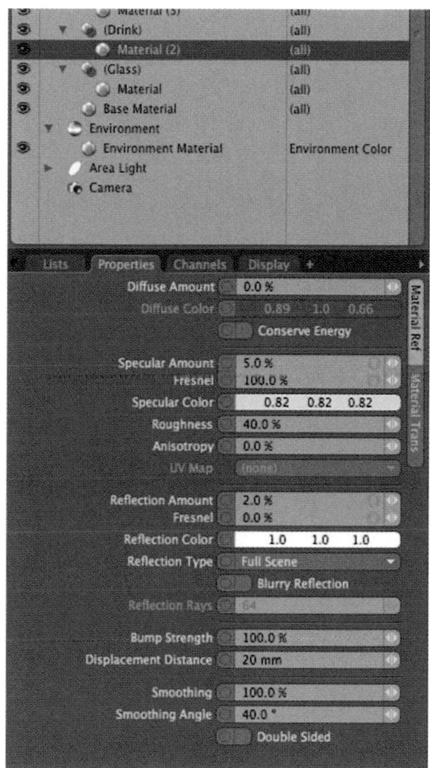

Figure 11.10
The surface settings for the drink's liquid are similar to the glass surface, though with minor differences.

22. Next, click on the Material Trans vertical tab. Set Transparent Amount to 100%. Absorption Distance should be only 50 mm. This is a small amount to give the drink more of the transparent color, since a ray won't have to penetrate very deeply to return the full transparency color. Lastly, set Refractive Index to 1.1.

23. One more setting to go. Change the Transparent Color setting in the Material Trans vertical tab to a very slight green, about 0.9, 1.0, 0.93. While it might not look like a very strong color, it will be vibrant in the surface of the model because of the low Absorption Distance setting. If you were to increase Absorption Distance, the green color would fade, as the transparent thickness falls off. Figure 11.11 shows the Material Trans tab settings along with a preview.

Figure 11.11 The last thing to change is the Transparent Color amount. With a very slight change to this value, the Absorption Distance value carries it through the surface.

As you can see, the glass and liquid are starting to look pretty good! Of course, you can vary these settings and watch the results, making the surfaces look any way you want. The idea here is that you get a feel for setting up surfaces, specifically glass surfaces, and, of course, understand what needs to be set to see decent results. There are a few other surfaces to apply, specifically the ice cubes.

1. Select the Material under IceCube in the Shader Tree tab. Then in the Properties tab, you can set up the surfaces in a similar fashion to the glass and liquid.
2. Set Diffuse Amount to 20%. Diffuse Color should be 1.0, 1.0, 1.0. Click on Conserve Energy. What this does is balance the specular light reflections and diffuse values. It's a filter of sorts, that suppresses the diffuse value as the reflection increases. It's a handy feature to help balance the surfaces in your scene.
3. Set Specular Amount to 45% and Roughness to 20%. Remember to balance the Specular and Reflection Amount values, especially when Conserve Energy is checked.
4. In the Material Trans vertical tab, set Transparent Amount to 100%, then set Absorption Distance to 10 m. Remember, this sets the transparency thickness, or better, the density of the transparency color. For ice, change Refractive Index to 1.8. This will really help sell the ice look.

5. Set Subsurface Amount to 50%.
6. Change the Subsurface Color setting to a very pale blue, about 0.87, 0.93, 1.0. The Subsurface Amount value adds to the diffuse values of your material. This setting helps balance the diffuse color values in your materials with the subsurface scattering amounts. Subsurface scattering then is the effect of light "inside" a surface. A good example of this is human skin or a candle.
7. Set Scattering Distance to 100 mm. Along with that, set Samples to 64. This sample rate controls the quality. Simply, the higher the value, the better the quality. But as with any setting, start low, test your model, and see how it looks. Then increase as needed. Figure 11.12 shows the ice cubes in the glass with these settings.

Note

On the book's DVD, be sure to check out the Subsurface Scattering video. This video is a clip from the 3D Garage.com modo 301 Signature Courseware. This is a major feature and writing about it here doesn't do it justice. It's best to see it in action, so watch the tutorial video for more information.

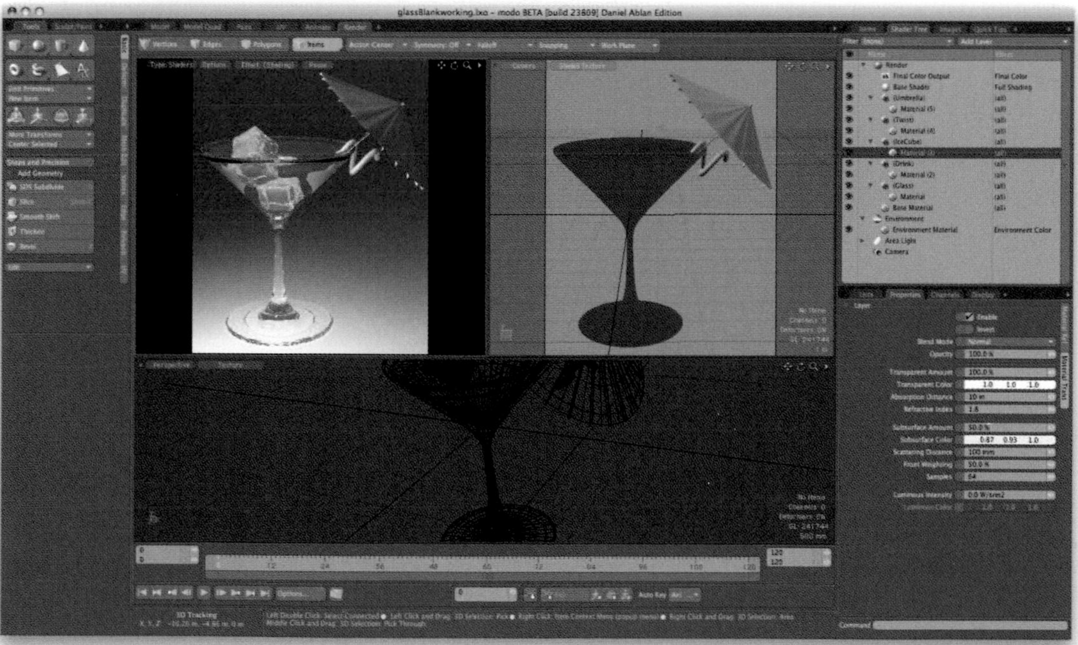

Figure 11.12 Using similar transparent settings as the glass and liquid, and then applying subsurface effects, the ice cubes are looking good.

8. The ice looks good in Figure 11.12, but it's a little bright. And it could use a little bit more than just shading. Making sure the IceCube material is selected in the Shader Tree, add a gradient from the Add Layer drop-down menu at the top of the Shader Tree. This gradient effect will help the surface reflections.
9. For the Effect variable of the gradient, right-click in the Effect column next to the Gradient listing and set it to Reflection Amount, as shown in Figure 11.13.

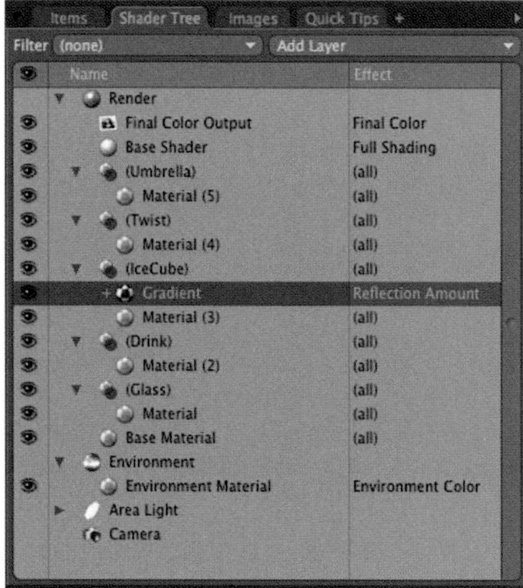

Figure 11.13 Apply a gradient to the IceCube material and set its effect to Reflection Amount.

10. In the Properties tab, click the Texture Layer vertical tab, and make sure the Blend Mode is set to Normal; for Input Parameter, choose Incidence Angle. The Incidence Angle setting will allow you to vary the amount of reflection based on the angle of incidence—the angle between the ray and the surface normal.
11. Click the Gradient Editor button. You'll see modo's Gradient Editor appear, as shown in Figure 11.14.

Figure 11.14 When a gradient is applied, you can open the Gradient Editor to set the values.

12. Click and drag the first keyframe in the graph down to the bottom left corner. This is 0% for both the amount and percentage of the input parameter you've chosen—in this case, Incidence Angle. The vertical value is the amount, while the bottom horizontal numbers are the percentage. To create an additional key, middle-click in the Gradient Editor. If you don't have a middle mouse button, use Ctrl and Alt at the same time while left-clicking. Then drag that key with the left mouse button to about 160%, to the right. Bring the key up to an amount of 50%. You can set these values numerically at the top left of the graph panel.
13. You'll see a small square with a line hanging out of the keys. You can click and drag these handles to change the outgoing and incoming curves for the keys. Figure 11.15 shows the graph with these settings.

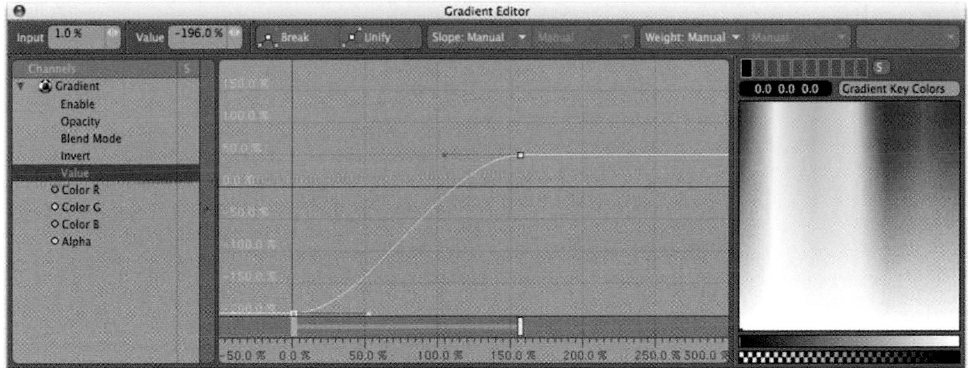

Figure 11.15
Create a key at the 160% percentage point, and adjust the slope of the curve for the 0% key.

Note

I've included a Gradient Editor video on the book's disc to help explain this cool feature of modo. You can find it in Chapter 11's Videos folder.

14. Close the Gradient Editor, and save your work thus far.
15. Back up in the Shader Tree, select the IceCube material, then click the Add Layer drop-down menu and choose Cellular. Set its effect to Displacement. This will help rough up the ice a bit.
16. In the Properties tab, click the Texture Layer vertical tab, and make sure Blend Mode is set to Normal. Opacity should be 10%. This will create just a slight displacement.
17. Cell Value should be 0%, while Filler Value should be 100%.

18. Type can be set to Angular, with a Cell Width of 60% and a Transition Width of 30%. What these values do is vary how this computer-generated procedural texture is used. You've already told modo that it's used to displace the object, but now you're telling it how it's applied.
19. Frequencies should be set to 1, and Bias and Gain can remain at 50%, as shown in Figure 11.16. Most of these values are the defaults, but double-check them to make sure.

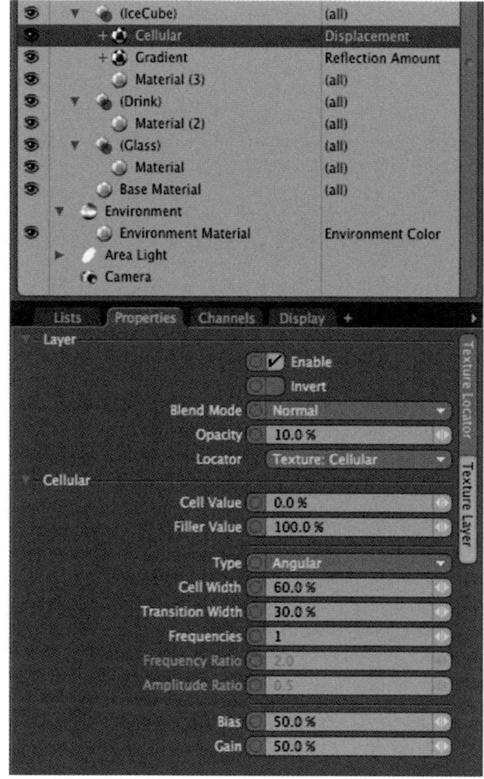

Figure 11.16
The Cellular texture is a cool looking procedural texture that also works well for random displacements.

20. Click the Texture Locator vertical tab, and change size to 5 mm for each the X, Y, and Z axes. Remember to use the gang select option to quickly change the values if you like.
21. Projection Type should be set to Solid. This applies the procedural texture directly over the entire surface.

> **Note**
>
> If your preview window slows down redrawing after you've applied the displacement to the ice cubes, you can click the Options button at the top of the preview window and turn off the Displacement feature. This turns off the displacement preview but does not change the surface settings.

22. Save your work. Figure 11.17 shows the scene thus far. You can see that the ice cubes are now looking pretty good!

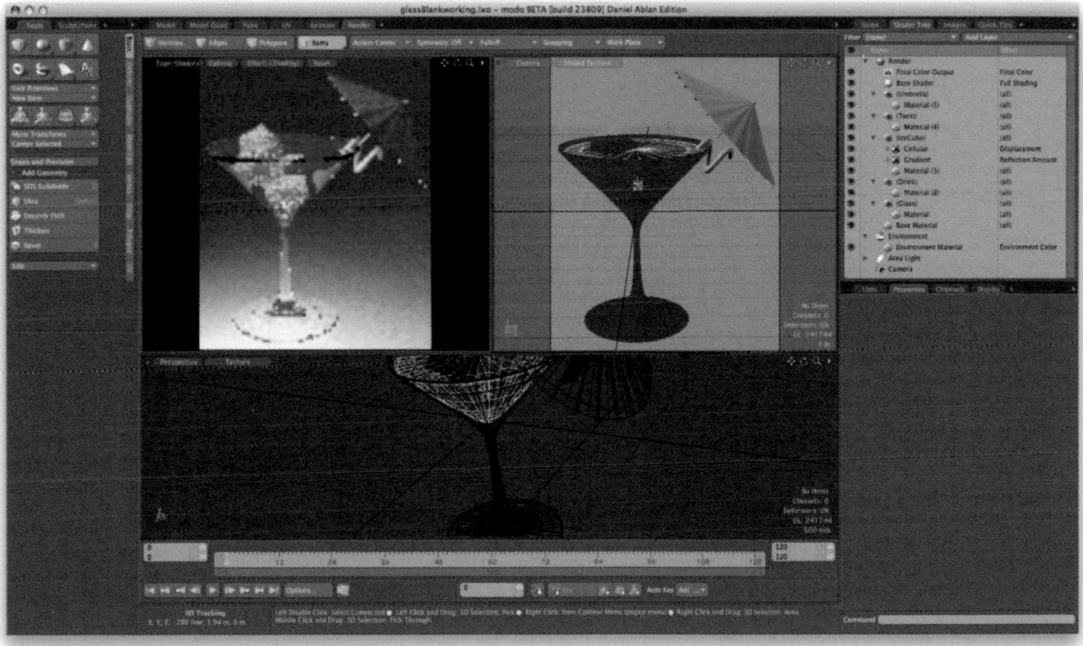

Figure 11.17 With a few more settings to the ice cube and adding a displacement, the surface looks good.

At this point, feel free to tweak and play with your scene as you like. Try adding another layer on top of the Cellular texture, perhaps a Noise layer, set also to Displacement. Save your project when finished. Now it's time to surface the umbrella. But rather than adding a typical material color or a procedural layer, you'll paint the surface!

Painting Surfaces

Painting surfaces is a cool technique that any 3D modeler can benefit from. You do not need to be an artist by any means. This next section will introduce you to the painting tools, how to set them up on a model, and how to use them. From there, you'll move on to the book's disc to watch video tutorials taking you further with painting and texturing. You'll use the traffic light model created in the previous chapter and finish what you started. After all, what's a good model without good textures? But before that, read on to learn about this slick modo feature.

1. Open up modo, and click over to the Tools tab. If you have a scene loaded, save it and then choose File, Save Incremental to save a new version.
2. Click the Sculpt/Paint tab, as shown in Figure 11.18.
3. Your previous scene has become complex with displacements, procedural texture layers, and global illumination; and since you want the best resources possible for feedback on your painting, right-click on the Items tab, and then from the popup menu, choose Viewport Settings, Auto Visibility, as shown in Figure 11.19.
4. In the Items tab, select the Umbrella mesh layer. Also, for working with the paint tools, change back to the Model view by clicking the first tab above the viewports.

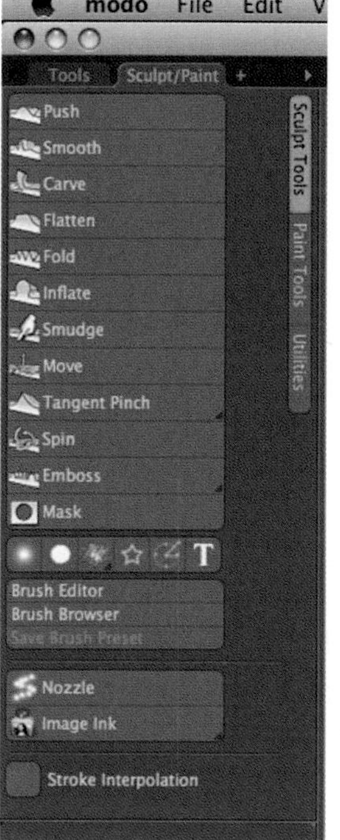

Figure 11.18
Open the Sculpt/Paint tab next to the Tools tab.

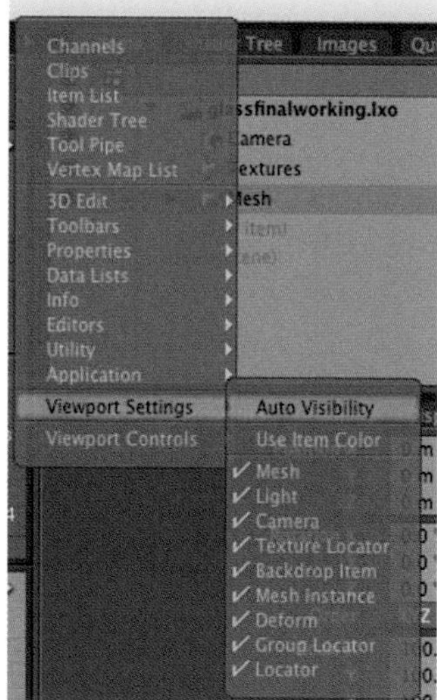

Figure 11.19
Activate Auto Visibility to isolate the selected mesh.

5. Within the Sculpt/Paint tab, click on the Utilities vertical tab. A the top of this tab, click the Add Color Texture button. The New Image dialog box will open asking you where you'd like to save the new image, as shown in Figure 11.20.

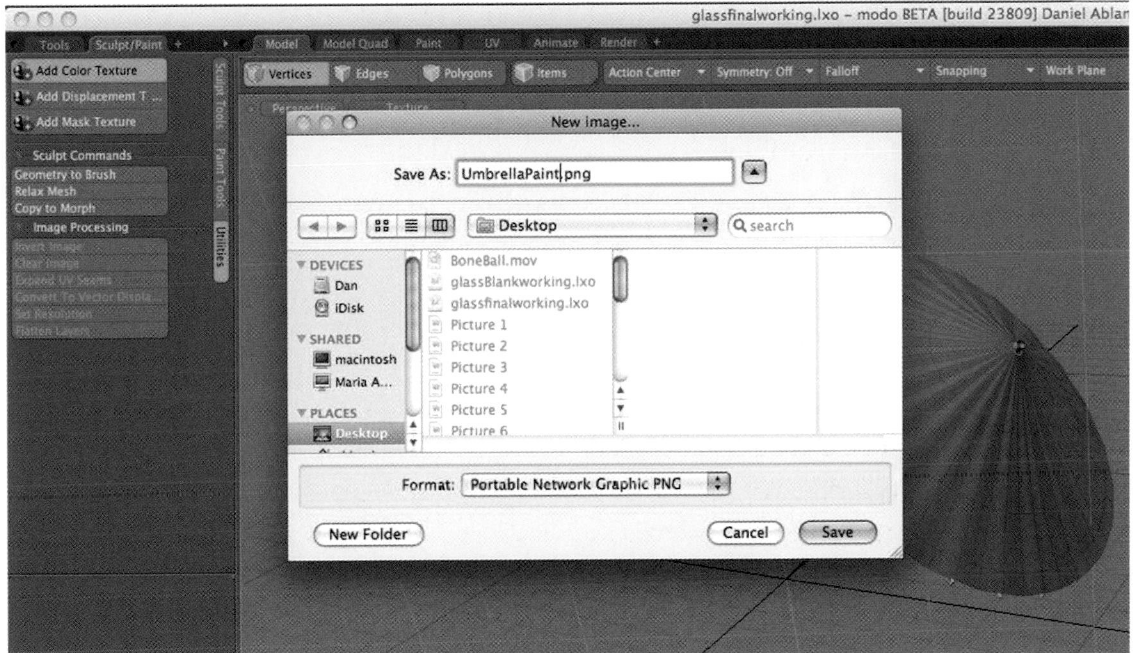

Figure 11.20 Choosing Add Color Texture from the Utilities vertical category first asks you where to save the image.

6. Give the image the name UmbrellaPaint and save it as a PNG or TGA, or whatever file format you like. PNGs are the image of choice for this book. Once you click OK, a New Still dialog appears, asking you some specifics of the image (see Figure 11.21). For this particular image, choose 1024 × 1024 for the Resolution setting. You can go up to 4000 for the image, but since the umbrella is not completely filling the scene, a 1 KB image works fine. You can choose RGBA for the Format setting. This is telling modo you're creating a color image with an alpha channel. Floating Point and Set Color don't need to be checked, but they can be if you'd like to set these. This image does not need to be a floating-point image. Essentially, a floating-point image is a 32-bit per channel image, which means it contains vastly more information than the standard 8-bit per channel image. It's mostly useful for displacements, lighting, and even reflections—anything that requires a lot of data. Since this is not a large image map you'll be painting, you don't need to apply this option.

Figure 11.21 Choose the resolution and format for your image.

7. Click OK. You've now set up an image to paint on. If you look at the Items tab, you'll see a new locator for texture image has been added.
8. To begin, click the Paint Tools vertical tab, which is in the Sculpt/Paint tab. Then, fill the umbrella with color. Do this by selecting the Fill tool, which is the paint can icon. When selected, you can change the FG Color (foreground color) to a bluish green. Then, click and drag slightly on the umbrella in the viewport. After a moment, your umbrella will be colored, as shown in Figure 11.22.
9. Coloring the umbrella is not a big deal, as this doesn't look much different than just setting a basic material color. Okay then, take it a step further. Back in the Paint Tools tab, select the Airbrush tool.

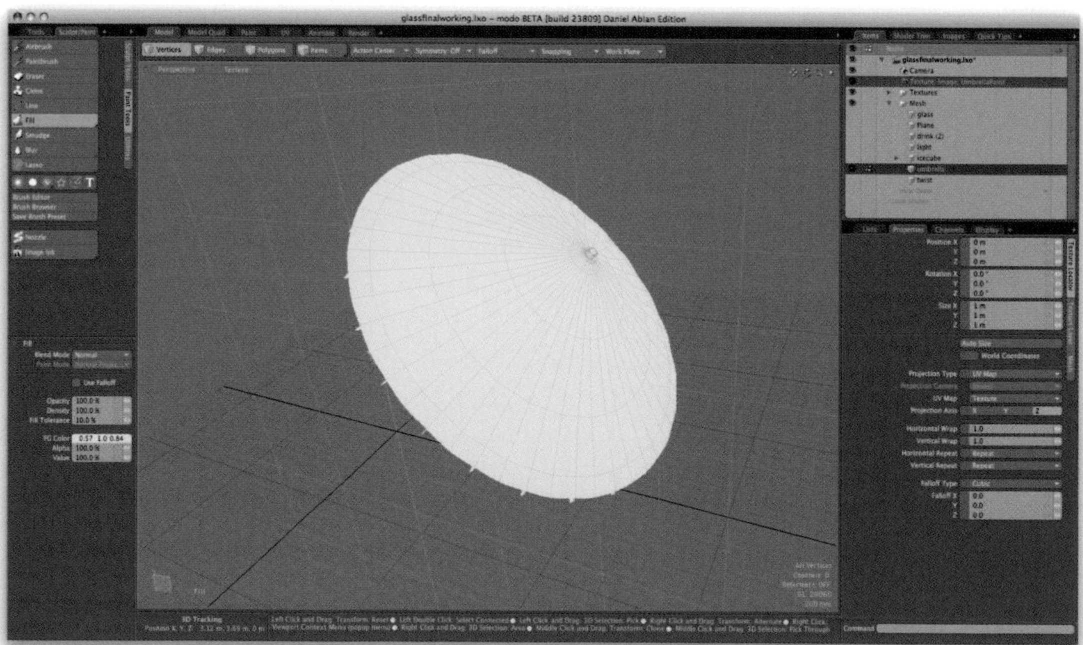

Figure 11.22 Using the Fill tool within the Paint Tools vertical tab, you can quickly fill an object with color.

> **Note**
>
> If you hold your mouse cursor over one of the paint brushes, after a moment, the name of that tool will pop up.

10. Then under the Brushes area, select the third brush icon, which is the Procedural brush (see Figure 11.23). If you click and hold this icon, you can choose yet another brush, the Sphere brush. The first brush is the Airbrush, which falls off to a soft edge from the center. The brush next to it, the Hard brush, is solid, but you can set a soft border in the Tool Properties panel. For now, the Procedural brush will work well, and it allows you to set some procedural noise in your paint.

11. Next, in the Procedural Brush properties underneath the Brushes area at the bottom, change the Type setting to Cellular. Remember that if you can't see the settings, click and drag between the windows to adjust them.

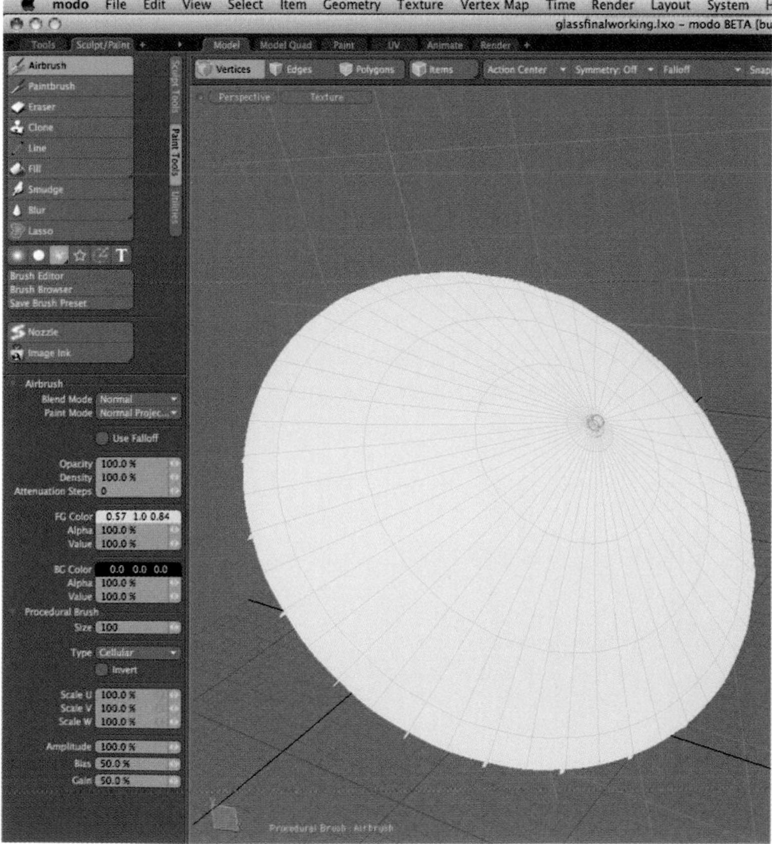

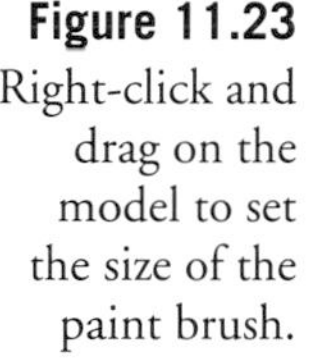

Figure 11.23
Right-click and drag on the model to set the size of the paint brush.

12. You won't use the Ink setting right now. However, this is where you'll be able to set images for painting. You'll do that in the video portion of this chapter on the book's disc.
13. With that all said, right-click on the umbrella and drag. This sets the size of the Procedural brush. Set it to about 100, which you can also do numerically in the Properties panel.
14. With the size set, change the FG Color setting in the Airbrush properties (see Figure 11.24). Pick a bright color, perhaps a dark blue. Then, using the left mouse button, click and drag on the umbrella. Voilà! You're painting on a 3D model! Now go further, and click the Paint Tools vertical tab at the top of the interface. Here, you can find the color picker, brush tips, and more. You'll find more tutorials in this area on the book's DVD videos.
15. What you'll find when painting is that you might want to redo it, often. Press Ctrl-Z (PC) or Command-Z (Mac) to undo your painting. Hold the Alt key, then click and drag the view around so you're looking more at the top of the umbrella. What you might find, however, is that as you paint, you get some weird offshoots of color, as shown in Figure 11.25.
16. As you can see, it's pretty easy to paint right on your models, but there can be issues at times. The solution to this painting error is to work more closely with UV maps.

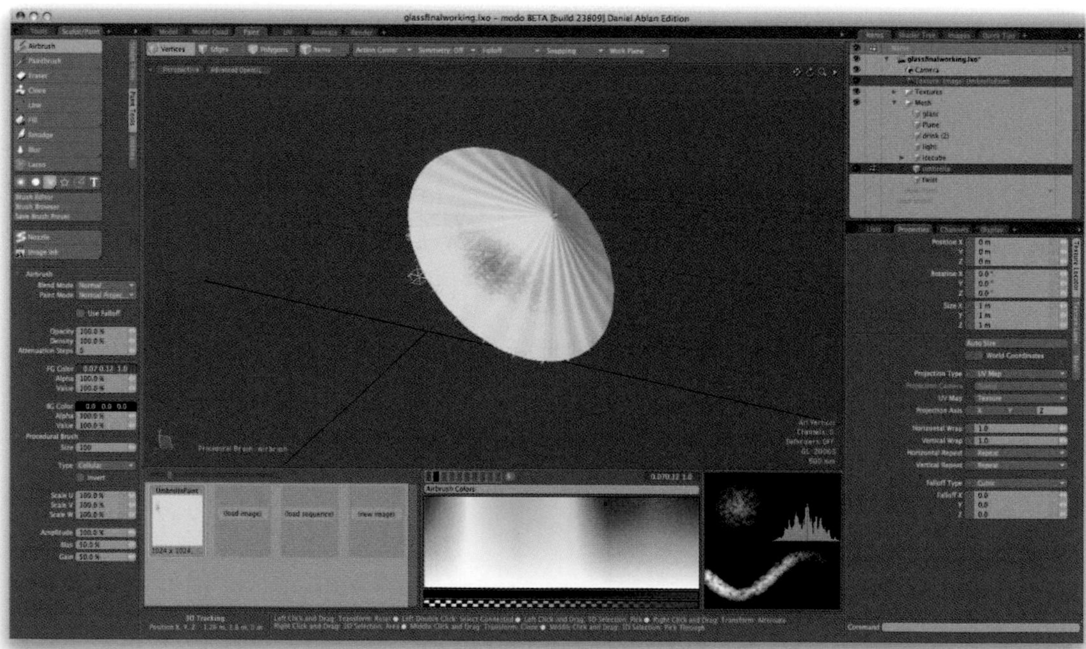

Figure 11.24 By clicking and dragging with the left mouse button, you're now painting on a 3D model.

17. At the top of the viewport, click the UV tab. You'll see the umbrella in the workspace on the right, and on the left, a weird red view. Figure 11.26 shows the screen.

    What you're seeing is the unwrapped UV map that was created when you first clicked Add Blank Texture Image. But you need to be more specific in the creation of your UV maps from time to time. Save your scene, and go to the UV Umbrella video on the book's DVD to see how to correct this painting issue.

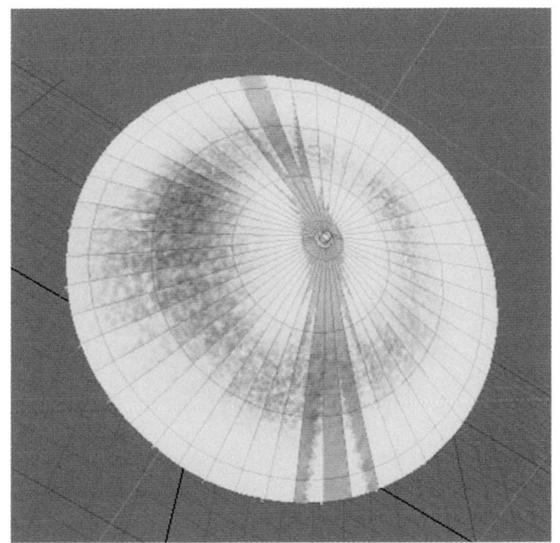

Figure 11.25 Painting larger areas can often lead to some unwanted results.

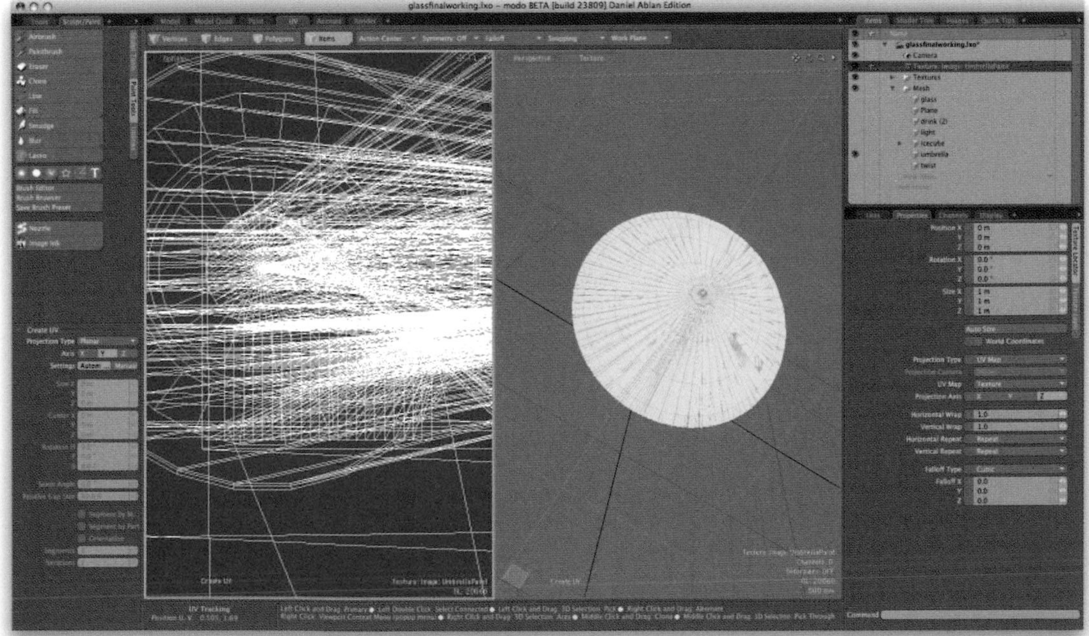

Figure 11.26 Using the UV view, you can see the map you're painting.

Note

The image you painted will not be saved simply by saving the scene. You have to choose Save All or Save all Images, or you can right-click on the image in the image list and choose Save.

18. Continue painting as you like, and even experiment. You can continually add different brushes and procedurals to make a very stylized umbrella. Perhaps write in your name or create bands of color. It's completely up to you.
19. Take a look at the Shader Tree. Your painted image might be above all of the other material layers, as shown in Figure 11.27.

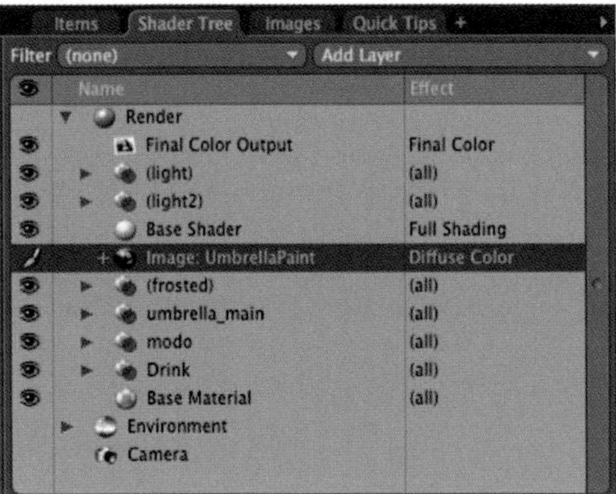

Figure 11.27 Your painted texture might end up on top of your other materials. If so, just drag it into the mask layer that it belongs to, in this case, the umbrella.

This only scratches the surface of modo's painting tools. In order to cover them properly, as mentioned, there are additional video training tutorials exclusively for this book from 3D Garage.com. And while 3DGarage.com offers a full modo 301/302 training course, the videos for this chapter have been created to match these projects. Additionally, you'll learn more about UV maps, how to unwrap them, and how to create additional surfacing techniques using the traffic light model created in the previous chapter.

12

Subdivision Surface Modeling

Throughout this book, you've used the modo toolset and created various objects. Some objects included the use of subdivision surfaces, and some did not. But I've yet to fully explain the workflow of subdivision surfaces, what they are, and how they work.

When you model an object, even just a ball or a cube, you're creating polygons. Polygons have faces, or *surface normals*. When you press the Tab key in modo, you turn an ordinary face polygon into a *subdivision* (or subdivided) surface. The polygons become smooth when converted to subdivision surfaces, also known as Sub-Ds. The goal of this chapter is to teach you how to model in Sub-D mode.

Understanding Sub-Ds

Sub-Ds, or subdivision surfaces, are an excellent choice for modeling characters because you can create a significant amount of detail without a lot of geometry. Why is this, you ask? Good question! You see, a subdivision polygon is dynamically multiplied. They are refined to as much detail as you specify. In fact, as with modo 201, modo 301/302 offers you the ability to have *micropolygon displacement*, which, when combined with subdivision surfaces, allows you to create models with the utmost physical detail. Subdivision surfaces are not only great for characters, but also for anything you can think of.

There are a few things you should be aware of before you begin modeling a character with Sub-Ds. The most important aspect is the flow of the geometry. The *flow* is the way the polygons in the mesh are aligned. For example, Figure 12.1 shows the ogre model with good flow. This model came with your modo software. Figure 12.2 shows the same model with bad flow.

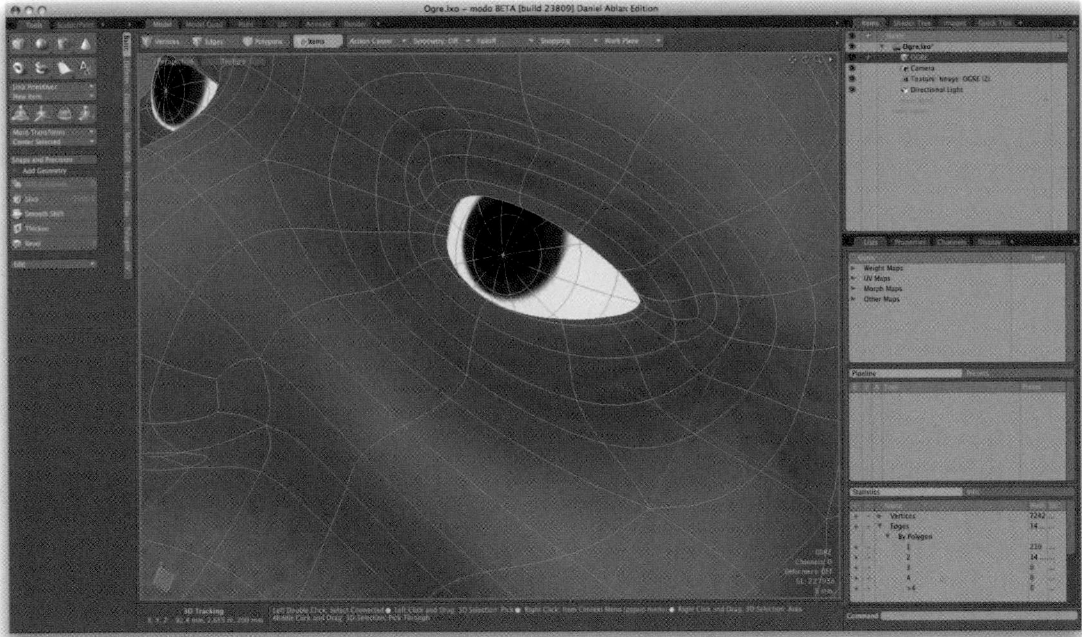

Figure 12.1 Using the ogre model from the modo content directory, you can see that the polygons in the mesh flow nicely, and the geometry is smooth and even.

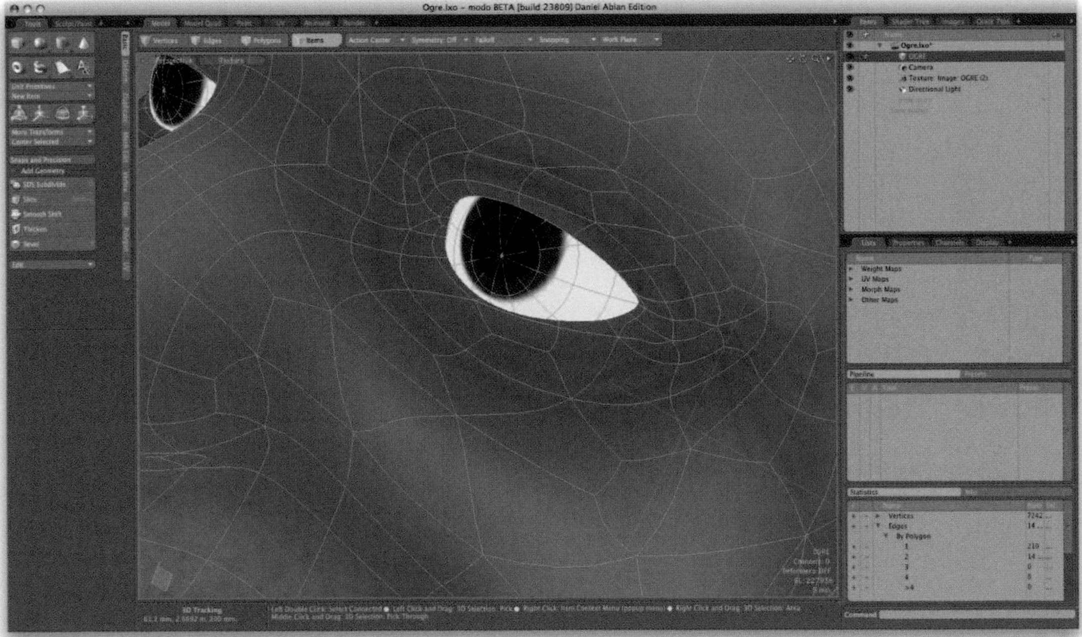

Figure 12.2 Using a variation of the ogre model from the modo content directory, you can see that the polygons in this mesh don't flow properly, resulting in a model that isn't as smooth as it could be. This can also result in shading and rendering problems.

Proper flow of your subdivision surface model is important to understand before you begin modeling. This way, you'll not only have more control over what you're building, but also better results when rendering. With that said, how about seeing it in action?

Building a Product in Sub-Ds

To begin creating this product, you're going to use a primitive shape. There are a few methods to modeling products and similar real-life objects. People often ask what the proper modeling method is for such an object. The debate rages on, but if you're busier using your 3D software than discussing it on an Internet forum, then you're already on the right path. You see, there is the *box modeling* method, where you start with a box and subdivide your model into shape, similar to an artist creating a beautiful sculpture out of ice. Another is the *point-by-point* method, where you build your geometry one point at a time using a background image. This is great for modeling characters from sketches or photographs. Another method is *spline-based* modeling. Splines are curves that you can align, then patch together to make a model. Which method is best? None of them! That's right. Now you can rest easy.

The point is, no one method is best for everything, be it modeling, surfacing, or rendering. It's completely up to you and what method you're comfortable using. The character in this chapter will benefit from simple geometric shapes, or the box-modeling method. And with that said, here's a little tip: In the end, it's the render that matters. You might often have artists ask you to see the "wires" or wireframe render of your model. What's important is the final render and whether or not your client/boss/director is happy. Does the model animate and render well? Then that's all you truly need to worry about. Figure 12.3 shows a cube, created by holding the Shift key and clicking the Cube primitive button. Next to it is the same cube after pressing the d key, which subdivides the cube. The third cube in the image shows it subdivided one additional time.

Looking closely at Figure 12.3, if you look at the edges of the third image of the cube, the one most subdivided, it's still rough. Pressing the d key only subdivided the mesh; it did not turn it into a Sub-D model, or a subdivision surface. It sounds confusing, but if you take a look at Figure 12.4, the image on the left is a subdivided cube, while the image on the right is a subdivision surface. This subdivision surface is toggled on and off by pressing the Tab key.

Note

Pressing just the d key creates a subdivision surface (also called SDS). If you press Shift and the d key, you can choose between a Faceted (flat) subdivision, Smooth, or SDS.

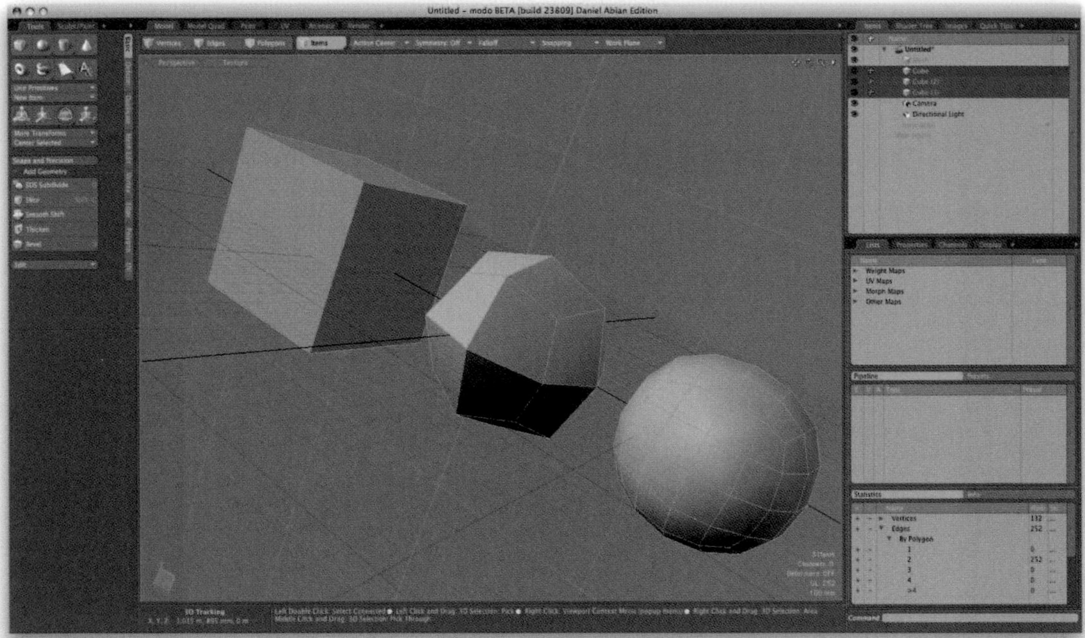

Figure 12.3 Starting with a simple cube, then pressing the d key two times, you can see how this basic shape becomes subdivided.

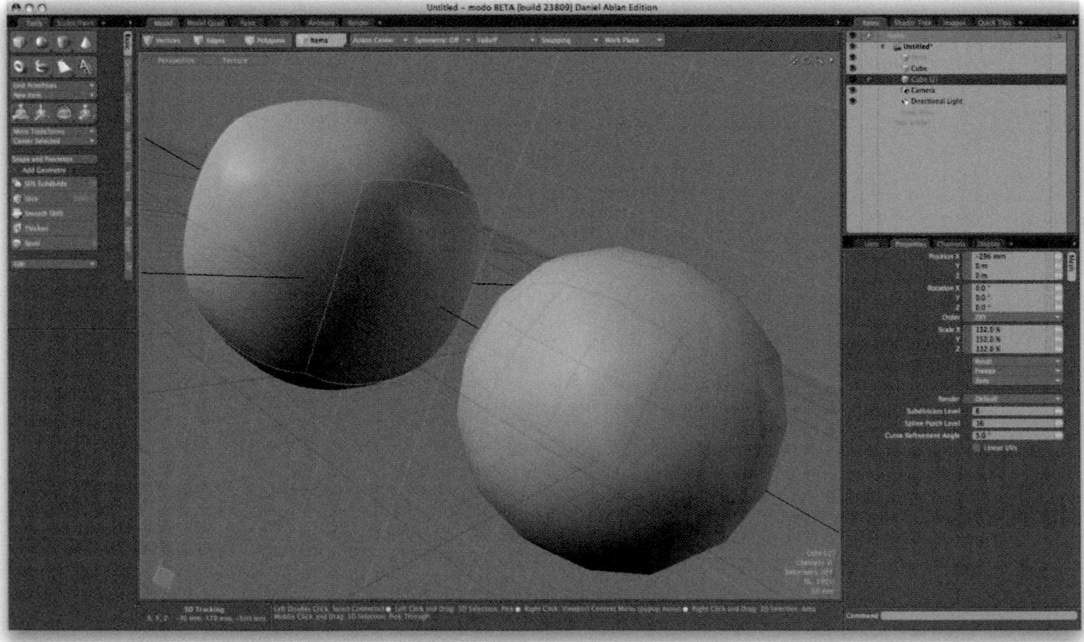

Figure 12.4 While subdividing the mesh, you can see that the image on the right is chunky. By pressing the Tab key and activating Sub-D mode, the image on the left is smooth.

Starting with a Cube for a Detergent Bottle

As you begin modeling this detergent bottle you may ask yourself, "Why is this crazy author making us create this?" First of all, no one is making you do anything. It's merely a suggestion. Secondly, the techniques you'll learn here are great for any kind of product like this, from bottles to cans to prototypes. You can branch out further to build lamps, ornaments, faucets, and other interior design elements. If you're adventurous, these same techniques will work for modeling automobiles. To begin, you'll use simple geometry and subdivide as needed, then convert the mesh to Sub-Ds along the way.

1. Open up modo, and click over to the Tools tab.
2. Select the Cube primitive.
3. Rotate the viewport so that the work plane is on the XZ axis, and make sure the positive Z axis is in front of you.
4. Draw out a flat box with two segments for both the X and Z axes, as shown in Figure 12.5.
5. Press the q key to turn off the Cube tool.
6. Press the Tab key to turn on subdivision surfaces.
7. Rotate the view a bit so that you're mostly looking down at the model, in a Perspective view.

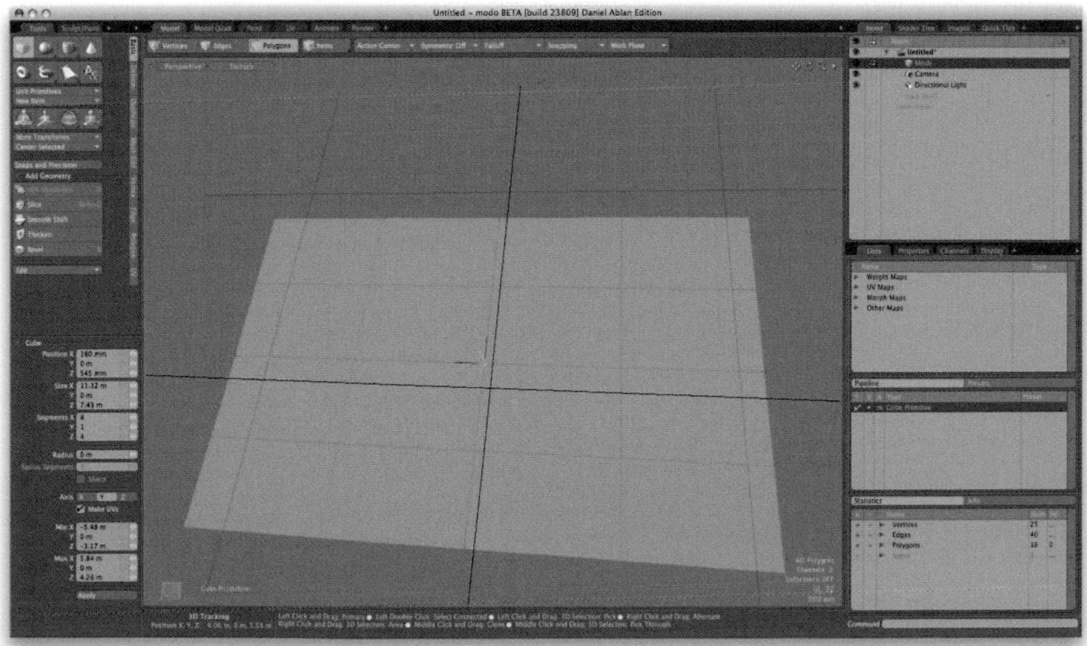

Figure 12.5 To begin creating the detergent bottle, start with a flat plane.

8. From the Basic vertical tab within the Tools tab, choose Center Selected, then choose All. This will center the model in the workspace.
9. Turn on Symmetry for the Z axis. Do this from the Symmetry menu at the top of the modo interface.
10. Then press the T key for the Element Move tool, and carefully click and drag on the rear center point of the flat plane. This is to round out the bottle, as shown in Figure 12.6.

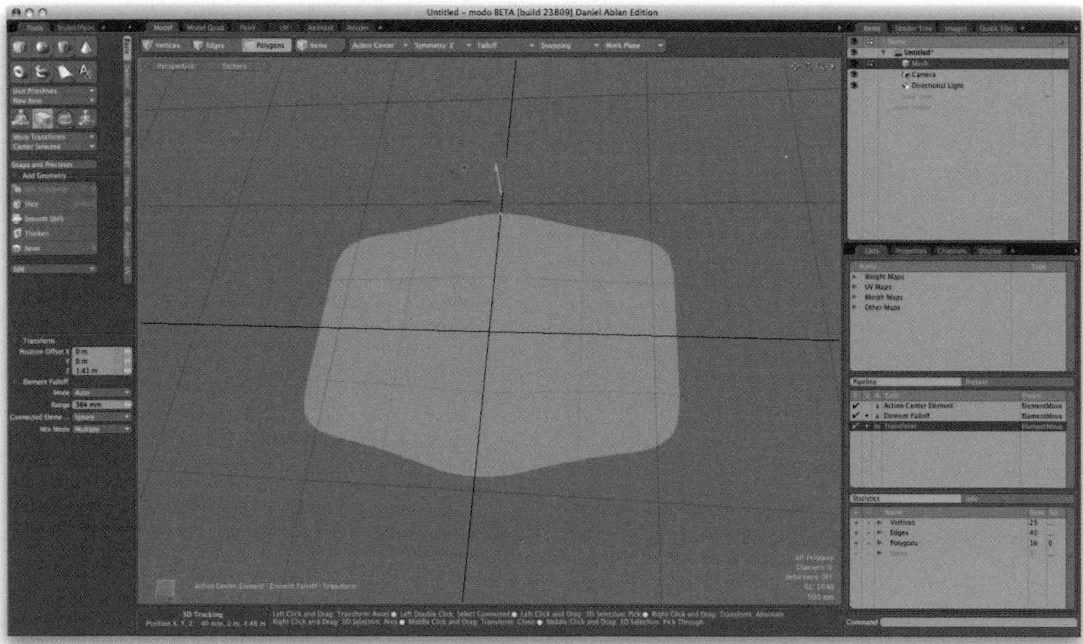

Figure 12.6 Using the Element Move tool, along with Symmetry for the Z axis, you can round out the flat plane.

> **Tip**
>
> If you're having trouble moving on a specific axis while using the Element Move tool, just click on the element, a point, edge, or polygon; then you'll see the axis handles. Use them to drag an element more precisely.

11. You can see that with subdivision surfaces on (Tab key), the simple flat cube already has a cool shape. So, using the same Symmetry setup as before, click and drag the other two points on the back of the model to even out the curvature, as shown in Figure 12.7.

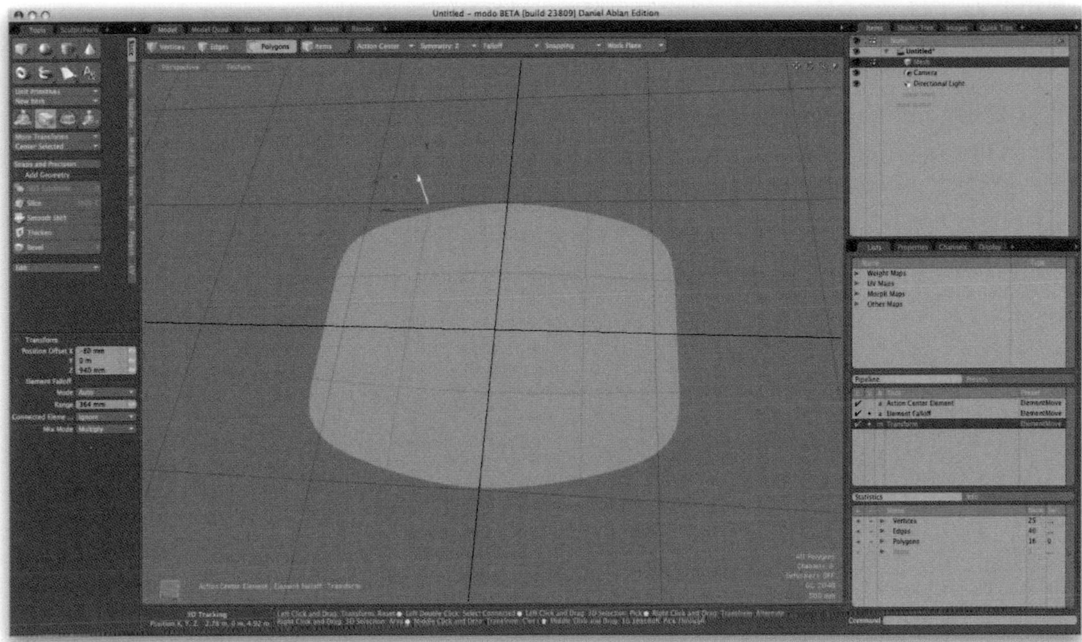

Figure 12.7 Using the Element Move tool, drag the remaining points on the Z axis to round out the flat plane.

12. Change the Symmetry from the Z to the X axis. As you did in the previous steps, press the T key, and use the Element Move tool to drag out the sides of the flat cube slightly to round them a bit. Figure 12.8 shows the example.
13. Save your work by pressing Command-S (Mac) or Ctrl-S (PC). Save it as Bottle_V001.lxo. You'll be saving your model incrementally with modo's Save Incremental option.
14. Switch to Polygons mode at the top of the modo interface and, using the right mouse button, lasso select the entire group of polygons. You're doing this so that as you bevel, you are only beveling one set of polygons.
15. With the polygons selected, press the b key to activate the Bevel tool. In the Bevel tool properties panel, make sure Group Polygons is checked.
16. Click once on the selection. The Bevel's red and blue handles appear.
17. Drag the red handle outward to change the Inset value. Then, click and drag the blue handle outward to bring the Shift value to about 120 mm. Figure 12.9 shows the operation.
18. Hold the Shift key and click on the selection to reset the bevel.

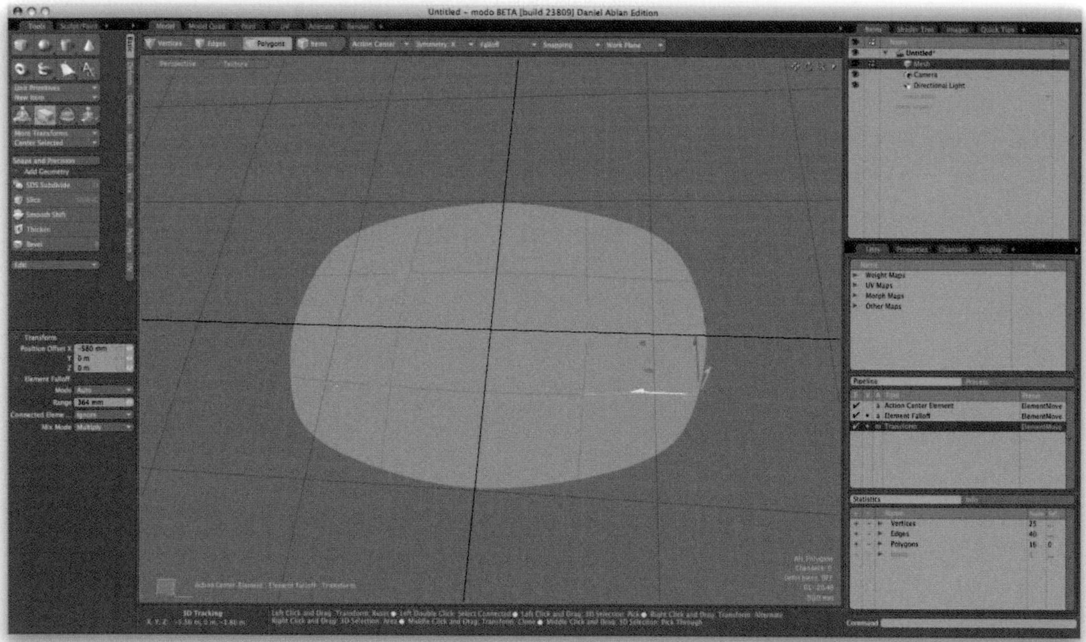

Figure 12.8 Use the Element Move tool on the sides of the flat plane to round it out slightly.

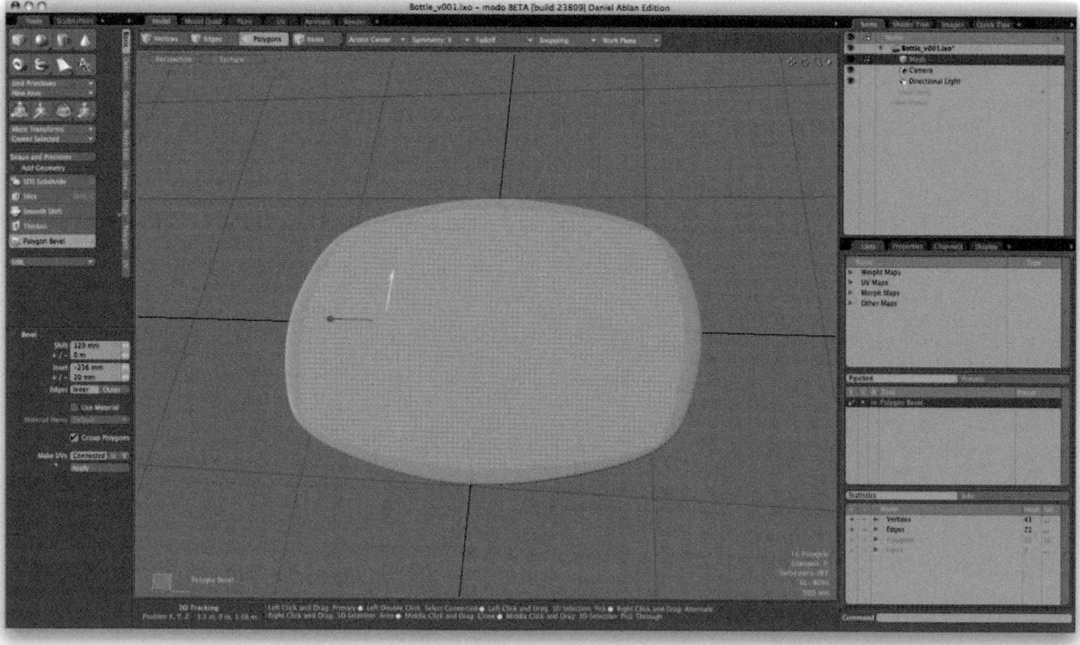

Figure 12.9 Click and drag the blue handle outward to adjust the Shift value for the bevel.

19. Click and drag the blue handle to shift the newly beveled polygons to about 1.75 m, as shown in Figure 12.10.

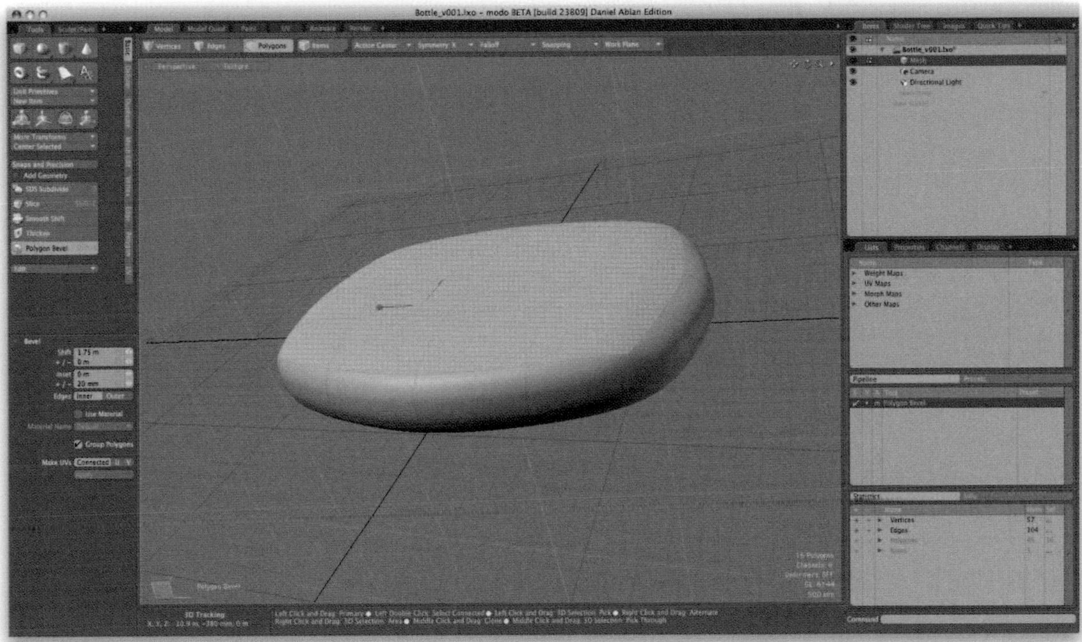

Figure 12.10 With a new set of beveled polygons, shift them about 1.75 m.

20. Repeat the previous two steps a few more times so that you have something similar to Figure 12.11.

> **Tip**
>
> Using the middle mouse button, you can exactly repeat the previous step.

21. Save your work, but this time, go to File, Save Incremental, as shown in Figure 12.12.
22. Hold the Shift key and click on the selected polygons to reset the bevel. Then bevel again, but only change the Inset value to about 3 m, as shown in Figure 12.13.
23. Click off of the model into an empty area of the viewport to deselect the polygons. You'll come back to these later to add the pour spout.

Figure 12.11 Repeat the steps so that you have a shape similar to the one shown here.

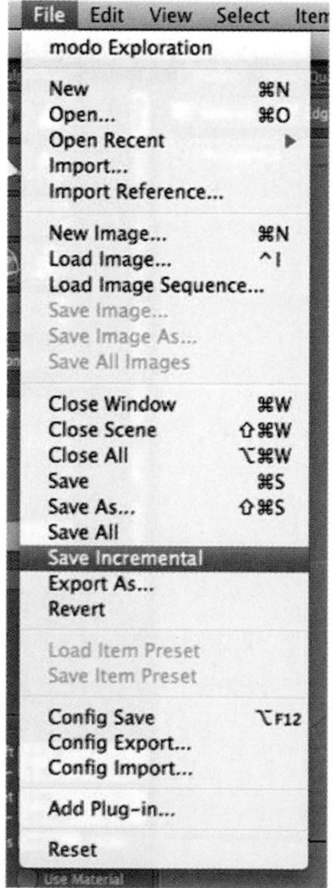

Figure 12.12 When building in modo, try using the Save Incremental option so that you always have the previous version.

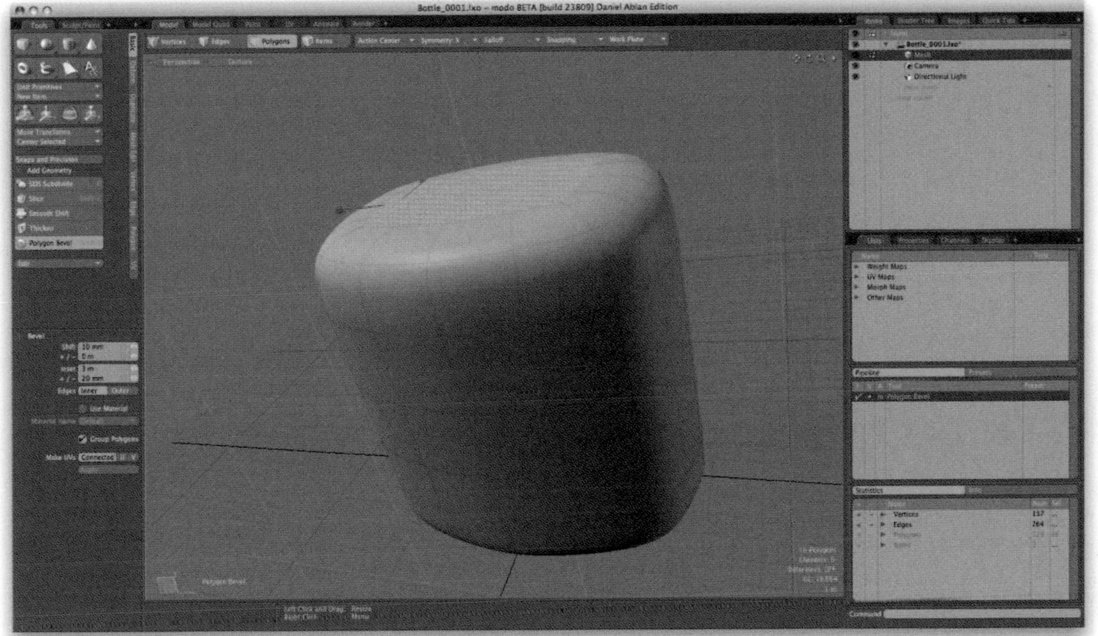

Figure 12.13 Inset the last set of polygons at the top of the bottle.

Sharper Edges with Subdivisions

One popular myth about working with subdivision surfaces is that they're only good for cartoon-like objects. Models that are soft and round are the only thing you can create. For models with sharper edges or more detail, people often think you can't use subdivisions. But that's not the case at all. This next section will show you a perfect use for subdivisions, something that is actually harder to achieve without subdivisions.

1. Picking up where the previous section left off, click over to the Basic tab within the Tools tab.
2. Click the Center Selected drop-down list and choose All. This will perfectly center the model on the 0 axis.
3. Then, at the top of the interface, choose Symmetry for the Z axis.
4. Select the 20 polygons that make up the face of the model. With Symmetry on, the opposite side of the model will be selected as well. However, if your original base model was not perfectly symmetrical when you used the Element Move tool, not all polygons will become selected. So, hold the Shift key and you can add to the selection. You should have 40 polygons total selected, 20 on each side, as shown in Figure 12.14.

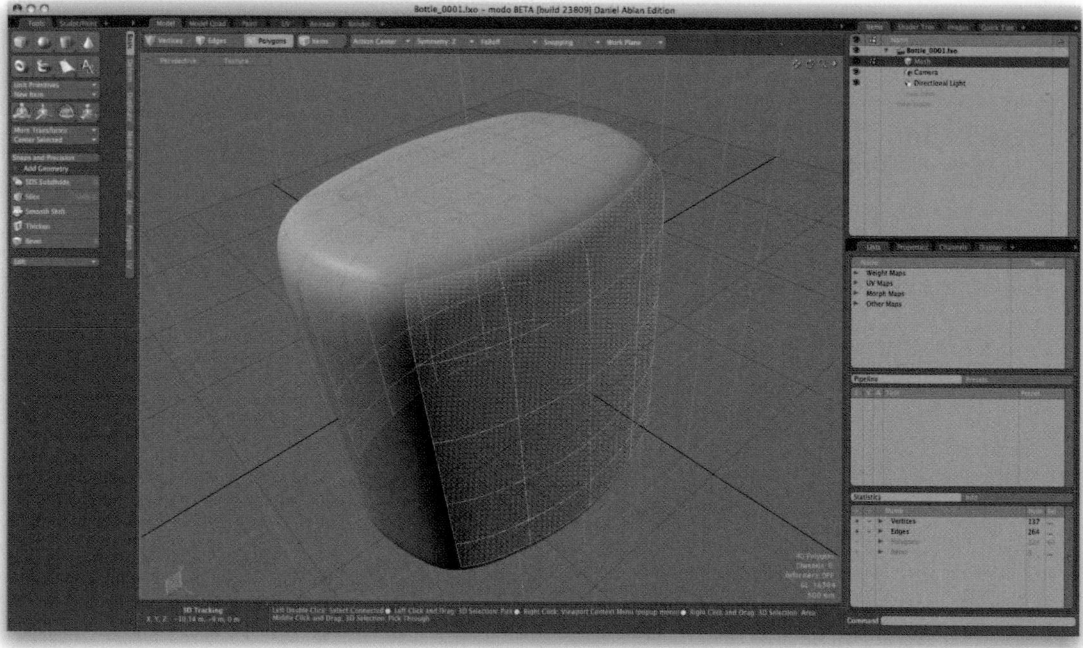

Figure 12.14 Select the polygons on both sides of the bottle.

5. With the polygons selected, press the b key again for the Bevel tool. Make sure Group Polygons is selected in the Bevel properties.
6. Click on the selection to activate the Bevel tool. Set the Inset and Shift values to 100 mm, as shown in Figure 12.15.
7. Hold the Shift key and click once on the selection to reset the bevel. You'll see the edges now really sharpen out. Almost a little too much! But you see, subdivision surfaces are like curves in Adobe Illustrator. A tighter curve yields more detail. By beveling two times, you've added extra geometry, thereby tightening the edge between the bottle and the selection.
8. Pull the Shift value out a bit to soften the edge slightly, as shown in Figure 12.16.
9. Deselect the polygons, and save an incremental version of your model.
10. Hold the Alt key, then click and drag in the viewport to rotate around to see the bottom of the bottle. Figure 12.17 shows the view.
11. A hole! Why is there a hole in the bottom of the bottle? It's not going to hold much this way. Because polygons are one sided, you had them facing up when you started beveling the bottle. So, the bottom now needs some geometry. Switch to Edges mode, then double-click the edge surrounding the open hole, as shown in Figure 12.18.

Figure 12.15 Set the first bevel to minor Shift and Inset values of 100 mm.

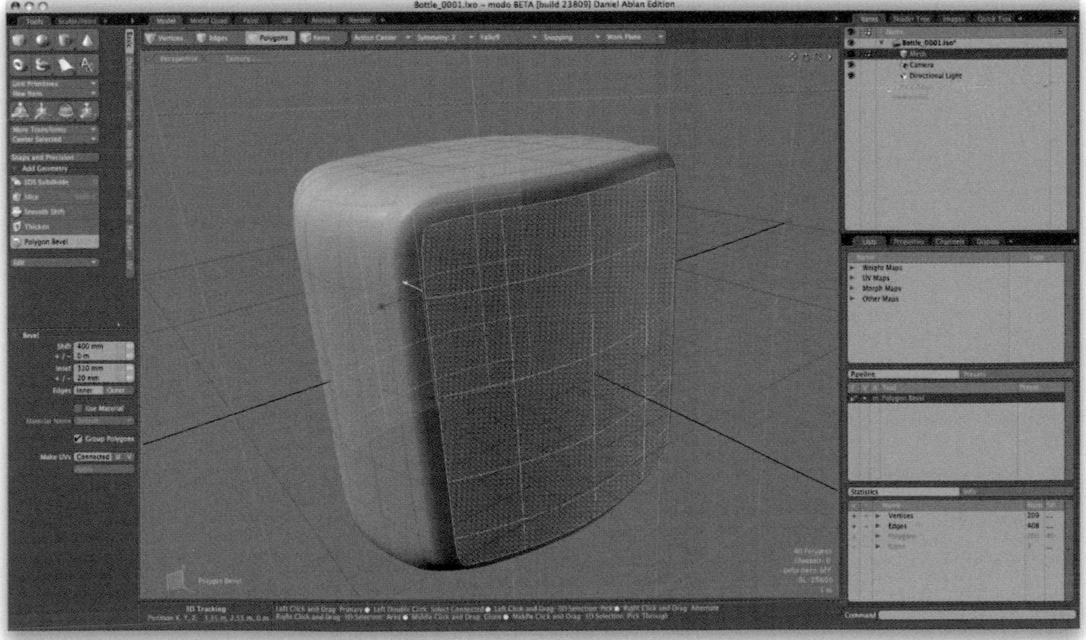

Figure 12.16 Extend the Shift value slightly to lessen the sharpness of the new bevels.

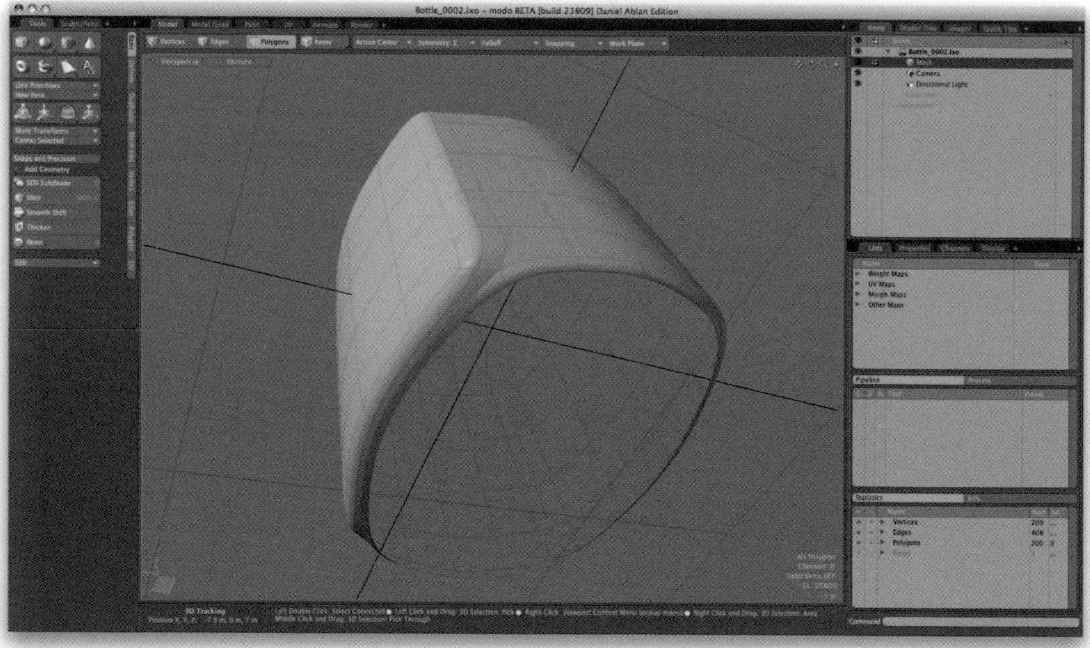

Figure 12.17 Rotate the view to see the bottom of the model.

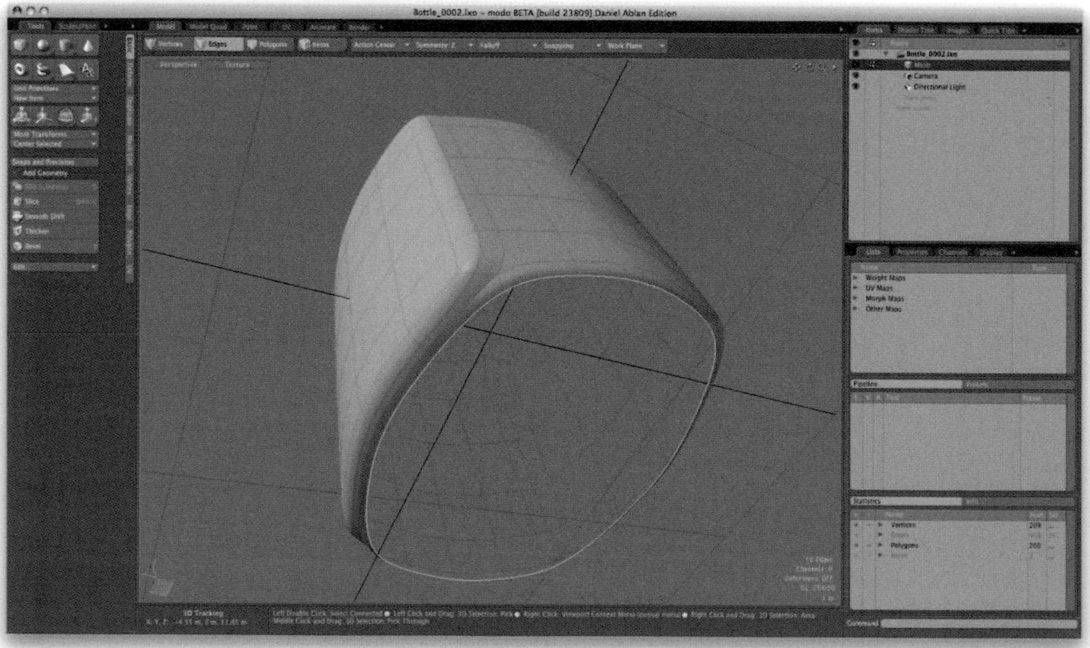

Figure 12.18 Double-click the edge surrounding the open hole of the bottle.

12. With the edge loop selected, press the p key to create a polygon and close the hole. Then, switch to Polygons mode. Press the b key and bevel the newly created polygon with a slight adjustment for the Inset and Shift values, as shown in Figure 12.19.
13. Deselect the polygon, and save your work!

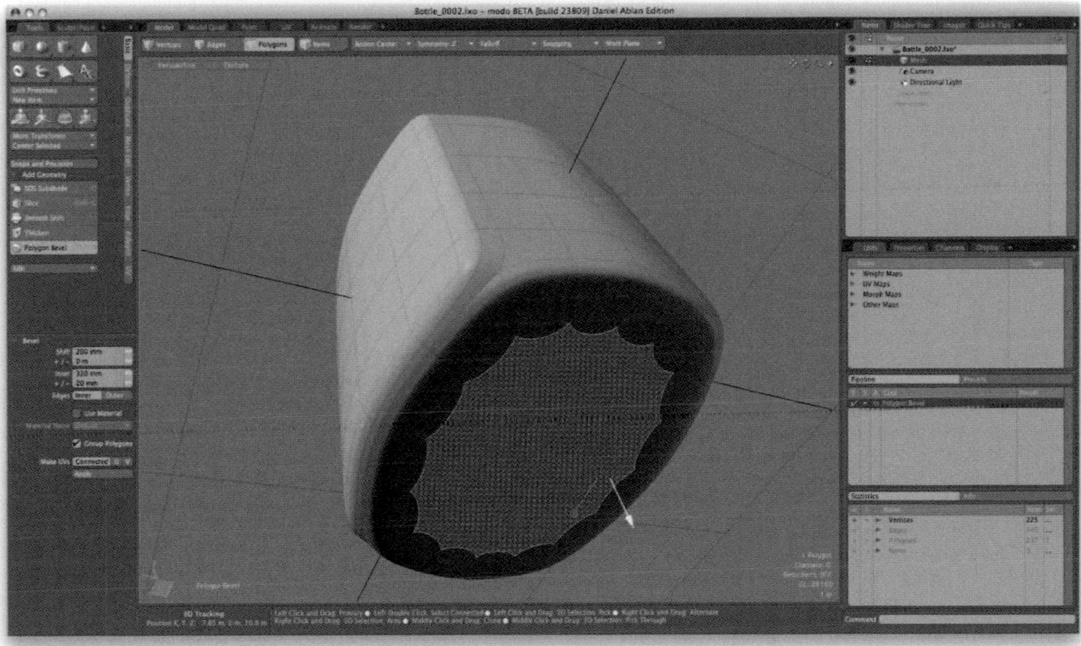

Figure 12.19 Bevel the newly created polygon a slight amount for both the Inset and Shift values.

Advantages of Subdivisions

At this point, you've not really made anything tremendous. C'mon, we know what you're thinking. But wait! There's more! This next section will show you how to create the handle for the bottle. Like most molded plastic today, such as a milk container, anti-freeze bottle, or a detergent bottle, the handle is blended, or part of the bottle itself. It's not a separate piece of plastic stapled to the top. So how would you go about building in a handle on an object that already has its base shape? This is where a subdivision surface model has advantages.

1. Continuing with the model you've been working on, switch over to Polygons selection mode. Note that you can use the Bottle_0003.lxo file on the book's disc if you like.
2. Save your object as a new incremental version, retaining the original model at that point.
3. On the right side of the bottle, select the top two polygons, as shown in Figure 12.20.

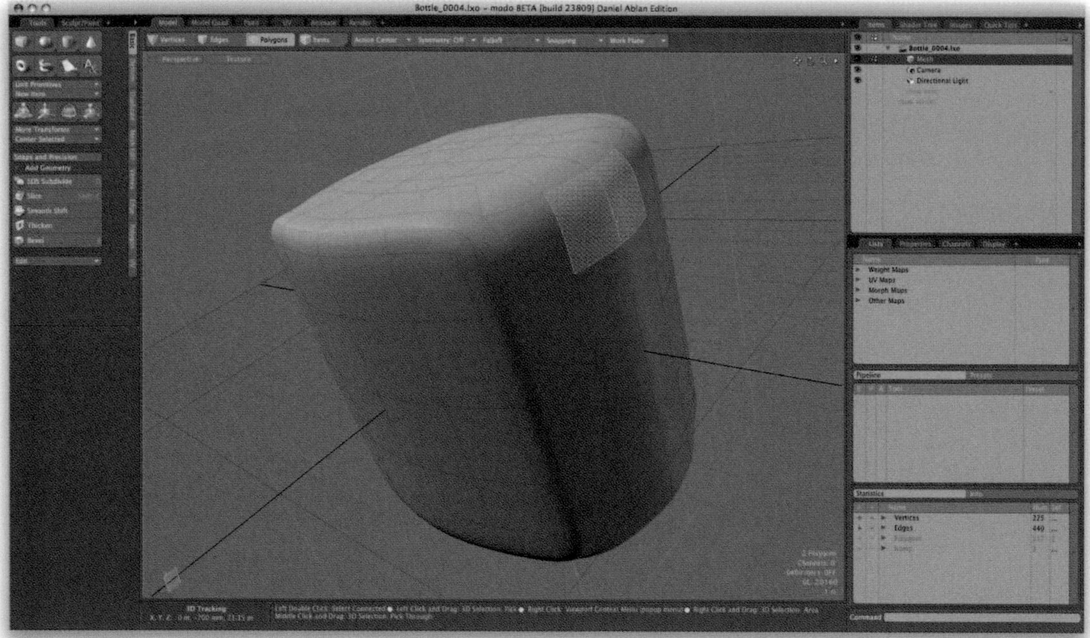

Figure 12.20 Select the top two polygons at the right side of the bottle.

4. Press the b key for the Bevel tool. Click on the selection to activate, and drag the Inset value to about 890 mm, as shown in Figure 12.21. This is where the handle will connect, and the initial polygon selection is a bit too large. By beveling, you create an additional, smaller selection.
5. Change your view to a Back view.
6. Then, in the Tools tab, select the Duplicate vertical tab.
7. Click on the Curve Extrude tool.
8. By going to a Back view, you'll ensure that your curve extrusion stays put on the Z axis. Trying to create this next step in a Perspective view can be awkward. With that said, click once in the middle on the polygon selection, then click again slightly outside of the selection, as shown in Figure 12.22.
9. You can see the handle starting, but it needs to be a bit longer. Click down on the Y axis a bit to begin curving the handle.
10. Then, click once more down toward the bottom third of the bottle.

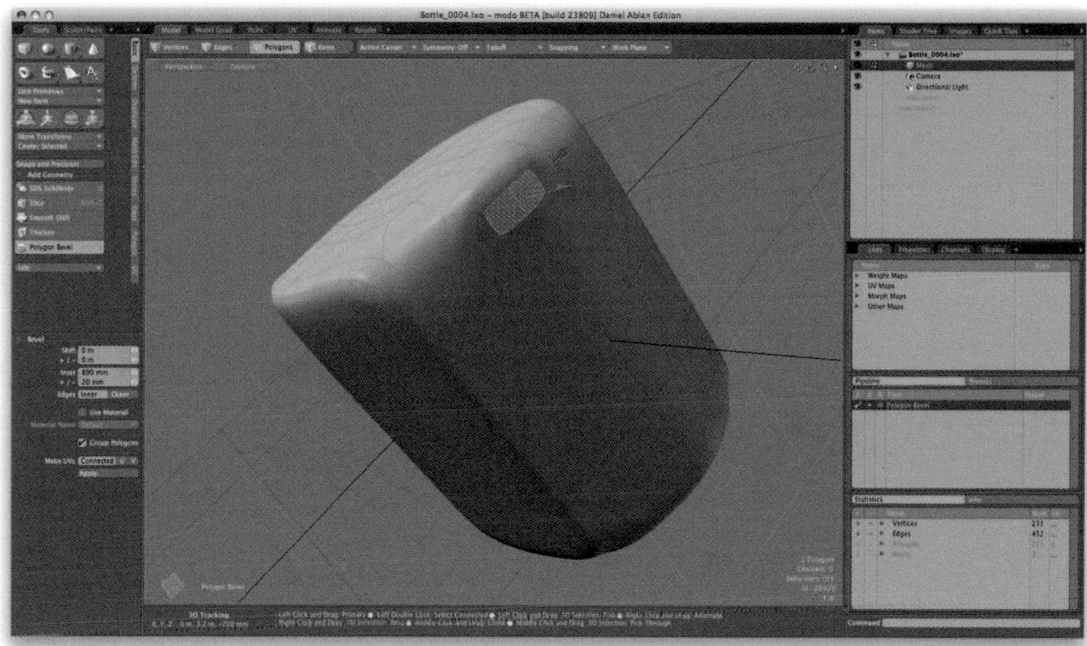

Figure 12.21 Inset the top two polygons with the Bevel tool.

Figure 12.22 Using the Curve Extrude tool in a Back view, you can begin creating the bottle's handle.

11. The handle is coming along, but needs a little tweaking. In the properties for the Curve Extrude tool, change the Steps option to 7. This lessens the amount of geometry created with the extrusion. Because this is a subdivision surface model, you don't need a ton of polygons.
12. Under Curve Path in the tool properties, change the Mode option from Add to Edit.
13. Click and drag on the points of the handle to shape (see Figure 12.23).

Figure 12.23 Using the Edit mode for the Curve Extrude tool, you can shape the handle.

14. Press the q key to turn off the Curve Extrude tool.
15. Switch back to a Perspective view, and press the r key for the Scale tool.
16. Scale the end of the handle up a bit (the two selected polygons you started with) to square it somewhat, as shown in Figure 12.24.
17. Switch to Edges mode, then double-click the edge just above the end of the handle to select the entire edge loop. Figure 12.25 shows which edge.

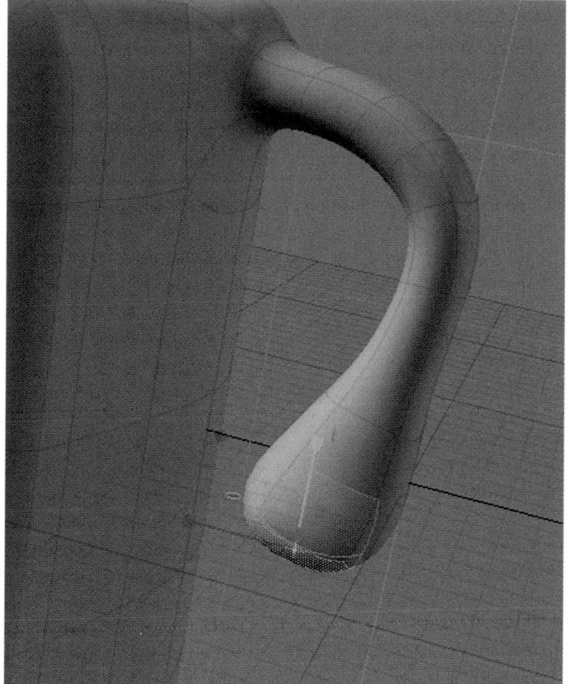

Figure 12.24 Using the Scale tool, size up the last polygons at the base of the handle.

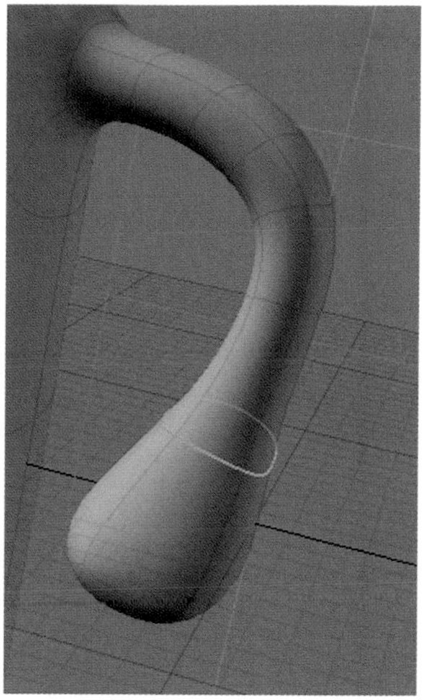

Figure 12.25 Select the last edge of the handle.

18. With the edge selected, press the r key and scale it up about 30%. You can see the percentage in the tool properties panel on the left of the interface.
19. Select the next edge up the handle and size this up as well (see Figure 12.26). You're just blending the larger sized polygons at the end of the handle with the smaller sized at the top.
20. Go back to Polygons mode. Deselect any selected polygons. Now, while you could just connect the handle to the bottle, you'd really have something more of a big square mug. You want the bottle to be a little more styled, or molded. So switch to a Back view.
21. Switch over to Vertices selection mode to work with points. Using the middle mouse button, select the bottom-right corner of points, including two rows above it, as shown in Figure 12.27.
22. It's important to use the middle mouse button for selecting so that you select "through" the model. Otherwise, you'll only select what's in front of you if your model is shaded. If you have no middle mouse, switch to Wireframe view, and then use the right mouse button. If you have no right mouse button, it's time to buy a new mouse.

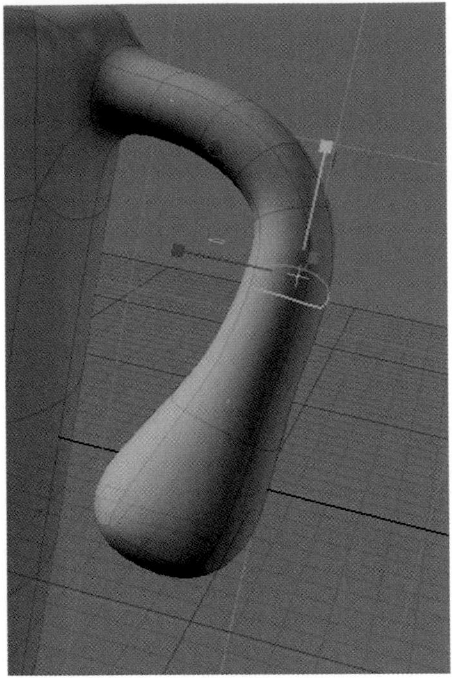

Figure 12.26 Size the next edge in the handle to balance the shape.

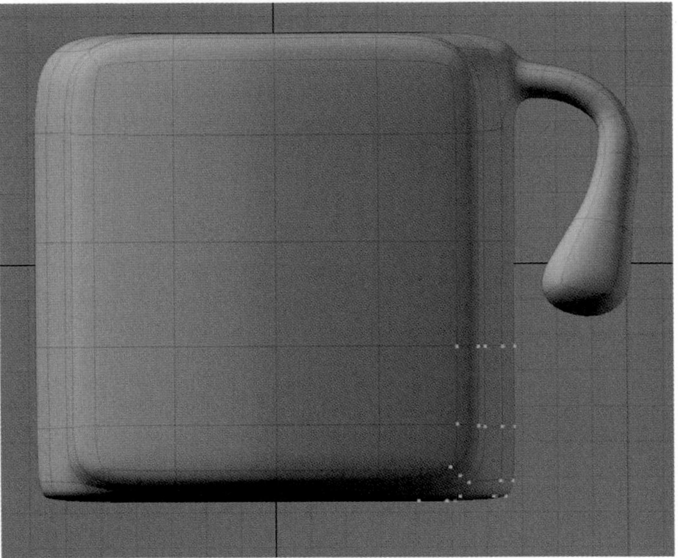

Figure 12.27 Select the points (vertices) that make up the bottom-right corner of the bottle.

23. With the points selected, press w for the Transform tool. Move the points out toward the handle, about 3 m or so. Figure 12.28 shows the move.
24. You can see that with subdivision surfaces on, the model has a nice flow to it. However, it might be a little too curvy at the base. Let's change that. Switch to Polygons mode. Select two polygons in order in the center of the model. Then press the L key to select the entire loop of polygons (see Figure 12.29).
25. In the Tools tab, click the Mesh Edit vertical tab. Then choose the Loop Slice tool. Alternatively, you can press Alt and the C key. Make sure the Count value is set to 2 in the tool properties, then click once on the selection. You'll see two new edges appear.
26. You can click and drag to create a new position for the new edges, or just enter in a value of 0.50% for the Position value in the tool properties. The position of the edges should be just at the handle and below it, as shown in Figure 12.30.
27. Press the q key to turn off the Slice tool. Save your model!
28. Switch to Edges mode, then double-click the top new edge just created, as shown in Figure 12.31.

Figure 12.28 Move the selected points out toward the handle with the Transform tool.

Figure 12.29 Select the entire row of polygons in the center of the bottle.

Figure 12.30 Using the Loop Slice tool, add new edges to the model for more control.

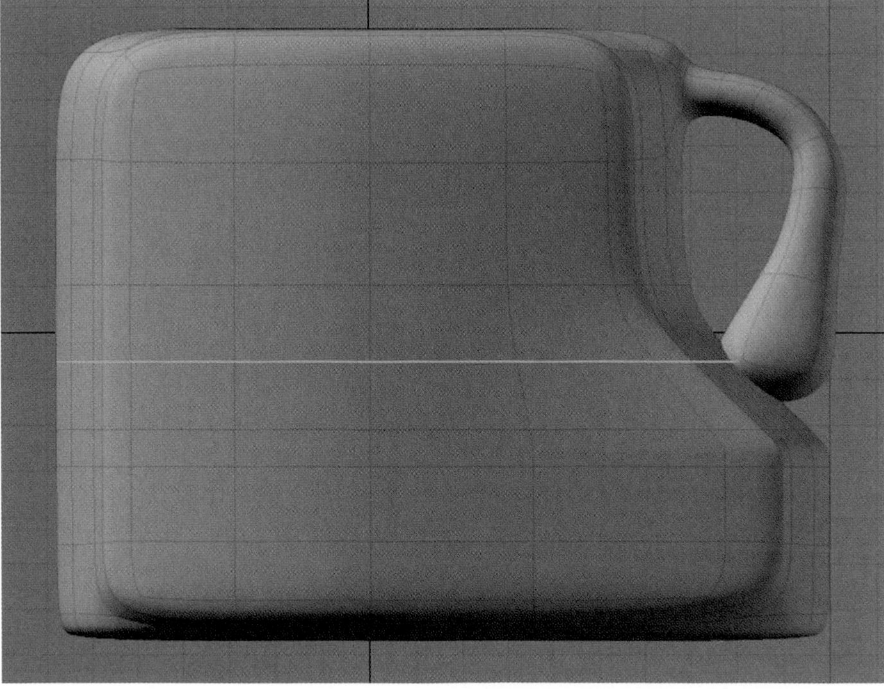

Figure 12.31 Double-click the newly created top edge to select it entirely.

29. With the edge selected, press w, and then move the edge up about 600 mm, as shown in Figure 12.32.

Figure 12.32
Move the edge up to tighten the curvature of the side of the bottle.

30. Press q to drop the tool. Deselect the edge, and switch back to a Perspective view. Figure 12.33 shows the model with the new edges. You see how a simple loop slice operation can change the model with subdivisions applied? The shape looks more complex than it really is.
31. Now it's time to connect the handle. First, select the two polygons at the bottom of the handle. You might need to move them up a bit so they're not intersecting the bottle. Figure 12.34 shows the selection repositioned slightly.
32. Drop the move tool by pressing q. Next, holding the Shift key, add to the selection and select the four polygons on the bottle directly beneath the handle, as shown in Figure 12.35.

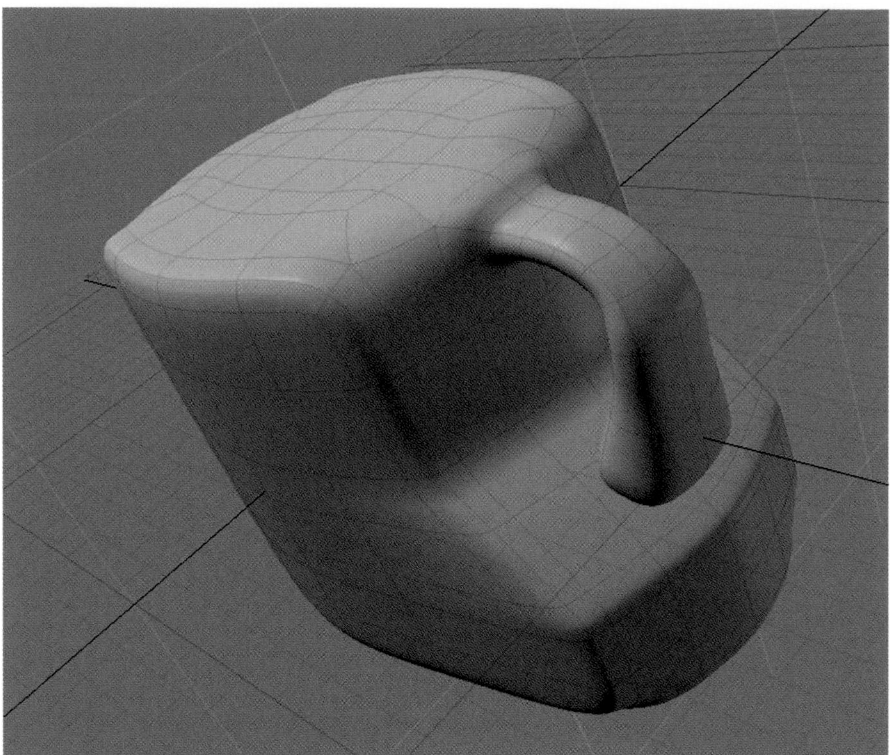

Figure 12.33
After adding some edges with the Loop Slice tool, the model starts to have a more custom shape.

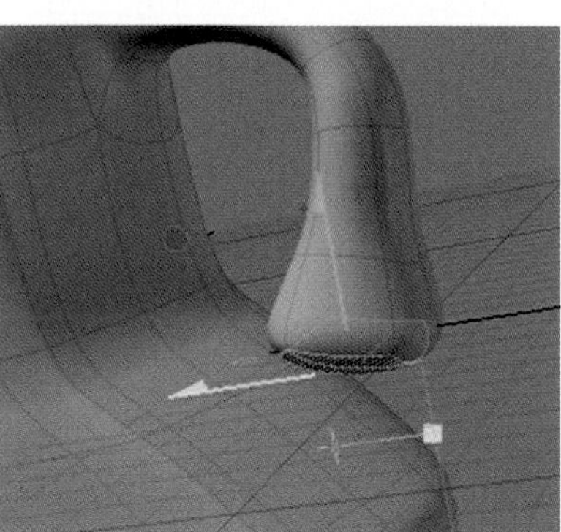

Figure 12.34
Select the two polygons on the bottom of the handle and reposition them slightly.

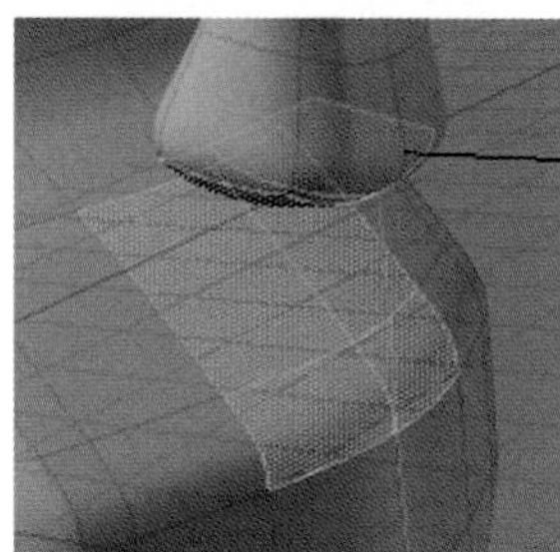

Figure 12.35
Select the four polygons beneath the handle on the bottle itself.

33. In the Tools tab, click the Polygon vertical tab. Turn on the Bridge tool. Then, click and drag on your model. Drag to the left so that you only bridge these polygons with one segment. Dragging to the right bridges them with more. You can also numerically enter the value in the tool properties panel. Your handle is now connected to the base. Figure 12.36 shows the result.

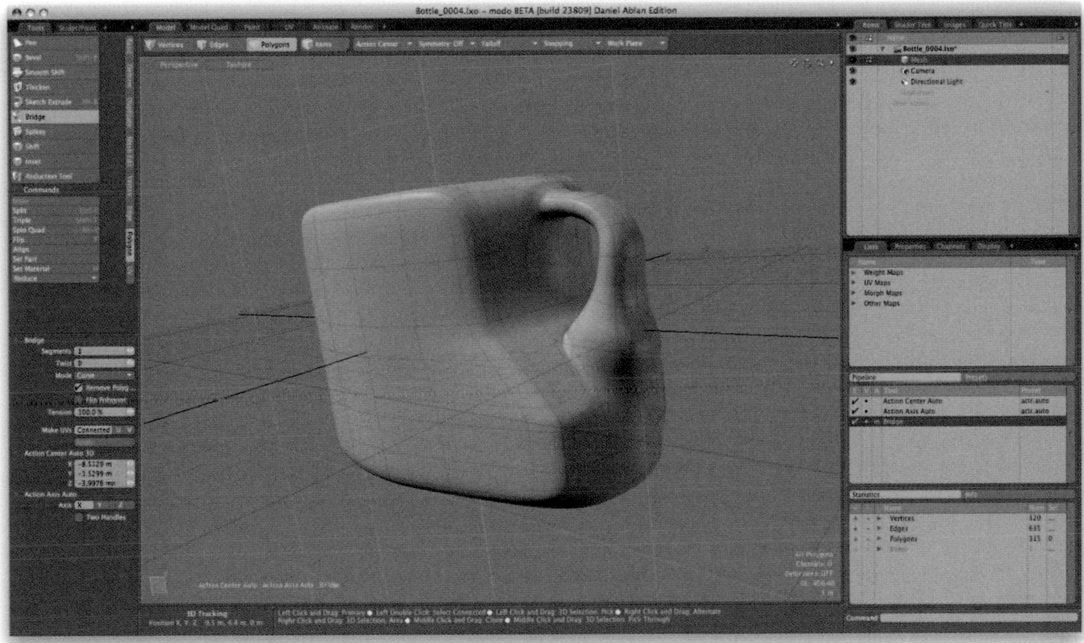

Figure 12.36 Using the Bridge tool, you can join polygons together.

34. You may find that the Twist operation will be helpful when using the Bridge tool. It allows the flow of polygons to remain intact. For the model in this chapter, a Twist value of 1 was applied.

35. You might find that the base of the handle where it connects to the bottle is a bit large. You can select the last edge of the handle, press the r key, and size it down a bit. Feel free to move it to your liking, as well. Figure 12.37 shows the Scale tool (r key) used on the last edge to size it down entirely; then by placing the tool on the outer edge, the X scale was adjusted. In order to place the tool in a different location, make sure Action Center option at the top of the modo interface is set to Automatic. This allows you to click a location to tell modo where a tool's "action" will happen.

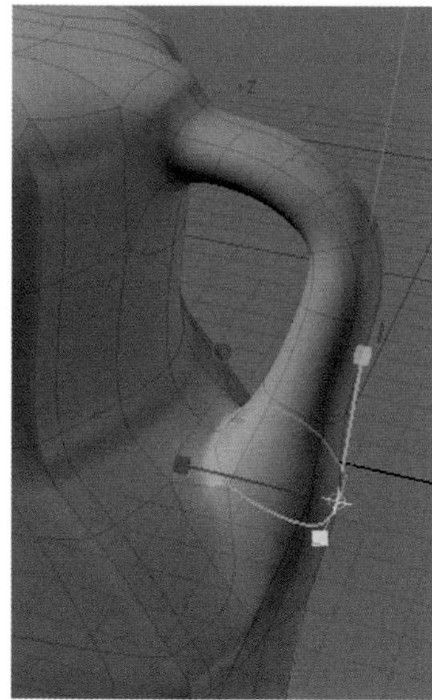

Figure 12.37 The Scale tool is used on the last edge to adjust the size.

36. Go ahead and use the Element Move tool (t key) if you'd like to modify or adjust any vertices, edges, or polygons. This doesn't mean you need to, but by using subdivision surfaces, you can always adjust your model and get instant results. This is why subdivision modeling often works better than some traditional spline-based modeling, which requires you to freeze your curves into polygons.
37. Save your work and marvel at your masterpiece.

The Next Step

As you can see, subdivision surface modeling is easier than you probably thought. And you can create some pretty amazing things, like detergent bottles! Okay, so it's not that exciting, but what *is* exciting are all the things you can create based on the steps in this chapter. But wait! There's more! On the book's DVD is a video showing you how to do more with this bottle, including building the spout and cap. And you'll see how a label can be applied. So pop in that DVD and finish this up. There's laundry to be done.

13

Sculpting Techniques

When it comes to modeling in modo, there really has been no limit to what you can create. That's even more true with modo 301's sculpting capabilities. This book is designed to show you all of the techniques available to you, through written word and visual examples on the DVD. This chapter will take you into another project in which you'll model a landscape. From there, you'll use modo 301/302's sculpting tools to shape it, then texture it, and later you'll add the environment. You'll see how modo's micro-polygon displacement works and how powerful it is.

Building a Landscape

Landscapes traditionally have been a chore for 3D artists. This is because to properly create them, you need a lot of geometry. A lot of geometry means a lot of polygons, and a lot of polygons means a lot of render time. But the team at Luxology introduced *micropolygon displacement* in modo 201, allowing you to create and work with simple objects but render with millions of polygons. How is this possible? The micropolygon displacement feature generates additional polygons at render time. The goal is that finer details can be achieved without physically modeling them into the base object.

You can then add to the details achieved through micropoly displacements and with modo's bump map capabilities to generate some terrific looking models. But how are these two techniques different? What determines the micropoly displacement over a bump? Let's say you build a landscape, such as the one shown in Figure 13.1. A basic model, which can be built from DEMs (demographic elevation maps) or just freeform with various modo tools. It's simple in the 3D workspace, but the render shows a more detailed model. In most cases, this will work well. The subdivision in this image comes from a procedural noise applied as a bump layer in the Shader Tree. Figure 13.2, on the

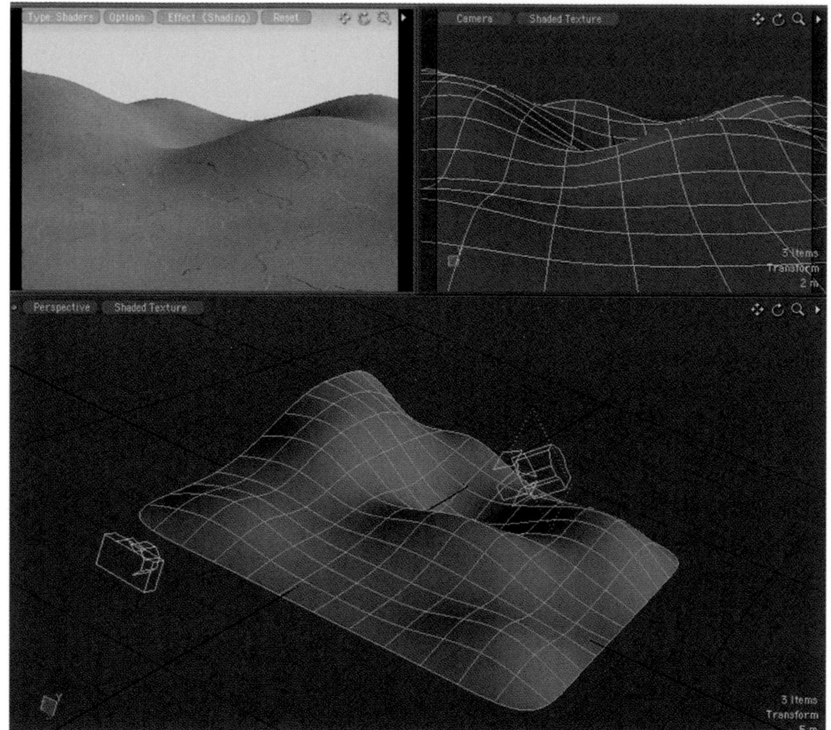

Figure 13.1
A typical landscape model, simple in the viewport, and then subdivided for the render.

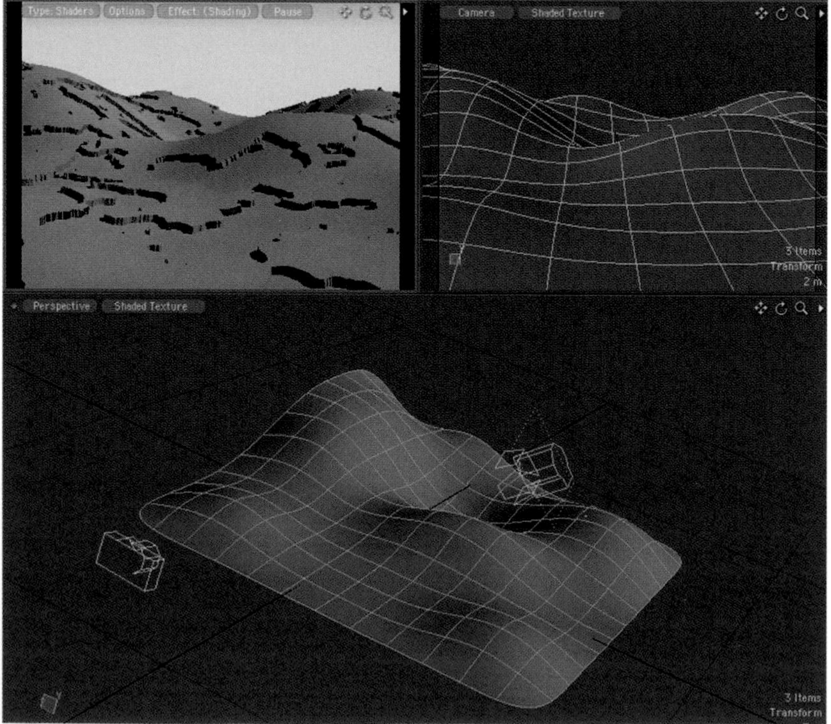

Figure 13.2
A typical landscape model, but with micropoly displacement turned on. Much finer detail is achieved.

other hand, is the exact same model with the same procedural noise applied as a layer. Micropolygon displacement is activated within the Render Properties panel in the Settings category. Notice the fine details in the image. These details are not bump maps, which are only a visual effect. Micropolygon displacements physically change the geometry. This allows you to create minute details that are almost impossible to achieve from modeling alone.

Creating landscapes can be an expression of your creativity or something more specific built from real-world references and data maps. This next project will show you how to create a landscape. It's simple in its approach, but the techniques will demonstrate that the possibilities are endless.

1. Clear out modo by selecting Reset from the File menu.
2. Add a 1-meter unit primitive plane to the workspace by holding the Shift key and clicking the Plane primitive in the Tools tab.
3. Press the a key to fit the plane to view. Feel free to rename the Plane listing in the Items tab to Landscape.
4. Make sure you're in Polygons selection mode. Then press Shift and the d key to subdivide the polygons. Choose Faceted, and click OK. Now repeat this three more times. You'll have something like what's shown in Figure 13.3.

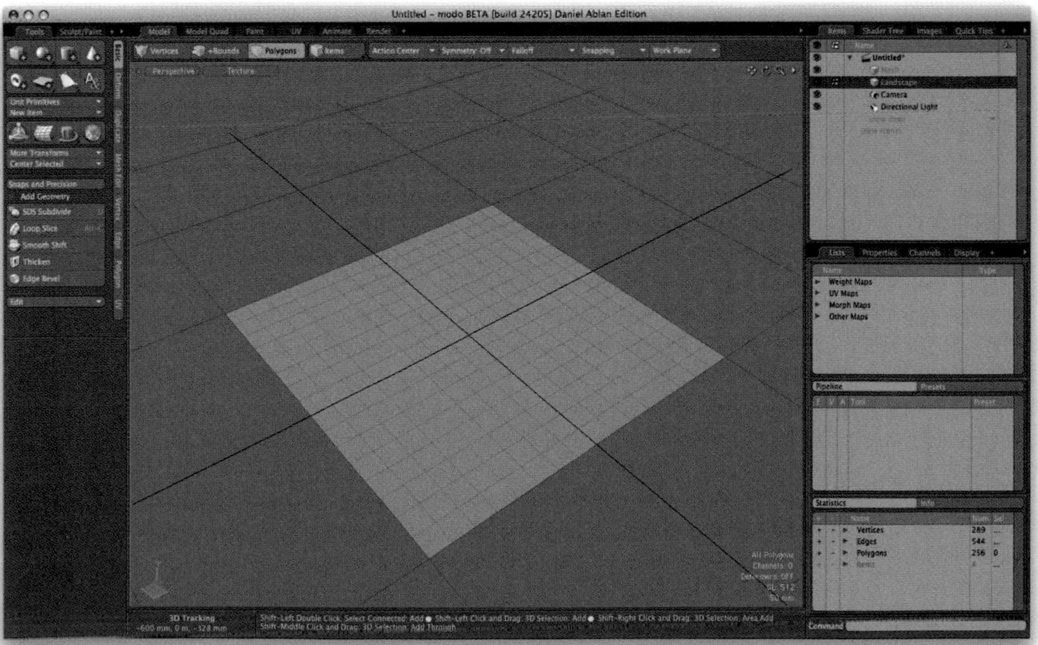

Figure 13.3 A flat plane subdivided four times will be the basis for a simple landscape model.

Note

Pressing Shift and the d key calls up the Subdivide Polygons command, which offers you a Faceted subdivision method for flat objects, Smooth for round objects, and an SDS Subdivide option. This method is very useful for subdivision surface–based objects that you need to subdivide. The SDS Subdivide option can also be directly chosen by simply pressing d in the viewport.

When building a subdivided plane, you can also do this: Draw out the flat plane rather than holding the Shift key and clicking to create a 1-meter unit. Then, after you drag out the plane, drag with the right mouse button to create multiple segments.

5. Press the Tab key to turn on subdivision surfaces for the model. While it doesn't look like much now, it will momentarily.
6. Now, you can very easily shape this model. You're going to use a combination of modeling tools for the general slopes, but then use displacements for the details. Select Sculpt from within the Scale Tools category on the Deform vertical tab within the Tools tab.
7. In the Tool Properties panel, change the Offset Mode to Absolute. Then, set the Offset Distance value to about 80 mm. The Smooth Amount value is fine at 30%. The Smooth Brush Size value should be set to 60. From there, click and drag on the model. You should see bumps appear, as shown in Figure 13.4.
8. Hold the Ctrl key, and click and drag. You'll set a negative distance.
9. To quickly change the Sculpt brush size, right-click and drag in the viewport. Then left-click to apply the tool.
10. Go ahead and shape out a nice landscape. When you're finished, save your work. Figure 13.5 shows an example.

Note

Another way to use and adjust the Sculpt tool, as well as other tools, is to work directly with the Auto-Haul Display. Open Preferences from the System menu at the top of modo. Under the Display heading, select Tool Handles. Change Auto-Haul Display to On. When a tool is selected, you'll see a visible measurement appear in the viewport. You can click and drag on it to adjust a selected tool's value.

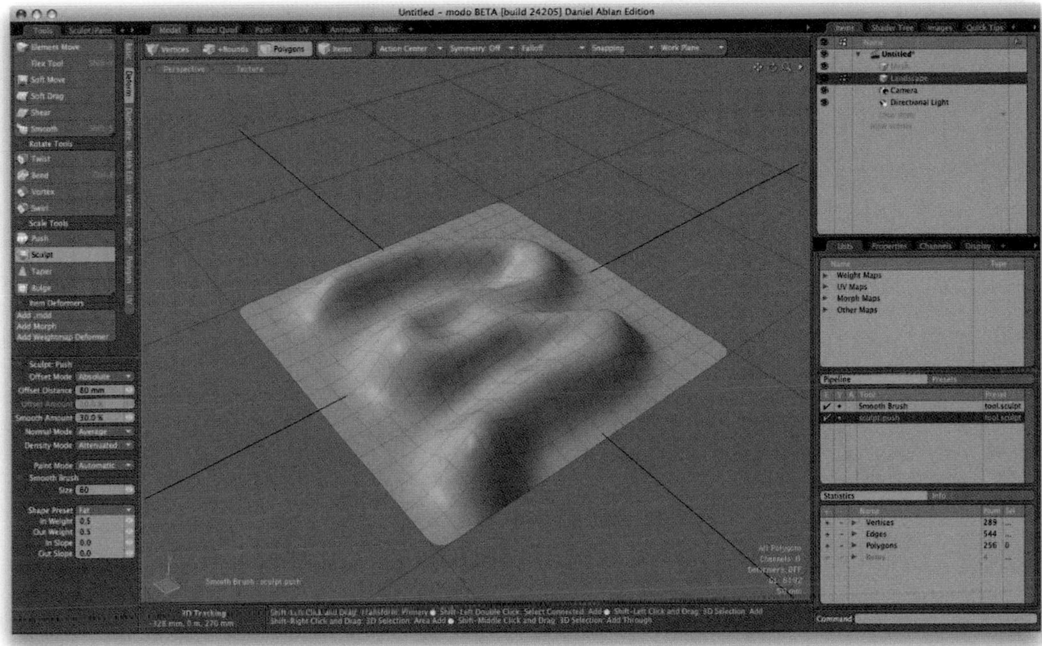

Figure 13.4 Using the Sculpt tool from the Deform vertical tab, you can easily deform geometry.

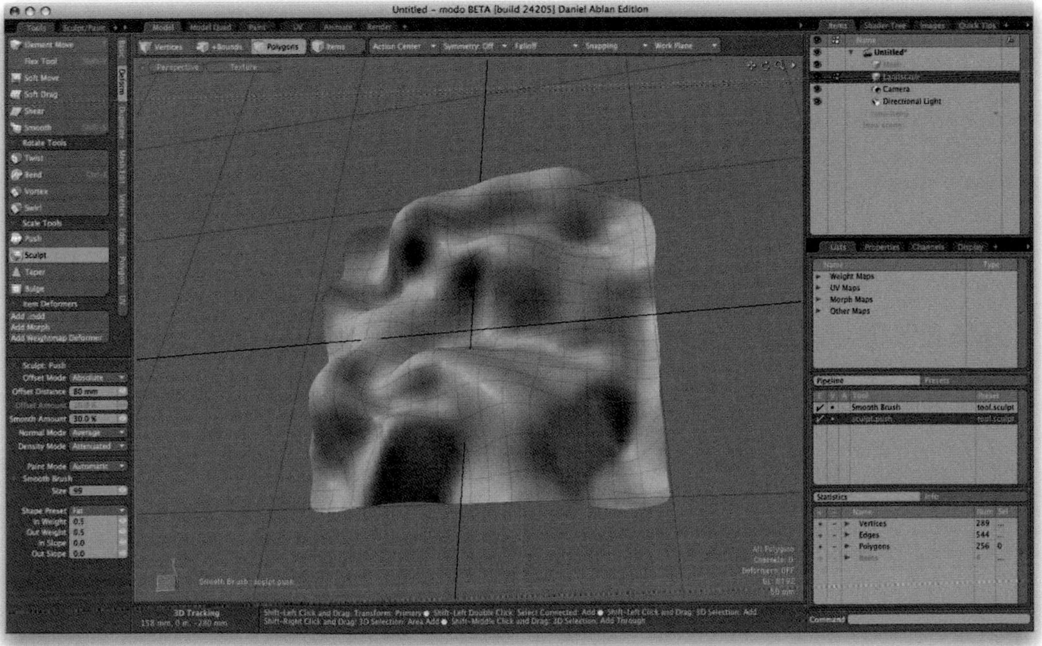

Figure 13.5 Applying a positive and negative distance on the subdivide plane, a simple landscape is created.

Note

If you want to change the distance of your sculpts, you can adjust the setting in the Tool Properties panel. However, doing so will change all of the sculpt operations you've already applied. So turn off the tool, turn it back on, then change the Distance value. The previous sculpt operations will remain as you set them. However, you could keep the setting at Adaptive, not Absolute, and adjust the strength on the fly with the middle mouse button. It's the best way to work.

Displacements

Building a Landscape such as this one is pretty easy to do, especially with subdivision surfaces and modo's Deform tools. But what will really make the details is the use of micropolygon displacement. This next section will show you how to apply this feature.

1. To begin, set up a good shot to see the model as it would appear when rendered. Switch to the Render tab at the top of the viewport so you have a three-window view.
2. The top-right viewport should be in Camera view. If it's not, make it so by clicking the options in the upper-left corner of that particular viewport.
3. Use the viewport tool controls to frame up the shot so you can see the model up close, as shown in Figure 13.6. You can do this in the top right of the viewport or use the keyboard equivalents of Alt/Option for Rotate, Alt/Shift for pan, and Alt/Ctrl for Zoom.
4. Over in the Shader Tree, under the Render Properties tab, expand the Environmental Material category. Make sure the Environment Type option is set to 4 Color Gradient. Make the Ground Color value the same as the Sky Color value. Change the Nadir Color value to a burnt orange or other sunset-like color. Change the Sky Exponent value to 20 and the Ground Exponent value to 3. This brings more of the blue sky down into the scene, as shown in Figure 13.7.
5. Save the scene at this point.
6. With the Landscape selected in the Item List, press m for Polygon Set Material and give the landscape a name of Landscape or something similar. You'll see the new material mask appear in the Shader Tree.
7. Select the Material listing under Landscape. Take a look at the bottom of the Render Properties tab for the Material. There is a setting for Displacement Distance. This setting will be the distance of displaced micropolygons when the Displacement texture value is at 100%.

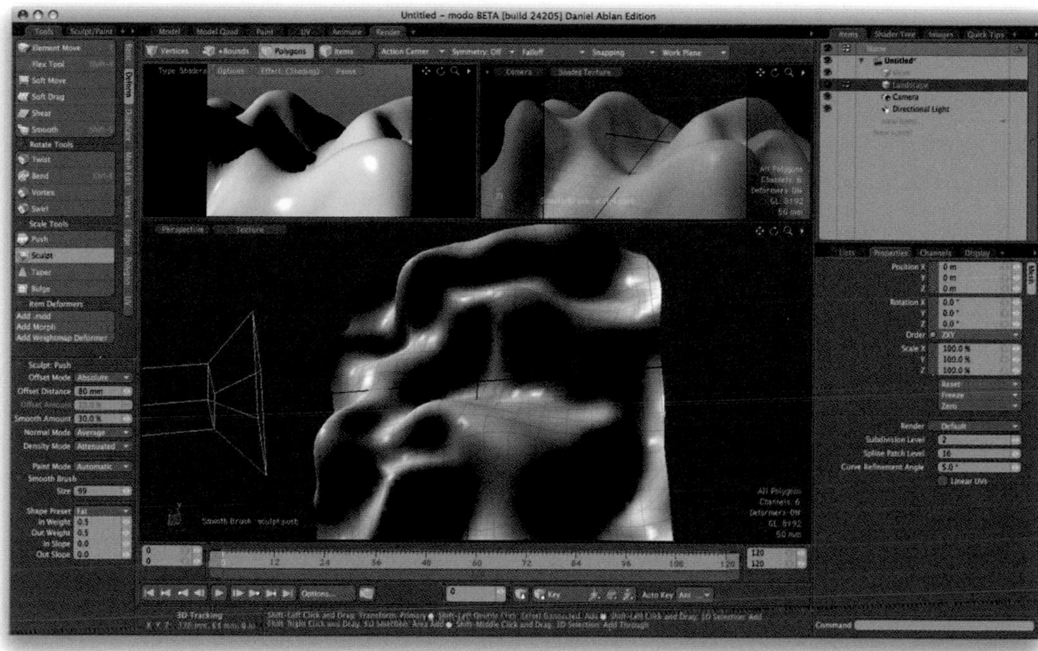

Figure 13.6 Position the camera to see the landscape and fill the frame.

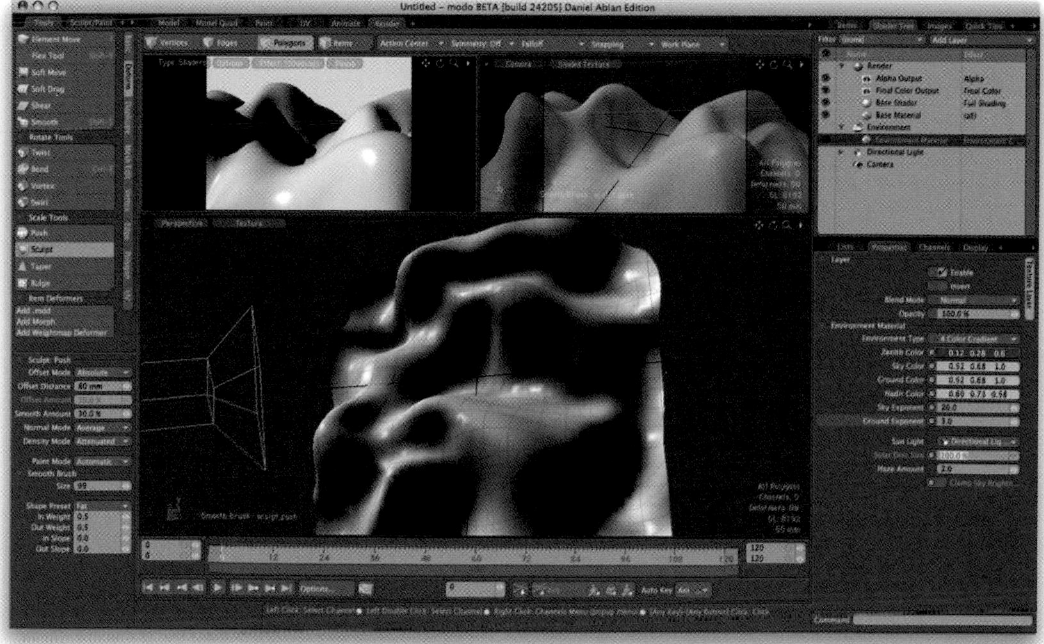

Figure 13.7 Changing the environment type to 4 Color Gradient, and making the ground color the same as the sky, you can create a soft background.

8. From the Add Layer drop-down list, choose Noise. You'll see a procedural noise pattern appear over the landscape, as shown in Figure 13.8. The default Effect setting of this Noise layer is Diffuse Color.
9. Right-click on the Noise effect and change it from Diffuse Color to Displacement. Figure 13.9 shows the update. Without much work, you've made snowy mountains.
10. If you're not seeing the displacement in the Preview window, make sure that Micropoly Displacement is checked. You can find this setting by clicking the Render listing in the Shader Tree. Then click the Settings vertical tab in the Render Properties panel. Figure 13.10 shows the selections.
11. You can change the look entirely with a few changes. Click the Material listing for the Landscape mask layer. Bring the Displacement Distance value up to about 100 mm.
12. Set the Diffuse Color value to a soft brown, about 0.75, 0.70, 0.65. Bring Specularity to 0%.
13. Now select the Noise displacement layer. In the Texture Layer vertical tab of the Render Properties panel, change the Type option to Turbulence. Then on the Texture Locator vertical tab, click Auto Size. Figure 13.11 shows the result. You've created sand dunes.

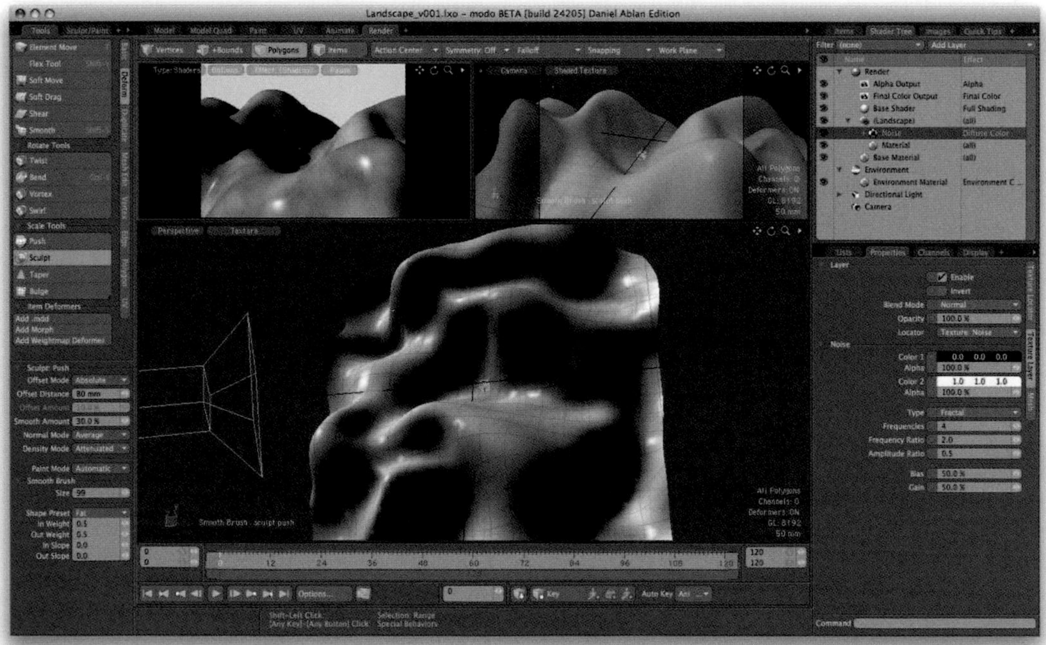

Figure 13.8 Add a noise layer to the Landscape material.

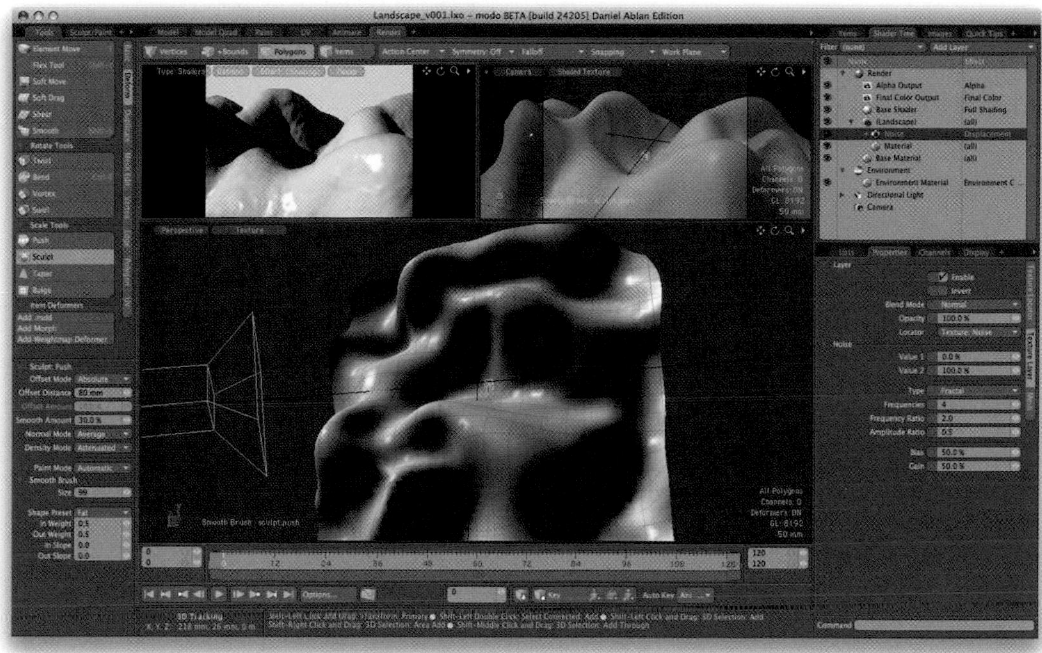

Figure 13.9 Changing the Noise effect to Displacement changes the model's look.

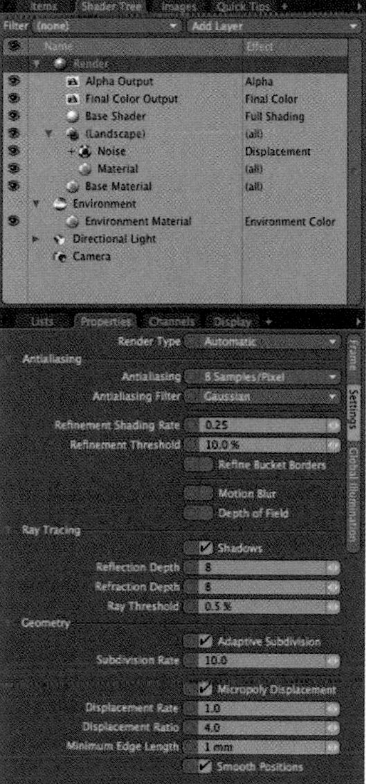

Figure 13.10 Micropoly Displacement should be active from the Render Settings vertical tab.

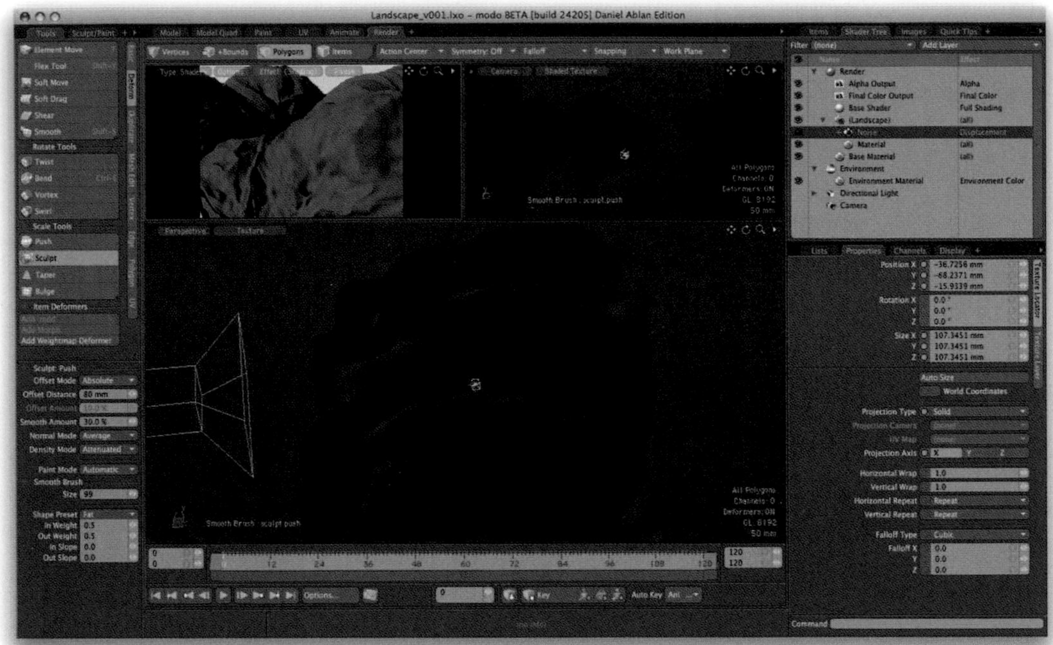

Figure 13.11 A few changes, and the snowy slopes are now sand dunes.

OK, so no big deal here, right? You see that modo is flexible. But here's what's cool about this technique you've been using so far: Go to the Camera view, and bring the camera in close to the object. Figure 13.12 shows the idea. Take a close look at the Preview window. The simple flat plane has intricate levels and smooth curves, thanks to micropoly displacement.

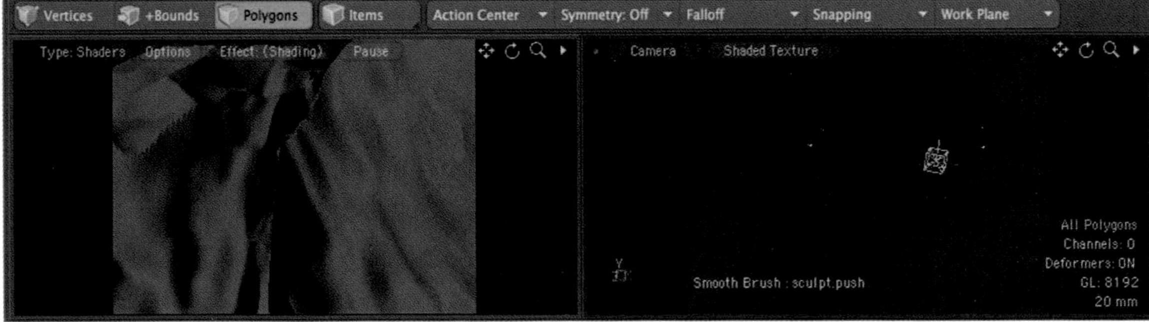

Figure 13.12 The bumps in the landscape are well defined when viewed up close thanks to micropoly displacement.

Morph Maps

Morph maps allow you to change the position of vertices on a model. You'd use a morph map to create various facial expressions on a character or different "poses" on inanimate objects. Be sure to check out the Morphing QuickTime video on the book's DVD to learn more about this feature. What's more is that you can use morph maps to shape objects, such as the landscape you've been creating.

Due to the embedded nature of the morph maps, many types of edits can be made to the base mesh without disrupting the morph shapes. This includes many forms of geometry addition and reduction. Morph maps can be added, selected, and deleted from the Lists tab under the Morph Maps category when the view is in its larger expanded mode, or under M when the view is collapsed to its compact view.

1. Continuing from your last landscape scene, make sure you're still in the Render tab. Figure 13.13 shows the setup.
2. Change to a Model view by clicking the Model tab at the top of the viewport.
3. Press the spacebar to toggle to Vertices selection mode.
4. Subdivide the landscape one time with an SDS subdivide (subdivision surface subdivide) by pressing the d key twice, which will give the model a good bit more detail. Figure 13.14 shows the change.

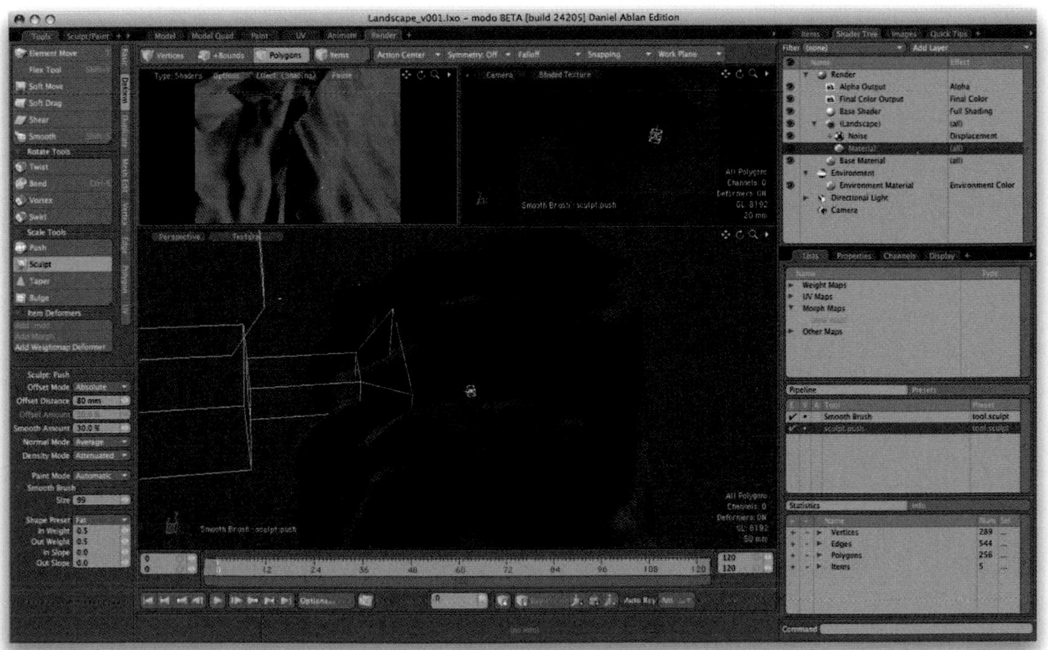

Figure 13.13 The current landscape as seen in the Render tab.

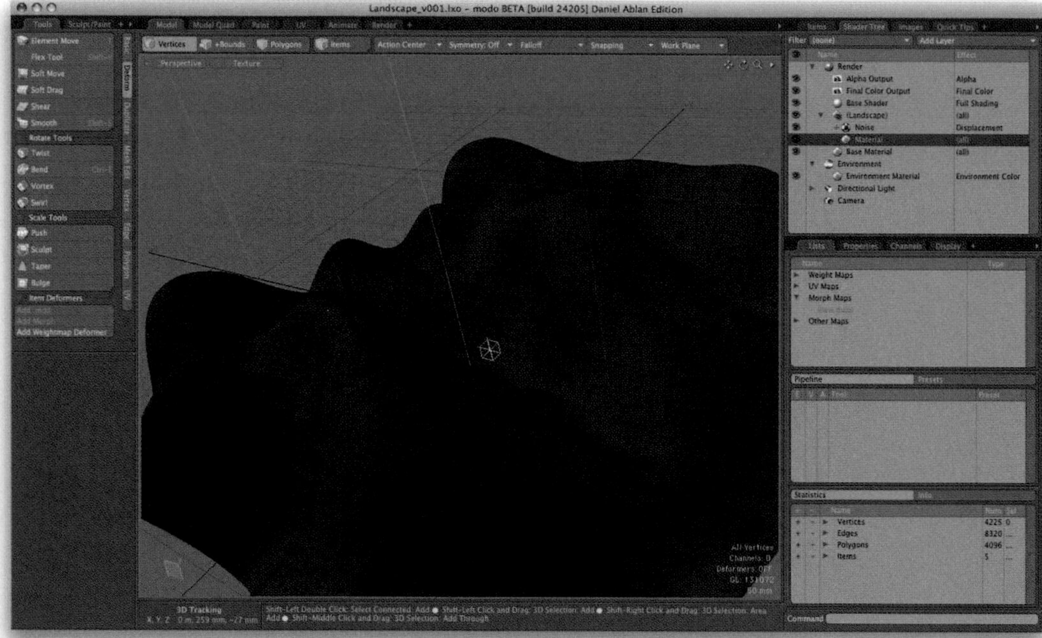

Figure 13.14 A single subdivision increases the polygon count, allowing even more deformation.

5. Select the Lists tab on the right of the interface. Expand the Morph Maps listing, and you'll see a ghosted choice for New Map, as shown in Figure 13.15.

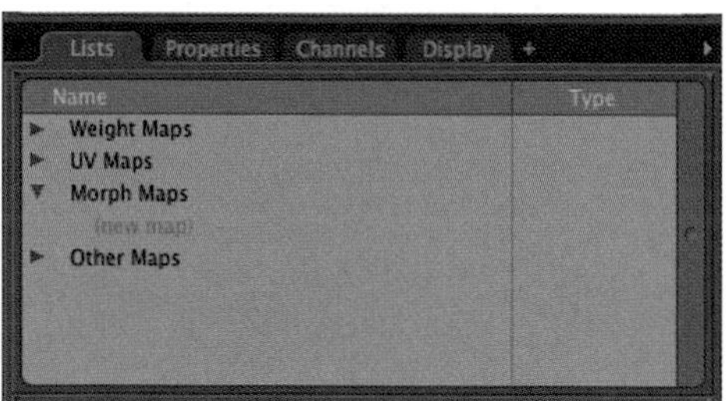

Figure 13.15 Select the Morph Maps listing within the Lists tab.

6. Click the New Map listing, and in the requester, enter the name NoiseMorph. The Create New Vertex Map panel will appear. Choose Relative Morph Map for the Vertex Map Type option. Leave the Value option set to 0, then click OK. You'll see a new morph map in the Morph Map section of the Lists tab.
7. Morph maps hold absolute positions, or offsets, which is a relative position. You can make changes to morph maps without affecting the model.
8. With the morph map selected, select a noise falloff from the Falloff drop-down menu at the top of the interface. Also, make sure Action Center is set to Automatic.

9. From the View menu at the top of the interface, select Show Falloffs, as shown in Figure 13.16. This will allow you to see falloffs represented by yellow to purple coloring on the vertices of your mesh.

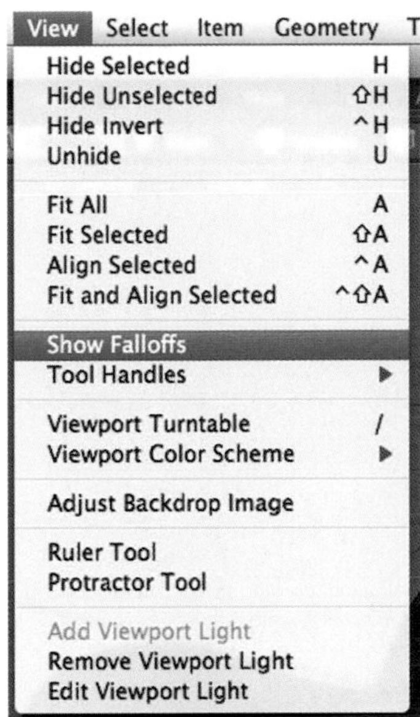

Figure 13.16
Choose Show Falloffs from the View menu.

10. In the Noise Falloff setting within the Tool Properties on the left of the interface, set the Scale value to 5% to make a smaller noise value. You won't yet see the vertices of your mesh turn to a yellow and purple color. Press the w key to activate the Move tool. However, if you're too close, you'll only see the colored vertices, so zoom out a bit and you'll see the actual noise falloff values, as shown in Figure 13.17.

> **Note**
>
> To create a split view like the one shown in Figure 13.17, hold the Ctrl key, click the thumb in the upper-left corner of the viewport, and swipe down.

11. Now, with the Move tool active, grab the green handle for the Y axis and drag up about 150 mm. Figure 13.18 shows the result.

> **Note**
>
> Remember that you can always see what tools and falloffs are active by taking a look at the Pipeline tab at the bottom right of the interface. You can click the check mark under the E column to turn on or off a desired tool.

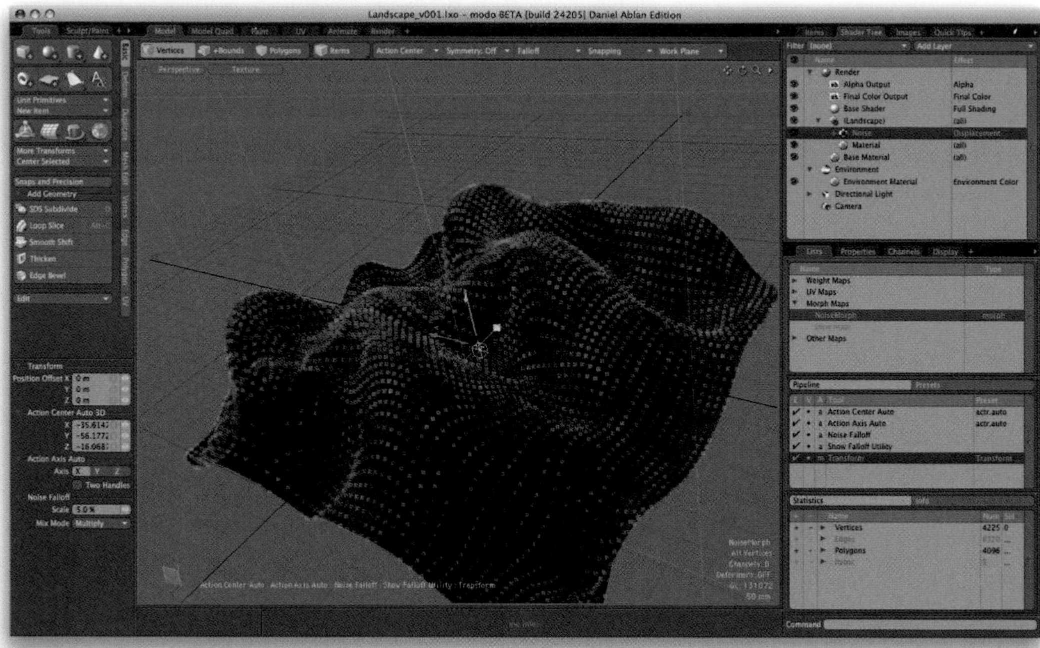

Figure 13.17 Here, a split view is shown to see the noise falloff close up and farther away.

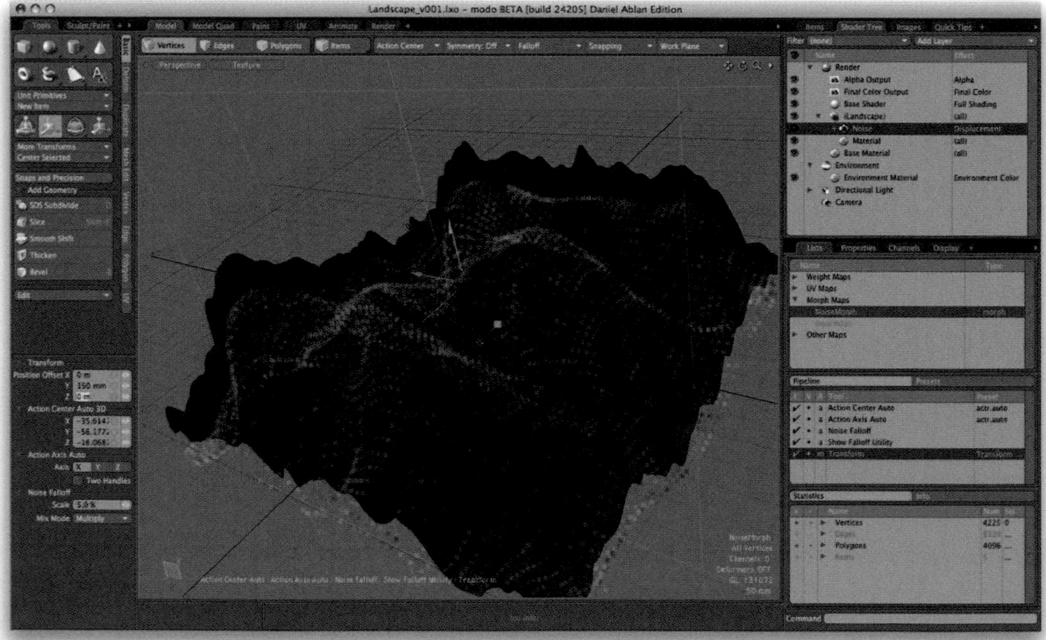

Figure 13.18 By applying the move tool with a noise falloff, only parts of the geometry are moved, resulting in bumps in the landscape.

12. Press the q key on your keyboard to turn off the Move tool.
13. Now if you click back up to the NoiseMorph listing you created as a morph map, you can toggle between two versions of your model, one with the newly applied noise falloff and one without. You can create as many morphs as you want. Why would you do this? Perhaps you need to animate a changing landscape over time, showing erosion. Perhaps you need to animate a dream sequence or a bad nightmare. Anything is possible!
14. Be sure to view the Landscape Morph QuickTime movie on the book's DVD to learn even more about this technique.
15. Back in the Shader Tree, change the Noise layer from a Displacement effect to a Bump.
16. Switch to a Render tab view if you'd like to see how the landscape looks now, as shown in Figure 13.19.
17. One more thing you can try before moving on. In the Lists tab, create a new relative morph map, and name it ShapeMorph. You'll see that you now have two morph map listings in the Morph Maps section: NoiseMorph and ShapeMorph. You'll also notice that when you create this new morph, the landscape loses all of the tight bumps created with the previous morph. That's normal.

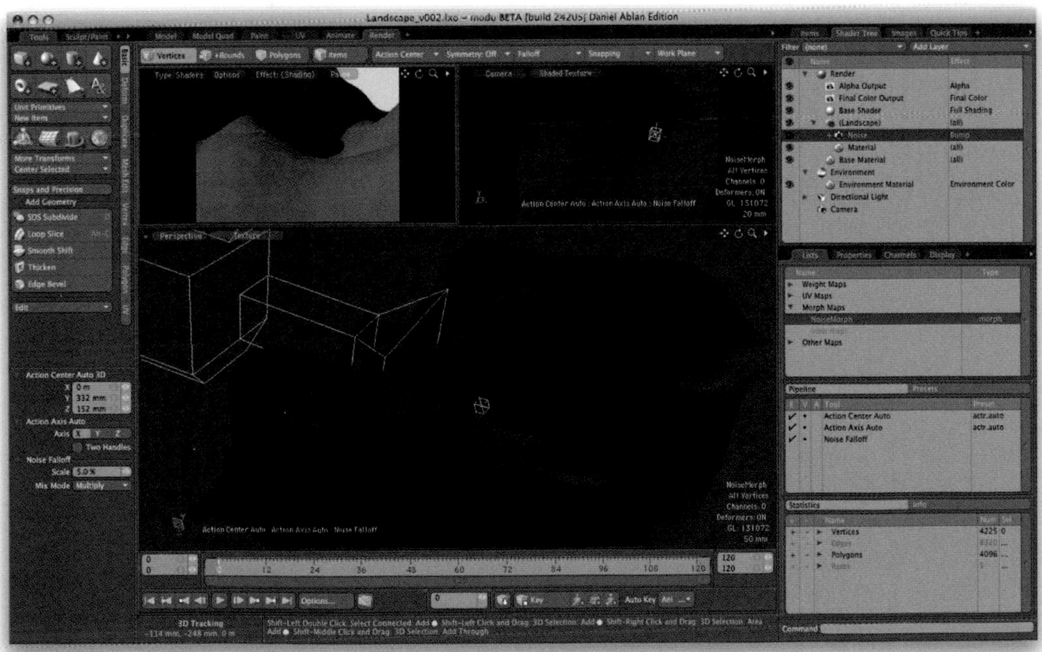

Figure 13.19 Now with a noise falloff and a noise bump layer, the landscape takes on a different shape entirely.

18. While the landscape is looking OK, the noise falloff used to apply the displacement is a little too even.
19. Once the new ShapeMorph is created, choose Vertices selection mode, and use the right mouse button to select a group of points in the center of the landscape, similar to what's shown in Figure 13.20.
20. With the center points selected, choose Apply Morph from the Vertex Map menu at the top of the modo interface. A requester will appear, asking you which morph to use. Since you only have one (which should be the NoiseMorph), go ahead and choose it. Set the value at 100%. Figure 13.21 shows the result.
21. Now, the edges of the landscape do not have the noise falloff applied, only the center selected vertices.
22. With the ShapeMorph selected in the Lists tab, select points across the model from the top view. That is, select points using the right mouse button in the shape of a crevasse. Figure 13.22 shows the selection.
23. With the points selected, press the y key, and click and drag the points down on the Y axis, about 250 mm or so (that's –250mm). You can drag them a bit farther if you like, and also feel free to press the r key to scale them. Deselect the points after you've moved them.

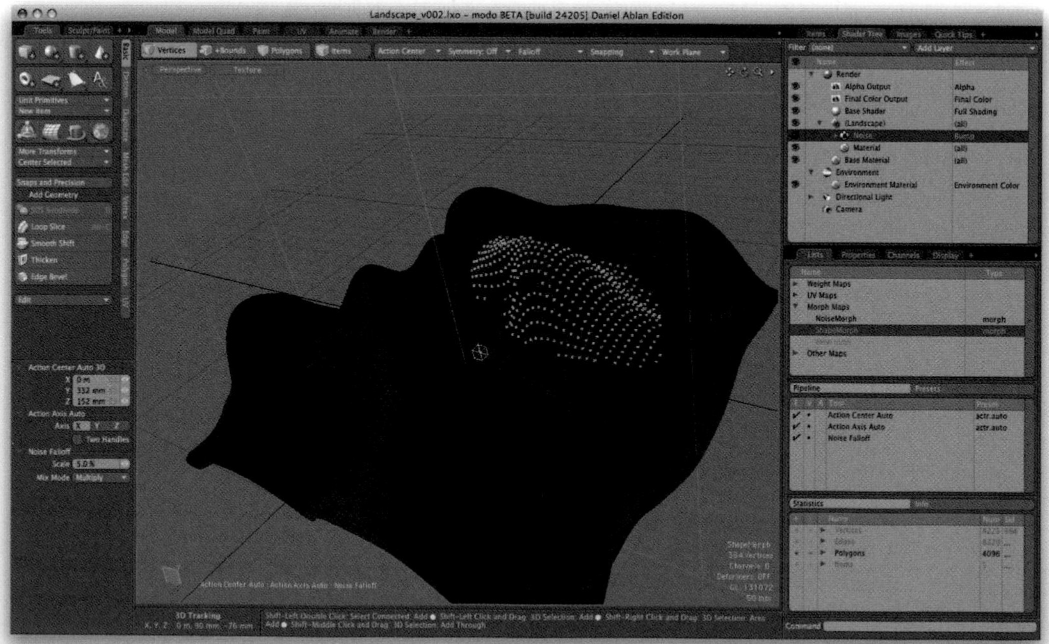

Figure 13.20 Select the points in the center of the landscape.

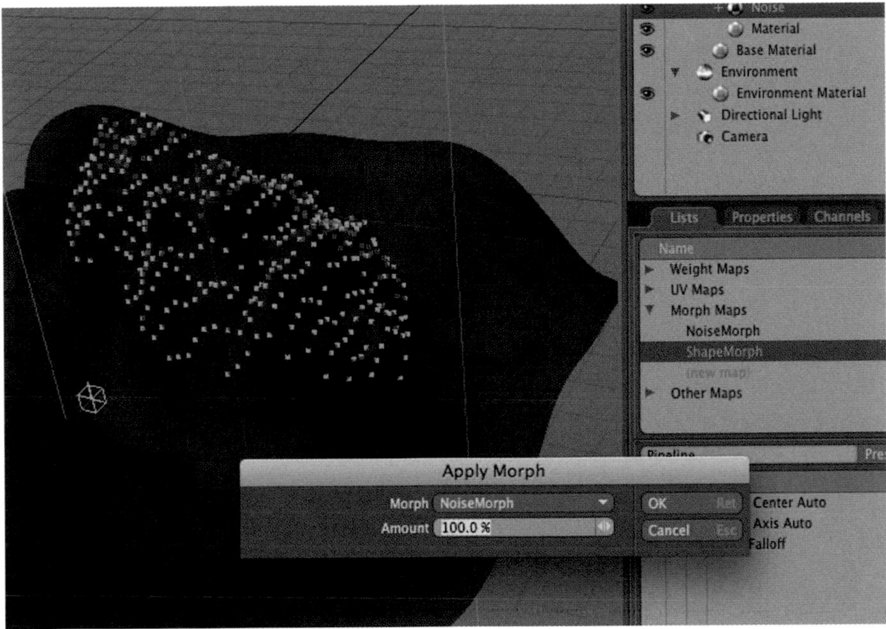

Figure 13.21 The Apply Morph feature allows you to apply a previously created morph to the current one.

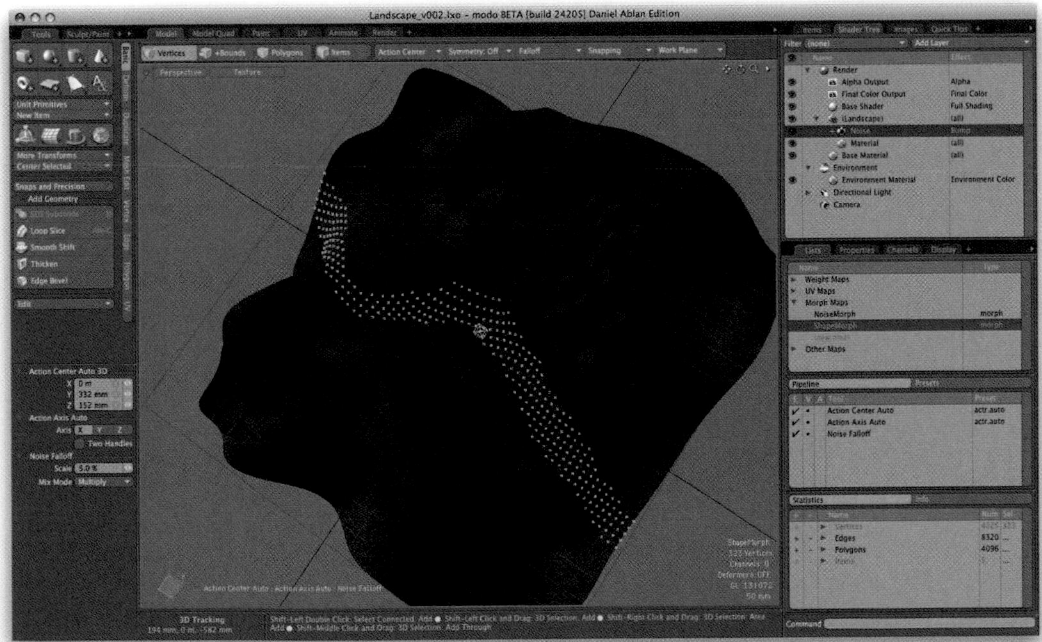

Figure 13.22 Select a group of points across the landscape model to make a crevasse.

24. Back up in the Shader Tree, make sure that the noise layer Displacement effect is now set to just Bump. Figure 13.23 shows the landscape, now more of a canyon with a slight manipulation to a few vertices.

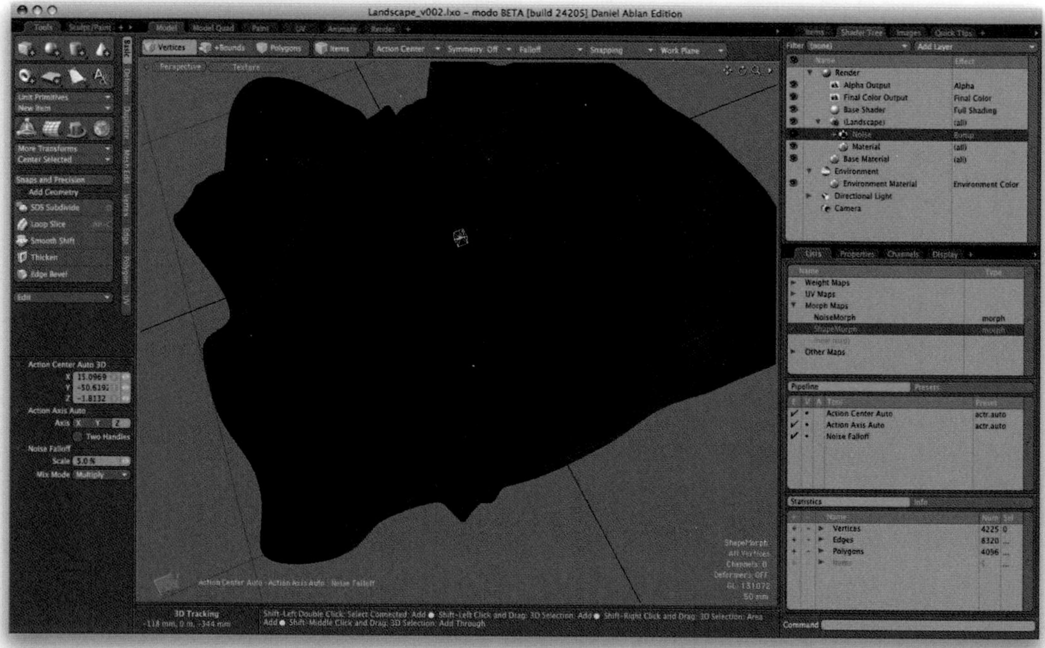

Figure 13.23 Move and adjust the points to create a crevasse in the middle of the Landscape.

25. Now when you click between the ShapeMorph and the NoiseMorph, you'll see the landscape change from one with all bumps to one with a deep crevasse.
26. Working with subdivision surfaces is pretty powerful, as you can see with just a flat subdivided plane. With a little more work, you can make a snowy mountaintop, soft rolling hills, or a mountain range with a deep crevasse.

The techniques here allowed you to see how much you can accomplish with micropoly displacements, as well as morph maps, and noise falloffs. And with modo's flexible Tool Pipe, all of these parameters can be used for anything you can think of. For example, all of the landscape project can be varied slightly to create an ocean. You can use morph maps to create a few tall waves, while maintaining an even amount of displacement and bump throughout.

It should also be noted the morph maps in modo, when exported, are "endomorphs" in NewTek's LightWave, and "blendshapes" in Autodesk's Maya. From here, you can create even cooler models with modo 301's powerful new sculpting tools.

Modeling with Sculpt Tools

Part of modo 301's main attractions, in addition to animation, are the new sculpting tools. Many 3D artists are familiar with ZBrush, a powerful 3D sculpting application from Pixologic. But while modo 301 does not have all the features of ZBrush, it is a tremendous addition to the modo toolset. The Luxology programming team has listened to users and created an entirely new set of tools that are most asked for and most often used.

This next section will introduce you to the sculpting tools with a simple project. From there, you'll head to the book's DVD for another sculpting project, shown to you as a video tutorial from 3D Garage.com.

1. Open up modo, then save and clear out any work you might have loaded.
2. Load the Flat_Land.lxo model from the Chapter 13 folder within the Projects folder on the book's DVD. This is simply a flat plane subdivided multiple times. Figure 13.24 shows the model loaded.
3. You can sculpt just about anything you want, as long as there's enough geometry to handle the amount of sculpting you desire. Click over to the Sculpt/Paint tab at the top left of the interface. Figure 13.25 shows the new tools, and you can see that there are additional vertical tabs on the right named Sculpt Tools, Paint Tools, and Utilities.

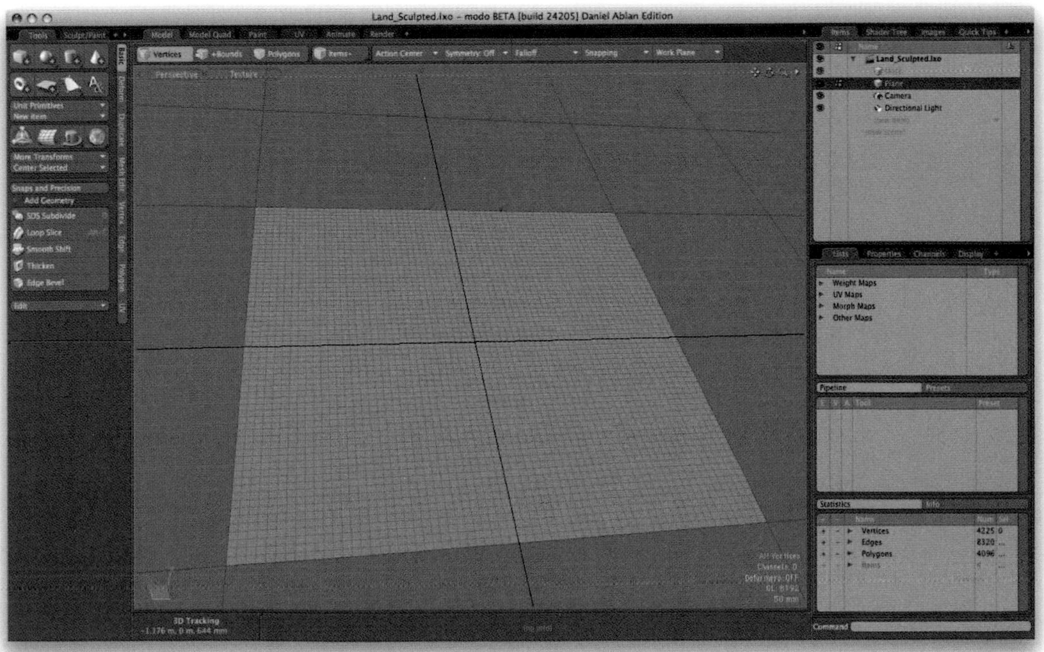

Figure 13.24 A flat, multi-subdivided plane will become a cool volcano.

Figure 13.25 The Sculpt/Paint tab is where you can find the new sculpting tools, as well as painting tools.

4. Save your loaded object as a new name, such as Land_Sculpted.
5. To begin sculpting a volcano, start by first creating some general deformation in the land. You'll then build up the volcano itself. Click the Inflate tool. Then select a procedural brush (the third brush icon).
6. Rotate the view to look down at the flat land. Click with the right mouse button to size up the brush to about 125. Then left-click and drag around the land, and you'll be brushing in small bumps, as shown in Figure 13.26.

Note

When sculpting, be sure to remember that you're building up your model. Small amounts of various sculpting tools applied over and over again can go a long way. In doing this, you should hold the Shift key and brush in some smoothness to a sculpted area.

7. Feel free to play around with the Inflate tool as you like. Next, select the Push tool from the Sculpt Tools tab.
8. Choose a soft edge brush. This brush is the first icon you see, directly under the Mask listing. Then set the Offset Distance value to 80 mm. The brush Size value should be about 100.

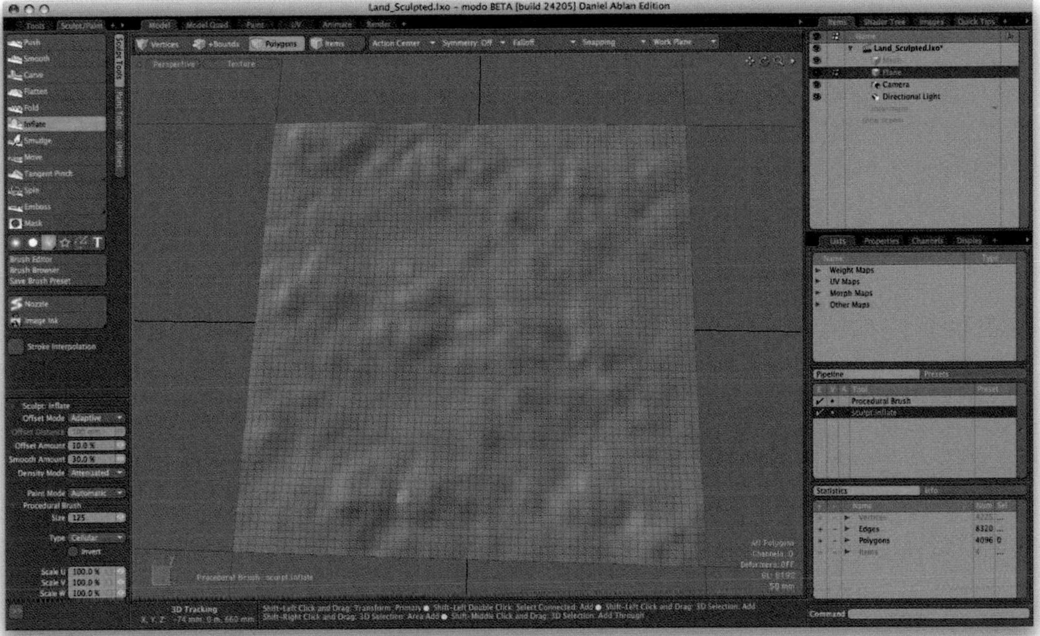

Figure 13.26 Using the Inflate sculpt tool and a procedural brush, you can rough up the land to begin creating the model.

9. Once your brush is set, click and drag on the center of the land object. Figure 13.27 shows the result. Create a mound in the center of the land, similar to the image.
10. Bring the Offset Distance down to about 40 mm, and set the brush tip to a procedural brush. From there, set the Size value of the brush in the tool properties to 50.
11. Push out the land area around the base of the volcano. Remember that at any point, you can press Command-Z (Mac) or Ctrl-Z (PC) to undo your steps, then resculpt your geometry. Figure 13.28 shows the example. Hold the Alt key, then click and drag in the viewport to rotate the view around to sculpt on all sides of the model.
12. When you're sculpting, you can vary the brush size, sculpt a little, vary it some more, sculpt some more, and so on.
13. Next, click the Inflate tool. Keep the same procedural brush and associated sizes from the previous steps. Now, the Inflate tool inflates your geometry. Duh! But here's a feature that works on all sculpt tools. Hold the Ctrl key, then click and drag. You will now invert the action. Do this on the center of the volcano to create a cavity in the model. Figure 13.29 shows the example.

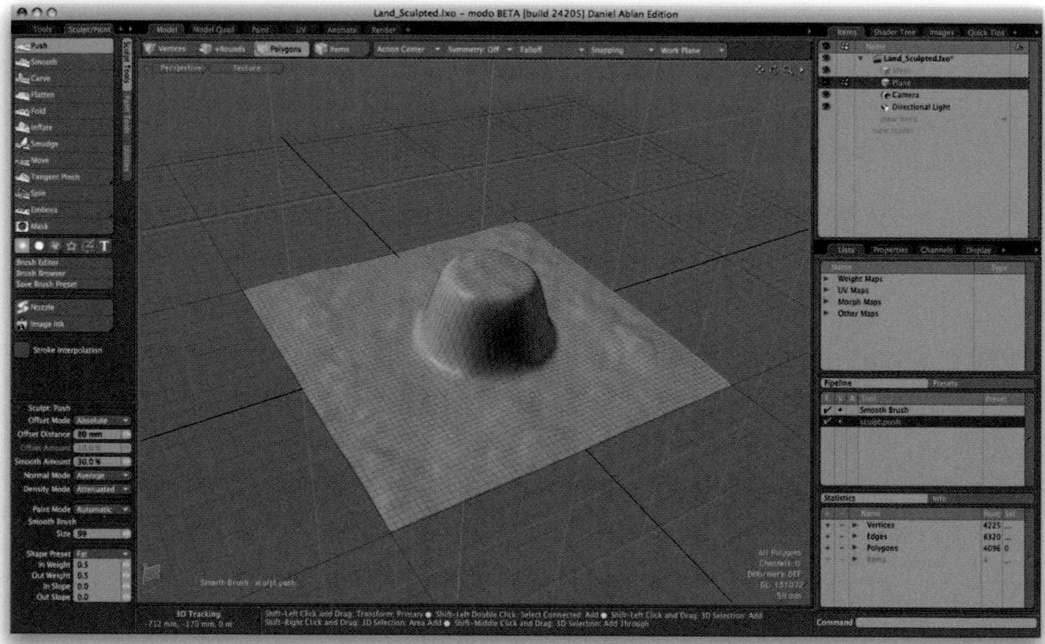

Figure 13.27 Use the Push tool to create a large mound in the middle of the land to begin building the volcano.

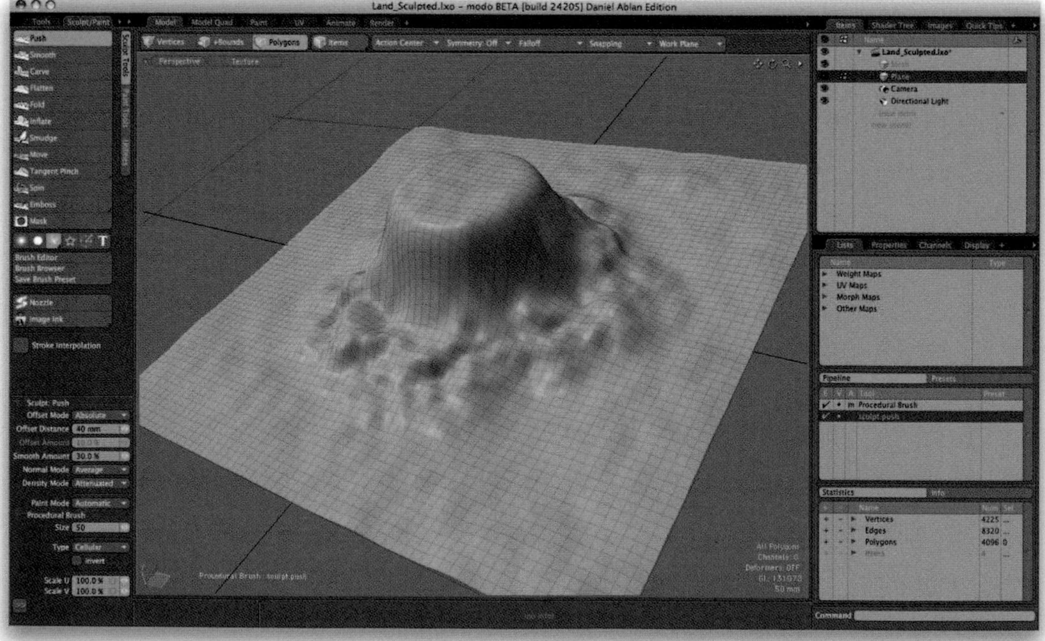

Figure 13.28 Push the land around the base of the volcano with a smaller offset.

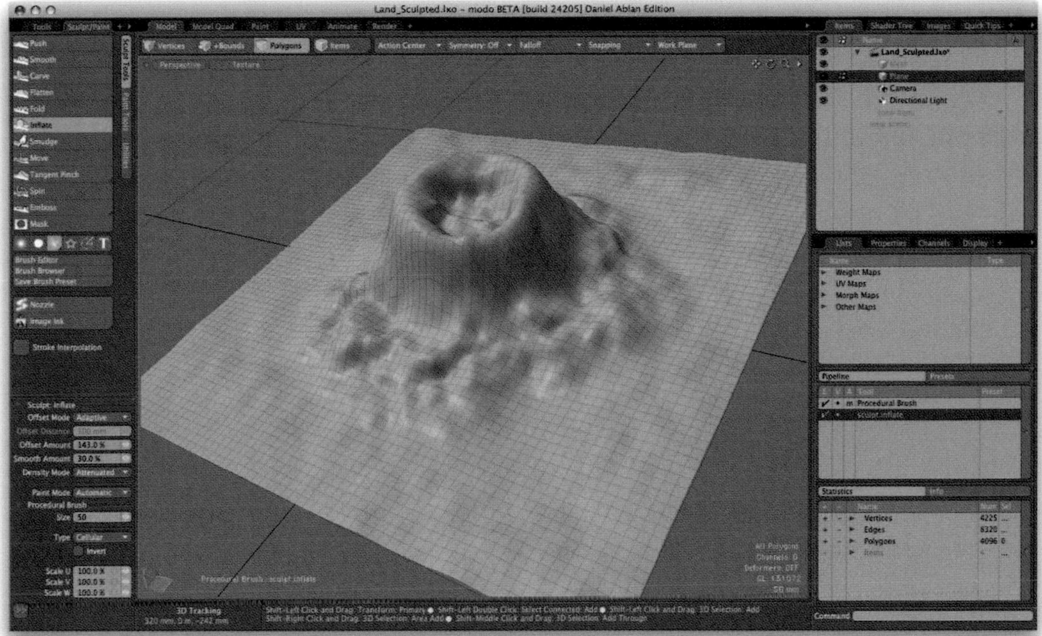

Figure 13.29 Holding the Ctrl key on any sculpt tool reverses its action. Here, the Inflate tool effectively deflates the center of the volcano.

14. At this point, save your model. It's coming along nicely. Now create those all-important grooves that allow the lava to run free. Select the Fold tool. As before, use a procedural brush.
15. Make sure the Offset Amount value is set to 100%, Smooth Amount to 30%, and Size to 20. You can leave all the other settings at their defaults, but feel free to experiment as you become more comfortable with the toolset. Now, click and drag up and down on the sides of the volcano to create cavities in the structure. Remember that you can hold the Ctrl key while doing this for a reverse effect. Sculpt with and without using the Ctrl key and see how you do. Figure 13.30 shows the example.

You can see that sculpting is pretty easy, especially on organic shapes like a volcano. Sculpting is a matter of choosing the right tool, setting a brush and a brush size, and going to work. Remember that you can set the brush size by using the right mouse button. It's an easy, interactive way to quickly change your brush size on the fly.

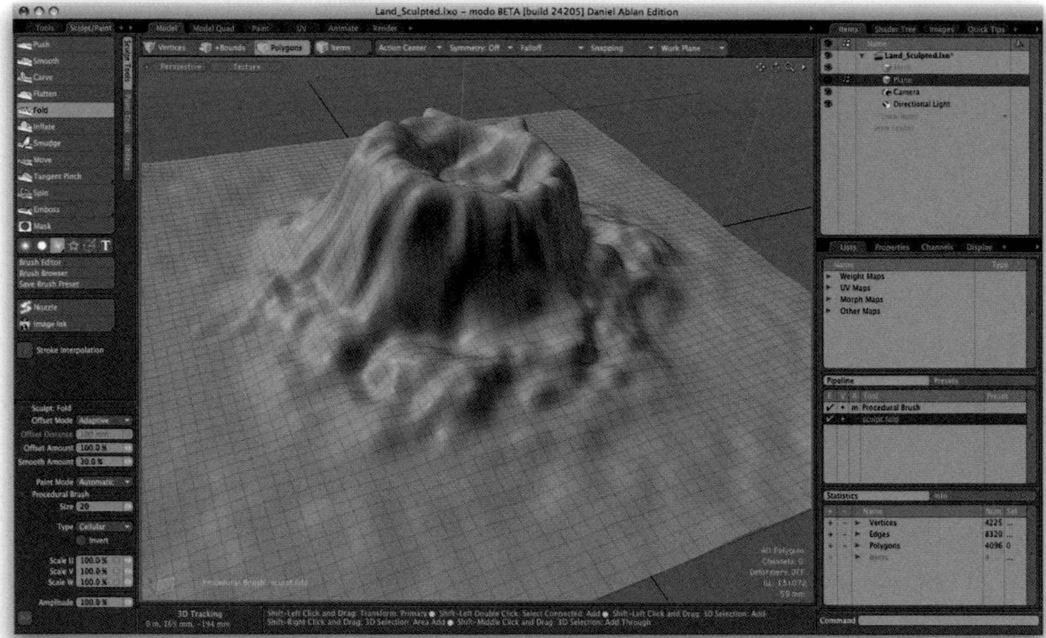

Figure 13.30 Use the Fold tool to create cavities along the sides of the volcano.

By no means are you done sculpting! But to understand the additional tools, and save room in the book for more chapters, take a moment now and head over to the book's DVD to continue practicing what you've learned in this chapter. Learn how to create more detail in the volcano with the sculpt tools, and find out about some other options not mentioned here in the text.

This chapter has guided you through more modeling tools, using various subdivisions, weights, noise falloffs, and morphs, and even used a cool tool like Edge Slice. And while it's been said throughout the book, it'll be said again here—all of these techniques can be applied to anything you like. For example, the subdivision landscape can be modified to build oceans or lakes. These concepts can be used to model any household item, desk item, and more. You'll see how the fine details are added in this chapter's video portion.

From here, turn to the next chapter to learn all about modo's top-notch render engine.

Part IV

Lighting and Rendering

14

Lighting and Rendering in modo

When modo was introduced, its strong points were, and still are, modeling and productivity. With the release of 201, and now 301/302, lighting and rendering have added to the functionality of modo without complicating the workflow. In addition, modo's lighting and rendering capabilities have not just added functionality, but also great appeal to this ever-expanding software.

This chapter will guide you through the use of lights in modo, then get you started with its powerful rendering engine. You'll use scenes you created earlier in the book as examples.

Lighting in modo

Before the projects begin, I'll show you a brief tour of the lights in modo and how they vary. Figure 14.1 shows a scene with two keys on a flat plane.

As you can see from Figure 14.1, the default directional light illuminates your scene and applies shadows. There's nothing glamorous about this light, and it's primarily good for outdoor situations when you need light from afar, such as from a sun or a moon. A directional light's position is not important, only its rotation. It will emit light from a distance, and this will vary only when you rotate the light, not move it. However, while a directional light's shadows are normally hard-edged, you do have the ability to soften them in modo by increasing the spread angle.

Figure 14.2 shows the same scene, but the light has been changed to a point light and moved to the middle of the scene. Can't see much there, can you? That's because the

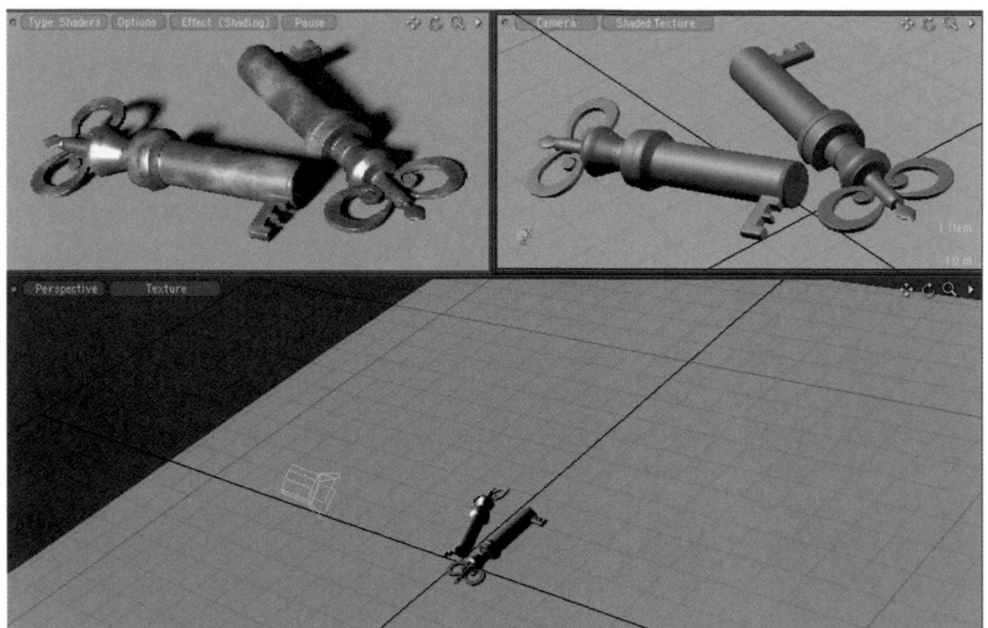

Figure 14.1
The default directional light has shadows and lights evenly.

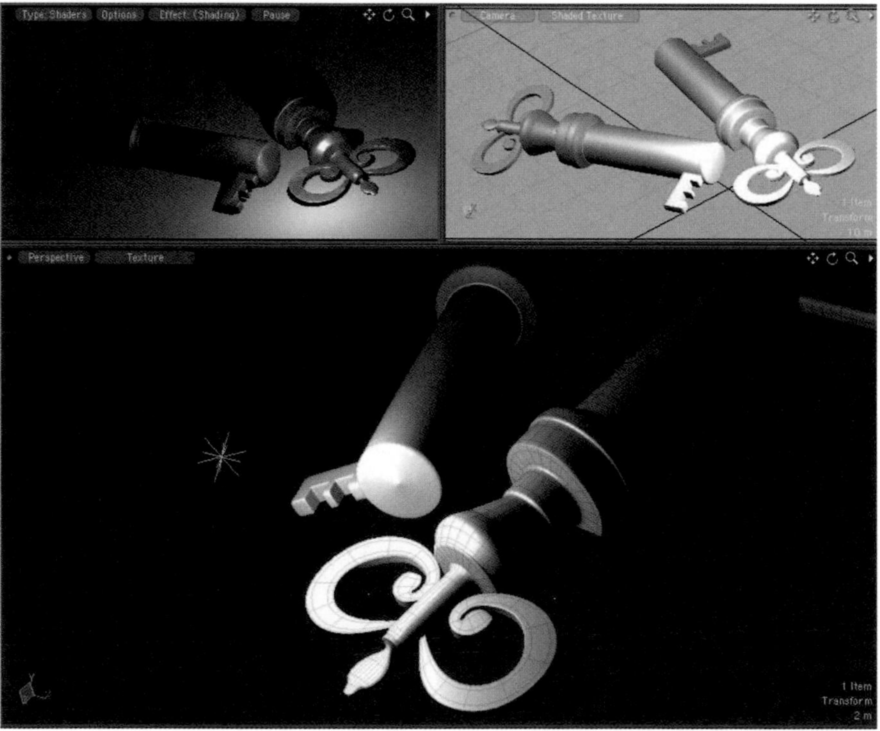

Figure 14.2
The point light, an omnidirectional light, emits light in all directions. Its rotational value does not matter in your scene.

point light emits in an omnidirectional fashion, and the Radiant Intensity value needs to be increased for the light to emit farther. A point light's rotation does not matter, only its position. Think of this light as the opposite of a directional light.

Figure 14.3 shows the same scene with a spotlight. With a spotlight, your scene can benefit from the light's position and rotation. Light is illuminated in the shape of a cone. You can vary the cone and also set a nice soft edge for the light. Spotlights are useful for all sorts of scenes, from headlights to flashlights to recessed lighting in architectural environments.

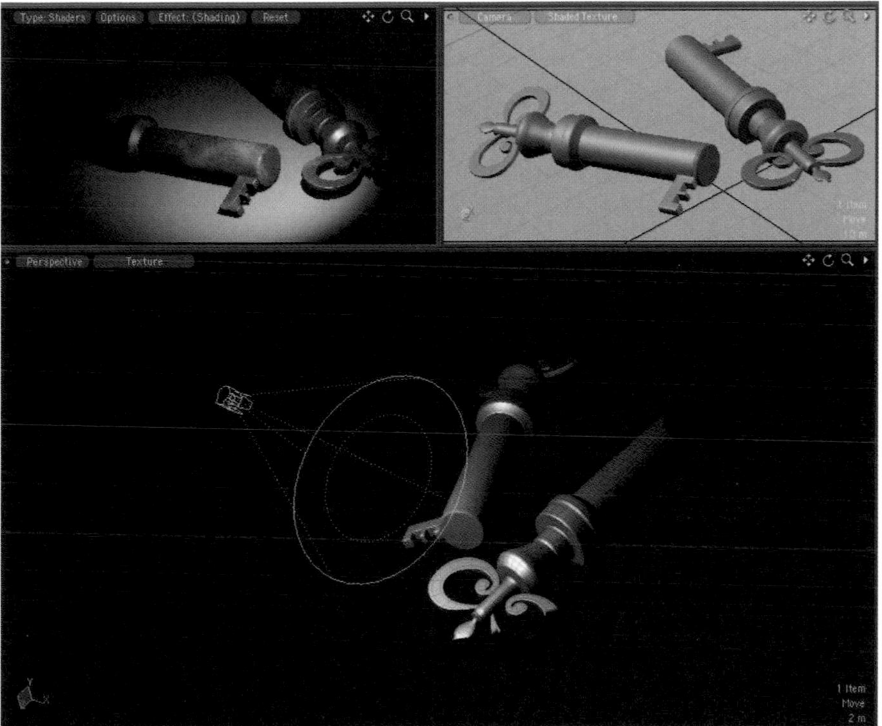

Figure 14.3 The spotlight offers you control over position and rotation for maximum flexibility.

Figure 14.4 shows a shot of the keys with an area light. Area lights are some of the best lights you can use because they offer realistic shadows, as well as greater control over intensity. They work this way because an area light simulates the size of a real-world light. In modo, you can press the y key and find two handles on an area light that will allow you to scale the area width and height. The light shape can be square, like a big soft light in a photography or video studio. They can also be oval in shape, which changes the throw of the light. You'll see this in a project a bit later.

Figure 14.5 shows the keys with a dome light. The look is similar to an area light with soft shadows, but rather than emitting from a directed source, the dome light emits from all over, simulating an environmental lighting situation.

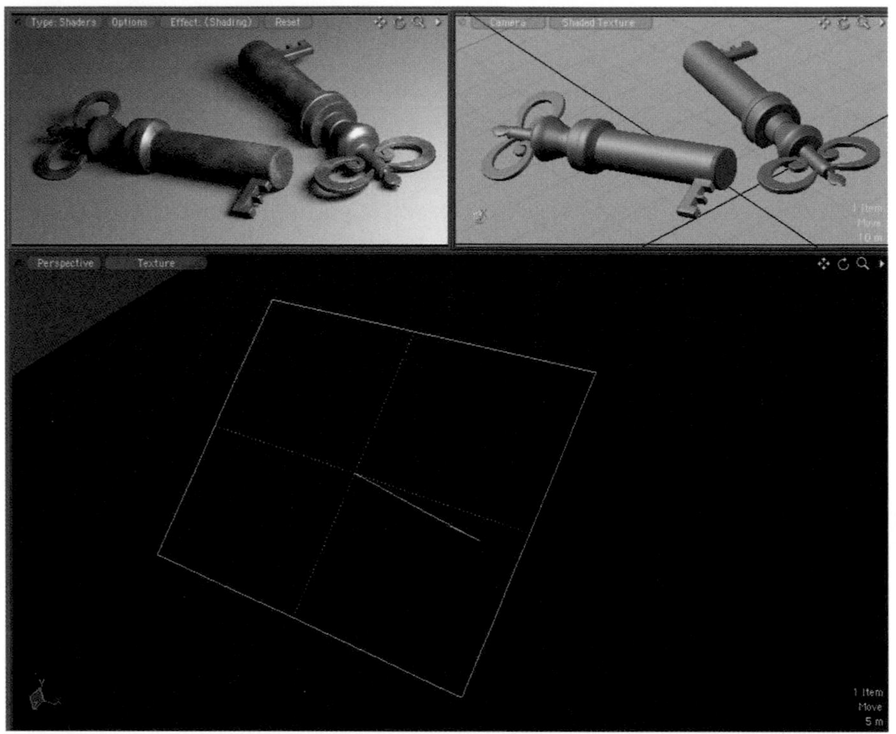

Figure 14.4
An area light allows you to create soft bright light in a directed fashion. Shadows are accurate and soft.

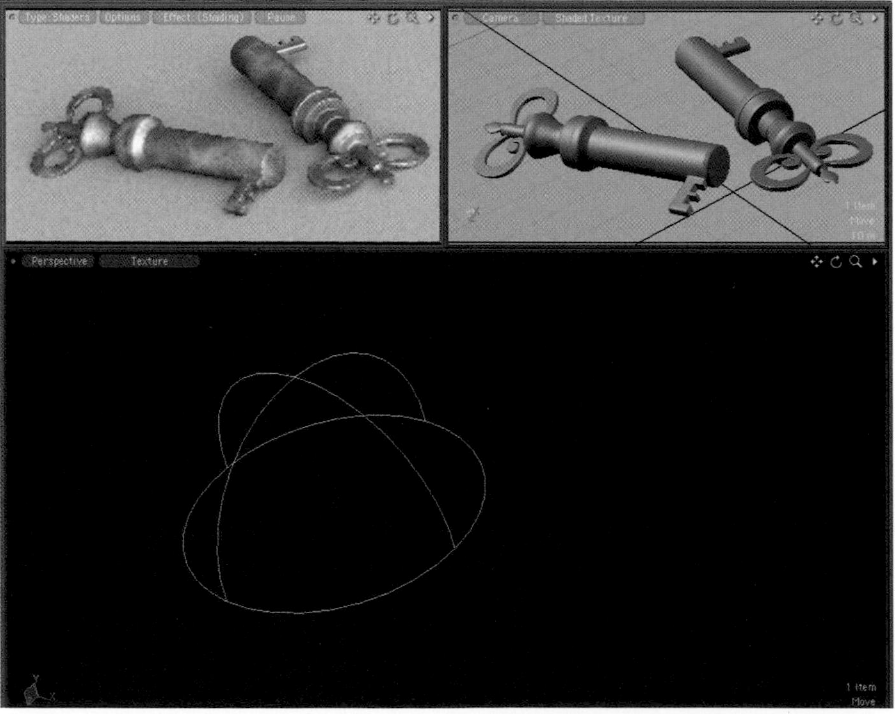

Figure 14.5
A dome light is a great way to light the entire scene, similar to an environmental light.

> **Note**
>
> While the dome light option is still available in modo, it's not often used much because of modo's fast global illumination. Additionally, modo 301/302's physical sky offers a real-world lighting situation that can trump any dome light setup.

Figure 14.6 incorporates a cylinder light, something that's very cool to use in your scenes. The cylinder light emits light in a cylindrical fashion, and it's great for setting concentrated light sources, perhaps in shots of medical imaging. With this light, you can change the length of the cylinder as well as the radius. Think of this light as a fluorescent tube.

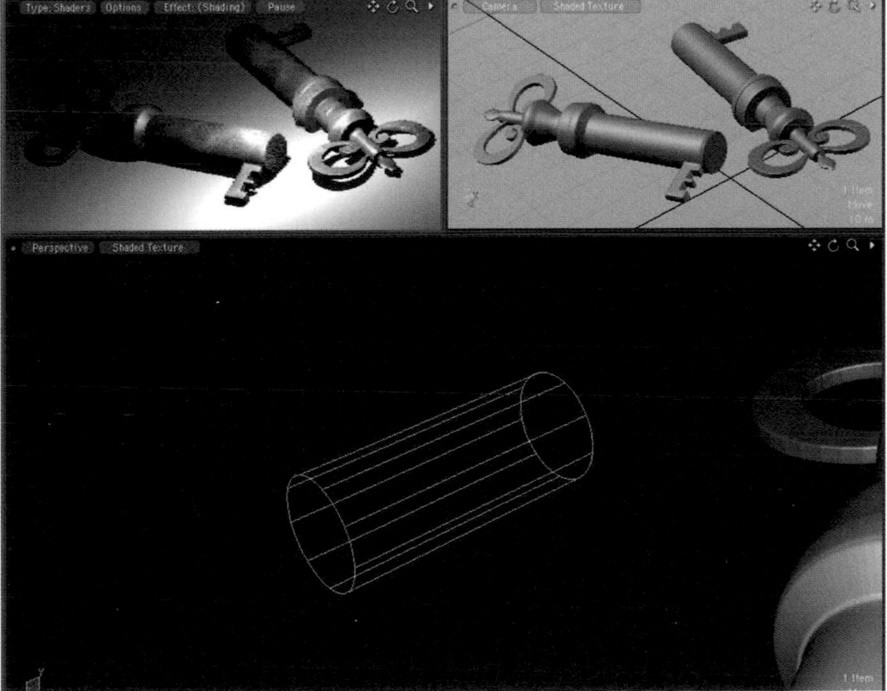

Figure 14.6 A cylinder light allows you to light your scene as if using a tube or fluorescent light.

You can use any light type in any way you see fit, but there are some basic principles that can guide you. Lighting in modo is a matter of preference, both in light type and attributes. But it's always a good idea to gain general knowledge of computer-generated (CG) lighting principles, which can apply not only to modo but to any 3D application.

There's one more type of light in modo 301/302, a photometric light. Also known as IES lights, these newly added lights offer you a light file that has been defined as a standard file type by the Illuminating Engineering Society of North America (IESNA). So what does that mean and how does it affect your scene? Good question. There's a video tutorial on the book's DVD, in the Chapter 14 folder, showing exactly how to work with this new light type, so check it out. It's called IESLights.mov.

Lighting Concepts

Light is everywhere. Light is everything. Unfortunately, many 3D artists don't consider light as an equal part of their scene. In fact, calling light an equal part of the scene might be an understatement. Light is part of our everyday world, in everything we do. While it's important to understand light theory and color, this chapter is geared more toward your working relationship with modo's lighting capabilities. There are tremendous books on lighting in 3D, such as Jeremy Birn's *Digital Lighting and Rendering, Second Edition* (New Riders Press, 2006), which you should definitely read and refer to on a regular basis. But without taking up too much time talking about all of the intricacies of CG lighting, take a look at Figure 14.7. What you're seeing is the visible spectrum of light we see everyday. Here, it's shown curved in the form of a rainbow. Look familiar?

Figure 14.7
The visible spectrum of light we see everyday.

Electromagnetic energy is all around us, and we perceive this in wavelengths that range from 400–700 nm (or wavelength), as visible light. Taking a look at the rainbow spectrum, on the left side you see blue. Electromagnetic energy in this range are X-rays and gamma rays. On the right of the spectrum is red, where you'll find radio waves. But how does this all relate to lighting in modo? This spectrum of colors is represented in the computer world as RGB, or red, green, and blue. These three colors are the primary colors of light, and mixing them is an additive approach that creates white. For example, if you take the RGB values in a color selector on your computer and drag them all up, you'll create the color white, 255 RGB. But why RGB? This has to do with the way our eyes perceive the visual spectrum. The receptors in our retinas respond to these values of the spectrum, but they also respond to the areas between these colors.

Quality of Light

You may not always think about the light in your 3D environment as something that has quality. But a light does have quality, and it's something you need to pay attention to. The quality of light refers to softness, angle, color, brightness, and throw pattern. The *throw pattern* is the shape of the light, and a good example of this is a square area light versus an oval area light. This is different from the light angle, which is more important for setting the mood of the scene. For example, a midday sun would be angled from above your 3D elements, or an evening sunset would be angled from low and to the side.

With modo, you might find yourself the victim of noise in your renders. While you might consider this a low-quality issue, it's really more a matter of properly setting the correct values. You'll perform a project that enables you to apply lights, render the scene, and then adjust it to see how the various settings change how a light affects the scene.

Other Light Sources

You've seen that you can choose from any of six lights in modo and put any combination of them into your scene. But there is a little bit more you can do to light your scene, using other types of light sources.

Figure 14.8 shows the key scene from earlier in the chapter lit without lights. That's right, no lights. The keys are lit by another 3D object.

You see, modo has the capability of global illumination (GI) . GI is the art and science of calculating the rays as they bounce in the scene. If an object is brighter, it will have a greater effect on the scene with global illumination. You'll set this up for yourself shortly.

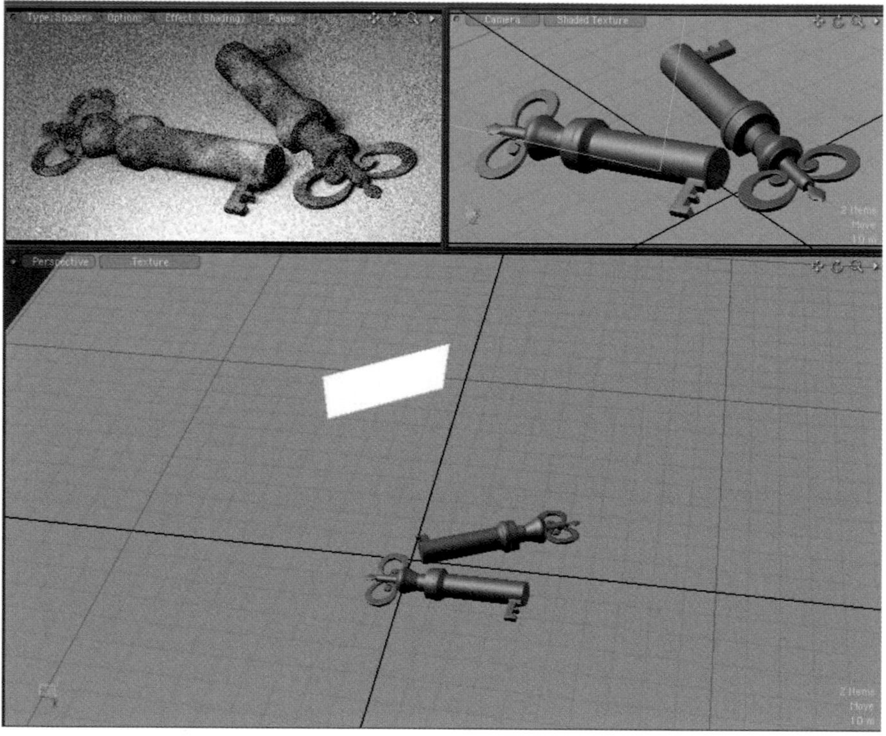

Figure 14.8
The key scene lit with one single polygon and no lights.

You can use any object as a light source. This is great for neon tubes, nighttime windows on a cityscape, or simply as soft light boxes, as shown in Figure 14.8.

Figure 14.9 shows the key scene with the Use Environment as Light option checked in the Render panel.

Here, your modo environment is used as a light source. So if you have a white background, modo carries those colors into your scene using it as a light from all directions. This of course is all based on the RGB values in the scene. However, like a dome light, it's not used as often because of modo's global illumination. Additionally, the global illumination option will render cleaner images.

Finally, modo also allows you to use HDR, or high dynamic range images. Computer screens can't display the full dynamic range of what lighting is like in the real world. The dynamic range is the ratio between the dark and bright regions of an image. But if a series of photos is taken at different exposures, then compiled in something like HDRShop or Photoshop CS3, a high dynamic range image is created. This type of image contains more data than you might think, enough to light an entire scene. Figure 14.10 shows the same key scene with an HDR image used as the only light source. This was a sample HDR image downloaded from Debevec.org. An important thing to note here is that modo can translate the pixel values of an HDR image into the same units of light energy that its lights use. Because an image has a high dynamic range, there are

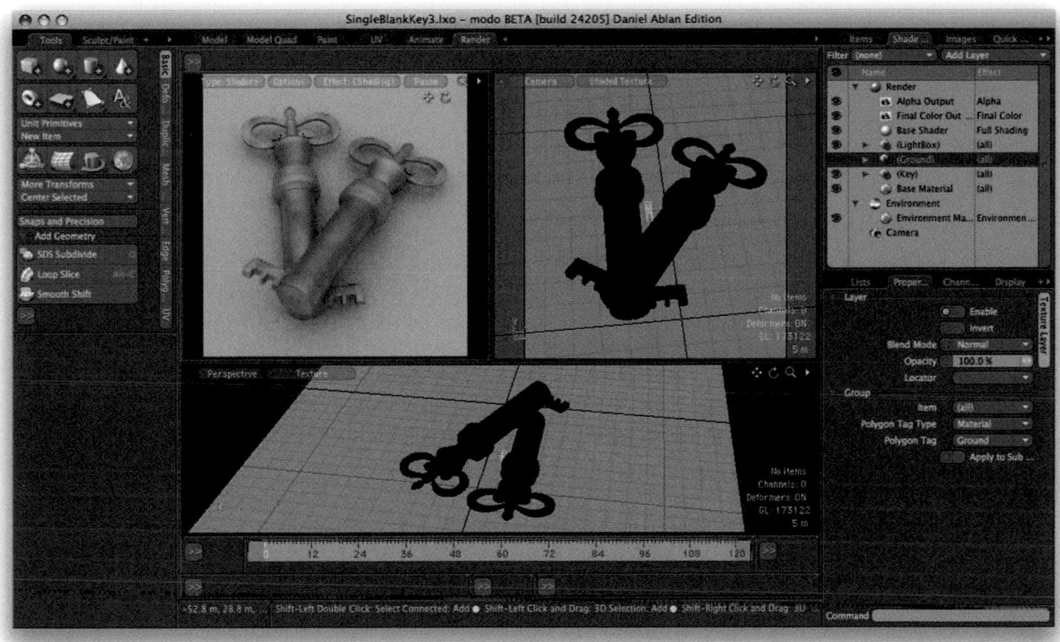

Figure 14.9 You can employ the environment as a light source in modo.

Figure 14.10 Incorporating HDR images into your scenes can produce very realistic lighting conditions.

values of great intensity (like a sun or room lights) that have pixel values much greater than 1. This allows subtle and realistic lighting.

The intensity of an HDR image allows a greater exposure in your 3D scene. In order for this to work, two things need to happen: The image must be an HDR, and you need to activate global illumination in the Render panel. In Chapter 15, you'll experiment with your own HDR images and set up a scene using them. For more information on this amazing science and technique, visit www.debevec.org. Paul Debevec was the pioneer behind merging high dynamic range imagery and computer graphics. Gregory Ward is credited with the being the founder of the HDR format.

Creating a Lit Scene in modo

Perhaps by this point in the book, you've tooled around enough to have created some decent looking renders. And perhaps you were adventurous and applied some various lighting effects to your scene. Tremendous! Experimentation is key. This next project will take you through the setup of a scene and how to apply different light sources. Along the way, you'll see explanations for various settings that might have eluded you up to this point.

1. Load the sonylcd.lxo scene from the book's disc. It's in the Chapter 14 projects folder.
2. Once loaded, click over to the Render tab. Figure 14.11 shows the scene.
3. This nice-looking setup was created and generously donated for use in this book by Mr. Philip Lawson. Thanks, Philip! You can see that you have an LCD monitor image mapped with a screen grab of modo. Also notice that there is just white all around the monitor. How is this scene lit?
4. Take a closer look at the Items tab. Mr. Lawson has created three groups: Models, Textures, and Lights. Figure 14.12 shows the Lights group expanded.
5. You don't want to save over the original scene, so resave it under a different name.
6. In the Items tab, expand and then select the three lights in the group, right-click on them and select Delete. When it asks if you want to delete child items, choose Yes.
7. Next, in the Shader Tree, select the Render listing. Then in the Properties panel, click on the Global Illumination vertical tab. Turn off Indirect Illumination, as shown in Figure 14.13.

   For now, you'll work just with modo's practical light types. In the next chapter, you'll work with HDR and indirect (global) illumination.
8. From the Items tab, click the New Item listing. It's ghosted and just below the last item in the list. Choose Area Light, as shown in Figure 14.14.

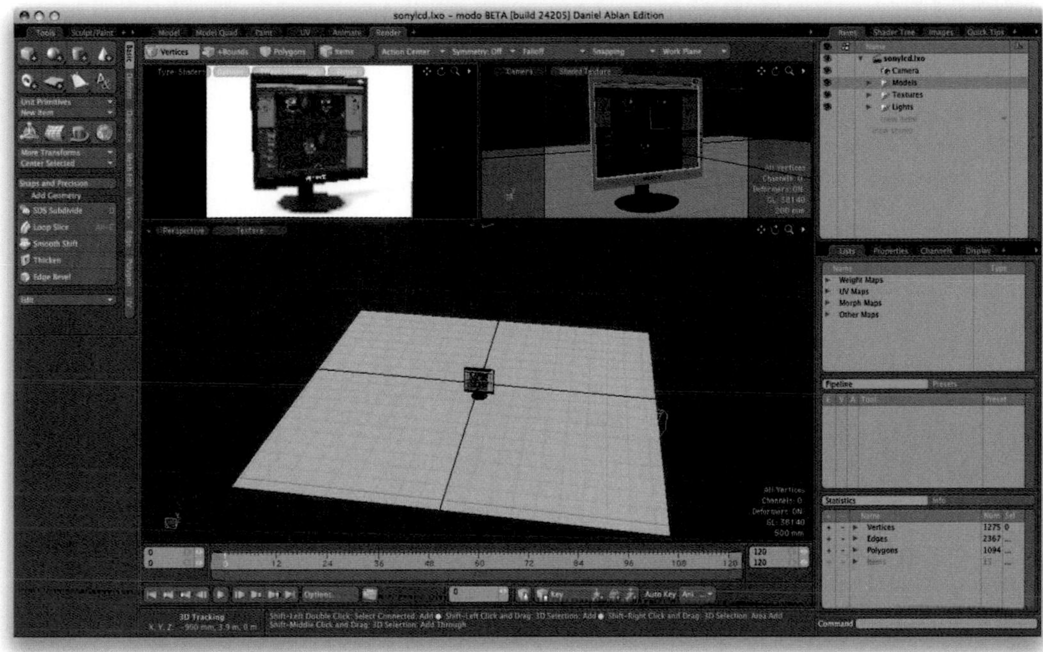

Figure 14.11 Load the LCD monitor from the projects folder on the book's DVD.

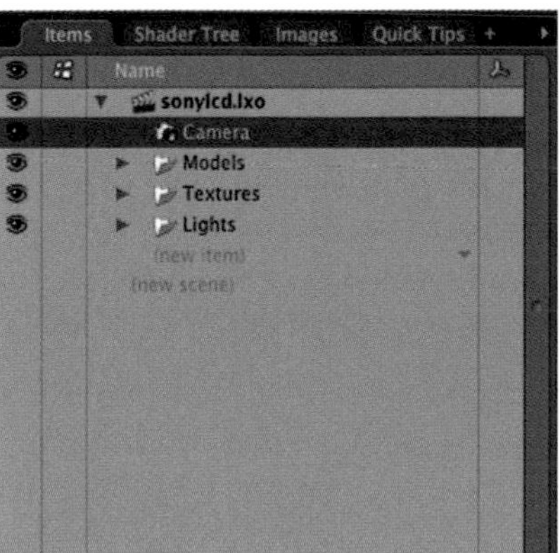

Figure 14.12 This default scene uses three directional lights. The result is an evenly lit object and a bright white set.

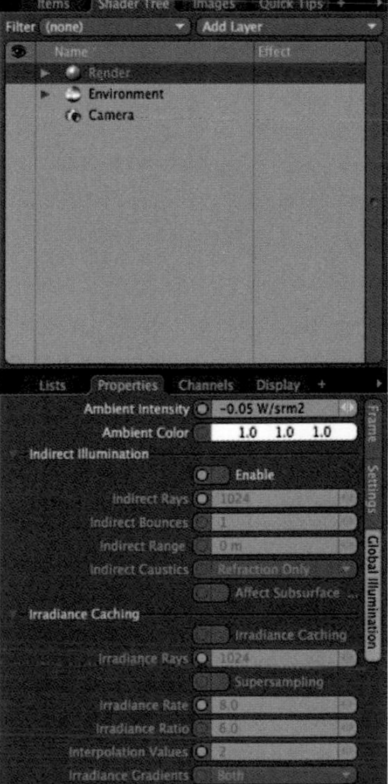

Figure 14.13 Turn off the Indirect Illumination option in the Render Properties tab.

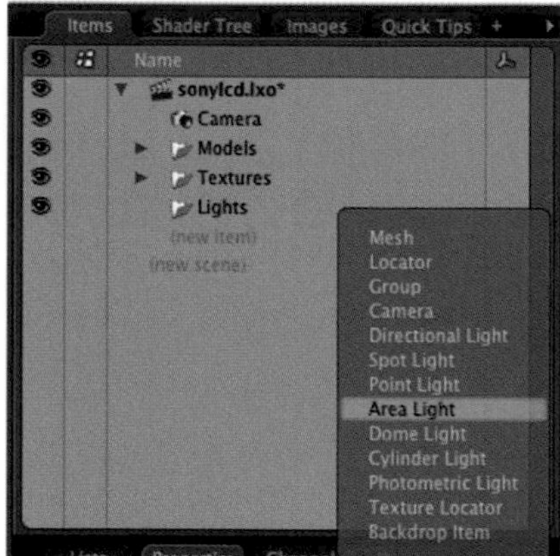

Figure 14.14 Adding a light to the scene is as easy as clicking the New Item listing in the Items tab.

9. Once the area light is loaded, it's plopped down right the middle of the scene, as shown in Figure 14.15.
10. Make sure the new light is selected in the Items tab, and check that you're in Items selection mode at the top of the modo interface. Next press the y key on your keyboard. While you can move the light by pressing the w key, the y key is ideal for an area light because you can move, rotate, and change the area width and height all in one tool.

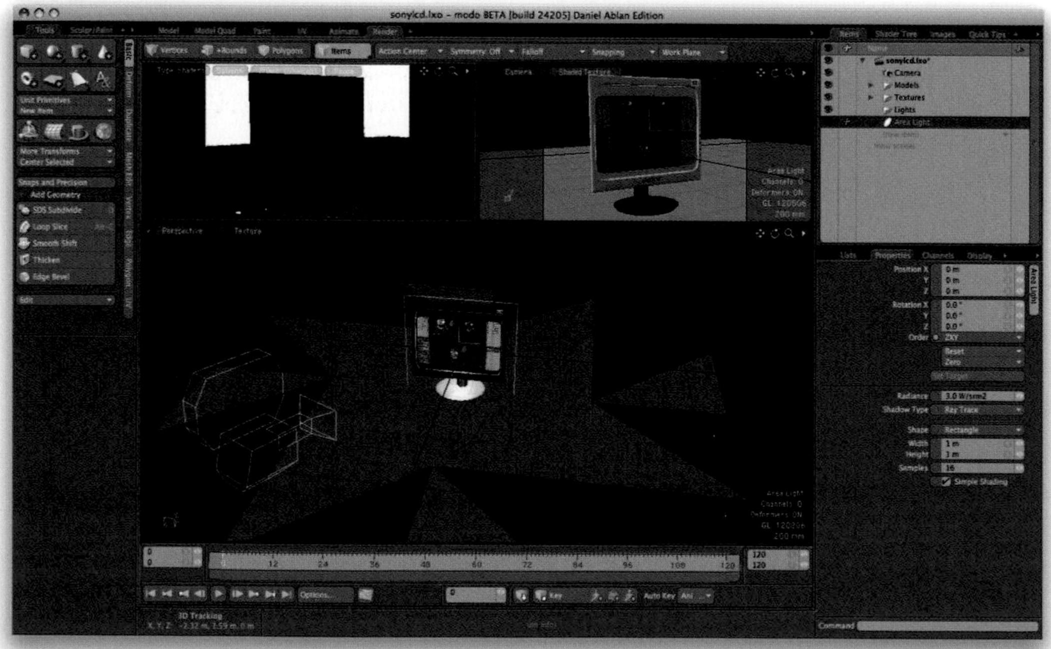

Figure 14.15 Adding an area light simply puts it in the middle of the scene. You'll need to move it into place.

Note

Action Center should be set to Automatic, although the Pivot Action Center can work as well.

Note

If you can't see the light in your scene, press the o key on the keyboard to open the Options panel. There, click the Visibility tab, and at the top of the panel, check on Show Lights. To close the panel, just move your mouse off of it. However, you've probably already accidentally done that!

11. Click and drag the green handle to bring the light up on the Y axis about 1 m. Remember that you can set the position on the item Properties tab on the right, and you can set the offset values for the currently active tool in the tool Properties panel on the left. You'll see the actual physical properties for the light in the Properties tab on the right side of the interface.
12. Now click the blue handle and drag the light on the Z axis to –1m. This will place the light in front of the monitor screen.
13. Click the red ring and drag the light about 35 degrees. What happens? Not much! You see, area lights have one direction. And because the light's direction indicator (the orange arrow) is now pointing up with a 35-degree rotation, you're not lighting the object at all. Rotate the light to –35 degrees, and the LCD monitor will now be lit, as shown in Figure 14.16.
14. Now, you see the light blue plus marks on the edge of the light? They'll appear when the light is selected and you press the y tool. Drag the right side square out to expand the Area Width value to 3 m. You can see the amount in the Properties panel. Then, drag the top square up to 2 m for the Height value. Figure 14.17 shows the change in light size and brightness.

    Notice in Figure 14.17 that the light is soft and well placed above the monitor. But the backdrop is awful, and the light falls off and doesn't light the set. When lighting your 3D scenes, there's more to it than just placing a light. The environment plays a key role in every scene you build. Here, the environment is just white, so change it.

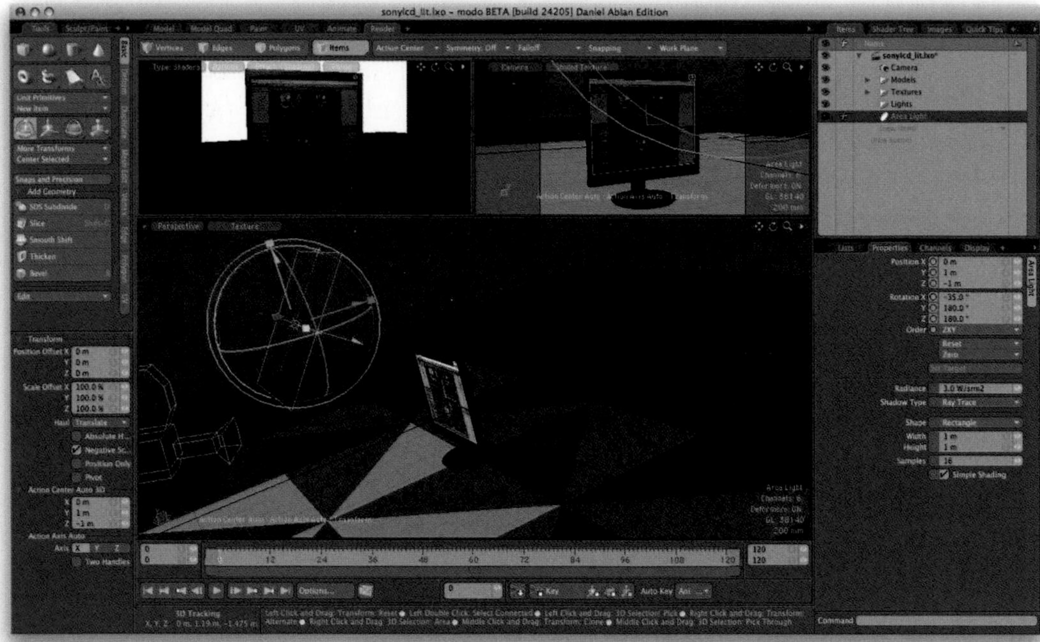

Figure 14.16 Rotate the area light to –35 degrees so the direction of the light faces the object.

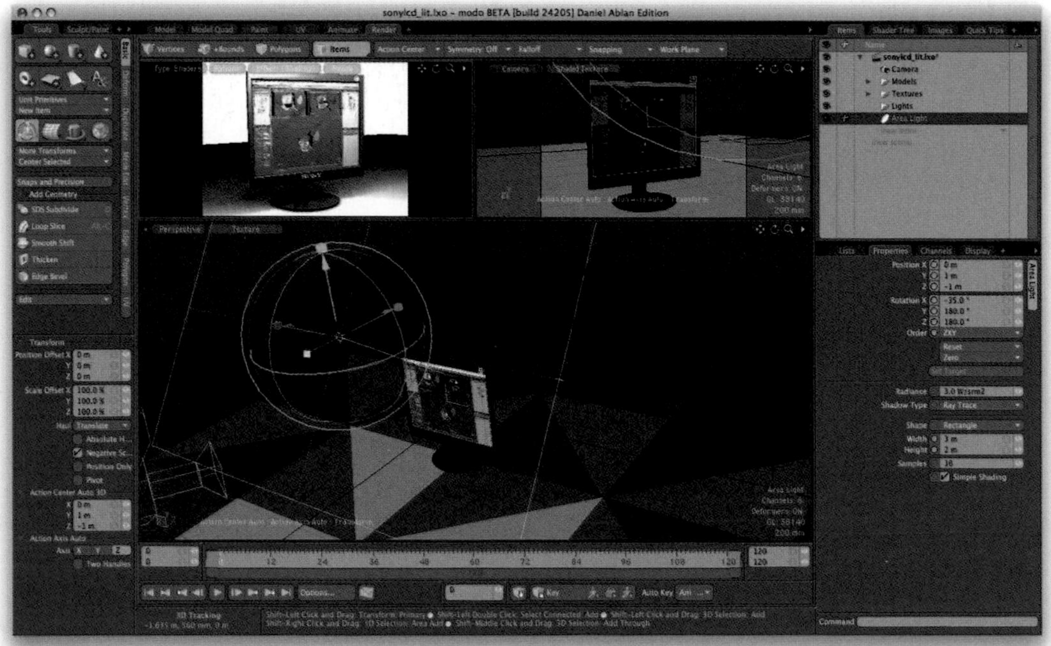

Figure 14.17 Changing the area light's width and height increases its strength.

15. In the Shader Tree, expand the Environment layer and select the Environment Material listing. In the Render Properties tab for Environment Material, notice that the Environment Type option is set to Constant. This sets one single color, which is currently white. How about something more dramatic? Change the Zenith Color option from white to black. You can do this quickly by holding the Shift key, clicking directly on the color values, and then dragging to the left.
16. Taking a look at the preview window in Figure 14.18, you can see that with the area light falloff and the black background, you've instantly changed the appearance of the render.

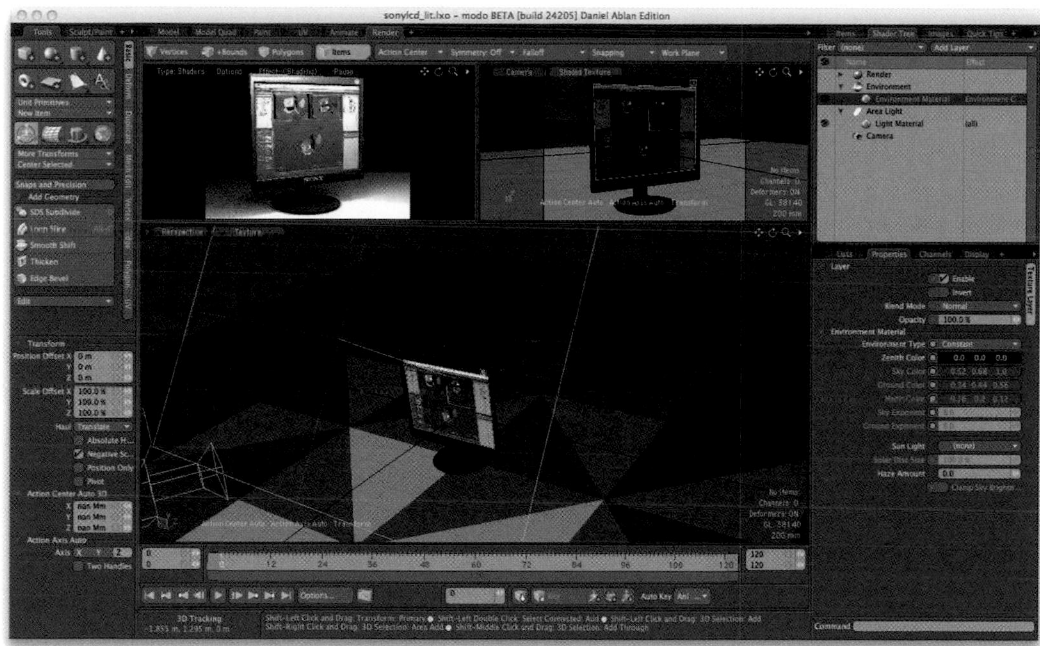

Figure 14.18 Change the Constant background to create a different mood in the scene.

17. You can go a step farther now to pull the object from the background. First, save your work. Then, in the Items tab, add a spotlight. Do this by clicking on New Item.
18. Drag the light to about 4 m on the Z axis, as shown in Figure 14.19. Notice something on the end of the cone? With the y Transform tool selected, there are move and rotate handles, as well as two small light blue squares, just as there was on the area light. Yet here, these two squares change the Cone Angle value (which is the spread of the light) and the Soft Edge value.

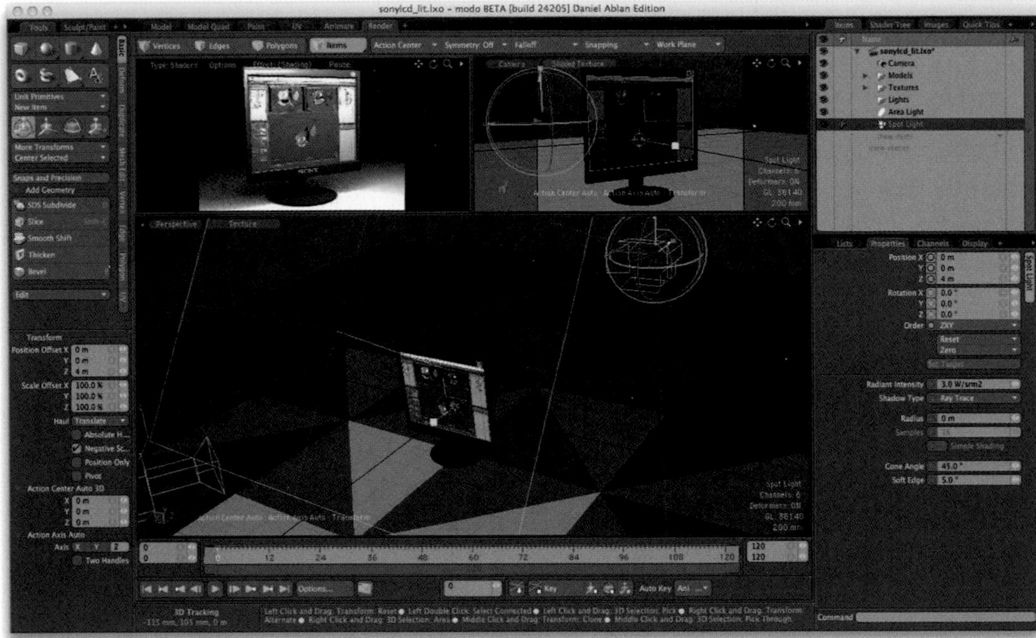

Figure 14.19 A spotlight can co-exist with an area light, no problem!

> **Note**
>
> So, let's say that you're having trouble navigating the scene because the light or camera icons are just too big. What do you do? To the right of the Properties tab is the Display tab. Select the desired item in the Items tab, such as a Light, and then change the Size value in the Display tab. One way to work is simply to change this value to 0. This will balance the size of the light or camera icon to match the scene.

19. Drag the Cone Angle value to 60 and the Soft Edge value to 80. By setting Soft Edge higher than Cone Angle, you can effectively pull the light away from the center spot. It's a nice effect for a light like this. Because this light is being used behind the subject and not as a main light, a softer edge works well.
20. Bring the spotlight up on the Y axis to about 1 m. Then grab the red ring and rotate the light about –24 degrees so that it's pointing at the back of the monitor.
21. In the Render tab, change the top-right camera view to Perspective. Then, change the main large view from Perspective to Light view. This way, you can see exactly what the light sees, making it easier to set up (see Figure 14.20).

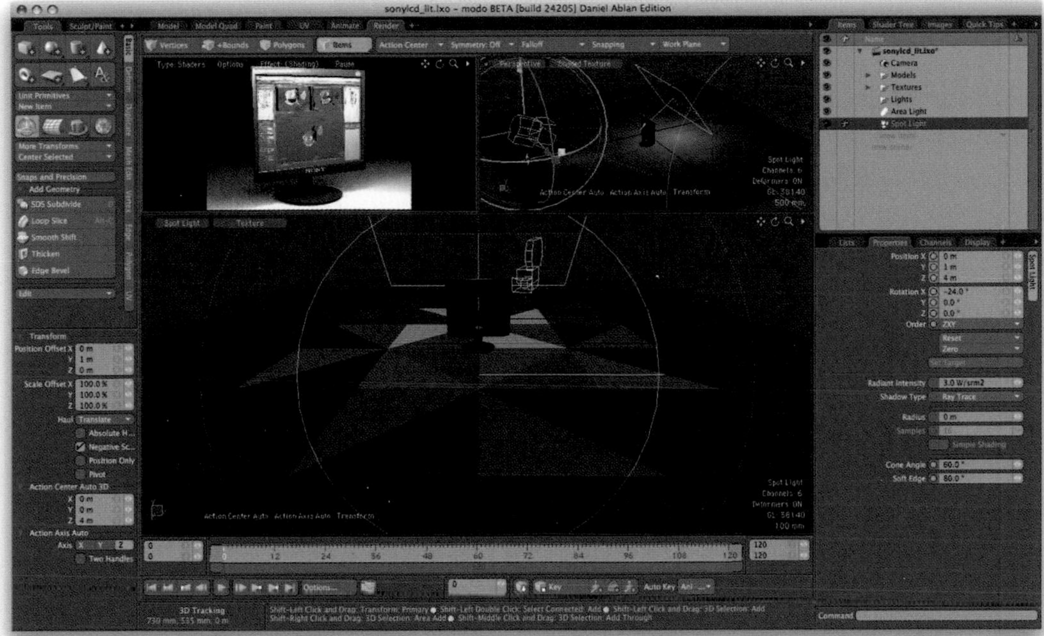

Figure 14.20 Change the views to incorporate a Light view to make it easier to set up the light.

> **Note**
>
> When working in Light view, you can move the light by holding the Alt+Shift keys, then clicking and dragging in the viewport. You can rotate the light by holding the Alt/Option key and clicking in the viewport. To zoom the light, hold the Ctrl and Alt/Option keys, then click and drag. To orbit the light, hold Alt and left-click; to rotate the light, hold Alt and right-click.

22. Position the light on your own to cast a back light on the monitor, maybe off to the side a bit, something like Figure 14.21.
23. The position is good, but the light itself doesn't seem to do much for the render, if you take a look at the Preview window. So click over to the Shader Tree, expand the Spot Light layer, and select the Light Material listing for it. Notice that in the Properties tab, the Color value is white, and the Shadow value is black. For now, the shadow color is fine, but you can change this if you like.

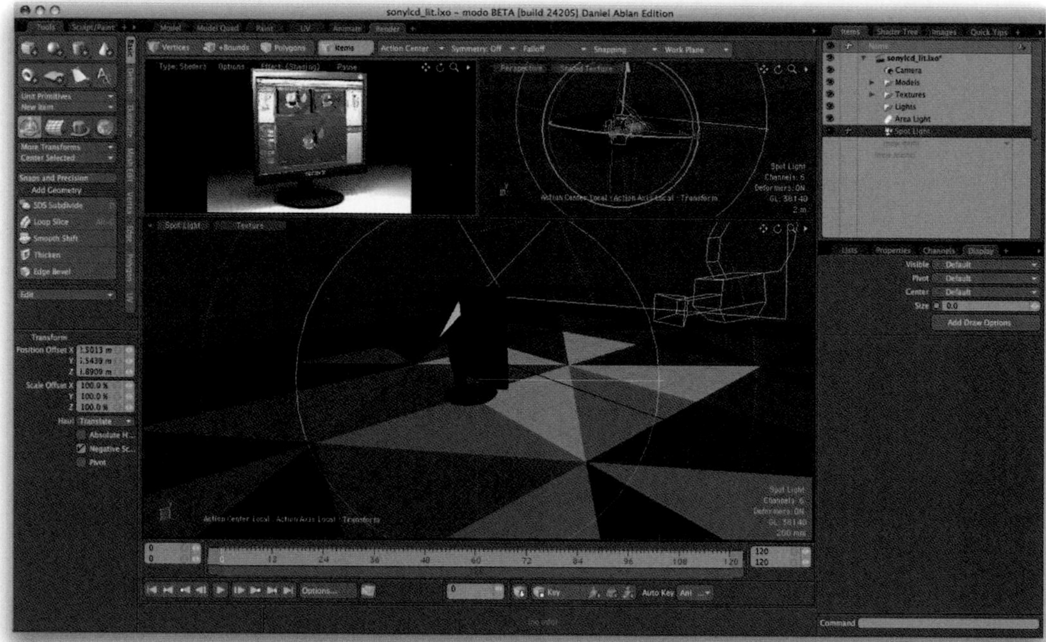

Figure 14.21 Position the light so that it's slightly above and to the side of the monitor.

24. Change the Color value for the light to a bright orange, roughly 1.0, 0.35, 0.07. You can click and drag directly on each of the Color values to change them. Select the Area Light in the Shader Tree and change the Radiance value from 3.0 to 1.5. Bring the Spot Light's Radiance value up to 6.0. Press F9 to render the frame. Figure 14.22 shows the render. Notice that there's not a soft warm color behind the monitor on the floor? The spotlight adds a bit of warmth to the scene and helps pull the monitor from the dark background.

25. To take this a step farther, change the Action Center to Selection. Press the y key, and then you can grab the blue handle to pull the light back on its own axis to fill more of the scene.

26. You can also change the Shadow Type option in the Render Properties tab, but in this case, a spotlight only has a ray traced shadow. Figure 14.23 shows the scene with the light moved and set to a brighter radiance, new position, and different color.

27. From here, try adding additional lights, such as a point light. Position it off to the far right side, and change its Radiance value so that the light acts as a simple fill for the scene. Often, this can be a very low value, just enough to pull some detail out of the shadows. Experiment!

Figure 14.22 Adding a colored spotlight behind the monitor helps give some warmth to the scene.

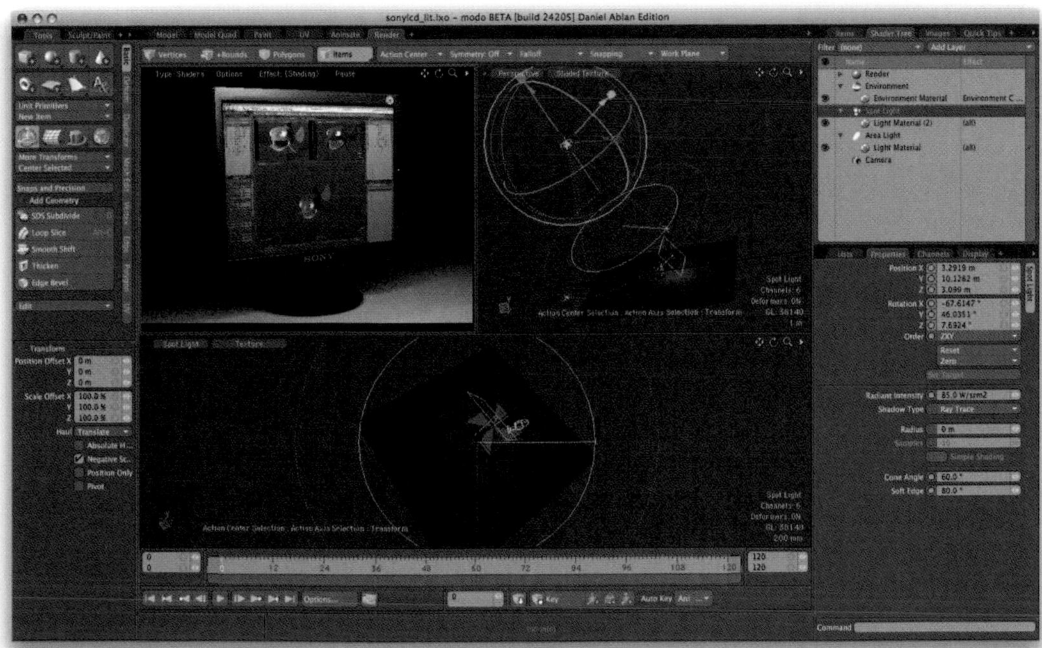

Figure 14.23 With the spotlight moved back and the radiance increased, the backdrop becomes even warmer.

Note

Other than a distant light, all of modo's lights use an inverse square law for their standard setting.

What you've set up here is similar to a basic three-point lighting shoot with slight variations. A three-point lighting setup requires a main key light (your area light), a back light (your spotlight), and a fill light to help balance dark shadows or lost edges, such as the left side of the monitor. This is what your point light is doing: In addition to helping light the model, these lights also enhance the overall mood and tone of your scene. So while Philip Lawson's original scene was great and very product-shot-like, the setup you've created is richer and takes on a whole different look.

Rendering Introduction

If you're from the modo 201 camp and have upgraded to 301/302, then you know that one of the biggest new features is the ever-improving modo render engine. With the incorporation of the render engine, modo now has advanced texturing capabilities, lights and shadows, and more.

As the next step in this next-generation program, modo incorporates a physically based shading model. This allows you to create some pretty stunning results quickly and easily. Figure 14.24 shows a render from the 3D Garage modo 301 Signature Courseware. Here, you can see that modo has done a great job with shadows, light color, falloffs, subsurface scattering, and reflections. But how does this all come together?

Note

Visit 3DGarage.com and type in the code **modo301book** to get a big discount on the full modo 301 courseware, now updated for modo 302. You'll learn how to create this candlestick scene from the ground up, as well as many more projects, including 15-plus hours of video training.

Take a look at Figure 14.25. What you're looking at is the Render Properties tab for this scene, accessed from within the Shader Tree.

Let's break down the settings, which will help demystify the myriad tools. When you select the Render listing in the Shader Tree, all of the necessary render parameters appear below it in the Properties tab. Easy enough, right?

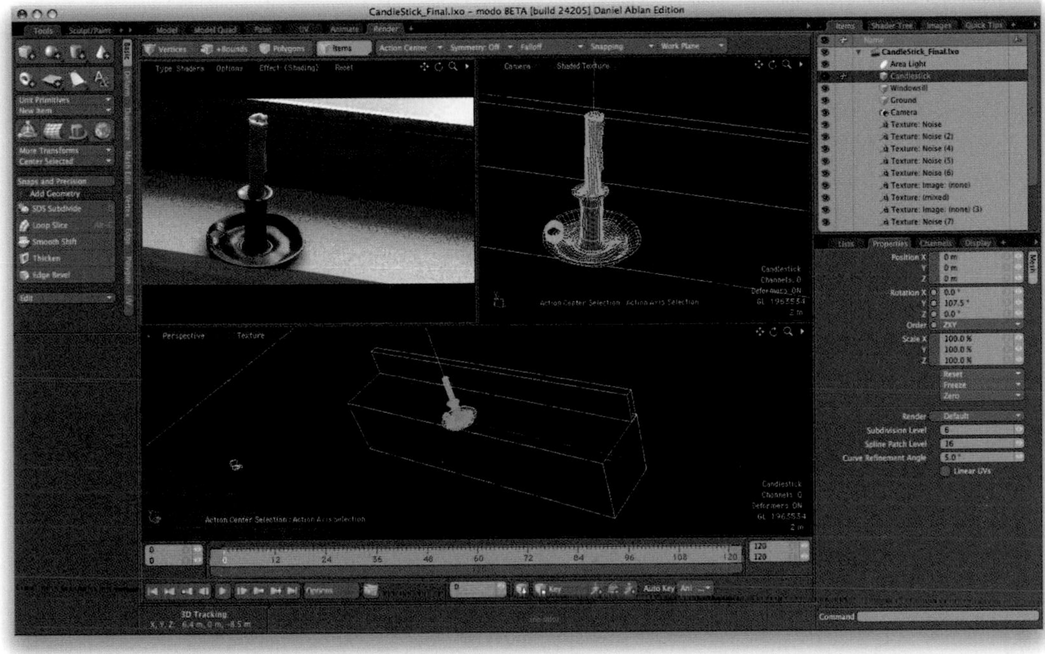

Figure 14.24 A candle by a window, waiting for the darkness. Simple but nicely rendered.

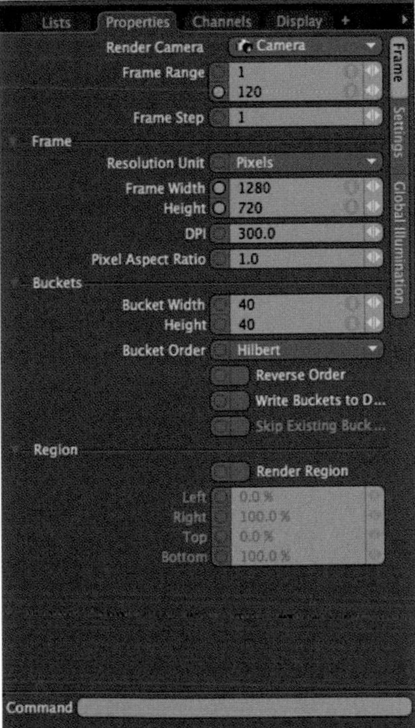

Figure 14.25 The Frame vertical tab in the Render Properties tab for the candle example.

Frame

Now, it's important to pay attention to the vertical tabs within the Render Properties panel. They are Frame, Settings, and Global Illumination. Refer back to Figure 14.25, which shows the Frame tab and its settings. At the top of the panel is the Render Camera option. Since you can have multiple cameras in modo, this setting tells the render engine which camera to render. From there, you'll see the next options. Frame Range is the first and last frame of your animation. Frame Step tells the render engine how to render the Frame Range values. By default, it's set to 1, meaning, render every 1 frame—that is, 1, 2, 3, and so on. You can set it to 2, or 5 if you like (or any value), and modo will render every second or fifth frame, respectively.

In the Frame tab, you can set the Resolution Unit option. By default, it's set to Pixels, the most common render type in 3D applications. But if you're rendering for print, you can change this to Inches. Beneath this setting is where you'll set the Frame Width and Height values. When you render your frame, this is the size of the image. You also have a DPI (dots per inch) setting, which defaults to 300, a typical setting when working in the print world. For video, DPI is irrelevant! DPI is only needed when rendering for print. The Pixel Aspect Ratio value is important to set properly, as it will change the look of your render. By default, it's set to 1.0 square pixel. This should be used for images staying within the computer, such as image processing in Photoshop, web sites, and so on. But, if your final render is going to video, the square pixel setting (1.0) won't look right. For standard definition D1 or DV video, you'll want 0.9, which sets a rectangular pixel. Further changes to the Pixel Aspect Ration value can be set for widescreen at 1.2 or 1.5.

In the middle of the Frame tab is the Buckets area. modo uses bucket rendering to render its frames. Basically, *bucket rendering* is a technology that separates the frame buffer into different regions, which are rendered independently. The result is faster rendering and more control over the process. But another cool thing about bucket rendering is that it significantly decreases the use of frame buffer memory, but the size of the buckets makes all the difference. By changing the Bucket Width and Height values, you can tell modo to use less memory when rendering, which can be important depending on the scene. Overall though, you won't need to change this for most renders. Each scene will vary, and the Luxology team has set the default Bucket Width and Height values to 40, a good working size. Using these settings helps you balance memory versus CPU consumption. The end result is that you have the ability with bucket rendering to render billions of polygons. Experiment with these settings and see what results you achieve. The Bucket Order option is also important when rendering with buckets, as this determines how the buckets (regions) are rendered. The Hilbert option is a mathematical function that finds a coherent balance for better memory management and speed. However, you can also set Bucket Order to Rows, Columns, Spiral, and Random.

Additionally, there is a Reverse Order option for the buckets. With Bucket Order set to Hilbert and Reverse Order checked, you can render your fame from the inside out.

Turning on the Write Buckets to Disk option tells modo to save the bucket data to a temporary space on your hard drive, helping ease the strain on your system's memory.

Lastly, you can choose the Render Region option. This simple setup allows you to render just a portion of your frame. Why would you use this? Let's say you've just rebuilt Rome and only need to see how one small building looks in the render. You can set up a render region for just that area, avoiding long render times with the rest of the frame. Time is money, people!

Setting

Just below the Frame vertical tab is the Settings tab, as shown in Figure 14.26.

At the top of the panel, you can tell modo to render in Scanline, Automatic, or Ray Trace mode. Scanline mode will use a scanline-based front end, while the Ray Trace setting employs a full ray traced render engine throughout your scene. For best results, keep this setting to Automatic, and let modo choose the right render settings for you.

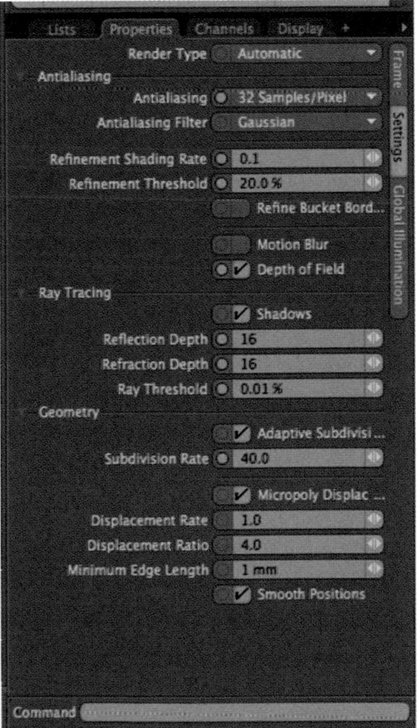

Figure 14.26 The Settings tab for rendering.

The antialiasing in modo works differently than what you might be familiar with. Here, modo uses samples per pixel. The default setting is 8, which means each pixel in your scene is broken down eight times. modo then creates an average for these samples and puts them together in the render for a clean, antialiased render. Different Antialiasing Filter options are available, such as Gaussian (default), Triangle, and Box. But you can tell modo how to process these pixels, and this is done with the Refinement Shading Rate value. This is a fine detail control for antialiasing. Leaving this set to 1, you're telling modo that your pixels do not need any help. This area is one of the most asked about parts of modo. The antialiasing settings are only working on geometric edges and material boundaries, but they also serve as motion blur and depth of field maximum samples. The Shading Rate value is what determines the quality of all interior shading, including shadows, reflections, and so on. The Refinement Threshold value is the rate at which to shade the pixels that fall within the refinement threshold. The refinement threshold determines which pixels are shaded at the shading rate and which at the refinement rate. The default of 10% means that pixels with more than a 10% difference in steps between them get shaded at the refinement rate. If they are less than 10% apart (pretty much the same color), they get shaded at the lower sampling rate of the shading rate found in the base shader.

You'll also find the Motion Blur and Depth of Field options here. Checking Depth of Field will help you achieve more photographic focus effects with your renders.

The Ray Tracing options are in the Settings tab as well, allowing you to turn the Shadows option on or off, set the Reflection Depth, Refraction Depth, and Ray Threshold values. For most of your renders, the default values will work just fine. But let's say you have a scene with a lot of water and glass—you might want to increase the depth values. In other cases, if only a small portion of your scene uses reflection or refraction, lower these values to save on render times. Test render first, of course, as changing the value too much might cause unnecessary render delays or render errors.

The Geometry section of the Settings tab allows you to set the Subdivision Rate value and turn on the Adaptive Subdivisions option. You should leave these values at their defaults, as this will definitely help your subdivided objects by calculating the additional geometry upon rendering. When using subdivision surfaces, this value picks a subdivision level for a given mesh item. The unit is pixels per edge. A lower value will subdivide more, since you will have an edge occupying fewer pixels. So an edge would be 4 pixels instead of 10, which means it subdivides more, not less. If you're creating really intricate scenes, such as detailed landscapes with displacement maps applied, you'll definitely want the Micropoly Displacement option active. This further subdivides your geometry, allowing very fine displacements. When turned on, you can control the Displacement Rate value, which determines the amount of polygons created during the render. It's important to note that setting a higher value will lower the polygon count.

So if you're looking to subdivide more, lower the value. The Minimum Edge Length option allows you to set a value so that when a micropoly displaced edge reaches that value, it will no longer be subdivided. This is important because if your polygons are continually refined, the render would never finish!

Note

One last important thing to note is the concept of *rates*. You might have a tendency to increase rates, thinking you're getting better quality renders. But, in fact, the opposite is true. Think of lower rates as finer settings, and higher rates as more course. And, because rates are pixel-based, you shouldn't have to change them if you change the resolution of your final render.

From this point, it's important to know that these basic lighting principles and render settings can apply to anything in modo. Their usage is the same, from adding to positioning and setting the radiance.

But modo is so much more powerful than what you've seen here, so instead of wasting pages with additional setup, you might really enjoy seeing more dramatic lighting examples. The way these can be achieved is with global illumination, a technique employed by most 3D applications today, but performed better in modo.

Turn to Chapter 15 to perform projects based all around on global illumination and advanced rendering.

15

Rendering with Global Illumination

A few years ago, the concept of using global illumination was foreign to most everyday 3D artists. Today, however, with the advances in computing power, memory capabilities, and powerful graphics cards, achieving the high-end render is quite possible.

Global Illumination

Global illumination uses algorithms that, when calculating light, take into account not only the light from a direct source, but also indirect light—for example, light that has originated from a 3D light source and bounced off of scene geometry or light coming from the environment and luminous geometry. In modo, when you select the Render layer in the Shader Tree, and view the Global Illumination tab within the Render Properties panel, you'll see a section for Indirect Illumination, as shown in Figure 15.1.

When you render with global illumination (with Indirect Illumination enabled), it will take more time, no question. However, the results are more than worth it. Also take into consideration that modo 301//302 is an animation program, so you're rendering multiple frames. Figure 15.2 shows a scene with typical lighting, similar to what you created in the previous chapter. Figure 15.3 shows the same scene lit entirely with the environment, using global illumination.

The funny thing about comparing Figures 15.2 and 15.3 is that both look really good! The render engine in modo performs so well that even what would be a boring, poorly lit scene looks good. But you can see that Figure 15.2 with global illumination active is softer and looks more realistic. This is because the global illumination is lighting the scene from all around, from the entire environment, rather than just from a single source. To further understand what's happening with global illumination, think of a room in your home. Imagine the morning light coming through the window. The room is lit up, and you can clearly see all around the room, even though the light is only coming in at one location. The reason you can see all over from this single light source is because the light is being diffused throughout the room. Each surface the light hits, the

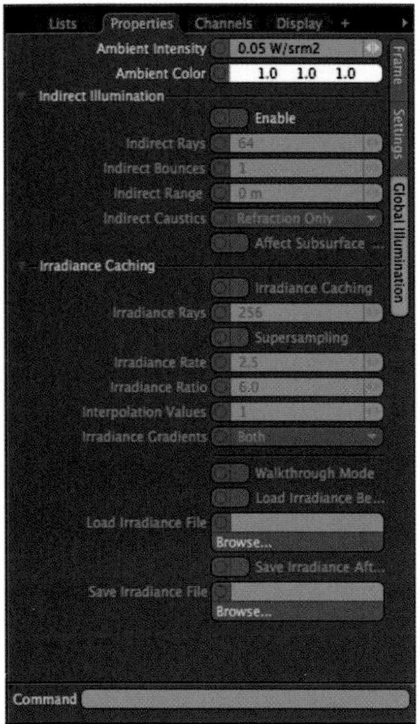

Figure 15.1
The Indirect Illumination category within the Global Illumination tab is found in the Render Properties tab.

Figure 15.2 An array of glasses lit with a single spotlight.

Figure 15.3 The same array of glasses lit with global illumination, using a white environment and a large white polygon.

floor, chairs, or cabinets, adds to the overall color and lighting. In the computer with a similar setup, unless global illumination is active with Indirect Illumination enabled, all you would see is the light coming through the window and hitting the floor or its subject. That's it.

It's important to understand that many things affect a scene using global illumination. Because the algorithm takes into account the brightness of everything in the scene, the environment you place your objects in makes a big difference in the way a scene renders. Reflection is also another factor in effective global illumination. That's not to say you need reflections, but in the example of the glasses in Figures 15.2 and 15.3, the added realism comes from reflections in the elements. Another example (see Figures 15.4 and 15.5) shows a simple object lit with global illumination; however, Figure 15.4 has no reflections, but Figure 15.5 does.

Figure 15.4 Three silver things don't look so silver, even with global illumination active.

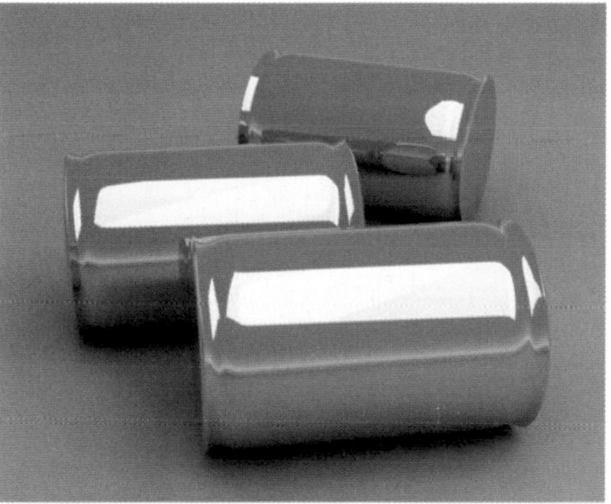

Figure 15.5 The same scene with only one change: reflection.

So while many of your scenes might not incorporate reflection (perhaps a dirty-looking wood crate or a soft and plush carpet), global illumination and surface properties all work together.

Ray Tracing

You might have heard the term *radiosity*, and you might even be familiar with it. Radiosity is simply an algorithm that is used in global illumination. You see, global illumination uses many different algorithms, such as radiosity, ray tracing, beam tracing, cone tracing, path tracing, and photo mapping. Many of these can be combined, and modo certainly uses ray tracing. You've been rendering with ray tracing throughout this entire book. In the mid 1990s, the introduction of ray tracing to 3D applications was a very big deal. Today, it's commonplace.

Ray tracing is when a ray of light travels within the 3D environment and reacts to what it hits. This ray of light is traced in a backward direction, and if it hits an object, a shadow is created. When this happens, a secondary ray is cast, and then a reflected ray is generated. That ray is then computed against other rays. What this all means is that ray tracing allows you to have accurate, realistic shadows and reflections. Figure 15.6 shows Philip Lawson's drink glass. It has no ray tracing applied. Figure 15.7 shows the shot with ray tracing.

Figure 15.6 Philip Lawson's drink glass without ray tracing.

Figure 15.7 The drink glass with ray tracing.

In Figure 15.6, the Base Shader option in the Shader Tree was selected, and in the Texture Layer tab, Cast Shadows was turned off as well as Receive Shadows. Also, the Visible to Reflection Rays and Visible to Refraction Rays options were also turned off. The result was a not-so-good-looking image. The reason this glass rendered black is because it's a transparent object that relies on refraction, or the bending of light as it passes through a surface. Ray tracing needs to be active to calculate that data, and by turning it off, you lose the surface. The umbrella, on the other hand, rendered just fine because it's a flat diffused surface.

> **Note**
>
> You can also quickly turn shadows on or off by selecting Render in the Shader Tree; then from within the Render Properties panel, under the Settings tab, you'll find the Enable Shadows option.

Advantages of ray tracing are that you can obtain very realistic situations with it, such as accurate shadows, soft shadows, reflections, and refractions for glass and transparencies. The disadvantage, however, is performance. Isn't that always the case? Even so, computer processors have become much faster, and the coding that goes into programs like modo has become smarter. The bucket rendering method discussed earlier is one way that modo helps make rendering faster, especially when it comes to ray tracing.

Ray Tracing and Global Illumination Combined

In this next section, you'll set up a lighting situation that will employ environmental light, traditional lights, and global illumination. You'll use ray tracing and render the final shot.

1. From the File menu in modo, select Reset to clear out modo.
2. Load the 8balls.lxo file. This is a scene that will help demonstrate the power of modo's render engine, combining ray tracing and global illumination.
3. Switch to a Render tab to see the preview.
4. Over in the Shader Tree, take a look at the variety of materials for the different balls. You have Plastic, Glass, Eggshell, and others. Each has been created based on what you've learned throughout the book, applying different color, variations in reflection and specularity, as well as transparency.
5. Select the material named Eggshell. This is one material that was intentionally left blank. Figure 15.8 shows the scene.

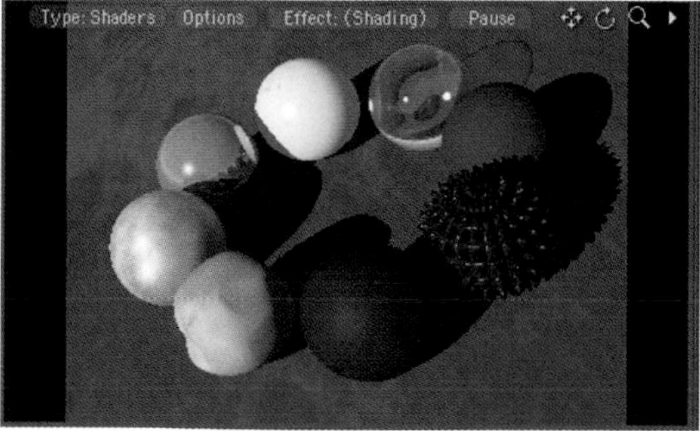

Figure 15.8 The 8balls scene is boring with a default distant light.

6. This scene as it stands has eight spheres set on a flat textured plane. There is one default directional light in the scene. To begin, in the Material Ref tab of the Render Properties panel, set the Eggshell material's diffuse color to white. Hold the Shift key, click on the color values, and drag to the right.
7. Choose Conserve Energy. This helps balance the reflection and color values.
8. Next, click the Material Trans tab in the Render Properties panel.
9. You don't need this material to be transparent, nor do you need to set up a subsurface scattering value. What you do need is the Luminous Intensity option.
10. Set Luminous Intensity to 6. The material will become fully opaque, as shown in Figure 15.9.

Figure 15.9
A very luminous object, the Eggshell material is now overpowering the other balls.

11. At this point, the bright white sphere just doesn't blend well in the scene, and perhaps the Luminous Intensity value is set too high. Before you make any changes, you're going to turn off the directional light and use global illumination to light the scene.
12. In the Items tab, right-click on Directional Light and choose Delete to remove it from the scene. Figure 15.10 shows the deal.
13. Back in the Shader Tree, click the Render listing. Then in the Render Properties panel, under the Global Illumination tab, enable Indirect Illumination. Let the Preview viewport update, and see what you get. Figure 15.11 shows the scene. Because the entire environment is now calculated as a light source, the bright white Eggshell material casts light onto the other balls. This gives the appearance of a light bulb. Imagine the variations you can make to this, perhaps creating neon tubes?
14. In the Shader Tree, change the Eggshell material's diffuse color to yellow: 1.0, 1.0, 0.0. Then in the Material Trans tab, set Luminous Intensity to 4.0. Figure 15.12 shows the result.

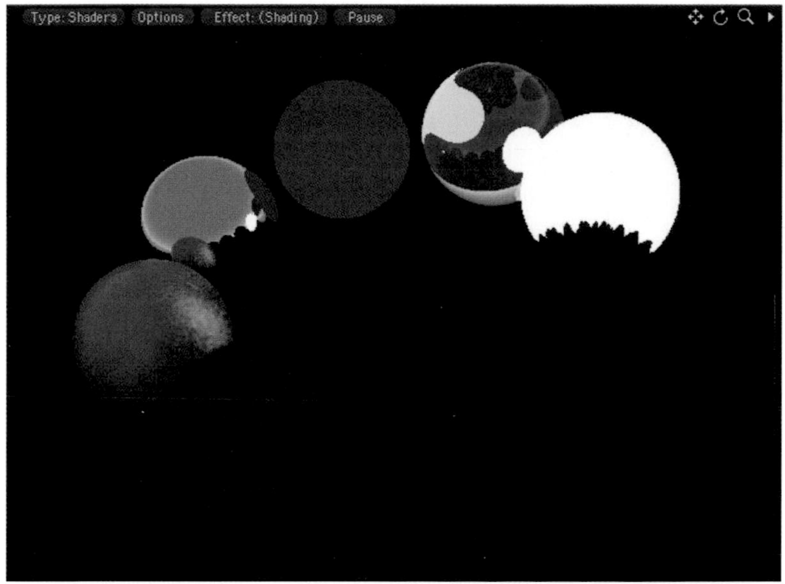

Figure 15.10 Without any light in the scene, various surfaces are still visible, but lack punch and realism.

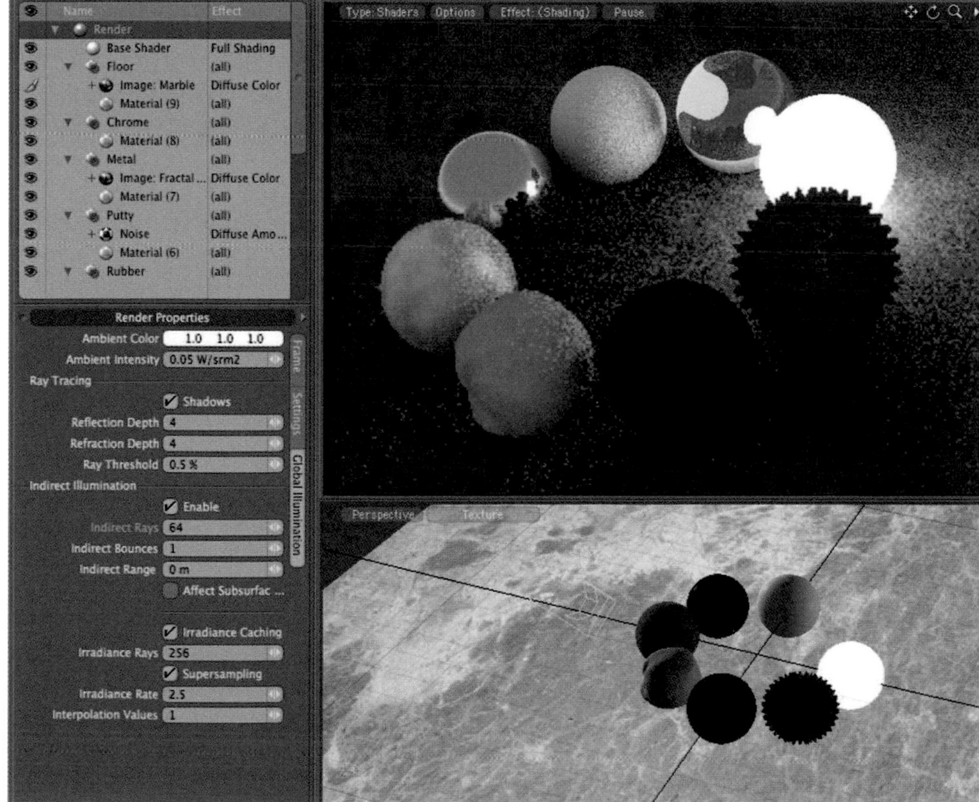

Figure 15.11 When the Indirect Illumination option is active, modo calculates the entire environment as a light source.

Figure 15.12
A slight change to the eggshell surface, and the scene takes on a different look.

15. As you look at Figure 15.12, what do you think of? Perhaps early evening at a beach? While you can think of the bright yellow sphere as a sort of campfire with the other spheres gathered around, what really makes this shot feel like it's early evening outdoors is the environment. Click on the Environment Material listing in the Shader Tree.
16. Looking at Figure 15.13, notice that Environmental Material is set to an Environment Type of 4 Color Gradient. The Zenith Color value (the color atop the 3D universe) is blue. Sky Color is a pale blue, and Ground Color is an evening blue. These colors are what give your scene its ambience. The Nadir Color value, set to a deep green, is the color at the bottom of the 3D universe that encompasses the scene. This color doesn't play too much of a role here because the ground plane object blocks it.
17. You can do a few things to change the environment surrounding the spheres. The Environment Type option can be set to Constant, which is one solid color. You can also choose a two-color gradient or simply make changes here to the four-color gradient.

Note

Setting the Environment Type option is also setting a background color in modo.

18. Set Zenith Color to 1.0, 0.95, 0.95. This creates a soft warm color. Apply this value to the Sky Color value as well.
19. Set the Ground Color value to a deeper version of the sky color, 0.90, 0.75, 0.40. Then, set the Nadir Color value to a reddish orange, sort of a sunset color, about 0.65, 0.25, 0.15. Figure 15.14 shows the change.

    What's more, you can change the Sky Exponent and Ground Exponent options. This will scale the colors closer together or farther apart. Also notice that the bright eggshell sphere is still luminous and affecting the scene, but with more environment color, brighter environment color, the eggshell sphere appears to have less impact.

    Because some of the surfaces on the spheres are reflective, such as the Chrome material, they reflect the environment colors, as well as the other objects in the scene. This happens because of the Ray Tracing option set within the Base Shader in the Shader Tree. The same goes for shadows.

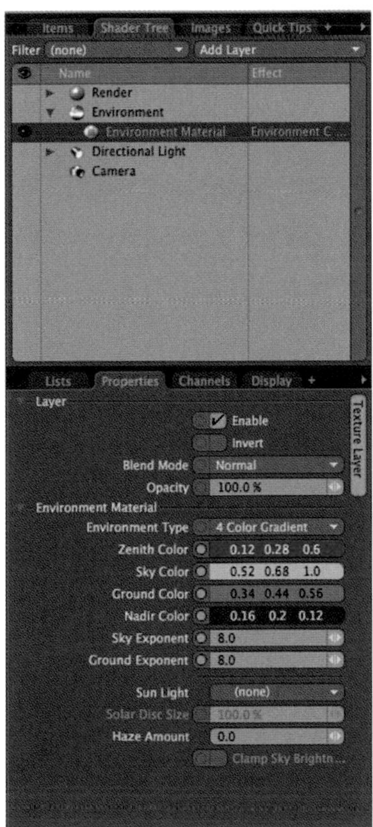

Figure 15.13 The Environmental Material colors are lighting the scene when global illumination is used.

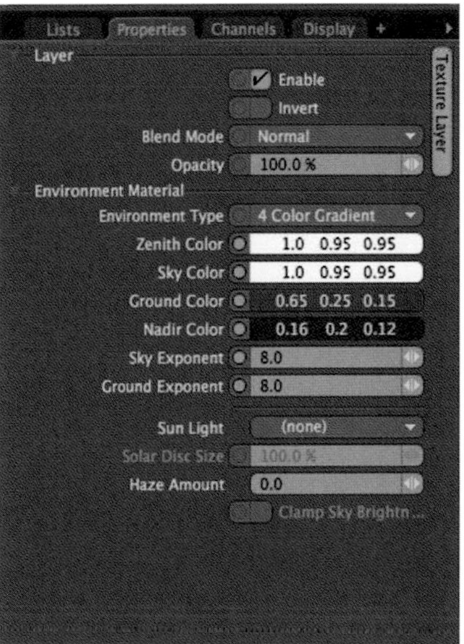

Figure 15.14 By changing the environmental colors and using global illumination, you change the entire look of the scene.

But what about combining more elements, such as a light or object? You've seen through various projects in the book that a luminous white plane can act as a light source. The principle is the same as the luminous sphere you're using here.

1. Add a 1-meter unit plane primitive to the scene. Do this by holding the Shift key and clicking the plane icon in the tool bar within the Basic tab.
2. The plane will be added directly to the middle of the scene, something like what's shown in Figure 15.15.

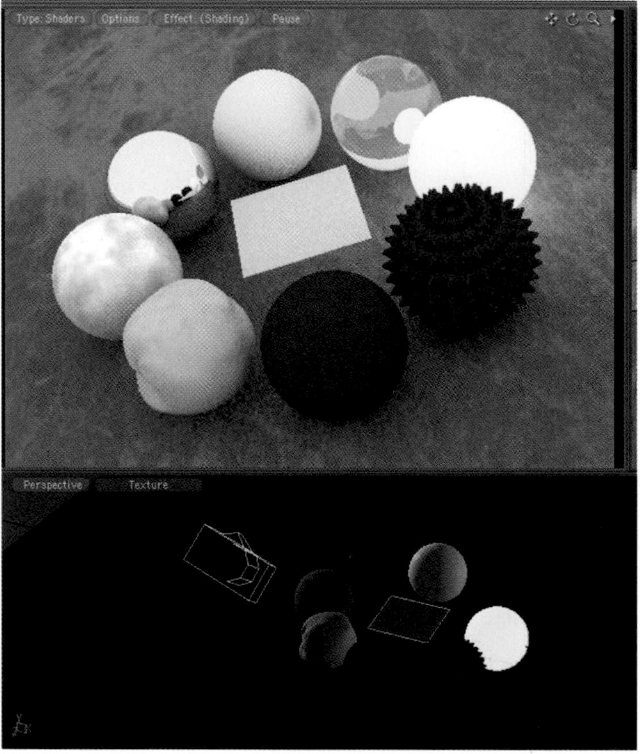

Figure 15.15 Adding a plane to the scene dumps it right in the middle of the spheres.

3. Select the plane in the Items tab. Press m to set a material name of LightBox.
4. With the new plane still selected, press the y key to activate the Transform tool, and then move the plane up and to the left of the spheres, as shown in Figure 15.16.

Note

So that things aren't too busy in your scene, press the o key on your keyboard for viewport options. For item visibility, turn off Show Cameras, if you like.

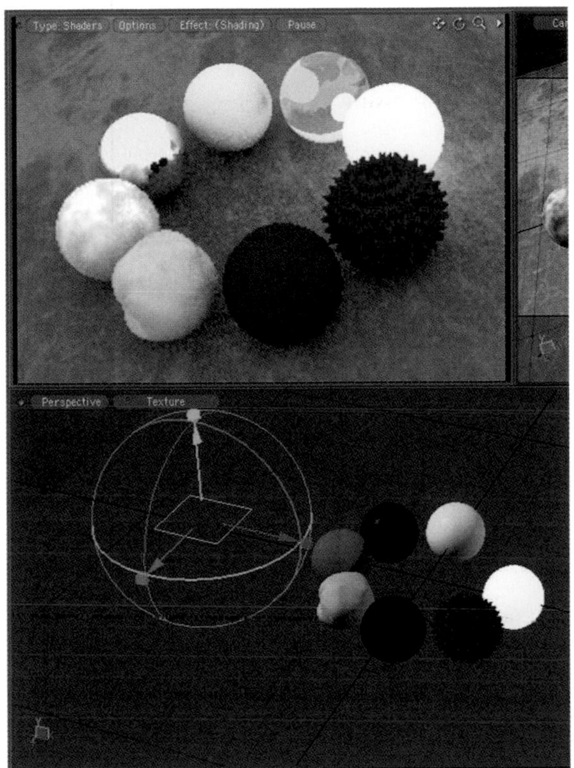

Figure 15.16 Move the LightBox plane up and to the left of the spheres.

5. Next, rotate the plane so it's facing down toward the spheres, as shown in Figure 15.17. Remember that when the plane is created, the surface normal is facing upward. You'll need to rotate it up and over (about 120 degrees) to have it face toward the object.
6. As it is now, this plane isn't doing much to the scene. Not a very good lightbox! Select the LightBox material in the Shader Tree and click on the Material Trans tab in the Render Properties panel. Bring the Luminous Intensity up to about 9. You'll see a light source appear from the front left, looking at the Preview viewport. Figure 15.18 shows the result.
7. If the eggshell sphere had Luminous Intensity of 4 and lit the entire scene, then why would a value of 9 for the plane not show up that much? The reason is because the size of the plane can change its effect. Make sure your Action Center is set to Automatic, then with the LightBox plane selected, press the r key for scale. Click and drag on the center light blue handle, and scale the object up to about 400%. You can view the scale by clicking the Mesh tab within the Render Properties panel.

   Now, the lightbox is too bright and overpowers the scene, as you can see in Figure 15.19.

Figure 15.17 Rotate the plane so it's pointing toward the spheres.

Figure 15.18 Adding a flat plane to the scene, making it luminous, starts to affect other objects, but not quite enough.

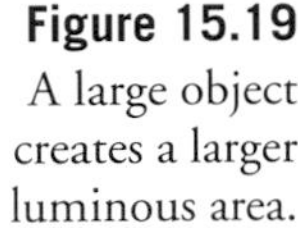

Figure 15.19
A large object creates a larger luminous area.

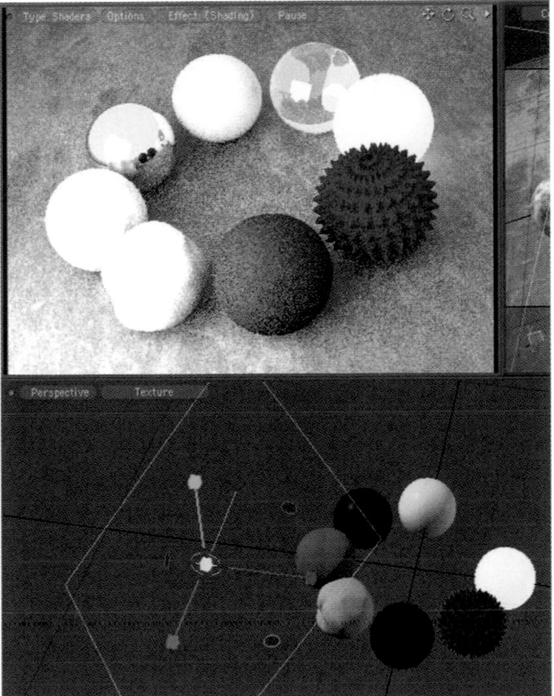

8. Back in the Material Trans tab, bring the Luminous Intensity down to 4.
9. In the Shader Tree, select Environment Material. Change the Environment Type option to Constant, and set the color to a deep brown—not quite black, but close. Figure 15.20 shows the change in the scene.
10. Figure 15.21 shows an F9 render of the scene. The spheres on the left are a little hot. Too bright. This is easily changed by adjusting their Diffuse values for the specific materials.

Lighting with global illumination in modo is a balance—a balance of color, light, luminosity, reflection values, shadows, and more. It's up to you to control this balance. You do this by studying other people's work. Find what you like, and more particularly, what you don't like. If you feel something is too bright or too dark, change it. Remember, you're the one driving.

Figure 15.20
With the object less bright and the environment a little darker, the look of the scene changes dramatically.

Figure 15.21
A full render of the scene lit with global illumination and ray tracing.

Try setting up one more render. This next project will use the corkboard you textured in Chapter 7.

1. Load the CorkboardTextured.lxo scene from the Chapter 15 project folder on the book's DVD. Click over to the Render tab. Figure 15.22 shows the scene.
2. This scene actually does have a light, but only a basic default directional light. Your goal is to light it so it's softer, like an interior light. To begin, change the current directional light to an area light. Right-click on the light in the Items tab and select Change Item Type.
3. With the light changed to an area light, you can immediately notice a difference, as shown in Figure 15.23.
4. There is a difference, but not necessarily a good one! First, the background has too much color, so you'll change that in a moment. Second, the light is not bright enough. If you remember the example of increasing the area width and height for an area light in the last chapter, you'll need to do that here. Select the light in the Items tab, and press the y key. Make sure you're in Items selection mode, too. Then, grab the light blue plus marks on the edges of the light (in a Perspective viewport) and drag it out. In the Render Properties panel, you'll see the area Width value increase. Bring it to about 5.8 m, as shown in Figure 15.24.
5. Increase the area Height value to about 2.4 m or so. Figure 15.25 shows the increase.

Figure 15.22 The corkboard scene from Chapter 7. Loaded but not lit too well.

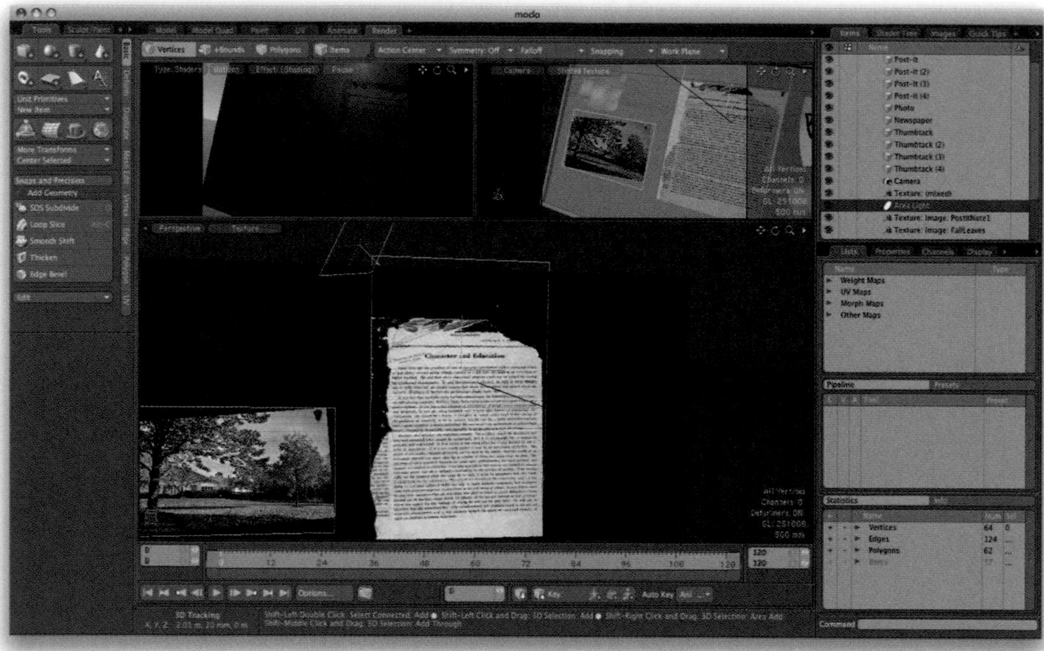

Figure 15.23 Changing the directional light to an area light changes the look of the scene.

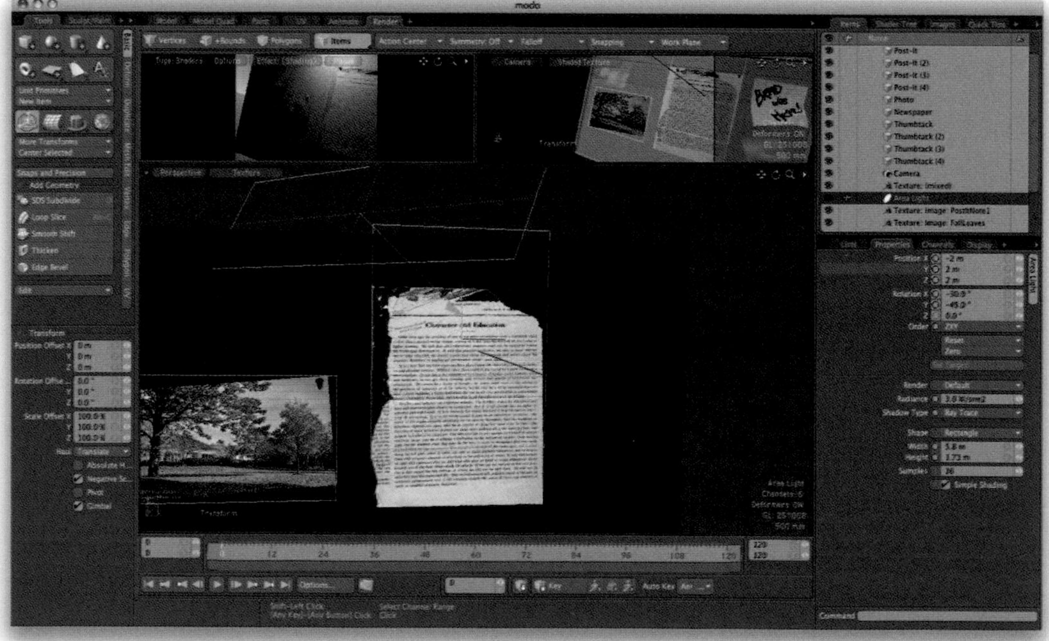

Figure 15.24 Increase the area Width value for the area light.

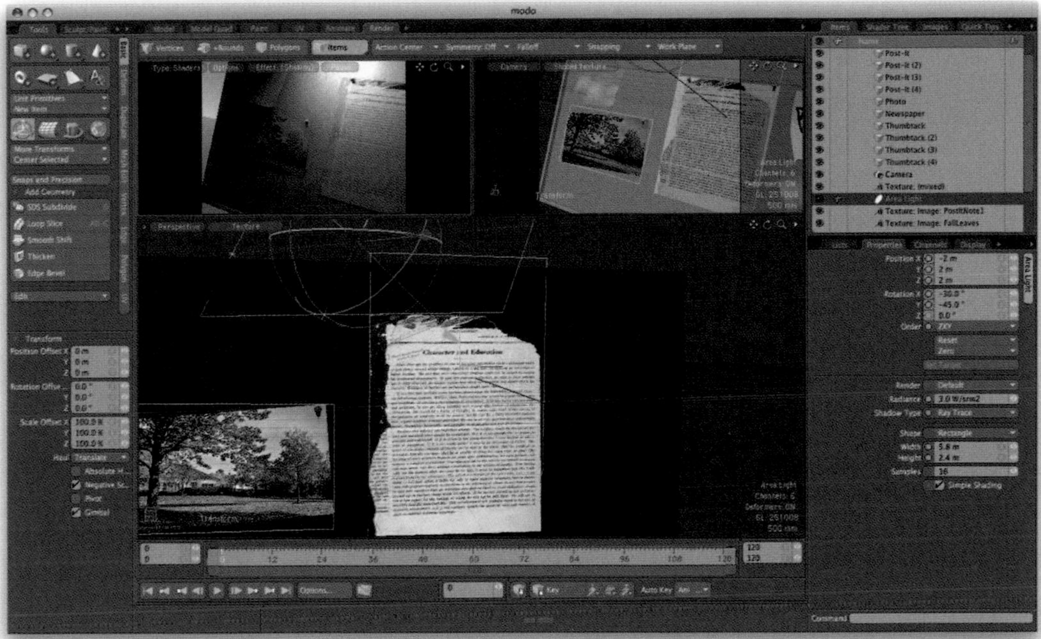

Figure 15.25 Increase the Height value for the area light, and the shot is well lit.

6. Position the changed area light back and up a bit from the corkboard. Then, in the Items tab, right-click on the area light and create an instance.
7. Select the instance and move it to the right side of the corkboard, opposite to the original. Position the area light to fill the side of the scene. Figure 15.26 shows the scene.
8. Change the backdrop color by selecting the Environmental material, just as you did previously for the 8balls scene. Choose the Constant option, and set it to black.
9. With the two area lights in place, you now have a corkboard lighting situation. What's that you ask? Where do you usually find a corkboard? Perhaps in an office or a hallway at a school. The two area lights help create that effect with a more diffused lighting look and softer shadows.
10. Press F9 to render a frame.

You can experiment with different lighting situations on your own and adjust the global illumination values for different types of looks. The next section outlines a few tips when setting up global illumination in modo.

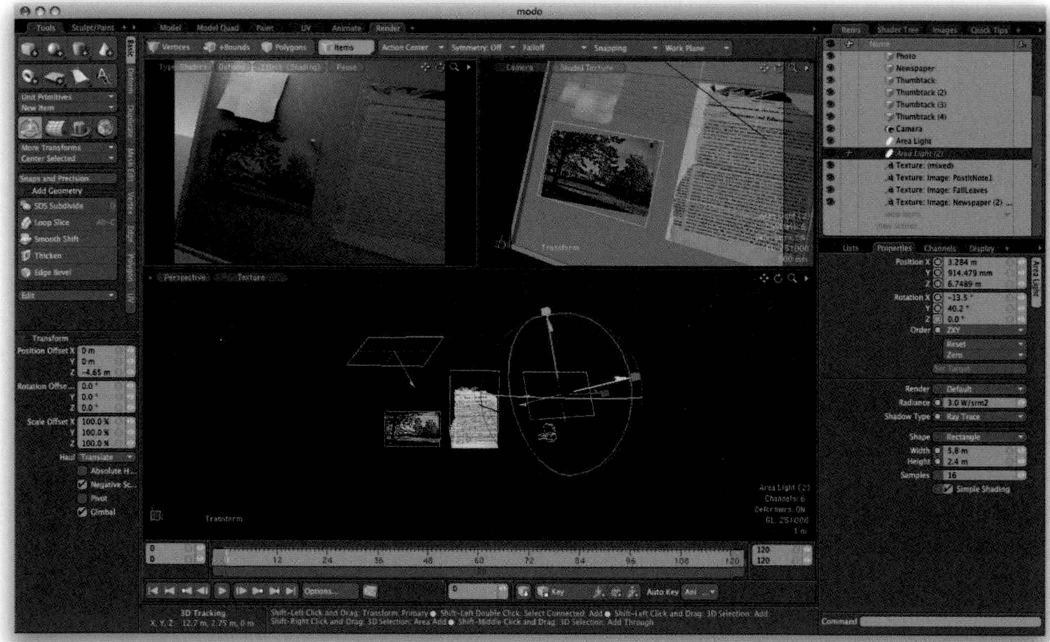

Figure 15.26 A copy of the area light helps light up the other side of the corkboard.

Noise and Render

A common problem users have with global illumination is *noise*. Some might call it *grain*, but it's actually noise (or variance). This happens when you try to estimate some sort of shading with not enough samples. Using area lights will cause grain, and the larger the light, the more samples you'll need to avoid noise in your render.

In addition, objects in the scene casting shadows can also aid in creating grain; to avoid this, you can increase the number of rays in the lights Properties panel for better quality. When you are using indirect light, as you did throughout this chapter, more rays will be needed when you have higher contrast and detail. You can control this by the Irradiance Rays setting in the Global Illumination panel. Irradiance Caching must be turned on to set this. This setting performs finer, or higher quality, evaluations of the scene. Irradiance rays are similar to indirect rays in that rays are fired out from a surface to calculate the indirect illumination. The higher this value, the more rays will be fired and the more quality you'll achieve.

If using a high contrast HDR image, you might find that increasing the minimum spot in the image map properties helps eliminate noise. The same goes for using blurry reflections—the more you blur, the more rays you'll need for a cleaner render.

You can remove noise from area lights if you set the direct illumination multiplier to a lower value in the Shader Tree properties.

What's Next

As stressed throughout the book, always experiment on your own. But as a recommendation when rendering, always perform one trick at a time. That is to say, set up your scene, then set up one light. Render and see how you like it. From there, set up another light or an environment variable, and then render and see how you like it. And, remember to use the Preview window as much as you can in order to work more efficiently. If grain appears, increase the rays and render again. Check out the Render video on the book's DVD, provided by 3D Garage.com, to learn a little more about rendering in modo 301/302.

3D is about time. It's about experimentation and trial and error. It's also about your creative talent, so remember to explore your ideas as much as possible.

Now, move on to the last chapter to learn a little bit more about rendering and how you can output your scenes and images.

16

Output Options

It's always interesting to follow user group forums and read the posts from people about 3D software. For whatever reason, the majority seem to be loyal to one 3D application only. Certainly, there's an investment in 3D, both in cost of the software and time to learn it. However, no one application can do it all. Each 3D application on the market today has its strengths and weaknesses, including Maya, LightWave, XSI, Cinema4D, Max, and even modo.

Does this mean that one software program is superior to another? Absolutely not! To ride the bandwagon of software favoritism is childish and something you shouldn't get wrapped up in. Truly, what is the point of getting a 3D application if you're going to spend all of your time whining on a public forum about which software is better or worse? You're better than that, and the Luxology team thinks so too. This is why modo is so flexible for your 3D Pipeline. It is a program designed to work well with other applications. Figure 16.1 shows the remapping section of the Preferences panel (also discussed in Chapter 1). Here, you can see that the Luxology team has graciously made modo to support other applications. While it's important to learn modo with its default settings, you can set the input presets to any major 3D application.

The input presets are just one way modo allows you to work well with other 3D applications. However, the input presets are not necessary to play well with others.

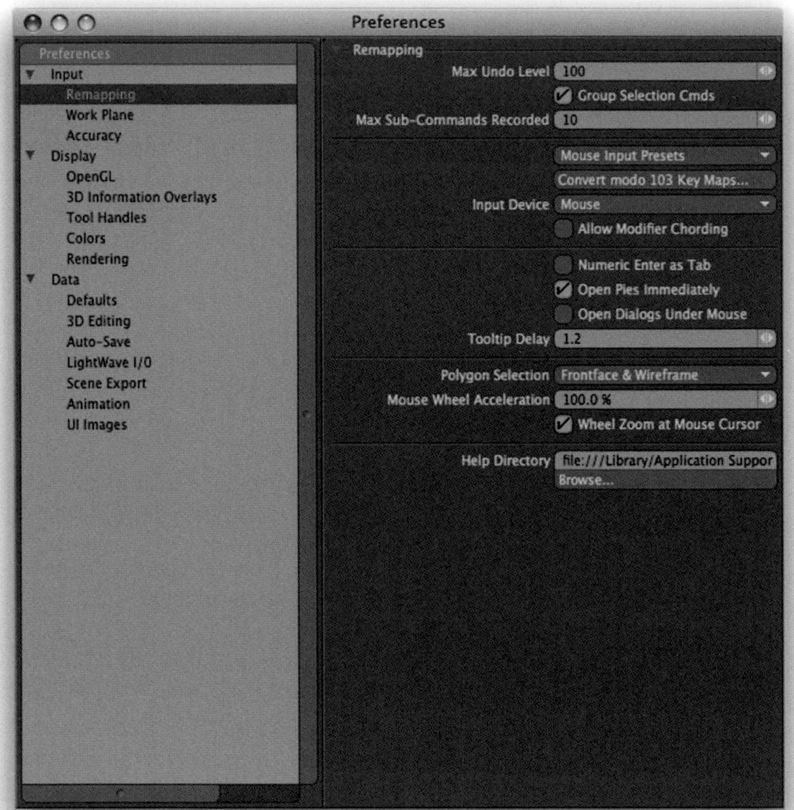

Figure 16.1
In the Preferences panel, modo offers a variety of input presets.

Animation

Until this latest version of modo, version 301/302, modo was a 3D modeling program, then a 3D modeling, painting, and rendering program. You, like many, don't just model, texture, and render for a living, but you also animate! The programmers at Luxology had a plan all along, and you are now seeing the fruits of their labors. This book introduced you to animation in modo, and there's even more to discover in the form of various videos on the book's DVD.

There's still one trick in modo that allows you to render your model in motion quickly and easily that you might not know about. Figure 16.2 shows the Render Turntable option, which is found under the Render menu.

This option allows you to do a quick turntable render of your model. You can't keyframe, but you can set up a few options. Selecting the Render Turntable option opens the settings shown in Figure 16.3.

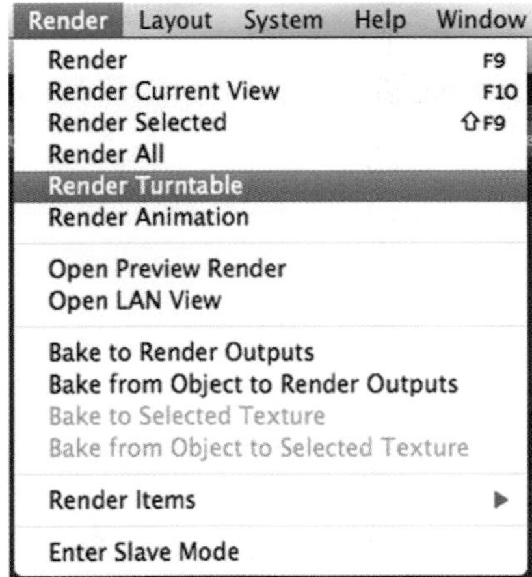

Figure 16.2 The Render Turntable option allows you to create a bit of motion, directly out of modo.

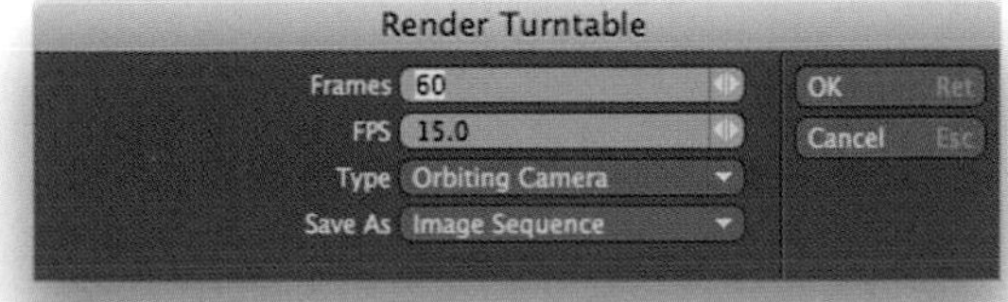

Figure 16.3 The Render Turntable feature offers a few options for saving an animation.

Here you can set the length of the render, as well as the frame rate. Additionally, you can save a movie or render in sequences. Part of the process also allows you to choose between an orbiting camera or simply spinning your model. And truly, that's the point of the turntable render—to spin your model. You can run this operation to preview your model from all angles and see how it reacts to light, reflections, and so on. This is also an excellent way to present your models to clients. Try it out!

When talking about render outputs, take a closer look at the options available in the Render menu. Figure 16.4 shows the full menu expanded.

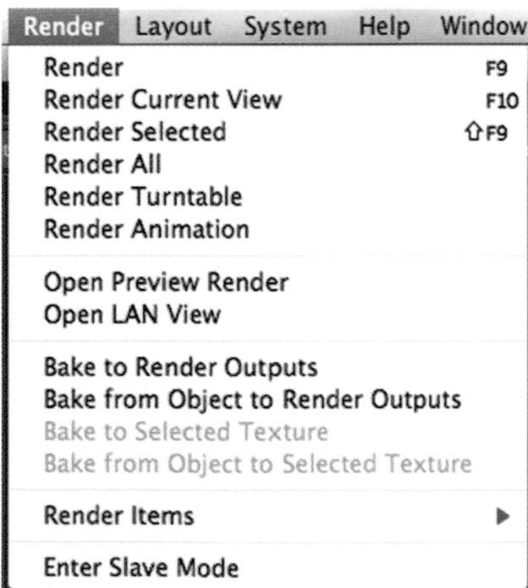

Figure 16.4 There are a few options for outputting your creations in the Render menu.

Render and Render Current View

The first choice in the Render menu is a full frame render, also accessed by pressing F9. You've done this throughout the book. But you can press F10 to render your current view. Let's say that you have a large scene and are using Auto Visibility in the Items tab. Pressing F9 will render your entire scene, regardless of what's visible or not from the Items tab. Pressing Ctrl-F9 will render just the visible items from the Items tab. Very handy!

Note

Auto Visibility automatically toggles items visible and not visible when selected. Right-click on the Items tab itself, and under the Viewport Settings listing, choose Auto Visibility.

Note

To manually make items visible or not in the Items tab, just click the eyeball icon in the left column next to the item you wish to hide. To clarify, this hides visibility and does not remove the item from the scene.

Render Selected

Similar to the Render Visible option, Render Selected allows you to select an item in your scene and, when pressing Shift-F9, you'll render just that selection. This is exceedingly handy because you don't need to worry about Auto Visibility in the Items tab. Just select an object, press Shift-F9, and go. The benefit of this is primarily for testing your render and saving time. Perhaps you're working on a complex scene and adding a new main element. As you continually tweak and update the textures, you don't want to waste time re-rendering everything in the scene just to see how this one element is coming along. And, rather than worry about changing visibility options in the Items tab, you can simply use the Render Selected option.

Render All

Similar to a simple frame, the Render All option will render all items in your scene. So if an item is not visible in the viewport, using Render All will draw it regardless.

Render Turntable

A quick down-and-dirty way to pump out a preview of a model is to use the Render Turntable feature. Perhaps you have a client that you're modeling for, and they need to see a preview of the model. So rather than moving the camera, rendering a frame, moving the camera again, rendering another frame, and so on, just use Render Turntable, and modo will pump out a rotation animation. Nice!

Render Animation

The title of this option pretty much says it all. Render Animation renders your animation. When you select this option, a panel appears, as shown in Figure 16.5. This allows you to set the first and last frame of your animation. You also can decide if you want to render a sequence of images or go straight to a movie file, based on the codecs installed on your system. Once you click OK, modo will ask you where you'd like to save the files. Choose the location, and you're animating. There are some other factors in setting up an animation, such as frame size, film back presets (new for modo 301/302), lens distortion, and a bit more. To really see this in action, I felt it best to create a learning video, which is included on the book's DVD in the Chapter 16 folder labeled RenderAnimation.mov.

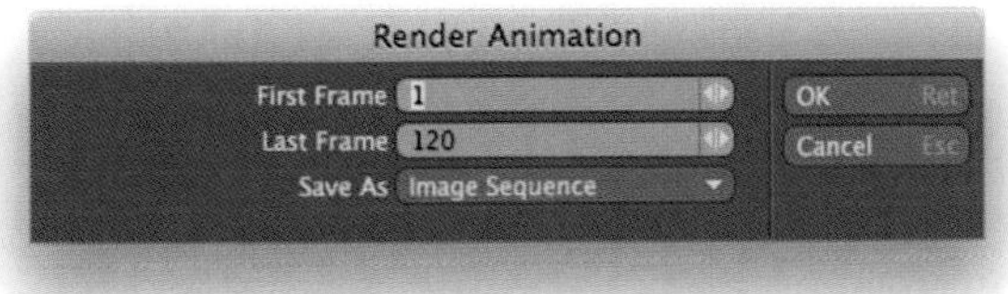

Figure 16.5 The Render Animation panel allows you to set the first and last frame of your animation, along with the file type for saving.

Open Preview Render

One of modo's great strengths is its real-time Preview window. You see it when you click over to the Render tab, as you have throughout the book. But let's say you're modeling in the Model tab, which is just one large model view, and you want to see a preview render window without jumping to the Render tab. Click the Open Preview Render option in the Render menu, and you'll see your real-time Preview window. You can move it around as you model, too, so it doesn't get in the way. You can also just press F8 to call it up.

Open LAN View

One thing I've not talked about throughout this book is modo 301/302's ability to network render. Essentially, with your modo license, you can install the program on multiple computers. When these computers are on the same network, perhaps one copy on a PC, and the other on a Mac, you can set one version up as a slave. This slave computer will render your scene in addition to your main computer, where your main animation lives. Selecting Open LAN View in the Render menu will show you the render slaves on your network. Visit the Luxology forums for more discussion and set up of LAN networks in modo 301/302.

Bake

There is also the option to bake in modo. You've probably heard the term *baking* when referring to many 3D programs. modo 301/302 now offers the options to Bake to Render Outputs, Bake from Object to Render Outputs, Bake to Selected Texture, and Bake from Object to Selected Texture. All of these are the process of precomputing texture and lighting information directly to an image map. This image map can then be re-imported into the 3D application and applied to the model. So rather than rendering every frame and having the computer calculate shadows, bumps, and reflections, it's already done and mapped onto the model. This is excellent for real-time environments, such as video games. The way this works is that complex shaders and lighting situations are often too complex to render in real time, but by having them precomputed to an image map, you can apply this rendered image to an existing UV texture.

In modo, render baking will render into the currently selected UV texture. Because of this, you need to make sure that you have the correct mesh layer selected, as well as the proper UV map. You can also bake directly to the Shader Tree. Baking textures from within the Shader Tree is beneficial for baking an effect, such as diffuse or color, into an image. Therefore, if you want to combine three image maps and two procedural textures into just one image map, you can do this by right-clicking on a new image and baking all the images below it (of the same texture effect) into the blank image. This differs from the Bake options in the Render menu in that the latter takes into account all lighting and texturing in the image.

Render Items

Also in the Render menu, you have the Render Items option. You can choose to select Render Item, Camera, and Environment. Typically, you would select your render items from the Shader Tree, and choose the appropriate render method as described previously, such as F9, F10, and so on.

Saving Single Images

When you render a single frame in modo, you'll see its progress, as well as the buckets rendering in the Render Frame panel shown in Figure 16.6.

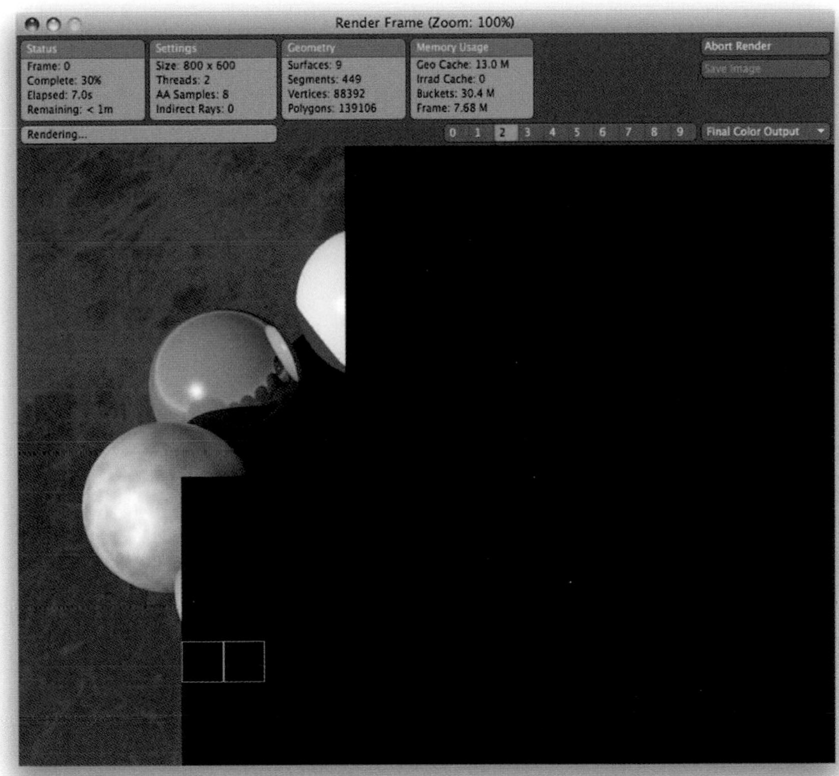

Figure 16.6 The Render Frame panel appears when you choose a render option, such as F9.

As you can see from Figure 16.6, as you render, the orange squares appear throughout the panel. These are the render buckets and will vary based on the settings you've set up for them, such as their size, bucket order, and so on. When your render is complete, the Save Image button will be active in the top right of the Render Frame panel. Click it, and you'll be able to save the rendered image, as shown in Figure 16.7. modo offers a wide variety of image formats, from TGA to TIF to XPM and OpenEXR.

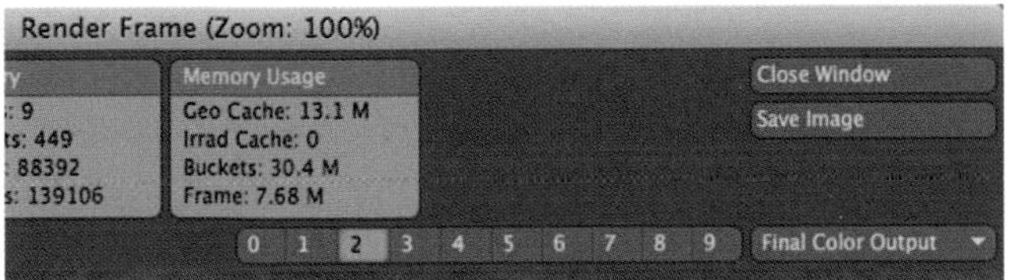

Figure 16.7 After you render a frame, you can click Save Image from the Render Frame panel.

It's very important to know that once you close the Render Frame window, either by choosing Close Window or pressing the Esc key on your keyboard, your render is gone. If you accidentally close the panel after rendering a frame, here's what you can do. Press F9 again to render a frame. As soon as you do, the Render Frame panel comes up. Then just click Esc to stop the render. This doesn't close the panel. And, if you look at the numbers along the top of the panel (you can see them in Figure 16.7), these are your previous renders. Each time you render, modo jumps to the next buffer and stores the frame for you on your hard drive. Click one of the numbers, and you'll see your previous renders. Then you can click the Save Image button to save that render to your hard drive. It's also good just for comparing renders. However, following is a trick you can use to automatically save an image after rendering, completely unattended.

Auto Save Single Frame Renders

Like many, you may press the Esc key on your keyboard simply by habit. Or by accident, you'll lose your rendered frame and, depending on what you're creating or how your memory cache is configured for the Render Frame panel, somehow you might have lost hours of work. So use the Render Animation option in the Render menu to save just one frame. In the options panel that appears, set the first and last frame to the frame you want to render, such as 0. What you're doing is telling modo to render just one frame. Then, choose Image Sequence for the Save As option. Click OK, and you'll be presented with a dialog box asking where to save the image. Give it a name, a place to be saved, and a format, such as TGA or JPG, and click OK. modo will then proceed to render the image and save it for you. This is extremely helpful if one of your images takes hours to render just a single frame.

Additionally, the Render Frame panel will still appear and, after the render is finished, you can select Save Image as a safety and save the image in a different format.

Outputting Models

When talking about working with other 3D applications and modo, it's important to understand how this application allows you to export your models.

From the File menu, you can choose Export As, shown in Figure 16.8.

When you select this option, modo offers you yet more options to bring your models to other 3D applications. Figure 16.9 shows the choices available to you.

You can choose from a variety of options, including X3D, a new web 3D standard formally known as VRML. If you're going to animate your model, you might be exporting to LightWave or Maya, and you can choose between LWO for LightWave or OBJ for Maya and others.

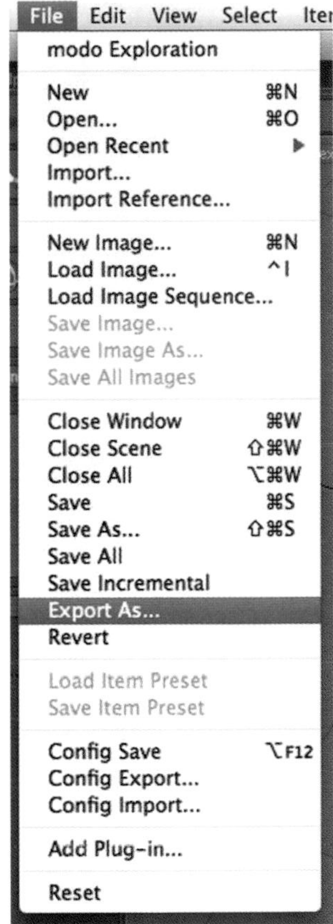

Figure 16.8 Choosing Export As from the File menu allows you to send your model to other 3D applications.

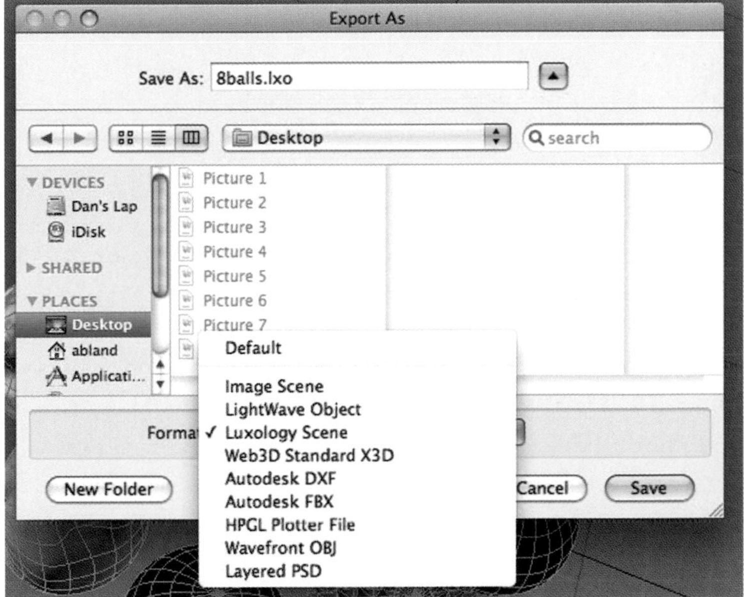

Figure 16.9 Once you select the Export As option, you're presented with various output choices.

When you import your exported model, depending on what format you choose, you might not be able to export all shading information. modo will tell you this as necessary. Next, open your 3D application and import the model. That's not to say your model will only export as a default white clay-looking object. It means that, depending on what you've assigned in modo, it might not be compatible with your chosen 3D application. Here, it's a matter of testing, depending on where you're sending your model. However, you can count on base shading to transfer quite well, including color, diffuse, specular, and so on.

If you've created image maps, either imported or painted, you can simply reapply those in your animation application. The UV data will stay with the model, so any UV maps you've created simply need to be reassigned. Again, each situation is different, and it's up to you to export your model and experiment with what works and what doesn't, based on your applications.

There are a few things to know about exporting models, beyond color and shading. Certain programs, such as LightWave, might not like how you create your model. For example, modo supports subdivision surfaces, or *n-gons*. This means that geometry can be subdivided by any number (that's what the *n* stands for) such as 3 or 5 or 9 vertices. LightWave through version 8.5 could only use subdivisions with 3 or 4 vertices. However, LightWave version 9 now supports Catmull-Clark subdivisions, allowing you to import models from modo that are subdivided beyond 3 or 4 vertices. Another aspect to know is that any edge weights you apply in modo will not transfer to LightWave.

Your Next Step

So now we've come to the end of the book. Hopefully, the information on these pages, as well all the videos on the DVD, have helped you grasp this amazing program. Be aware that modo is constantly evolving, and you should check the Luxology web site often for updates.

From here, you can experiment on your own and tackle just about any modeling project. The challenge with any 3D application is to forget about the buttons and panels and concentrate on your model. The goal of this book is to help ease your pain in learning a new application so that you're spending more time creating and less time trying to get a tool to work or figure out what it does. While there are many technical aspects and intricacies within modo that are spelled out in the modo manual, the goal of this book has been to help you use the program. The modo manual and this book make a great combination, and you should refer to the modo manual often for definitions of terms and concepts. To further enhance your learning, check out the appendices for links to key web sites focused around modo and general 3D. Be sure to view the videos to see modo 301/302 in action, and remember that you can use discount code "modo301book" for a full copy of the 3D Garage 16-hour modo 301 Signature Courseware, with updates for 302 (available at www.3DGarage.com).

Thank you for supporting this book! Your commitment to 3D and modo is appreciated.

Part V

Appendixes

A

Reference Materials

No matter how complete any software product might be, and no matter how thorough a book is, there is always room for more information.

Because of that, I've put together a list of resources that not only relate to modo, but to 3D as well. It's important to gain as much knowledge of 3D modeling, 3D space, color, light, and cinematography as you can. All of these real-world principles can play a role in your quest for the perfect modo creation.

Web Sites

Listed here are some modo-related web sites for discussion and information.

Luxology.com for tips, tricks, and tutorials
www.luxology.com

Luxology's own forums
http://forums.luxology.com/discussion

3D Garage.com for video training
www.3dgarage.com

Vertex Monkey for scripts and info
www.vertexmonkey.com

CG Talk for discussions
http://forums.cgsociety.org

Modo Mode, Japan
http://popover.blogzine.jp/weblog

Yahoo Groups
http://groups.yahoo.com/group/Luxology

CG Architect
www.cgarchitect.com/vb/129-modo

CG Focus
http://cgfocus.com/forums

Lighting
http://3drender.com

Animation and effects
www.vfxworld.com

Studies on various topics
www.pixelcorps.com

Paul Debevec
www.debevec.org

Reflection Properties

Table A.1 presents a good mix of materials and their basic reflective properties. There are many factors that affect an item's reflectivity, so use these values as a starting point.

Table A.1 Percentage of Incident Light Reflected by Various Materials

Material	%	Material	%
Aluminum	45	Graphite	20
Aluminum Foil	65	Green Leaf	21
Asphalt	14	Iron	15
Brass	40	Linen	81
Brick	30	Marble, White	53
Bronze	10	Mercury	69
Chrome	70	Paper, Newsprint	61
Copper	71	Paper, White	71
Earth, Moist	08	Pewter	20
Gold	84	Platinum	64

Table A.1 Continued

Material	%	Material	%
Porcelain, White	72	Stainless Steel	37
Quartz	81	Steel	55
Rubber	02	Tin Can	40
Silicon	28	Vinyl	15
Silver	90	Wood, Pine	40
Slate	06		

Refraction Properties

Table A.2 displays an extensive list of items and their refraction properties. Certainly you won't use all of these properties, but they're a good reference to have just the same.

Indices of refraction for various elements, materials, liquids, and gases at STP (standard temperature and pressure) in visible light are listed.

Table A.2 Indices of Refraction

Material	Index	Material	Index
Vacuum	1.000 (Exactly)	Amblygonite	1.611
Acetone	1.360	Amethyst	1.544
Actinolite	1.618	Amorphous Selenium	2.920
Agalmatoite	1.550	Anatase	2.490
Agate	1.544	Andalusite	1.641
Agate, Moss	1.540	Anhydrite	1.571
Air	1.000	Apatite	1.632
Alcohol	1.329	Apophyllite	1.536
Alexandrite	1.745	Aquamarine	1.577
Aluminum	1.440	Aragonite	1.530
Amber	1.546	Argon	1.000

Table A.2 Indices of Refraction (Continued)

Material	Index	Material	Index
Asphalt	1.635	Chalcedony	1.530
Augelite	1.574	Chalk	1.510
Axinite	1.675	Chalybite	1.630
Azurite	1.730	Chlorine (gas)	1.000
Barite	1.636	Chlorine (liquid)	1.385
Barytocalcite	1.684	Chrome Green	2.400
Benitoite	1.757	Chrome Red	2.420
Benzene	1.501	Chrome Yellow	2.310
Beryl	1.577	Chromium	2.970
Beryllonite	1.553	Chromium Oxide	2.705
Brazilianite	1.603	Chrysoberyl	1.745
Bromine (liquid)	1.661	Chrysocolla	1.500
Bronze	1.180	Chrysoprase	1.534
Brownite	1.567	Citrine	1.550
Calcite	1.486	Clinozoisite	1.724
Calspar1	1.660	Cobalt Blue	1.740
Calspar2	1.486	Cobalt Green	1.970
Cancrinite	1.491	Cobalt Violet	1.710
Carbon Dioxide (gas)	1.000	Colemanite	1.586
Carbon Dioxide (liquid)	1.200	Copper	1.100
Carbon Disulfide	1.628	Copper Oxide	2.705
Carbon Tetrachloride	1.460	Coral	1.486
Cassiterite	1.997	Cordierite	1.540
Celestite	1.622	Corundum	1.766
Cerussite	1.804	Crocoite	2.310
Ceylanite	1.770	Crown Glass	1.520

Table A.2 Indices of Refraction (Continued)

Material	Index
Crystal	2.000
Cuprite	2.850
Danburite	1.633
Diamond	2.417
Diopside	1.680
Dolomite	1.503
Dumortierite	1.686
Ebonite	1.660
Ekanite	1.600
Elaeolite	1.532
Emerald	1.576
Emerald, Synth flux	1.561
Emerald, Synth hydro	1.568
Enstatite	1.663
Epidote	1.733
Ethyl Alcohol (Ethanol)	1.360
Euclase	1.652
Fabulite	2.409
Feldspar, Adventurine	1.532
Feldspar, Albite	1.525
Feldspar, Amazonite	1.525
Feldspar, Labradorite	1.565
Feldspar, Microcline	1.525
Feldspar, Oligoclase	1.539
Feldspar, Orthoclase	1.525
Fluoride	1.560
Fluorite	1.434
Formica	1.470
Garnet, Almandine	1.760
Garnet, Almandite	1.790
Garnet, Andradite	1.820
Garnet, Demantoid	1.880
Garnet, Grossular	1.738
Garnet, Hessonite	1.745
Garnet, Rhodolite	1.760
Garnet, Spessartite	1.810
Gaylussite	1.517
Glass	1.517
Glass, Albite	1.489
Glass, Crown	1.520
Glass, Crown, Zinc	1.517
Glass, Flint, Dense	1.660
Glass, Flint, Heaviest	1.890
Glass, Flint, Heavy	1.655
Glass, Flint, Lanthanum	1.800
Glass, Flint, Light	1.580
Glass, Flint, Medium	1.627
Glycerine	1.473
Gold	0.470
Hambergite	1.559
Hauynite	1.502
Helium	1.000

Table A.2 Indices of Refraction (Continued)

Material	Index	Material	Index
Hematite	2.940	Malachite	1.655
Hemimorphite	1.614	Meerschaum	1.530
Hiddenite	1.655	Mercury (liquid)	1.620
Howlite	1.586	Methanol	1.329
Hydrogen (gas)	1.000	Moldavite	1.500
Hydrogen (liquid)	1.097	Moonstone, Adularia	1.525
Hypersthene	1.670	Moonstone, Albite	1.535
Ice	1.309	Natrolite	1.480
Idocrase	1.713	Nephrite	1.600
Iodine Crystal	3.340	Nitrogen (gas)	1.000
Iolite	1.548	Nitrogen (liquid)	1.205
Iron	1.510	Nylon	1.530
Ivory	1.540	Obsidian	1.489
Jade, Nephrite	1.610	Olivine	1.670
Jadeite	1.665	Onyx	1.486
Jasper	1.540	Opal	1.450
Jet	1.660	Oxygen (gas)	1.000
Kornerupine	1.665	Oxygen (liquid)	1.221
Kunzite	1.655	Painite	1.787
Kyanite	1.715	Pearl	1.530
Lapis Gem	1.500	Periclase	1.740
Lapis Lazuli	1.610	Peridot	1.654
Lazulite	1.615	Peristerite	1.525
Lead	2.010	Petalite	1.502
Leucite	1.509	Phenakite	1.650
Magnesite	1.515	Phosgenite	2.117

Table A.2 Indices of Refraction (Continued)

Material	Index	Material	Index
Plastic	1.460	Shell	1.530
Plexiglass	1.500	Silicon	4.240
Polystyrene	1.550	Sillimanite	1.658
Prase	1.540	Silver	0.180
Prasiolite	1.540	Sinhalite	1.699
Prehnite	1.610	Smaragdite	1.608
Proustite	2.790	Smithsonite	1.621
Purpurite	1.840	Sodalite	1.483
Pyrite	1.810	Sodium Chloride	1.544
Pyrope	1.740	Sphalerite	2.368
Quartz	1.544	Sphene	1.885
Quartz, Fused	1.458	Spinel	1.712
Rhodizite	1.690	Spodumene	1.650
Rhodochrisite	1.600	Staurolite	1.739
Rhodonite	1.735	Steatite	1.539
Rock Salt	1.544	Steel	2.500
Rubber, Natural	1.519	Stichtite	1.520
Ruby	1.760	Strontium Titanate	2.410
Rutile	2.610	Styrofoam	1.595
Sanidine	1.522	Sugar Solution (30%)	1.380
Sapphire	1.760	Sugar Solution (80%)	1.490
Scapolite	1.540	Sulphur	1.960
Scapolite, Yellow	1.555	Synthetic Spinel	1.730
Scheelite	1.920	Taaffeite	1.720
Selenium, Amorphous	2.920	Tantalite	2.240
Serpentine	1.560	Tanzanite	1.691

Table A.2 Indices of Refraction (Continued)

Material	Index	Material	Index
Teflon	1.350	Variscite	1.550
Thomsonite	1.530	Vivianite	1.580
Tiger eye	1.544	Wardite	1.590
Topaz	1.620	Water (gas)	1.000
Topaz, Blue	1.610	Water 100°C	1.318
Topaz, Pink	1.620	Water 20°C	1.333
Topaz, White	1.630	Water 35°C (room temperature)	1.331
Topaz, Yellow	1.620	Willemite	1.690
Tourmaline	1.624	Witherite	1.532
Tremolite	1.600	Wulfenite	2.300
Tugtupite	1.496	Zinc Crown Glass	1.517
Turpentine	1.472	Zincite	2.010
Turquoise	1.610	Zircon, High	1.960
Ulexite	1.490	Zircon, Low	1.800
Uvarovite	1.870	Zirconia, Cubic	2.170

B

What's on the DVD

The accompanying DVD has been provided as an additional bonus to the book. The following sections contain descriptions of the DVD's contents and how to use the content included for the tutorials in this book. In addition, video tutorials have been included just for this book direct from 3D Garage (www.3dgarage.com). These video tutorials will aid in the modo 301 learning process.

DVD Contents

I've packed the DVD with video to enhance your learning. On the DVD, you'll find video tutorials to complement the chapters, exclusively from Dan Ablan and 3DGarage.com.

Video List

Chapter 2

ActionCenters.mov

WorkPlanes.mov

Chapter 7

Shader Tree video

Chapter 8

Key tutorial

Chapter 9

Animation basics

Animation – Pivots

Animation – Graph Editor overview

Chapter 10

Thicken video

Stoplight video

Chapter 11

Painting video

Using Image Ink

UV umbrella video

UV unwrap

Subsurface video

Gradient Editor

Chapter 12

Bottle model

Chapter 13

Morphing video

Landscape morph

Volcano sculpt video

Chapter 14

IES light basics

Chapter 15

Physical sky basics

Chapter 16

Render animation movie

Using the Video Files

In order to play the 3D Garage video tutorials supplied on the book's DVD, you'll need a DVD-ROM drive in your computer. This is not a DVD video, and it will not play in your DVD video player. The videos have been recorded using the Apple QuickTime H.264 codec, and they will work on both PC and Mac. To play the video files, you'll need QuickTime or a QuickTime-compatible player. The video tutorials are supplements to the chapters, some of which coincide with the tutorials in the book, and some stand on their own. Be sure to check them out for additional tips and tricks.

For more video training and full modo 301 courseware, visit www.3dgarage.com, with free updates for modo 302.

System Requirements

This DVD was configured for use on systems running Windows XP, and Macintosh OSX.

I've worked hard to make sure the contents on the DVD are just as useful as this book. The combination of the two makes this a tremendous resource. Enjoy!

Index

NUMBERS

3D

editing, data preferences, 41
information overlays, 38
Model views, 5–7, 27
orientation icon, 6

8balls scene, 383

A

Absorption Distance value, 284

accessing

Camera view, 14
controls, 188
Form Editor, 46
Input Editor, 51
Preferences panel, 31
Quick Access Selection bar, 74–76
viewports, 7

accuracy, input preferences, 34–35

Action Centers, 52–56

lighting, 365
selections, scaling, 147

Add Color Texture button, 295

adding

area light, 364
beveling edges, 179
depth, 157, 200
detail, 104, 136
displacements, 293
edges, 324
flat planes, 390
geometry, 61, 69, 104–109, 266
image maps, 202
item masks, 217
layers, 197
lighting, 364
materials, 194
mesh, 162–166
noise, 225, 334
planes, 388
properties, 217
scenes from Items tab, 170–180
to selections, 146
spotlights, 371
surface controls, 282
tabs, 18
textures, 200
Tool viewports, 23
windows, 22, 28

Add Layer list, 197

advantages of subdivision surfaces, 315–326

Airbrush falloffs, 87

alternate primitives, viewing, 162

Animate tab, 234

animation

channels, 237–238
configuring, 239
controls, 233–236
data preferences, 42
Graph Editor, 244–246
interfaces, 233–236
keyframes, 238–244
output, 400–404
overview of, 233–238
tools, 234
Transform tool, 241

Antialiasing filters, 376
Apple key, 124
applying
Bevel tool, 95
Color Gradient settings, 285
Convert selection option, 100
distance, 331
image maps, 203
Linear falloffs, 173
macros, 140, 143
Move tool, 340
Shader Tree, 182–212
surfaces, 228
transparent settings, 289
Apply Morph feature, 342, 343
area light, 356
adding, 364
rotating, 366
spotlights, coexisting with, 368
assigning
material masks, 282
materials, 194
selection sets, 145
Attribute properties, 45
attributes, viewing surfaces, 196
Automatic Action Centers, 55
automating with macros, 133–143
Auto-Save options, data preferences, 41
auto-saving single frame renders, 406
axis
moving, 306
work planes, 56–58, 169

B

backgrounds
colors, configuring, 386
Constant, modifying, 367
layers
using as references, 166–170
viewing, 150
baking, 404
bars, Quick Access Selection, 74–76
Base Material listing, 187
beam tracing, 381
Bend tool, 165
beveling
edges, 252
polygons, 254, 256
Bevel tool, 61, 63
applying, 95
edges, 99
rounding, 127
selecting, 132
resetting, 175
subdivision surfaces, 317
bias, 227
Birn, Jeremy, 358
blank viewports
creating, 22. *See also* viewports
3D Model views, converting, 27
blending
geometry, 104–109
materials, 225
Blend Mode setting, 227
blocks, building, 121–133
Boolean function, 150
box modeling method, 303
Bridge tool, 325
brushes, paint, 297
bucket rendering, 374
building
blocks, 121–133
macros, automating with, 133–143
shapes, editing, 143–148
hard-surface modeling, 251
landscapes, 327–332
in layers, 155–162
products in Sub-Ds, 303–326
Bump effect, 200, 201
buttons
Polygons, 57, 60
Viewport Style, 6–7

C

caches, Irradiance Caching, 396
calculating math, 198
calling. ***See also*** **accessing**
  commands, 47
  Quick Access Selection bar, 75
cameras
  Items selection mode, 73–74
  Items tab, navigating, 154
  positioning, 333
  scenes, navigating, 368
Camera view, accessing, 14
Capsule tool, 90
Catmull-Clark subdivisions, 408
Cellular texture, 198, 292
center points, selecting, 275
changes, tracking, 128
channels
  Graph Editor, 245
  keyframes, 237–238
  Position, 242
characters, subdivision surfaces, 301–326
clearing interfaces, 21
Color Gradient setting, 285
colors
  Add Color Texture button, 295
  backgrounds, configuring, 386
  Display preferences, 39
  Environmental Material, 387
  modifying, 111
  objects, filling, 296
  two-color gradients, 190
  values, modifying, 227
commands
  calling, 47
  Form Editor, 48
  Record Macro, 134
  Reset, 65, 213
  Scale, 182
  Show Falloff, 339
  Spin Edges, 131
  Stretch 3D, 262
  Subdivide Polygon, 330
Command-Z (Mac), 347
Common Properties, 45
concepts, lighting, 358–359
cone tracing, 381
configuring
  animation, 239
  color backgrounds, 386
  Color Gradient setting, 285
  Element Action Centers, 54
  Fresnel, 283
  interface configuration, 3–4
    overview of, 4–30
  interfaces, 89
  lighting, 369
  Linear falloffs, 172
  materials, 109–117, 194–201
    images, 202–206
  measurements, 34
  modo configuration files, 42–44
  polygon materials, 282
  properties, 204
  rendering, 372–377
  Roughness, 283
  Tool viewports, 24
  Visibility option, 15
  work plane axis, 169
Constant background, modifying, 367
Constructive Solids Geometry (CSG), 150
controls
  accessing, 188
  animation, 233–236
  keyframes, 236, 237–238
  surfaces, adding, 282
converting
  blank viewports into 3D Model views, 27
  edges to polygons, 70
  nontabbed viewports to tabbed, 17
  selections, 69

Convert selection option, 100
coordinates, rounding, 34
copying
images, 209, 210
items, 124
objects, 215
viewports, 9–11
corkboards, creating, 156
Create Alternate Command dialog box, 49
CSG (Constructive Solids Geometry), 150
Ctrl-Z (PC), 347
Cube primitive, 121
cubes, selecting edges, 126
Curve Extrude tool, 105, 106, 317
Curve Path Mode setting, modifying, 107
customizing
layouts, 12–20
Preferences panel, 31–42
viewports, 8
Visibility option, 15
cutting shapes, 148–152
cylinder light, 357
Cylinder tool, 90, 93

D

data preferences, 40–42
3D editing, 41
animation, 42
Auto-Save options, 41
defaults, 40–41
LightWave I/O, 41
Scene Export, 42
UI images, 42
decreasing opacity, 201
default data preferences, 40–41
default directional light, 354
default layouts, 122
default modo 301/302 interface setting, 89
default settings, viewing, 215
default Shader Tree tabs, 187
defining
landscapes, 336
regions, 83
deformation
geometry, 331
of objects, 81
deleting, 97
edges, 102
horizon lines, 190
items, 124
selections, 102
viewport changes, 10
DEMs (demographic elevation maps), 327
depth, adding, 157, 200
deselecting polygons, 264
details
adding, 104, 136
hard-surface modeling, 268–277
micropolygon displacement, 332–336
detergent bottles, modeling, 305–311
dialog boxes
Create Alternate Command, 49
Item Name, 159
Merge Vertices, 262
Polygon Set Material, 219, 267, 282
Save Layout, 19
Vertex Map, 222
diffusing materials, 199
***Digital Lighting and Rendering, Second Edition,* 358**
directional light, 363
selecting, 191
displacements
micropolygon, 301, 327
random, 292
sculpting, 332–336

Display preferences, 35–40
3D information overlays, 38
colors, 39
OpenGL, 35–38
rendering, 39–40
tool handles, 38
distance, applying, 331
dome light, 356, 357
dragging
models, 297
objects, 181
points, 307
to scale up, 101
Drink mesh layer, 282
dropping images, 206
duplicating
images, 210
items, 124
objects, 215

E

Edge Bevel, 160
edges
adding, 324
beveling, 252
Bevel tool, 99
deleting, 102
editing, 94–97
Element Move tool, 82
highlighting, 98
horizontal, 178
loops, 68, 160, 177
modifying, 97–104
moving, 323
multiple, selecting, 101
rounding, 127
scaling, 273
selecting, 103, 126, 130, 221, 258, 319
selections, 70
sharpening, 311–315
Edge Slice tool, 350
Edges mode, 129, 139
Edges selection mode, 97
Edge Weight tool, 261
editing
3D, 41
geometry, 97–104
materials, 110
shapes, 94–97, 143–148
Edit mode, 318
curve paths, modifying, 107
Editors. *See also* tools
Form Editor, 44–50
Gradient Editor, 290
Graph Editor, 244–246
Input Editor, 50–52
effects
Bump, 200, 201
masks, 207–212
modifying, 211
Reflection Amount, 290
tapering, 173
Eggshell material, 384
Element Action Centers, 55
Element falloffs, 84
Element Move tool, 49, 53, 82, 167, 306
elements, 52
Items tab, navigating, 154
pulling, 83
selecting, 68
shaping, 83
elevation, demographic elevation maps (DEMs), 327
English measurements, configuring, 34
Environment Material, 189, 285
colors, 387
environments
as light sources, 361
modifying, 333
Environment Type option, 386

expanding
Render listings, 187, 193
selections, 253
Export As option, 407
exporting
interface configuration, 30
Scene Export, 42
Extrude tool, 251, 252

F

faceted subdivision surfaces, 303
falloffs, 76–85
Bend tools, 165
Linear
applying, 173
configuring, 172
Noise falloff, 339, 341
Show Falloff command, 339
Tool Pipe, 85
File menu, Reset command, 65
files, modo configuration, 42–44
Fill tool, 296
filters, Antialiasing filters, 376
Find Form function, 48
flat cylinders, 92
Flatness of Perspective value, 36
flat planes
adding, 390
subdividing, 329
fluorescent light, 357
Fold tool, 350
formatting
images, 296
interfaces, 22
mesh, 124
Selection Sets, 71
tubes, 139
Form Editor, 44–50
frames, animation, 235
Frame tab, 374–375
Fresnel, configuring, 283
full frame render, 402
functions. *See also* commands
Boolean, 150
Find Form, 48
Macro, 142

G

Gang select feature, 92, 93
geometry
adding, 61, 69, 104–109, 266
beveling edges, 179
blending, 104–109
CSG (Constructive Solids Geometry), 150
deforming, 331
editing, 97–104
highlighting, 61, 98
Lasso tool, 152
materials, assigning, 194
rendering, 109–117
surfaces, 109–117
Tool Pipe, 87
GI (global illumination), 359
noise and render, 396–397
overview of, 379–381
ray tracing, 381–396
rendering with, 379–397
turning on, 285
glass materials, 284
global illumination. *See* GI
Gradient Editor, 290
gradients
Color Gradient setting, 285
two-color, 190
Graph Editor, 244–246
Ground Color, configuring, 387
Group Polygons, 64
groups, 218, 228–232
creating, 229
masks, 225
points, selecting, 343

H

- **handles**
  - falloffs, 77
  - moving, 159
  - rendering, 164
  - tools, Display preferences, 38
- **hard-surface modeling**
  - details, 268–277
  - overview of, 250
  - references, working from, 250–267
- **HDR (high dynamic range), 360**
- **heads-up display (HUD), 61**
- **height, modifying lighting, 366**
- **highlighting geometry, 61, 98**
- **hollow shapes, 151**
- **horizon lines, deleting, 190**
- **horizontal edges, 178**
- **HUD (heads-up display), 61**

I

- **IceCube material, 290**
- **icons**
  - Cylinder, 90
  - Plane, 162
  - playback, 235
  - Zoom, 112
- **IESNA (Illuminating Engineering Society of North America), 358**
- **Illuminating Engineering Society of North America (IESNA), 358**
- **image maps, adding, 202**
- **images**
  - copying, 209, 210
  - dropping, 206
  - formatting, 296
  - hard-surface modeling, working from, 250
  - HDR (high dynamic range), 360
  - high dynamic range (HDR), 360
  - inverting, 211
  - loading, 205
  - mapping, 36
  - materials, configuring, 202–206
  - saving, 405–406
  - UI, data preferences, 42
- **Images tab, loading, 205**
- **Indirect Illumination, 380, 385**
  - turning off, 363
- **Inflate tool, 347**
- **inner edges, selecting, 265**
- **Input Editor, 50–52**
- **input preferences, 32–35**
  - accuracy, 34–35
  - remapping, 32–34
  - Work Plane, 34
- **interface configuration, 3–4**
  - custom layouts, 12–20
  - exporting, 30
  - interfaces, rolling, 20–30
  - overview of, 4–30
  - viewports
    - overview of, 4, 5–8
    - splitting, 9–11
    - tabbed, 11
    - tools, 7–8
- **interfaces**
  - animation, 233–236
  - configuring, 89
  - Form Editor, 44–50
  - Shader tree, 186
- **inverting images, 211**
- **Irradiance Caching, 396**
- **Irradiance Rays setting, 396**
- **isolating mesh, 294**
- **Item List, 18**
- **Item Name dialog box, 159**
- **items**
  - masks, 213–219
  - Shader Tree, 186
- **Items mode, 240**
- **Items selection mode, 73–74**

Items tab, 124
- navigating, 153–184
- scenes
  - adding, 170–180
  - merging, 180–184

J

joining polygons, 108

K

keyframes
- animation, 238–244
- channels, 237–238
- controls, 236
- motion between, 243

keys
- Apple, 124
- creating, 291
- Shift, 127
- Tab, 125

L

landscapes
- building, 327–332
- defining, 336
- morph maps, 337–344
- points
  - modifying, 344
  - selecting, 342

Lasso tool, geometry, 152

Lawson, Philip, 280

layers, 153
- adding, 197
- backgrounds
  - using as references, 166–170
  - viewing, 150
- building in, 155–162
- groups, 218
- image maps, adding, 202
- Items tab, navigating, 153–184
- materials, 226–228
  - naming, 230
  - selecting, 196
- mesh, adding, 162–166
- noise, adding, 334
- textures, selecting, 195

layouts
- customizing, 12–20
- default, 122
- recalling, 20
- saving, 19
- tabbed viewports, 11

LCD monitors, loading, 363

Leuenberger, Greg, 155

LightBox plane, moving, 389

lighting, 353–358
- Action Centers, 365
- adding, 364
- concepts, 358–359
- configuring, 369
- Directional Light, selecting, 191
- GI (global illumination), 359. *See also* GI
  - turning on, 285
- Items selection mode, 73–74
- Items tab, navigating, 154
- light sources, 359–362
- points, 354
- polygons, 360
- positioning, 370
- quality of, 359
- ray tracing. *See* ray tracing
- scenes, 362–372
- surfaces, 385

Light Unit System, 34

Light view, 369

LightWave, 408
- data preferences, 41

Linear falloffs, 80
- applying, 173
- configuring, 172

listings
- Base Material, 187
- Morph Maps, 338
- New Map, 338
- Render, expanding, 187, 193
- selecting, 188
- Weight Map Texture, 225

loading
- images, 205
- LCD monitors, 363
- objects, 214
- scenes, 181

Local Action Centers, 55

loops, edges, 68, 160, 177

Loop Slice tool, 322

M

Macintosh modo configuration files, 42–43

Macro function, 142

macros
- applying, 140, 143
- automating with, 133–143
- saving, 141
- starting, 134

manipulating models, 94–97

mapping
- demographic elevation maps (DEMs), 327
- morph maps, 337–344
- photo, 381
- textures, 36

masks, 195
- effects, 207–212
- groups, 225
- images, adding, 203
- item, 213–219
- materials, assigning, 282
- polygons, 219–221
- Shader Tree, 213–226
- textures, creating, 210
- vertex, 221–226

materials
- adding, 194
- blending, 225
- configuring, 109–117, 194–201
- depth, adding, 200
- diffusing, 199
- edges, selecting, 221
- editing, 110
- Eggshell, 384
- Environment, 189, 285, 387
- glass, 284
- groups, creating, 229
- IceCube, 290
- images, configuring, 202–206
- Landscape, adding noise, 334
- layers, 226–228
  - naming, 230
  - selecting, 196
- masks, assigning, 282
- naming, 137
- polygons
  - configuring, 282
  - item masks, 213–219
- previewing, 198
- sizing, modifying, 232
- TopKey, 218, 219
- viewing, 193

Material Trans tab, 285, 391

measurements
- configuring, 34
- viewing, 158

menus
- File, Reset command, 65
- Render, 401

Merge Vertices dialog box, 262

merging scenes in Items tab, 180–184

mesh
creating, 124
images, moving, 206
isolating, 294
Items selection mode, 73–74
layers, adding, 162–166
renaming, 159, 167
subdividing, 304
message boards, creating, 155
method selections, 65–73
metric, configuring, 34
micropolygon displacement, 301, 327
details, 332–336
models
detergent bottles, 305–311
dragging, 297
hard-surface modeling. *See* hard-surface modeling
Items selection mode, 73–74
landscapes, 327–332
manipulating, 94–97
ogre, 302
output, 406–408
preparing, 89–93
scaling, 149
sculpting, 345–350
sharpening, 259
subdivision surfaces. *See* subdivision surfaces
viewing, 257
modes
Edges, 129, 139
Edit, 318
Item, 240
Scanline, 375
Modifiers listings, 50
modifying
area light, 366
blank viewports, 27
colors, 111
values, 227
Constant background, 367
Curve Path Mode setting, 107
effects, 211
elements, 83
environments, 333
falloffs, 78
items, 124
materials, sizing, 232
models, 94–97
noise, 335
options, 167
points, 344
Sculpt tool, 330
selection modes, 69, 72
Shift values, 96, 308
surfaces, 97
Tool Pipe, 87
Transparent Color amounts, 288
tubes, 144
viewports, 8, 152, 223
views, 369
visibility, 256
modo configuration files, 42–44
morph maps, 337–344
motion between keyframes, 243
Mouse Input Preset setting, 33
Move 3D tool, 183
Move tool, 76, 182
applying, 340
moving
area light, 366
axis, 306
edges, 323
handles, 159
images, 206
LightBox plane, 389
lighting, 364
models, 297
objects, 168, 181
points, 307, 321, 344
spotlights, 371
Tool Properties viewport, 26
Tool viewports, 24
viewports, 29
views, 113

multiple edges, selecting, 101
multiple layers, using as references, 166–170
multiple selections, 142

N

naming
items, 124
layouts, 19
materials, 137, 230
mesh, 159, 167
polygons, 220
navigating
Graph Editor, 244–246
Items tab, 153–184
scenes, 368
selections, 71
tools, 46
Work Planes, 56–58
negative distance, 331
New Map listing, 338
New Palette option, 23
new scenes, creating, 171
New Tab option, 18
n-gons, 408
noise
adding, 225, 334
falloffs, 341
GI (global illumination), 396–397
modifying, 335
Noise falloff, 339
nontabbed viewports, converting to tabbed, 17
normals, surfaces, 301

O

objects
Action Centers, 53
building blocks, 121–133
copying, 215
editing, 94–97
Extrude tool, 252
filling, 296
Items tab, navigating, 154
layers, adding, 162
loading, 214
moving, 181
positioning, 255
rendering, 90
resizing, 182
rotating, 81
rounding, 308
scaling, 168
shapes, creating, 171, 174
Transform tool, 163
viewing, 28
ogre model, 302
opacity, decreasing, 201
OpenGL Display preferences, 35–38
opening Properties tab, 111
Open LAN View option, 404
Open Preview Render option, 403
operating systems, modo configuration files, 42–44
options. *See also* customizing; preferences
Convert selection, 100
Environment Type, 386
Export As, 407
Indirect Illumination, 385
modifying, 167
New Palette, 23
New Tab, 18
Open LAN View, 404
Open Preview Render, 403
output, 399–400. *See also* output
Render All, 402
Render Animation, 403
Render Items, 404
Render Selected, 402
Render Turntable, 401, 403
Save As, 406
Save Incremental, 310
viewing, 156
viewports, 8
Visibility, 15
Work Plane, 34

Options button, timelines, 236
organization of groups, 229. *See also* groups
Origin Action Centers, 55
outer edges, selecting, 265
output
animation, 400–404
images, saving, 405–406
models, 406–408
options, 399–400

P

paint tools, 280–293
surfaces, 294–300
panels
Preferences, 31–42, 400
Properties, 237
Render Properties, 329
Tool Properties, 13, 64, 149, 269
path tracing, 381
PCs, modo configuration files for, 43–44
perspective, Flatness of Perspective value, 36
Perspective view, 13, 269
photo mapping, 381
Photometric measurements, 34
pie menus, modifying selection modes, 72
Pipeline, 85–87
Pivot Action Centers, 55
Plane icon, 162
Plane primitives, rotating, 164
planes
adding, 388
LightBox, moving, 389
rotating, 390
scaling, 113
playback icons, 235
point-by-point method, 303
points
editing, 94–97
groups, selecting, 343
lighting, 354
modifying, 97–104, 344
moving, 307, 321
selecting, 342
polygons
beveling, 175, 254, 256
deselecting, 264
joining, 108
lighting, 360
masks, 219–221
materials
configuring, 282
item masks, 213–219
naming, 220
Quick Access Selection bar, 74–76
scaling, 147
selecting, 105, 128, 144, 220, 253
Polygons button, 57, 60
Polygon Set Material dialog box, 219, 267, 282
Polygons selection mode, 95
Position channels, 242
positioning, 167. *See also* moving
cameras, 333
lighting, 370
Move 3D tool, 183
objects, 168, 255
slices, 267
spotlights, 355
Tool Properties viewport, 26
values, 242
viewports, 29
Position X, 237
positive distance, 331
preferences
data, 40–42
3D editing, 41
animation, 42
Auto-Save options, 41
defaults, 40–41
LightWave I/O, 41
Scene Export, 42
UI images, 42

Display, 35–40
colors, 39
3D information overlays, 38
OpenGL, 35–38
rendering, 39–40
tool handles, 38
Form Editor, 44–50
input preferences, 32–35
Preferences panel, 400
customizing, 31–42
preparing models, 89–93
presets, 33
Action Centers, 54
previewing
materials, 198
regions, 235
Preview viewport, 13
primitives
alternate, viewing, 162
Plane, rotating, 164
Torus, 239
properties
adding, 217
configuring, 204
Render Properties panel, 329
Tool Properties panel, 269
Properties panel, 237
Properties tab, opening, 111
Properties viewport, 18
pulling elements, 83
Push tool, 348

Q

quality of light, 359
Quick Access Selection bar, 74–76

R

Radial falloffs, 77, 78
Radiant Intensity values, 355
Radiometric measurements, 34
radiosity, 381
radius, 92
random displacements, 292
ray tracing, GI (global illumination) and, 381–396
recalling layouts, 20
Record Macro command, 134
references
background layers, using as, 166–170
hard-surface modeling, working from, 250–267
input, 32–35
Reflection Amount, 290
regions
defining, 83
falloffs, 84
previewing, 235
remapping input preferences, 32–34
removing. *See* deleting
renaming
items, 124
mesh, 159, 167
Render All option, 402
Render Animation option, 403
rendering, 90, 372–377
bucket, 374
Display preferences, 39–40
Frame tab, 374–375
geometry, 109–117
with global illumination (GI), 379–397
handles, 164
lighting, 286
Settings tab, 375–377
troubleshooting, 302
Render Items option, 404
Render listings, expanding, 187, 193
Render menu, 401
render preview, viewing, 14
Render Properties panel, 329
Render Selected option, 402
Render Tri viewport, 13, 14
Render Turntable option, 401, 403
Reset command, 65, 213

resetting
Bevel tools, 175
tools, 64
resizing objects, 182
resolution, selecting, 296
RGB values, 359
rolling interfaces, 20–30
Rotate tool, 81, 184
rotating
area light, 366
Plane primitives, 164
planes, 390
spotlights, 355
viewports, 169
views, 113, 314
Rotation Y, 237
Roughness, configuring, 283
rounding
coordinates, 34
edges, 127
objects, 308
Round Level value, 104, 160

S

Save As option, 406
Save Incremental option, 310
Save Layout dialog box, 19
saving
images, 405–406
layouts, 19
macros, 141
Scale command, 182
Scale tool, 172, 319, 325
scaling
edges, 273
models, 149
objects, 168
planes, 113
selections, 147
Scanline mode, 375
Scene Export, data preferences, 42
scenes
8balls, 383
creating new, 171
HDR images in, 361
item masks, 213–219
Items tab
adding, 170–180
merging, 180–184
Items tab, navigating, 154
layers, adding, 162
lighting, 362–372
navigating, 368
planes, adding, 388
viewing, 181
Screen Action Centers, 55
sculpting, 327
displacements, 332–336
landscapes, building, 327–332
models, 345–350
morph maps, 337–344
Sculpt/Paint tab, 294, 346
Sculpt tool, modifying, 330
searching forms, 45
segments, building blocks, 123
Select Connected feature, 72
selecting
Action Centers, 54
center points, 275
Directional Light, 191
edges, 103, 126, 130, 221, 258, 319
horizontal, 178
loops, 160, 177
geometry, 97–104
listings, 188
material layers, 196
multiple edges, 101
points, 342, 343
polygons, 105, 128, 144, 220, 253
resolution, 296
texture layers, 195
Selection Action Centers, 55

Selection Center Auto Axis Action Centers, 55
selections, 59–85
adding to, 146
converting, 69
deleting, 102
edges, 70
expanding, 253
falloffs, 76–85
Items selection mode, 73–74
methods, 65–73
multiple, 142
navigating, 71
Quick Access Selection bar, 74–76
scaling, 147
working with, 60–65
selection sets
assigning, 145
creating, 71
settings. *See also* configuring; options; preferences
Irradiance Rays, 396
OpenGL, 35–38
rendering, 372–377
Settings tab, 375–377
Shader Tree
applying, 182–212
default tabs, 187
Environment material, 189
groups, 228–232
images, loading, 205
masks, 213–226
materials
editing, 110
layers, 226–228
overview of, 185–191
polygon masks, 219–221
properties, adding, 217
texture layers, 211
vertex masks, 221–226
shading
troubleshooting, 302
Vertex Map, 223
Shading panel, 67
shapes
cutting, 148–152
editing, 94–97, 143–148
hollow, 151
objects, creating, 171, 174
starting, 122
subdividing, 304
shaping elements, 83
sharing interface configuration, 30
sharpening
edges, 311–315
models, 259
Shift key, 127
Shift values, 96, 159, 308
Show Camera, 14
Show Falloff command, 339
Show Lights, 14
SI (system internationale) measurements, 34
sizing
materials, modifying, 232
textures, 201
slices, 97
positioning, 267
Slice tool, 266
smooth models, creating, 255
Smooth Shift tool, 269
smooth subdivision surfaces, 303
sources, lighting, 359–362
spectrums, visible, 358
Spikey tool, 275
Spin Edges command, 131
spline-based modeling, 303
splitting
viewports, 9–11
views, 339

spotlights, 355. *See also* lighting
adding, 371
area light, coexisting with, 368
starting, 21
macros, 134
shapes, 122
tools, 61
Stretch 3D command, 262
Subdivide Polygon command, 330
subdivision surfaces, 301
advantages of, 315–326
edges, sharpening, 311–315
models, viewing, 257
Sub-Ds, 301–326
turning off, 130
turning on, 125
surfaces
applying, 228
attributes, viewing, 196
controls, adding, 282
geometry, 109–117
glass materials, 284
hard-surface modeling. *See* hard-surface modeling
images, adding, 203
lighting, 385
modifying, 97
normals, 301
paint tools, 294–300
subdivision, 257. *See also* subdivision surfaces
switching selection modes, 61
system internationale (SI) measurements, 34

T

tabbed viewports, 11, 17
Tab key, 125
tabs
adding, 18
Animate, 234
default Shader Tree, 187
Frame, 374–375
Images, loading, 205
Items, 153–184
adding scenes, 170–180
merging scenes, 180–184
Material Trans, 285, 391
Sculpt/Paint, 294, 346
Settings, 375–377
Visibility, 154
tapering effects, 173
Texture Locator, 208
textures
Add Color Texture button, 295
adding, 200
Cellular, 198, 292
layers, selecting, 195
mapping, 36
masks, creating, 210
overview of, 279
paint tools, 280–293
sizing, 201
surfaces, 294–300
Thicken tool, 261
timelines, 234
controls, 236
Options button, 236
Tool Pipe, 55, 85–87
Tool Properties panel, 13, 64, 149, 269
Tool Properties viewport, 25
tools, 90
animation, 234
Bend, 165
Bevel, 61, 63
applying, 95
edges, 99
edges, rounding, 127
edges, selecting, 132
resetting, 175
subdivision surfaces, 317
Bridge, 325
Capsule, 90
Curve Extrude, 105, 106, 317
Cylinder, 90, 93
Edge Slice, 350

Edge Weight, 261
Element Move, 49, 53, 82, 167, 306
Extrude, 251, 252
falloffs, 76–85
Fill, 296
Fold, 350
Gradient Editor, 290
Graph Editor, 244–246
handle Display preferences, 38
Inflate, 347
Loop Slice, 322
Move, 76, 182
applying, 340
Move 3D, 183
navigating, 46
paint, 280–293
Pipeline, 85–87
Push, 348
resetting, 64
Rotate, 81, 184
Scale, 172, 319, 325
Sculpt, modifying, 330
sculpting, 345–350
selections, 59–85
Slice, 266
Smooth Shift, 269
Spikey, 275
starting, 61
surfaces, 294–300
Thicken, 261
Transform, 148, 163, 241
Weight, 223
Work Planes, 58

Tool Properties viewport, moving, 26

Tool viewports, 7–8
adding, 23
configuration, 24
moving, 24

TopKey materials, 218, 219

Torus primitive, 239

Toy Block, 149

tracking changes, 128

transformations, Action Centers, 55

Transform tool, 148, 163, 241

Transparent Color amounts, modifying, 288

transparent settings, applying, 289

troubleshooting image maps, 203

tubes
creating, 139
lighting, 357
modifying, 144

turning off
Indirect Illumination, 363
Record Macro command, 136
subdivision surfaces, 130

turning on
Global Illumination, 285
subdivision surfaces, 125

two-color gradients, 190

types of lighting, 357

U

UI images data preferences, 42

Unit System settings, 34

unweighted power, 34

UV view, 299

V

values
Absorption Distance, 284
colors, modifying, 227
Flatness of Perspective value, 36
positioning, 242
Radiant Intensity, 355
RGB, 359
Round Level, 160
Shift, 96, 159, 308

variables, viewing, 33

Vertex Map dialog box, 222

vertices
editing, 94–97
masks, 221–226
modifying, 97–104

viewing
alternate primitives, 162
default settings, 215
layers, backgrounds, 150
materials, 193, 198
measurements, 158
models, 257
objects, 28
options, 156
scenes, 181
Shader Tree, 186
surface attributes, 196
variables, 33
View panel, 67
viewports
3D Model view, 5–7
custom layouts, 12–20
modifying, 152, 223
moving, 29
options, modifying, 167
overview of, 4, 5–8
rotating, 169
Shader Tree, 186
splitting, 9–11
tabbed, 11, 17, 18
Tool Properties, 25, 26
Tools, 7–8
adding, 23
configuration, 24
moving, 24
Viewport Style buttons, 6–7
views
Camera, accessing, 14
Light, 369
modifying, 369
moving, 113
Perspective, 13, 269
rotating, 113, 314
split, 339
UV, 299
View Type option, 156
visibility, modifying, 256
Visibility option, 15
Visibility tab, 67, 154
visible spectrum, 358

W

wedges, creating, 175
Weight Map Texture listing, 225
Weight tool, 223
width, modifying lighting, 366
windows, adding, 22, 28
Windows XP, modo configuration files, 43–44
Work Plane, 56–58
axis, configuring, 169
input preferences, 34
Y axis, 91

Y

Y axis, 91

Z

Z axis, 264, 307
Zenith Color, configuring, 387
Zoom icon, 112

License Agreement/Notice of Limited Warranty

By opening the sealed disc container in this book, you agree to the following terms and conditions. If, upon reading the following license agreement and notice of limited warranty, you cannot agree to the terms and conditions set forth, return the unused book with unopened disc to the place where you purchased it for a refund.

License:
The enclosed software is copyrighted by the copyright holder(s) indicated on the software disc. You are licensed to copy the software onto a single computer for use by a single user and to a backup disc. You may not reproduce, make copies, or distribute copies or rent or lease the software in whole or in part, except with written permission of the copyright holder(s). You may transfer the enclosed disc only together with this license, and only if you destroy all other copies of the software and the transferee agrees to the terms of the license. You may not decompile, reverse assemble, or reverse engineer the software.

Notice of Limited Warranty:
The enclosed disc is warranted by Course Technology to be free of physical defects in materials and workmanship for a period of sixty (60) days from end user's purchase of the book/disc combination. During the sixty-day term of the limited warranty, Course Technology will provide a replacement disc upon the return of a defective disc.

Limited Liability:
THE SOLE REMEDY FOR BREACH OF THIS LIMITED WARRANTY SHALL CONSIST ENTIRELY OF REPLACEMENT OF THE DEFECTIVE DISC. IN NO EVENT SHALL COURSE TECHNOLOGY OR THE AUTHOR BE LIABLE FOR ANY OTHER DAMAGES, INCLUDING LOSS OR CORRUPTION OF DATA, CHANGES IN THE FUNCTIONAL CHARACTERISTICS OF THE HARDWARE OR OPERATING SYSTEM, DELETERIOUS INTERACTION WITH OTHER SOFTWARE, OR ANY OTHER SPECIAL, INCIDENTAL, OR CONSEQUENTIAL DAMAGES THAT MAY ARISE, EVEN IF COURSE TECHNOLOGY AND/OR THE AUTHOR HAS PREVIOUSLY BEEN NOTIFIED THAT THE POSSIBILITY OF SUCH DAMAGES EXISTS.

Disclaimer of Warranties:
COURSE TECHNOLOGY AND THE AUTHOR SPECIFICALLY DISCLAIM ANY AND ALL OTHER WARRANTIES, EITHER EXPRESS OR IMPLIED, INCLUDING WARRANTIES OF MERCHANTABILITY, SUITABILITY TO A PARTICULAR TASK OR PURPOSE, OR FREEDOM FROM ERRORS. SOME STATES DO NOT ALLOW FOR EXCLUSION OF IMPLIED WARRANTIES OR LIMITATION OF INCIDENTAL OR CONSEQUENTIAL DAMAGES, SO THESE LIMITATIONS MIGHT NOT APPLY TO YOU.

Other:
This Agreement is governed by the laws of the State of Massachusetts without regard to choice of law principles. The United Convention of Contracts for the International Sale of Goods is specifically disclaimed. This Agreement constitutes the entire agreement between you and Course Technology regarding use of the software.